CARIBBEAN PORTRAITS

Essays on Gender Ideologies and Identities

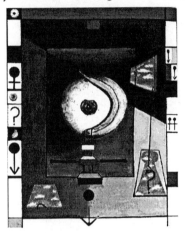

*My ancestors are nearer
than albums of pictures*

Olive Senior

CARIBBEAN PORTRAITS

Essays on Gender Ideologies and Identities

edited by

Christine Barrow

Ian Randle Publishers
Kingston

in association with

The Centre for Gender and Development Studies
University of the West Indies

First published in Jamaica, 1998 by
Ian Randle Publishers
206 Old Hope Road, Box 686
Kingston 6

ISBN 976-8123-56-7 paperback

A catalogue record for this book is available from
the National Library of Jamaica.

Cover and book design by Robert Harris
Set in 10/14 Stone Informal x 27

Cover painting: *The Flying Chamber of Enigmas* by Helen Carnegie

Printed and bound in the USA

Contents

Acknowledgements

This collection owes its greatest debt of gratitude to the editorial board –
to Eudine Barriteau, Jane Bryce, Jeniphier Carnegie and Nan Peacocke –
all of whom contributed papers and who were unfailing in their enthusiasm, dedication and support throughout its genesis. They join me in
thanking the contributors, especially those who also reviewed papers.
Kathleen Drayton deserves special mention for her thorough reviews and
valuable suggestions for the volume.

Appreciation for funding goes to the Centre for Gender and Development Studies at the University of the West Indies and its regional coordinator, Elsa Leo-Rhynie. To Helen Carnegie many thanks for a front cover
which vividly captures the central themes of the collection and to Cyrilene
Walcott and Ann Taylor gratitude for their technical expertise on the
computer. And very special thanks to Jennifer and Geoffrey for their
'caring labour' for the duration.

Christine Barrow
November 1996

Ancestral Poem

Olive Senior

I
My ancestors are nearer
than albums of pictures
I tread on heels thrust
into broken-down slippers.

II
My mother's womb impulsed
harvests perpetually. She
deeply breathed country air
when she laboured me.

III
The pattern woven by my
father's hands lulled me
to sleep. Certain actions
moved me so: my father
planting.

When my father planted
his thoughts took flight.
He did not need to think.
The ritual was ingrained
in the blood, embedded
in the centuries of dirt
beneath his fingernails
encased in the memories
of his race.

(Yet the whiplash of my
father's wrath rever-
berated days in my
mind with the inten-
sity of tuning forks.
He did not think.
My mother stunned wept
and prayed Father
Forgive Them knowing not
what she prayed for.)

One day I did not pray.

A gloss of sunlight through
the leaves betrayed me so
abstracted me from rituals.
And discarded prayers and
disproven myths
confirmed me freedom.

IV
Now against the rhythms
of subway trains my
heartbeats still drum
worksongs. Some wheels
sing freedom, the others
Home.

Still, if I could balance
water on my head I can
juggle worlds
on my shoulders.

Introduction and Overview[1]
Caribbean Gender Ideologies

Christine Barrow

After a relatively delayed start, Caribbean feminist scholarship has, since the late 1970s, moved rapidly to become established as an exciting field of epistemological, theoretical and methodological advance. It did not emerge in isolation from mainstream studies. The United Nations Decade for Women (1975-85) was the catalyst and much stimulus came from European, American and African feminist studies. At the same time, local scholars were clearly uncomfortable with prevailing knowledge: Caribbean women just did not fit received images and rhetoric. They were not 'marginalised' in the same way as their Third World counterparts, they could not be accommodated into private/public dichotomies which confined them to home, domesticity and motherhood, and, though constrained by patriarchal ideology and practice, they did not suffer the same subordinate status in relations with their menfolk.

Images of women have multiplied in the literature. The 'respectable wife and mother' stereotype of the 1960s was replaced by that of the 'powerful matriarch' at the centre of an extensive kinship network of support. This, in turn, was challenged by studies revealing the poverty and vulnerability of women's lives, especially those who head households. Shifting focus more recently to add Indian, white and 'coloured middle-class' women has created a veritable mosaic of Caribbean feminine portraits and blurred the identity of the 'Caribbean woman'. This begs the question: What, if anything, do Caribbean women share in this arena of plural race, class, culture and gender ideology and practice? Paradoxically, having searched for her for the past two decades, feminists struggle to avoid the conclusion that perhaps 'Caribbean woman' does not exist.

Studies of Caribbean men lag behind. Dismissed as 'marginal' in early anthropological studies and subsequently sensationalised as 'at risk' and 'in crisis', as they are presumed to be overtaken by girls and women at school and at work, men have re-emerged only recently as the academy turns its attention to Caribbean masculinity. The central question is: How are black and Indian masculinities constructed in a world pervaded by the prescriptions of white racism and patriarchy?

Caribbean feminist and gender studies have come a long way in two decades. Imported theories, archaic, patriarchal assumptions, gender stereotypes and misconceived policies have been problematised and challenged and the process of reinterpretation and rejection through the lens of engendered indigenous knowledge is well underway. This book makes its contribution by focusing on the issues of gender ideology and identity. The essays in this collection ask simple, fundamental questions: Who are Caribbean women and who are Caribbean men? How do gender ideologies and stereotypes define them and how, in turn, do they respond? How are gender identities and relations moulded and how, in the process, do the dynamics of imperialism, capitalism, racism and sexism and the plural constructs of race, class and culture intersect?

Caribbean Island Countries

The anglophone Caribbean island chain curves southward from the Bahamas, a few miles from the coast of Florida, to the twin island state of Trinidad and Tobago, off the South American coast. Aligned historically and economically are the South American mainland country of Guyana (formerly British Guiana) and Belize (formerly British Honduras) in Central America. Geographical proximity masks environmental and social heterogeneity. The volcanic peaks and rain forests of the majority contrast with the flat, cultivated, coral stone surface of Barbados. Physical size ranges from Guyana, with a land area of nearly 215,000 square kilometres, to the small island colony of Anguilla with 91 square kilometres. Jamaica's 2.5 million people and Guyana's low population density of 3.4 persons per square kilometre, contrast with the low head count of under 9,000 persons in Anguilla and the very high density of Barbados, at over 600 persons per square kilometre.

Caribbean populations also differ in ethnic composition and culture, reflecting variations in the historical experience of migration and colonial dominance. All were, during their early days of settlement, rigidly strati-fied into white elite, brown middle class and poor black. The subsequent arrival of new immigrant groups, especially the mass immigration of East Indians as indentured servants after the end of slavery, has altered the composition of Trinidad and Guyana in particular. Many white colonial officials and planters departed over the years and those remaining have replaced racial endogamy with a cautious and selective intermarriage, changing elite colour composition to 'high brown' and 'pass for white'. Political independence, educational and occupational opportunities and black upward mobility made their mark on the colour/class hierarchies, creating dual elites, combining a black political directorate and a local white or brown, wealthy business and professional group. In countries such as Trinidad and Tobago, St Lucia and Dominica, controlled by the French or Spanish at some time during their colonial history, the addition of Catholicism, Creole language (Kweyol) and Carnival distinguishes them from Barbados, for example, continuously dominated by Britain and reflecting European culture with surviving sub-cultural Africanisms. Nevertheless, Caribbean countries share a heritage of colonialism, slav-ery, migration, plantation structures and global periphery status, all of which have combined to shape contemporary cultural patterns, including gender identities, relationships and ideologies.

The Men and Women of the Caribbean

The modern social history of Caribbean men and women begins with European settlement and African enslavement in the 1620s. By this time or shortly thereafter the indigenous peoples and cultures of the Caribbean – the Kalinago (Carib) and the Arawak – were eliminated. Only a few small settlements remain in Dominica, Guyana and Belize. Plantation slavery has been described as 'part of a precocious experiment in social engineering' (Hart 1989: 2). To fulfil the demands of imperialist expan-sion, artificial societies were created by migration. First to arrive were the whites from Europe who settled as wealthy planters and as indentured servants. They were followed by the Africans, abducted and transported en masse as slave labour to generate the enormous sugar fortunes which fed European industrial capitalism and supported the lavish lifestyles of the white elites.

Although Caribbean slavery was one of the most iniquitous, exploita-tive system ever to have existed, it did generate a remarkable level of gender equality among the slaves and, together with inherited African

patterns, laid the foundation for contemporary female economic autonomy. The majority of slave women worked side by side with their menfolk
in the plantation fields and were treated as equals within a system which,
in denying their humanity, also obscured their gender. It was only during
the amelioration period, the last phase of slavery, that reproduction and
motherhood were encouraged and rewarded and the system began to
acknowledge a black female identity. Meanwhile, slave men have been
portrayed as rebels and runaways, as emasculated and irresponsible
'husbands' and parents. Rightly or wrongly, contemporary male behaviour is often attributed to this slave past. The gender identities and
relationships of the East Indians, Chinese and other migrant groups were
also reconstructed. Under the conditions of East Indian indenture, for
example, especially the sex imbalance and female scarcity, women resisted the Indian traditions of seclusion and familial patriarchy. On many
occasions, their husbands reacted with extreme violence.

In another bold experiment at social engineering, this time to build
'free', 'civilised' societies, the colonial government introduced measures
to recast black and Indian women as submissive housewives and mothers,
while socialising their partners as responsible workers and family men.
The combined forces of State, school and church were marshalled in the
process. The school, that major agent for socialisation, social control and
the preservation of the status quo, taught boys gardening and other
manual skills necessary for an obedient, industrious workforce, while girls
were socialised for refinement and domesticity through recitation, needle-
work and cookery. In turn, the function of the church was to encourage
marriage and wholesome family life structured according to the European
nuclear ideal.

The conversion of women was more successful, though not fully so,
among East Indians as the feminine and masculine ideals fitted quite well
with their own patriarchal traditions. For black men and women, the
colonial blueprint not only contradicted their established gender identities
and relationships, but was impossible to implement in practice. The
overall strategy was riddled with ambivalence: black men were taught the
values of a Euro-centred responsible manhood in circumstances of high
unemployment, dehumanising poverty and persistent white male promiscuity with black women. Women were imbued with the virtues of home
and family, while the system gave them no choice but to enter the
workforce to support their children and other dependents. The anomalies
became glaringly apparent when, with the collapse of sugar in the late
nineteenth century, survival depended on the mass emigration of men.

This was especially apparent in those countries without land for peasant development. In Barbados, for example, the 1921 sex ratio was upset to only 679 males for every 1,000 females and women experienced full employment. In Trinidad, while Indian women remained at home in the rural areas working in agriculture, many black women migrated to town to seek employment, mainly as dressmakers and domestics. By the early 1920s, however, women were joining men in migration and assuming their pivotal positions in transnational family networks. These factors combined to reinforce, in post-emancipation and early twentieth-century Caribbean society, the high proportions of working mothers and grandmothers, female headed households and matrifocal families.

The modernisation of the economies and societies of the Caribbean from the 1960s had a profound effect on the labour and lives of men and women. An important development was economic diversification from plantation to mixed economies, with the addition of tourism and manufacturing and the expansion of the service sectors. Whereas only one or two of the previous generations gained social mobility as policemen, clerks, teachers and nurses, now men and women could and did take full advantage of a much wider range of occupational opportunities. However, sex stereotyping persisted. To this day, women predominate in traditionally female jobs as nurses, teachers, secretaries, dressmakers and domestic servants and, during periods of economic downturn, it is they who are forced out of waged work and back into the home, or into small-scale agriculture and the informal sector where their work is uncertain, poorly remunerated and unprotected by state social security provisions. In the new international division of labour, women are chosen as a cheap, docile and easily tapped source of labour in Export Processing Zones (EPZs) that have been eagerly 'invited' in by Caribbean governments. Unemployment rates for women are consistently higher than for men. However, much of the contribution of women remains invisible due to the inadequacies of official data collection and their own propensity to obscure informal income generating activity by representing themselves as 'housewives'.

Another important development is the spread and success of birth control since the late 1950s. Fertility rates have declined significantly and the impact on women's lives, in particular, has been far reaching. Unlike their mothers and grandmothers who believed they were destined to bear their biologically allotted number of children and for whom child bearing was a way of ensuring an, albeit tenuous, economic insurance in old age, for the new generation of Caribbean women, another child is more likely to be perceived as an additional burden. By postponing child birth, Caribbean women began to experience an adolescence. They reduced the number of children they bore and shortened their childbearing span. Motherhood remains central to their lives and identities as women, but it is controlled in the interests of improved health, education, employment and quality of life.

A parallel development is the expansion of secondary and tertiary education and the influence of an ideology of equal opportunity on the basis of gender, in addition to class and race. With education perceived as the only gateway to escape poverty and deprivation, parents fully encouraged both their girl- and boy-children. Indeed, the enrolment and achievement of girls have outpaced boys, prompting a public outcry declaring boys to be robbed of their masculinity and rightful place and calling for a return to single sex schools.

Although both men and women have participated fully in education and employment, the same cannot be said of national politics which remains dominated by men. Only a few women have reached the top, notably Dame Hilda Bynoe and Dame Nita Barrow, as governors general of Grenada and Barbados respectively, and Dame Eugenia Charles, as the past prime minister of Dominica. Although there is some indication of greater female participation as candidates in national elections, women's politics has operated outside the formal arena and adopted various forms and ideological perspectives. From the 1920s, middle-class women as pillars of the church and community, were charitably concerned to alleviate the extreme poverty and deprivation of those less privileged than themselves. The participation by women in more radical solidarity has also been part of the Caribbean political scene since the days of slavery. In the mass rebellion which spread throughout the Caribbean in the late 1930s and in the labour movements which emerged subsequently, women played their part in strikes and other forms of active resistance.

Caribbean countries have ratified the 1979 UN Convention on the Elimination of All Forms of Discrimination Against Women (CEDAW) and established women's desks, bureaux and, on occasions, ministries to oversee and coordinate activities for the promotion of women's rights. High on their agendas are legal reforms in the areas of equal pay, maternity leave, abortion, sexual harassment, domestic violence and the status of common law wives and 'illegitimate' children. In the forefront of feminist politics today are Caribbean NGOs such as Red Thread of Guyana, Sistren Theatre Collective of Jamaica and the Women and Development Unit (WAND) based in Barbados, but with a regional focus.

Through these agencies, the women's policy agenda has shifted emphasis from 'integration' to the 'empowerment' of women and the traditional female concerns of welfare, family and consumer issues, have been expanded to include reproductive health, the rights of women to control their bodies and the fight against all forms of violence and oppression against women.

For the last two decades or so, Caribbean economies have been in trouble. Much of the proud record of achievement in health and nutrition, literacy and education, employment and social services, gender empowerment and political stability is being eroded. International Monetary Fund structural adjustment programmes in Guyana, Jamaica and Trinidad and Tobago have mandated repeated currency devaluations. These, along with privatisation and other fiscal and monetary measures, have resulted in an escalating cost of living. Economic downsizing and public sector layoffs have increased unemployment rates, especially among women and youth, and migration no longer offers a safety valve. Women suffer disproportionately as social services are repatriated to the household. Not only do they provide the bulk of the labour in these sectors and therefore become prime targets for layoffs, but, as family care givers, they are also become primarily responsible for securing basic needs. Crime rates have increased, especially drug trafficking and domestic violence, a so-called 'subculture of violence' has developed among gangs of young men and there is evidence of street children in some Caribbean countries. Environmentally, these small island states are fragile and subject to ongoing degradation, and seasonal hurricanes which in the last decade or so have wrought devastation on many countries of the region.

In summary, the Caribbean social-gender system has been built on an insecure and ambivalent foundation. Throughout slavery, colonialism and even today, the system imposed an ideology of masculinity and femininity while simultaneously refusing to build the socio-economic structures required to support it in practice. The quality of life of Caribbean men and women, enhanced by modernisation and development, is now threatened by economic crisis, a crisis which will inevitably impact on Caribbean gender identities and relationships.

Caribbean Gender Research

Caribbean men and women first appeared on the research agenda after the Report of the West India Royal Commission (1945). The Commission investigated social and economic conditions in the British Caribbean in an effort to devise and implement reform policies to prevent a recurrence of the 1930s riots. An important research focus which emerged was black family life which was denounced as 'abnormal' and 'dysfunctional' as the cornerstone of morally and socially integrated, stable society. Although families were labelled 'matrifocal', the reality of women's lives was much distorted by stereotypes of wives and mothers, confined to home, fully occupied with domesticity and child care, submissive to their 'husbands' and conforming to mainstream cultural prescriptions for social acceptance and mobility. Nevertheless, given this intensive focus on family, women from the start became the centre of attention in Caribbean research; men were defined as 'marginal' to family life and virtually invisible in these ethnographies.

Although anthropological and demographic studies of family and fertility maintained a focus on Caribbean men and women, the primary effort of Caribbean research during the 1960s was devoted to the construction of macro-level models which highlighted race, class and ethnicity and paid scant attention to sex and gender. It was not until the advent of the regional Women in the Caribbean Project (WICP) in 1979 that women and gender systematically reappeared in Caribbean scholarly discourse.

The WICP is, to date, the most extensive and ambitious project of its kind. It was designed to fill a knowledge gap in the social realities of Caribbean women's lives; to devise a theoretical framework for the analysis of women's roles; to develop guidelines for a cohesive social policy for women; to identify appropriate mechanisms for the dissemination of research results and to train a cadre of women in self-confidence and 'female-centred' research skills to make a meaningful contribution to Caribbean development (Massiah 1986: 1-2). Based at the Institute of Social and Economic Research at the University of the West Indies in Barbados, the project gathered together a multi-disciplinary team of over 25 researchers and numerous interviewers and conducted research in several Caribbean countries. Coverage was deliberately extended to accommodate variations in ethnicity, race and class (Massiah 1986: 12), but, operating within the discourse of 'women's studies' and specifically designed to make women visible, the project merely tacked on men in small scale, single country, group interviews (Barrow 1986). Despite several constraints, not least the reluctance of male colleagues to become fully involved in what they perceived to be 'female-segregated' research (Massiah 1986: 21-212), the project generated a large volume of documented evidence and provided the impetus for the formation of the

Women and Development Studies Groups (renamed the Gender and Development Studies Groups) located at each of the three campuses of the University of the West Indies.

The approach taken by the research team was to 'let Caribbean women speak for themselves', thereby clearing the analysis of premature allegiance to prevailing Eurocentric and androcentric theoretical perspectives (Anderson 1986: 291; Massiah 1986: 1). The general aim was not to 'stir in' Caribbean women, but by a thorough epistemological reconstruction, to create a truly indigenous understanding of their lives. The project questioned imported formulations of race and class, redefined several concepts such as 'work' and 'employment' in the lives of Caribbean women, refuted models which conceptualised women's place as private or domestic and explored theoretical perspectives through core concepts such as 'invisibility', 'autonomy' and 'equality' (Massiah 1986: 11, 22; Safa 1986). The project retrieved Caribbean women from the periphery of intellectual discourse, but, ultimately, did not fulfil its theoretical goals (Barriteau 1992: 8; Reddock 1993: 45-46; Safa 1986: 4).

The WICP generated a set of findings which were labelled 'contradictory', 'ambiguous' and 'inconsistent' (Anderson 1986: 314-318; Le Franc 1983; Safa 1986: 16). These were interpreted as evidence of theoretical newness, pointing to 'the need to push the theoretical analysis further' and implying that 'a complete integration of the findings will depend on the next phase of analysis' (Anderson 1986: 292). The project ended thus, with the conviction and the challenge that an integrated model of 'Caribbean woman' would be achieved with further conceptual and theoretical sophistication. Furthest from the minds of the researchers was the notion that this might be impossible. Convinced at the time not only by binary assumptions that women are different from men, but that, as Caribbean women, they have a unique identity – some integrative thread of experience – such a thought would have constituted an admission of theoretical helplessness and failure.

It is on this note that this collection picks up the story. The empiricist character of research on Caribbean men and women has persisted and the essays in this volume come from multi-disciplinary perspectives to lay the groundwork for Caribbean gender theory. The authors reject borrowed grand theory, especially neo-liberalism, and voice their distrust for meta-narratives of gender. They are, nevertheless, fully aware of Caribbean realities in which body and sex referents persist and are (mis)used to define as 'natural' and thereby to strengthen prevailing divisions of power, labour and sexuality. Essentialising 'the female' reinforces disadvantage and subordination, while the masculine counterpart sets stand-ards which not all men have the resources or power to match. Binary, confrontational gender ideology operates in the Caribbean to condemn men as 'marginal', put women in their place, constrain the lives of both and confuse gender relationships. In addition, although the language of this collection moves towards post-modernism and reduces the urgency of gendered policy formulation, this has not altogether disappeared.

The shift from 'women only' to 'woman and man', and from 'women's studies' to 'gender studies', has directed attention to gender as a social and cultural construct. This introduces into theory the notion that gen-dered identities are multiple and mutable, sub-culturally specific and historically variable. They are also mutually influential and overlapping, even interchangeable. However, despite the swing to gender, a feminist lens has been maintained in this collection. Studies of Caribbean mascu-linity and gender relations from a masculinist consciousness and view-point are appearing slowly, but much of the initiative has been taken by women scholars. The one regret of this collection is the relative lack of response from male colleagues, only three ultimately submitting essays and two of them jointly.

Gender ideologies are patterns of ideas which shape beliefs and atti-tudes about appropriate identities and behaviours of men and women. They also explain and legitimate these identities within the cultural milieu of particular societies. Feminists may argue that gender is a social con-struct, but dominant ideologies reinforce patriarchy by justifying gen-dered identities and power relations as natural and universal, and there-fore fixed and unquestionable. However, gender essentialism is partial and selective. In the Caribbean, it is contradicted by the lived realities of men and women which shape and are moulded by their own gender knowledge and ideas which, in turn, retain the cultural symbolism of Africa, Europe, India and China. In addition, Caribbean gender ideologies articulate with others such as imperialism, capitalism or racism. When Afro-Caribbean or Indo-Caribbean women challenge received femininity, therefore, they confront the triple subordination of race, class and sex. Their menfolk may maintain domestic patriarchy on essentialist grounds, but they face race and class barriers, and are relegated to the periphery by a masculine ideology which is not their own. Thus, reductionist essentialism persists despite the variety, complexity and fluidity of Carib-bean masculinities and femininities. Caribbean gender studies continue to search for theoretical consistency within the diversity of race, colour, class, culture and life cycle, acknowledging Caribbean gender ideologies and identities as products of the convergence and articulation between all of these variables.

This collection has been divided for convenience of reading into five sections. However, the volume did not emerge with essays pre-categorised into specific themes. As a result, the division here is somewhat arbitrary and individual essays may speak to more than one theme.

Section One

The Political Economy of Labour Force Feminisation, Women's Work and Gender Relations

During the years of economic crisis, structural adjustment and impoverishment, women in the Caribbean, as elsewhere, have become increasingly visible in the labour market, while the participation of men has declined. Girls are also out-stripping boys at school and university. But, ask Klaus de Albuquerque and Sam Ruark, does this signify the ascendance of women? Are men 'at risk' or are women simply catching up? The analysis of official statistical evidence for selected Caribbean countries clearly confirms women's advance but, obscured by the highly aggregated data, are the details of persistent discrimination against women in employment, occupational status and remuneration. Although women have some way to go, it is incumbent on feminist researchers to evaluate their progress, rather than cling to the well-worn themes of economic marginalisation and exploitation.

The feminisation of the labour force is due, at least in part, to an employer preference for women based on patriarchal assumptions of a labour reservoir of daughters and wives, whose employment and earnings are merely supplementary to family welfare and who possess the required docile, malleable personality type. However, as Carla Freeman points out, the new high-tech informatics industry in Barbados has refashioned its labour profile in accordance with local gender images. To the international stereotype of 'docile girl', satisfied with 'pin money' and unencumbered by family responsibilities, is added a new ideal worker, the 'matriarch' – the hard-working, dependable mother, household head and family manager. In comparison with her, the school leaver is frivolous, self-indulgent and unreliable. The Barbados experience also refutes the high-turnover, foot-loose global assembly line stereotype. The employment strategy is to retain and develop a semi-permanent cadre of workers, socialised to maturity and loyalty within the company.

The fluid and adaptable gendering of work is also evident in definitions of appropriate employment. On occasions, women may even move into 'man's work' as illustrated in Alissa Trotz's examination of the private security sector in Guyana. Pervasive authoritarianism, militarisation, social and economic deterioration and escalating crime have contributed to a high demand for security services. With households in crisis, more women have entered the labour market and numerically dominate the security services. They are welcomed as more trustworthy, reliable and, because of their own sexual vulnerability, more vigilant. Nevertheless, their presence in what is clearly signified as male employment provokes resistant outbursts, calling on 'natural' female attributes. Women are too hysterical and indecisive to be armed and in action. Working alone and at night, they must be neglecting homes and children, and either exposing their bodies to the risk of attack or soliciting sexual favours. Thus women remain on the lower ranks of the service, as domestic guardians of other people's homes and children.

For Lynn Bolles, the study of women in the Caribbean trade union movement requires a 'multiple theorising guide' which addresses the 'matrix of domination' by combining an appreciation of the triple oppression of race, class and gender. She defines a reflexive anthropological role for herself, that of 'facilitator', enabling younger, female trade unionists to listen to and learn from their predecessors, some of whom carry memories and experiences of the movement from its genesis in the 1930s. Women in the labour movement have internalised gender stereotypes and suffered the effects. They have little confidence in themselves or each other and are frustrated and critical of their own involvement in what they know to be highly patriarchal associations. They are bypassed in critical contract negotiations, deprived of resources and training, and what influence they have had has been confined to routine matters of office management, social welfare and support services. A woman who challenges this is an 'upstart', who 'must be put in her place'. And yet, Bolles concludes that without women, the Caribbean labour movement would have 'come to a sudden halt years ago'.

Families and households are not immune to global and national economic processes. Marietta Morrissey endorses the recent theoretical shift to the political economy of gender relations which exposes the inter-relatedness of women's and men's labour market experiences. Women's numerical predominance in the labour force reinforces male economic marginality and signifies a reduction in real wages. Families are further impoverished as women resist a conjugality which increasingly signifies submission, restriction and added domestic responsibility. Morrissey urges the adoption of policies in which State and interest groups provide employment and social services to empower all working people – men women and their families – marginalised by recent economic trends.

Section Two

Hegemony, Patriarchy and the Creation of a Caribbean People's Culture

Hilary Beckles' paper centres women in the making and re-making of gender during slavery. Caribbean slave society experienced the encounter of a West African and a European gender ideology which clashed, but which also shared some general principles of masculinity and patriarchy. To this the Caribbean system added its own unique features. In their justification of female slave labour, West Indian planters were fully aware of African codes defining agriculture as woman's work and placing them in positions of lowest status. They also added a defeminised black female identity of 'brutish chattel'. Later, as the political economy of slavery required the breeding as against the buying of slaves and as the abolitionist campaign centred its challenge on the woman's condition, female slaves were recast as women, especially as mothers. Beckles concludes that feminist knowledge, theory and liberation is best served by a history which understands how evolving communities thought about and practised gender, along with race and class, in changing social, economic and ideological contexts.

The theme of the post-emancipation reconstitution of rural villages and a people's culture in the context of plantation economies and land monopolisation is being reworked through a gendered lens. While acknowledging pan-Caribbean perspectives, recent research also highlights specific country and village features of the colonial/Creole encounter in shaping and engendering Caribbean peasantries. In Barbados, for example, as Janet Momsen shows, women's land ownership and agricultural productivity, though facilitated by formal legal equality, was restricted, even reversed in accordance with dominant ideologies of domestication and respectability. In this ecology of extreme land scarcity and marginalised female farming, women developed their own ideology of land as a social and symbolic, rather than an economic resource. Their minuscule plots – their kitchen gardens and family yards – were sites of independence from the plantation and symbolised their own special space of resistance.

Noting that neither the 'female focus' nor the 'male bias' of anthropology captures gender ideology in Caribbean peasant villages, Jean Besson advances the unitary theme of 'gender complementarity' within dynamic Caribbean culture building. Her research in eight post-emancipation Jamaican communities, reveals diversity and a shift between gender symmetry and a male or female orientation. This is featured in land holding and transmission, in kinship, in marketing roles and rotating credit associations, in ritual identities and in the ancestral heroes and heroines of village oral history.

According to the paper by Diane Austin-Broos, Pentecostal churches offer to Jamaican women a redefinition of their life's condition by providing the opportunity for creative autonomy, for the exercise of ritual and social skills and for leadership, dignity and status. At the periphery of national politics and labour movements and morally outcast as unmarried household heads by orthodox Christianity and dominant feminine ideologies, women respond by valorising their suffering and circumstance in pentecostalism. Neighbourhood churches represent for the mature woman a place for rebirth as a 'bride of Christ' and a source of healing, support and solidarity. But, while pentecostalism offers the milieu for autonomous creative resistance, it also harbours the hegemony and racialism of North America.

Section Three

Acquiring Gendered Identities: Socialisation and Schooling

Gender is acquired, not inherited. It is a social construct, not an innate quality. But, as Monica Payne points out, the process by which gender is acquired and enacted remains somewhat obscure in the Caribbean and awaits the contribution of a gendered psychology. The advantage is that Caribbean psychology starts with a relatively clean slate, unencumbered by the neutral, standardised universals of Western positivism and hegemonic discourses of gender. The way forward, as Payne sees it, requires the establishment of an empirical data base, the full acknowledgement of the social context of gender domination and the embrace of certain of the possibilities of social constructionism.

Women are socialised into 'caring labour' which, though essential for the quality of human life, is undervalued. Drawing on journal entries and dreams, Nan Peacocke's personalised narrative reflects her family's experience of her father's last five years with Alzheimer's disease. By a process of subjective reinterpretation and self-repositioning, she comes to disavow her earlier feminist stance, which sentimentalised and subordinated female social reproduction, and to exalt the occupation of caring. She finds identity and power, motivation and agency in the experience and urges that men enter the relational space of caring labour.

Barbara Bailey's literature review points out that gendered research in Caribbean education remains predominantly grounded in the language and concerns of liberal feminism. The dominant theme of sex role socialisation is evident in stereotypes of anxious, uncertain girls, selecting safe 'feminine' courses of study and sexism in textbook images. Institutionalised invisibility, subordination and isolation from decision making is the lot of women in educational professions. Assuming the State to be benevolent and just and the educational system essentially 'good', Caribbean educational research remains preoccupied with identifying and eliminating the barriers to full female integration. Bailey, however, recommends that the research and policy agenda for the future adopts a radical, transformational theoretical approach.

Rhonda Ferreira Habersham returns to gender ideology and practice in Caribbean colonial education, filling in the gaps left by history with the personal literary perspectives presented in a selection of Caribbean novels. School girls – Tee, Laeticia, Anjanee, Beka and Angel – lead double lives. Education promises them an escape to an exotic world of blond hair, spring, orchards and operettas, of virgin purity and happy families. But the interplay of these idyllic images with their own devalued home lives, compounded by the triple jeopardy of sex, class and race converge in the young girls' psyches. Shame, alienation and breakdown are the result. As Anjanee's suicide demonstrates, the contradictions between the East Indian patriarchal family and female educational achievement can destroy a young girl. Only the few, like Angel, break through to rediscovery in the university domain of gender equality and revolution.

Elsa Leo-Rhynie examines a pioneering project on gender socialisation in Dominica, Jamaica and Guyana. The results reveal a pervasive and disturbing essentialist polarisation in Caribbean gender images. Fathering is defined as material and disciplinary, not interactive and emotional, while woman's identity centres on motherhood and the close mother-child bond. Space is gendered and separate – girls belong inside the house and yard, while boys' territory lies beyond. But women challenge ascribed femininity by enhancing economic autonomy and conjugal authority, boldly initiating sexual liaisons and turning to lesbianism. Men adopt an aggressive masculinity and homophobia. Conjugal relations are confron-

tational, even violent. Leo-Rhynie proposes interventions in gender socialisation for positive male/female relationships and nation building.

Section Four

Representations of Femininity and Masculinity: Embodiment, Sexuality and Family

Drawing on a range of feminist and post-colonial theorisations of the
body, Denise deCaires Narain focuses on the different representations of
the black female body in the texts of three Caribbean women writers –
Grace Nichols, Erna Brodber and Marlene Nourbese Philip. In these
literary texts, the body functions at thematic and aesthetic levels as a site
of contestation, resulting in a series of diverse, often contradictory, inscriptions and strategies for recovery. Her paper also interrogates the connections between sexuality and textuality and between sexuality and power.
She concludes with the challenge that critical practice should avoid
privileging any one interpretation, but should recognise these diverse
articulations as exemplifying the 'complexity and infinite inscriptability'
of the woman's body itself.

Caroline Allen tackles the complex interplay between gender and race
as reflected in embodied representations of masculinity and femininity.
Body image produces and reproduces definitions of self and others, but is
also a target and tool of social control. An elaborate series of binary
oppositions, based on an assumed primary distinction between mind and
body, project colonial, patriarchal and racial constructions by claiming
moral ascendancy for the white male mind. The black and the female are
objectified and debased. The recent 'fitness culture' of bodily care both
reproduces and resists these constructions. Contestations of feminine
identity centre on the body, dress and place – the madonna construct of
sexual purity and repressive respectability is challenged by public, shameless displays of Carnival 'wining'. Allen suggests that resistance should
celebrate the 'hybridity of Caribbean culture', but warns that present day
image-building professionals and advertising manipulate bodily anxieties
in men and women and, in the process, transform and commodify the
politics of resistance into consumer style.

From her review of Caribbean women writers, Evelyn O'Callaghan
concludes that they subscribe to 'compulsory heterosexuality'. Heterosexuality is represented as normal, while homosexuality is deviant, abhorrent and silenced. Raised by her mother under the rule of heterosexu-

ality, a young girl is required to sever female bonds and fantasies for real sex with men. As a woman, she is the opposite of a man and incomplete without him. A lesbian, therefore, is not a woman; her sexuality is 'unnatural' and must be suppressed. And yet, the female heterosexual experience is portrayed either as a sordid event leading to inevitable pregnancy, downfall and destitution or as an emotionally empty act of submission to a male predator. O'Callaghan asks: Is the problem hetero-sexuality itself? Is not heterosexuality integral to an institutionally con-structed femininity of shame, constraint and subordination? Cosmopoli-tan tolerance abroad frees 'newer' Caribbean women writers to explore the range of 'lesbian experience' – the renewal of mutual tenderness and sensuality and the recovery of motherland. Male homosexuality, on the other hand, continues to be linked to dysfunctional motherhood – to maternal abandonment and damnation.

Sharing the view that popular culture contributes to shaping gender identities, Jane Bryce exposes the gap and explores the tension between Ideal and Real man and woman in the romantic fiction series, Caribbean Caresses. The authors reclaim the reality of the Caribbean woman by indigenising the heroine: the artificial femininity of the slim, submissive Lady is replaced with the dark-skinned, successful businesswoman. The theme of overcoming obstacles to achieve love, tenderness and fidelity is a Caribbean reality, but the local formula does not require women to passively accept typical male behaviour. In addition, a revisionary hero appears – sensitive, caring, trustworthy – though the heroine is not always fully convinced by the transformation. Most 'unReal' of all in these Caribbean novels is the conformity to editorial prescriptions for sexual reticence and morality.

Functionalist images of Caribbean masculinity encoded in 'margin-ality' and 'reputation' persist virtually unchallenged. Through the narratives of Barbadian men, Christine Barrow revisits men and family by foregrounding extended family roles, by reassessing the perform-ance of fathers and conjugal partners and by relocating masculinity, at least in part, within the family and gender relationships. Binary models which reduce Caribbean masculinity to socio-economically determined 'marginality' and 'irresponsibility' are replaced by mascu-linity defined as multiple, mutable and ambivalent. Conjugal relation-ships may be problematic, male symbolic space may be 'outside' the household and manhood valorised in 'deviant', peer group perform-ance, but masculinity is not entirely separate from nor opposed to femininity, the family or the State.

Section Five

Women's Power in a Man's World:
Contestations of Race and Culture

Marina Warner explores the place, and the power, of the native woman in the ambiguous alliances of inclusion and exclusion forged during the early years of the colonial encounter. Madame Ouvernard, a Kalinago (Carib) woman who married Sir Thomas Warner, the first English governor in the West Indies, and bore him many children, is a most ambivalent figure. She is obscured in the master-narrative of empire and silenced by British colonial justice which refuses her testimony and denies the identity, paternity and fratricide – at the hands of his white half brother – of her son 'Indian' Warner. Invisible though she is in history, she nevertheless features vividly in mythology. Like her counterpart, Uma, in Robert Louis Stevenson's short story, Madame Ouvernard belongs to two worlds – a hyphen, disrupting the boundaries between the indigenous nature/forest and the coloniser's civilisation/plantation. The native woman is the beguiled lover of the invaders, treacherous betrayer of her people and the land. But, beautiful and enchanting while young and revered in naked, bent extreme old age, she is also the 'female savage', soucouyant and cloven-hoofed diablesse – sexually and magically potent, mysterious and untameable.

From the childhood foundation that 'woman talk' has provided in shaping her personal experience and consciousness as a writer, Merle Collins interrogates theoretical and political issues. These 'vinegar-honey' stories are private narratives of apparent resignation in a world that is male and white, but they also socialise and empower. However, although race and class are issues for open discussion, women find it difficult to translate their secret codes to confront gender issues in the public arena, for example, in the politics of revolutionary Grenada. As gender concerns are globalised in public fora, Collins urges that we appreciate the subjectivity and multi-dimensional experience of race, class and gender.

Patricia Mohammed's paper traces the formulation of a united Indian mythology, which overwrote historical and religious variation, to serve the interests of a reconstituted classic Indian cultural tradition and gender identity in Trinidad. Pivotal is the myth of Ram and Sita. Ram represents the masculine prototype, while Sita embodies feminine purity, chastity, duty and devotion. Male and female identities are intertwined – her virtue preserves his honour – and her sexuality must therefore be controlled.

Through religious festivals and prayer meetings, film and folktale, it was Indian men who promoted these ideals. Women have generally colluded, but rebellious indentured ancestors and some young women of today contest the Sita model and the chains of Indian femininity and, in doing so, threaten masculinity.

Rhoda Reddock examines four decades of nationalist contestation in which Indian and African, lower and middle class, high and low caste, male and female in Trinidad and Tobago have struggled for authenticity and representation in national culture and national identity. The challenge centres on the predominantly Creole symbols of Mas (carnival masquerade), calypso and pan (steelband). The Indian response has varied – from outright rejection of Creole forms as obscene; to the creation of Indo-Trinidadian alternatives in 'Chutney' music and dance; to a tentative and predominantly male participation. Reddock suggests that Creole Carnival and the Indian 'spring' festival of *Holi* or *Phagwa* share a common origin in pre-Christian and pre-Hindu celebrations which link agricultural productivity with female sexuality and fertility. And yet, women's public participation is 'debauchery and obscenity' and provokes much protest. Middle-class creole women are being 'led astray', while their Indian counterparts 'stain sacred womanhood', forsaking purity for 'sex, wine and easy money'. Despite these stereotypes, Reddock identifies a special political responsibility for women to engage in this discourse which, she fervently hopes, will provide the foundation for a truly inclusive national culture and identity.

Eudine Barriteau disputes the inheritance of enlightenment liberalism in Caribbean state ideology and gender relations. The division of society into male-public and female-private domains and the subordination of the latter continue to generate contradictions in women's lives. In Barbados, state policy has successfully altered the material relations of gender by expanding women's public participation and relevance. But the ideological premises of a 'natural' female inferiority and private patriarchy remain unchallenged. Liberal philosophy cannot accommodate women's equality. The situation provokes a misogynous outrage, which holds women accountable for the problems experienced by boys and men, predicts a conspiracy to establish a matriarchal society, opposes women's citizenship and calls for their return to their proper, private place.

Gender Ideologies and Identities

As small island states with virtually no indigenous peoples and cultures, with imported populations 'seasoned' and acculturated by slavery and indenture, and with open societies and economies, Caribbean countries have experienced not only the longest, but also the most penetrating form of colonialism and imperialism. Together with the exercise of power and force, the imperialist project centred its domination on an ideological complex combining liberalism, patriarchy and racism. In the Caribbean, the grand liberal principles of individual freedom, equality and democracy were overwritten by an essentialism of race and gender. The social domains of inclusion and exclusion, ambiguous and flexible enough during the early colonial encounter to allow individuals like Madame Ouvernard and Sir Thomas Warner to traverse the boundaries (Warner), were increasingly concretised. Thus, racial and gendered identities of all men and women became clearly modeled and prescribed.

Imperialist ideology defines a world of opposites. The categories 'woman' and 'man', 'black' and 'white' are biologically determined; they are natural, unequivocal and fixed. The white male mind is at the centre of the universe; the 'black', the 'female' and the 'body' are defined in relation to and below him (Allen). From a gender perspective, the woman is opposite or complementary, and invariably inferior: she is his deficient other. She is programmed to be cooperative, dependent and emotional; he to be individualistic, autonomous, and rational (Bailey, Payne). She, therefore, is best suited to the nurturing, caring roles of mother and homemaker and belongs at home, while he has the innate talents to venture into and succeed in the public domain of work and politics as breadwinner and authority figure. The logic is familiar, quite simple and, by prescribing a system which is promoted as functioning harmoniously and ensuring social stability, has wide appeal, even today.

Complications and challenges arise when attempts are made to translate these gender prescriptions into practice. Imperialist gender ideologies have never been operationalised in pure form either at home or abroad. Liberal rhetoric articulates with and is compromised not only by the tenets of racism and sexism, but also the demands of capitalism. In effect, capitalism is deprived of a source of cheap labour to exploit if the model for women is motherhood, domesticity and home confinement. Conversely, depriving men of employment opportunities or paying them low wages undermines their prescribed roles as family providers and household heads.

Furthermore, the colonial encounter is invariably shaped by local ideas and conditions. The western 'natural' gender identities are, in fact, unnatural to the majority of the Caribbean population; they are integral to the privileged colonial ideology and alien to African and Indian gender patterns. Black women, in particular, live the contradictions of a Euro-derived ideology of female subordination and the African woman-centred tradition (Bolles). Away from home, patriarchal ideologies may even shift to an 'apparent gender neutrality' evident, for example, in the Barbadian laws relating to land holding (Momsen). Several dominant local groups, defending a variety of interests, may also make their input. The results are graphically illustrated in Caribbean post-emancipation society where the efforts of the colonial state to engender and properly socialise the ex-slaves were riddled with contradictions as colonial officials, planters, clergymen and employers pursued their different agendas. Even within each group, ambivalent attitudes and behaviour prevailed, contesting gender ideology and capitalist practice. Planters, for example, generally supported the domestication of women, but they also preferred female labour and, having employed women, proceeded to criticise them for neglecting their children (Momsen). What is amazing overall, is the capacity of dominant males to live with and manage the turbulence of paradox and contradiction that characterises their world (Beckles).

Despite this ambivalence, the principles of liberalism and patriarchy were 'absorbed uncritically', even 'proudly maintained' (Barriteau), and the process of essentialising masculinity and femininity in the service of 'civilised' society was relentlessly pursued. The contribution of dominant social institutions – religion and education in particular – was harnessed. The role of the school was to promote the sex role socialisation and gender asymmetry fundamental to the reproduction of social hierarchy and order (Bailey). In the socialisation of Indian girls and women, imperialist patriarchy was reinforced by Indian tradition. The model for Indian gender in Trinidad was provided by a selective reinterpretation of Hindu legend and mythology, invoking the ideals of Ram and Sita (Mohammed) and silencing the powerful Goddess Kali (Reddock).

Powerful as these imperial gender ideologies were and are, cultural diffusion is not a one-way, top-down domination which silences all other voices. African symbolism, beliefs and practices have survived to contribute to a reconstituted Creole culture (Austin-Broos, Besson, Momsen) and, as mentioned, Indian traditions and mythology have been consciously revived (Mohammed, Reddock). Neither was the white population isolated from African and Creole folk norms (Reddock). In other words, the imperialist blueprint was not translated into practice in the Caribbean, even among the white populations, far less the black and Indian.

Caribbean Gender Identities

The social construction of gender identities involves an understanding of how men and women interpret their world and their place within it; of how they have creatively moulded their identities as they accept, reshape or resist gender stereotypes – including the received imperialist images of ideal man and ideal woman. The essays in this collection make a contribution by exploring the way in which Caribbean masculinities and femininities are defined, acquired, expressed and changed as men and women negotiate the tensions between the Ideal and the Real (Bryce). The summary that follows deals first with the theme of work and space, and then resistance and power.

Work and Space

The concept of a 'male public domain' has been rewritten from a post-modernist perspective as 'male symbolic space'. Caribbean masculinity is confirmed 'outside' – as a 'man among men' in rum shop and street corner performances (Barrow, Reddock). This arena also constitutes the training ground for the socialisation of boys (Leo-Rhynie), for the affirmation of masculine controlling behaviour (Peacocke). Boys adopt behaviour and attitudes contrary to the school ethos (Bailey). They forsake higher education to move into the world of work and consumer durables – the status symbols of masculinity (de Albuquerque and Ruark). Despite the expectation that men will 'settle down' and take on family responsibilities as they mature, black masculinity is firmly centred in virility (Barrow), on pride in the belief that black male heterosexual prowess is superior to that of other all ethnic groups (Reddock). Even as Caribbean men are praised for good parenting and conjugal sensitivity (Barrow) and, even as new masculine images of romantic heros (Bryce) and 'spiritual redeemer figures' (deCaires Narain) appear, any display of emotion or move to the 'inside' threatens masculinity. Emotion and vulnerability are masked by physical fitness and body building – by the masculine signifiers of 'size' and 'hardness' (Allen). With homosexuality condemned in the Caribbean, especially in the virulently homophobic culture of Jamaica (Leo-Rhynie, O'Callaghan) but also in the Barbadian climate of reluctant tolerance (Barriteau), the dangers to the masculine image are all too real.

The public arena continues to be defined as male space into which not all women move easily. In general, the right of Indian women to physical mobility and 'working out' is severely constrained (Mohammed, Reddock, Trotz). In addition, the lives of middle-class women are more tied to the etiquette of 'tea time' (Bolles) than those of their lower-class counterparts. As they venture into the man's world of trade unionism, they must be seen to put their responsibilities as mothers, wives and homemakers first (Bolles). The younger female generation is also more spatially confined. Their play is more sedentary (Allen) and instilled into them at puberty is the precept that the territory beyond the house and yard represents a place of danger – of sexual assault, pregnancy and downfall (Leo-Rhynie). Women's physical exercise takes place inside – to be outside is to be the object of sexist taunts and to risk assault (Allen).

What physical mobility women have, should take them into church and school, that is into other domains symbolising orthodox morality and social order. Indeed, education appears to be fast becoming a feminine space of success and social mobility (Bailey, de Albuquerque and Ruark), although within the ethos of a colonial education system their progress is not without its costs. As young girls negotiate the chasm between their own 'backward' home and village lifestyles and the lure of exotic school textbook images, they lose their own identity and space – they move up but no longer have any place to go (Ferreira Habersham).

Women of the Caribbean – native, exslave or Indian – have never really stayed in their allotted place (Mohammed, Reddock, Warner). Afro-Caribbean women have never been confined to the 'domestic domain'. Income generation is integral to their identities as mothers and their very survival and that of their children has always depended on their ability to juggle multiple roles at home and at work. In Trinidad, even middle-class women have contested the boundaries of private seclusion and taken over masquerade, though not without public censure as they break with decency and motherhood in a 'wave of abandon' and 'vulgar bawdy Africanism' (Reddock).

Appropriate work for men and women is also prescribed by essentialist doctrines. Occupations requiring physical strength, mental ability and leadership aptitude are delineated as 'male', while jobs stereotyped as 'female' are those which extend a woman's 'natural' disposition for caring and homemaking. Status considerations also distinguish work by gender. Slave men objected to menial agricultural labour which their West African cultural heritage defined as women's work. Because the work of women is devalued relative to that of men, it is also cheaper – this despite the absence of any 'weak feminine' black female stereotype (Collins). Economic development in the Caribbean has taken full advantage of women's labour, biologically and psychologically programmed to be dexterous, docile and sit still for long hours of tedious work. Furthermore, by selectively accommodating local gender myths, corporate capitalist logic cleverly manipulates labour force composition. The high-tech industry of Barbados, for example, exploits the popular Caribbean stereotype of the 'strong black matriarch'. It makes more economic sense to retain a loyal work force of these mature mothers and household heads than to follow the global pattern by hiring and firing young girls at will (Freeman). Similarly, because the Guyanese woman's self-image identifies security work as appropriate, so, in the absence of men, the service calls on their labour (Trotz). Thus, as economic enterprise willingly recruits, accommodates and exploits a local female workforce, profit maximisation is not compromised and may even be enhanced (de Albuquerque and Ruark, Freeman, Morrissey, Trotz).

To jump to the conclusion that the preference for female labour signifies Caribbean woman's ascendancy is to ignore high female unemployment rates and low wages, glass ceilings and pervasive occupational discrimination (de Albuquerque and Ruark). The feminisation of the workforce signifies the lowering of labour market standards. This and the repatriation of social services to the household are gendered effects of Caribbean economic recession and structural adjustment. They are indicators of households in crisis and demand policy reformulation (Morrissey).

To the chagrin of essentialist thinkers, the division of labour by sex does not result in a clear and simple separation between male and female work. The contradictions of gendered work and space are most evident in situations where women contest their socio-spacial boundaries and enter the arenas of politics, trade unionism and man's work (Bolles, Reddock, Trotz). To do so, not only are they required to have higher qualifications and prove their competency to be as good as or better than that of men (de Albuquerque and Ruark, Bolles, Reddock, Trotz), they must also confront a constant barrage of sexism. When, for example, Guyanese women as security workers invade the ultimate male territory — the public arena at night – they carry with them a feminine essentialist burden which is used against them – to put them in their place. Even as the security service in Guyana becomes stereotyped as work for women and old men, the women continue to be harassed and humiliated, at home and on the job (Trotz). In the domain of trade unionism, a woman is similarly stereotyped. She is allowed in, but as a women, psychologically second class and therefore suited to supportive, social positions. Women in the Caribbean labour movement, 'stayed inside and did the clerical work', functioning as the 'right hand' to the 'born leader' (Bolles). Similarly, women who enter politics are relegated to the 'arms' and 'branches' of men's national parties (de Albuquerque and Ruark). Thus the subordination of women's work in Caribbean labour markets and political arenas is justified as 'natural', and the message to women is that, if they must work and leave home at all, as good wives and mothers, they should avoid unfeminine activities.

While cleverly manipulating the perceived strengths of Caribbean womanhood, the system, however, acknowledges feminine identity only so far. A worker may be preferred because she is a woman, a mature mother and household head, but as a worker on the job she is expected to leave these identities and responsibilities at home. One or two governments and industrial establishments may provide paid maternity leave and job security after child birth, but this is rare, as is the provision of child care facilities. The paradox of 'supplementary' wages for mothers and household heads and 'pin money' for young girls whose income is integral to the household budget (Freeman); and the contradiction of firing a security guard for returning to her children when the guard for the next shift fails to turn up (Trotz) are disregarded. Once again, the realities of women's lives are distorted and devalued by convenient myths and stereotypes.

Resistance and Power

Caribbean men and women have repeatedly contested the received gender identities of dominant regimes. Slave women subverted the de-feminisation project through their adornment and dress, their mothering and sexuality and their marketing activities and revolutionary struggles (Beckles). At the other extreme, they have also resisted the Victorian femininity of modesty and submission imposed on them after emancipation. Feminist writers contributing to this volume have taken issue with this version of femininity as it was captured in the value complex of 'respectability' and opposed to a Caribbean male 'reputation' (Wilson 1969). Among other things, Caribbean women were stereotyped as passive and accommodating supporters of orthodox morality and the social hierarchy. The feminist critique privileges Caribbean women's integral and equal part in cultures of resistance (Besson) and, despite restrictions on female resource control, in the creation of their own 'resistant symbolic space' in small scale land ownership (Momsen). Even Caribbean romantic fiction has challenged and indigenised the heroine by subverting the Ideal desirable lady and replacing her with the Real independent career woman (Bryce). Women also challenge the patriarchal order in brazen public Carnival displays (Allen, Reddock) and in lesbianism and resistance to conjugal authority (Leo-Rhynie). Their involvement in Pentecostal ritual is reinterpreted as an arena of 'female reputation', where women valorise their own life experiences without dependence on a man. Although women's activities, in Pentecostalism for example, may simultaneously reinforce a hegemonic status quo, resistance is no longer perceived as an exclusive privilege of men (Austin-Broos).

Any power that women have exists in contradiction to patriarchal ideologies. And, although these essays contest the outdated female images of passive and powerless 'respectability' and the themes of 'marginalisation', 'subordination' and the 'victim syndrome' (de Albuquerque and Ruark, Barriteau, deCaires Narain, Morrissey), they also recognise that women's power continues to be circumscribed. Women find their political voices within the boundaries of specified social units – in the NGO movement (de Albuquerque and Ruark), in Pentecostalism (Austin-Broos) and in matrifocal families (Morrissey). Feminist analysis may have redefined politics to encompass the personal and 'vinegar-honey stories' may empower women, but they are private narratives of gender, not translated on to the public political agenda (Collins). Caribbean women may be perceived as 'matriarchs' (Freeman), but since their authority does not transcend domestic space, those who head households are among the poorest and most destitute in Caribbean societies (de Albuquerque and Ruark, Morrissey). Women who enter the formal political and corporate arena are marginalised and, on the occasions that they raise their voices in public and assume power like men, they are labelled 'lesbian' and 'feminist', that is women who are out to emasculate men (Barriteau).

Women's power is portrayed as a relational power, not a power to change. The relationality of their 'caring labour', generally viewed as women's subordinate work, is reassessed as a source of empowerment and a doorway to rebellious consciousness (Peacocke). Women's power is also is described as non-sexist and democratic (Bolles). But it can be destructive. Women have a compelling hold on their children and enforce an obligatory heterosexuality on their daughters and sons (O'Callaghan). Although the relationship with her sons is usually emotionally close, mutually supportive and enduring (Barrow), it is she who viciously rejects her homosexual son with devastating effects (O'Callaghan).

Mythology and literary narratives locate women's power in orality, sexuality and the wild. With one foot in nature, women maintain a subversive power through their voices, their bodies and their sexuality. The Creole cacophony of women's tongues, representing sexuality and survival, subverts and will not be silenced by the arid, coldness of elite patriarchy and colonialism (deCaires Narain). Moreover, the black female body, once representing decay, pain, shame and oppression, has been rewritten as a vehicle for empowerment and healing (deCaires Narain). It is significant, therefore, that a central strategy of colonial settlement was the acquisition, assimilation and control of women. Masculinity may be deviant and men may be runaway maroons, but they are more amenable to domestication and civilisation – convertible to genial 'Uncle Toms' (Warner). In Hindu mythology also, Kali is the powerful, black, aboriginal goddess of death and destruction who represents 'a major spiritual threat to Hindu patriarchal orthodoxy' (Reddock). Women's power, therefore, is mythically potent, subterranean, often 'destructive'. But, although women may disrupt boundaries by contesting patriarchy and manipulating and undermining men, it seems they still have little power to change the world they live in.

Male and female empowerment interlock. The status of the lower-class, black man, already eroded by generations of white patriarchy and imperialism, is further threatened by the educational success of girls and the feminisation of the labour force within economic recession and crisis. The public reaction borders on hysteria — boys are deemed to be victimised, emasculated and devoid of male role models as women take over the teaching profession (Bailey). Alarm buttons are sounded and women take the blame for the 'crisis' of Caribbean masculinity (de Albuquerque and Ruark, Barriteau). Within gender relationships, for as long as masculinity means control over women, women have the potential to disrupt male identities. In the Indian community in Trinidad, male honour is dependent on female virtue. When she transgresses the limits of Indian femininity, she has a devastating effect on his self-esteem (Mohammed).

To be a Caribbean man is to be in control, especially of women. Politically peripheral, economically eroded and confronted by partners who increasingly resist public and domestic patriarchy, Caribbean men seek to re-establish control with the only resource they have left – physical force (Allen, Leo-Rhynie, Trotz). Indian men have in the past, vented their rage in the mutilation and murder of women or turned their frustration in on themselves and committed suicide (Mohammed). Paradoxically, as women make their way in the world of education, work and politics, domestic patriarchy may be forcefully re-established. The home may be her space, but it is his castle. Although the present generation of men may define gender equality, communication and sensitivity into their lives (Barrow), male/female relationships continue to be portrayed as a 'battle of the sexes' (Reddock). Interventions are necessary to change established patterns of gender socialisation and identity and to reverse conjugal double standards, distrust, discord and abuse (Leo-Rhynie).

The final note returns to the central theme of multiple gender ideologies and identities. The essays in this volume highlight the problem – maybe the impossibility – of constructing a Caribbean theoretical perspective representative of the multiple and changing portraits and experiences of all men and women of the region. Paradoxically therefore, in denying the unitary constructs, biological and social, of 'man' and 'woman', the discourse loses sight of Caribbean men and women just as they are becoming visible (Payne). However, from an alternative viewpoint, this cultural and ideological variety celebrates resilience in the face of persistent hegemonic pressure to mould Caribbean gender identities to conform to the binary ideologies of imperialism and nationalism, patriarchy and racism. That the contributors to this collection recognise this collage of masculinities and femininities is not a reflection of theoretical immaturity or failure but a challenge, and that they do so without silencing the common material realities of gender subordination, male and female, is a tribute Caribbean gender scholarship.

Note

1. Comments by Klaus de Albuquerque and Evelyn O'Callaghan on the first draft of this introduction are gratefully acknowledged.

The Political Economy of Labour Force Feminisation:
Women's Work and Gender Relations

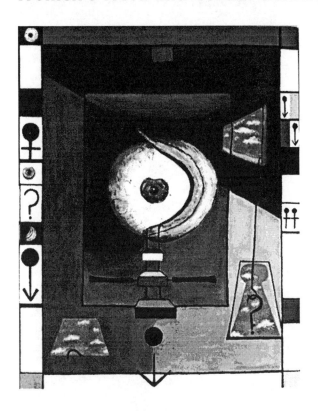

1

'Men Day Done':
Are Women Really Ascendant in the Caribbean?

Klaus de Albuquerque and Sam Ruark

Introduction

Errol Miller (1991: 283) proclaims that the third millennium belongs to women ('women will hold most of the positions of power with men as their lieutenants'). He contends that men in Caribbean societies, particularly those in the lower-strata, have become progressively marginalised. As evidence he points to 'boys' declining participation and performance in the educational system, the decline in the proportion of men in the highest-paying and most prestigious occupations and the decrease in men's earning power relative to women's' (Miller 1991: 93). Patterson (1993) writing in a somewhat similar vein lays to rest the sociological trope of the double/triple burden of African-American women and repeats the now familiar litany of statistics demonstrative of African-American females better life chances and higher educational attainment relative to their male counterparts. Unlike Miller, Patterson does not see this as a global phenomenon presaging a *fin de siecle* 'men day done'.

Not surprisingly, both Miller and Patterson have earned the ire of feminist scholars, although to be fair to Miller, many Caribbean feminists have misread his marginalisation hypothesis which locates the conflict, not between the genders, but between 'men of different groups'. In other words, Miller's marginalisation has to do with class rather than gender, with propertied males (many of whom are members of visible ethnic minorities) replacing lower-strata males with more compliant and harder working females. Miller (1991: 279-280) asserts further that women 'frustrated by the ceiling placed on their progress may find common cause with marginalized males' to depose powerful men, and that if and when this occurs, 'women would have had better education, experience, contacts, general exposure and confidence in matters of state, than the men. The commanding heights of power would therefore rest mainly with women.'

Miller's propitiary *Men at Risk* ('it would be good for humanity to have men languish at the margins for a while' (Miller 1991: 283) is based on minimal empirical data focusing largely on gender differences in the Jamaican educational system. However, it has served as a kind of clarion call, with the Vice-Chancellor of the University of the West Indies, and other prominent males throughout the English-speaking Caribbean, raising concerns about 'men falling behind'. But are men really falling behind or are women simply catching up? After all, the literature on Caribbean women continues to encapsulate their experiences under a few familiar themes, none of which suggests a significantly improved status for women. These themes include, marginalisation from the public domain (Anderson 1986; Dagenais 1993; Peake 1993), the invisibility of women's work, continued economic marginalisation i.e. women confined to small-scale farming and the informal sector (Anderson and Gordon 1989; Barrow 1993; Brierley 1993), the feminization of the tertiary, the exploitation of women in the informatics and offshore manufacturing sectors (Safa 1981; Gomez and Reddock 1987; Pearson 1993), and so on.

How can Caribbean women (we are referring to women in the English-speaking Caribbean in this paper) be ascendant and at the same time marginalised and exploited? Does this ascendancy have a class basis, with middle- and upper-class women narrowing the gender gap? Have Caribbean scholars, weaned on ethnographic studies of small communities and marginalised women and men, and trapped within their particular gender ideologies, fallen victim to the error of reductionism and failed to recognise the larger structural changes occurring around them? There certainly seems to be a penchant among some scholars studying gender in the Caribbean to eschew macro-level evidence in favour of a kind of subjective, anecdotal approach. It is one thing to point out, as Massiah (1986) and Senior (1991) have done, that earlier censuses tended to underestimate women's contribution to economic activities, but quite another to blithely ignore new and improved official statistics, including census data, that underscore the changing status of women and men in the Caribbean.

Since 1970, most English-speaking Caribbean states have made significant progress towards greater gender equality – most notably, the Bahamas, Barbados, Guyana, Jamaica and Trinidad and Tobago (these are the states for which the UNDP reports data on gender-related development and gender empowerment). Barbados, for example, ranks 11 in terms of its gender-related development index (GDI), above such countries as New Zealand, the United Kingdom, Belgium, Switzerland, and the Netherlands (the GDI, a variant of the human development index (HDI), measures life expectancy, educational attainment, and income of women relative to men). The 1995 Human Development Report notes that there is less gender inequality in the Caribbean than other regions in the world. Relative to the HDI, the GDI in Barbados is only two per cent lower, in Cuba six per cent, and in the Bahamas, seven per cent (UNDP 1995). The Caribbean also does well with regards to gender empowerment (GEM), which measures women's participation in economic (female share of earned income), political (percentage share of parliamentary representatives) and professional (proportion of women in administrative, managerial, professional and technical positions) terms. Barbados ranks 12 overall in terms of GEM, the Bahamas 14, Trinidad and Tobago, 15, and Cuba, 16, above such countries as Switzerland, the United Kingdom, Belgium, and France. Clearly, as far as aggregate measures are concerned, Caribbean women are doing better than their counterparts in more industrialised countries.

The question this chapter attempts to address is simple. Are Caribbean women really doing as well as the highly aggregated data that is used to compute the GDI and GEM would suggest, or are women still experiencing continued economic marginalisation and political disenfranchisement? As a corollary, we will also attempt to address if Caribbean men are 'at risk' as Miller and others have contended.

Data and Discussion

Census data can provide us with some answers and Tables 1.1-1.3 present data on labour force participation, education, occupation, income and households, by gender. Reasonably comparable census data between 1970 and 1990-91, were available only for Barbados, Dominica, St Lucia, and St Vincent. The census data should be interpreted with the usual caveats regarding content and coverage errors and lack of strict comparability of definitions and categories (e.g. occupational groups) from one census to another. Nevertheless, our concerns are with relative differences between the genders rather than absolute differences.

There is one area, namely economic activity, where current census questions may lead to error. Caribbean women, in general, do not report themselves as 'unemployed' if they are by default engaged in 'home duties' or other non-remunerative labour. Yet if a reasonable wage/salary job became available, many would willingly accept it. So hidden unemployment is much greater among women than men, especially women in older age cohorts (this explains the lower official unemployment rates for 40-59-year-old females in Table 1.1). In addition, women are much more likely to be involved in the informal sector, and therefore often missed in official employment statistics.

Despite these caveats, female labour force participation rates (LFPRs) show significant increases for all four islands between 1970 and 1990-91, while male rates have declined marginally (Table 1.1). Falling participation rates for men (except St Vincent) cannot be blamed on women entering the labour force in proportionately greater numbers (there is no zero sum calculus as Errol Miller and others imply), but rather on the changing structure of the economies of all four islands, particularly the declining contribution of agriculture to the gross domestic product (McElroy and de Albuquerque 1990), growth in the manufacturing sector (now stagnating), and rapid expansion in the tertiary (services) sector.

Women have also experienced greater occupational diversification. In all four islands the percentages of all employed women in 'professional and technical' and 'administrative and managerial' positions has increased significantly (Table 1. 2). The fact that in both 1970 and 1990-91, there were proportionately more women employed in 'professional and technical' fields, should be interpreted with caution, since this aggregated category masks the fact that men continue to dominate the higher paying and more prestigious occupations of medicine and law while women dominate nursing and teaching. The category of 'administrative and management' provides a somewhat better gauge of the improved occupational status of women. In Dominica, St Lucia, and St Vincent, the proportion (though not numbers) of women employed as administrators and managers exceeds that of men. Women have clearly made strides in this area, from negligible participation in 1970 (less that one per cent of all employed females) to a high of 9.7 per cent in Dominica. Proportionately, there are now more females employed in administrative and management positions in Dominica, St Lucia, and St Vincent, but we

Table 1.1 Labour force participation, unemployment and educational attainment by gender 1970 and 1990-91

Island, Year and Age Group		Labour Force Participation Rate[a] (%)		Unemployment (%)		% Population 15+ by Highest level of Education			
						Secondary[b]		University	
		M	F	M	F	M	F	M	F
Barbados									
1970	20-39	95.7	61.2	4.8	5.7	85.2	85.2	2.3	1.2
	40-59	94.1	47.8	1.6	1.0	63.5	60.4	1.8	0.8
1990	20-39	92.2	77.9	8.6	9.9	61.0	63.9	5.4	5.5
	40-59	90.8	65.0	3.6	2.8	31.6	31.2	8.1	4.7
Dominica									
1970	20-39	96.3	48.7	3.3	3.3	11.2	9.7	1.5	0.7
	40-59	92.6	40.6	1.1	0.5	4.3	3.4	1.9	0.6
1991	20-39	89.7	53.3	8.2	5.8	16.0	27.7	2.9	2.0
	40-59	87.9	43.7	3.2	1.3	8.0	7.4	4.6	2.5
St Lucia									
1970	20-39	95.3	43.2	5.6	3.9	1.9	0.6	14.6	6.6
	40-59	91.5	35.6	3.2	1.1	1.6	0.3	3.6	3.3
1991	20-39	91.9	63.7	5.5	4.1	3.0	2.2	22.6	32.5
	40-59	90.3	50.9	2.8	0.9	5.1	2.2	6.8	7.2
St Vincent									
1970	20-39	95.2	43.8	6.4	4.2	10.3	8.1	1.3	0.4
	40-59	91.3	36.9	3.2	1.0	4.6	3.6	1.6	0.2
1991	20-39	95.3[c]	60.9	15.8	13.4	n.a.	n.a.	n.a.	n.a.
	40-59	91.9	47.9	10.2	3.9	n.a.	n.a.	n.a.	n.a.

Sources: 1970 Population census of the Commonwealth Caribbean, Barbados, Dominica, St Lucia and St Vincent.
1990 Population and housing census, Barbados, Vol. 1.
1991 Population and housing census, Commonwealth of Dominica
1991 Population and housing census, St Lucia Vol. 2 and Vol. 6
1991 Population and housing census, St Vincent and the Grenadines, Vol. 2

Notes: a. 12 months before the census
b. Does not include post-secondary or pre-university
c. Week before the census

Table 1.2 Occupation and Income by Gender, 1970 and 1990/91

| Island and Year | Occupational group[a] (adults 14 years and older not attending school) | | | | | | | | | | Mean Annual Income[b] | |
| | Professional and Technical (%) | | Administrative and Management (%) | | Clerical (%) | | Sales and Services (%) | | Production and Trades (%) | | | |
	M	F	M	F	M	F	M	F	M	F	M	F
Barbados												
1970	9.4	9.4	2.1	0.4	6.2	13.7	17.5	46.0	38.9	12.7	2,423	1,510
1990[c]	25.8	33.5	5.0	3.5	2.4	27.3	11.5	16.5	51.2	16.7	16,424	12,410
Dominica												
1970	4.4	11.4	1.0	0.3	3.4	9.1	7.3	36.6	26.3	9.7	1,767	926
1991	8.9	17.6	4.2	9.7	2.6	18.3	5.3	13.6	28.2	21.0	8,743	8,941
St Lucia												
1970	5.1	12.7	1.1	0.5	3.3	10.1	7.7	33.1	32.2	13.0	1,478	914
1991[c]	9.8	15.1	4.4	5.8	3.0	14.8	8.8	17.1	38.6	17.7	14,372	11,015
St Vincent												
1990	6.7	13.0	1.0	0.2	3.3	8.3	11.5	34.5	33.7	12.9	1,234	687
1991	9.0	18.4	4.8	6.4	3.2	15.7	8.3	16.1	30.2	7.2	8,708	7,811

Sources: See Table 1
Special tabulations for Dominica, St Lucia and St Vincent

Notes: a. By current employment unless where indicated. Percentages do not add up to 100 because of the exclusion of some occupations.
b. In Bdos$ and EC$. 1991 mean annual income for Dominica was computed only on the native-born population. 1991 mean annual income data for St Vincent was estimated indirectly.
c. Occupation for which trained.

would venture to guess that they are employed at lower levels in administrative hierarchies.

Women continue, however, to dominate 'clerical' and 'sales and services' occupations, and men, 'production and trades' and 'agriculture'. Interpreting 20- year declines for women in the sales and services sector (Table 1.1) can be misleading because of the lack of strict comparability in this occupation group between the 1970 and 1990-91 censuses. Disaggregated data show that women have moved away from domestic services to tourism and the infomatics sector, particularly in Barbados. Also, data reported from the Barbados Statistical Services *Labour Force Reports* (Coppin 1995) do not show any 20-year declines in the percentage of women in sales and services (this is the inevitable problem that arises when comparing data from two different types of surveys).

Census data on employment in 'agriculture and related occupations' (not shown on Table 1.1), indicate that females have left agriculture in proportionately greater numbers than males. For example, in 1970 and 1991, 'agriculture' in St Vincent accounted for 30.1 per cent and 17.6 per cent of male employment respectively. The counterpart figures for females were 20.3 and 6.2 per cent (1970 and 1991 Population Census for St Vincent and the Grenadines). In other words, the proportion of men employed in agriculture in St Vincent declined by less than half between 1970 and 1991, while the proportion of women in agriculture declined by greater than two-thirds. Similar gender differences in declines in employment in agriculture occurred in St Lucia and Dominica, and to a lesser extent in Barbados. It would appear that the 'direct displacement' (the siphoning of labour from agriculture to the more lucrative tourism and related services sector) reported on in an earlier paper (McElroy and de Albuquerque 1990), disproportionately effects women. This does tend to call into question the 'feminisation and refeminisation of agriculture' theses (Momsen 1987), although these theses more correctly refer to small-scale farming (evidence from the Dominica and St Vincent agricultural censuses show that male small-farm operators continue to outnumber female operators).

Have greater occupational diversification and increased LFPRs for women translated into significant declines in the income gender gap? The evidence here appears mixed. In Barbados and St Lucia, women have made some income gains, increasing from 62 per cent of men's earning power in 1970 to about 75 per cent in 1990-91 (Table 1.2). Yet, all the evidence indicates that women in both these islands are still confined to lower wage tertiary sector jobs with fewer opportunities for advancement.

In Dominica, average annual income for women has risen from 52 per cent of that of men, to 102 per cent. We would advise caution in interpreting this surprising finding since the income data were derived from special tabulations that have not been rechecked or officially approved (the tabulations were prepared for the senior author by the Dominica Central Statistical Office). Nevertheless, absolute income values aside, women in Dominica and St Vincent have significantly narrowed the gender gap in income. This is corroborated by the significantly improved occupational status of women in these two Windward islands.

Household data by gender of household head (Table 1.3) also reveal some unexpected results. Besides Barbados and St Lucia in 1970, the differences in household size between male and female headed house-

Table 1.3 Household headship, Size and Income by Gender, 1970 and 1990/91

Island and Year	Household Headship (%)		Average Household Size (Persons)		Median Household Income[a]	
	M	F	M	F	M	F
Barbados						
1970	57.1	42.9	4.6	6.3	1,543	955
1990	56.3	42.7	n.a.	n.a.	12,361	8,889
Dominica						
1970	n.a.	n.a.	4.8	4.2	1,018	664
1990	63.1	36.9	3.8	3.9	11,291	8,961
St Lucia						
1970	59.1	40.9	3.6	4.5	1,014	616
1991	59.6	40.4	4.0	4.1	13,000	10,471
St Vincent						
1970	54.6	45.4	5.2	4.9	907	412
1991	60.7	39.3	n.a.	n.a.	7,062	4,599

Sources: See Table 1.1
Special tabulations for Dominica, St Lucia, and St Vincent

Notes: [a]In Bdos$ and EC$. 1991 data for Dominica and St Vincent are reasonably close estimates computed indirectly from special tabulations.

holds is marginal. Median household income, however, follows the expected pattern, with female headed households having significantly lower incomes. Indeed, the poorest households on all four islands are disproportionately female headed. On the surface, the household income data for Dominica and St Vincent in 1991 would seem to contradict the data on mean annual income by gender. However, it must be remembered that male headed households are much more likely to have multiple income earners than female headed households. It is on the educational front that Caribbean women have made the greatest gains. Table 1.1 shows that between 1970 and 1990-91, female educational attainment (secondary school level), caught up, and in some islands (Dominica and St Lucia), surpassed, male educational attainment. There were still proportionately more male university graduates in both age groups in Dominica and St Lucia in 1991. However, data in Tables 1.4 and 1.5, show that female university graduates have begun to outnumber male graduates.

Total student registration by gender at the University of the West Indies (UWI) shows a disturbing downward trend in male enrolment, with women in 1994-95 making up 61 per cent of all students (Table 1.4). Only in St Augustine (Table 1.5) are there more male registrants, and this primarily, because of the male dominated Faculties of Agriculture and Engineering. Even the Faculties of Medical Sciences, Natural Sciences and Law, long the preserve of males, have shown significant increases in female registrants. In all three campuses, the Faculty of Law is dominated by females. Female students from all Commonwealth Caribbean coun-

Table 1.4 University of the West Indies enrolment by gender, 1950/51-1994/95

Year	Total Number	% Male	% Female
1950-51	141	73.8	26.2
1960-61	977	67.2	32.8
1970-71	5,016	61.8	38.2
1980-81	9,089	51.8	48.2
1990-91	12,628	43.2	56.8
1994/95[P]	16,191	38.9	61.1

Source: The University of the West Indies, Official Statistics 1993-94

Note: [P] Provisional

Table 1.5 Full-time University of the West Indies Student Registration by Programme, Faculty, Campus and Gender, 1993/1994

Programme and Faculty	CAMPUS								
	Cave Hill			Mona			St Augustine		
Undergraduate	n	%M	%F	n	%M	%F	n	%M	%F
Agriculture	–	–	–	–	–	–	234	65.4	34.6
Arts & Gen. Studies	201	20.0	80.0	900	18.2	81.8	433	22.9	78.1
Education	19	21.1	78.9	224	23.7	76.3	46	22.7	78.3
Engineering	–	–	–	–	–	–	783	81.6	18.4
Law	322	32.6	67.4	39	30.8	69.2	41	24.4	75.6
Medical Sciences	49	55.1	44.9	522	46.4	53.6	576	54.9	45.1
Natural Sciences	362	57.5	42.5	1,151	50.2	49.8	612	48.4	51.6
Social Sciences	624	33.7	66.3	1,231	34.4	65.6	638	38.1	61.9
Total	1,577	37.7	62.3	4,067	36.3	63.8	3,363	52.4	47.6
Higher Degree									
Agriculture	–	–	–	–	–	–	43	51.2	48.8
Arts & Gen. Studies	4	50.0	50.0	70	19.4	81.4	15	33.3	66.7
Education	3	100.0	0.0	19	15.8	84.2	10	30.0	70.0
Engineering	–	–	37.5	–	–	–	44	63.6	36.4
Law	24	62.5	37.5	–	–	–	–	–	–
Medical Sciences	11	81.8	18.2	154	51.3	48.7	7	57.1	42.9
Natural Sciences	45	51.1	48.9	80	37.5	62.5	23	43.5	56.5
Social Sciences	9	66.7	33.3	483	38.1	61.9	179	51.4	48.6
Grand Total[a]	1,751	38.7	61.3	4,731	36.0	64.0	3,628	52.0	48.0

Source: See Table 4; Note: a. – Includes Diploma, Advanced Diploma and Certificate students

tries, including Barbados, Dominica, St Lucia, and St Vincent, are in the majority in both the Cave Hill and Mona campuses.

Some of the difference in registration by gender at UWI is due to the fact that females are outperforming males in secondary school and therefore have higher admission rates. There are several reasons for the gender difference in academic performance in secondary school, but one interesting reason being bruited about the region, is that young males are more likely to opt for wage/salary jobs or enter business for themselves upon leaving school. They therefore do just enough to pass a few CXC subjects and view university education as a postponement of their potential to earn the income necessary to purchase stylish clothes, jewellery, consumer durables, and the much sought after automobile. The suggestion here is that the social capital offered by a university education is less appealing to Caribbean males.

Does men's declining educational attainment relative to women, signify that they are at risk? It is one thing for Caribbean women to outperform their male counterparts at all levels of education, but quite another for this superior educational achievement to bring with it commensurate rewards. We are convinced that if we could control for education, that Caribbean women university graduates in medicine or law, for example, would have lower incomes than their male counterparts. Additionally, disaggregated census data show that many Caribbean female university graduates are underemployed (in positions requiring lower qualifications). On the political front, female parliamentarians and ministers are much more likely to be expected to have higher educational qualifications to enter this male arena. We cannot think of any Caribbean female in a high level political position who is not well educated, while there are several men with minimal educational qualifications in these positions.

Nowhere is this lack of congruence between women's educational attainment and occupational prestige more apparent than in the university itself. In 1993-94, only 18.8 per cent of the full time academic staff was female (7.0 per cent of the Professors and 8.1 per cent of the Senior Lecturers). The proportion of females among senior administrative staff was slightly better – 27.0 per cent (UWI 1995). This in a university where over 60 per cent of student registrants are female!

Although the university has been probably slower to change than most other public institutions, it is not unreasonable to expect that well-educated Caribbean women are also subject to a glass ceiling elsewhere in the public sector. But what about Caribbean women in general? The gains we have reported in this paper seem to have primarily affected middle- and upper-middle-class women (the gains are much more noticeable in Dominica and St Vincent than in St Lucia and Barbados). We would venture, that while the majority of Caribbean women have significantly improved life chances over their mothers, gender discrimination is still pervasive, especially on the economic and political fronts.

Senior (1991: 153) and others (Henderson 1988; Giacalone 1994) stress that women are very poorly represented in the highest reaches of political power in the Caribbean, and are most often assigned subordinate roles as party workers, or relegated to 'women's arms' or auxiliaries of national parties. Giacalone (1994: 228) notes that women have begun to seek out alternative forms of organisation like cooperatives, community organisations, NGOs, workshops, etc. Yet the 1990s has seen a movement towards the inclusion of more women in the English-speaking Caribbean in high political office, Barbados being a case in point.

Conclusion

Although the 1995 UNDP Human Development Report indicates that women in the Caribbean have made great progress towards gender equality, they still have some way to go. The data on Barbados, Dominica, St Lucia, and St Vincent, presented in this paper, indicate, that while women have entered the labour force in greater numbers, they continue to have significantly lower rates of participation than men. The data would also seem to indicate that occupational segregation has diminished drastically, with proportionately more women than men being employed in 1990-91 in 'professional and technical' and 'administrative and man-agement' positions. However, as we indicated, this is misleading since disaggregated data show women employed at lower levels in professional, technical and managerial fields. On the income side women have made some gains in Barbados and St Lucia, and in Dominica and St Vincent they appear to have closed the gender gap. However, female-headed households are still more likely to be in poverty, with households headed by females having significantly lower median incomes.

Caribbean women as a group, are as well, if not better educated, than their male counterparts, but are significantly under represented as large business proprietors and managers, as university lecturers, in trade un-ions, parliaments, the judiciary, and other bastions of power. So while some lower-class men may well be at risk, Caribbean women still have a way to go before they can fulfil Miller's prediction of claiming the third millennium. Yet, as the data in this paper show, they have made great strides in the last two decades, and it is up to scholars interested in gender to evaluate how the changing educational and economic status of women is transforming Caribbean societies, rather than tenaciously clinging to some rather static portrayals of Caribbean women.

2

Island-hopping Body Shopping in Barbados:

Localising the Gendering of Transnational Workers[1]

Carla Freeman

Within the carpeted recess of Data Air[2]'s warehouse-sized production facility, amidst eye-catching skirt suits and fashion accessories there is not a single man in sight. These new off-shore data entry operations in Barbados embody the region's newest experiment in export production. Far transcending garments and electronics which preceded them, the 'informatics' industry strikes its new employees and passersby alike, with plush, office-like working environments and the most potent sign of modernity itself – sophisticated computers and satellite communications – as the technological hub. For the student of global capital and labor movements, this sight is striking. The clean and high-tech setting suggests skilled white collar work, and stands in marked contrast to the dust fumes of many an offshore garment or computer chip assembly plant. It is the glamorous adornment, however, and not the predominance of women alone in the data-processing workplace that sets it apart from other labour-intensive industries. Parades of young women workers rushing to and from their shifts in such factories across the globe are not only a familiar, but indeed, an expected component of such export enclaves. Not only has offshore production in many traditional areas become synonymous with female workforces, but a very specific sort of feminine profile has typically been defined and recruited.

This article explores the specific case of the new informatics industry to investigate how these transnational patterns have emerged, and identifies ways in which they are also contested and changing. As such, it will probe locally specific notions of gender, work, and identity in the Caribbean context. By investigating the personnel demands of international capital and the Barbadian locale where stereotypes of the ideal worker are negotiated, the analysis will reveal some surprising paradoxes in the beliefs held by both managers and workers regarding long-established archetypes of ideal workers as young, pliable and feminine. These paradoxes are related to specific and changing aspects of Barbadian social life, the pattern of industrialisation, household formations and gender ideologies, and illustrate the complex manner in which prescriptive and adaptive capacities of the international market reshape themselves in the face of cultural difference.

Why do women make cheap workers?

Some excellent studies of the new international division of labour (e.g. Nash and Fernandez-Kelly 1983; Fernandez-Kelly 1983, 1985; Kelly 1987; Sassen 1988; Safa 1990; Ward 1990; Ong 1987) have shed light on the requirements demanded by foreign companies setting up offshore industries in developing countries. Among these are generous tax holidays, political stability, docile trade unions, subsidised rents and modern factory shells. In addition, multinationals have tended to opt for establishing operations in areas where industrial, community, and family life is strongly influenced by traditional patriarchal relations. Development officers representing countries seeking to recruit foreign investment often stress the ready availability of female workers who comprise what is frequently described as a large and previously marginalised reservoir of adaptable workers. Indeed, cheap labour in the form of young women workers has been the single most important factor in the international movements of labour intensive industries (garments, electronics, etc.). Gender therefore plays an integral role in constituting vast labour forces around the world.

Women's youthful and strong bodies are believed to be well suited for meticulous work and long hours of tedious labour; their fingers are described as nimble and dexterous, and used to fine detail work. Women's innocence, inexperience, and eagerness to learn are said to give them a temperament that is ideally suited as well. They have been brought up in 'traditional', often rural households, where patriarchal relations dictate obedient behavior on the part of daughters, and their employment may even have been arranged by a male member of the family. Their status, as 'daughter,' furthermore implies that while their wage will contribute to the household economy, it is not the primary source of support; and their single and childless status ensures their availability and an undivided sense of allegiance to work for their employer. In a nutshell, these young women, both as individuals and in relation to their family, community, and the international marketplace, have stood to represent the quintessential offshore assembly worker across the globe.

There is a long historical precedent for hiring women workers as reserve armies of labour. Following Marx's lead, Braverman (1974: 383) used this notion to describe the process of capital accumulation, whereby an industrial pool of labour can be incorporated or discarded as wage workers as required by capital. Braverman argues that with increased rationalisation of a wide range of work (both in industrial and service areas) as well as increased geographical mobility of these jobs, larger numbers of workers become a part of the workforce in this way. The reserve army therefore functions as a flexible reservoir of labour that responds to the demands of capital and serves as a cheap labour source for expanding service industries. However, until recently little attention has been paid to the fact that women rather than men have systematically been drawn into these footloose industries. Braverman (1974: 385) noted that 'women form the ideal reservoir of labour for the new mass occupations. The barrier which confines women to much lower pay scales is reinforced by the vast numbers in which they are available to capable'. Women are presented as constituting massive pools of labour, patiently waiting for the tides of capital to pull them into wage work for the first time. And, by definition women as *low-wage* workers are logically concentrated in those industrial sectors of the economy undergoing rationalisation or new expansion. This argument has formed the core of several works by anthropologists specifically addressing the incorporation of women workers in multinational factories around the world (Fernandez-Kelly 1983). Without problematising the notion of women as cheap labour, however, we risk repeating a persistent tautology that fails to get to the crux of the question – women make up a natural source of low wage workers because women are paid less than men.

As a number of historical analyses of labour and households have pointed out, the incorporation of women workers into low wage, labour-intensive jobs is not a new phenomenon. Textile mills and factories of the early nineteenth century revealed similar patterns and rationales for hiring large numbers of women, as young 'mill girls' or 'married operatives' formed prototypic wage-earning women in expanding industrial enclaves (Tilly and Scott 1978: 63). The relationships, however, between international, local, and household economies, as well as between the state and individual, family, cultural and corporate conceptions of female labour are historically and culturally specific (Hartman 1976; Westwood 1985; Beechey 1987). This work explores areas of continuity and similarity across cultural and historical contexts as well as those aspects of the information industry in late twentieth-century Barbados that reveal particular relationships and apparent contradictions surrounding women's experience as high-tech off-shore workers and the gender ideologies that underlie their incorporation as low-wage workers.

The basis for my persistent questioning along these lines in Barbados was twofold. One area of concern was whether this new high-tech industry would recruit any differently from that or its traditional industrial predecessors. Given the clerical 'white collar' nature of this computer-based work, I wondered if higher educational levels and skills would be demanded, and additionally, whether the emphasis on youth and first-time work status would hold as well. There has also been some suspicion that clerical workers represent a different (higher) class of workers than factory workers, though the official placement of the data entry sector under the same rubric of traditional export industries would seem to counter this claim.[3] Furthermore, the fact that in some other countries (e.g. Ireland and the Dominican Republic), data entry was not a strictly female domain, posed a strong invitation to set the gender question straight for the Barbadian context.

The second line of thinking had to do with the specific context of Barbados and the different gender categories and ideologies that permeate its culture. From the kinship literature of the West Indies, as well as the poetry and fiction written by and about Afro-Caribbean women, not to mention a multitude of popular calypsos with various (if often unflattering) portrayals of women, I hardly imagined the 'docile and malleable' feminine stereotype to hold much weight in the Barbadian context. If anything, the strong and independent black matriarch seemed a much more pervasive cultural stereotype within the region at large. Even though under-represented in seats of political and corporate power, Barbadian women are widely believed to provide the backbone of the family and the society in general (Barrow 1988; Senior 1991). Indeed, while numerous studies of women's work and family life demonstrate the onerous and multi-dimensional responsibility women – especially heads of households – face trying to piece together a living, popular rhetoric and corporate rationales frequently persist with an idealised stereotype of the powerful matriarch. I set out, therefore, to establish a general 'worker profile' first to identify more precisely *which* women have been incorporated into the information industry, and to parse out the inconsistencies between companies' conceptions of 'ideal' workers and the realities presented by the women themselves, and secondly, to look more closely at the interrelationships between women's household and family lives and their work in the information industry and the ways in which these challenge and reshape the ideal profiles.

Real and Ideal Profiles of Pink Collar Workers

In Barbados' export processing enclaves, women are simultaneously and paradoxically described as strong, selfless and hardworking, frequently the main breadwinners for their children, in short, the backbone of society; and alternatively they are depicted as materialistic consumers obsessed with fashion and appearances, clever and even mercenary in their strategies for piecing together a living, and essentially not in dire economic need of these jobs. 'Even in women's own minds,' a labour representative said, 'they're not considered the prime breadwinners, although often in reality they *are*. Certainly in the workplace you're not seen as a main breadwinner.' The rationale for this, she explained, relates to the social organisation of Barbadian family life. 'One man may have three women so his $100 got to go to three households; but a woman's same $100 stays within her own family. In the back of people's minds, this is part of the rationale for employing men – that the money you pay him gets disbursed further.' She adds that women's critical consciousness of themselves as 'second-class workers' is growing, and that they 'have changed a lot in their thinking. Women are conscious of their money wage. They're supplying themselves with houses and cars – their material things are very important to them'.

These contradictory images emerge within the off-shore informatics industry, and in many instances are heightened by allusions to the hyper-modern high-tech appearance of these enterprises. When adopted into company rhetoric, these opposing profiles of women workers take on particular importance. On one hand as implied above, and contrary to the traditional off-shore industries in other countries, where the systematic profile of the multinational assembly worker is a young, single, first-time worker, managers often argued that hiring women who have children (married or single heads of households or not) creates a more reliable and hardworking labour force. (Peña 1987:132). These women are believed to work harder and generally take their jobs more seriously because, regardless of the assistance of their extended families and 'child fathers', *they* are the primary breadwinners for their children. One manager of a data entry operation contemplated hiring women for four shifts to encourage those with children to take the jobs. He thought that the shorter workday would ease their childcare burden, and at the same time enable the employment of these superior, more responsible workers. In contrast to the traditional argument for a family wage, where a male head of household is paid at a higher rate on the basis of his breadwinning role, these female heads of household, however, are paid low wages in exchange for their higher levels of responsibility and job commitment.[4] On the other hand, like their counterparts in other countries, local managers were also frequently heard describing the work force as consisting ideally of young girls, in their first job who are working essentially for pocket money.[5] In short, this is the familiar 'pin-money' argument so often used to describe women's work and to rationalise the low wages they receive.

One development officer specialising in the promotion of the off-shore information industry in Barbados described the predominance of women as a matter not of deliberate selection, but due to the nature of the production process itself (labour demands) as well as the educational and cultural climate, and biological make up of the operators (labour supply factors).

Women tend to do light assembly work which involves sitting and manipulating fine objects. Some persons claim that men don't have the good coordination . . . I think it might more be a matter of aptitude, and aptitude is probably cultivated by your society and so on. A man is seen in movies and in real life doing things, moving and so on. A man is never seen sitting . . . especially on a line manipulating fine things. And he may not have the practice . . . women have had practice manipulating needles and doing fine intricate things, embroidery or cake icing, or being more delicate. And also they have smaller hands, so if you're going to manipulate fine things their physical structure may have some impact . . . Whatever the reason is, it so happens that women tend to do data entry, garments, electronics assembly, and men tend to do heavier work.

Arguing from the perspective of the labour supply, on the other hand, a Barbadian manager of a small data entry company gave the following comment to explain women's predominance in the industry,

. . . one of the factors is that there are about three or four women to every man in Barbados. (after hesitating) . . . maybe you should check that out with the statistical department, but I think that's true. Many of the people out there are females that are unemployed, fairly intelligent people, and typing is a skill that somehow seemed to fit into a female society.

In fact, women do slightly outnumber men in Barbados (1.6 women to every man); however, this manager's gross exaggeration relates more to his sense of the 'cheap reservoir' of female labour[6] created, of course, more by women's economic vulnerability than numerical disproportion. As in many other developing countries, women between the ages of 19 and 25 represent the highest proportion of the unemployed labour force.

Workers and managers alike concur that these enterprises are filled with women because women know how to type since typing is a prerequisite for the job, it is logical that the companies hire women workers. This 'supply side' rationale was frequently bolstered with arguments about the gross representation of women in the Barbadian population, as well as women's greater tenacity in looking for work in order to support their children.[7] Many of these discussions were permeated as well by gender stereotypes about women's natural predisposition toward fine, meticulous, sedentary work, and corollary notions about men's natural inclination toward heavier physical work and the need to 'move around.'

More often than not, women workers themselves offer the supply side rationales by saying simply that women are the ones who learn to type and since these jobs require typing, men don't bother to apply. The logic seems self-evident; in Barbados, like most places, typing is considered a feminine activity (higher-level computer work, incidentally, is not). Therefore, according to management and workers alike, the industry is not really selecting women per se, they select themselves insofar as they fall into a 'naturally' female domain of work. As one woman put it, the reason the industry is filled with women is 'because one of the stipulations for applying . . . was knowing how to type. I know in my time, I don't think a guy would be caught dead typing'. Another added, 'I suppose the men got frustrated just sitting there keying all the time; most men like to know they're moving around or delivering something.' These gender stereotypes, and others relating to women's roles within the family/domestic arena, permeate their entry into the data entry industry.

The general manager of Data Air presented the following worker profile as representing the core of his operation:

I would guess off hand that they are largely still living at home with parents . . . [and] that at least 50% or more have at least one kid. I know that largely speaking, they do not *need* . . . this job . . . this whole question of clothes and jewelry and entertainment and that type of thing, they seem to work a lot for that. We watch their savings patterns and we encourage membership in the credit union . . . we practically sponsored a credit union in-house, and one of the complaints we get from the credit union is that as soon as the savings hit . . . they go back for it. They're taking it and you can see very conspicuously how they are spending it . . . I think the wages *are* crucial *to them*, and the more the merrier . . . but very frequently, you'll almost get threatened 'I'll stay home, then' and I think it really has to do with the feeling that 'I can be no worse off if I stayed home' — that 'I will get all of the basic things that I need' — and that largely therefore, 'I can give up that job.'

His remarks are revealing on several fronts, both in terms of the basic demographic portrait of his employees and his sense of the importance of these jobs in their lives. Living 'at home' (i.e. with one or both parents or guardian) is viewed as insuring a certain basic level of support, and this manager implies quite clearly that regardless of the presence of a woman's own child, or the particular circumstances of her family, if she lives at home her wage is supplemental to the household budget. In effect, this is the old 'pin money' rationale for why women's wages are lower than men's. The misconception, however, lies in the assumption that living 'at home' ensures basic subsistence and therefore places one's earnings into the category of supplemental or extra income. While this may be the case for some of the data entry operators, it clearly does not reflect the reality for the majority. In fact, one could argue, as I do elsewhere, that the perception of these women as working for pocket money, and the pressure to dress and appear as a 'professional' worker, lends added economic as well as social duress to the work experience when their wages are indeed integral to their household economy.

Unlike the global trend in which workers are hired and then quickly let go (Safa 1990:80), the low attrition rates (two per cent at Data Air) imply that the vast majority of their Barbadian data operators have tended to keep their jobs well beyond the international trend in other off-shore industries of two to three years. In fact, according to Data Air's general manager, of the original workers hired in 1983 a majority are still with the company. Among those workers employed from the start and still with the company the age range is now between 27 and 35. Within the newer areas of the company, which began in 1990 and continues to hire new recruits, the average age still hovers between late teens and early twenties. In essence, there has emerged a two-tiered workforce: young 'school leavers' on one hand, and the 'old guard' on the other. These two 'generations' relate closely to contradictory portraits drawn between the hardworking and mature single mother and the frivolous school leaver. Graphic stereotypes offered by management and workers alike, about work ethics, demeanor and dress act to distinguish between the two groups as well. The young school leavers, for example, are considered by their older compatriots to be less committed to the 'mission of the company' and more intent simply on making money. The implication is that they spend their money exclusively on their own frivolous whims, and that their earnings are not integral to household support. Social interaction and cliques of friends who regularly meet for lunch, dinner, or shift breaks, tend to parallel these generational differences, in part because work areas become age stratified based on hiring wages and length of job tenure. For example, when the insurance claim division opened at Data Air, new recruits were young school leavers. Entire shifts in this new division, therefore, are made up of the younger generation of workers, and logically they socialise with one another.

Grouped together both within the workplace and outside it, then, the style and overall look of these school leavers becomes especially pronounced. Upstairs, in the airline ticket processing area the presence of the old guard is more evident. Reflecting on the difficulty in pinning down a single worker profile or even an average age, the general manager described the situation well, ' . . . we have two companies, really; the claims operation, where the average age is probably 20 or even younger, and our airline division where it is probably 25 or even higher, 27 or 28'. One member of the 'old guard' who began working for the company when it opened in 1983 and is now 30, illustrates the divide in describing the 'young' workers as follows:

They do not think like the people of before. That's the basic bottom line. They don't have the same serious minded approach to a job, like, say what I had when I started. They treat it like school, like they think they can come and go as they please and you really have to rail-road them to get them to think straight.

Another operator, aged 28, remarked:

You will find that an old person like me will concentrate on the errors (maintaining higher accuracy) cause we are working for Data Air, right? But they're not. They are strictly thinking about money. So if you lose it in incentive [earned through accuracy], make it up in overtime.

Younger workers describe their annoyance with the strict rules regulating each minute of the workday and all procedures, from those related to the job itself, to going to the bathroom or using the telephone. Indeed they complain that 'it's just like being back in school', and having just left school, with its uniforms, bells and regulations, they find the similarities confining. From the management point of view, on the other hand, coming directly from school, young girls are accustomed to following instructions and are considered well suited for the discipline of the 'open office'. A manager of one of the smaller locally run data facilities said that young school leavers with no prior data entry experience are ideal because they are eager to work on a computer and are not faced with re-learning or 'un-learning' another system. From this perspective, prior work experience in other data entry facilities makes an applicant less attractive, and youth becomes associated with eagerness to learn and receptivity to the enculturation of the company.

Indicative of their awareness of these two distinct 'generations' of workers, and revealing the company's concern for those values and work ethics that have become associated with their 'older' more mature workforce, an experiment was initiated by the personnel department of Data Air. Ten women were hired who fell into the age bracket of the 'old guard' (between 24 and 30) with the belief they would be 'more mature and reliable' workers than the young 'girls' generally hired directly out of school. However, the personnel manager was deeply disappointed when she learned that the majority did not survive the three- month probationary period. Their low productivity was accounted for by a lack of familiarity and general anxiety surrounding computers, which have only recently been introduced to some of the secondary schools. Additionally cited as a reason for their failure was a reluctance to take direction from supervisors who were often younger than themselves. Only one member of the experimental group remained employed after the three-month trial period.

What this experiment seemed to imply, therefore, was that age alone was not the key ingredient to a 'mature' and 'ideal' worker. Rather, age associated with experience and socialisation within the company became preferred characteristics. Preference for the 'mature' worker reflects a shifting priority associated with the company's identity, which along with its workforce, has evolved over its nine years of operation. The companies, therefore, are not recruiting a qualitatively different workforce since young school leavers continue to be the favored candidates; however by retaining its workers for long durations, the profile of the ideal operator has consequently matured. Whereas mandatory pregnancy tests and compulsory dismissal have been the norm in many export plants in Asia and along the Mexican border zones, in Barbados more and more women in data entry have become mothers, returning to their jobs as guaranteed by the national maternity leave policy. Women's decision to remain in these jobs through different stages in their life cycle has itself shifted a widespread characteristic of multinational industries around the world to hire and fire at will, and has given a new look to the companies' own life cycles.

In light of the persistence of static gender stereotypes, and internationalised rationales for a specific feminine workforce, it is noteworthy that in Data Air's sister plant in the Spanish speaking island of the Dominican Republic, roughly 40 per cent of the operators are men performing virtually the same data entry jobs as their Barbadian counterparts. This is an intriguing fact, given the well entrenched pattern of gender segregation in traditional multinational factories in the Dominican Republic (e.g. garments, electronics, food processing). Managers and workers in the Dominican Data Air speculated that the draw of the computer technology along with increasing unemployment and underemployment rates accounted for the presence of young men in this special case of 'free zone' work. They also added that a high proportion of these young men are students in technical or university programmes, and perceive these jobs as a temporary vehicle for getting experience with computers and earning money to help pay for school books and supplies.[9]

Also distinguishing the Barbadian Data Air from its sister in Santo Domingo, is a radically divergent pattern of attrition. Data entry workers in the Dominican Republic tend to stay with their jobs for two years on average, and the general manager of this plant cited two years as the optimum life span for a data operator. Unlike the Barbadian managers who hailed the superlative commitment and productivity of their 'old guard', she remarked that productivity levels begin to decline after the second year of employment. Safa (1990:78-79) notes the attrition rates are high in multinational factories in general in the Dominican Republic, as a result of both labour practices which hire and fire quickly, as well as factors related to the labour force itself. While young women recently have begun to express a desire to resume employment after marriage or childbirth, traditionally young single women work for a few years up until they experience these milestones. Citing yet another factor, Safa adds that higher job stability in Puerto Rico, denoted by long-term employees of 20-30 years, is attributed to higher rates of unionisation across the export sector. The extent to which culturally specific gender ideologies and practices influence different patterns of labour recruitment and longevity, *and become bound up in corporate rationales for these patterns* has been little mentioned in accounts of transnational corporate enterprises. These striking exceptions to the overwhelming trend in which women have been targeted and positioned along the global assembly lines demand that we look more critically at the localised circumstances, demands, and rationales used to explain corporate strategies across widely diverse contexts. The singular profile of young, unwed, childless, docile, dexterous woman worker is not only inadequate as a transnational generality, but it also obscures a closer understanding of the manner in which workers are incorporated and disciplined by particular industry designs.

In terms of labour supply factors, Barbados presents a distinct context for women's incorporation into these new industries. While the 'office-factory' is a relatively new phenomenon in Barbados, women's entry into the labour force is not, and in fact their active participation in 'low-tech' factory jobs in both local and foreign-owned operations long precedes the emergence of the off-shore information sector. The particular implications of this new high-tech enclave have to do with the specific nature of the industry, the work at hand, as well as the distinct style of management and uniquely office-like style of the operations, than with the fact that women are for the first time incorporated as wage earning workers. Bound up in the complex of market forces influencing the demand for and supply of labour are powerful and contradictory cultural stereotypes and gender ideologies among workers and their employers.

Contradictory as it may seem, corporate heads in the information industry continue to argue that young Bajan women constitute the ideal workforce for this high detail, computer-based industry though, as we have seen, they are known to utter alternate female stereotypes – both the 'international' as well as 'Barbadian' versions – to defend their selection. These contradictions reflect negotiations and readjustments that are continually taking place between various levels of international corporate management and local cultural practice. In Barbados, a dialectical relationship has emerged between the maturing labour force – which moves into different life stages and ceases to conform to the original young, single, childless profile – and the corporate expectations for what its workforce ought to look to maximise productivity. Through the 'maturation' process, which encodes not simply more advanced age but also deeper indoctrination into the corporate ethics and expectations of the operation, workers adopt a serious and committed approach to their job, and exhibit work habits which the employers come to identify as preferable to those of the younger 'school leavers'. The old guard 'matriarchs' furthermore, by the very nature of their mature position and their combining work with motherhood and household responsibilities, have come to guarantee the companies a productive, secure and loyal workforce.

Simultaneously, as women have managed to maintain their dual work and family roles, they, in turn, alter what has become a well entrenched pattern by similar multinational operations to hire and fire quickly. They were hired as young, single women who fit the international prescription, but altered it by staying in these jobs and shifting into another stage in their life cycle – that of the 'powerful matriarch.' Contrary to popular belief, therefore, those apparently monolithic internationalised gender stereotypes that multinationals transplant from one production site to another around the globe, may actually reveal nuances and contradictions that are shaped by cultural distinctions within the countries that host them. As Barbadian gender ideologies and the West Indian family structure in general have resisted the confines of international capital's 'traditional' family (in its nuclear, patriarchal form), level international industrialists have incorporated an awareness of these differences into their longer term management strategies. In essence, neither of the ideal types – 'docile girls' or 'powerful matriarchs' – fully describe the complex of realities that constitute these women's lives. They do reveal, however, both the attempt by corporate managers and national governments to type and barter for workforces in a competitive world market, as well as to reshape them and mould them to fit the needs of their changing industry. The imposition of static internationalised portraits of a singular 'ideal' worker have failed to apprehend the specific nature of Barbadian gender identities and multitude of family constellations that inevitably shape the profile of its labour force. By gradually attending to the specificities of Barbadian family/household life, some companies have come to view the 'powerful matriarch' (vs. the 'docile girl') as an alternative ideal. However, the implications of changing household formations and decreasing guarantees of support from the extended family will undoubtedly place greater pressures on women in their attempts to juggle their multiple roles. Just as the 'docile girl' stereotype has long misrepresented women workers around the world in the interest of highly mobile corporate capital, the idealisation of the 'matriarch' runs similar essentialising risks that distort the realities of Barbadian women's lived experience.

Notes

1. Acknowledgments. This article is based on fieldwork conducted in Barbados between 1989 and 1992. The research was generously supported by grants from Fulbright, the National Science Foundation, the Wenner Gren Foundation for Anthropological Research, and the Organization of American States. Many thanks to Sherri Grasmuck, Rosario Espinal, Gul Ozyegin, Helen Safa and Maria Patricia Fernandez-Kelly for their insights and suggestions on various stages of its revision. The longer work in which the research is presented is forthcoming from Duke University Press as *High Tech and High Heels in the Global Economy*.
2. 'Data Air' is a pseudonym.
3. I take up this slippery question of class in more detail elsewhere (Freeman, forthcoming).

4. There has been a historical trend of wage differentials between typically male and female arenas of work in Barbados. For example between jobs of comparable skill, a machine attendant and a 'light' industry assembly operator, the former performed by men received a median wage of US$119 per week and the latter, by women, US$75 per week.

5. Continuing along these lines, one manager said he had heard (and counted on the fact) that Barbadian women would make good workers because they bear the bulk of responsibility for their children alone, and therefore must be responsible to their employers. However, he argued instead that the matriarchal and extended family seems to provide young people with a guaranteed safety net, thereby obviating precisely the autonomy and sense of responsibility he had hoped to find.

6. The argument that women far outnumber men in Barbados, has at some moments in history had greater truth than at others, due largely to labour migration trends.

7. As noted earlier, the argument about a disproportional number of women was used frequently by Barbadian men to account for their 'need to have more than one women at a time'. 1990 census figures cite a male population of 123,000 and a female population of 135,000.

8. This is not so for the sister plant of Data Air in Santo Domingo. There, workers tend to stay with their jobs for two years on average, and the general manager of this plant cited two years as the optimum lifespan for a data operator.

9. It is noteworthy that the *maquiladora* industries along the Mexican border, long known for their recruitment and high turnover of female workers, (Fernandez-Kelly 1983, Ruiz and Tiano 1987) have recently been hiring significant numbers of men, claiming a shortage of optimal female labour. These examples point to ways in which the gendering of work is a dynamic and fluid process, and that there is not a single transnational profile impermeable to local conditions, demands and circumstances. I am proposing here that negotiation is at work that often involves local state cores, transnational corporate interests, as well as those of the workers themselves.

3

Guardians of our Homes, Guards of yours? Economic Crisis, Gender Stereotyping and the Restructuring of the Private Security Industry in Georgetown, Guyana[1]

D. Alissa Trotz

Introduction

Current economic trends and the adoption of structural adjustment prescriptions from international financial institutions have prompted increasing emphasis on the gendered impact of the new global neo-liberal orthodoxy on the developing world (Bakker 1994; Benería & Feldman 1992; Standing 1989). In the Caribbean, attention has been paid to the reorganisation of labour markets through the growth of export-processing zones (Freeman 1993; Pearson 1993; Safa 1994); the dynamics of household strategies under structural adjustment (Antrobus *et. al.* 1990; Bolles 1981); and the effects of migration on the creation and maintenance of 'transnational' families (Andaiye 1993; Wiltshire 1986).

Through an examination of the private security industry in Georgetown, Guyana, this paper is intended to contribute to the discussion by focusing on yet another emerging – and oft unintended – consequence of adjustment measures, namely the visibility of women in non-traditional employment sectors. By non-traditional as it is used here I mean jobs which are dominated by and represented as suitable only for men. Thus export-processing, while new in certain contexts, created a demand for female labour and a corresponding delineation of the work required as feminine, and does not fall within this category (Laurie 1995).

It is now commonplace in the literature on gender and employment to find reference to terms like 'traditional female occupations'; 'jobs which are sex-typed as female' and so on. Such phrases are shorthand for commercialised replications of women's domestic responsibilities. Yet there is a clear disjuncture when women (or groups of women) become increasingly involved in 'male' work, highlighting the instability and problematic universality embedded within our own representations.[2] Accounting for these disjunctures and carefully historicising stereotypes requires paying attention to how gendered images and activities are produced, circumscribed and sanctioned.

At first glance, the security business would appear to be a largely masculine occupation. Specific and culturally endorsed linkages exist between strong, male bodies and the work involved: patrolling grounds, foiling prospective and often violent criminals, brandishing weapons. Moreover, this is a society in which the military have been a pervasive aspect of people's lives in the post-independence era. Yet Guyanese women are becoming increasingly visible and even numerically dominant in the private security industry, giving rise to the common local perception that 'is women taking over the guard service now'.

This paper will examine the factors responsible for the erosion of traditional barriers to women's entry, and consider the implications of a growing female presence for representations and relations of gender within this occupational division.[3]

Feminisation: Some conceptual notes

'Feminisation' must be placed in the context of the burgeoning literature on gender and/in development, although the terms of the debate have shifted. Issues today revolve not around whether women are incorporated – the preoccupations of earlier writers of whom Boserup is perhaps the most well known – but rather the terms of their inclusion. The jury is still out on whether employment in export-oriented factories under the New International Division of Labour benefits or marginalises women even further, even if discussions are far less likely to operate with universal stereotypes of the female factory worker that existed in earlier research on the subject (for discussion see Pearson 1986). In keeping with this trend, Guy Standing (1989) extends the discussion of feminisation beyond an emphasis on women's recruitment into the labour market. For Standing, feminisation refers not simply to the increasing visibility of women in the workforce, but to the general lowering of labour market standards to resemble the devalued and inferior conditions previously associated exclusively with occupations in which women were concentrated. He identifies this as a necessary corollary to supply-side policies and their corresponding emphasis on export-oriented industrialisation. In addition to precipitating the movement of women into the waged workforce, intensified deregulation of local labour markets tends towards the substitution of women for men in many instances.

While undoubtedly this approach refines our understanding of the gendered effects of adjustment, it is argued here that it needs to be broadened to allow for the variety of ways in which this trend might be manifested across and within countries. Standing concentrates on the potential demands of employers (private and public sector, local and multinational) as if these are always and necessarily satisfied, but there is not a global, undifferentiated body of women and men who are simply recruited or marginalised. Of equal importance are the ways in which categories of work and their associations with appropriate behaviours (according to gender as well as class, race, age and ethnicity for instance) are invested with meaning and significance 'on the ground', so to speak. Indeed Standing alludes to the reluctance of men to remain in jobs now stripped of their advantageous status, although he does not develop this insight further. An analysis along these lines entails situating 'feminisation' within the cultural contexts under which masculinities and femininities are produced within and beyond the labour market.

The preceding discussion of feminisation in the contemporary international arena can fruitfully be applied to the present case-study of change within the service sector. Although it does not immediately appear to be linked to patterns of global restructuring, Guyana's private security industry is an indirect beneficiary of the real and anticipated social consequences of structural adjustment in the form of increasing polarisation and crime against property. Moreover the industry has attracted international interest and there are now two foreign owned companies in operation. Adjustment policies have also created and reinforced opportunities provided by foreign investment as well as in the informal and internationalised trading sector. In most cases men have been most able to exploit these openings. This has left the security industry with a potential workforce that is predominantly female in a specifically Caribbean context in which work constitutes an integral aspect of women's identity. As we shall see below, that employers were for the most part reluctantly confronted with predominantly black female applicants (as opposed to actively recruiting women) underscores the need to foreground our research in an analysis not only of the labour market, but equally of the households from which employees have been recruited.

In this respect, feminist debates offer critical insights about the household which will be taken up in this paper. In the first place, domestic divisions of labour are no longer seen as the outcome of natural and harmonious utility-maximising strategies. Neither entirely the site of women's oppression nor haven of egalitarianism, the domestic domain is seen as a locus of political activity constituted through relations of conflict, mutuality and compromise. The second important issue concerns the critique of the public/private split. This dichotomisation obscures the interconnectedness of the two domains, and the power relations which interpenetrate these various processes (Bruce and Dwyer 1988; Folbre 1994).

The advantage of this position is that the household is presented not as a domain which produces fixed social identities, but rather as an economic and cultural configuration which is made meaningful through the activities of its members linked in various ways to the world without. By seeing the domestic domain as constitutive of – and not just constituted by – wider relations of power, it becomes possible to investigate how micro-level changes might 'influence larger scale social, economic and political processes' (Moore 1994:88). Applying this to the present case-study generates the following questions: what precipitates women to enter into domains from which they have been excluded; how do the dominant 'ways of seeing' work to include women while nullifying the challenges thus raised; and how are these realignments resisted?[4]

The preceding discussion provides a perspective which is extremely pertinent to the concerns of this paper and the Caribbean context in which it is situated. For a start, the recognition that the household does not exist in isolation finds immediate resonance in ongoing Caribbean concerns that an exclusive household focus imposes artificial closures which ignore the visibility of women in the economy as well as articulations between domestic, local and global processes (Berleant-Schiller 1993; Brodber 1975).

Secondly, the rejection of the notion of categorical social identities offers a useful framework for reflecting on Guyana, a society allegedly riven along lines of plurality between the two main ethnic groups, Afro-Guyanese and Indo-Guyanese.[5] It also provides welcome respite from the more rigid variants of pluralist theory which portray Caribbean societies as a composite of non-overlapping cultural segments, each of which is ascribed sovereign status. The point, in short, is that an exclusive focus on the representations of difference can obscure the ways in which these are continually cross-cut and undermined by the experiences and subjectivities of Guyanese women.

Finally, women's increased visibility in labour markets under conditions of economic crisis finds comparative ground in a region undergoing
profound structural change in the 1990s. Admittedly female wage-earning, although not continuous for certain groups of women (especially
Indo-Caribbeans in the post-indentureship period), is by no means a new
phenomenon in the Caribbean. Nonetheless, it would be an oversight to
underestimate the salience of gender as an organising principle of these
societies (Barriteau-Foster 1992; Momsen 1993; Senior 1991). Not only
do women continue to be subordinated within largely segregated labour
markets, but these inequalities are presented as natural. As I hope to show
below, the contradictions manifested under crisis conditions reveal the
unnaturalness of such distinctions. The task is to consider the possibilities
and limitations which these junctures provide.

Research

The research on which this study is based was carried out in the summer
of 1995 in Georgetown, Guyana's capital. Out of a possible 14 security
companies identified in Georgetown, eight were selected. Due to limited
time and resources, an exhaustive survey of employees was ruled out,
although one company made its entire employment records available.
Twenty persons — five of whom were men — were interviewed. Contact
was made by visiting firms' headquarters at the beginning of shifts when
roll calls were made. Additionally, a meeting with twenty-five employees
from one firm was held, and I attended a session hosted by one of the
companies to allow workers to air their grievances with management.
Finally, I had a discussion with a representative from the Ministry of
Labour on the status of labour legislation relating to the private security
industry.

Militarisation, Authoritarianism, and
Economic Crisis in Guyana

Military institutions have been a pervasive feature of Guyanese society
over the last two-and-a-half decades. The proportion of GDP allocated to
military expenditure in Guyana between the end of the 1970s to 1986
was with the exception of Nicaragua the highest in the entire Latin
American and Caribbean region (Ferguson 1995). Apart from the security
forces set up in the colonial period, a variety of paramilitary services were

established after independence in 1966. Thus, between 1965 and 1976, in addition to extending the existing unit into the Guyana Defence Force, the Government created two paramilitary organisations, the Guyana National Service and the People's Militia. It also had its own security service, the National Guard Service, which was incorporated into the police force in 1993.[6]

Ostensibly this strategy was rationalised in the name of defending the country's borders against territorial claims and incursions by Venezuela and Suriname. In fact the extent and shape of the militarisation process was integral to the development of authoritarianism in a society politically divided along ethnic lines by the 1960s and where widespread discontent was evident from the late 1970s. After taking office in 1964 by a constitutional sleight of hand, the Afro-Guyanese dominated People's National Congress (PNC) remained in power for the next 28 years despite an obvious demographic disadvantage.[7] This was made possible through the holding of fraudulent elections, the expansion of the powers of the presidency and the party over the governmental process, and the adoption of a co-operative socialist agenda which effectively provided the state with massive resources for political patronage. In this context, the military as the watchdog of civil society was a necessary corollary to the consolidation of authoritarian political power (Danns 1984; Thomas 1988). Thus, it is no surprise that there was a direct relationship between the overall level of deterioration in the social and economic fabric and the percentage of GDP devoted to the military, which grew from 3.2 per cent in 1971 to 12.4 per cent by 1986, when the country was teetering on the verge of economic collapse (Ferguson 1995).

The racialisation of Guyanese politics also explains the disproportionate numbers of Afro-Guyanese in the police and military forces. In historical terms, this bias has been mainly explained by the concentration of Indo-Guyanese in rural areas and occupations and late arrival into the urban and public sector job market where most of the recruitment continues to take place. Despite constituting 51 per cent of the total population in 1965, Indo-Guyanese were just 20 per cent of the security forces (Danns 1984). By 1970, only 25 per cent of the personnel in the police and defence forces were Indo-Guyanese (Hintzen 1989: 92). The persistence of this imbalance after independence has been attributed to the need for the Afro-Guyanese political elite to entrench its hold on power by recruiting personnel along ethnic lines, as well as to the refusal by Indo-Guyanese of the methods and implications of recruitment (Poynting 1987; Premdas 1996).

Military officers were predominantly men. The PNC's official policy of gender equality has co-existed with gender-stereotyped and welfarist orientations (Peake 1993), with beneficiaries often determined by party membership and loyalty. While women are highly visible in the work-force, they tend to be confined to segregated and inferior corners of the labour market. The military is a good example of this tendency. To be sure, some women were recruited, but mainly among the lower ranks. Women have been more visible in the National Service and People's Militia, which operate as reserve supports for the traditional forces. The latter, mainly a part-time organisation, predominantly drew its volun-teers from the lower ranks of the civil service, most of whom were again Afro-Guyanese. An emphasis on partisan loyalty belied the representation of the military as a symbol of national unity against territorial aggressors, revealing it to be the state's need to defend itself against the population in whose name it illegitimately claimed the right to govern.

Notwithstanding distribution of patronage, the government had lost widespread support by the end of the 1970s on account of the economy's poor performance and the illegitimacy of the political regime. The col-lapse of the Guyanese economy dates back to the mid 1970s and was precipitated by a combination of internal and external factors: continued dependence on primary exports; the use of the state sector for patronage and as a channel of accumulation for the political elite; unsustainable state expansion under a co-operative socialist agenda; and mismanage-ment of the economy all combined to create a situation which became untenable in the aftermath of the global oil price rise in the early 1970s. Between the 1960s and the 1980s, growth rates fell from 3.6 per cent to 3.3 per cent. The visible trade balance, which registered a surplus in 1971, moved to a position of deficit by 1981, while the external debt escalated by some 111 per cent between 1980 and 1985. The crisis was passed on to the population in the form of massive retrenchments and wage cuts, a rapidly rising cost of living and a deterioration of public services and basic infrastructure.

In 1985, following the death of the president and the declaration by the IMF that Guyana was ineligible for further assistance, the government embarked on a new strategy which entailed the abandonment of co-op-erative socialism and economic and political liberalisation. In 1990, a standard structural adjustment programme was adopted which included the removal of price controls, devaluation, divestment, restructuring of the public sector and the opening up of the economy to foreign investment (Ferguson 1995). The SAP has continued unabated following the transfer of political power in 1992 under the first democratically held elections in 28 years.

While output and investment have risen over the last five years, the SAP has delivered increasing levels of pauperisation to a population already feeling the brunt of 20 years of economic decline. The burden of adjustment has been shifted to the households of those least able to afford it. Maternal and infant malnutrition and mortality rates have escalated beyond the average in the wider Caribbean while life expectancy has dropped from 70 to 65 years between 1985 and 1991 (Boyd 1989: 10-12). It is estimated that over 60 per cent of the population live below the poverty line; some put the figure as high as 75 per cent (Ferguson 1995: 109). Migration rates have soared such that Guyana is one of the few countries to experience negative growth rates; between 1980 and 1992 the reported population had declined from 760,000 to 730,000 persons. The exodus constitutes a critical survival strategy and source of support for those left behind (IADB 1994).

The Expansion and Feminisation of the Private Security Industry

Both the expansion and internal restructuring of the private security industry over the last ten or twelve years can be linked to the crisis outlined above. The widening income gap – made more visible by the propensity of many whose businesses have benefited under the SAP to indulge in conspicuous consumption – has precipitated a surge in the demand for security guards from businesses, diplomats and the middle class, anxious for protection against anticipated social consequences of economic im-miseration. Between 1980 and 1993 there was an increase in reported burglaries and larcenies[8] (IADB 1994). While much of this takes place in villages in the rural areas – where 'kick down the door banditry' prevails – and certainly in low-income communities, the services continue to be primarily available in Georgetown and its environs to those who can afford them.

Initially, the expansion depended heavily on migration from the defence industry. If the economic crisis produced a greater official empha-sis on militarisation, it also attracted underpaid and disaffected military officers into the private security business and other avenues of employ-ment. Almost all of the businesses were started by ex-officers from the police and army, and they targeted a specifically male labour market. Yet over the last decade, this has virtually been supplanted by the influx of predominantly Afro-Guyanese female applicants, a major proportion of whom have work experience but no military training. This change must be set against the backdrop of economic liberalisation and its concomitant effects on the structure of the labour market.

As in other countries undergoing structural adjustment measures, Guyana has witnessed a dramatic rise in the numbers of women seeking jobs. Female labour force participation rates rose from 20 per cent in 1970 to 39.2 per cent by 1992. This is less a reflection of a growing demand for female labour than an indicator of households in crisis. In 1992, women accounted for 53 per cent of the unemployed, despite constituting only 34 per cent of the total labour force. There is also considerable underemployment, most noticeably within the informal sector which has experienced an exponential increase over the last decade and which largely consists of irregular and seasonal work.[9]

Notwithstanding some diversification, women have not been equally integrated into the economic sectors as men, who remain far more predominant in agriculture, construction, electricity, mining, quarrying, transport and communications. The vast majority of women remain in commerce and service-oriented jobs. The latter area, in which women were already highly visible owing to the expansion of the state bureaucracy during the 1970s, has seen an even greater concentration of females as men exited as a consequence of retrenchment and an effective downward adjustment of wages (Andaiye & Shiw Parsad 1994).

Interestingly, it is in the context of a feminisation and devaluation of services in general that the security industry has become an attractive choice. In most of the companies a fortnightly wage – especially when combined with overtime – easily equals or outstrips the monthly earnings of many in the private and public sectors, such as junior clerks, domestics, and even unqualified teachers and nursing assistants.[10] If relative wage levels make security work attractive for lower-income groups, limited job opportunities render it among the most viable options for women. Men who might have previously applied or worked in security have been able to take advantage of the employment opportunities presented by the structural adjustment programme in the construction, transport and mining sectors. At least two of the security companies had experienced a severe attrition of their male workers in the wake of foreign investment in mining and timber concessions in the country's hinterland regions. Additionally, self-employment – especially in the informal and transnational trading sector which brings products from the Caribbean, Latin and North America to Guyanese urban sidewalks and stores – is now an integral feature of the contemporary Guyanese landscape, and despite the risks and uncertainty men can still hope to earn more than they would as a security guard. This is an area in which women have also become increasingly involved but as their activities tend for the most part to be confined to the lower end of the scale, their earnings are far lower than men's (Holder 1989). Moreover, if the initial impetus for men to leave the workforce was largely economic, the changing gender balance also seems to act as a dissuasive force on prospective male applicants; in short, the symbolic association between security work and men is being displaced by the presence of women.

The predominance of Afro-Guyanese employees is also significant. In keeping with wider Caribbean patterns, Afro-Guyanese women have always displayed high levels of participation in the paid labour force, the result of migration in the post-slavery era to urban areas, early access to job opportunities there and the high incidence of female-headed households. Indo-Guyanese women in contrast, although always highly visible in unpaid agricultural work, have had a far less continuous relationship wtih the waged labour force in the post-indentureship years. This derives from a number of interconnected factors which include their marginalisation from the sugar industry in the 1960s, their concentration in rural areas with little access to jobs, the domination of the public sector by Afro-Guyanese and greater domestic prohibitions against women working. In the contemporary period, however, one can discern closer convergences in women's labour force patterns. Whereas many of the early female recruits were from within the Afro-Guyanese dominated public service, today employees come from the private and self-employed sectors, and several have not worked before. With increasing numbers of Indo-Guyanese moving to the urban centre (and those on its outskirts travelling to the city in search of employment), the ethnic occupational balance appears to be slowly changing.

A Profile of the Security Industry

The age of the businesses varied from 27 years to three companies set up in the last six years. Although most of the industry is locally owned, two firms have recently opened, with parent companies and branches in the Caribbean, Latin America and the United Kingdom (one American firm opened briefly but soon closed after apparent recruiting and employee problems). Given the diversity of resource profiles, companies range from those well equipped with vehicles, communication equipment, canine and armoured divisions and boasting a clientele which includes diplomatic missions and prominent businesses, to firms which rely exclusively on government offices, small businesses and residents for their income. Larger businesses have between 300 to 450 employees, while smaller ones vary from a low of 66 to about 250 workers. Most pay weekly or fortnightly, and there are also some incentive and bonus schemes. It is clear that the provision of security services has become a highly competitive business and some smaller companies have scaled down and closed in recent years as clients were lost to more competitive tenders. Most of the employees are drawn from the city and the wider metropolitan Georgetown area.

Entry requirements are fairly straightforward. Applicants are required to produce police clearance certificates. Previous work experience is desirable but not necessary. Literacy and numeracy are stressed, but employers assert that stringent rules were frequently relaxed on account of the collapse of the formal educational system. Successful applicants are given rudimentary classroom type training which lasts for about one week and includes lessons on writing up log books, incident reports, deportment and customer service. Armed officers are trained in firearms by the police, the costs of which are borne by the employer. Officers did not appear to undergo any other defense training.

Of the two ethnic groups – Indo-Guyanese and Afro-Guyanese – most visible in the workforce, Afro-Guyanese officers predominated.[11] There were intra-industry ethnic disparities, ranging from a low of five per cent to a high of 50 per cent Indian employees. Those companies in which Indo-Guyanese were most likely to be found were either headed by an Indo-Guyanese (two) or had several Indian employees at the management and personnel levels. The numbers of Indian women were also far lower than men throughout. In one firm, for instance, Indian women accounted for 10 per cent of the female labour force while Indian men comprised 20 per cent of the male workforce.

In most of the firms surveyed, women constituted roughly half of the workforce; the two exceptions were one company with 10 per cent and another with 70 per cent women. Significantly, the former offered the lowest wages and hired mainly older men (over the age of 60). In keeping with wider Caribbean trends, there was a substantial number of young mothers in the workforce. In one firm, the average number of children for female employees was three. Forty-eight per cent of the women had infants under six-years- old, while 73 per cent had children between the ages of six and fifteen years. Generally speaking, most of the respondents were single parents in need of a regular income, while others had partners, not all of whom were working or had regular jobs.

Households, Labour Markets and the Supply of Female Labour

The figures above tell us little of the processes involved in the changing gender composition of a traditionally male occupation. Older firms experienced the process of feminisation some ten years ago, when the country was on the verge of both economic collapse and the formulation of the Economic Recovery Programme. Interviews suggested that only Company 'A' had adopted a deliberate policy of recruiting women from its inception. More often, preferences continued to be expressed for more male applicants. One firm advertised vacancies for 80 males, 20 females in the daily newspaper while my research was continuing. Such quotas, it was hoped, would deter women from coming forward.

That the incorporation of women was in fact *not* an employer initiative requires attention to the broader context which helps constitute the supply of different types of labour for employment. The relative ease of entry combined with salary levels attracts women to security work: 'It has to do with finance and Government jobs are not paying and it's easier, you don't have to go running around begging people for jobs.' Respondents described opportunities as being far more class-specific for women, with options severely circumscribed at the lower levels where inadequate formal educational qualifications prevailed. When asked what job they would apply for if they left their present employment, women overwhelmingly identified domestic and service jobs; in contrast, men chose carpentry, supervisory and trading occupations. Twelve of the 15 women interviewed had never entered or completed secondary school. Technical training placements were a possibility for men: 'Men can find a faster fit in a job. A woman got to have papers [qualifications], but a man can always just apprentice.' However, the presence of three women with qualifications up to and beyond the secondary level – one of whom had recently left her job as a nurse at a public hospital – testifies to the growing pauperisation of previously protected categories of workers as a result of the crisis.

The household is also an important factor in its designation of rights and responsibilities. Women in particular have been most affected by the repatriation of social services to the household during adjustment and recession (Benería & Feldman 1992; Deere *et. al.* 1990). If one of the effects is broadly acknowledged as increasing female labour force participation, this case-study suggests that women's centrality in the domestic domain may also manifest itself in their willingness to seek entry to non-traditional areas of work which offer greater remuneration (Laurie 1995). In short, what we are witnessing is women seeking new ways of satisfying old/traditional roles. All of the respondents explicitly referred to their familial responsibilities as the principal reason behind applying for a security position, and commented more generally that this accounted for the high numbers of female relative to male officers. Considerations of status were clearly more important for men; and while some women admitted that they were initially ashamed of applying for a security job, and their own families often objected, they could not afford to let their pride impede their need for a regular income to support their homes:

The first thing, the man would look to see if they friend would see them in the work clothes, it would be the last work they would do . . . the women will come out because they have the responsibility, but you will hardly find the man saying that.

According to accounts, men were more prepared to take risks for quick money or to opt for unemployment in lieu of badly paid or unsegregated jobs which eroded the material and symbolic basis for enactments of masculine superiority. It also appears that in the contemporary period men may be more likely to forego jobs considered to be low in wages or status, particularly where women are becoming increasingly visible. It was noteworthy that the male officers interviewed claimed that security work was most appealing to older men who had retired, were unable to take the risks associated with independent businesses or to maintain their positions as skilled tradesmen. It was presented by some as a sedentary occupation, involving little or no effort. In the words of a 65-year-old male officer who had trained as a carpenter: 'If I was a younger man, I wouldn't be a security guard, I would be doing my own sort of trade.' In one company, the average age of male employees was 45 years, and 33 years for women.

The ethnic imbalance in the labour force (with mostly Afro-Guyanese applicants and workers) is also striking. Motherhood for Afro-Caribbean women is inextricably linked with income earning; what is new in this study is the fact that women now seem increasingly prepared to assume new roles in the labour force to fulfil these duties. Given the vast majority of female applicants who worked previously, it can be argued that the transition from a typical to an atypical job, while raising questions of suitability, does not challenge the right of such women to work in the first place. The situation is quite different for Indian women with little or no previous work experience, and for whom female employment per se has been a far more contested domain vis-à-vis both their households and the labour market.

Another issue concerns the representation of the labour market in Guyana as a site of ethnic demarcation and production. I have mentioned previously the massive under-representation of Indo-Guyanese in the military, a fact which disadvantaged potential – male – Indian recruits in the formative years of the private security industry when men with prior military training were actively recruited for employment. That relatively fewer Indo-Guyanese apply for such jobs today may well be related to discriminatory factors on the part of the employers, but it is equally the case that the perception of the job as the preserve of one ethnic group may act as a disincentive to others and particularly to Indian women, since in both gender and ethnic terms the position is controversial. Certainly this idea of employment as a signifier of ethnic identity appeared time and again in conversations with employees. As one Afro-Guyanese woman commented:

The Indian man nowadays very particular with the wife, and when they got to go out and mix with black man, specially when night come, they wouldn't allow it. When they come into contact with black man is one of the worst things for them, on the face of the earth. The black man would trust the women them more.

At the same time as we recognise ethnic disparities, we must be wary of accounting for them in terms of an ahistorical and unchanging cultural plurality. Economic immiseration has resulted in a rapid reconfiguration of gender relations within Indo-Guyanese households, such that paid employment is increasingly becoming a legitimate sphere for female activity. What is equally striking, therefore, is not the small numbers of Indo-Guyanese (predictable to many), but rather their growing visibility in the service.[12] Moreover, the predominance of female heads among the employees indicates that women living with partners face constraints which cut across ethnic lines. As several respondents pointed out, both Indian men as well as women are occupying a profile that is growing within the companies, and among employees ethnic divisions are muted and continually undercut by the conditions facing all workers, and women in particular.

Guarding the Guards: Gendering Representations and Practices within the Service

Given that employers were forced to recognise the contemporary reality, what did the process of adaptation entail? There was overwhelming acknowledgment by employers that women have 'proven' themselves to be a worthwhile if unavoidable investment. Explanations hinged on traditional representations of female domesticity. In the first place, women's responsibilities as mothers restricted them far more than men to finding and keeping a secure job under crisis conditions. Secondly, women's vulnerability to sexual violation obliged them to be perpetually on their guard. These twin attributes – good mother/sexual subordinate – produced high attendance, low levels of absenteeism, respectability and alertness. Most of the problems – alcoholism, turnover rates, sleeping on the site, absenteeism, sloppiness and thefts – were identified with men.

Notwithstanding employers' recognition that 'women are as good as and even better than men', one can trace various levels of resistance to the challenge posed by female employment. That employers continue to assert that women are assuming positions which should have been men's suggests that the denotion of security work as a masculine identifier – as well as the sovereignty of certain spaces within it is – retained. Generally speaking, women were predominantly portrayed as good mothers with little alternative to 'unfeminine' jobs.

That this is so is demonstrated by practices within the workplace. As Table 3.1 illustrates, there is widespread vertical segregation.

Table 3.1 Positions held in security firm 'B'

Division	Males	Females
Baton	0	0
Inspectors	14	0
Principal guards	65	17
Senior guards	50	42
Regular guards	44	45
Armoured	58	3
Driver	6	0
Total	237	107

Source: Compiled from records of Security Firm B, Georgetown, August 1995

Senior officers earn higher pay rates and are required to work for less hours before earning overtime pay. Hourly cash incentives are also given to the armoured division. In another company, women accounted for almost three-quarters of the labour force. In all, 19 per cent of the female employees were security supervisors, as opposed to 36 per cent of the male employees. This was not related to educational disparities, as proportions of men and women who had received primary and secondary schooling were exactly similar. However, prior military or security experience did appear to be a differentiating factor; 37 per cent of the female supervisors and 78 per cent of the men had previously worked in the security forces.

To be sure, military experience provides men with one advantage over women in chances for promotion, but it is not a sufficient explanation. Employers uniformly relied on naturalised attributes to explain women's unrepresentativeness within higher echelons. Almost all voiced their reluctance to consider women for armed training on the grounds that they were prone to hysteria. Paradoxically, this qualified women for sites where 'early warning signals' were needed. In other words, female officers are deterrents against potential criminals but ineffective against the actual demonstration of illegal intent, portrayed as unable to handle a gun or cope with situations requiring objective and spur of the moment decisions. Significantly, none of the employers provided any examples from past experience (or even saw the need to do so) to substantiate their claims that men were better with firearms than women. Women were also described as not being aggressive enough in the competition for promo-tion, or refusing to accept greater responsibilities. The resulting cultural logic is that responsible mothers make good guards, but women are not responsible enough to trust themselves (or be trusted) with positions of authority.

In fact these attributed characteristics are selectively manipulated by employers, resulting in a climate in which the personal safety and well being of employees are often low on the list of priorities. For example, employers transgress their own defined boundaries by putting women on the night shift, but traditionalise it by refusing them adequate protection on the grounds that they are unsuited to carry weapons. Working alone – a frequent occurrence unless the site was a large business which required more than one officer – without arms and adequate/any communication equipment meant that women often felt vulnerable to possible sexual and other types of assault. Additionally, an apparent recognition of women's domestic responsibilities does not mean that employers are likely to make women's shifts more flexible. If motherhood is essentialised, the conditions under which it is carried out must nevertheless be kept invisible, separate from the workplace and subordinate to its demands. Single mothers with young children were most affected by the double shift, which frequently occurred when a replacement did not appear at the end of a seven-hour workday. Two of the women had lost earlier jobs for leaving a site unprotected after working for 14 hours without relief and with no knowledge of whether any provision had been made for their children in their absence.

The ambivalence and biases of some of the management staff is reinforced by the difficulties they frequently face in placing female officers. Security companies are in a very real sense intermediaries who ultimately depend on *their* employers, the clients. A gendered demand could be discerned in that where officers had to perform receptionist duties, execute manual security checks on visitors, or be stationed at a household in which young children were present, females were specifically re-quested. Some clients also believed that men were prone to criminal activity, whereas women would prove to be more trustworthy (there have indeed been reports of crimes committed by or in collusion with officers, although whether only male guards were involved is open to question). In this regard, one can perhaps argue that there is not so much a dissolution of 'traditional' barriers as an extension of the belief that women, as nurturers and guardians of their own homes, are well suited to protect other people's children. As the extended comments made, by an employer aptly illustrate below, there is still considerable discomfort with the general idea of the female security guard:

Almost all clients will stipulate that they want a male. Even those that don't stipulate, give them a couple of weeks with a woman and they will always, still find a fault with her. Mostly it's on women's appearance, 'they don't look as tough' or 'they're not good enough'. What some clients have done in order to strike a balance is to say I can have a woman, but only in the day, not at night.

Ultimately, given the logic of profit maximisation, it is the women whose hours, location, incentive pay and even recruitment are affected. As one employer succinctly stated, 'What are we going to do? The bottom line, at the end of the day, is that we have to provide a service for our clients'.

Guarding the Guards: Of Co-workers and Partners

At the level of the workplace and household culture, antagonism towards the visibility of female guards was evident, highlighting the uniqueness of the internal restructuring of the security industry, as the employment records of one company demonstrate in Table 3.2.

As can be seen much of the labour supply is the result of migration within services, although women and men were concentrated in different occupations. Men were predominantly employed previously as defence personnel; 64 per cent of all the male employees had received military training. In contrast, 24 per cent of the women had military/security training, and most of their previous service jobs consisted of domestic and counter attendant work. In other occupations, male/female distinctions were also reinforced. Far more men worked in craft related jobs as masons, electricians and carpenters; with the exception of one female mason, women worked as seamstresses. The second highest category for women was as unpaid labour within the home.

The high proportion of officers with immediate prior experience of segregated jobs suggests not only that employees negotiate the terrain of non-traditional work against the backdrop of a society which continues to operate along traditionally stratified lines, but also that there is an available and hegemonic repertoire of ideas which naturalises and legitimises the power relations inherent in these inequalities. Within the companies, women described direct and indirect efforts to maintain a working environment in which gender divisions were prevalent. Most of the men interviewed believed that women and men were best suited to perform different tasks, and that female security guards were doing a job

Table 3.2 Job held prior to security appointment

Jobs	Women		Men	
	No.	%	No.	%
Professional*	6	4.2	3	4.9
Craft	7	4.9	10	16.4
Sales	8	5.6	–	–
Service	65	45.5	38	62.3
Manual	13	9.1	9	14.8
Home/Unemployed	44	30.8	1	1.6
Total	143	100.0	61	100.0

*Nurses and Teachers

Source: Compiled from records of Security Firm A, Georgetown, August 1995

which did not come naturally to them, regardless of how capably they performed their duties.

As other studies have shown, expressions of male hostility are likely to occur where women are held responsible for involuntary male marginalisation in a particular industry (Cockburn 1983; Walby 1986). The present case is slightly different in that women are not deliberately substituted for men; on the contrary, it is men who are not offering themselves in sufficiently large numbers. Nonetheless, the content of security work retains an association with maleness which resonates with the meanings given to physically demonstrative work in wider society, although it is clearly problematic to reconcile this with the contemporary reality. While most of the respondents voiced the view that male colleagues were adapting to their presence, and many had experienced no direct discrimination, women believed that they were not fully integrated into the industry, and felt that they were scrutinised as *female* workers. Some women stated that they felt pressured to perform twice as well as their male counterparts to justify their positions. Others cited instances of men refusing to have women work on a site with them. Not surprisingly perhaps, many voiced their reluctance to be considered for promotions, but not necessarily as a result of any inherent bias against meaningful responsibility, as suggested by the employers above. Rather, women stated that they could only expect problems from officers – men as well as women – who would have difficulty in accepting orders from a female supervisor.

The main problem faced by women related to sexual harassment, predominantly identified with the supervisory staff. It took the form of jokes, references to women's inability to perform, and sexual overtures in exchange for relief of duties. Men freely acknowledged that this was a problem for women in the industry, citing it as one reason for their reluctance to allow their partners to take jobs as security officers. While men's behaviours were freely acknowledged, they were dismissed as natural and expected. On the other hand, it was women who needed to be protected from the male gaze, or upon whom the onus was placed to behave in a manner which discouraged male advances.

Within their households, women frequently encountered resistance from husbands and partners. A fundamental aspect of this discussion concerns the production of derogatory images of women who transgress their socio-spatial limits. The predominant stereotype is that only sexually irresponsible women put their bodies on the line. Security work is an extreme example as it involves patrolling public places at night – the ultimate masculine space. Such women, the tale goes, use their job as a cover to meet paramours, friends, and generally escape their domestic duties. Given such representations, it was not surprising that most of the men, including those who in principle agreed that women could be security guards, were exceedingly ambivalent when the question assumed personal overtones, as indicated by the following comment by one officer on whether his wife could become a guard: 'Who? What? She got to be crazy. What she doing now giving she enough money. Even if she not making enough, I wouldn't let her. No explanation to be given.' The conflict that takes place between a female guard and her partner as a result of this ambiguity often results in severe domestic violence. Of the 12 women interviewed who had partners, five faced no opposition from their spouses, with the remainder experiencing initial or ongoing resistance. Several of the women concerned had suffered intensified emotional and physical abuse after taking security jobs. Faced with the problem of defining women who do male jobs, particularly in an area where the male body itself remains *the* primary signifier of suitability, men resorted to disciplining the subversive feminine body. One respondent suffered frequent blackouts after suffering concussion from a blow she had received from her husband. Another said of her partner:

He tells me I am going places, even though I have on my uniform. Before I live with him, I used to carry the children out, but now as soon as I want to go, he says I going to reach this body and that body [person]. Sometimes I find myself so frustrated, but I have to stay with him for the children, because the area that I live in is not safe.

Nor was battering confined within the walls of the home. Women were also humiliated at their places of work and several accounts were given of women beaten by husbands in the presence of other officers, or forced to leave their site by the appearance of an estranged partner.[13] Indian women were also accused of going to meet black men. Employers pointed out that the opposition of a male partner was one of the principal reasons for women leaving the job.[14] Through these performances, men publicly seek to enact and re-establish a masculinity eroded by the rising cost of living. It is hardly surprising then, that for Indo- and Afro-Guyanese women alike, female heads were most likely to be found in security positions. At the same time, the pervasiveness of violence reminds us that many of these women are in visiting relationships and face similar threats as those who live with men (Danns and Shiw Parsad 1989).

Women were also expected to fulfil their domestic responsibilities by both employers and partners. Companies asked questions about childcare only of women; in one firm grandmothers, sisters and older children were predominantly named as the carers. Few partners helped out in the home, and many of the women had little choice but to leave their children unattended. That this has become more common indicates that while extended female networks have long been critical in enabling Caribbean women to work, these informal mechanisms are being attenuated in the current climate in which increasing numbers of women are entering the job market. Perversely, women are blamed if domestic duties are seen to be neglected. In one extreme example, the partner of a female guard raped her daughter while she was away on night duty. Notwithstanding condemnation of the rapist, the view of many implicated the woman as well for being an irresponsible mother by choosing to protect other's property instead of her own domestic domain (personal communication, Karen de Souza, Red Thread Women's Collective, Georgetown Guyana, May 3rd, 1996).

Experience and Subjectivity

So far we have looked at the context in which female guards operate. Yet the visibility of women in this domain begs the question of how they are affected by their performance of purportedly masculine work, in the process drawing our attention to the fact that their daily lives exceed the categories imposed upon them. In other words, efforts to exert control over the representation of the occupation as well as the actions of female guards signify not closure but rather an inability to ever fully enclose the experiences and subjectivities of the women employed therein. This tension should not be overstated, lest we unproblematically attribute to women an unfailing and heroic ability to resist over and above the constraints in, through and against which they constitute themselves (Abu-Lughod 1990). If recognition of incompleteness opens up possibilities for analysing the conditions under which social change occurs, it is also the case that participation does not take place in a vacuum, but rather operates complexly within structures of legitimation/dominance.

Nina Laurie (1995) suggests that in Peru, low-income earning women employed in symbolically masculine work relied on what she terms a 'moral economy of difference'. They partially accepted the dominant representations which portrayed female roadsweepers as vulgar, gossips, lesbians and adulterers in order to distance themselves from such images and create the space within which they could justify their own employment in such areas to their menfolk and families. Similarly, the women in this study identified with the hegemonic images of female security officers as women who exploited their sexuality to meet men on the job and elicit favours from their superiors, while simultaneously reiterating that they were simply good mothers, female heads, older women and loyal partners out to bring in a needed income. As one woman stated: 'Men bother women all the time, that's a norm with them. And the women take them on as well. But not me. It just depends on how you carry yourself.' These stereotypes of domesticity echo wider, class-specific ideas about female respectability.

Locating oneself within hegemonic discursive structures in order to ameliorate the disjunctive effects of women doing men's work is often a necessary (and sometimes unsuccessful) subterfuge where disapprobation can lead to job loss and extremes of physical violence. It helps maintain the space as one which women can have access to, in a situation where there are precious little alternatives to earn a livable income. At the same time, participating in and experiencing the destabilisation of gendered work divisions did appear to affect women's self-definitions. All of the female interviewees felt that women and men were equally capable of doing similar work, while recognising the pressures this placed on them to prove themselves:

When I first started security I had a hard time getting in, because they say they more looking for male than for female. Look, my company put me on a location and the client said we requested a male. I said whatever a male puts out, a female can do it too. I am a female, yet I got to be much more than the male.

Additionally, broader differences in wages were identified as discriminatory. As one respondent asserted: 'Women should do the same job as men because the woman does always earn less than the man when she does different work.' Another said: 'When you have equal rights with men, it doesn't mean that you want to do everything that a man do, is whatever you're capable of, is about allowing you to give of your best.' These responses contrast with an earlier survey (1992-93) in which respondents in segregated occupations were ambivalent on the question of whether they could perform similar tasks as men (Trotz 1995: 268-71). Notably, when asked what types of jobs they wanted for their daughters, women stated that security work was not one of their options, but the reasons given were largely class-specific (low wages, job insecurity); there were no suggestions that it was unsuitable work for women.

Women also articulated the relationship between their domestic and work lives which they felt were not respected by security firms. At one staff meeting I attended, management complained that employees were uncommitted, often refusing to work at short notice when staff shortages were severe. Disagreeing, several of the women emphasised that employers were insufficiently cognizant of the difficulties young mothers faced in finding suitable support systems. The comments of one woman forced to leave evening classes because her employer refused to consider rescheduling her timetable, are fairly typical of the resentment voiced by others:

Is like you begging for a job. Is like some of them don't care about you, don't go out of their way to cater for single mothers, like giving them flexible shifts, not making them do double shifts just like that. They only cater for the money. Is quite disheartening, is like they don't mean to go nowhere to meet you.

Nor did women simply accept this state of affairs. According to a representative from the Ministry of Labour, female employees frequently registered complaints. These revolved around sexual harassment and discrimination against pregnant women, who are rarely allowed to work and are sent on unpaid maternity leave.[15] Most persons making individual complaints to the Ministry were women, despite the fact that many of the discriminatory factors operating in the workplace affected men as well, such as the lack of protection against summary dismissals. This might well indicate any one of three possibilities: that women are more likely to lose their jobs; that men have more choices in alternative job opportunities or can better afford the time-lag involved in moving between jobs; or that men's responses are more likely to involve some form of collective action. In the case of the latter, women are also visible, although efforts of the workforce to come together across gender divisions are gravely hampered by the inadequacy of legal mechanisms, as well as the view of many of the employers that it is illegal for a uniformed officer to strike. The labour representative noted three instances in which an unsuccessful attempt was made to form a union; in each case, the employees all lost their jobs.[16] As far as could be recalled, the initiators of the unions were men. Given that these attempts were stopped in their infancy, it is not possible to assess the extent to which the specific interests and grievances of women were incorporated.

Conclusion: Same old story?

This article has explored the reasons for and implications of female employment in non-traditional work. It argues that the increasing trend towards feminisation (in numerical terms) of the private security sector in Guyana is less an index of gender equality or employer incentive than an outcome of the limited choices that low-income women face over the sale of their labour power. It involved changes at the micro-level (the household) which in turn affected the composition of the labour market. Motherhood, a salient symbol, has become not only more explicitly linked across ethnic lines with employment, but increasingly necessitates the willingness of women to enter areas traditionally closed to them. This is not to say that there are no barriers to entry. On the contrary, it is precisely the lack of an available male workforce that has left employers with little choice but to hire women. Despite security companies' accommodation of growing numbers of female applicants, women do not have equality of access to all posts and face continued problems at lower levels.

The rapid influx of women does not appear to have fully dislodged dominant notions of appropriateness: it is women's natural motherhood which makes them natural protectors. In a somewhat more cynical and sinister twist, it is their sexual vulnerability which makes them vigilant (for they are on guard against their own violation, not just the violation of the client's property), but their ascribed emotional instability which leaves them unarmed against potential perpetrators of crime.

Additionally, if private security work in the early days was the only escape route from the public sector for men, today informality, mining or construction beckon. With so many women, this occupation has now partly become a symbolic marker of declining male status – for some men, it is better to be unemployed. Thus, far less men apply and security work is spoken of as something which women and older men do (despite the presence of many young male officers). This is not to say that men accept that the job is a feminine one, or the consequences of that ambivalence. At the level of the household, many women constantly confront threats to their physical safety and most experience precious little change in the domestic division of labour.

Nor have the anachronisms of the security industry been allowed to infect the body politic, particularly as it manifests itself in a global arena. Ironically, security work now seems to traverse a public/private divide. Official policing and military institutions remain dominated by men, and were drawn on to maintain public order in the 1992 elections which heralded the country's return to electoral democracy. The armed forces also represent the nation to the outside world, most recently as members of an international peace-keeping unit stationed in Haiti. Women, meanwhile, remain in charge of homes – their own and other people's. They are in a service which remains supportive of and ultimately subordinate to the national security force.

Are we to conclude then that what we are witnessing is simply an addition to Guyanese women's repertoire of 'traditional' jobs and a reiteration of well worn gender and ethnic stereotypes? A few observations must give us pause, all of which deserve future research. Firstly, whatever the patterns of class and gender discrimination within individual firms, and despite domestic problems, the fact remains that women continue to apply for and remain as security guards. As we have also seen, they express themselves as equally capable as men, and in some cases have been able to (with Indian women) take their case to government officials and (with men) to struggle for union representation. Secondly, divisions other than gender are also shifting and there are now a growing number of Indo-Guyanese employees, for whom the matter of survival is similarly a desperate one. Finally, all of the women claimed that they wanted jobs for their daughters on grounds that were class but not gender related. It awaits more detailed and longitudinal study to determine whether there are intergenerational changes in the types of jobs that both women as well as men apply for.

As I suggested at the beginning of the chapter, levels of analysis are interdependent but not functional. That is to say, society does not simply reproduce itself, and conflict, accommodation and negotiation characterise the process of change. It is meaningless to elide women's visibility within male domains with the erosion of gender inequalities or to locate women's practices and self-presentations outside of dominant structures and representations. It would also be an oversight not to address equally efforts to reimpose patterns of dominance, to reconfigure stereotypes and the exclusions that they entail. Attention to both these aspects highlights the fluidity and unnaturalness of such stereotypes, and allows us to trace potential spaces and possibilities for positive change.

Notes

1. This study was made possible by a research grant from the University of Cambridge Travel Expenses Fund, supported by the Centre of Latin American Studies, Cambridge. I am indebted to a number of people, especially the women of Albouystown and Red Thread Women's Collective, whose experiences first provided the ideas in this chapter, and the employers and employees of the various security companies who gave so freely of their time two years later when I had the opportunity to carry out this research. Nina Laurie has generously shared her work with me. I also wish to thank Andaiye, Karen de Souza, Geoffrey Hawthorn, David Lehmann, Linda Peake, Jacqui Quinn-Leandro, Terry Roopnaraine, Verena Stolcke and an anonymous reviewer for their comments on various drafts, for their advice, and for their time. An earlier version of this chapter was presented to a graduate seminar on the sociology of politics and development at Cambridge University, and to the Caribbean Studies Association Conference, San Juan, May 27-31, 1996. As usual, I take full responsibility for the arguments presented.

2. For example, census figures for Guyana between 1881 and 1911 show that clerks and shop assistants were predominantly men (Rodney 1981: 237); yet these are two areas which today have become almost exclusively associated with women, and which moreover are represented as timelessly so.

3. Gender as it is used in this chapter refers to a cultural construction through which the categories of male and female are constituted in relation to each other and to other social divisions in specific contexts. While it uses biological – sex – differences as a referent, it cannot be reduced to these since the ways in which the precisely through essentialising the relationship between the body and its representation that divisions of labour, power and sexuality which disadvantage women are reinforced as natural (Floya Anthias and Nira Yuval-Davis, *Racialized Boundaries: Race, Nation , Gender, Colur Class and the Anti-racist Struggle* (London: Routledge,1992); Jane Collier and Sylvia Yanagisako, *Gender and Kinship: Essays toward a Unified Analysis*, (Standford University Press, 1987).

4. For an excellent account of these issues in the context of women's employment in emergency work programmes in Peru originally designed for men, see Laurie (1995).

5. The contemporary descendants of African slaves and Indian indentured labourers.

6. Observers have commented that the NGS was a political arm of the ruling party paid for out of public funds, and never explained in Parliament.

7. According to the 1980 Population Census, Indo-Guyanese accounted for 51 per cent of the population, while Afro- and mixed-Guyanese constituted 42 per cent. The remaining seven per cent is comprised of Amerindians, Chinese and Europeans.

8. There has also been a perceptible increase in violent and spectacular crimes, although much of this tends to be confined within competing interests in organised crime – drug and people trafficking. The latter refers to the lucrative business in counterfeit passport and alien resident cards to the United States which are sold for huge sums to would-be migrants.

9. These figures have been taken from the 1970 and 1980-81 Population Censuses of Guyana and preliminary figures from the 1992 Household and Income Expenditure Survey. Given gender biases in official definitions and measurements of work, these figures must be taken as conservative estimates and not as adequate reflections of the extent and complexity of women's work.

10. The prescribed hourly wage was set at G$22/hour. This was increased to G$30/hour under the Minimum Wages (Watchman) Amendment Order, 1993. Although a few smaller enterprises have been investigated by the Ministry of Labour for breaching the legislation, most firms – including all of those interviewed – pay wages above the minimum rate (at the time of the interviews, $US1 = G$145).

11. In one company, there were only two Amerindian employees. Chinese and Portuguese officers were completely absent; this is fairly typical of the industry as a whole.

12. It should be noted that if the current economic situation is pulling more Indo-Guyanese into security work, some – men in particular – have also left for other jobs. Such was the experience of one company which had partially relied on a rural Indo-Guyanese labour force. It recently witnessed the return of many of its employees to the sugar industry following the institutionalisation of a joint management contract between the government and a subsidiary of the pre-nationalisation conglomerate, the Booker Tate Group.

13. Several respondents – both male and female, when asked whether any guards had been killed on the job, referred to an incident in which a female guard was killed by her husband. Whether or not this is true (I was unable to corroborate it), this story has become part of the narrative of women's experience of 'guard work'. The client's space (often domestic, as women predominantly guard homes) becomes proscribed public space for female guards. The primary danger they face is not just (or even) from

would-be intruders, but from partners intent on returning them within their socio-spatial limits, even at the cost of life itself.

14. One employer recounted how he had been forced to discipline the husband of a female guard who arrived at head office one morning and proceeded to drag his wife out of the muster line and beat her. Tellingly, the employer was offended not by the fact of male brutality, but rather by the disrespect demonstrated by this public – and working-class – brawl; implicit in this was that such matters should be dealt with at home (as the employer said, 'I told him you can do whatever you want to do at home, but don't bring it to my place of work'). The irony here, of course, is that it is precisely the 'effort' of the woman's husband to return her to the home that precipitated his beating her in public in the first place.

15. As one employer stated, 'Our clients would complain, what is a woman guard going to do when she is walking around sticking out? How is she going to protect the place?'

16. This appears to be an area of contention. According to the Ministry's labour representative, police and auxiliary members of the police force cannot strike, but this does not apply to supernumerary constables who constitute the bulk of the private security force. In October 1994, the attorney-general was asked for advice on the interpretation of the law relating to the right of supernumerary constables to unionise and strike, but no answer was received at the time of the interview.

4

Working on Equality:
Commonwealth Caribbean Women Trade Union Leaders

A. Lynn Bolles

As the world dramatically changes from day to day and year to year, anthropologists find themselves as keepers of knowledge of the 'old ways,' and as analysts, documenters and interpreters of the effects of social change and social upheaval. My work with women trade union leaders in the Commonwealth Caribbean chronicles the combination of roles anthropologists play in their contemporary research. It also recounts the roles scholar/activist feminists anthropologists play. The work increases the understanding of the social construction of gender in cultures and societies whose very being was based on inequality exacted at a tremendous price. It analyses the dramatic effects of social movements for freedom, self-governance and self-determination. And, it interprets a specific social formation – organised labour, which meshes politics and the economy.

A number of factors facing anthropological/social inquiries are addressed in this work. First there are issues concerning methodology. How did I come to do this research on women, and organised labour in the English-speaking Caribbean? How did I actually carry out the project? Second, the analysis incorporates the social construction of gender, and social inequities found in seven societies – the location of the action – of the Commonwealth Caribbean spanning a period of 50 years. During those years, the countries underwent a transition from being the British West Indies (islands and mainland rim colonies) to independent nation-states. The majority of peoples in the Commonwealth Caribbean are descendants of slaves. The social structure, including economics, and social organisation are framed by the plantation modes of production. And finally, there is the perspective of standpoints – my own and that of the women trade union leaders.

Women's leadership experiences in the labour movement have made substantive contributions to the 50-year history of trade unionism in the region. They have played critical roles in these vital organisations – as political entities and mass social movements. However, women have been ignored, made invisible or underestimated by those recording the events of the region – scholars, politicians and trade unionists. In the research, stories of older women trade unionists who were on the scene in the early years of the labour movements (1930s-50s), women who were active during and after the years of national independence (1960s -70s), and those designated as the movement's future women leaders. A combination of personal narratives, historical accounts, and descriptions of everyday activities are used to draw attention to the work and lives of these women as agents of social change. Women leaders from mainstream trade unions in Jamaica, Barbados, Guyana, Antigua, Montserrat and St Vincent are represented.

Throughout my career as an anthropologist, I have been completely steeped in and a practitioner of responsible research. The moral responsibilities of conducting research came together full force in the late 1960s, in the discipline of anthropology and the institutionalisation of African-American studies. The responsibility of the researcher included paying attention to publications, to persons or organisations given access to materials, to the accountability of the anthropologist to the people under study, and the context of the work when it is translated into other languages. Moreover, as powerless people are made into subjects by research, specific safeguards should be in place to prevent political and economic manipulation by those who would do them harm (see Gwaltney 1981; Jones 1970; Willis 1974; Valentine 1972). Carrying out one's moral responsibilities is more than assuaging a sponsor agency. For me, the most significant component in doing responsible research rests on the relationship between the fieldworker and the folk (see Bolles 1985).

The positioning of the women trade union leaders' standpoint is a critical element in this endeavour, because of the past history of colonialism, US hegemonic relations between countries of the region, the varying levels of female subordination in the Commonwealth Caribbean, the invisibility of women in the region's labour history, and the region's status as a testing ground for a variety of research, experiments and fieldwork for North American academicians. It is my intention to express and to interpret the women trade union leaders' standpoint, and not to determine for them the meanings and goals of their lives. Writing about the experiences of African-American women, and black feminist thought, Patricia Hill Collins (1990: 750) discusses the interdependent nature of the relationship between the two. She writes, 'While black feminist thought articulates the taken-for-granted knowledge of African-American women, it also encourages all black women to create self-definitions that validate a black woman's standpoint.' Black feminist thought's potential demonstrates more than that black women can produce 'independent specialised knowledge'. It offers black women a different view of themselves than that offered by 'the established social order'. The consciousness of difference and identity already existed among black women. But by black feminist's re-articulating those values and traditions, which validates and acknowledges their differences and identity, African-American women have another 'tool of resistance to all forms of their subordination'.

Aihwa Ong (1988) argues that western feminists objectify non-western women by relegating their status to that of the 'Other'. In western philosophical constructs, women are subordinated by the patriarchy in such terms that they have no voice, and no concept of self than 'Other', i.e. not a part of the tradition of male authority which assigns, categorises and evaluates who and what someone is or is not. Ong (1988: 80) states that 'feminist voices in the social sciences unconsciously echo this masculinist will-power in its relation to non-western societies'. Further on she writes 'when feminists look overseas, they frequently seek to establish *their* authority on the backs of non-western women . . . the claim to common kinship with non-western women is at best, tenuous, at worst, non-existent'. Before many white feminists took stock that their notion of global sisterhood was a goal to strive for, not one already in place, my own ethical stance and personal position was a self-determined standard.

For me, some of the dilemmas that I encountered doing research in the Caribbean resulted from my identity as an African-American, and my middle-class origins. The latter point had distinctive meanings for the two groups of women with whom I have worked. For the working-class women, I was a woman of incredible privilege, but not perceived as elitist as their own upper-classes (see Bolles 1985). The middle-class women, who were represented among the trade union women leaders, viewed me as not being *really* middle class, since I did not belong to their own, and did not have the entry from birth or through West Indian channels of qualification, i.e. their 'proper' education, job and civic and/or church affiliations. Plus, who had ever heard of a member of the black American middle class, unless it was a person of West Indian descent who had done well after he or she immigrated to the US? My native, multi-generational African-American middle- class circumstance was an unknown to many, therefore 'suspect until proven otherwise'.

From my position as a black feminist, I envisioned a way to provide Caribbean women in the organised labour movement with another tool of resistance to all forms of their oppression. In the alternative way of presentation, where their standpoints would be expressed through their own voices, they would also be actively involved in the production of the work. My role was to facilitate that process, because they did not have the time, money and energy to do it for themselves.

Overall there is a recurring question that guides the larger work as well as this one. It asks: How did a people's struggle for self-government and social change end up being another case of male domination, female subordination and social hierarchy? Answers to that question are examined in four parts. The discussion begins by presenting the compilation of theories used as guides for understanding the women trade union leaders' position. This is followed by situating West Indian women in the mainstream organised labour movement, particularly in respect to constructs of gender, class and power. Next, I recount the methodologies used in the work that underscore the intellectual authority of the women trade leaders themselves. Finally, there is an analysis of the discussion with women trade union leaders and their views on organised labour and gender relations.

Ways of Understanding

One of the attributes of feminist scholarship has been its willingness to assess old theories, re-engage them in a gendered fashion, or try out new modes. Not all attempts of forging new theories have been successful. But no one can criticise feminist scholars of whatever 'political' persuasion, of not challenging the status quo or of experimenting with new concepts and ideas. Black feminists theories are predicated on the mutual importance of gender and race alongside other aspects of social systems. As a result, the work in black women's studies contends that black women have a self-defined standpoint on their own oppression which suggests that they experience a different world than those who are not black (or non-white) and female (Collins 1989: 747). The concept is helpful in understanding Caribbean women, the majority of whom are of African descent. Other theories examined here look at women in the context of social reproduction, class and power relations within and outside of the domestic sphere.

Most feminist studies concerning women place primacy on gender relations. Gender is the fundamental aspect of social relations of power, individual and collective identity, and the fabric of meaning and value in society (Morgen 1989). This perspective challenges the majority of available literature, written from the dominant masculine perspective. For example, the majority of studies on Caribbean marriage and the family focused on women, in terms of how disorganised and abnormal they were, compared to the 'norm' because they were woman centred. The reality is, of course, that the majority of family forms found in the region do not fit the 'norm' of the male dominated model (Bolles 1988).

In societies, like those in the English-speaking Caribbean, all classes of women are taught two kinds of histories and aspirations to guide them in their walks of life. One is the traditional African heritage rooted in the experiences of slavery. From it come the struggle, activism, collectivity, and community spirit which are the elements that support women, men, and children in their survival. In addition, both women and men engage in the social, cultural and economic activities which value the contributions of people regardless of their gender. Likewise, due to the variation in mating relationships and the constraints of division of labour, the majority of women in the region find themselves, for better or for worse, as the centre of many social and cultural arenas.

'The realm of familial responsibility' (Durant-Gonzalez 1982: 3) guides the daily lives of the majority of women in the Caribbean, and requires reciprocal obligations to kin and friends, which is often extended to community, church and work activities. Although the sentiment is shared by both sexes, women are the ones most encouraged to be responsible for others and for themselves through those domestic networks which constitute most women's strategies for survival.

The second type of history and culture learned, is based on a Eurocentric model which is part and parcel of the legacy of British colonialism, and the division of labour on which capitalism is founded. Simply, in this patriarchal view, men are the breadwinners and women are the housewives. Men deal with the world of wage labour, politics, social affairs, and are ordinate to women. Women deal with the world of biological reproduction, family, domestic labour, and are subordinate to men. Through the constructs of the capitalist system, men's labour is valued, and women's labour is devalued. The wage labour of people is encoded by gender whereby jobs that women perform are based on their 'natural' suitability, such as sewing, cleaning, tending to the sick and housekeeping. Needless to say, since men are the 'biological' family breadwinners – whether engaged in work demanding physical strength or mental aptitude – they receive greater compensation for their work than women do. Even though the slave system had men and women working side by side, in the modes of production which directly followed emancipation to modern times, men's and women's labour is sexually divided, inequitably valued, and differentially compensated.

In the region today, women and men deal with male domination, female subordination and the sexual division of labour in their productive lives and incorporate this ideology, of male domination and female subordination, into their perceptions of the way things ought to be (Anderson 1986:320). Men, as the dominate gender are seen as 'born leaders', regardless of their class origin. Of course, ruling class membership is an additional attribute for doing what is considered a male inclination. The image of the proper role for women, regardless of class, is that of homemaker and wife. In reality however, most West Indian women do not fit that image, though by clinging to the ideal, they believe they can aspire to this correct state (Ford-Smith 1986:156).

In the societies of the Americas, the nature of social and economic inequality was and still is measured by the status of one's birth and in some regions, the colour of skin and/or race. The legacy of slavery provides the backdrop as to how social and economic inequalities have been manifested throughout the years using skin colour as an ascriptive measure for class position. More importantly, it should be clear that whatever gains were made in the social and economic well being of peoples of African descent, the nature of racism continues to chart its overt and covert course. For women of African descent there is the added dimension brought about by both racism *and* sexism. The double oppression takes on a variety of meanings mitigated by class and colour in the Caribbean and Latin American context.

Even in the Caribbean today, there are some instances in which to be black and poor places one in a situation not much changed from the days of slavery. The social hierarchy, critical to the success of European colonialism, has been maintained by the ruling classes, and in contemporary times, by the economic agents of wealth and power. To be middle class implies the continuation of the privileging of colour and class. National independence did improve the access to education and employment for blacks and East Indians, who took advantage of those opportunities. And though the current economic crisis has dealt a blow to the Caribbean middle class, with their ordained positions they have more options to explore for their survival in hard times.

Most of the literature concerning the West Indian middle classes comes for studies looking at class relations, where the emphasis is on the majority – the working classes (e.g. Austin 1986; Brathwaite 1955; Smith 1965; Smith 1967; Stone 1980). A few studies have focused on West Indian elites, particularly in reference to their share of economic and political power (Alexander 1976; Phillips 1977; Wilson 1973; Bell 1964). Most of the middle class in the West Indies have a cultural heritage of the African-based tradition which forms ways of survival and resistance for the majority of the folk. However, in the Caribbean, a commercial middle class is privy to ethnic groups – Chinese, Christian and Jewish Lebanese, and recently East Indians. Many members of the service middle class, which includes private and public sector managers as well as owners of capital, are predominantly black or brown skinned. The class position of an individual is based on recognition of kin ties, employment, education, political activity and is circumscribed by the size of the island. In large countries, one's skin colour often changes on the basis of one's class in the eye of the working-class beholder. According to a study of class relations in Jamaica, being a member of the middle class includes the material base that the term class implies, and a perception of their own life as a matter of individual achievement. Members of the middle class have a strong sense of moral propriety and sense of cultural superiority that is characterised as 'education' (Austin 1986). Furthermore, the sense of morality and propriety is a product of British middle-class civility which was the colonial model for 350 years. Therefore, for women understanding race and class raises other consequences.

Class, as an economic relationship expressing productive and social reproductive relations is embedded not only with race, but also gender. Black feminists (Collins 1990; Brewer 1993) refer to this set of relations as 'the matrix of domination'. The matrix is the multiplicative nature of race, class and gender relationships that requires theorising that is both historical and contextual as Patricia Mohammed (1994) reminds us. In Caribbean societies, the use of the matrix of domination can be a valuable concept because of women's divergent economic and racial and ethnic situations. The matrix is also helpful when examining power relations and women's access to power in various domains of society.

Patricia Anderson (1986: 320) argues that in the Caribbean, female power seems to exist at a somewhat subterranean level, especially in regard to kinship and the family. However, she says, women's power is severely curtailed in terms of sex-segregated activities, e.g. duties and occupations with their inferred low status.

In his ethnography on Trinidadian women factory workers, Kevin Yelvington (1995: 15-16) defines power as a determined casual property achieved by means of resources that are hierarchically distributed. Power is derived from scarce resources (e.g. time, money, commodities), where the control over these resources by a social entity (an individual, a group, a class) is based on relations between that social entity and the resources. When using the matrix of domination, subterranean familiar power, and relational definitions of power as guides, women's power is clearly constrained by all of the limiting forces in a particular society. Women also critically exercise power available to them under those social conditions. For middle-class women and men, there is more of a striking discord than seen in the literature on the poor and working classes.

Peggy Reeves Sanday (1974) observes that antagonism between the sexes may be noted in societies where female power exists in contradiction to the dominant ideology. Preliminary findings on research on Jamaican middle-class women supports this concept (Rawlins 1987). In this case, the upper classes are advocates of the tenets of a patriarchal ideology even though women exert familial power. The key to understanding the matrix of domination here, is to determine in what domain women have power, and the ideological web of relations used at home, at the office, and in organisations.

Middle-class women have the responsibility of maintaining that sense of propriety and socialising children in that mode. Women are to be keepers and managers of the home. They are never to permit wage employment to interfere with child bearing and rearing. These unwritten rules resulted partly from the division of labour derived from the legacy of slavery, and partly from the availability of domestic workers. They have been socialised to carry on the tradition of propriety, civility, and 'teatime' in various forms. Moreover, many members of the middle class maintain the colonial privileged ideology of the class/colour system in regards to their perceptions of women of poor and working-class backgrounds.

Here, the use of the matrix of domination provides some understanding of the apparent contradictions of Caribbean middle-class women's lives. The dominant prescription of patriarchy moves back and forth between the cultural meanings of middle-class women's familial power and other arenas of women's activities, especially in other settings, such as in the workforce. Since the jobs that middle-class women occupy are class based, the matrix of domination of race, class and gender takes on other nuance features of inequality. When middle-class women become conscious of the multiplicative nature of the relationships, they come to realise how these structures affect them and other women as well. Subsequently, from the ranks of the middle class have come some of the region's most committed women activists for social change. Likewise, some of vital forces of female leadership in the organised labour movement have middle-class origins.

The concept of varying levels of women's inequality, or the nuances of the matrix of domination, leads to another theorising guide that is instructive to understanding Commonwealth Caribbean women trade union leaders. In their article 'Toward a unified analysis of gender and kinship,' anthropologists Sylvia Yanagisako and Jane Collier begin with the premise that social systems are, by definition, systems of inequality.

Using multifaceted strategies as a framework, an understanding of the genesis of symbols and cultural meanings finds itself in the historical analysis of the society, which informs the contemporary scene of social and cultural changes over time. Ideas and actions are rooted in the evolution of culture and clarify the very process of how inequality is organised. By examining what people do, say, fear, explain, influence, etc., as they create relationships, one interprets the cultural meaning of these actions and ideas. Through this type of analysis one grasps the balancing act which exists between the interpretation of the way structures shape people's experiences, and of how people's actions are coded by structures (Yanagisako and Collier 1987: 43).

How to interpret the way people redirect the formations of inequality within specific parameters of a society is the challenge facing social scientists who map out the discourse, and those planners and policy makers who stand on the frontline to implement new courses in practice. Such is the situation facing the women trade union leaders who want to reconstruct their organisations so that they will be more democratic, less hierarchial, non-sexist and politically and economically meaningful in this changing world. What is required in this reconstruction, or upending the matrix of domination, is to perceive of alternative methods of exercising power.

Howard L. Smith and Mary Grenier (1982) analysed how men and women achieve and exercise power in organisational settings. They focus on the organisational's source of power and analyse its relevance for women. Similar to Yelvington's working definition, Smith and Grenier define power as a combination of the ability to influence others, determine others' behaviour, and the potential to achieve goals. Specifically, a powerful person may directly as well as indirectly influence others through structural avenues, such as decision channels or resource control. In the end, the structural context of the organisation will shape and be shaped by the behaviour of the women themselves and that *structure and behaviour together* determine power.

Smith and Grenier suggest three basic and overlapping sources of power: (1) Participation in central essential activities of the organisation; (2) Participation in activities that set the future agenda; and (3) Access to and control over resources. Sub-divisions of the degrees of centrality refer to the way activities are interrelated within a system. These are: the structural mechanics of the operation and decision-making process; the separations between line and staff personnel departments (activities essential to the organisation's existence); the chain of command, a direct or indirect line to the top; the division of labour within each department. For women to advance, Smith and Grenier argue, they must understand these complexities and their interrelationship to the organisation as a whole.

Coping with uncertainty is a critical structural category to consider because it is often used against women in their upward mobility within organisations. The ability to take risks and to assess probabilities are among the psychosocial factors, thereby women must 'prove' their competency while men are assumed to be competent until proven otherwise. Sub-divisions within this category include the degree of formalisation, i.e. how policies and procedures are officially specified; degrees of routinisation, meaning who performs jobs with more or less predictability; the degree of environmental complexity in decentralised situations or stringently hierarchical ones; and the position of hierarchy in which the more ill-defined, non-routine, future oriented a job is the more power it wields.

Control over resources is the last category in this theoretical framework of sources of power. Having control over resources includes not only a person's ability to channel funds and resources, but it also refers to the degree of access a person has to future information and resources. Like the other two structural categories, a chain of command, span of control, and degree of formalisation are important components which impede or assist one's rise to power.

Depending on the setting and situation then, both structural and behavioural strategies would be emphasised for women to gain, exercise and maintain positions of power. A wide array of structural strategies exist and can be taken in the accumulation of power. However, as the over-arching discourse of the matrix of domination is in operation, women still face sex-stereotyping, 'old boy' rules of entry and conduct, and other impediments to restrict and contain their access to organisational power.

This section began with a declaration – multiple theories must be used to best understand the lives and experiences of Caribbean women. As one theory after another showed, the multiplicative nature of race, class and gender demands such an approach. The collective body of theorising Caribbean women's differences underscored the need for historical and contextual roots. The contradictions between the Euro-based ideology of female subordination and the Afrocentric position of women centeredness are the subjects of feminist historical analyses (Mair 1974; Reddock 1984; Shepherd *et. al.* 1995). With this collective body of theories we can start to examine the general cultural meanings of power embedded in struc-tures of Commonwealth Caribbean trade unions and how it is expressed by the behaviour of the men and women involved.

The Setting

The general strikes and worker insurrections which blazed across the English-speaking Caribbean in the 1930s gave rise to two things: a more self-confident working class in demanding its rights and trade unions. These two factors spurred on a course of social change unseen in the region since the abolition of slavery. Between the end of slavery (1838) and prior to the advent of World War II, the working and living conditions of the masses of people in the then British Caribbean changed very little. The population grew, but there were few employment opportunities, a huge reserve of unskilled labour, and high levels of under and unemployed labour. Furthermore, three centuries of British colonialism and vestiges of a plantocracy made the effects of the Great Depression even more devastating in the West Indies. It was this kind of general economic and socioeconomic crisis which gave rise to the modern Caribbean labour movement.

From the beginning, the nexus of mobilising workers and forming political constituencies was the guiding force behind trade unionism and what would eventually be – once enfranchisement was granted – electoral politics in the English-speaking Caribbean.

After World War II and the realignment of world power, anti-Commu-nist sentiment influenced trade unionism and politics in the region. Trade unions with socialist leaders were stamped out and their political influ-ence squelched. Labour organisations not targeted in the Red scare, moved forward with their trade union activities and political agendas. From the 1950s to the 1970s, former trade union all-island supervisors were sworn in as heads of state, and trade union members were labelled 'the aristocracy of labour'. However, by the late 1970s and through the 1980s, trade unions found their friends in national governments not in favourable situations to help out in negotiating workers' working condi-tions and livelihoods. The debt crisis, balance of payment problems, IMF (International Monetary Fund) agreements, restrictive CBI (Caribbean Basin Initiative) contracts, and sluggish economies, etc., placed organised labour in a poor bargaining position to protect, demand, and provide for its members. Rank and file members began to question the institution of trade unionism in general, and their disaffection was noticeable at the ballot box.

At the same time as trade union members were expressing their misgivings about their organisations, women – both members of the rank and file and leaders – raised their voices in dissatisfaction. The UN Decade for Women (1976 - 1986) helped to heighten the consciousness of women as individuals and as members of groups. In the late 1970s, it was not uncommon to hear rank and file women speak of sexism on the job and on the part of the male organiser who was representing them. There were a host of job-related grievances, but those who were clearly sex-specific were placed alongside of, and with parity to, the others already on the table. Women trade union leaders spoke of the sexism within their organisations and were frustrated at their inability to help their trade unions through the crisis, which showed no signs of ending.

Women leaders' internal conflicts took on two forms: one focused on the organisational structure of trade unions in the Commonwealth Car-ibbean, and the other was self-criticism. At the institutional level, women trade union leaders cited sexism as the reason for a number of inequities, including the fact that no woman could claim to be the Chief Executive Officer (CEO) of a trade union; that rarely did a woman engage in collective bargaining; or even know the rudimentary procedures of nego-tiations; and that, although they performed a wide range of functions, most of these involved clerical, secretarial and catering services.

But, self-criticism also played a major role in the women leaders' critique of their organisations. Many of the very vocal women were angry at themselves for the way they helped create and maintain such a male-dominated institution. Women in decision-making positions wielded a certain amount of power within the hierarchy of their organisations, but they went along with the structure. For the most part, they did not have the self-confidence, knowledge and political savvy necessary for commanding respect, much less securing institutional change from their male peers. Perhaps the best example of this type of situation that many women trade union leaders found themselves in is the case of the executive secretary of a trade union whom I met in the late 1970s in Jamaica.

The CEO's executive secretary, a highly articulate, gifted young woman, served as an administrative assistant, although at that time, she had neither the title nor the salary to fit the work load. She *acted* as an officer of the organisation and was a committed trade unionist. The executive secretary's mobilising, counselling, teaching and secretarial skills were valued by the CEO and used without recourse in almost all institutional matters. Other members of staff included secretaries, an accountant, an office maid and a handyman.

Direct appeals to the CEO by the executive secretary granted me institutional support in the research I was doing at the time. One of the ways I reciprocated was to be this young woman's sounding board for the anger and disgust she felt concerning her situation in the organisation. Her grievances had numerous points. She was well qualified, well educated and more importantly, had earned the right to be an officer of the trade union. Furthermore, she deserved to be awarded certain perks that went with the position, and to be a recipient of advanced training offered overseas. Rightly, the executive secretary wanted to be compensated for her 50 to 70-hour work weeks which impinged on her family and personal life. The rank and file had already acknowledged her work individually and as groups from different places of work. However, the accolades she received from shop delegates (shop stewards) were in reference not to her personal endeavours, but to her position as the CEO's 'right hand'. How ironic, the working-class trade union members understood her merit, while the middle-class men with whom she worked with everyday – her peers and her boss – failed to recognise her valuable work to the labour movement.

Often the variety of ways women deal with social inequality included demonstrations, protests or personal intervention. Ordinary women, took responsibility in these kinds of acts of repudiation of the status quo, by engaging in traditional cultural acts of resistance to oppression. There are the deeds of exceptional women who inspired others, names not recognised outside of their communities, but who helped improve the conditions of peoples' lives. Or, there are still others, whose names are inscribed in official histories and documents, or are associates with civic duty and national pride. These include Nanny, the leader of the Maroons; Una Marson and Amy Ashwood Garvey of Jamaica, Elma Francois, of St Vincent/Trinidad; and Audrey Jeffers, from Trinidad and Tobago (see Ford-Smith 1986; Reddock 1988; Haniff 1988). For those women who lead public lives as leaders, up until recently they did so only as 'extensions' of their domestic lives, as e.g., social workers, teachers, nurses and so forth.

So the clash of the Eurocentric ideal and the Caribbean reality frames the configurations of the multifaceted Caribbean (Nettleford 1974). However, the clash is more than a colonial binary redux. It is a reverberation of the matrix of domination in a Caribbean framework. Individual and societal variations do surface, but they are based on the theme of why and how women and men negotiate gender, race and class in a particular context. Consequently, the social construction of the matrix of domination is embedded in institutions, such as the Commonwealth Caribbean labour movement.

Trade unionism, which found its way as an institutional structure in the region was based on a British model. And like many other models which were replicated in the colonies, the inherent gender bias remained unchallenged, even in situations where human resources were scarce. Moreover, the class nature of the early trade union leaders was in keeping with the Eurocentric notion of male domains of work and politics. Women leaders, representing every class, whose socialisation made them ideal trade unionists, were locked into a system which rendered them invisible. Thus, the trade union movement reflected the gendered stratification found throughout the West Indies. This stratification was based on class, race, and ethnicity and determined who assumed leadership positions, as well as prescribed 'the proper role' for women. What have women trade union leaders done to challenge their circumstances in the organised labour movement, while they still fight, as women and as members of their societies, for the elimination of the social conditions which keep them oppressed, exploited and powerless?

A standard joke that circulates in the Caribbean academic community makes fun of the often repeated phrase 'But you must realise, the Caribbean is a very complex area!' The variety of social differences in the region makes it hard for an easy explanation to satisfy all situations. And never has that often-repeated understatement been more true than in the situations surrounding women trade union leaders in the Commonwealth Caribbean. The complex and varied experiences of these women leaders in organised labour figure significantly in positions they hold in key institutions found at every level of society. Furthermore, the extent of women's contributions – those deemed 'indispensable' as well as those that are sex stereotyped and marginalised – contribute to the lack of recognition and esteem accorded them by their peers, scholars, politicians and those who record events. And finally, there are the issues of a personal nature. What role has trade union work played in these women's personal lives as citizens, mothers, mates and kinspersons?

Personal Location and Participant Participation

My research plan was simple. I would elicit the help of the women trade union leaders I had met over the years, who had been participants in a training and development programme designed and organised by a team of women trade union leaders from Barbados, the Bahamas, Jamaica and Trinidad and Tobago in the early 1980s. I hoped that the former Project participants would be interested in meeting and talking with the older women of the labour movement of their country, since they too were interested in the unheralded pioneers of the early years (1930s-50s) depending on the country. From my previous experience I knew that personal brokerage was the only way to meet people in the Caribbean. Personal introductions also made sense in terms of mutual respect and mutual personal integrity.

The key role that the women trade unionists played in this research was as 'participant participators'. Participant participators form a category of indigenous researchers who offer more than just an 'insider's perspective' on the body of data being collected and clearly more than indigenous fieldwork assistants. A participant participator is actively engaged in the work, is steeped in its merits and will stand by the outcome of the study which will bear her name. Thus, there will be long-term value for those participating as researchers.

In the beginning of the research, ten women trade union leaders expressed their willingness to interview past, contemporary and future women leaders of organised labour in their respective countries. We met on an individual basis, where we discussed the ways of doing interviews, collecting life stories, or if they knew the person well, to doing a life history which required a tremendous amount of time and energy. These meetings were conducted in five countries on at least three occasions. One woman volunteered to write up the socioeconomic and political history of her country which would frame the narratives. Confidentiality, safety and compensation for time, supplies and mileage were discussed and provided. Tapes of the interviews were copied and deposited in labour union libraries back in their respective countries. Women whose stories were collected could receive copies of their interviews if they so desired. The tapes were transcribed in the region, so as to appease the fear that a North American would not comprehend various West Indian vernaculars. But above all, credit would be given where it was due. Women's names as interviewers or interviewee would be cited if they had given permission.

Even though they were presented with an alternative research strategy to capture their own positions and that of their peers and friends, most of the materials collected by the participant participators did not stray outside of the basic questions to help guide discussion for collecting narratives and life stories. In some instances, those inquiries evolved into a questionnaire. Only one woman participant participator spent hours and days collecting life stories from a set of early generation women trade unionist from her country. Although they all agreed that to seize the moment to claim their standpoints in their work and lives, there was just not enough time, money and energy to go around to do the work. The disappointment was genuine for most of the women, who felt the need to do this research for their self-edification and for their organisations. And as a witness to their struggles and works, I recognised when it was time for me to amend the original plan and to become the friend, the academic and then the fieldworker, in that order. Because of my proven ethical stance, my democratic agenda in developing the research design, and my Jamaican identity (earned through fictitious adoption), the lack of time translated into money and energy were not recounted as fabrications. The fashion in which materials are presented in the larger work suggests the multiplicity of their origins. However, letting the women literally 'speak for themselves' remained the primary objective. My role became one of a facilitator and director of the production.

Trade Unions and Women Leaders

The trade union movement in the English-speaking Caribbean relied on the two-fold premise of meeting the worker's needs and of practising electoral politics. Managed for the most part, by middle-class male leadership, the organising principles follow the prescribed notions of gender relations, i.e. the dominant ideology of female subordination. The gender inequality in labour unions/political parties was inherited/modeled after the labour groups in Britain and the United States. Such inequitable relations between the genders devalues, oppresses, subordinates and restricts women's activities. According to a 1979 International Labour Organization (ILO) report, executive positions in the Commonwealth Caribbean were held by men at a ration of 3:1. Over the more than ten years since that report was written, things have changed in a positive direction, but the number of women CEOs is less than a handful in the entire region. Since middle-class men direct this movement, they operate with the dominant ideology which places women's labour, of any class background second, and overtly devalues the contribution of women whether or not it is in their best interest to do so to maintain a sense of control.

The roles that women played in the early days, and do in contemporary times as movement leaders and expressed by them here, reflects the reality of the situation. That reality is that women with skills and leadership abilities are desperately needed in trade unions because they play vital parts in the survival of these organisations. Also a part of women trade unionist reality is the result of the impediments to their receiving proper recognition and advancement within their organisations. For some of the elderly women leaders, social location also was a key to the temper of their activities.

Mrs Maggie Peters is a 93-year-old political/labour leader from Montserrat. I arranged to meet Mrs Peters at her home through the help of a young woman trade unionist whom I had met while she was participating in a workshop at the Barbados Labour College. To say that Mrs Peters is well known is an understatement. When I got in the taxi to go to her house, I gave the street address, and the cab driver said to me, 'Oh, you are going to visit Mistress Peters.' Maggie Peters also holds the ultimate respect of all trade unionists in the Leeward Islands.

Mrs Peters was quite bent, gnarled and frail looking. But what a wit! At our first meeting, she was refreshed from taking a long nap. She talked for two hours straight with only her nurse interrupting her to tell her to take a rest, and 'Mother' Peters taking the time to dismiss her. Finally in the third hour, I fatigued. Plus, I had to fly back to St Maarten that afternoon. When I said that I had to end our conversation because I had a plane to catch, this 93-year-old woman said 'but my dear, I have much more to tell you. I have only gotten up to 1953'.

Maggie Peters came from a solid African-Caribbean middle-class background. Her father was the headmaster of the colonial schools in Montserrat. He also was a small landowner. Her mother was a homemaker. Maggie Peters went through primary schools in Montserrat, and went to boarding school in neighbouring Antigua and was sent to England to finish her studies.

When she returned home to Montserrat, Maggie Peters became a school teacher, but also found herself in the anti-colonial struggle surrounding workers' rights and labour conditions on sugar estates on the island. In her classroom, she taught home economics. And in the cane-fields, in her yard, and in meeting places Mrs Peters taught cane workers their rights as workers and as people. Because of the influence of her father and the militancy of her husband, Maggie Peters' life career was that of an agitator. Only during World War II and when she was having babies, was Maggie Peters not on the front lines. She was never elected an officer of the trade union she helped to found, nor held a political position. Mrs Peters did not see that as her role. However, many things would not have happened if she had not been there.

Another woman who was on the frontlines in the late 1930s was the Hon. Lady Bustamante, widow of Jamaican National Hero, Sir Alexander Bustamante. Not promoting her own position, she says, 'I was secretary to Sir Alexander Bustamante for three years before the start of the BITU'. The BITU (Bustamante Industrial Trade Union) was formed in 1939. So for 50 years and more she had been a member of that organisation. When asked if more women were in leadership positions, would Caribbean trade unionism be different, Lady Bustamante replied that 'Yes, because women can manage very well since women put their minds to what is needed.'

Another elderly Jamaican trade unionist is Miss Halcyone Idelia Glass-pole, former office manager of the National Workers Union in Jamaica. Her brother was a trade union man and one of the founders of the modern labour movement in Jamaica. In 1988, when Miss Glasspole was interviewed, her brother Florizel Glasspole was the governor general – the Queen's representative of Jamaica. Miss Glasspole (she never married) entered union work in 1938 because of her brother's involvement.

Everybody decided that we were going to form this big organisation, the TUC (Trade Union Congress). And so it was formed and we carried along. We only had a few female workers who did just the clerical work. We weren't interested in the organising part of it, because it was terrible uphill work, and the men did that part of it, and we stayed inside and did the clerical work. And we struggled along, as I told you, it was a terrific fight, fighting the employers and we went right along until around 1945 when we decided to call a strike at the mental hospital . The Bellevue Hospital now, and that was why you had the terrific upheaval.

That struggle goes on today, 'And we were threatened to be sent to jail and that was hard, particularly for my brother because he was the general secretary so he was the mainstream of the struggle.' Asked if this was how she got involved, she replied, 'Yes, this [was] how I became involved.'

Miss Glasspole was not free with information because she *still* sees herself as one of the few confidential and competent persons to have served in the early Trade Union Congress and the National Workers Union. She is *still* very willing to give service, loyal and faithful to the labour movement.

The fashion in which women operated in the movement benefits from the Smith and Grenier (1982) analysis of women, power and organisations. The three sources of power – centrality, control of uncertainty, and access to resources – have great relevance for understanding the leadership positions of Commonwealth Caribbean women in the trade union movement. These three themes frame the following discussions of trade union and women leaders in general terms. Differences between organisations are quite apparent due to political, economic and chronological factors. For argument's sake, generalities will be the medium for analysis.

Centrality

Clearly, one of the tremendous restrictions facing women who wanted access to trade unionist power are the structural mechanics of labour organisations and the decision-making process. Overall, trade unions are extremely hierarchial and the chain of command is direct. In some cases, however, the executive council (composed of officers and elected members of the rank and file) do have a voice in the course of action taken on behalf of the trade union. But the ultimate decision comes from the general secretary or president, depending on which office wields the power. Officers with titles of 'president' or 'general secretary' are not equal in terms of power and duties from one trade union to another. Depending on the organisational flow chart, the president may be the pinnacle decision-maker, or that power may rest with the general secretary. Usually, if one office has the power, the other has the duties which usually include office management. And more often than not, the top female executive holds the 'management officer' position, a.k.a. secretarial functions, while the top man holds the power. Therefore, a woman can be president or general secretary, but the organisational flow chart indicates the direction of influence.

Women from St Vincent and Guyana had this to say about the opportunity for advancement, and what kinds of discrimination women experienced. These women clearly recognised the limitations both in society and in themselves: 'Not many women were interested in advancing. They avoided the hard work that was associated with the leadership position'; 'There are a number of women who still feel that men can handle the situation better than the women.'

In the departments where women do exert power – in office management and social welfare divisions for example – their positions are not questioned or challenged. However, because their line to the top may be different (i.e. indirect) women's power may be checked. Moreover, if their departments are viewed as support services, the centrality (as opposed to 'marginality') of the activities is questioned and devalued. They are not considered necessary for the survival of the organisation.

Likewise, the division of labour within trade unions is quite sex segregated. Women are rarely organisers, rarely represent the executive side in contract negotiations, and are rarely considered appropriate to handle such duties. The inability of women to carry out the responsibilities of a labour organiser is reinforced by the sex stereotyping of women's behaviour; they are non-aggressive, defer to men, and are incapable of making a decision of their own. Not only do most men hold this opinion, but also a good number of women show a total lack of confidence in the leadership abilities of other women. 'Peggy White' of Barbados, one of the women trade union leaders interviewed, says this about that situation, 'Somewhere along the line, they look at you as an upstart, a strife-maker and an aggressive woman who wants to be put in her place, at the right time, I sometimes get that feeling.'

On the office management side though, if women were not in the critical position of bookkeeper, comptroller, and executive secretary, then the trade union movement would have come to a sudden halt years ago. It is because of the technical skills, leadership capabilities, and innovative financial wizardry of the majority of women trade union leaders in office management that their organisations survive and continue to operate. But, that division of labour totally conforms to sex-segregated job dictates. It does not challenge the centralised position of power. This is clearly seen when the gallant efforts of many a committed woman trade unionist tend to go unrecognised in any form or manner.

Coping with Uncertainty

According to Smith and Grenier, the coping with uncertainty category is one used most often against women in their efforts to advance within their organisations. Risk taking is not put in the hands of women trade unionists. What responsibilities occupy the majority of the women leaders are routine and predictable. Again, this relates to the centralised structure of most Caribbean labour organisations – the stringent hierarchy which maintains those structural postures, and the reinforcement of sex stereotypes concerning women power and organisations. 'Margaret Paul' from Guyana tells it this way 'As a branch secretary I encountered both male and female members of the union and at times I felt challenged and the male tried to make me feel incapable of making representations because they wanted to keep me out.' A trade union leader from St Vincent, Sylvia Findaly-Scrubb notes:

I realised that as a rank and file member, there was very limited scope. After being involved in a few training sessions locally, there was this urge to become more committed to the cause of the working class. As a result, I was nominated for executive position at our biennial convention. My defeat did not mar my future involvement it only made me more determined to try.

Other women echo this position: 'You may fight very hard and be very well educated if you are to attain these positions and men in the unions have not been superbly educated in terms of academic ability'; 'Very often men did not support me because I was a woman. They felt I was playing a man because it was felt that trade unionism is for men.'

Control over Resources

The critical point in this aspect of sources of power within an organisational structure, is not necessarily a person's access to channel funds and resources, but the degree a person has to future information and resources. On a low level, women trade union leaders have been able to assert some control over resources, especially in the daily operations of their departments. Comptrollers can squeeze a bit of money to cover unexpected costs for the organisation, or break or bend a rule to assist an individual through a difficult financial period. But the majority of women leaders' positions are restricted according to the first two structural categories just discussed – centrality and uncertainty. Therefore women's access to resources is also restricted in terms of wielding a large measure of organisational resources and financial power.

In addition to these structural and behavioural impediments keeping women from leadership positions in the region's labour movement, a lack of adequate training and development as trade unionists on par with their male colleagues also inhibits their rise to power. The Project for the Development of Caribbean Women in Trade Unions initiated two courses of study and training to undo this almost 50 years of neglect in terms of trade union education for women. The inequitable position women find themselves in at present is a point of redress for the future. As Claudette Joseph, a Guyanese woman trade unionist, says:

In the trade union movement you would find the male would tend to say "Well women really shouldn't have positions in the trade union movement", but then without the women there is nobody there to see the rights of the women and to get proper representation, so I think there is room there for us in the trade union.

High on the list of priorities for women leaders is how to gain power and access to resources. One woman said the following:

There is room for advancement and opportunity for both genders. But as we know in the trade union world many of the members are men and they can't but to work with men, so we, the women in the organization, have to speak out and show where we also need opportunities to advance our knowledge, our abilities.

Another said:

I think that somewhere along the line there is still this traditional feeling that men must operate more readily in the positions I think women have to prove too much that they have a super ability to be given the post first off-hand. You will not be given it as readily as if a man had come in and showing the kind of ability.

In addition to the three sources of power, there are other inevitable drawbacks facing women in the labour movement. One issue women leaders face is the lack of confidence of other women. As one leader put it, 'The discrimination within the trade union is just like within any other organisation because the men and women, sometimes I would even say more so the women feel that men can handle the situation better than the women.' Another commented, 'I know that they look at you as an upstart, strife-maker and why pay her sufficient attention that she'll think she's important, that is how I feel.'

Another issue has to with fulfilling domestic responsibilities. A female member of the Barbados Workers Union (BWU) for 15 years was asked if her parents approved of her joining the labour movement. She said, 'Well just being a member was no problem. At Executive level, especially when I had to go to the "Exec meetings", my mother kept a lot of noise because it meant staying out late 'till one o'clock some mornings and she didn't like that at all, she quarreled until I came off.'

A BWU colleague analysed the complications of being female and a trade union leader.

You cannot be satisfied; you have to keep educating the women, keep getting behind the women to do things for themselves and then break them out of that whole pattern, that whole traditional role if possible. There will always be some women who will not change, but those of us who recognise that what benefits can be derived on a personal level from breaking away from the past in terms of what we are accustomed to, what is expected of us, what we have to do is to work on our children and work on other women where possible to get them to break out of the tradition, to take up things that are not necessarily seen as "women things", get into areas which are not seen to have traditional women areas, see themselves as individuals and try to improve themselves as a person and try to take up more, be more ambitious in their goals, in their careers, take up more challenging roles. I would like to see women being recognised as proper equals not behind men nor out in front of men. Equality will preserve all through life.

Conclusion

There are numerous reasons why black feminists do corrective research. One follows what Audre Lorde called using the master's tools to dismantle the master's house. In that spirit, this work with women trade union leaders from various parts of the English-speaking Caribbean attempts to do just that. It makes visible what organised labour does not: the tremendous importance of women's leadership throughout its history. By using a range of methods of theorising, we can use what is necessary to explain and analyse the lives and experiences of women in particular historical and social contexts. As Caribbean, and other women of colour build their own feminist theories, it is critical to build that work on not only the academic world, but also the world of experience coming from the ranks of women, who may not call themselves feminists, but in all ways of female empowerment, do grassroots politics on a daily basis. Some of those women are trade union leaders.

5

Explaining the Caribbean Family:

Gender Ideologies and Gender Relations

Marietta Morrissey

Introduction

Since the 1930s the Caribbean family, in particular the woman-headed family, has been the subject of continuing scholarly attention. Social science research and analysis have reflected gender and other current political ideologies. They have also been narrow in their focus on issues of social legitimacy and on the influence of men or women in the creation of woman-headed families. Caribbean studies have recently presented another approach, grounded in the political economy of gender relations. It is a novel and critically significant perspective, moving beyond a male or female focused point of view and offering a rationale for a gender-integrated approach to job creation and social service provision.

This paper begins with a brief examination of the work of early social scientists and their influence on colonial and related policies directed to family organisation. I consider as well how scholarship took a more empirical and nationally-focused turn as social scientists considered male economic marginalisation and its contribution to 'matrifocal' households. This paper then turns to feminist influences in the social sciences that have highlighted Caribbean women's economic autonomy and its relationship to the maintenance of their families.

Finally, I review recent social science literature on gender relations suggesting that the tendency for women to maintain families is related to both men's and women's labour market experiences. This perspective recalls the work of an earlier generation of social scientists who stressed the rationality of woman-headed families in economies that deny male occupational opportunities. But it also calls attention to women's entry into the formal labour force, their informal labour market activities, and how these experiences influence women's interests in family organisation and household economies. Further, this approach raises questions about how recent trends in Caribbean political economies have marginalised poor men and women and their families and the need for regional states to respond.

Describing the Caribbean Family: The Early Social Science Literature

Much early social science discussion of Caribbean families reflected debate about the origins of family forms that appeared to be different from Western norms. E. Franklin Frazier (1939) argued that slavery had continuing negative consequences for families of African origin in the Americas, resulting in large numbers of woman-headed families.[1] Melville and Frances Herskovits contended that African traditions and customs continued in the Americas. Their observations of Suriname (1936) and Trinidad (1947) and Melville Herskovits' study of Haiti (1937) suggested that West Indian religion, music and family organisation owed much to the African origins of the region's peoples and were thus socially legitimate.

Those who followed Frazier defined the Caribbean family as the source of more general social and political problems. Academic observers were particularly troubled by two dimensions of Caribbean family organisation (Henriques 1953, 1949; Herskovits and Herskovits 1947, 1936; Herskovits 1941, 1937). First, consensual unions often took the place of formal marriage. Nevertheless, these unions could be stable and long-lasting, with high degrees of commitment on the part of both men and women to each other and to the children of their unions. Second, many conjugal unions were not stable and long-lasting. Their relationships appeared to the European observer to be casual and characterised by promiscuity on the part of women and an uncertain commitment to the relationship and to resulting children on the part of men. There were gradations in mutual economic and emotional commitment and obligation to children in Caribbean families. These corresponded to a large degree to social class and to the age of the couple: as couples aged and had control of more resources they were more likely to enter into stable unions, or to legalise or in some other way increase the level of mutual obligation in existing relationships.

Social science of the period contributed other insights about Caribbean families that persist in much current discussion. For example, Herskovits and Herskovits (1936: 23) noted that despite the origins of some of Suriname's former slaves in patrilineal descent groups, '[e]mphasis is always placed among these people on the ties towards the mother and her family, and that the responsibilities held binding are those which bear upon relationships through the mother'. Others, such as Henriques (1949), described the relative status of women, particularly among the poor where woman-headed families were most common. 'The Jamaican lower-class woman both in social and in family affairs has a prominence which is absent in the equivalent European society' (Henriques 1949: 36). He commented further on the 'strong sense of kin beyond the immediate family' (Henriques 1949: 36). However, in the end he declared West Indian societies in a state of disequilibrium, owing to the continuing destructive consequences of slavery.[2]

Colonial policy makers utilised social scientists' work as a means to buttress their own disapproval of many aspects of local social organisation (Matthews 1953; Simey 1946). Simey, for example, argued that stable, indeed marital relationships, were most often found among the British West Indian middle and upper classes. These patterns were often associated with high levels of economic development. On the assumption that these styles of family organisation in fact contributed to economic development, they seemed worth imitating in the West Indies (Proudfoot 1953). Simey noted further that while West Indian children were valued and loved by mothers and fathers, they lacked the discipline that resulted from living in a family setting with a patriarchal father. Children appeared to be free to wander among households. The Caribbean pattern of fostering children reinforced the image of children without a single set of dominant or authoritative parents socialising them for economic and social success.

While much policy-related discussion emanated from colonial offices and focused on the British West Indies (Bolles and D'Amico-Samuels 1989), prescriptive messages were equally strong in other settings. In Puerto Rico, for example, physicians, public health workers and church groups sent powerful messages to women about the importance of appropriate familial relationships, reproduction and the socialisation of children (Colón 1993; see for example Clark 1930). In the French West Indies, the Catholic Church discriminated against women who were not legally married and the children of unmarried mothers. As elsewhere in the region, religious figures tried to persuade couples to marry, even when they lacked the economic means to establish households (Beauvue-Fougeyrollas 1979).

The Origins of Woman-headed Families

The next generation of social scientists were less interested in judging the Caribbean family than in understanding the terms of economic interest and exchange that influenced the formation of various patterns of organisation (Bolles and D'Amico-Samuels 1989). By the late 1950s and the 1960s ethnographies, community studies and surveys illustrated the tendency for landlessness and extreme poverty to produce woman-headed families, with nuclear families more likely to result in more prosperous circumstances[3] (see, for example, Blake 1961; Clarke 1957; Cumper 1958; Safa 1965). Anthropologists also debated the extent to which cultural expectations framed by economic circumstances had an equally strong impact on the removal of men from the residence of women companions and their children (see review of debate between R. T. Smith and M. G. Smith in Clarke 1957). This was an important issue because some groups, for example, East Indians in Trinidad and Guyana, who lived in conditions that could be said to be propitious for the development of woman-headed families, in fact generally lived in patriarchal families (Smith 1956).

As the role of culture in defining marital and paternal expectations became clear, some anthropologists suggested that the Caribbean lower-class family form constituted a type that was not necessarily unique to the region. Rather, in many poor areas, economic circumstances were such that men could not fulfil the traditional economic role associated with patriarchy (Lewis 1966, 1959; Rodman 1971). This family type was best termed 'matrifocal': social life revolved around the mother, who helped her children economically as she could (González 1970, 1969, see 1984 for further discussion; Smith 1956, 1973; Tanner 1974). As the only adult in residence, she was generally part of a large network of woman-headed families. In these circumstances, unemployed or marginally employed fathers were a drain on resources. The family ultimately benefited from the father's absence. Matrifocal families were thus economically rational, indeed, economically optimal. Such families were in fact as much woman-focused as they were mother-focused. Often several generations of women lived together, raising children and attempting to assist young men as much as possible in establishing economically viable relationships with women and children. But when men failed, women and their children could often return to the family origin, without stigma or other negative consequences. Moreover, given the likelihood of economic failure in these discouraging circumstances, there was little reason for men or women to invest in marriage or other economically demanding institutions or customs. Non-marital births were common in societies with large numbers of matrifocal families.

The expectations of men in these circumstances were thought to be conditioned by the support of mothers, grandmothers, sisters and other women. Men could generally support themselves with the assistance of female relatives and engage in competition among themselves for the attention of women. The lack of employment opportunities gave men time for the development of networks of friendship and competition. But, as Brana-Shute (1976), Wilson (1973) and others observed, these were usually young men's networks. Older men were often in a better position to contribute to the support of women and children, although many older men settled into companionable relationships with women who continued largely to support themselves.

The focus on men's inactivity obscures the fact that male migration was often a factor in the creation of woman-headed families. In this situation, men were absent, often for years, sending home money whenever possible to support their families (Massiah 1983). Nevertheless, the household was matrifocal still because of the mother's strong influence on familial relationships and her continuing management of the household economy.

The matrifocal typology suffers theoretically in two other ways. First, while men may not reside with their companions and children, matrifocality suggests that men's influence over women and children is slight. The empirical record suggests otherwise, with children often involved with their fathers' kin and emotionally attached to their fathers and to their lineages (Smith 1988).[4] The extent to which this is true depends of course on the economic circumstances, the local culture and individual histories and proclivities. Nevertheless, definitions of matrifocality need to be qualified to acknowledge the emotional and social contributions of fathers, even when economic contributions may be slight or may be absent. Moreover, while male authority may be lacking in some matrifocal families, male authority embodied in the patriarchal family is often an ideal in so-called matrifocal societies (Massiah 1983; Momsen 1993; Smith 1956).[5]

Second, families move in and out of the culture of matrifocality. Men and women often try to establish nuclear families, sometimes succeed and sometimes fail. To a large extent, the age of the individuals is a factor in success. In this sense, matrifocality exists in a kind of symbiotic relationship with other family forms, generally the nuclear family, and remains in the early literature an expression of the failure of the nuclear family to succeed in many economic environments.

Finally, the matrifocal family rests on presumed male failure to succeed in economically difficult circumstances. It is assumed that if men could find jobs, they would do so and other forms of family life and organisation would develop. Many ethnographies of the period from the late 1950s through the 1980s reflect this male-focused point of view (Dagenais 1993:103). However, implicit in this perspective is the understanding that male absence granted women more status in the home; more power over her children and other members of her extended family; and more influence in her community (Austin 1984; Rodman 1961; Rubenstein 1987; Slater 1977 for ethnographic elaboration of these phenomena). Moreover, women's work responsibility may not increase greatly as a result of heading their families; other relatives, friends and the children themselves assume more responsibility (Justus 1981; Sutton and Makiesky-Barrow 1981). More recent work (see for example Morrow 1994) suggests that male violence against women may be less intense in matrifocal communities as well. Thus, built into the concept of the matrifocal family was an understanding of women as intelligent and often powerful actors an understanding that would emerge more fully in later woman-focused research on Caribbean families.

Focusing on Women

In the late 1970s and 1980s a literature emerged in Caribbean studies that focused on women's actions and interests in the heading of families. Some scholars now described women as agents of their emotional choices and the organisation of their families rather than as victims of men's lack of employment.

Many works from this era focus on women as conscious and able economic actors (Massiah 1983; see also collections by Hart 1989 and Ellis 1986). Some suggest that while women may not choose to head families, their economic strength and flexibility gave them options and allowed them to approach family headship with some confidence (Massiah 1983). Some scholars recognise more explicitly that when women have economic strength they need not settle for relationships in which males partners fail to carry out their economic responsibilities (Brown 1975; Moses 1981).

This important empirical work on the Caribbean reflected and contributed to theoretical trends in the study of gender elsewhere in the world. Blumberg (1977, 1975) tried to establish the conditions under which woman-headed families are frequent in a setting, including women's access to jobs and income at a level fairly equivalent to men of their social class. Chant (1985) observed that in Latin America women who head families may have greater access to income than those in conjugal families, where patriarchal husbands/companions are unwilling to share resources and income with conjugal partners (see also Bryden and Chant 1989). Buviníc, Youssef and Alier (1978) called our attention to the measurement problem, arguing that the true number of women heading households in many Caribbean settings is unclear. Definitions of women heading households technically include women living alone and woman-headed households that include children, although the needs of the two groups are quite different. Moreover, women in stable conjugal relationships but who are not married may claim to head a household. And while women may be the sole breadwinners in a household, their unemployed male partners and companions may claim to be household heads. Finally, households and families are often grouped together, when in fact the household and family heads may be different people. While their notion of potential woman-headed households addresses only some of these problems, it challenges social scientists to refine their survey techniques to address to the ever increasing range of family and household types found throughout the world as gender relations change.

Perhaps the most important contribution of the woman-focused literature on Caribbean women heading families is that which explores the potential power that women have in local communities as they take principal responsibility for the socialisation of their children and the management of their families. For example, Senior (1991) explores in general terms the tremendous strength and moral authority West Indian women hold in large part because of their profound historical impact on production and social reproduction. Kerns (1989) takes another approach in considering the way in which the absence of males has established women as the keepers of local cultural customs among the Garifuna in Belize. The worship of ancestors involves a complex set of beliefs, rituals and related tasks that women now perform.

As our understanding of Caribbean women's multifaceted lives and how they vary by social class, nation and community has grown, it also became clear that we lack a systematic explanation for why women's tremendous influence and achievement has not translated into greater economic and political power. As González noted in 1970 in writing about the consanguineal family, women's domestic power does not translate into political, economic or jural power. And, in fact, given the relationship between poverty and large numbers of women heading families, domestic power may be an indicator of economic, political and jural weakness. Nevertheless, there is a contradiction between giving women control over communities, in particular, over the socialisation of young people, and their economic and political powerlessness. Indeed, a society that allows women to nurture, educate and control future generations of workers – or of the unemployed – is ceding them a tremendous influence. Is it then an indicator of women's latent influence and power that they manage the socialisation and social control of children? Or is it an indicator of the insignificance of socialisation and social control of some economically marginalised groups? While these important questions remained latent in woman-focused analyses of women heading families, the latter laid the groundwork for the more highly integrated work on women heading families that has recently begun to appear.

The Political Economy of the Woman-headed Family

In focusing first on men's and then women's labour market experiences and related social responses, past theories of the origins of woman-headed families have failed to consider fully how men's and women's economic statuses are related and how they have changed in recent years (Morrissey 1989).

If in poor communities men's historical lack of labour market opportunities have led to their abandonment of families, men's economic circumstances have deteriorated in recent years throughout the world (Joeckes 1987; Safa 1995). Male formal labour force participation is down worldwide, a function of earlier male retirement and employer preferences for female labour. Women's formal labour force participation is increasing, along with their attendance in secondary and post-secondary institutions. In the Caribbean area these trends are reinforcing women's relative historical economic strength and men's labour force marginalisation.

These tendencies in labour market participation and educational achievement suggest that there may be no single explanation for family organisation to the extent that it is related to economic, specifically labour market, status. Rather, there is a relationship between men's and women's economic activity that bears on social institutions. The corollary to this principle is the notion that at the cultural level men's and women's expectations and behavior are symbiotic. For West Indian women to enjoy honour, prestige and power in their communities may mean that men are held in a different cultural position than we would associate with highly patriarchal societies (Safa 1995). In short, more recent work shifts our focus from men's or women's positions to gender relations.

The most significant research on gender relations is on men's and women's relative and mutually impacting labour market experiences. Safa (1995, 1993) has recently done extensive research on this theme in both Puerto Rico and the Dominican Republic, reporting on how women are preferred in light manufacturing (see also Monk 1993; Perez Herranz 1990; Ríos-González 1990). While women have not displaced men in these jobs, it is true that the entry of women into this sector of the labour force *is associated with* men's less visible presence in work. This raises the question of why employers have sought women workers for some jobs. The larger research literature suggests that employers perceive women as more compliant and willing to work for less. As Sutton and Makiesky-Barrow (1981: 476) found in reporting employer preferences for women in a Barbados community, 'the wage structure effectively discriminates against women employees'.Hence women's entry into the formal labour force and men's departure signal an overall decline in real wages. The average woman household head earns less, even with participation in the formal labour force, than do male family heads generally.

However, it is important to note that when we talk about male and female family heads we are not talking about individuals with the same level of education or engaged in the same types of work. Women family heads generally have less education than do their male counterparts. They are more likely to work in the informal sector. They are also more likely to be impoverished (Massiah 1983). However, within formal work settings that draw unskilled women workers, there may be a dispropor-tionate share of woman who are family heads.

The impact on conjugal relationships of women's labour market entry and men's withdrawal is profound. Safa (1993: 18) notes that 'two-thirds of the female heads of household in our sample would prefer not to remarry. They see men as restricting their freedom rather than assisting them with the responsibility of raising a family'.

At the cultural level, the elaboration of patriarchy is contingent in part on the gender division of labour and control of income (Safa 1995). For example, in Trinidad, when British colonial policies mandated women's withdrawal from the labour force and the creation of the housewife/consumer, patriarchy was reinforced along with a strict gender division of labour and of power (Reddock 1989). Skelton (1989) found that in Montserrat gender relations varied with the degree of commitment and stability expressed in the union. 'Gender relations in marriage and cohabiting unions were strongly patriarchal; those in visiting unions were either egalitarian or weakly patriarchal.' Gearing (1988) describes for St Vincent a similar dialectical relationship between men's capacity to support their families and gender relations. If a man gave too much support to a woman, it hurt his capacity to compete with other men for respect as a free and unencumbered individual; but if he offered too little support, his female companion would leave him.[5]

Future Research: Families, Gender and the State

While the economic positions of men and women are key to understanding the origins and dynamics of woman-headed families, we must turn our attention as well to Caribbean states and how they can and will manage the impoverishment of families given women's relative invisibility and lack of influence in political decision making bodies. And while women in poor countries have more often depended on private voluntary and cooperative assistance on than on the direct help of the state, national governments create incentives and obstacles to private group organisation (Bolles 1993; Peake 1993). Moreover, there is increased pressure on Caribbean states to contain the negative social consequences of poverty and inequality in ways that have profound effects on women and their children.

Ann Orloff (1993) has outlined how government would serve women's needs had they a commitment to do so. She suggests that women need labour market protections, assistance with the care of children, social security and other benefits also needed by men. If women are to remain out of the workforce because of their commitment to dependent children they are in need of still another type of state protection, one generally not available to men. And if women as a class, because of discrimination and other factors, cannot earn the same salary as men, they require supplementary assistance.

This ideal type is useful as a guide for what women might usefully seek in their communications and negotiations with governments. But it also stands as a kind of model against which to measure government plans and programmes. And it makes clear that worldwide government efforts to privatise industries and to reduce governmental commitments hurt women and reflect their lack of political power.

In poor countries, including those of the Caribbean, there is relatively little history of state commitment to social security, public health, or assistance targeted to single women and their children (Boyd 1988; Massiah 1983).[6] There is little reason to expect a change along these lines now, but problems of poverty and underdevelopment have worsened. And, at the same time, states are pressured to control the consequences of public neglect. This bears on women, especially those who raise their children alone and who are vulnerable themselves to both a lack of social control and the often aggressive efforts of the state to create public order.

As women's political influence grows in the Caribbean they must assert a new definition of the role of government and the need to protect women and children. But it is a mistake to isolate these political concerns as women's issues for several reasons. First, women cannot be politically successful without the support and assistance of traditionally male-focused groups, including labour unions and political parties and movements. More important, at the conceptual level women's political marginalisation is inseparable from the marginalisation of many male voices. An agenda that advances the interests of women and children must be linked to those that reinforce the political power of working people in general and seek to provide all people with decent jobs and adequate public services.

Summary and Conclusions

Throughout the second half of the twentieth century the large number of Caribbean woman-headed families has generated much research by students of the region. Scholars have argued that on one hand, the woman-headed family reflects and reinforces the relatively high status of Caribbean women and the extensive networks of mutual support that surround Caribbean families. On the other hand, women's maintenance of families reflects high levels of poverty and contributes to familial poverty to the extent that a single adult is earning the greater part of the family income and is disadvantaged in the labour market because of gender-based wage and employment discrimination.

While in the past the region's governments saw male employment and the reinforcement of patriarchal, bourgeois male responsibility as an antedote to women's maintenance of families, more recent observers have attempted to focus public attention on the needs of single mothers and their dependent children (Massiah 1983; Reddock 1989). Women's groups have worked hard to develop governmental and privately funded programmes to improve the life chances of women who head their families. This approach remains of vital interest to women, but should not be separated from efforts to bolster workers' rights in general and to force area governments to attend to the needs of those marginalised by international, regional and national economic trends. In the current climate of enhanced Caribbean government interest in international investment and trade and the resulting impoverishment of growing numbers of people, the struggle for public support of any marginalised group is challenging. Coalitions of historically male and female interest groups representing working people may be the most effective vehicles to force states to create and enforce laws and budgets that protect men, women and their families.

Notes

1. Much literature on woman-headed families uses the terms household and family interchangeably. This is of course in error, as households may include more than one family or none at all. At the same time, families may inhabit several households or only one. In fact, most households in the Caribbean are made up of families, and occasional other adults and/or children. As one or more kinship units are usually embedded in households, I use the term 'woman-headed family', unless I am referring to survey research that has specifically measured households, with no indication of or assumptions about the kinship relations of household members.

2. Henriques' (1949) concern about disequilibrium in the West Indian family reflected the dominant functionalist view among anthropologists, especially those influenced by British social anthropology. If social institutions seemed in some way out of order, or seemed to produce consequences for individuals that could be termed pathological, they were said to be in disequilibrium. The influence of individual prejudices and cultural norms in judging institutions was considerable, no less so in the case of the West Indies where anthropologists' judgements were often negative.

3. Woman-headed families can also be found independent of these conditions (Kundstater 1963).

4. Herskovits and Herskovits (1936) make the same point. Another significant variable in a man's economic and emotional attention to families in the number of relationships, children and households he has formed and where each falls on a continuum of social respectability and legitimacy (Bryden and Chant 1989). In fact a man may be married and live in a household with his wife and children while maintaining another household.

The latter is likely to be a secondary household and to receive fewer resources from the man than do his wife and legitimate children.

5. Momsen (1993: 1) refers to a 'double paradox: of patriarchy within a system of matrifocal and matrilocal families; and of domestic ideology coexisting with the economic independence of women'.

6. Cuba forms the most significant exception to this pattern in the region. In the cases of Puerto Rico and of Martinique and Guadeloupe, the US and France respectively provide some governmental resources to the poor who are disproportionately women and children (Dagenais 1993; Safa 1995).

Hegemony, Patriarchy and the Creation of a Caribbean People's Culture

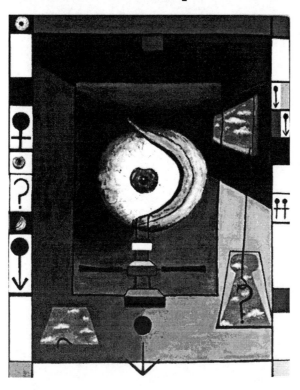

6

Centreing Woman:
The Political Economy of Gender in West African and Caribbean Slavery

Hilary McD. Beckles

Mapping the origins and itinerary of gender in Caribbean history enables us to sharpen our focus specifically on slavery as a constantly changing system of socio-sexual exploitation and control of women, and generally to penetrate its internal dynamism as a mode of labour extraction. Gender, as a social construction that determined and reflected the sexual division of labour within the slave mode of production, constitutes a clear vista through which the cultural working of patriarchy as well as challenges to it at diverse levels of everyday life can be illuminated.[1]

In some ways 'modern' slave societies in the Caribbean facilitated a revolutionary restructuring and magnification of traditional gender representations while producing unique features of their own. For sure, the institutional design of Caribbean slavery, particularly its cultural specificities, significantly affected the (re)making of gender identities of males and females. Individuals evolved self-identities within the contexts of the gender order they encountered, and often contested. A wide range of strikingly unstable circumstances gave rise to gender as organised ideology. The constant reordering and redefinitions of conditions and terms of social living – and dying – determined that gender representations were oftentimes perceived as paradoxical and contradictory. This circumstance, in turn, indicates the considerable fluidity of ideological readings of slavery, and constitutes a barometer of the turbulence internal to the construction of the gender order.[2]

The methodological approach chosen here to explore the evolution and movements of gender identities and representations, and their ideological effects, is to utilise historical evidence to examine the macrocosms of slavery by penetrating the microcosms within. The proposal is that visits be made to three historical sites where gender discourses seemed most advanced and determining of social relations and popular perceptions of identity. First, the gender order of pre-colonial West Africa is examined within the context of pressures exerted upon it by forces endemic to the wider Atlantic political economy. Second, the ideological constitution of gender identities within the Caribbean plantation complex is explored in so far as it affected and determined the nature of work and reproduction. Third, the instability of gender representations under increasingly adverse circumstances of sugar production and the global political challenge to the legitimacy of slavery in the early nineteenth century, are presented as causes of reforms to women's relations to production and reproduction and the creation of a new gender order.

An objective of this exercise is an attempt to make a contribution to feminist theorising in the Caribbean, albeit from a masculinist conscious-ness, by examining how gender relations were historically constituted and experienced, and ought therefore to be thought about. By adopting a historical approach, critical conceptual distance can be achieved to assess and alter contemporary gender arrangements. The specific empirical focus on women's history is intended to illustrate how men have suc-ceeded in maintaining the domination of women, despite their subversive actions and visions; also, to participate in the forging of a closer analytical relation between the study of women's history and gender history within Caribbean subaltern historicism.[3]

Most slaves in West Africa during the period 1500 to 1800 were female. This was also the case in the older sugar plantation colonies of the West Indies between 1800 and 1833. Prior to 1800, however, West Indian slavery was overwhelmingly male biased. The mid eighteenth century witnessed the transition in demographic structure. There was nothing paradoxical about it; the specific focus on the female in the conception, design and reproduction of these slave systems was the result of discern-ible social and managerial imperatives.[4]

Sex distribution patterns within the Atlantic slave complex had as much to do with the working of gender in traditional West African societies as with modernist discourses of work, gender and social life in colonising Europe. After the 1750s, the established Caribbean custom of male preferencing in the purchase and retention of slaves gave way to a pro-female trend that fundamentally transformed the sex structure and modified gender discourses. Barbados had attained the unique status of having a female majority in the slave population since the end of the seventeenth century; it shared this characteristic with the Leeward Islands by the end of the eighteenth century. Sugar planters in these colonies gradually moved towards the privileging of females as part of a revised strategic plan to promote the natural reproduction of the labour force. The effects of this demographic shift on gender representations and identities were considerable. Important insights into the causes and nature of conflict and instability in slave societies therefore necessitate the creation of gender-derived forms of knowledge.

New World slavery represented something altogether unfamiliar to African males and females. It confronted, rejected and restructured the gender attitudes and identities legitimised by their traditions. The working of labour ideologies in most West African societies distinctly gendered certain types of work and relations of power; these were exploded and reconfigured within the Caribbean context. It is therefore problematical to propose fundamental continuity in forms of slavery and legitimisation for Africans between traditional experiences and the New World encounter. The gender implications of West Indian plantation slavery for Africans furthermore were culturally transformative. Initially, the Caribbean gender order as it related to types of work was peculiar to males in part but more familiar to women in general. It is important, then, that the nature of these confrontations be identified, and their implications for gender roles and identities understood and explained.[5]

Analyses of Atlantic slavery have tended to revolve around criteria that indicate the degree of intensity and type of involuntary servility that constitute slavery. The property relations criterion in particular has received greater attention as one way to differentiate between modernist Caribbean chattel slavery and traditional forms of slavery in Africa. In addition, notions of kinlessness, marginalisation, exclusion, and subjection to others, have been privileged by cultural anthropologists who have drawn attention to the importance of comparative treatment of the subject over space and time in different and the same societies in Africa. In neither approach, however, has it been stated that these criteria have produced mutually exclusive categories. Rather, the tendency has been to identify what may reasonably be described as 'principal' and 'secondary' characteristics within the dominant mode of production.[6]

In West Africa during the period of Atlantic slavery the majority of persons described as slaves were female. The explanation for this circumstance has to do with the functions performed by women within the gender order of these mostly patriarchal societies. There was a considerable internal slave market on which the demand was mostly for women and children. Women were also traded through the Sahara into the North African Muslim labour markets, while the non-African Atlantic market was supplied mostly with males. One compelling explanation for this pattern is that West African societies did not easily absorb male slaves. A general tendency was for males captured in intercine warfare to be executed by the State; another trend was to retain limited numbers of men for military rather than agricultural or industrial purposes. As a result of warfare, and other forms of political conflict, however, the majority of captives retained and integrated into local socio-economic systems were woman and children.[7]

The development of this pattern of sex specificity has to do with the greater local demand for females as slaves. This is reflected in the prices paid for female slaves in coastal and interior societies. Philip Curtin has shown, for example, that whereas in Senegambia African traders supplied men and women to European buyers at the same price, in the interior agricultural belt women slaves sold for twice the price of male slaves. An often stated explanation for this trend is that women slaves were preferred because of their biological reproductive functions. This is only a minor part of the explanation. African men with property did demand wives and concubines who were kinless within their immediate social space, and whose progeny had little or no property rights or status claim within the inheritance system. But such kinless women and their children were secured directly by patriarchal elites primarily as workers, and were marginalised mainly because of their alienability as marketable labour.[8]

The ability of the patriarchal system to absorb, assimilate, and subjugate greater numbers of kinless women is the critical part of a more systemic explanation. The more expansive the economic system, the civil society, and the state apparatus, the greater was the demand for female slaves. The wide range of possible forms of absorption of kinless women magnified the numbers any society could carry. In most West African societies wealth was accumulated principally by means of the recruitment and retention of such labour. This was as true for the State as it was for individuals. As a result there was enormous pressure upon women in most societies to maintain the 'free' status. Even within the kinship system there was significant pressure to alienate women for social offences thereby creating situations that could easily lead to their enslavement. While it was possible for some slave women to gain their freedom through gradual assimilation into a kinship system, a greater tendency existed, on account of the demand for female slaves, for free women to be denied kinship rights and marginalised into the pool of transferable slaves.

The principal objective of this process was to generate servile female labour for productive functions. Slavery, concubinage, and patriarchal dominance, assured that the woman was centred as the principal productive agency within the gender order. Women worked, and the majority of their labour hours were dedicated to agriculture. This was the case in the period of Atlantic slavery as it is now. A recent survey shows that in the sub-Saharan region women still contribute between 60 and 70 per cent of the labour within the agricultural sector.[9] They planted and harvested crops, looked after animals, and generally engaged in all labour intensive work such as crafts and domestic service. Importantly, women were expected to perform agricultural labour which was prescribed and understood within the dominant gendered division of labour as 'woman work'.

Since material development in most West African societies was based upon agricultural activity it followed that production and productivity expansion necessitated the aggressive integration and engagement of women slaves. Meillassoux has shown, for example, that in these economies 'women were valued above all as workers'. Robertson and Klein have argued that increasing production depended more on acquiring female labour, since 'women's work in Africa was generally the less desirable labor-intensive, low status work'. They conclude that in these contexts 'the value of women slaves was based on a sexual division of labour which assigned much of the productive labour to women'.[10] In these societies the progeny of female slaves were claimed by their owners. Female slave owners could also secure the right to the labour of slaves' children when the fathers were outside of their sphere of legal influence. The implication of this process was not always as clear, however, when the father of children born to slave women was himself a slave owner or a man of influence within the society. The biological reproduction of slaves that centred around women, therefore, was as complicated a process as its ideological reproduction within the gender order.

Such female slaves were used in miscellaneous economic activities in addition to supplying their owners with socio-sexual benefits. Many were traders, maids, cultivators, craft workers, and concubines. In addition, they were expected by male and female elites to reduce the demand for the intensive labour services of free women, and contribute towards the biological reproduction of the unfree labour force. Hard labour, then, of the intensive low status kind, came to be considered by West Africans as woman work, beneath men's social standing within the gender order. With respect to agricultural labour, therefore, West African men considered themselves privileged, and female slaves were gendered the 'lowest creatures on God's earth'.[11]

Caribbean slavery launched a direct assault on traditional West African gender orders. To begin with, significantly fewer black women entered the Atlantic slave trade than black men. The available records of European slave traders demonstrate this point forcefully. Klein's comprehensive analysis of the records of Dutch slave traders, who in the seventeenth century also supplied French, Spanish and English colonies, shows that only 38 per cent of Africans shipped were female. The adult sex ratio for Dutch traders was 187 men for every 100 women, and the child ratio was 193 boys for every 100 girls. Danish records yield a similar 36 per cent female cargo with an adult sex ratio of 186 men to 100 women and 145 boys to 100 girls. Using a broader based sample of British slave trade records, Klein found a similar pattern of discrimination against females (See Table 6.1).[12]

The general pattern, therefore, was clear. Between 65 per cent and 75 per cent of all slaves shipped from West Africa were males with only slight variations across the West African coast from Senegambia to Angola. This pattern indicates the tendency for West African economies and societies to retain traditional commitments to the dominant gender order in which men were considered more dispensable to internal processes of social and economic activity.

Table 6.1 Average sex ratio of adults shipped in the English slave trade to the West Indies, 1791-98[13]

Region in West Africa	Males per 100 females	No. of shipments
Senegambia	210	5
Sierra Leone	210	29
Windward Coast	208	15
Gold Coast	184	26
Bight of Benin	187	2
Bight of Biafra	138	79
Congo-Angola	217	60
Unknown	188	56
Average	183	272

The Atlantic Slave Trade, however, carried to West Indian plantations not only measurable units of labour, but also gender identities and ways of thinking about gender. On early West Indian plantations enslaved African men, the social majority, were pressed into labouring activities which were gendered as 'woman work' . The social implications of this development was that the Caribbean became a site that witnessed an early modern encounter and clash of two formally contradictory gender orders – one European and one West African. Managerial power was held decisively by the European male, and the potency of African gender ideologies was tested against the background of the productive needs of colonial capitalism. The European male held clear views with respect to gender and the sexual division of labour that differed from those of the African male; both sets of men, however, shared many common gender values and attitudes with respect to masculinity and the relation of 'woman' to patriarchal power.

Englishmen, in particular, pursued coherence in the articulation of gender representation, different categories of women and work. White women described as 'ladies' were not expected to labour in the field or perform any demeaning physical task. This was clearly a class position since the thousands of female indentured servants imported from the British Isles between 1624 and 1680 worked on the cotton, tobacco and sugar plantations in gangs alongside their male counterparts, as well as with enslaved Africans. It was not until the late seventeenth century that English planters, thinking of gender more in terms of race than class, finally implemented the policy that no white woman was to work in plantation labour gangs. This ideologically driven initiative to isolate white womanhood from plantation field work, however, had much to do with the social needs of patriarchy to idealise and promote the white woman as a symbol of white supremacy, moral authority, and sexual purity. The patriarchal ideology of white supremacy conceptually re-quired the social isolation of all white women, irrespective of class, from intimacy with the black male to minimise the dread of miscegenation.

The space vacated within the labour ranks had to be filled. White men believed that black men were best equipped to the physical task of frontier plantation construction, but suggested that black women were better prepared for the subsequent maintenance of efficient production. Criti-cally, they did not share the black male's view that field work was female work. Colonial managers, therefore, recognising the context of the gender orders, used the brutality of the death threat to enforce a work regime upon black males that ran counter to their gender identity and consciousness. Black men found the reversal of sex roles a major challenge to their masculine identity, and reacted with both outright violence and the negotiation of demand for entry into prestigious, non-agricultural occupations. By the mid eighteenth century, the artisanal, supervisorial labour aristocracy was male dominated; so too was the visible organisational military vanguard of plantation based, anti-slavery rebellions.

As the frontier receded, the centreing of the black woman within the slave complex took shape in two stages. First, by the mid seventeenth century slave owners had legislated the principle of matrilineal reproduction of the slave status. This approach provided that only the offspring of a slave woman would be born into slavery. All children at birth took the same legal status as their mothers. Womanhood, as a gendered formulation, was therefore legally constituted as a reproductive device that offered the slave system continuity and functionality. Slave owners were also in legal and philosophical agreement that the white race could not be reduced to chattel slavery. This meant that the gender identity and ideological praxis of the white woman could not be linked to enslavement, and only the offspring of black and 'coloured' women could be born into slavery. African women, then, on arrival in the West Indies, were placed strategically in the labour supply mechanism, and used as the restrictive instrument to broad based social access to freedom. By seeking ideologically to distance the white woman from the black man as a principal objective of race discourse, and at the same time socially exposing the black woman to all men, free born children from the black race would always be a very small minority.

The second stage relates to the natural reproduction of slaves as an important supply strategy. The minority status of women within the slave trade, and the fact that many of them 'had already used up some of their potential fecundity by the time they had arrived', meant that slave populations in the Caribbean 'could only have experienced a negative growth rate'.[14] This fact was not emphasised, or understood by slave owners. Over time, however, they problematised the negative growth rates of blacks and produced an expansive discursive literature. As they debated demographic trends and patterns, and concluded from colony to colony that natural reproduction was cheaper and more politically consistent with 'progressive' managerial policies, the slave woman was further targeted and bombarded in an ideological frenzy of new gender representations.

Plantation slavery, therefore, was not all about material production and human reproduction. Work and social relations on the estates were particularly relevant to the reproduction of significant social categories such as 'male' and 'female'. Work constituted the context within which the normative expectation attached to labour was gendered. That is, the work regime had as much to do with the production of sugar and other agricultural commodities as it did with the reproduction of the gender order. Field work came to be viewed by black males as slave work, rather than woman's work, which included all blacks and excluded white women. In addition, field work, and other forms of unskilled manual labour, were promoted as consistent with the 'essential nature' of blacks, an ideological construct that finally created an escape hatch for the landless white males. This shifting of class, race and gender relations within the division of labour is indicative of West Indian planters' distinct capacity for conceptualising the nature of their social world and formulating hegemonic ways to manage its paradoxical and contradictory tendencies.

African arrivants, therefore, were subjected to a process of physical acclimatisation as well as re-genderisation, generally referred to as 'seasoning'. During this initial phase of two to three years, they were inducted to a new gender culture and protected from the physical rigours of plantation life. The objective of this policy was to allow slaves time to recover their physical and psychological strength, build up some immunity to the new diseased environment, and learn the political economy of the gender order. It was at once an ideological, biological and labour apprenticeship.

Slave owners in the West Indies were familiar with the gender traditions of agriculture in West Africa. They understood at once that black women could be thrown into the deep end of the labour regime, and be productive. This explains in large measure their refusal to shelter these women from the most arduous physical task, as well as the suggestion that productivity differentials did not exist between the sexes. Mature women hoed the soil, dug drains, cut and bundled canes, planted new canes, carried baskets of manure to the fields and performed other physically demanding tasks. Younger women did what was considered light work, such as weeding, grass picking, tending cattle, and miscellaneous plantation tasks. Female children, looked after stocks, carried water to the fields, as well as other tasks.

The egalitarian labour regimes women experienced provided the context within which gender ideologies were conceived as constructions designed to promote the political economy of the colonial enterprise. The gender representation of black women was formalised in ways that offered coherence to the relations between sex, labour productivity, and capital accumulation. The colonial gender discourse confronted and assaulted traditional concepts of womanhood in both Europe and Africa, and sought to redefine notions of black feminine identity. The black woman was ideologically constructed as essentially 'non-feminine' in so far as primacy was placed upon her alleged muscular capabilities, physical strength, aggressive carriage, and sturdiness. Pro-slavery writers presented her as devoid of the feminine tenderness and graciousness in which the white woman was tightly wrapped. Her capacity for strenuous work was not discussed in relation to the high mortality rates and incidence of crippling injuries that characterised enslavement. When mention was made of such circumstances, it was done to portray her as clumsy, brutish, and insensitive to the scientific nature of bodily functions. As such, she was represented as ideally suited to manual labour as part of a wider civilising social experience. Edward Long, eighteenth-century pro-slavery ideologue of Jamaica, had no doubt that she was the perfect brute upon which the plantation's future rested. Her low fertility for him was an additional feature that indicated her essentially non-feminine identity.[15]

The defeminisation of the black woman, recast as the 'Amazon', allowed slave owners to justify within the slavery discourse her subjugation to a destructive social and material environment. It was said that she could 'drop' children at will, work without recuperation, manipulate at ease the physical environment of the sugar estate, and be more productive than men. These opinions, furthermore, constituted an ideological outlook that, when articulated by white males, seemed contradicted by the evidence of commonplace miscegenation. Long's text reveals evidence of the ideological subversion that resulted from white men's sexual attraction to black women. The 'goatish embraces' invariably produced a 'tawny breed', he said, who in turn tantalised like sirens all categories of gentlemen.[16] Long was aware that the socio-sexual reality of Jamaica could readily produce a gender reading of ethnic relations that exposes the contradictory nature of the race discourse. The discursive mechanism he adopted, as a protective cloak, was the invention of white feminine degeneracy that threatened, if left unattended, the future of the white male colonising project.

Long's pro-slavery text, furthermore, could be read as part of the discourse of feminine subversion to hegemonic representations. The sexual embrace of the black woman as metaphor speaks to the black community's claim to an irrepressible humanity that gave life to and nurtured a morally imploded conquistadorial elite. Miscegenation, of course, was a double-edged sword within the context – evidence of human sexuality to recognise itself as such and transcend crudely constructed ideological boundaries, as well as an indication of the fragility and private irrelevance of the race discourse. Enslaved black women's protection and publication of their feminine identities, therefore, took many forms, from their insistence on procuring fine clothing and decorative jewelry, love and care for their kith and kin, pursuit of market engagements through huckstering, leadership and involvement in revolutionary struggle, to loving white men into a kind of oblivion by producing coloured children with them that took their names, and more importantly, their properties. Gender, then, was socially contested in several ways, but as a relation of power, its role in the reproduction of masculinist class and race rule was critical.

The ideological defeminisation of the black woman, furthermore, contributed to a gender order that negated black motherhood and devalued maternity. Before the 1780s slave women were given a short respite from labour in the advanced stages of pregnancy. When William Dickson arrived at Barbados in the early 1770s, he reported being,

astonished to see some women far gone in pregnancy, toiling in the field, and others whose naked infants lay exposed to the weather sprawling on a goat skin, or in a wooden tray. I have heard with indignation, drivers curse both them and their squalling brats, when they were suckling them.[17]

The expression of hostility to pregnant women reflected planters' perception that it was cheaper to buy than to reproduce slaves naturally. This, however, is not how it was explained in pro-slavery texts. Slave-owners spoke instead about black women's disregard for motherhood and nurturing, and explained this as further evidence of their brutishness and lack of femininity. Since it was 'natural', they argued, for women to desire motherhood, black women's apparent low fertility within the context of an alleged sexual promiscuity, suggests a certain kind of moral undevelopment rather than physical inability.

Subversive resistance to these gender representations by women invariably incurred punishments. Slave drivers had the authority to use the whip to enforce conformity to the social implications of the gender order. African- born women did not expect to work during advance pregnancy nor in the three months after childbirth. Those who resisted the new regime were punished as part of the gender retraining. Richard Ligon described the mid seventeenth century plantation regime in Barbados:

The woman is at work with her pickaninny at her back . If the overseer be discreet, she is suffered to rest her self a little more than ordinary, but if not, she is compelled to do as others do. Times they have of suckling their children in the fields, and refreshing themselves, and good reason, for they carry burdens on the back, and yet work too.[18]

The unfamiliarity of this labour culture to Africans contributed to the low fertility levels and high infant mortality rates that rendered the black population unable to naturally reproduce itself.

Eighteenth-century records placed depletion rates (the excess of a population's crude death rate over its crude birth rate) as high as 50 to 65 per cent, while modern historians using case study analysis place it much lower. Estate records for Jamaica in the third quarter of the eighteenth century suggest depletion rates of about 20 per cent, while slave import-re-export records suggest 30 per cent between 1700 and 1750, and 25 per cent between 1750 and 1775. The depletion rate for Barbados in the first half of the eighteenth century seemed worst than that of Jamaica; 49 per cent between 1701 and 1725 and 36 per cent from 1726 to 1750, but falling to less than 12 per cent between 1775 and 1800. The demographic experiences of the Leewards approximated those of Barbados with depletion rates of 40 to 50 per cent up to the 1760s and less than 15 per cent in the last quarter of the century. By the time of the general registration of slaves between 1814 and 1818, and the collapse of slavery in the 1830s, depletion rates in Barbados and the Leewards were between three and four per cent.[19]

It was commonplace for visitors to the island in the eighteenth century, who were unfamiliar with the gender order of plantation slavery, to express horror on observing the physical brutalisation of females, and slave-owners' disregard for black motherhood and maternity. Accustomed to a gendered culture in which women were perceived as being constantly in need of social and moral protection from male tyranny, some individuals who remained pro-slavery during the debate on abolition, were moved to support policies for radical reformation of slave women's condition. To such observers, it was in relation to gender that slavery was most vile, unjust, and corrupting of civilised values. Not surprisingly, therefore, abolitionists after the 1780s used evidence of corporal punishments inflicted on females, splitting up of black families, and disregard for domesticity, to make their principal moral charge against slavery. In so doing they encouraged West Indian planters to address as a separate issue the matter of slave women's social and domestic conditions. An important effect of this political campaign was the reformalisation of gender representations. For the first time in the Caribbean the notion of the black woman as a member of the 'gentler sex' – hence physically inferior to males – became the basis of policy initiatives in slave management.

Abolitionists, furthermore, used the rate of natural decrease, or depletion rate, as proof of the unnatural character of the hegemonic gender order. They claimed that it was hostile to slave women, their domestic lives, and destroyed their natural tendency to be mothers. Centreing the slave woman within gender representations as the principal victim of nutritional deficiency, Kiple considers high infant mortality the single most important factor in explaining the high depletion rate. Mothers were often helpless as their children suffered and died of lockjaw, yaws, worms, and a bewildering array of unfamiliar infections and diseases. Most of these diseases, Kiple argued, were related to malnutrition which was an endemic consequence of consciously applied gendered policies.[20]

Bennett's account of Codrington Estates in Barbados during the eighteenth century highlights the personal aspects of women's daily social experience with high infant mortality rate. Assessing the effects of underfeeding and overworking pregnant and lactating mothers, he describes their experiences with child rearing on the estates as follows:

In 1745, Joan's daughter was born on February 7 and died on May 12; Occo's daughter began life on February 13, and died July 13; Molly's boy was born on July 7 and died on July 14; Bennebah's daughter lived only from October 3 to October 10; Arnote's son Cudgoe, lived only to 1748, and Moll's baby daughter, Moroat, lived only to 1748. Mercy's daughter, Mary, was the only one of the seven youngsters born in 1745 who survived at least three years. One of the three children born in 1746 died in the same year. The two children born in 1747 outlived their second years, and six of the seven babies born in 1748 lived past December 31 of that year – thus ten of the twenty three children born in the years from 1743 to 1748 died before the close of the period.[21]

This account offers a glimpse into the horror experienced by enslaved women. This was the personal emotional world of women that existed behind the aggregate statistics of depletion rates. Women watched their children die in quick succession, and buried more than those who lived to become adults. It was spiritually and emotionally crippling for many, but for most the experience enabled them to find subversive ways to survive and to maintain and define their feminine self-identities. 'Monk' Lewis, a Jamaican planter in the early nineteenth century, provides piercing insights into this social world of slave women with regards to gender identity, child rearing, and motherhood. Consistent with the dominant slave owners' representation of black women in the age of 'amelioration', he describes the women on his estate as 'kind-hearted creatures' who were 'particularly anxious to rear children'.[22] He details the reaction of a woman whose child had caught cold and showed the 'symptoms of a locked jaw':

The poor woman was the image of grief itself: she sat on her bed, looking at the child which lay by her side with its little hands clasped, its teeth clenched, and its eyes fixed, writhing in the agony of the spasm, while she was herself quite motionless and speechless, although the tears trickled down her cheeks incessantly. All assistance was fruitless at noon today it expired. This woman was a tender mother, had borne ten children, and yet has now but one alive: another, at present in the hospital, has born seven, and but one has lived past puberty; and the instances of those who have had four, five, six children, without succeeding in bringing up one, in spite of the utmost attention and indulgence, are very numerous.[23]

Despite the agony of high infant mortality, Lewis argued that the rearing of children, domesticity and family life, exerted a steadying and maturing influence upon slave women. To him, slave mothers appeared more moral, less sexually promiscuous, and more conforming.

The caring of children, the promotion of motherhood and domesticity, were therefore raised as sociological as well as economic fine tuning aspects of managerial imperatives. Gender representations were de-established and reconstructed to offer coherence to new reproductive policy initiatives. By the late eighteenth century, there was widespread commitment to pro-natal policies in an attempt to encourage natural reproduction as an important method of ensuring a labour supply in the long term. This development meant that a 'woman policy' had to be conceived, formulated and implemented on the estates. Traditional managerial attitudes and actions towards slave women had to be reconsidered and reshaped in a manner conducive to higher fertility levels. It was the beginning of a broad-based initiate to celebrate and promote black motherhood that resulted in the representation of the black woman as a natural nurturer – everyone's nanny, granny and auntie.

It should be stated, however, that slave owners had no direct evidence to prove that their females had been consciously imposing restraints upon their fertility, or that hegemonic gender representations helped towards its suppression, even though some believed it to be the case. No one considered that the slave woman, constructed as Jezebel, could possibly practise sexual abstinence (gynaecological resistance), but some believed that they possessed deep-rooted hostility toward child rearing in slavery, especially within the context of hostility to motherhood. Slave owners proposed to minimise the degree of female indifference and resistance to child rearing by systematically offering socio-material incentives and reshaping the ideological aspects of the gender order.

This fundamental managerial departure centred the woman as nurturer and meant that new gender ideas had to be formulated, carefully tested and evaluated. As a consequence the pro-slavery cause found itself the recipient of an upsurge in literature which addressed directly aspects of slave breeding policies. Most contributors, many of them posing as experienced authorities on slave management, sought to encourage this trend, conceiving it as representative of new progressive organisational thought. Also, successful reproduction was considered a political strategy to take wind from the sails of abolitionists who argued that the endemic ill-treatment of slave women sprang from conceptual sources deep within the gender order.

One influential work, a pamphlet published in London in 1786 entitled 'The Following instructions are Offered to the Consideration of Proprietors and Managers of Plantations', was written by a prominent absentee Barbadian planters. Printed in bold, capitalised letters in the introduction is the central thesis:

THE INCREASE IS THE ONLY TEST OF THE CARE WITH WHICH THEY ARE TREATED.

The Barbadians had already achieved natural growth and were now offering for emulation the key features of their success to other less fortunate planters. The critical factor, of course, was the attainment of a female majority in the slave population. Barbados led in this regard (See Table 6.2), and attributed their success to the effects of their demographic restructuring.

The pamphlet emphasised the need for planters to implement a series of pre-natal policies to assist pregnant women to deliver healthy babies. Most importantly, it stressed the need to protect fertile women from the tyranny of overseers. In addition, emphasis was placed on the need for post-natal facilities to assist lactating mothers in lowering the high level of infant mortality. These policies meant, in addition to marginal reduction of labour hours for pregnant and lactating field women, and improved material care, the representation of black women as graduant members of the 'gentler sex' whose fragility required specific policy

Table 6.2 Slave sex ratios in the British West Indies c. 1817 and c. 1832[24]

Colony	Males per 100 females	
	c. 1817	c. 1832
Barbados	83.9	86.3
St Kitts	92.4	91.9
Jamaica	100.3	94.5
Nevis	95.3	98.1
St Vincent	102.1	95.2
Trinidad	123.9	112.6
Demerara/Essequibo	130.9	110.2

protection. In effect, the authors recommended a significant reconstruction of the gender order.

Tinkering with gender by way of finding methods to remove as many irritants as possible from women's sexual and domestic oppression was considered necessary. Slave owners were urged to encourage young slaves to form Christian-style marriages as monogamous relations were considered more conducive to high fertility than African polygyny. The nuclear family structure, as an institutional arrangement, was encouraged by slave owners and considered suitable to attaining the objective of high levels of reproduction. On many estates, then, Christian-style married slaves were found living in single households. Also, the use of financial incentives as stimuli to reproduction was institutionalised by slave owners. By the 1790s, evidence from plantation account books shows that financial payments were commonplace.

'Monk' Lewis of Jamaica could not be satisfied with crude systems of monetary and material rewards for the creation of life. Money was important, but for him it was insufficient and brutally inadequate when offered as an incentive to motherhood. He needed something more philosophical, befitting the nature of the new, moral, gender order. Slave women, he believed, were entitled to 'honour' as mothers in their heroic struggle against nature. Respect was due to them, and such values, he believed, were necessary to encourage fertile women who were altogether too few on his estate. Lewis outlined his woman's policy as follows:

I then gave the mothers a dollar each, and told them, that for the future they might claim the same sum, in addition to their usual allowance of clothes and provisions, for every infant which should be brought to the overseer alive and well on the fourteenth day; and I also gave each mother a present of a scarlet girdle with a silver medal in the centre, telling her always to wear it on feasts and holidays, when it should entitle her to marks of peculiar respect and attention, such as being one of the first served, and receiving a larger portion than the rest; that the first fault which she might commit, should be forgiven on the production of this girdle; and that when she should have any favour to ask, she should always put round her waist, and be assured, that on seeing it, the overseer would allow the wearer to be entitled to particular indulgence. On every additional child an additional medal is to be affixed on the belt, and precedence is to follow the greater number of medals. I expected that this notion of an order of honour would have been treated as completely fanciful and romantic; but to my great surprise, my manager told me, that he never knew a dollar better bestowed than the one which formed the medal of the girdle, and that he thought the institution likely to have a very good effect.[25]

This 'belly-woman' initiative was just the kind of counter-offensive West Indian slave owners needed to protect their regime from the moral assault of metropolitan anti-slavery campaigners. The notion of 'an order of honour' was intended to complicate the charge of abolitionists who described 'reforming' slave owners as vulgar materialists for using sexual manipulation and exploitation as necessary approaches to finding an adequate labour supply. The offering of money to slave women for the delivery of infants was depicted by abolitionists as a more degrading action than the purchase of the mother in the first instance, and constituted proof of the cultural and moral degeneration of the gender order within the slave owning community.

Abolitionists, therefore, also centred the slave woman with respect to their campaign strategies, propaganda, and analytical critiques. The slave woman was placed at the core of a contradictory discourse that sought, on one hand to protect and prolong slavery, and on the other to undermine and destroy it. The discourse was transatlantic in nature. On the estates in the West Indies increases in the slave woman's fertility was hailed the deciding factor in the 'good treatment' thesis. In Europe, the slave woman was depicted as the tragic and principal victim of the worst system of masculine tyranny known to the modern world.

The debate over the slave woman was part of a wider gender discourse that sharpened opinion on both sides of the Atlantic and focused attention on the nature of slavery as a particular kind of gender power. The promotion of the paternalist idea in European discourse of the 'woman' as the gentler sex placed tremendous ideological ammunition in the hands of the anti-slavery movement. Campaigners sought to portray the evil of West Indian slave society as resulting from its bias – both in terms of the sex structure of labour gangs and its emphasis upon natural reproduction in the wake of the abolition of the slave trade in 1807. While, therefore, some hardline pro-slavery advocates continued to defend female corporal punishment in terms of 'the Amazonian cast of character' of the black woman, anti-slavery forces believed that they had discovered in gender – eventually – the soft, vulnerable underbelly of the slavery structure.[26]

Slave owners, therefore, found themselves placed in a difficult and paradoxical position with respect to the gender discourse. While they made claim to possession of an egalitarian ideology, within which black women were not recognised as inferior or subordinate to black men – as demonstrated in their labour productivity – there was no intention on their part of weakening dominant patriarchal systems to which the black male also subscribed and was partially empowered and privileged. The subsequent conceptual imprisonment of the black woman within a re-structured gender representation that promoted notions of difference and inferiority had the effect of supporting her claim to legal emancipation but at the same time deepening her victimisation within the gender order. Slave owners, however, while promoting gender egalitarianism under the whip, sought to defeminise her in this way by inferring a sameness with males.

The abolitionist discourse, furthermore, needed to cross a few turbulent rivers before it reached a comfortable resting place with respect to the objectification of the black woman. Was she in fact a woman, and if so, what did her femininity look like? In what ways, and to what extent, was she different from the white woman? Should she be regarded as a 'sister' by white women, or subsumed within the category of chattel and brute? Was she victim not only of white tyranny but also black masculine tyranny – a kind of malehood that saw all women as 'less than', and 'other'? The answers to these questions would have policy implications for the movement, particularly with respect to issues such as the separation of children from mothers, attitudes toward family life, corporal punishments, and the general nature of sex, gender and work.

By the mid 1820s both males and female English abolitionists were satisfied that the 'woman card' was their strongest in the struggle to win the hearts and minds of a seemingly indifferent public that, according to John Bull, was 'almost sick of this black business'. Throughout England, middle-class white women formed anti-slavery organisations and campaigned against slavery by promoting the 'feminine' characteristics of the black woman who was their 'sister' in the search for a new moral, Christian order.[27] In most cases white female abolitionists claimed a special understanding of the plight of black women, and slaves in general, derived in part form their 'essential nature' as female. The author of *A vindication of female anti-slavery Association*, argued that their movement was part of a general struggle against human misery, social oppression, and moral injustice. Elizabeth Heyrick, a popular anti-slavery campaigner, stated in her pamphlet, 'Appeal the Hearts and Conscience of British Women (1828)', that the woman on account of 'the peculiar texture of her mind, her strong feelings and quick sensibilities, especially qualify her, not only to sympathise with suffering, but also to plead for the oppressed'.[28]

The strategy of the British female anti-slavery movement, furthermore, was to construct a gendered trinity composed of woman, child, and family, that slavery had destroyed and denied black people. Without the emotional, spiritual and institutional bonds to enforce the viability of this trinity, they argued, civilisation was not possible in the West Indies and those responsible for its absence were guilty of contributing to the pool of human misery and backwardness. 'Hell' was depicted as a place where men enslave and beat women, alienate them from their children, place a market price upon infants at birth, and deny them the right to religion, education, and moral guidance; and it was portrayed as a place not dissimilar from a West Indian slave plantation.

Gender, then, also resided at the core of concepts and discourses of slavery and freedom in modernity. Extracted from West Africans by the slave trade and deposited in the Americas in considerably lesser numbers than men, women constituted initially a minority in frontier Caribbean societies. Minority demographic status gave way to numerical majorities as socio-economic formations matured and were rationalised. Significant gender implications resulted from the fact that the entire system of slavery was female focused, as enslaved black women constituted the conduit through which black infants acquired at birth the slavery status. As a consequence, successive gender representations of black women developed around the need to align changing sex compositions and demographic requirements with the political economy of efficient resource use. This was illustrated by the empirical evidence and conceptual articulations of the late eighteenth century when slave owners shifted their labour supply policy from 'buying' to 'breeding'. As the slave woman featured centrally in changing methods of slave reproduction, gender representations reflected the rationalisations of choices. Likewise, the politics of anti-slavery in Europe privileged the gender discourse to illustrate and emphasise slave women's relatively greater exploitation and brutalisation. Abolitionists, further, used gender representations of black women to highlight the extreme moral and social oppressiveness and backwardness of societies based on slavery, and the degeneracy of elites that maintain and defend it.

The considerable turbulence in the gender journey of slavery requires that events and processes be examined and historicised with the view to obtaining critical forms of feminist knowledge about male domination. Feminist theorising is best served by readings of history that illustrate how evolving communities actually thought about gender and formed opinions within changing social, economic, and philosophical contexts. As an historical moment, slavery was characterised by considerable internal turmoil that enable us to map the contours of the complex interactions between gender and relations of race and class. An understanding of the 'enterprise of the Indies' as a project of modernity, therefore, requires the creation and organisation of knowledge about gender as socially constructed relations of domination. The praxis of gender, and liberation from its capacity to socially differentiate for the purposes of domination, then, should begin and be guided by an understanding of how and why we came, over time, to think about things we think and do not think about.

Notes

1. See Hilary McD. Beckles, 'Sex and Gender in the Historiography of Caribbean Slavery' in Verene Shepherd et. al. (eds), *Engendering History: Caribbean Women in Historical Perspective* (Kingston: Ian Randle Publishers, 1995) pp. 125-140; also in this volume, Bridget Brereton, 'Text, Testimony, and Gender: An Examination of Some Texts by Women on the English-speaking Caribbean, from the 1770s to the 1920s', pp. 63-94; and Rosalyn Terborg-Penn, 'Through an African Feminist Theoretical Lens: Viewing Caribbean Women's History Cross-culturally', pp. 3-19.

2. Kamau Brathwaite, 'Caribbean Woman during the Period of Slavery', 1984 Elsa Goveia Memorial Lecture, University of the West Indies, Cave Hill; Rhoda Reddock, 'Women and Slavery in the Caribbean: A Feminist Perspective', *Latin American Perspectives*, 40, (12:1), pp. 63-80. Hilary McD. Beckles, *Natural Rebels: A Social History of Enslaved Black Women in Barbados* (New Brunswick: Rutgers University Press, 1989); Marietta Morrissey, 'Women's Work, Family Formation and Reproduction among Caribbean Slaves', *Review*, 9 (1986), pp. 339-367.

3. See for the wider relevance of this discussion Hilary McD. Beckles, 'Black Masculinity in Caribbean Slavery', Women and Development Unit, University of the West Indies, Cave Hill, *Occasional Paper* 2:96 (1996); Lindon Gordon, 'What's New in Women's History', in Teresa de Lauretis (ed.) *Feminist Studies/Critical Studies*, (Bloomington: Indiana University Press, 1986) pp. 20-23; Louise M. Newman *Journal of Women's History* 2:3 (1991); Mary Poovey, 'Feminism and Deconstruction', *Feminist Studies*, 14, (1988).

4. See Beckles, *Natural Rebels*; Arlette Gautier, 'Les Esclaves Femmes aux Antilles Francaises, 1635-1848', *Reflexions Historiques*, 10:3, (1983) pp. 409-35; B. W. Higman, 'Household Structure and Fertility on Jamaican Slave Plantations', *Population Studies*, 27 (1973) pp. 527-550; *Slave Population and Economy in Jamaica, 1802-1834* (N.Y.: Oxford University Press, 1976); H. S. Klein and S. L. Engerman, 'Fertility Differentials between Slaves in the United States and the British West Indies', *William and Mary Quarterly* 35 (1978) pp. 357-374; Michael Craton, 'Changing Patterns of Slave Families in the British West Indies', *Journal of Interdisciplinary History*, X:1 (1979) pp. 1-35.

5. The protracted violent war between Africans and Europeans on the sixteenth- and seventeenth-century Caribbean frontier has been well documented, but the contribution of changing gender identities and roles to social turbulence and instability has not been accounted for despite the considerable evidence found in slave owners' texts. See Hilary McD. Beckles, 'Caribbean Anti-Slavery: The Self-Liberation Ethos of Enslaved Blacks', *Journal of Caribbean History* 22:1 and 2 (1988) pp. 1-19; Bernard Moitt, 'Women, Work and Resistance in the French Caribbean during Slavery, 1700-1848' in Shepherd et. al. (eds.) *Engendering History: Caribbean Women in Historical Perspective*, pp. 155-175; Barbara Bush, *Slave Women in Caribbean Society, 1650-1838* (Bloomington: Indiana University Press, 1990); Marietta Morrissey, *Slave Women in the New World: Gender Stratification in the Caribbean* (Kansas University Press, 1989).

6. See David Brion Davis, *The Problem of Slavery in Western Culture* (Ithaca: Cornell University Press, 1966); also, *Slavery and Human Progress* (New York: Oxford University Press, 1984); David Eltis and James Walvin (eds.) *The Abolition of the Atlantic Slave Trade: Origins and Effects in Europe, Africa and the Americas* (Madison: University of Wisconsin Press, 1981); Thomas Hodgkin, 'Kingdoms of the Western Sudan', in Roland Oliver (ed.) *The Dawn of Africa History* (London: Oxford University Press, 1961); Jan Vansina, *Paths in the Rainforest* (London: James Currey Publishers, 1990); Philip D. Curtin, 'Africa and the Wider Monetary World, 1250-1850' in John F. Richards, (ed.) *Precious Metals in the Later Medieval and Early Modern Worlds* (Durham: Carolina University Press, 1982) pp. 231-68; John Fage, 'The Effects of the Export Trade on African Populations' in R. P. Moss and R. J. Rathbone (eds.) *The Population Factor in African Studies* (University Press of London, 1975), pp. 15-23; Joseph Inikori, (ed.) *Force Migration: The Impact of the Export Trade on African Societies* (London: Hutchinson, 1981); Ray Kea, *Settlement, Trade and Politics in the Seventeenth Century Gold Coast* (Baltimore: Johns Hopkins University Press, 1982); Claire Robertson and Martin Klein (eds.) *Women and Slavery in Africa* (Madison: University of Wisconsin Press, 1983) Claude Meillassoux, 'Female Slavery' in Robertson and Klein, *Women and Slavery*, pp. 49-66; Walter Rodney, 'African Slavery and Other Forms of Social Oppression on the Upper Guinea Coast in the Context of the Atlantic Slave Trade', *Journal of African History* 7: 3, (1966) pp. 431-443; 'Gold and Slaves on the Gold Coast', *Transactions of the Historical Society of Ghana* 10 (1969) pp. 13-28.

7. Claire C. Robertson and Martin A. Klein, 'Women's Importance in African Slave Systems', in Robertson and Klein (eds.) *Women and Slavery*, pp. 4-5.

8. *Ibid.*; see also Martin Klein 'Women in Slavery in the Western Sudan' in Robertson and Klein, (eds.) *ibid.*; pp. 67-92.

9. See Robertson and Klein 'Women's Importance', op. cit. p. 9.

10. Meillassoux, 'Female Slavery', op. cit. p. 49; Robertson and Klein, 'Women's Importance', op. cit. pp. 10, 11.

11. See Robertson and Klein, *ibid.*, p. 18. See also, J. D. Fage, 'Slave and Society in Western Africa, c. 1455-1700', *Journal of African History* 21 (1980) pp. 289-310; M. Klein, 'The Study of Slavery in Africa; A Review Article', *Journal of African History*, 19 (1978) pp. 599-609; I. Kopytoff, 'Indigenous African Slavery: Commentary One', *Historical Reflections* 6 (1979) pp. 62-77; I. Kopytoff and S. Miers, 'African "Slavery" as an Institution of Marginality', in S. Miers and I. Kopytoff (eds.), *Slavery in Africa* (Madison: University of Wisconsin Press, 1977).

12. Herbert S. Klein, 'African Women in the Atlantic Slave Trade', in Robertson and Klein (eds.) *Women and Slavery*, op. cit. pp. 29-32.

13. Ibid., p. 33 (Table 2.6).

14. *ibid.* p. 37.

15. Edward Long, *The History of Jamaica* 3 vols. (London 1774) pp. 274-276, 327-328, 330-31.

16. Ibid., p. 328.

17. William Dickson, *Letters on Slavery* [1789] (Westport: Negro University Press Reprint, 1970) p. 12.

18. Richard Ligon, *A True and Exact History of the Island of Barbados* (London 1657) p. 48.

19. See J. R.Ward, *British West Indian Slavery, 1750-1834: The Process of Amelioration* (Oxford: Clarendon Press, 1988) pp. 121-122.

20. See K. F. Kiple, *The Caribbean Slave: A Biological History* (Cambridge: Cambridge University Press, 1981); K. F. Kiple and V. H. Kiple, 'Slave Child Mortality: Some Nutritional Answers to a Perennial Puzzle', *Journal of Social History* X (1979) pp. 284-309; 'Deficiency Diseases in the Caribbean', *Journal of Interdisciplinary History* XI: 2, (1980), pp. 197-205.

21. J. H. Bennett, *Bondsmen and Bishops: Slavery and Apprenticeship on the Codrington Planta-tions of Barbados, 1710-1838* (Berkeley: University of California Press, 1958) p. 55.

22. M. G. Lewis, Journal of a West India Proprietor, Kept during a Residence in the Island of Jamaica (London 1929 edition), p. 87.

23. *ibid.*

24. B. W. Higman, *Slave Populations of the British Caribbean, 1807-1834* (Baltimore: Johns Hopkins University Press, 1984) p. 116.

25. Lewis, *Journal of a West Indian Proprietor*, pp. 108-109.

26. Report on the Debate in Council on a Dispatch from Lord Bathurst to Governor Warde of Barbados (London, 1828) pp. 21-23.

27. See Clare Midgley, *Women Against Slavery: The British Campaigns, 1780-1870* (London: Routledge, 1992) pp. 93-117; Louis Billington and Rosamund Billington, '"A Burning Zeal for Righteousness": Women in the British Anti-slavery Movement, 1820-1800', in Jane Rendall (ed.) *Equal or Different: Women's Politics, 1800-1914* (Basingstoke: Macmillan, 1985) pp. 82-111; Bill Hooks, 'Sisterhood: Political Solidarity between Women', *Feminist Review* 23 (1986), pp. 125-138.

28. A Vindication of Female Anti-slavery Associations (London: Female Anti-slavery Society, [n.d.]) pp. 3-4; [Elizabeth Heyrick], *Appeal to the Hearts and Conscience of British Women* (Cockshaw, Leicester, 1828) p. 3. Also cited in Midgley, *Women Against Slavery*, p. 94.

7

Gender Ideology and Land

Janet Henshall Momsen

Contemporary ecofeminist and 'women, environment and development' (WED) work emphasises a special relationship between the environment and women as its users or managers, but here I argue that links between gender identity and ecology, far from being timeless, as the ecofeminists assert, were often constructed and altered in the politics of the colonial encounter. Recent feminist-environmentalist research in India (Nesmith 1991; Agarwal 1994), East Africa (Moore and Vaughan 1995; Schmidt 1992) and West Africa (Leach 1994; Brown 1994) has undermined ecofeminist meta-narratives of women's agricultural marginalisation under colonialism and highlighted the variability in experiences of colonial and post-colonial land use change in the light of local cultural and political contexts and different ecological possibilities. We have also become more aware of the importance of gender relations in land and labour use and the ways in which the dynamics of household formation interplay with regional political issues. But gender has yet to receive serious consideration in environmental history overall (Leach and Green 1995) and gender aspects of environmental issues have been virtually ignored in Caribbean historiography.

Ecofeminism has tended to conflate 'Nature' and 'Environment' and to assert that the woman-nature connection is a universal, biologically based, ideological construct. But studies in many parts of the world have revealed that this women-nature link in Western thought, when seen in a global context, is a contingent rather than a necessary relationship

(Croll and Parkin 1992). Shiva (1989) takes this further and cogently argues that Western images of the dichotomies of nature and culture, female and male, in which the former are subordinated to the latter, have been imposed on indigenous societies through capitalist development during and since the colonial period. Many researchers have found these views difficult to reconcile with the environment in which they work (Joekes, Leach and Green 1995).

Women, seen merely as a single category in their relationship to the environment, form a chaotic concept, given the wide range of social, economic and cultural differences both within and between communities and places. The United Nations Conference on Environment and Development (UNCED) held in Rio de Janeiro in 1992, presented women's interests in relation to the environment as united and did not question whether this dominant view really represented the voice of women in non-Western cultures (Braidotti 1994). Within any society viewing 'women' as a unitary category ignores differences linked to class, ethnicity, age, education and marital status. Ecofeminism also fails to deconstruct 'men' as a category, seeing all men as patriarchal, powerful exploiters of 'nature'. In the WED literature, on the other hand, men are invisible while women are considered to be the only ones capable of sustainably managing the environment (Leach 1992; Momsen 1993).

The conceptualisation of the environment in WED/ecofeminist thought can also be criticised. Ecofeminism, grounded in Western ideas of binary opposition, tends to conflate ecological aspects of the environment with the natural biological needs of human beings in its concept of 'nature'. In a similar fashion, in WED literature generalised references to 'environmental sustainability' or 'environmental crisis' are common. But equating the 'environment' with 'nature' and making non context-specific generalisations 'can obscure the historical and continued shaping of landscapes by people' and 'the plurality and the politics of environmental perceptions' (Leach, Joekes and Green 1995: 3-4).

The core of the concept 'environment' is land which has three major constructs: land as property, land as usufruct and land as territoriality. All three resonate with gender relations in different ways, but all form the basis of power in most societies so ensuring that women's access to land is limited and controlled by men. A focus on the intersection of gender and property relations interprets women's relationship with land very differently from the approach taken by ecofeminist histories.

In the post-emancipation plantation economy of the Caribbean land was seen as the pivot of a pre-Fordist agrarian restructuring from vertically integrated industrialised farming with a permanent workforce of field gangs based on physical strength and experience rather than gender, to a system which included small family farms, outsourcing and gender-differentiated contract labour. Land became a point of both negotiation and contestation as planters attempted to create a flexible but stable labour force and the former slaves sought access to cultivable land as a livelihood strategy. Land was the basis of the reproduction of the workforce but to retain use of the controlled workforce that the imperialist project of abolition had forced them to give up, the plantocracy had to limit access to this vital resource. Thus, the Caribbean experienced one of the first attempts to develop a model of industrial labour control for a semi-proletarianised agricultural workforce.

In Barbados, where women had been the main field workers under slavery and also the main producers of local foodstuffs, this post-emancipation project had a clear gender focus. This focus became confused by tensions between conflicting gender ideologies of Church and State, imperial and planter legislatures, and patriarchal households and employers all operating within changing global and local economic relations. Small- scale agriculture developed in the spatial, economic, and social interstices of the plantation landscape, 'the excess or left-over spaces of their world' (Anzaldúa 1987: 20). Women farmers were even more peripheralised by the patriarchal attitudes of colonialism and religion reinforced by class and race. Agarwal (1994: 13) argues that women's emancipation is dependent on their control of property but gender ideologies about women's needs, roles and capabilities can restrict women's abilities to exercise their property claims. Those who own property can exert control and influence over the institutions that effect ideology and the impact of these ideologies on women will vary according to the class and economic standing of the household. Thus 'gender ideologies and associated practices are culturally specific, historically variable, and dialectically linked to property ownership and control' (Agarwal 1994: 16).

Legal discrimination against women's ownership and inheritance of land is widespread throughout the developing world (Mehra 1995). In many countries religious or customary law prevails over constitutional law inhibiting women's rights. Even where there is no legal discrimination, since women in most societies are disproportionately poor, they are at a disadvantage when obtaining land as competition for this limited resource intensifies. While policy makers in Asia and Africa are attempting to devise strategies to encourage the equal involvement of both men and women in agriculture, in the Caribbean the process is being reversed by the undermining of traditional gender equalities in land ownership and agricultural production.

In many parts of the Caribbean, the oldest colonial region of the world, women have had equal rights to land ownership and inheritance of property from the earliest days of European settlement in the seventeenth century. Since the late nineteenth century even married women have had the right to own property separately from their husbands. Yet today, paradoxically, although some one-third of small farms are operated by women in the Commonwealth Caribbean, these farms are smaller and both environmentally and economically more marginal than those of men (Momsen 1984). Yet capitalism, in the form of the slave plantation, did not marginalise slave women by confining them to the domestic sphere but, on the contrary demanded that their productive roles in the cane fields take priority over biological and social reproduction. This treatment gave black women a remarkable degree of personal autonomy and equality in relation to their menfolk which continued in their post-emancipation work of producing and marketing foodstuffs (Barrow 1993). The post-emancipation adoption of gender ideologies of female domestication that marginalised women farmers, despite longstanding legal equality in land ownership while, at the same time, women's perceptions of land as a source of family survival and territory rather than as a major economic resource have led them to cling to minuscule plots.

This paper explores the causes underlying this paradoxical reduction of women's entitlements despite apparently gender neutral colonial attitudes. It examines the interplay of different institutional externally-created gender ideologies in a local context of female-headed households and high levels of female participation in agricultural labour. It specifically focuses on changes in the gendered nature of patterns of land ownership in the immediate post-emancipation period. These changes were constrained by the economic structures established during the period of slavery and reflected in their perturbations, the tensions between the economic and sexual needs of individual planters on the one hand and the sometimes conflicting ideologies of the colonial power and local legislatures, on the other. It is suggested that the post-emancipation redistribution of farmland had both gender and environmental dimensions which laid the foundation for the contemporary agricultural situation in the region.

Nineteenth-century Barbadian women smallholders did not leave written narratives concerning their attitudes to land so we are forced to depend on the documents of the elite: missionaries, colonial and local officials and planters. These documents comprise both factual accounts and social representations of the situation and above all are both andro-centric and ethnocentric. I have tried to contextualise these discourses and highlight the tensions between them so that I might build up an interpre-tation without removing all ambiguities (See Moore and Vaughan 1994, for a discussion of the difficulties of using similar data).

Gender and land in the Caribbean

In the seventeenth century many Caribbean islands became archetypal plantation colonies based on the production of sugar by African slaves. There was no traditional peasantry although Sidney Mintz (1974: 132-133) has argued that slaves who were allowed to cultivate 'provi-sion grounds', gardens that provided most of the local food supply in these colonies (Patterson 1967: 18), could be considered 'proto-peas-ants'. These gardens were only permitted on the fringes of the planta-tions, on land unsuitable for cane cultivation, but played an important role in maintaining the labour force and reducing food imports. In some cases they had the unplanned effect of enabling slaves, especially the women who marketed the produce, to build up enough capital to buy their freedom. Thus usufruct rights to land were seen as a means of resistance to colonialism, slavery and the plantation (Mintz 1974: 132-133).

However, gender roles among the proto-peasants have been disputed for while Mintz (1976: 38) 'could find no evidence that provision grounds were granted to women', Lucille Mathurin-Mair (1986: 10) also writing on Jamaica notes that 'Female slaves like male slaves, enjoyed customary, and after the 1792 slave legislation, legal entitlement to their provision grounds.' In Martinique, where the idea of provision grounds had been introduced by Portuguese expelled from Pernambuco in the seventeenth century, the Royal Ordinance of 1846 regulated the existing practice and declared that each adult slave, male and female, over 14 years-of-age had equal rights to plantation provision grounds (Tomich 1990: 267). The underlying ideology of this legislation on the eve of emancipation, was to prepare the slaves for freedom by giving them property and so a stake in society. Olwig (1985: 41) shows that in St John both male and female slaves had rights and a strong attachment to land.

Colonial land allocation at the time of settlement in the British West Indian colonies, was also relatively non-discriminatory (Satchell 1995).

When Jamaica was taken from the Spanish in 1655 'Oliver Cromwell, Lord Protector of England, proclaimed that all would-be settlers would be granted land by letters patent at the rate of 12 acres for each male over 12 years old and 10 acres for females and males under 12 years' (Satchell 1995: 215). In 1662, the gender specification in total area of land to be granted was removed and the amount raised to 30 acres of land for any would-be settler irrespective of age (Satchell 1995: 215). Large land grants of between 200 and 500 acres were commonly made to both men and women (Claypole 1970). Gradual consolidation of land grants into even larger holdings still left women represented as major landed proprietors (Satchell 1995). In common with many colonial frontiers of settlement, male planters often travelled in search of alternative economic opportunities leaving wives in charge of the family plantation. When it came to inheritance it is clear from many of the seventeenth- and eighteenth-century wills in the Barbados archives that men considered their wives capable of actively running their plantations and their daughters worthy of inheriting land equally with sons.

However, there was one limitation to this picture of apparent legal equality. Under Law 43 of 1663, married women in Jamaica were precluded from owning property. When a woman landowner married, her land had to be vested in her husband as trustee at the time of her marriage. Not until the Married Woman's Property Act of 1870, with an additional amendment in 1882, was this 1663 law annulled in Jamaica. Thus after 1882, women could retain their property on marriage, have sole right to property acquired during marriage and participate in the local land market. In Barbados an Act to Amend the Law relating to the Property of Married Women was passed on August 22, 1879 (Goodman and Clarke 1912-13). Under this law, property inherited after marriage, rents from inherited freehold property, wages, salaries and income from artistic or literary skills were all to be considered property for her separate use. The same law, however, made a married woman liable for support of an indigent husband. In 1880, on October 18, a law relating to real estate was passed extending all rights under the Law of 1853 to married women. Under this law a married woman was allowed to dispose of her own or joint property as long as her husband concurred, but this right did not extend to property settled on her on the occasion of her marriage (Goodman and Clarke 1912-13). Suffrage was based on property, income or professional training but was limited to men who were allowed to vote on the basis of their wives' property (Barbados Government 1913). Not until 1943 were women, owning property worth at least £25, granted the vote in their own right, with universal adult suffrage following in 1950 (Beckles 1990: 178,186).

During colonial times, in the French West Indies, women had the right to inherit land (Lefort de Latour 1782) and in the Dutch West Indies, among the Sephardic Jews of Curaçáo, inheritance was matrilineal (Abrahams 1993). Women's access to land in both these areas has declined as their societies became more open in the twentieth century and migration of both men and women to the metropole increased (Abrahams 1993; Poirier and Dagenais 1986).

Slavery was also a fairly gender neutral institution. Divisions of labour were based on strength and endurance and so reflected life course rather than gender. Although at first planters had sought male slaves for the hardest field work, with women being assigned to domestic tasks, by the end of the eighteenth century the slave sex ratio was in balance and with the cessation of the slave trade, women soon came to outnumber men in the slave workforce (Beckles 1988). On many plantations, women became a majority among the field slaves while male slaves held most of the elite skilled positions (Beckles 1988). Beckles (1988: 17) suggests that because West African women were accustomed to agricultural tasks 'Planters could not develop a sexual division of labour among field cultivators based upon production or productivity differentials.' Moitt (1995: 157) notes that 'though women were generally outnumbered by men for most of the slavery period, they performed proportionately more hard labour than men'. Thus at emancipation there was a tradition of active female involvement in agriculture both as workers and managers.

Post-emancipation Gender Ideology

Missionaries in many of the islands towards the end of the eighteenth century introduced a gender ideology of respectability. They provided land for free villages and often the only schools available to ex-slaves and made formal marriage a prerequisite for church membership. They sought a pious peasantry and, unlike the planters, the missionaries did see Afro-Caribbean people as potentially equal in humanity to Europeans provided they adopted a suitable lifestyle (Olwig 1995). Part of this lifestyle involved the ideology of the male breadwinner as an essential element for social progress and the reconstruction of 'civilised society' in the post-slavery period. Thus there was social pressure for the development of nuclear families in which gendered roles were established and the woman played her Victorian role as housewife and mother. With the ending of apprenticeship in 1838 many female former slaves sought the private sphere previously denied them and retired from the fields to the duties of the home (Morsen 1841). Children were also removed from agricultural work and it was noted in the 1839 magistrates' reports for Barbados that 'parents are determined that the girls shall be brought up as sempstresses and the boys to trades' (Parliamentary Papers 1842: 164).

Although the plantocracy generally supported this ideology, economic pressures undermined it and led to some ambivalence: for 'while the planters criticised mothers for neglecting their offspring, they preferred to hire females, whom they considered more regular than males in their work habits' (Levy 1980: 113). Similar reactions were found in Jamaica where it was felt that even if the men gave sustained labour after abolition it would still be 'quite impossible to continue sugar cultivation to give any remuneration to the proprietors unless the females also be induced to labour regularly' (McNeil quoted in Mair 1986: 10). Male migration, leaving many women as the sole support of their children, combined with rising food prices in the mid nineteenth century, forced many women back to agricultural labour. Furthermore, the individualisation of work as a slave was carried over into the wage labour system and wage rates were established which differentiated on the basis of gender, with women being paid less than men despite the equality under slavery. By the end of the nineteenth century women constituted a majority of the workforce in Barbados.

Indian indentured labourers, brought into many islands after 1845 to replace the emancipated slave workforce, were at first treated in the same gender neutral manner as the slaves had been. They were offered land as an alternative to repatriation after they had completed their period of indenture. Women who emigrated as single persons were entitled to the same amount of land as male indentured workers (Shepherd 1995: 254). Under this equitable allocation in Jamaica, 48 Indian women in 1904 and 38 in 1906 were granted ten acres of land each. In 1891, there were 62 Indian peasant proprietors in Jamaica of whom only three were women, but by 1921 women made up one-quarter of the Indian peasant farmers and 36 per cent of small rice farmers (Shepherd 1995: 251-522).

Under labour-rent systems, whereby access to land was dependent on providing labour to the plantation, all members of the family had to participate, which mitigated against the missionary ideal of the male breadwinner. The former slaves resented the planters' attempt to bind them to the estates through control of access to their provision grounds which had become a customary right under slavery. In St John in the

Danish West Indies, although most land purchased after slave emancipation in 1848 was in the name of men, upon death it passed to the heirs as a group, both men and women (Olwig 1981). This land was considered *family land*, a concept known widely throughout the region (Besson 1987). As in the British colonies, St Johnians kept the customary right, established during slavery, to cultivate estate land not being used by the owner. In St John this seems to have been more a form of sharecropping than the Barbadian system of formally linking access to land with work as a plantation labourer. 'Women had, of course, as much right to use estate land as had men' (Olwig 1981: 69).

Conflicts over land and labour led to strikes in several islands after 1838. Eventually a few concessions were gained: small wage increases, guarantees of rights to standing crops in cases of eviction and, as a reflection of the new gender ideology, a shorter working week for women (Marshall 1979). At first the colonial power supported the plantocracy in their efforts to ensure a continuing steady, cheap supply of labour. But towards the end of the century, as West Indian sugar became less important in imperial trade, a peasant-based colonial policy was forced on the local legislatures.

Gender and Land Ownership in Barbados

In the post-emancipation Caribbean,

freehold land was not only of obvious economic importance to those ex-slaves who managed to obtain it, giving some independence from the plantations and a bargaining position for higher wages when working on them, but it also had considerable symbolic significance to a people who had not only once been landless, but property themselves. For such land symbolised their freedom and provided property rights, prestige and personhood . (Besson 1987: 18).

A place of their own also enabled the ex-slaves for the first time to separate residence and workplace. But, unlike the situation in many of the larger islands such as Trinidad, Jamaica and St Lucia, in Barbados there was no unclaimed land on which the ex-slaves could cultivate crops and raise animals. Access to land was limited by both the land market and the changing and sometimes conflicting gender ideologies of the imperial power, the local plantocracy, missionaries and the new society created by the former slaves.

Given the longstanding equal legal rights to land ownership for men and single women and for married women after 1879, women's involvement in agriculture and more women than men in the population, it might be expected that the proportion of women land owners would gradually increase following emancipation in 1838. Satchell (1995), in his study of land transactions and peasant development in Jamaica for the period 1866 to 1900 calculated that women gained 2,005 acres of land between 1866 and 1869, but had a net loss of 156,832 acres over the period 1870 to 1900. He concludes that 'such widescale transfer of landholdings seems improvident in an agrarian society where land indicates socio-economic power and prestige' (Satchell 1995: 229). In this parallel study of Barbados land ownership, I seek an alternative explanation to that of mere improvidence.

Barbados has long had a higher proportion of women in the population than most Caribbean islands and at emancipation had the lowest proportion (2.9 per cent) of African-born slaves of any British West Indian colony (Beckles 1990). Thus the creation of a peasantry in Barbados was least influenced by African traditions and more clearly a female project than elsewhere in the region. As early as 1673 over half the slaves were female and by the early eighteenth century the gender balance of the slave population had settled to 48 per cent male and 52 per cent female (Beckles 1990: 51). By 1801, the proportion of females in the slave population had risen to 54 per cent. There were also poor white women and free coloured women involved in agriculture as well as women planters. In 1844, the sex ratio in Barbados was 118 women for every hundred men rising to 125 per 100 in 1891 (Massiah 1984). On farms of less than ten acres women made up 56 per cent of the operators in 1963 (Henshall 1969) and 41 per cent of operators of farms of less than four hectares in 1989 (Barbados Ministry of Agriculture 1991).

Drawing on the annual parish rate books, supplemented by other land records in the Barbados Archives, it is possible to trace the changing gendered basis of land occupance. At emancipation all farmland was occupied: 'there is not in the whole island a spot of wasteland for cultivation, and as the land is principally divided into plantations, the proprietors are not likely to sell off small plots for that purpose; and there being no public lands available, it is plain that freeholders to any extent cannot be established in this country' (Parliamentary Papers 1842). Yet in 1847 Barbados had, excluding the parish of St Andrew, 2,501 freeholders of whom one-fifth were women (Table 7.1). Of these landholdings, 1,631 were between one and ten acres in size, an increase of 464 since 1840. Women made up 26 per cent of owners of farms of between one and ten acres, ten per cent of farms 10 to 99 acres and three per cent of estates of over a hundred acres. The overall average size of farm was 38 acres, but the average size of women's farms was just under ten acres. Women made up a substantial proportion of the new freeholders of the 1840s probably from gifts given to former mistresses or to the children of such liaisons by planters.

This explanation is reinforced by the changes over the next few years. Virtually all land was controlled by the plantocracy and it was the policy of both the local and the imperial government to create from the slave population a landless proletariat rather than a peasantry (Beckles 1990: 114). Land prices in Barbados were the highest in the British West Indies, especially for small lots, and small parcels of land were rarely offered for sale. Yet, 'the coloured race have a great desire to possess land and are ready to pay high prices for small portions.' (Davy 1971: 148). Davy, writing in 1854, went on to note: 'Of the large number of the labouring class who have purchased freeholds September 18, 1997 the space of ground they have been provided has generally been too small and its quality so inferior (the poorer lands being sold to them) as not to suffice under culture for the support of themselves and family, being little, if any, more than they were allowed to have under slavery' (Davy 1971: 397, 405). In this way estate labour remained essential for survival for most of the former slaves.

The sugar industry in Barbados maintained profitability until the 1880s by improving technology, increasing economies of scale by amalgamating estates and by cutting wages. Only those people with special skills as craftworkers or successful traders could afford to buy land. Women received lower wages than men and the gender ideology of domestication made it difficult for them to work as entrepreneurs. Until 1885 only about half-a-dozen women were licenced traders in St Philip, from 1885 to 1890 there were eight but in 1891 the number rose suddenly to 17 and to 25 in 1893. In 1875 women owned 133 more holdings of one acre and over than in 1847 (excluding St Andrew parish) but the amount of land they held had fallen by a quarter with a consequent decline in the average size of their holdings (Table 7.1).

Only in the rapidly urbanising parish of St Michael and the neighbouring parish of Christ Church did women's share of land and/or of holdings of less than ten acres increase between 1847 and 1875 (Table 7.1). This trend suggests that women were choosing to move out of low-wage agriculture into urban based occupations such as domestic service, dressmaking, baking and trading and were able to obtain plots near their work. These small pieces of land were sufficient for some subsistence production and provided dwelling space for mothers and their adult children.

Table 7.1 Women landowners in Barbados, 1847 and 1875

Parish	Number of holdings		Acres in holdings	
	1847 %	1875 %	1847 %	1875 %
St James	31 (16.9)	28 (14.0)	332.5 (4.3)	103.3 (1.4)
St Thomas	33 (16.5)	23 (11.9)	382.5 (4.5)	319.0 (3.8)
St Philip	96 (23.9)	100 (16.5)	589.0 (4.0)	383.6 (2.6)
St Michael	43 (15.5)	73 (24.4)	339.0 (7.8)	378.6 (5.0)
Christ Church	93 (21.3)	78 (16.1)	780.7 (5.6)	1095.5 (8.2)
St George	48 (20.6)	38 (12.6)	616.4 (4.5)	401.0 (3.8)
St John	15 (11.8)	10 (8.3)	129.0 (1.5)	55.1 (0.6)
St Joseph	37 (16.7)	184 (13.6)	474.0 (7.8)	65.0 (1.1)
St Andrew	– –	36 (16.4)	–	603.8 (7.5)
St Peter	27 (19.4)	26 (15.7)	651.0 (8.2)	351.2 (4.6)
St Lucy	64 (22.6)	60 (18.8)	405.0 (4.8)	402.6 (4.9)
Total	487 (19.5)	656 (21.7)	4699 (5.0)	4158.5 (4.1)

Sources: Police Magistrates Returns to the Governor's Private Secretary. List of property owners of one acre or more, 1847. Barbados Archives Accession # 67.

Return of Persons Liable to Militia Tax for the Year 1875. Minutes of the Assembly

Land Ownership in St Philip

To understand the way in which a new landholding system evolved after the end of slavery it is necessary to look in detail at one parish. The parish of St Philip has the longest continuous set of parish records with rate books in which taxes on land and houses and licences granted to traders are recorded from 1874. Using these data, ownership changes in individual plots can be traced from year to year.

The parish of St Philip lies in the south-east of Barbados, has thin rocky soils, less than 1,500 mm of rain per annum, and a November to July moisture deficit. It is constantly swept by the trade winds carrying salt spray inland. This parish was one of the few areas on the island where smallholdings operated by poor white farmers survived and these may have formed nuclei around which the ex-slaves could find land. John Davy, writing in 1854, noted that 'The culture of the aloe, which is confined to the small farmer entirely, and carried on chiefly in the parish of St Philip, towards the seashore where the soil is scanty and dry, at times has been very profitable' (Davy 1971: 150). This combination of negative and positive attributes explains the growth of small farms in this part of the island. By the 1880s St Philip had more new villages than any other parish in Barbados (Momsen 1988).

In 1847 St Philip had the most women landowners (Table 7.1). They owned one-third of the holdings of one to ten acres and eight per cent of the larger holdings but only four per cent of the land. By 1875, St Philip had more small holdings than any other parish but the proportion held by women had fallen to 21 per cent for holdings between one and ten acres and seven per cent of larger holdings and included only 2.6 per cent of the land (Table 7.1). The parish rate books give slightly different figures and are more inclusive. These records show that in 1875 women owned 124 lots of less than one acre, 105 of one to ten acres and only eight larger holdings of which two had been inherited from husbands, one from a father, and one was held jointly with her husband, a vicar. The largest of the remaining four was only thirty acres and women owned barely four per cent of the land in holdings over ten acres. By the mid 1880s the number of women owners had begun to increase again as the sugar industry depression deepened. In 1895 half the smallest lots of less than one acre were in women's hands, 40 per cent of those three to five acres and 30 per cent of those five to ten acres. Even among the larger holdings, although the total number fell, the proportion owned by women increased from 10 to 25 per cent.

Thus as sugar production became unprofitable, women were able to obtain farmland as a result of both falling land prices and reduced competition for this very limited resource. The average size of farms fell steadily from 1874 to 1895 (Table 7.2) but between 1887 and 1895 the number of holdings owned by women doubled and the amount of land in their hands increased almost as much (Table 7.2). Prices fell precipitously from £65 to 70 in 1884 to £25 to £30 in 1887 per acre (Beckles 1990: 132). Parish land taxes rose to raise funds to support the increasing number of paupers from one shilling and sixpence in 1874 to three shillings and sixpence in 1883. Writs issued for non-payment of taxes reached a peak of 239 in 1886 but declined as the land taxes were reduced from 1885. The number of freeholders rose from 1,078 in 1875 to 1,142 in 1880. Whites owned 12,500 acres of land and blacks and coloureds 2,450 acres in St Philip in 1876 and, based on this property, there were 80 registered white (male) voters and 104 registered black and coloured (male) voters. Women freeholders were not seen as politically threaten-

Table 7.2 Women landowners in St Philip, 1874-95

Year	Holdings			Acres				
	Under10 acres	10 acres plus	Total No.	Under10 acres	Mean size	10 acres plus	Mean size	Total acres
1874	235	9	244	365.1	1.55	348.5	38.7	713.6
1877	268	11	279	387.8	1.40	591.5	53.9	979.3
1880	270	11	281	370.8	1.37	622.5	56.6	993.3
1884	287	10	297	385.3	1.34	715.5	71.6	1100.8
1887	296	8	304	406.3	1.37	645.8	80.7	1052.1
1895	588	20	606	643.2	1.09	1117.8	59.5	1761.0

Source: St Philip Parish Rate Books, 1874-95.

ing, especially as very few owned enough property to enable their husbands to vote. Although married women could own land in their own right after 1879, it is doubtful if this had much influence on the desire of women to obtain small plots of land.

The Development of Land Tenure Systems in Barbados

Land rights emerged as a central theme in the development of free villages in the post-emancipation British West Indies. Such a move into real estate could be considered 'improvident' if farmland was being considered purely in terms of short-term profits and output. Nor could miniscule plots of land grant prestige as Satchell suggests but they could give partial food security in the face of falling wages and widespread malnutrition. Greenfield (1960) argues that the primary value of land in Barbados was to free its owner from the restrictions of the located labourer system). He further suggests that because there was so little land available to the former slaves it was always seen as secondary to men's off-farm jobs as a source of income and as they had to travel widely for work they 'had little time-or inclination-to till their land themselves' (Greenfield 1960: 170). Thus small-scale farming came to be seen as a task for women and an extension of her domestic sphere of work.

Access to land was almost always dependent on plantation land being made available. Thus farmsteads and villages were widely dispersed and particular locations became associated with specific families. In many cases Afro-Caribbean women do not formally marry until late in life, if at all, and the family focus is often the yard, around which the mother and her adult children live (Pulsipher 1993). This concept of land as territory for the matrifocal family and as a site of resistance and independence from the plantation rather than as an economic resource became central to the development of small holdings.

This concept also underlay the development of a customary tenure system and pattern of land transfer. Legal freehold provided the foundation of most free communities in Barbados but customary rights of tenure and transmission soon emerged as a prime basis of family stability as they had been in the proto-peasant past (Besson 1987). Edith Clarke (1966) saw such customary tenures in Jamaica as derived from Ashanti kinship system and supportive of the survival of female-headed households. Greenfield (1960) working in Barbados with its highly creolised population, accounts for Barbadian family land in terms of English cultural heritage. Besson (1984) argues that such island-specific explanations are inadequate for such a pan-Caribbean institution and sees family land as a dynamic Caribbean cultural creation forged by the peasantries themselves in resistant response to the plantation system.

To understand the workings of this system and the central role of women in it, it is helpful to look at individual cases. Of the 95 women owners of more than one acre of land in St Philip in 1847, only 26 could be identified in 1875. Identification is made more difficult because not only did women landowners change names on marriage and sometimes transfer their land into their husband's name, they also adopted aliases and changed first names. The naming of individual locations also was in flux during this period as plantations were subdivided or amalgamated and villages created. Until 1891 land titles did not have to be registered which contributed to the ease with which land could change hands at this time. It may also explain why it often took many years after an owner's death for land to be registered in the tax records as belonging to a new owner. It is also clear that the belief, which is still found today, that whoever pays the land tax owns the land, developed very early. All these problems make it difficult, despite the detailed nature of the parish records, to be certain of anything more than broad trends in the gendered pattern of land ownership.

Of these 26 plots belonging to women in 1847 and still owned by them in 1875, six were still registered in the same name in 1895 despite one of the owners having died before 1874. This last mentioned property plus another which had been passed to a daughter in 1885 were the only two whose acreage had not changed over the 48 years. Five had become smaller while one had grown from 1.75 acres in 1847 to six acres in 1874, and seven in 1877 before falling to 6.5 in 1885 and 5.5 acres and 20 perches in 1895. Two women sold their holdings and three plots passed to children. One owner changed her name to an alias. Most of these holdings just disappear from the records in the 1880s probably because of the owner's inability to pay the land taxes.

Cases of both consolidation and fragmentation of land are common in the records. Sometimes land is inherited from different family members and on many occasions land is divided equally among all the heirs, both sons and daughters. The results of this can be seen in the clustering of names in certain areas: there were 15 plots owned by Gittens family members in 1847 and 30 in 1875. The land was often divided into very small plots: in 1874 eight members of the Carter family each inherited 23 perches of land near Mount Ebenezer. Three sisters amalgamated their plots, one brother sold his to a sister and one sister to a brother and one sold it outside the immediate family and one became only a housespot so that in 1895 only one of the 23 perch plots remained. Greenfield (1960) sees this type of inheritance pattern as being a way of creating inalienable *family land* which protected one's heirs, both legitimate and illegitimate, from the vagaries of the located labourer system. With a change in the law in 1925 and the ending of the located labourer system in 1937 this type of inalienable land transmission became not only illegal but also less necessary.

Another way to keep land within the family even when the owner does not wish to use it, is to rent it out with or without formal payment. This situation in which land is owned by one individual but is in the possession of another can be seen from the tax records to have become popular during the 1890s. In 1895 of the 588 holdings in St Philip of less than ten acres on which women paid tax, 94 (6.3 per cent) were occupied rather than owned. One-fifth of the larger holdings was in the possession of women. Of the 98 holdings held 'in possession', 71 per cent were holdings owned by women, 22.5 percent were holdings owned by men and the remainder were women's plots occupied by men. Three-quarters of all the holdings so occupied were registered to deceased owners. This evidence suggests that in most cases this development of the 'in possession' form of land occupance in Barbados represented a backlog of inherited land awaiting the formal transfer required after 1891, rather than a formal recognition of usufruct versus ownership rights and a customary means of making land available to women for subsistence. In general, Barbadians have preferred legal freehold to customary tenure. In 1963 only eight per cent of smallholder plots were reported as family land (Momsen 1969) and the most recent agricultural census recorded only 6.6 percent of both male and female operated farm parcels consisted of family land and less than one per cent were rented for other than cash (Barbados Ministry of Agriculture 1991).

Conclusion

After an immediate post-emancipation surge, there was a 24 per cent decline in the amount of land occupied by women between 1847 and 1875 (Table 7. 1) but at the same time there was an increase of 27 per cent in the number of woman landowners, excluding the parish of St Andrew for which there are no 1847 figures. This was a relative increase from 19.5 per cent to 21.7 per cent of total landowners as well an absolute increase. The 1847 and 1875 lists do not include holdings of less than one acre which was the median size of women's holdings. The parish records show that women moved into land ownership, of both large and small holdings, very rapidly as soon as land became more affordable. From Table 7.2 it can be seen that the acres owned by women in St Philip increased by two-thirds in just eight years between 1887 and 1895. These figures suggest that in Barbados women did not improvidently dispose of land, as Satchell (1995) describes for Jamaica, despite the much higher land prices in Barbados, but rather indicate a continuing land hunger.

These contrasts between the two countries reflect their different ecological possibilities and emphasise the need for context-specific studies. The differences may also relate to the archival sources used, as the Barbadian parish land tax records give a picture of overall land ownership rather than the dynamic view provided by the data on Jamaican land transactions used by Satchell. It is also likely that both sources undercount the amount of land farmed by women as it is clear from the parish records that many women landowners transferred title to their husbands on marriage (even after 1879) or to other men who paid the land taxes for them. This type of transfer was easily done before 1891 when registration of title became required.

At the end of the nineteenth century in Barbados, economic crisis combined with gender specific migration led to changes in official gender ideologies. Nuclear families dependent on a male breadwinner were clearly not possible for the majority and the legislature's perceived population problem became one of overpopulation rather than controlling the workforce. These changes enabled the reversal in the 1880s of the mid century trend out of female land ownership in Barbados, similar to that noted for Jamaica by Satchell (1995). Today 39 per cent of farmers in Barbados are women and they occupy 6.1 per cent of the farmland which is more than in 1847 or 1875. But over half the women farm operators work less than 0.1 hectares of land while only 13 women operate farms of more than four hectares (Barbados Ministry of Agriculture 1991). Most holdings farmed by women are in the environmentally marginal parishes of the rugged Scotland District and in the dry northernmost parish of St Lucy. This paradoxical combination of legal rights to land and economic and environmental marginalisation may be explained in terms of gender differences in the ideology of land ownership.

For a group who had been considered property themselves only a few years earlier, even the smallest plot could give prestige and family security, especially in an island where land was such a scarce resource. These smallholdings served the practical needs of poor women by providing a source of subsistence and their strategic needs by reducing their dependence on the plantation and supplying a piece of territory for an intergenerational family base. Thus, I would argue that women clung to these micro-holdings because they considered land to be more a cultural, symbolic, and social resource rather than a possession having economic utility. Above all, many of these women see their land as a resistant response to the dominant culture and, with bell hooks (1990: 341, 343), accept marginality 'as much more than a site of deprivation [as] one of radical possibility, a space of resistance a space I choose'.

8

Changing Perceptions of Gender in the Caribbean Region:

The Case of the Jamaican Peasantry

Jean Besson

Introduction

Two related paradoxes have typified the anthropology of the Caribbean region. First, although the Caribbean is the oldest colonial sphere, anthropology marginalised this frontier (Trouillot 1992). Second, while mainstream anthropology moved from male-bias to Women's Studies then Gender Studies (e.g. Ardener 1975; Moore 1988), there was a contrasting movement in the Caribbean context from a preoccupation with the 'matrifocal family' to the study of 'marginal men' before turning to feminist analysis. This chapter examines these changing perceptions of gender in the Caribbean region, through a case- study of the Jamaican peasantry.

I first discuss the swing from female-focus to male-bias in Caribbean anthropology, and suggest that neither of these perspectives adequately reflects Caribbean gender ideologies.[1] Using data from eight peasant communities in west-central Jamaica, I then show that an analysis of both genders is essential for understanding the identities, relationships and roles of Caribbean women and men. Moreover, in addition to identifying a unitary theme of gender-complementarity, the case-study reveals diversity in gender ideologies even within this one area of a single Caribbean territory.[2] This suggests the need for a comparative gender perspective rather than discrete, binary or confrontational gender categorisation, and indicates that such analysis should be empirically based.

From Female-focus to Male-bias

The dominant theme in Caribbean anthropology for many decades was the so-called 'matrifocal family' and its interpretation. Condemned from a colonial perspective as unstable, the matrifocal family was explained by anthropologists as either an African survival or a deviation from European norms. While Olwig (1981) critiqued the matrifocality approach, focusing instead on ego-oriented bilateral kinship networks of male and female relatives on both parental sides, R. T. Smith (1988) recasts the matrifocal family within the contexts of bilaterality and hierarchy. However, by overlooking ancestor-focused cognatic or nonunilineal descent systems traced through both women and men, neither Olwig nor R. T. Smith fully explored gender ideologies in the sphere of kinship. Another female focus, with a sounder basis, emerged with the study of women's roles in Caribbean peasant marketing systems (e.g. Mintz 1960).

In an attempt to rectify the preoccupation with the matrifocal family and women, Wilson (1969, 1973) advanced his influential but male-biased theory of 'respectability' and 'reputation'. Respectability is derived from colonial culture and social stratification; while reputation is a creole counter-culture based on equality and personal worth, reflected for example in customary landholding, kinship, orality, entrepreneurship, creole religion and procreation. Wilson contended that respectability and reputation are differentially subscribed to in terms of class, gender and age: elites, women and older men adhere to respectability; while young lower-class men are the vanguard of reputation. He asserted that lower-class Afro-Caribbean women uphold colonial values, because of their historical association with the master class as concubines and domestic slaves. He argued that to achieve true autonomy and development, Caribbean peoples (especially women) must shift from respectability to reputation. The impact of Wilson's analysis is reflected in a range of studies (e.g. Dirks 1972; Brana-Shute 1979); while his gender-bias was parallelled by Horowitz's (1967) portrayal of male decision-making in Caribbean peasant conjugality.

Despite my critique of Wilson's theory (Besson 1993), showing that Caribbean peasant women do not subscribe to respectability but participate in reputation, and that female slaves resisted the master class, Littlewood (1993: 295 n42) reasserted Wilson's thesis and suggested I had misread Wilson:

Jean Besson has pointed out that the respectability-reputation dichotomy undervalues the very real idea of resistance by black women against slavery my own reading (and

I think that of Peter Wilson) is that his bipolarity is to be read as polythetic: women are respectable, not as a fixed characteristic but relative to men.

However, my critique questioned Wilson's and therefore Littlewood's reading of respectability-reputation precisely as defined by Littlewood.[3]

This chapter, based on continuing fieldwork among the Jamaican peasantry, develops my earlier perspective regarding the complexity of gender in the Caribbean region. I explore gender ideologies in relation to landholding, kinship systems, oral tradition, ritual, entrepreneurship, migration and tourism in eight communities in the parishes of Trelawny and St Elizabeth. These communities represent significant variations of Caribbean post-slavery peasantries. Five of these settlements (The Alps, Refuge, Kettering, Granville and Martha Brae) are Baptist 'free villages' in Trelawny, established by former 'proto-peasant' slaves at the vanguard of the post-emancipation flight from the estates (Mintz 1989: 151-152, 157-179; Besson 1984b, 1992, 1995d). The sixth community, Accompong Town in St Elizabeth, is the oldest surviving post-treaty corporate Maroon society in African-America (Price 1979; Mintz 1989: 152-53; Besson 1995a, 1995f). Aberdeen in St Elizabeth is the closest non-Maroon village to Accompong, and has even more direct continuity with the proto-peasant past than the Trelawny villages. Zion in Trelawny has been established on 'captured' plantation land during the period of my fieldwork (1968-95), and is a variant on the theme of 'squatter peasantries' (Mintz 1989: 147-148; Besson 1995a).

Land and Gender among the Jamaican Peasantry

Access to land lies at the heart of the eight peasant adaptations, which are encompassed by persisting plantations, and both women and men are significant in landholding in all of the communities.[4] However, the communities reflect variations on this theme due partly to their historical origins. Among the Jamaican proto-peasantry both male and female slaves appropriated and transmitted customary land rights, and former proto-peasants of both genders purchased land in Trelawny's post-emancipation villages; this being preceded by squatting in the case of Martha Brae, which was established on the site of a former planter town. In the five free villages studied (The Alps, Refuge, Kettering, Granville and Martha Brae), various legal and customary tenures have evolved in relation to house yards and provision grounds, which are measured in square chains. Both men and women participate in these tenures, which include 'bought land', 'rent land', 'lease land', 'free land' and 'captured land'.

In addition, at the heart of these villages is a core of 'family land' often typified by family burial grounds.[5] Family-land rights are transmitted from the original land purchaser through unrestricted cognation to all descendants regardless of gender, age, legitimacy and residence; while new family land is created out of purchased land. Women and men therefore participate equally in the institution of family land. I have analysed the family-land institution (which is widespread in Caribbean peasant communities) in detail elsewhere, highlighting its symbolic as well as economic role and showing how it perpetuates village communities. I have argued that this tenure rooted in the proto-peasant adaptation is not a survival from either Africa or Europe, but is instead a cultural creation by Caribbean peasantries in response and resistance to land monopoly by plantations, mining and tourism. I have also shown how this customary tenure articulates with colonially derived agrarian legal codes (e.g. Besson 1984a, 1984b, 1987a, 1988, 1995d, 1995e).

In contrast, all land is insecurely held as captured land in Martha Brae's satellite squatter settlement of Zion. Zion was founded in 1968 by a tenant couple (man and woman) from Martha Brae, who moved their chattel cottage to reside near a 'No Squatting' sign on land owned by the Trelawny Parish Council on part of neighbouring Holland plantation. Following attempted eviction, the squatters were permitted to relocate their cottage on the land, where they created a house yard as in the proto-peasant and post-emancipation past. By 1979 there were about 30 households at Zion, and in 1995 there were some 70 households on around 30 acres of captured land. The Parish Council has recently surveyed the settlement with a view to taxation and land sales, measured in square metres, to both male and female household heads. Some squatters have family-land rights in Martha Brae or elsewhere. Therefore in Zion, as in Trelawny's free villages, both genders participate equally in landholding

In marked contrast to Zion, and even to the free villages of Trelawny, land rights in Accompong have an older engendered history. Accompong is the only surviving community of the Jamaican Leeward Maroon polity, and is located in the precipitous forested southern area of the Cockpit Country Mountains in northern St Elizabeth. The village was consolidated over 250 years ago, after the First Maroon War (1725-39), by a treaty between Colonel Cudjoe, the Leeward Maroon leader and the British colonial government, forced to sue for peace.[6] This treaty granted the Maroons their freedom and 1,500 acres of marginal common land. However, since the Maroons Allotment Act of 1842, four years after emancipation, the colonial government and subsequently the Jamaican state have attempted to deprive the Maroons (including the Windward polity in the east of the island) of their status and commons. The firmest resistance to these attempts has come from Accompong, and Kopytoff (1979) documented border and tax disputes up to the 1970s. Such disputes continued throughout my fieldwork up to 1995.

Common land in Accompong incorporates both genders, though the early Maroon community suffered from a shortage of women (Kopytoff 1978: 301) reflecting both the constraints of marronage for female slaves with children and the significant role of women in proto-peasant communities. The commons with their community burial grounds provide the basis of Maroon corporate identity, which is further reinforced by an elected Maroon colonel, his deputies and a secretary of state, all of whom are male, and a Maroon council comprising both women and men. However, during the period of my fieldwork (1979-95), a cognatic land-holding system, transmitting usufructory rights to an individual's male and female descendants, was emerging in relation to house yards and provision grounds in the inner zone. This process of kin-based incorporation of portions of Maroon land is being reinforced by an emergent pattern of yard burial, more typical of family land in non-Maroon communities. Such land transmission is consolidating pre-existing overlapping unrestricted cognatic family lines, traced through both genders from the 'First-Time Maroons'.[7] The reputed origin of this cognatic descent system, based on gender complementarity, is symbolised by the Leeward Maroons' appropriation of 'Nanny', the 'Windward Maroons' ritual leadress, who is said by Accompong Maroons to have been Cudjoe's sister.

Accompong Maroons further claim that the neighbouring non-Maroon community of Aberdeen in St Elizabeth was established on Leeward Maroon treaty lands; a view supported by Aberdonians, some of whom have ties of marriage, kinship and descent with Accompong. My research suggests that the old core of the dispersed mountainous community of Aberdeen was established after emancipation by former proto-peasant slaves from Aberdeen Estate (bordering the Maroon commons), initially by squatting on plantation backlands south of Aberdeen Estate and then through government land retrieval, registration and land sale; augmented by some Maroons who left Accompong to live nearer to the plains. By the late nineteenth century, a Moravian station had been consolidated in the Aberdeen community. Unlike Accompong Maroons, Aberdonians pay land taxes to the Jamaican state and their range of tenures, including family land, are similar to those in the Trelawny free villages where gender equality pervades landholding. As in Trelawny, family land in Aberdeen is held by cognatic descent groups, traced through both men and women, and symbolised by family burial grounds.

Kinship and Gender in the Maroon and Non-Maroon Communities

In all eight communities, kinship and marriage are based on gender complementarity reflected in: cognatic descent, traced from an ancestor or ancestress through males and females and incorporating both women and men; bilateral kinship, reckoned from each person through both sexes on mother's and father's side; and serial polyandry and serial polygyny, that is, sequential husbands and wives. However, differences as well as similarities exist. In the Trelawny free villages (The Alps, Refuge, Kettering, Granville and Martha Brae) 'Old Families' or cognatic descent groups originating from ex-slaves overlap not only within, but also among, communities; while personal bilateral kinship networks interweave within and between communities as was the case among the proto-peasant slaves. On the Jamaican slave plantations an exogamous 'complex' or open marriage system[8] with sequential unions based on varying commitment and age-related status, was also created maximising conjugality and affinity among the slaves. This dynamic marriage system, forged from the atom of the incest taboo in the fictive-kinship shipmate bond, persists within and among Trelawny free villages. These three dimensions of descent, kinship and marriage also stretch from the free village of Martha Brae to its satellite squatter settlement of Zion. This three-dimensional family system and its gender-symmetry, is reflected in Hawaiianised-Eskimo kinship terminology (Besson 1995f).[9]

In contrast, in the Accompong Maroon community in St Elizabeth the overlapping cognatic descent lines integrate the corporate Leeward polity. This incorporation is strengthened by the dense bilateral kinship networks within this isolated peasant adaptation. Like the Trelawny peasantry Accompong Maroon men and women both practise serial polygamy, but in contrast to Trelawny the Maroons display tendencies towards community endogamy and cousin-conjugality, similar to 'elementary' marriage systems which perpetuate recurring alliances among kin.[10] These marriage practices further incorporate the community, and are reinforced by the belief that marriage alliance among the First-Time Maroons transcended 'tribal' rivalries between Congos and Coromantees.[11] This system of consanguinity and affinity, in which both men and women have considerable status and autonomy as the descendants of rebel slaves, is reflected in the Maroon sayings 'We are all One Family' and 'We are Royal Family'.[12] Maroon kinship, marriage and descent are also symbolised by the 'Kindah Tree': a fruitful mango tree, with a sign proclaiming 'We are Family', that is at the centre of the sacred 'Kindah' grove (discussed below) at the edge of the residential zone in Accompong (Besson 1995f).[13] However, as noted previously, the Leeward Maroons experienced a short-age of women during marronage[14] and today migration exacerbates the vulnerability of the Maroon adaptation. Paradoxically, in addition to reinforcing cousin-conjugality, this has led to the incorporation of outsid-ers of both genders through marriage to augment the Maroon polity. Such incomers are known as 'bye-Maroons' and are granted Maroon status and land rights.[15]

By the incorporation of outsiders through marriage, and by the 'coming out' of Maroons who migrate from the community, Accompong is linked especially to the neighbouring non-Maroon village of Aberdeen, which evolved from the slave community on Aberdeen estate. Accompong Maroon oral history states that this relationship existed as far back as the era of marronage, when the Leeward Maroons sought assistance for plantation raids from Aberdeen proto-peasant slaves (Besson 1995a). While Aberdeen (in St Elizabeth) manifests patterns of kinship and marriage similar to the Trelawny free villages, the distinction between non-Maroons and those of Maroon descent is an important aspect of internal differentiation in post-slavery Aberdeen. This is mirrored in Aberdeen's central Old Family, which traces its eight-generation cognatic descent line through males and females from a male African-Prince Maroon, who is said to have been brought on a slave ship to Jamaica and to have escaped from a plantation on the plains into Accompong.[16] His descendants are said to have 'come out' from Accompong and to have acquired land in Aberdeen. In Aberdeen this Maroon descent group, with its family land and burial ground, overlaps with a non-Maroon cognatic descent line of Afro-Scots origin.[17]

In all eight communities both virility and fertility are highly prized within the contexts of these systems of kinship, marriage and descent. Thus children are 'poor men's riches' (Wilson 1973: 74) for women as well as men; being significant bases of status, symbols of both womanhood and manhood, and the beginning or continuance of cognatic descent lines. This is illustrated by the case of the Accompong Maroon community in St Elizabeth, where the largest family line traces descent from Nanny; where an elderly male Maroon (aged 90 in 1995), who claims descent from Nanny, proudly states that he has followed the biblical decree to 'go forth and multiply' and that he knows all of his fifty children by name; and where the fruitful Kindah Tree symbolises procreation by both genders, as manifested in the Myal ritual discussed below.

Engendered Oral Traditions

Oral tradition is a rich resource in all eight communities, with origins varying from slavery, marronage and the flight from the estates to the recent accounts of the founding of Martha Brae's satellite squatter settlement of Zion. In all of these communities such oral history is engendered (cf. Besson 1996). This is reflected in accounts of ancestor-heroes and ancestress-heroines, and parallelled in the current creation of such gendered symbols of hidden history including the male and female founders of Zion. Both genders also create and transmit oral history, with women being especially significant in this respect in the domestic domain.

The oldest oral tradition exists in Accompong (the community in St Elizabeth descended from rebel slaves), reaching back to the First Maroon War (1725-39) and focusing on the male warrior ancestor-heroes: Colonel Cudjoe and his captains (Quaco, Cuffee, Johnny and Accompong). The Kindah Tree at the edge of the residential zone is said to have been Cudjoe's 'War Office', where he and his captains sat on the boulders beneath the spreading branches to plan guerilla tactics; and much oral history has been recounted to me in this public domain by male Maroons sitting on these stones.

Oral history further states that Colonel Cudjoe is buried at another sacred grove about a mile away: at his 'headquarters' at 'Old Town'[18] in a valley beneath a jutting 'Cockpit' mountain covered with cocoon vines, which are said to have provided both camouflage and food (giant bean pods) for the warrior Maroons. The captains are reputedly buried in an intermediate grove where, like Cudjoe's symbolic resting place, their graves are marked by boulders. Nanny, the ritual ancestress-heroine appropriated from the Windward Maroon polity in the eastern mountains of Jamaica, is said to be buried next to her 'brother' Cudjoe at Old Town, where stones likewise mark her reputed grave. Other First-Time Maroons, both men and women, are recounted to be buried in African ethnic burial grounds (Congo and Coromantee), which are marked by cairns and boulders, at the Kindah grove. The 'Peace Cave', a hollow rock between Accompong and Aberdeen, where the treaty is said to have been signed is a further symbolic landmark; as is the adjoining 'battle ground' where the Maroon warriors reputedly ambushed the enemy. With the notable exception of Nanny, therefore, Accompong oral tradition is male-oriented. In neighbouring Aberdeen, the oral history of the African-Prince Maroon is a variation on this gender-specific theme.

In Trelawny's free villages women (and children) feature more prominently in oral tradition, along with men, reflecting greater gender symmetry rooted in proto-peasant and post-emancipation peasant adaptations. However, in two cases (The Alps and Granville) ex-slave ancestor-heroes are highlighted in relation to the establishment of villages, on the basis of either the greater occupational mobility available to male slaves or as a result of Baptist Class-Leader status.

In The Alps, Trelawny's first free village, established in 1838 on a former coffee estate in the northern foothills of the Cockpit Country Mountains, the central Old Family traces its ancestry and lands through male and female links to Archibald (Archie) Campbell The First who, with his wife, is said to have been a slave on nearby Mahogany Hall cattle pen. Oral tradition states that this emancipated slave purchased several acres of land from the Reverend Dexter, who established this village in the year of emancipation under the sponsorship of the Baptist missionary William Knibb.[19] This suggests that Archie Campbell The First had been a slave of relatively high occupational status, who may have had access to more extensive provision grounds resulting in the significant accumulation of capital from marketing activities (see Mintz 1989: 159, 180-213; Patterson 1973: 57-65, 151). The son of these ex-slaves, also named Archibald Campbell, is interred in the family-land burial ground where his tombstone states that he was born in 1813 and died in 1924; indicating that he was 21 at emancipation and died at 111. Their descendants whom I interviewed included an elderly grandson (a cultivator-marketer born in 1892, aged 91 in 1983) of Archie Campbell The Second. My informant's late mother (who with her son and his wife had been a peasant marketer) was one of this ex-slave's 13 children. This grandson knew his maternal grandfather (Archie Campbell The Second), 'who used to wear long shirt' and who told of his experience as a slave boy in a hog-meat gang (see Patterson 1973: 59).

In similar vein, oral tradition in Trelawny's free village of Granville (founded by William Knibb in 1845) recounts the subdivision of village lands by 'Sergeant Wallace', Knibb's 'land butcher' or surveyor, said to have been a mulatto,[20] a police sergeant and a Class-Leader in the Baptist church. Oral history states that Sergeant Wallace retained the largest and most fertile piece of land, and this is consistent with the Wallace family land at the edge of Granville (Besson 1984b: 11-12). In 1995 I interviewed the male family-land trustee, a returned Baptist migrant from England, who confirmed that he is the great-grandson of this ancestor-hero. However, there is also a significant ancestress-heroine: Granville villagers speak of 'Mother Lawrence', who was known to older villagers and who was a slave girl at emancipation. Mother Lawrence's mother is said to have been a slave on neighbouring Merrywood Sugar Estate, a participant in the emancipation celebrations, and one of the ex-slave settlers of the village who obtained half-an-acre from Knibb. This has been transmitted as family land through six generations of female and male descendants.

Oral history in Trelawny's free village of Refuge (established in 1838 by Knibb), focuses equally on women and men. The ancestress-heroine, Elizabeth Bell-Merchant nicknamed 'Queenie', her brother nicknamed 'Hard Time',[21] and their close male and female kin, all feature in the oral history of the Bell Old Family, one of the two central landholding family lines. Queenie's tomb can be identified in Refuge and many of the elderly villagers are her grandchildren. Oral tradition states that Queenie's father cooked 'freedom dinner' on Oxford Sugar Estate, bordering Refuge, at emancipation. His mother is said to have been one of the ex-slaves from Oxford who settled in Refuge, and who acquired two small plots of land from Knibb one of which remains as family land. Queenie's paternal grandmother is also reputed to have been one of three sisters brought on a slave ship from Africa to Jamaica, and separated on different plantations. These ex-slave ancestors and ancestresses not only passed down freehold land rights to their male and female descendants, but also accounts of slavery. The other main landholding family line is traced to an African-born slave couple and their son 'Old John Lyon, an old slave fellow', who was a Creole slave on Hyde Hall Estate (Besson 1984b: 14-15).

Similar gender equality typifies oral history in Kettering, a Trelawny free village founded in 1841 by Knibb on a former pimento estate. For example, the Scott Old Family traces its family land five ascending generations, through male and female links, to the ex-slave Emanuel Scott who is buried on the land; while another family line is traced to Sarah Wilson, who was known to elderly villagers and who told them of her experience as a slave girl in a hog-meat gang. She is said to have been 12-years-old at emancipation and to have lived to the age of 105. Oral history also tells of a pregnant slave ancestress who was whipped, for refusing to work, on Harmony Hall sugar plantation adjoining Kettering.

Oral tradition in Martha Brae (where Baptist ex-slaves established a free village around the 1840s on the ruins of a colonial planter town) likewise recounts emancipated slave ancestresses and ancestors, from Irving Tower and Holland sugar plantations bordering the village, who acquired land in Martha Brae; some of whose names can be identified in the 1876 Trelawny Land Tax Roll. Such engendered symbols of hidden history include 'Nana Green' (the paternal grandmother of an elderly female family-land trustee born in 1910 and aged 85 in 1995), who is said to have died as a very old woman in 1922 and to have been a slave girl who carried lunch trays on her head to field slaves on Irving Tower Estate. In Zion, similar oral history is currently being created regarding the first male and female settlers who captured land and created house yards in this recently established peasant community.

Men, Women and Ritual

In the older communities, especially the Accompong Maroon society in St Elizabeth and the Trelawny free villages, ritual interweaves with oral tradition in reinforcing land rights and kinship systems. Like these dimensions of village life, ritual is variously engendered but with more gender specific roles. In Accompong, a Presbyterian (now 'United') church has existed since the late nineteenth century, and its cemetery has become a symbol of the creole Maroon community. There are also Revival and Pentecostal churches, which include both men and women, and a male Rastafarian network. However, it is Myalism that is at the heart of the Accompong community, brought from the slave plantations and transformed by marronage. Myalism was the first creole spirit possession religion forged among the Jamaican slaves from African cosmologies, and the Myal Dance was performed to protect the plantation slave communities from external and internal harm (Schuler 1980; Besson 1995b). In contemporary Accompong, the Myal Dance is performed each year around January 6 at the sacred burial groves, to commemorate both the peace treaty and Cudjoe's birthday, and to protect the community through perceived possession by the spirits of the male warrior Maroons.

The annual Myal ritual is engendered and hedged by taboos and rules, ordering communication with the First-Time Maroons (Besson 1996). A feast is held at the sacred 'Kindah' grove, cooked on jutting cockpits, from which sacrificial food is taken to Old Town and the intermediate grove. The cooks are male and prepare gender-specific and colour-coded food, representing the traditional economy of the black warrior maroons. Male pigs and fowls are sacrificed, and even the yams are male; while the hogs and cocks are black.[22] The ritual return from Old Town likewise highlights the maleness of the warrior-heroes, the Maroons being armed with sticks and battle camouflaged in cocoon vines. The presence of policemen and male bodyguards accompanying the representatives of the Jamaican state, further underlines the themes of masculinity, warfare and alliance. At the Myal Dance or 'Play', performed around the Kindah Tree, the drummers and Abeng blower[23] are also male. However, the culmination of the dance focuses on women, with the perceived possession of entranced females by the spirits of the warrior-heroes. This spirit possession, enacted directly beneath the fruitful Kindah Tree, highlights the central role of scarce but precious women in reproducing the Maroon polity. The symbol of the Kindah Tree, with its sign 'We are Family', incorporates the generational links and the male and female identities, relationships and roles perpetuating the corporate Maroon community and embedded in its systems of kinship, marriage and descent.

Pentecostalism co-exists with the Moravian church in Accompong's neighbouring non-Maroon community of Aberdeen and with Baptist churches in Trelawny's free villages. However, in Trelawny it is Revivalism, rooted in the Myalism of slavery and in the related Native Baptist Movement and the post-emancipation Great Revival, that continues at the heart of these communities and which has spread to the squatter settlement of Zion. In these rural areas women have a central place as 'Mothers' in Revival ritual and healing, while men play a supporting role as pastors and deacons, with drummers being male and female (Besson 1993, 1995b). Thus female-focused Revival is not 'a disappearing religion' being replaced by patriarchal Rastafari as Chevannes (1978, 1995) suggested. However Rastafarianism, originating in Ethiopianism on the slave plantations and consolidated in the twentieth century by Garveyism in Jamaica and the crowning of Ras Tafari in Ethiopia, is spreading through Trelawny's towns and villages and impacting Zion. In Trelawny, Rastafarianism remains patriarchal and its adherents are mainly men: young, middle-aged and old. Dreadlocks, challenging the 'white bias' and representing masculinity and the Nazarites, are the dominant ritual symbol; and it is men who reason together in the Rastafari network weaving through the parish and beyond.

Gender and Development

The preceding dimensions of peasant life are all rooted in the culture building of the Jamaican slaves and their descendants, but – with customary land tenures and small-scale agriculture – peasant marketing and rotating savings and credit associations (ROSCAs) have a central place in sustainable development. In marketing and ROSCAs gender ideologies are not only significant, but also reflect continuity, change and current transformation. In this context data from the eight communities advances Mintz and Price's (1992: 80) thesis of dynamic Caribbean culture-building, rather than theories of passive African retention, in the region's peasant marketing systems. I first briefly outline the controversy on the African heritage and gender differentiation in Caribbean peasant marketing, and then show the significance of my comparative data for understanding dynamic and varying gender ideologies in this sphere of peasant life; and in the related Jamaican ROSCA 'partners', which has parallels throughout the Caribbean region (Besson 1995c).

The predominance of female marketers and higglers in the contemporary Caribbean has been attributed to African influences (e.g. Herskovits 1937: 260; Herskovits and Herskovits 1947: 292). However, in assessing the role of the African heritage Mintz asserts that, while women dominate Haitian and Jamaican post-slavery markets as in West Africa, complementing a primarily male-cultivator role, reports of proto-peasant marketers provide no evidence that women outnumbered men and family groups, and men probably outnumbered women in such marketing activities. Moreover, the first marketplace in Jamaica was not African, but English (Mintz 1960: 114, 1989: 210-212, 216, 223-224; Mintz and Price 1992: 77-80). Simmonds (1987: 32) concludes that, in a context where gender division of labour by the latter part of the eighteenth century in Jamaica was more marked among urban slaves than plantation slaves,[24] 'the rural component [of trading] was at best shared between the sexes, with the possibility of the men being the principal cultivators, while urban marketing was dominated by females'. She also suggests African influences on the marketing roles of urban female slaves (Simmonds 1987: 32), consistent with Higman's (1984: 53-54) view that plantations rather than towns were the vanguard of creolisation.

Nevertheless, Mintz's (1989: 217) observation for Jamaica that 'divorce among the slaves was consummated by tearing in two the *cotta*, or headcloth' (used by Trelawny market women until the 1980s), and his 'guess that this practice signified the breaking in two of a symmetrical economic relationship between male cultivator and female marketer' does suggest some gender differentiation among plantation slaves paralleling the female emphasis in urban trading. Moreover, urban and rural sectors were not isolated even during slavery and the marketing network linked plantations and towns. However, while Mintz (1989: 216) had 'no evidence that land use was ever afforded other than to male slaves', we now know that Afro-Caribbean women have had access to land and cultivated yards and grounds since slavery days (Besson 1992, 1995d; Bush 1990: 49; Momsen 1988). A synthesis of the evidence therefore suggests some gender divisions of labour in relation to male cultivation and female marketing among the proto-peasantry, but within a wider context of flexible gender differentiation in these spheres in contrast to more distinct gender ideologies among urban slaves.

After slavery there were increasing tendencies towards male cultivation and female marketing in rural areas, as gender divisions of labour in agriculture replaced the age and health distinctions of the slave-plantation fieldwork gangs (Patterson 1973: 59-61; Momsen 1988: 84, 92). Marketing and higglering provided women with opportunities for autonomy, mobility, flexible entrepreneurial roles and an alternative source of cash to domestic service (Mintz 1989; Durant-Gonzalez 1983). Mintz and Price (1992:77) note that in post-slavery Haiti and Jamaica 'women emerged as the overwhelming majority of marketers'; while Mintz's (1960, 1989) research revealed the persisting predominance of female marketers and higglers in contemporary Haiti and Jamaica complementing a male emphasis in cultivation. Mintz and Price (1992: 80) therefore argue for dynamic Caribbean culture building in these gender roles, with African cognitive orientations regarding gender autonomy being 'reinforced by the plantation experience', rather than for passive African retention (cf. Bush 1990: 50).

Comparative data from the eight peasant communities in west-central Jamaica advance this thesis of Caribbean culture building by revealing not only continuing tendencies towards male cultivation and female food marketing, deriving from the slavery and post-emancipation periods, but also current transformation towards undifferentiated gender roles in dry goods higglering. Such dry goods higglering is escalating as a transnational post-modern mode of sustainable development, which is especially impacting the Trelawny peasantry, and the related flexibility of gender differentiation parallels the interchangeability of male and female economic roles among the proto-peasantry.

Within these contexts, I turn to commonalities and differences in marketing among the eight communities. In the Accompong Maroon village in St Elizabeth, and in neighbouring Aberdeen which evolved from a proto-peasant adaptation, gender tendencies in cultivation and food marketing show continuity with gender emphases in the slavery and post-slavery past. These mountainous communities have more extensive land than the Trelawny peasant adaptations, especially those on or near the North Coast plantation-tourist plains (the free villages of Refuge, Kettering, Granville and Martha Brae, and the squatter settlement of Zion). In Aberdeen ground provision cultivation for household use and for peasant marketing is a mainly male activity, reinforced by cash cropping in bananas and sugar cane for nearby Appleton Estates; while women may go to market at Maggotty and Santa Cruz on the northern plains of St Elizabeth. Aberdeen is also a rich source of food supply for higglers from the plains. In more isolated Accompong a male emphasis in production likewise persists; reinforced by the predominance of men in marronage, the precipitous topography and banana production for the world economy,[25] and symbolised in the Myal ritual by male cooks and masculine 'pot food'. Primarily female Maroon marketers and higglers, assisted by a male van driver, go from Accompong to market at Maggotty and Southfield on the northern and southern plains of St Elizabeth; while, like Aberdeen, Accompong is also now a source of ground provisions for higglers from the plains.

In Trelawny, peasant marketing has focused on the Falmouth market-place since the late eighteenth century, when Falmouth eclipsed the planter town of Martha Brae and proto-peasants flocked to the urban Sunday market from the surrounding slave plantations (Besson 1987b: 120; cf. Simmonds 1987: 34-35). Around 1840, two years after emancipation, the classic lithograph of a Jamaican Market from a daguerreotype by Duperly immortalised the Falmouth market situated around the large stone water tank in Market Square. From this lithograph can be discerned both male and female marketers, but a clear preponderance of women. In 1896 the Albert George Market was built in Market Square and the Trelawny peasantry frequented this marketplace until 1982, when women still dominated marketing activities. By 1982 the market, held on Wednesdays, Fridays and Saturdays, had so expanded that larger premises were built on the eastern edge of Falmouth, and this 'New Market' is still used by the Trelawny peasantry; including those in the free villages of Granville and Martha Brae, and the squatter settlement of Zion, communities all less than three miles from Falmouth.

As in St Elizabeth, peasant cultivation in Trelawny is mainly (though not exclusively) a male domain, and in 1995 women marketers and higglers continued to dominate food marketing on Fridays and Saturdays in the Falmouth marketplace. This continuity from the slavery and post-emancipation periods is reinforced by an islandwide network of mainly female food marketers and higglers who come to Falmouth from throughout Jamaica, facilitated by the staggering of market days. In addition to such periodic markets elsewhere in Trelawny (for example, at Jackson Town near The Alps, at Duncans adjoining Kettering and at Clarke's Town near Refuge), weekly markets are held on various days in Kingston (Jamaica's capital), and in other parochial capitals and smaller towns throughout the island. Mainly women food marketers and higglers in the Falmouth marketplace include traders from the parishes of St Ann, St James, Hanover, St Elizabeth and Manchester as well as from Ulster Spring, Albert Town and Jackson Town in Trelawny.

In contrast to this continued female emphasis in the marketing of ground provisions, which has been the backbone of Jamaica's domestic economy from slavery days (Mintz 1989: 198-201), Falmouth's Wednesday dry goods 'Ben' Down Market'[26] is undergoing significant transformation which is impacting gender ideologies. Since the late 1980s the Falmouth Ben' Down Market has become Jamaica's largest rural market, linked through networking to informal commercial importing which is a new variant of marketing, circulatory migration and sustainable development. Large numbers of male as well as female higglers from throughout the island commute by air to Curacao, Panama, Miami and New York, buying dry goods retail and wholesale for resale in Jamaican markets including the Falmouth marketplace. For example, in 1995, such higglers came from the parishes of Clarendon, St Catherine and St Thomas, as well as Kingston. The main dry goods are clothes and shoes, bales of cloth, and brightly coloured plastic pails and bowls, but combs, cosmetics, jewellery, and household goods (pots, pans, crockery and electrical appliances) are also sold. Despite airfares and import tax, such higglers of both genders maintain profitable retail market stalls. This transformation in dry goods marketing, and the related change towards undifferentiated gender higgler roles, co-exists with the continuing sale of homemade clothes by women marketers and higglers from Trelawny peasant communities such as the free village of Martha Brae and its satellite squatter settlement of Zion. By 1995 young male Rastafari from such communities were also selling Rastafarian clothes and crafts, which they had knitted, in the Falmouth marketplace.

Within these contexts of continuity, change and current transformation in the marketing system, the traditional Jamaican ROSCA 'partners' has been both reinforced and transformed as a further dimension of sustainable development.[27] Partners enables capital to be raised for large items of expenditure and has been reported as a mainly female institution, including its use by female higglers to purchase goods for marketing (Katzin 1959; Austin 1984: 50; Harrison 1988: 113). Partners is still a thriving institution among women in the free villages of Trelawny and the squatter settlement of Zion. However, both the scale and role of partners have escalated in the Falmouth dry goods Ben' Down market, where male as well as female higglers now use this ROSCA to raise much larger sums of capital for informal commercial importing (Besson 1995c). This is paralleled by the increasing participation of men in ROSCAs in Trelawny's peasant communities.

Male and Female Participation in Migration and Tourism

In addition to continuity and change in marketing and ROSCAs, migration and tourism have impacted the peasant communities. The tourist industry has reinforced the land monopoly that constrains these peasant adaptations;[28] while participation in migration and tourism, by men and women in various ways, is an aspect of the occupational multiplicity that is an increasing dimension of the peasant economies. In the non-Maroon communities an overseas migration tradition reaches back to the aftermath of emancipation, paralleling the flight from the estates and earlier marronage. Such freedom of movement to varying destinations has represented a quest for identity, as well as a response to economic constraints (Thomas-Hope 1986); while family land has enabled return and circulatory migration, which in turn has facilitated purchases of land.

The Trelawny free village migration tradition can be illustrated by the case of Martha Brae, where work histories and oral histories from both genders reveal migratory patterns as far back as the nineteenth century. Five engendered migratory trends can be identified. First, oral tradition tells of nineteenth-century migrations to Central America among the former slaves. This migration, shaped by labour demand for construction work in Panama on the trans-Isthmian railway and canal and on the Costa Rican banana-plantation railroad, was mainly male. It is symbolised by the ancestor-hero William Minto, an ex-slave (who with his emancipated parents founded the village's central family line), who migrated to Costa Rica and returned to consolidate landholdings in the village. The second migration was to Central America and Cuba in the early twentieth century. This typified older villagers, whose work histories and oral traditions I recorded early in my fieldwork, who are now deceased. Both genders participated in this migration, but this still had a male emphasis due to labour demand for Panama canal construction, Costa Rican banana plantations and Cuban sugar estates. The third trend was also mainly male, with migration to the United States to work in the Manpower schemes of the World War 11, reinforced by subsequent migrations on the post-war Farm Work Scheme.

The fourth movement followed the US' 1952 restrictive McCarran-Walter Act, being the major migration to Britain in the decade 1952-62. Both men and women participated in this migration, sent remittances and sometimes visited; and with maturing pensions some migrants have returned to settle in the 1990s. The fifth and current trend has been further migration to North America, since the 1962 British Commonwealth Immigrants Act and the revision of immigrant regulations in Canada (1962) and the US (1965). Typically, young women have migrated to Canada on the Household Helper Scheme; while young men have resumed recurrent migration for farm labour in the USA. Migration continues to contribute to the peasant economy, to transnational kinship relations and to the definition of engendered identities.

In the Accompong Maroon community in St Elizabeth, freedom of movement was achieved well before emancipation with marronage and the treaty of 1739. However, since the building of the road to Accompong in the 1940s, overseas migration has become an increasing dimension of Maroon society and economy. Maroon transnational networks of women and men stretch especially to London and Bradford, England, though Maroons also migrate to North America. Common tenure enables return and circulatory migration, particularly for the Myal ritual. Similar migratory trends exist in relation to family land in the neighbouring non-Maroon community of Aberdeen. Since World War II, rural-urban migration to Kingston has involved both genders in all the seven older communities (the Trelawny free villages, Accompong and Aberdeen).

Like urbanisation, tourism has been a major theme of social change in Jamaica since World War II particularly on the island's north coast. This imposed tourist development has differentially impacted the eight communities, with the free villages in the northern coastal area of Trelawny being most affected; especially Kettering in the vicinity of resorts at Duncans Bay, and Martha Brae near Trelawny Beach Hotel and Montego Bay. Coastal tourism provides some employment for men as waiters, chefs, bellhops and builders; while some domestic service is available for women. However, such employment is seasonal and competitive. In Martha Brae, there is the added impact of Rafters' Village, the island's second river rafting project, opened by the Jamaica Tourist Board on the Martha Brae River in 1969 soon after the beginning of my fieldwork. Rafters' Village is on the former sugar plantation of Southfield one-and-a-half miles up-river from the free village of Martha Brae, with rafting terminating at the river bridge at the edge of Martha Brae. By 1995 this project had expanded, with 92 male rafting captains including men from Martha Brae. A few villagers of both genders work as ground staff at Rafters' Village, while some Martha Brae women sell cooked food at the river bridge.

The Accompong Maroon community in St Elizabeth provides a further variation on the tourism theme, namely, appropriation of the tourist industry. Since the 1970s Accompong has presented itself as a tourist attraction, to bring income to the community, and when I began my fieldwork there in 1979 there was already a Visitors Book and a 'Cockpit Country Tour' run by a Maroon from a hotel in Montego Bay in the neighbouring parish of St James. By 1991 hotel tours had increased, and the Maroons circularised hotels advising that the Maroons themselves would conduct the tours in Accompong. By 1994, the Maroon Council included a Minister of Tourism and Culture and there are now Maroon tourist guides. Such tourism is male-oriented: the Minister and guides are men, and a male ex-colonel has built a house for tourist-rental. However, the annual Myal ritual, which has a male emphasis but incorporates both genders, is becoming the most significant tourist attraction, as well as a symbol of Jamaican nationhood.[29]

Conclusion

This chapter has identified a swing in Caribbean anthropology from a preoccupation with the 'matrifocal family' to the study of 'marginal men', preceding feminist analysis; developments that contrasted with trends in mainstream anthropology, which marginalised the region. I have argued that neither a female-focus nor a male-bias adequately reflects Caribbean gender ideologies. Through a case-study of the Jamaican peasantry, I have shown instead that an analysis of both genders is essential for understanding the identities, relationships and roles of Caribbean women and men. Moreover, in addition to identifying a unitary theme of gender complementarity, the case-study, based on eight communities in west-central Jamaica, reveals diversity in gender ideologies even within this one area of a single Caribbean territory. This suggests the need for a comparative gender perspective rather than discrete, binary or confrontational gender categorisation, and indicates that such analysis should be empirically based.

In all eight communities gender complementarity emerges as a central theme. Both men and women are equally involved in land acquisition, whether this be through land purchase, as in the free villages of Trelawny and post-slavery Aberdeen; land capture, as in the recently established squatter settlement of Zion; or treaty rights to land, as in the Accompong Maroon society. In the seven older communities both genders also transmit land rights: either in the context of post-emancipation family land, as in the Trelawny free villages and Aberdeen in St Elizabeth; or within common tenure, as in Accompong. In all the communities the family system likewise reflects gender equality and autonomy through cognatic descent, traced through males and females and incorporating women and men; bilateral kinship, reckoned from each person through both sexes on maternal and paternal sides; and serial polygamy, with sequential husbands and wives.

In addition, in all the communities both males and females have significant economic and ritual roles and feature in oral tradition, though in these spheres there is more gender specificity. For example, in the peasant economy complementary gender emphases towards male cultivator and female food marketing roles occur. In the Trelawny communities (the free villages and the squatter settlement of Zion) there is a gender distinction within Revival ritual; while in the Accompong Maroons' Myal ritual men and women have different roles. In the oral traditions of Accompong and Aberdeen in St Elizabeth, and of the Trelawny free villages (The Alps, Refuge, Kettering, Granville and Martha Brae), ancestor-heroes and ancestress-heroines are differentiated; a theme in the making in the recently established squatter settlement of Zion.

However, the non-Maroon peasant adaptations, especially in Trelawny, show greater gender symmetry than Accompong Maroon society which is more male-oriented. This contrast results in part from differing gender ideologies originating in Maroon and proto-peasant/post-emancipation histories, and partly from recent change. For example, in the Trelawny communities both males and females established family land (in the free villages) or captured land (in Zion), and both genders feature prominently in Revival ritual and oral history; whereas Accompong's common tenure was consolidated in a treaty forged by male warrior

Maroons, as reflected in contemporary political organisation, Myal ritual and oral tradition. Likewise while tendencies towards male cultivation and female marketing typify the Trelawny communities as well as Accompong (and Aberdeen), dry goods marketing reflects increasing gender symmetry in the Falmouth marketplace. Aberdeen, at the non-Maroon/Maroon peasant interface, straddles some of these contrasts in gender ideologies between Trelawny and Accompong: as in Aberdeen's male-focused oral tradition of the African-Prince Maroon embedded in the gender symmetry of post-emancipation cognatic family land.

However, even in Trelawny variations in gender ideologies exist. In The Alps and Granville, oral history regarding the establishment of these free villages has a male emphasis (like Accompong and Aberdeen) focusing on Archibald Campbell The First and Sergeant Wallace respectively, despite the general gender symmetry in these communities' oral traditions. In the other three free villages of Refuge, Kettering and Martha Brae, and in the squatter settlement of Zion, oral history is more equally engendered. However, in Martha Brae involvement in tourism is more male-oriented than in the other Trelawny communities, due to river rafting. This male focus parallels the situation in the Accompong Maroon society in St Elizabeth, with its male tourist guides and Minister of Tourism and Culture.

In addition, Martha Brae's migration tradition reflects variation in gender ideologies over time within the same community and even in the same institution; for the early male-focused movements have been increasingly reinforced by female migrations. Likewise, dry goods higglering in the Falmouth marketplace has been transformed from a primarily female role to one of gender symmetry.

Therefore even among the peasantry of west-central Jamaica, Caribbean gender ideologies show diversity and change. Yet an underlying unity exists in the significance of both women and men in culture building and sustainable development, in this core area of the Caribbean region,[30] from the days of slavery to the 1990s.

Notes

1. I use the concept of 'gender ideologies' to refer to systems of ideas articulating with, and reflected in, gender identities, relationships and roles.
2. My fieldwork in Jamaica (1968-95) was funded in part by the Jamaican Ministry of Education, the Social Science Research Council (UK), the Carnegie Trust for the Universities of Scotland, the University of Aberdeen, and the Nuffield Foundation.

3. Moreover, in the book in which my article appeared, four contributors critiqued Wilson's thesis (see Momsen 1993: 6).

4. Persisting plantations include Long Pond and Hampden Estates in Trelawny, and Appleton Estates in St Elizabeth. I use the concept of 'peasantry' as defined by Mintz (1989: 141), a definition highlighting the significance of access to land.

5. For a discussion of variations in burial patterns among the Trelawny villages see Besson 1984b.

6. The Leeward Maroon Treaty of March 1739 included Trelawny Town/Cudjoe's Town and Accompong Town. The Trelawny Town Maroons were deported after the Second Maroon War (1795-96).

7. As Kopytoff (1979: 52) notes, 'First-Time Maroons' refers to the Maroons who won the treaties rather than to the first runaway slaves.

8. Levi-Strauss (1969) distinguished two types of exogamous or out-marrying systems: 'elementary' and 'complex' (see also Fox 1967: 175-239). Elementary systems specify required or preferred classes of spouses (various types of cousins, such as a man's father's sister's daughter or mother's brother's daughter), thereby perpetuating marital alliances among kin (comparable to marriage alliances among European royalty, see note 12 below).

   Complex marriage systems have no such prescribed or preferential rules, specifying only which relatives one may not marry. Complex systems therefore have no recurrent marital patterns among kin, but result in alliances being forged in numerous directions (as is usually the case among commoners in Euro-American societies). On Jamaican slave plantations and in contemporary non-Maroon communities, a complex marriage system is elaborated by the fact that both men and women may have several sequential non-patterned conjugal unions. This dynamic marriage system is therefore more 'complex' then even Levi-Strauss envisaged.

9. 'Eskimo' kinship terminology reflects bilateral kinship and the nuclear family (modified in Jamaica to highlight serial polygamy and half-siblingship), while 'Hawaiian' kin terms reflect cognatic descent. For a discussion of Hawaiianised-Eskimo terminology in Jamaica see Besson 1995f.

10. See note 8 above.

11. Coromantees and their descendants dominated the Leeward Maroons in the eighteenth century, and 'Congo' runaways settled 'deep in the western woods' after the treaty (Kopytoff 1976: 38, 40). The Accompong Maroons in fact relate intermarriage among three 'tribes' – Ashantis, Congos and Coromantees – but then qualify this statement by the accurate observation that Ashanti and Coromantee coincide: 'is the same thing' (see e.g. Patterson 1973: 119, 135, 138). Maroon cousin-marriage therefore approximates to Levi-Strauss' model of 'direct exchange' or 'symmetrical alliance' between two groups (cf. note 8 above and Fox 1967: 175-207).

12. The saying 'We are Royal Family' draws a parallel with marriage alliances among European royal families.

13. The word 'Kindah' seems to derive from the German *Kinder* or children, but I have yet to uncover the origin of this word in Accompong.

14. Kopytoff (1978: 301-304) notes that both the Leeward and Windward Maroons suffered from a shortage of women in their early history, and contrasts the sharing of rights to women (thus enhancing fertility) in Leeward Maroon society with exclusive rights to women among the Windward Maroons. As outlined in this chapter, the explicit emphasis on fertility among the Leeward Maroons is symbolised in Myal ritual.

15. R. T. Smith (1988: 40) notes of West Indian kinship that 'Those who have "come into the family" may also be called "bye family," a term derived, apparently, from the old English meaning of "bye" as secondary or subsidiary.'

16. This oral tradition is consistent with Price's (1979: 20, 24) historical observations that early Maroons were often recently enslaved Africans, and that the first Maroon leaders tended to claim African royal descent.

17. St Elizabeth, like Trelawny, was a parish of significant Scottish colonial settlement.

18. 'Old Town' refers to Cudjoe's Town (see note 6), symbolically relocated at the edge of Accompong.

19. Oral tradition on the founding of The Alps (originally named 'New Birmingham') is reinforced by archival research, see Besson 1984b: 17-18.

20. My research suggests that the father of 'Sergeant Wallace' was from either the planter or overseer class.

21. Wilson (1973: 151, 156) interprets titles and nick-naming as reflecting male reputation, but these typify both genders in Jamaica.

22. Nowadays, a white fowl is also sacrificed where whites will cross a path – as at Kindah for the Myal ritual.

23. The Abeng is a cowhorn, which was blown to communicate in Maroon guerilla warfare. Abeng blowing now includes spiritual communication with the First-Time Maroons. The line of succession to the sacred office of Abeng blower is male.

24. Simmonds (1987: 31-32) notes that on the plantations, while male slaves dominated the higher status roles of drivers and artisans with females filling domestic occupations, the majority of field slaves were given the same work regardless of gender – the gang system being differentiated only by health and age. In contrast, in the towns – where there was a preponderance of women, slave-holding females and African female slaves (rather than males and Creoles) – slave women were mainly engaged in domestic work and marketing; while male slaves were generally assigned skilled occupations (cf. Higman 1984: 50).

25. The oral tradition of the Accompong Maroons tells of plantation livestock raids on Aberdeen Estate and clandestine trading at Maggotty Market during marronage, complementing cultivation, hunting wild hogs and gathering cocoon beans (Besson 1995a). In 1941, while hunting was waning, peasant marketing by mule transport still complemented cultivation. With the construction of the first dirt road to Accompong in the 1940s, the Maroons diversified into cash cropping bananas and sugar cane in the 1950s and marijuana in the 1970s, though banana production declined in 1981 due to vulnerability in the world economy (Barker and Spence 1988). However, during my fieldwork in 1995 the Accompong Maroons signed a contract for renewed banana export production; while reports of marijuana cash cropping in the community continue (Earle 1996).

26. The Ben' Down Market is so called because stalls are often on the ground and buyers and sellers have to bend down. The transformation of such dry goods marketing in Jamaica through informal commercial importing is encapsulated in Ginger Knight's Jamaican play, *Higglers!*, also performed at Lewisham Theatre in London, England, in December 1995.

27. For a discussion of Caribbean ROSCAs in relation to the African heritage and creole institution building, see Besson 1995c: 274-77.

28. For example, while land in the Trelawny free villages is measured in square chains, it has been surveyed in square metres in the recently established squatter settlement of Zion.

29. However, non-Maroons are not allowed beyond the Kindah grove.

30. Jamaica is the Caribbean plantation tourist society par excellence, with pronounced peasant adaptations. The parishes of Trelawny and St Elizabeth are at the heart of the island's persisting plantation-peasant interface.

9

Women and Jamaican Pentecostalism

Diane J. Austin-Broos

Although it is very likely that religion plays a prominent part in the lives of many Caribbean women, there is relatively little written about this involvement except, perhaps, as part of the discussion of Caribbean respectability (see for instance, Wilson 1973; Olwig 1993: 69-89; cf. Austin 1981, 1984: 103-118, 1987). Older characterisations of Caribbean women as confined to the yard and the church that ignore their participation in the workforce have been criticised, and appropriately (see for instance Ellis 1986; Momsen 1993). Consistent with these latter accounts is Besson's (1993) critique of Wilson's portrait of a Caribbean society in which men sustain a reputational culture of 'resistance' while women sustain a status quo rooted in religion that is European-derived. Besson observes quite correctly that women compete for 'reputation' in many domains of their lives, including church participation. She also proposes a view that I will not pursue, that nonconformist or sectarian churches within Jamaica have been part of a culture of 'resistance'. Certainly she points to the radical simplifications in Wilson's account that, whilst containing some acute observations, has served to mislead as much as it enlightens.

In one particular respect, Raymond Smith's (1987, 1988) recent writing on Caribbean kinship and marriage may seem to support Wilson's portrayal. In these works, Smith proposes to interpret Jamaican society in terms of a 'dual marriage system'. Historically, this has been a system that included both concubinage and legal marriage. Initially, in plantation society, white men married white women of similar status whilst they sustained non-legal relations with women who were brown or black and judged to be of inferior station. Moreover, this pattern was indicative not only of white and non-white relations, but also of powerful male slaves and their spouses. The former 'might marry – either legally or according to some customary form but they would also have "outside" unions, and those usually with women of lower status in the racial hierarchy' (Smith 1987: 177; Higman 1976: 146-147, 1984; cf. Austin 1979). In this way, Smith proposes, marriage became appropriated as a sign of relatedness between status equals who were also superior in status to others. With the advent of Crown colony rule, Smith proposes that the system moved down a register to concern, not the white expatriate elite, but rather the middle class in their relations with lower-class Jamaicans (Smith 1987: 183; see also Douglass 1992). More important for this discussion, is Smith's assertion that the alternative forms of concubinage and marriage so evident in the lower classes is in fact a further permutation of this system. Smith (1989: 189) remarks that 'the structure was compressed within the confines of the lower-class in such a way that a lower-class man could use any status factor, even masculinity itself, as the basis for insisting upon casual rather than a legally sanctioned union'. Smith (1987: 188) remarks that the major impact of this system is now felt by 'the lower class woman of limited means attempting to raise several children, forced to work if and when she can, and often passing through a series of unions'. These women, Smith proposes, are likely to believe that they 'cannot do better' or, in the words of Judith Blake, believe that 'the man — must ask' (Smith 1987: 169; Blake 1961: 134).

This account aligns with Wilson's to the extent that it seems to propose that women rather more than men favour and look for marriage as much for status as for economic reasons. Smith proposes, nonetheless, that it is a cultural logic beyond the explicit and individuated intentions of women, or men, that actually allows the men to manipulate marriage in such a way that it remains a mere alternative, and one often engaged only late in a couple's life. These larger implications of Smith's account show him in fact on a different track from Wilson, for Smith is at pains to underline that lower-class women suffer most due to the dual marriage system. Wilson tends to align not only respectability and femininity, but also associates these traits with a middle-class status. Smith's analyses of kinship and marriage clearly break this nexus apart to focus on the real struggle in which so many women are involved. Yet, in doing so, Raymond Smith's portrayal of lower-class women takes on a sometimes abject quality in which it seems that these women have very little control in their lives.

In the following discussion, I intend to indicate some aspects of the historical and contemporary significance of Pentecostal churches to Jamaican women. I will propose that one dimension of these churches' popularity pertains to the complex Smith describes. The churches offer women a redefinition of their circumstances which they readily grasp. For the women who remain involved, the churches provide one way in which they can actively respond to a larger hierarchical order that intersects with their gender relations. I would be most disinclined to figure this as a type of 'resistance' for, like all other Christian churches in the Jamaican environment, the Pentecostal milieu is a complex and ambiguous one. It harbours elements of creative practice and also hegemonic dimensions. Nonetheless, it provides for women an arena in which to negotiate a circumstance that is often defined by analysts simply in terms of domestic life and workplace participation. The arena of the church in fact gives women a greater scope to re-present themselves and redefine their social position. This repositioning and redefining has practical impacts in women's lives to which they themselves attest.

Women and Pentecostalism

It is established clearly in an ample literature that Pentecostal organisations are populated in the majority by women who, at least in independent churches, often take leadership roles as well (see Austin 1981, 1987; Cucchiari 1990; Gill 1990; Hollenweger 1969; LaRuffa 1980; Rose 1987; Smith 1978). Jamaica is no exception and yet it is important to understand the particular cultural modalities in which this pattern recurs. One role of churches in Jamaica has been to act as an alternative organisational base to both the plantation and the state in the course of Jamaican history. Free villages certainly proposed an alternative to the plantation system and churches have also been a form of collective organisation for many Jamaicans who remain beyond the domain of organised labour and its forms of association (see Austin 1991-92, 1992, 1996; cf. Mintz 1974a, 1974b). For many Jamaicans not incorporated into proletarian milieux, or into an ethos of secular politics, issues of suffering, malaise, and healing are as real, and sometimes more real, than issues of class interest and conflict (cf. Comaroff 1985). Such Jamaicans, in the present and the past, have had recourse to Jamaica's religions whether in the form of orthodox denominations, Zion Revival, or Pentecostalism.[1]

That women have been incorporated more slowly than men into a secular politics of the state, and its attendant organisations, may explain their continuing and large-scale turn to the church. Certainly, churches have provided alternative avenues for status, 'reputation', and the power of local and extra-local organisation. Churches, and the everyday support they provide, both practical and ideological, have also been attractive to women lacking male partners and raising children while they work.

As a consequence, many Pentecostal churches, especially in Kingston's urbanised milieu, appear almost as women's clubs that provide an organisational base for solidarity in a neighbourhood (Austin 1984: 103-115). In terms of Smith's analyses, they are organisations that confirm for women that they can and should do better than remain dependent on the decisions of men. It is therefore not unusual, especially in an urban milieu, to see women pass from a situation in which they will endorse aspects of the 'sweetheart life' to one in which, as they mature and need to look to their dependents, they give their worries 'over to Jesus' and join a Pentecostal church. As women who are 'born again', and can become 'saints' and 'brides of Christ', these women sustain a superior status within a local milieu. If they become dedicated practitioners within one of the larger churches, they may have the opportunity for extra-local organisational roles, and even, international ones. These options involve only a minority of women, but for the majority, the churches can offer consolidated local networks that facilitate daily assistance in domestic tasks and especially child minding and rearing (Austin-Broos 1991-92, 1996 in press). The church is one course that women can take to sustain autonomous lives of hope because they can redefine the unmarried household head as a virtuous exemplar in her milieu. Because Pentecostal churches are reluctant to accept common-law relations, they also support women in their request that a conjugal relation be sanctified (and legalised). In the following discussion I give attention to two aspects of Pentecostalism in Jamaica: changes in the socio-racial order that have made Pentecostalism a popular recourse; and some meanings of Pentecostal rite that make it especially attractive to women even when many pastors are men.

A Changing Socio-Racial Order

Generally, it is not appreciated that Pentecostalism became established in Jamaica during the 1920s (see Conn 1959; Austin-Broos in press; cf. Wedenoja 1980). Neither is it well known that Pentecostalism has become Jamaica's most prominent popular religion. During the post-war period, it has wrested that status from perhaps a dual folk allegiance to orthodox Baptist practice and to Zion Revivalism. The latter unorthodox companion to an orthodox Baptist faith has been important in folk healing, a perennial and central component of Jamaican Afro-Christian practice (cf. Schuler 1980). The appeal of Pentecostalism through the twentieth century has been in no small part that it aligns a powerful healing practice, albeit solely through the Holy Ghost and not through balm yard cures, with an institutional church. Along with Pentecostal enthusiasm in worship, which practitioners compare with the 'straight' orthodox Baptists, this healing focus has appealed to the people and helped to build a major movement. By 1982, adherents subsumed under the census categories 'Church of God' and 'Pentecostal', included close to a quarter of Jamaica's population (see Table 9.1).[2]

This radical 'sea-change' in Jamaican religion is integral to a shifting regional hegemony that has seen North American influence prevail over the declining influence of Europe. This shift first became evident with the rise of Jamaica's banana industry, the sea routes it opened up, and the lines of communication it allowed. During the 1880s and 1890s, at least eight different trading companies secured themselves in ports along Jamaica's northern shore. In the same period, the number of steamship lines out of Jamaica expanded from one to seventeen. Among other ports, these lines sailed to New York, New Orleans, Philadelphia and Boston (Hall 1964: 72-73). During the 1910s and 1920s, some of these would be the routes that east coast Pentecostal churches, such as the Church of God from Cleveland, Tennessee, would travel to Jamaica. Pentecostalism only emerged as a distinctive American faith during the 1910s (Anderson 1979). With its strong evangelising thrust, the Caribbean was an early port of call (Conn 1959).

Elsewhere I argue that the rise of Pentecostalism in this regional milieu should be set beside the emergence of unionism, nationalism, and Rasta-farianism (Austin-Broos in press). Each has been a major social movement in Jamaica responding to particular circumstances. And the circumstances relevant to Pentecostal growth have pertained especially to the position of women confined to the Jamaican scene, facing a local hierarchy, and largely ignored by unionism. This is not to suggest that Pentecostalism has been women's only response (see French and Ford-Smith n.d.). It was, however, a prominent one that would shape the feminine culture of Jamaica's lower class and leave its imprint on the whole society.

The early decades of the twentieth century were a period of labour migration in which men travelled in the region to Panama, Costa Rica,

Table 9.1 Population by Religious Affiliation, by Sex – All Jamaica

Religious Affiliation	Total	Male	Female
Church of God	400,379	175,140	225,239
Baptist	217,839	98,700	119,139
Anglican	154,548	71,287	83,261
Seventh Day Adventist	150,722	67,129	83,593
Pentecostal	113,570	47,974	65,596
Roman Catholic	107,580	50,769	56,811
Methodist	68,289	30,770	37,519
United Church	58,938	27,154	31,784
Moravian	31,772	14,924	16,848
African Methodist Episcopal Zion	30,530	12,761	17,769
Jehovah Witness	25,016	10,991	14,025
Brethren	22,961	10,029	12,932
Rastafarian	14,249	11,661	2,588
Salvation Army	11,131	5,040	6,091
Disciples of Christ	8,483	3,706	4,777
Moslem/Hindu	2,238	1,311	927
Jewish	412	202	210
None	385,517	244,191	141,326
Not stated	243,614	122,834	120,780
Other	125,091	56,889	68,202
Total	2,172,879	1,063,462	1,109,417

Source: 1982 Population Census (Final Count). Statistical Institute of Jamaica.

and Cuba (Newton 1984; Knight 1985; Lewis 1987). Although the successful 'Colon Man' was celebrated in Jamaican song, the euphemism 'a silver man' recalled the experience of segregation in impersonal labour markets dominated by the United States and condoned by the British colonial regime. Predictably, it was the Panamanian arena which constituted a shared experience for a number of Jamaicans who became leaders of popular movements within Jamaica itself. Amy Jacques Garvey maintains that her husband's travels through Costa Rica, Panama and Ecuador radicalised Garvey's view of the black man in the New World: 'he saw the awful conditions under which they laboured – no protection from the British Consul and no efforts for their welfare' (Garvey 1970: 7; cf. Lewis 1987:557- 565). Bustamante travelled extensively within this same region (Eaton 1975: 13-15). Unionism for Bustamante meant popular mobilisation, not to bring down the regional order, but rather to harness its wealth for the benefit of the people. To operate in this new system, Jamaica had to overcome the arbitrary political barriers of the remnant British regime (Hill 1976).

Bustamante grasped the mood of the nation and was ultimately successful in his quest, becoming Jamaica's first prime minister elected by universal suffrage. Yet, by underlining possibilities in the region, Bustamante glossed over its many constraints. These constraints were embodied in the racialism of the United States and in the stratification of labour that continued under its influence. Alexander Bedward, the early religious radical, was a returnee from Central America as was each of the founders of Rastafarianism (Smith et. al. 1960: 6-9; Hill 1983: 39). Bedward is known for his announcement of the imminent destruction of the white populace and the firing of Kingston as the 'black wall' of his followers confronted the 'white wall' (Chevannes 1971: 49). It was this sense of being encapsulated in a white world, of being confronted by a white wall that gave an impetus to Garvey's United Negro Improvement Association (UNIA) and the Rastafarian movement that would prove so influential in Jamaica.

The Moralisation of Women's Position

Notwithstanding these initiatives in Pan-African politics, unions had become, by the late 1930s, the principal form of popular organisation. This process occurred at a time when women were leaving a rural workforce finally subject to some unionisation (Phelps 1960; Post 1978: 238-261; French 1986). Women had moved from agriculture to service occupations at the turn of the century in the face of stagnation in the rural sector. In the 1910s, and particularly in parishes that combined sugar cane and peasant cultivation, women moved back to the land to replace migrating men. From the 1920s and into the 1930s, however, as migrating men returned to resume their places in agriculture, women moved en masse into service occupations, especially vending and domestic service (Lobdell 1988; Higman 1983; Roberts 1957: 158-164).

The women who became vendors were yet to organise, and for women moving into domestic service there were no unions available. Whether they were men or women, the small farmers who stayed on the land still had only limited representation. These Jamaicans faced events that involved the emergence of nation state structures, but structures to which they had limited access and also gave only limited salience. Their view of the world at the turn of the century was at once, local, magical, and infused with a creole cosmology (cf. Chevannes 1994). Religious rite was a response to suffering and also a means to a better life. In addition, these peoples' experience of racialism was local and domestic rather than regional and proletarianised. The 'Back-to-Africa' movements relied for their appeal on a sense of a regional industrial order infused with racial prejudice. They did not address immediately the more subtle stratifications involved in a maid's encounter with her mistress, or even the hierarchy of rural village life (cf. Brodber 1984). The situation of those who sustained this position between a local, rural, and ritual world and a secular political one, is epitomised by women entering domestic service in the first three decades of the twentieth century.

As domestics, women received average money wages of less than £40 a year which was well below wages for comparable work both in Britain and the United States (Higman 1983: 1291-30). Their material situation was a little better than those involved in rural labour, for in addition to money wages they received accommodation and some payment in kind. They experienced, however, strong symbolic statements of their subordinate position. Servant accommodation was often in rude huts separate from the employer's house, and even when incorporated within the house, seldom was there direct access from these quarters to the main living area. Servants were to be separated and kept in their position even in the modest houses of clerks and shop assistants. For these women and a number of their menfolk, the world of labour and associated movements was still a distant one.

A sense of these women's lives is gained from Herbert G. de Lisser's account of their position. De Lisser was a leading advocate for Jamaica's banana industry, editor of the Jamaican *Daily Gleaner*, for a time co-leader of the conservative Jamaica Imperial Association, and a publicist for Jamaica. He was among Jamaica's conservatives; a politically prominent spokesman for the planter class. Yet as a young man he had Fabian sympathies and wrote as a novelist-observer of local life (Carnegie 1973: 162-177). In the first decade of the century he was already writing about Jamaica's new army of female employees. In his novel, *Jane's Career*, he made justly famous the social personality of a young rural woman who became a domestic servant in Kingston. In 1913, de Lisser made the following comment on Jamaican society.

It will be apparent that if out of a population of less than nine hundred thousand, most of whom serve themselves, the number of domestics is forty thousand, almost everybody who has the slightest pretensions to be considered anybody employs a servant. In fact you are not respectable if you have not a servant (de Lisser 1913: 97).

This affirmation of the status concerns of a newly confident middle class underlines one important cause of the dramatic restructuring of female labour that occurred in the course of the early twentieth century. De Lisser proposed that a mother's concern for her daughters' physical and moral well-being would encourage her to support their employment in domestic milieux (de Lisser 1913: 96-100). This was a preference, however, that also coincided with a rural economy that had reached its limits. The flow of feminine labour to the towns would be magnified in the coming decades as men returned form overseas (Roberts 1958: 152-154, 158-164; Lobdell 1988; Higman 1983). Women moved both to Kingston and St Andrew and to the larger market towns, and often this involved a movement away from kinship networks of rural life so that living, and mating, in urban areas became a more precarious affair (cf. Smith 1962: 242, 1966: xxiii-iv). De Lisser himself described a possible life cycle for the domestic as she matured.

the possession of children may compel her to give up a comfortable room in a big and fairly sanitary yard, and may oblige her to rent a little place in an insanitary yard, playing the rent out of the scanty wages she receives. Periodically she comes into possession of a 'friend', and then, for the time, her burden may be lightened. But as her family grows, grows also the necessity for her to work harder and more steadily. Then someday, her eldest girl goes off to 'look a living' for herself, or her biggest boy departs to carve out an independent career . If she lives to be old, she will probably become a regular member of a church, and her children will see that she and their father do not starve (de Lisser 1913: 104-105).

There is no reason to believe that these conditions which began in the first decade of the twentieth century, changed very much in the following thirty years. Edith Clarke's (1966: 93-96) account of the economic situation of women moving into sugar towns in the 1930s is equally austere. Clarke's account, like de Lisser's, points to the economising of sentiment that was involved in a woman's attempts to acquire a male earner for her household. And yet this was not the mere economising of sentiment. Notwithstanding their economic position, women often endorse the 'sweetheart life'. Reflecting on her life in service, a Kingston woman once remarked to me, 'Me have four or five children den, han' I'm livin', they call it "sweetheart life", not livin' wid my husband, jus free han' quiet.' Being 'free han quiet' signified a release from a troubled domestic environment in which a husband, himself beset by unemployment, proved unreliable and at times aggressive. Even when it is initially sought by women, marriage is not always a condition happily sustained in a lower-class milieu (Sobo 1993: 190-196). The consequences are readily recognised however: 'Say I goin te church. They don' accept me as much as they would accept you that have six, seven children han' married'. The conjuncture of public and private conditions in the early years of the century, and even now, has allowed ample scope for the respectable to denigrate the lives and morals of their servants, and legitimise their own position through appeals to Christian piety. Churches, as de Lisser observes, have been institutional mainstays for lower-class women in conjunction with their immediate kin. Yet churches have also been a major voice condemning them for their life's condition. The ritual resolution of this dilemma is present in Pentecostalism; a Christian practice that would circumvent the denigration of orthodox religion.

The spate of reports and commissions that followed the labour rebellion of 1938 reflect the moralisation of women's position. A strong focus on land settlement schemes and extension services for farmers addressed the interests of the rural men. The landless male would be catered to through further development of trade unions. Where women were concerned, however, there was little discussion of their work and extensive comment on welfare measures to improve their home making skills (Moyne 1945: 220-221). The only measure proposed to address the situation of Jamaica's domestics was the construction of hostels in major towns to accommodate working women. Yet this proposal was never acted upon (French 1986: 13). Instead, the wife of the governor, Lady Huggins, launched a Mass Marriage Movement in 1944-45 to regularise the families of Jamaican workers. After some early impact, this initiative proved largely unsuccessful (Smith 1966: iv-v).

The report of the Moyne Commission was particularly adamant concerning the need to constitute proper families in Jamaica with a male income earner at the head. These recommendations were made as part of aspirations to promote the economically vulnerable: lowly paid women and their dependent children. There was little attempt, however, to see these women as a significant component of Jamaica's labour force. Rather, the presence in the workforce of women with children was seen as an inadvertent outcome of profligacy. Even the policy adviser, T. S. Simey, who was careful to caution against coercive moral measures to cope with the 'economic evils of promiscuity', remained within the bounds of these conventional understandings (Simey 1946: 182-191, 224-6).

During the slavery period and throughout the nineteenth century, there is little evidence of gender being used as a criterion to debar women from agriculture or other forms of physical work. There was an evident stratification in relation to trade and field occupations, but certainly women were judged to be fully part of the manual labour force (Higman

1976: 187-201). Within the peasant milieu of the post-emancipation period, the position of women planters was equally established. The expansion of the middle class at the end of the century, however, promoted the idea that women should not work 'out'. This was but one moment in the ideological delineation of classes according to levels of education, mores, colour and social style (Norris 1962; de Lisser 1913). The fact of women working 'out' became representative of a moral failing in the women, in their class, and in their cultural tradition. Hence the focus on promiscuity as a serious social issue.

Pentecostalism's appeal to Women

In the 1930s and 1940s, women and men who remained on the land or migrated into towns were progressively encompassed in a larger nexus of market relations and regional patterns of race and class. Concurrently they were subject to the local moralising of their position. And to this particular Jamaican discourse they brought the practice of a rural creole people. Their experience of a moralised hierarchy they interpreted in a religious mode that made their suffering and circumstance an index of their capacity for holiness. Pentecostalism, a popular religion opposed to the ecclesiastical mores of the middle class, and endorsed by representatives of a powerful white America, became a vehicle for women and politically peripheral men to valorise their experience.

The religion included in one organisation healing and enthusiastic rite, the power to marry followers, and to become a secure and institutionalised church. As women moved into towns and away from the rural milieux that harboured orthodox denominations and folk Revival with its balm yard traditions, this amalgam was attractive. In the older religious synthesis Zion Revival leaders were not licensed to marry and in the denominational churches those who had lived in concubinage often commanded lesser status. Pentecostalism's powerful doctrine of the Christian 'born again' to a radically new life allowed believers to re-position themselves within this part of Jamaica's status order. As a consequence of these factors, women from the pre- and post-war generations turned rapidly to Pentecostal churches.

A large proportion of the congregations, however, are also women from succeeding generations in a different position again from their mothers. While over a third of women in the workforce worked in domestic service in 1943, by 1984 this proportion of women had dropped to a mere 16 percent (Gordon 1989:72). Women were mobile into the middle strata of various clerical positions and also into the 'mass professions' of teaching and nursing in particular (Gordon 1987: 15-16). These occupational movements are indicative of a relative educational success for lower-class women in relation to lower-class men (cf. Miller 1986, 1990). Yet, the situation of women is modified by the meagre incomes in these occupations, the greater pressure on women to work, and the high unemployment rates they experience (Gordon 1989: 72, 75-77). At all points in the educational spectrum men in the workforce receive greater returns for their education than women (Gordon 1989: 76, 1991). Moreover, the mobility of women, mainly structural mobility, means that they are almost twice as likely as men to find a position that is different from that of the women of their natal home (Gordon 1987: 17, 1989: 77-78). The Pentecostals provide for these women well organised and powerful churches that support them in their difficult position.

Through the century, Jamaican women as well as men have experienced a marked dislocation and constant re-adjustments to their position. Manifest in rural to urban migration, these changes were precipitated by regional labour re-organisation and structural change within Jamaica itself. These processes have intervened and radically changed a local rural milieu in which the early mission churches and Zion Revival had become ensconced. The people affected by these changes have not always been drawn into labour or national movements that sought to address the changing conditions. With increasing urbanisation and the moralising of women's position, the proposal of Pentecostalists, that the black lower class could become Christian saints, and their women 'brides of Christ' within a large regional church, has been an attractive truth. For these Jamaicans, Pentecostalism has been a way to contest the status quo and also draw on the power of a new and expanding regional presence. Its focus on becoming a saint and living holy in the grace of God, a condition that is manifest through healing and speaking in tongues, has allowed many of these Jamaicans to place themselves 'on the victory side' even in a changing milieu. It has marked in the twentieth century a major Jamaican response to the demise of Britain's colonial order and the ritual modes that its missions bequeathed.

Pentecostal meanings for Jamaican women

Given the integration of the older mission churches with Jamaica's colonial order (see Stewart 1992), it is not surprising that Jamaican women would look for a new church, especially as they urbanised. There were, however, others in the field besides Pentecostalism. These included the Salvation Army, whose representatives first arrived in 1887, and the Seventh Day Adventists, established in Jamaica in 1894.[3] Neither of these movements has equalled Pentecostalism's popularity, although the Adventist church is now a prominent one in Jamaica and possibly second only to the Pentecostals in its rate of expansion in this century (see Table 9.2). Pentecostalism has become embedded in the lives of many Jamaican men and women because it carries forms of ritual meaning readily adapted to a Jamaican environment. Moreover, as they are articulated in rite, some of these meanings have a special significance for women who are household heads or residing with children in non-legal unions.

Pentecostal rite promises to women a radical inversion of a status defined through the socio-racial order. The rite is concerned with a transition that changes a person into a saint. It involves a 'sanctification' realised through Holy Ghost possession and signified by speaking in tongues. Only glossolalia confirms that a person has been filled by the Holy Ghost. But glossolalia also only hails an initial working of the Spirit that may be repeated again or not, depending on the Spirit's design. Healing and the assumption of morality signal, on a more regular basis, that both the body and soul have changed to become a 'perfect' saint. They are indicative of a change completed, and not a mere apprenticeship to grace. In this context, morality becomes metonymic for perfection. It is not the totality of faith but rather a sign of a completed faith.

The morality that is relevant to Jamaican saintly perfection bears on an understanding of the body as a vessel for the Holy Ghost about to conjoin with the body of Christ. The soul's transformation in the body involves its assimilation to the logic of Spirit but such a soul can only inhere in a body that is undefiled. The salient signs of Pentecostal transformation,

Table 9. 2 Adherents for Selected Faiths

	1921	1943	1960	1970	1982
Baptist	205,483	318,665	306,037	319,730	217,839
Church of God	1,774	43,560	191,231	305,412	400,379
Seventh Day Adventist	5,416	27,402	78,360	117,059	150,722
Pentecostal	–	4,907	14,739	57,055	113,570
Rastafarianism	–	–	–	–	14,249

Source: Jamaica, Department of Statistics, Census of Jamaica: 1921, 1943, 1960, 1970, 1982

a moral healing of the self, are signs of cleanliness concerning the body. One set of signs involves health itself. Pain often signifies spiritual anxiety and healing through the laying on of hands re-asserts the dominance of Spirit. Many Jamaicans employ an idiom of health and pain to signify their general state of being (cf. Sobo 1993). To make the observation that a person is 'hearty' is almost always to say as well that the person is spiritually content. To experience 'pains' in 'meh inside part' is also an expression of incorporeal unease. If a person is a member of a church this unease will precipitate a prayer request to try to set the matter right. In this idiom Jamaicans affirm the experiential complex of affliction that sees moral and physical malaise conjoined. Sobo captures the situation well:

People who 'lived good' cannot, ideally, be caught by socially precipitated sicknesses: sickness instigated in a response to perceived affronts by an animate being (a neighbour, a demon, God or a duppy [ghost] sent by a 'science man' hired by a 'grudgeful' villager). In an ideal world, a moral sociable person could never anger anyone enough to attack. And should anyone really want to 'sick' a physically and spiritually 'clean' person. God and his angels provide protection (Sobo 1993: 294).

To be hearty, then, is to be spiritually at peace and although not all forms of malaise are seen as indicative of moral failing, it is generally assumed that a morally clean body will also be a healthy one.

Women frequently come to church with back pains and pains in muscles and joints. Very often these pains are indicative of muscular or spinal strain from heavy work, or else the early onset of arthritic pain that often comes with repeated and prolonged cold water laundering. Saints have headaches as well, some of which clearly come from stress. To this repertoire of pain that is integral to environment is added the cultural construction of pain as an obligatory manifestation of saints' need of the Lord. Feeling pain and requiring its cure is a manifestation of holiness that has not become arrogant and over-confident. The curing that comes to terminate pain is a major sign of saintly status and allows women to deploy an idiom familiar in their daily lives to constitute an assertion of saintliness. Though men participate in this idiom, the close association of pain and spiritual malaise, and its relief which allows spiritual elevation, is focussed in a feminine milieu of lower class, usually service work (cf. Ong 1987).

Another set of signs of spiritual transformation are the moral signs of the saved. These signs revolve around sexuality and around the idea that any sexual practice not sanctified in marriage will sully a vessel and make it unclean. Manifesting the moral state thus becomes the active rejection of 'fornication', and the rejection of other practices that independently make the body unclean or else may lead to fornication: the rejection of dancing, smoking, drinking, jewellery, cosmetics, swearing, and of engagement with the unsaved. For Jamaicans these restrictions have also involved a ban against straightening curly hair, and in the case of women, once involved leaving the hair uncut. A purified life that sustains clean bodies is central to the Pentecostal progress. It provides the saved with two related statuses that are integral to being a saint. One is to be, as part of the church, a bride awaiting the Bridegroom's approach. The other, as part of the 'body of Christ', is to be the vessel for His Holy Spirit. As embodied vessel for the Holy Ghost, both beyond and around his Holy essence, it is imperative that the saint be clean.

A saint may express a jealous sentiment, be angry, lie, say 'bad words', or even perpetrate a violence that demands a penance and prayer to God. A saint may remain unemployed for years and never demonstrate that duty in a calling indicative of the ascetic Protestant. But even one act of fornication would signify a fall from grace. Likewise, if a saint went to dance halls, started smoking, or drinking liquor this would be a sign of 'backsliding', of resuming the fallen state. It would signify beyond any doubt the reversion of the vessel to an unclean state, separation from the body of Christ, and departure of the power of the Holy Ghost. While other failures or transgressions can be construed as failings of the flesh that merely frustrate the capacity for perfection, these moral signs are signs of defilement that mean that capacity for perfection is lost.

Second- or third-generation Pentecostal women often relate that their mothers counselled them that they were 'too young' to receive the Spirit when they attended church in their teenage years. According to Pentecostal doctrine this could never be the case provided that the person knew the gospel message and was able to perform the acts of contrition involved in signifying repentance. For young Jamaican women, however, this youth pertained to the likelihood that they would bear children out of wedlock prior to settling with a partner. It was less momentous for a woman to be pregnant who was saved and not sanctified or not saved at all, than it was for a saint to actually fall and for a time, be suspended from the church. An older saint addressed on this observed that 'The young gal' do not like t' fast han' tarry. Dey are too young t' open de'r heart t' Jesus.' Consistent with this pattern of expectations, it is more often older women, over forty years, who have placed their child-bearing time behind them, who are richly imbued with spiritual gifts and leaders in evangelism.

Nonetheless, if younger unmarried women wish to become sanctified saints, and *inter alia* bring their child bearing period to a close, this can be done in a positive way with the support of the church. Certainly, women are provided with a powerful ideology that allows them to expect of men that a union will be sanctified. Sometimes men succumb to this force without becoming Pentecostalists themselves and thereby provide women with a domestic order integrated with the church. For women without a common-law partner who have borne children in their youth, the process of becoming a saint, and more importantly a bride of Christ, can allow a redefinition of the self along with access to an organisation that often offers pre-school support and a structuring of everyday life that can supplement over-extended kin relations.

In these ways women redefine the central nature of their being and move sometimes in a definite way to exchange a procreative being for a spiritual being within the church. In this latter role they mentor neophytes so that they may be 'born again'. Whilst child bearing more than sexuality itself seems central to definitions of femininity, it is, perhaps, the persona of prolific practitioner that is central to at least some men; that more than one 'oman 'ave pickney fe we' (cf. Chevannes 1985; Sobo 1993: 173-243; MacCormack and Draper 1987). In addition, smoking and drinking are activities that bind men together in groups that meet after work at a street corner, a domino game, or a small rum bar (Manning 1973; Wilson 1973; Austin 1984: 119-130). Gambling is also a Pentecostal taboo, and gambling on Chinese number games, domino games and the horses is integral to men in groups. This very pursuit of 'reputation' is integral to a masculine identity that must be transformed within the church and thereby discourages many men from its highly organised milieu. Men who become Pentecostals often pursue a leadership role at least as deacon or elder in the church that through its assertion of a patriarchal status mitigates the loss of these masculine signs. For women, however, the transition from a procreative status to one of giving birth to other saints is a less troubled passage that allows women through their bodies to assume in powerful ways the status of vessel for the Holy Ghost and saints of superior religious standing. The churches thereby act as major arena of feminine 'reputation' that also challenges some aspects of the cultural logic involved in Jamaica's dual marriage system. Women can redefine themselves without reliance on a man and can do so in a way that is supported by large trans-regional organisations that have grown in influence through the century. This recourse appears to be a major attraction not only for many Jamaican women today but also for some generations past who have experienced the society's rapid transformations.

Conclusion

Many Jamaican women use Pentecostal churches creatively to reposition themselves within a lower-class milieu. Especially in some independent churches, women are pastors and evangelists and provide through their congregations important feminine milieux beyond the workplace and domestic domain. In these milieux women find means to reconstitute their being that allow them a creative autonomy that is not confined by low position in the workforce or by a union status in which they 'caan' do better' and must simply wait on the man 'to ask'. Accounts of lower-class women's position in Jamaica and other Caribbean societies will be less than comprehensive if they do not address this arena as other than a mere 'status quo'.

Nonetheless, it would be mistaken to interpret these arenas as forms of 'resistance'. Indeed, they demonstrate the limitations of analyses that accept domination-resistance as their principal axis. Like the established denominations that began as mission churches in Jamaica, Pentecostal churches reflect the hegemony of metropolitan power. Though most Jamaican churches are self-financing today, the cultural influence of America is potent, as British influence was also potent in the nineteenth century mission churches (cf. Stewart 1992). Pentecostals in Jamaica are very aware of the racialism that infuses many churches in North America. Whilst they are critical of the situation, they are limited in their capacity to change it. And while they offer a reconstitution of the self to a committed believer, they cannot, in a Rastafarian style, sustain a critique of a Euro-Christianity's racial dimensions.

Yet the churches offer to Jamaicans, and especially to Jamaican women, large-scale organisations in which, especially within Jamaica, they are able to experience an autonomy of worship and organisational practice. Certainly where women are concerned, the churches can be vehicles for the autonomous articulation of spiritual and social skills. In sum, they are ambiguous domains, part of a larger regional order that carries similar complexities. Analyses that proceed simply in terms of domination *or* resistance cannot capture the import of these milieux for women which often allow an ostensibly constrained position to be lived with some dignity, and with some ritual flair.

Notes

1. Among these popular religions I do not mention Rastafarianism because one of its major divergences from a previous Afro-Christian tradition has been to focus on 'reasoning' or critique rather than on healing the body as a way of reconstituting the world. In this sense, Rastafarianism is an eminently 'modern' or rationalist religion notwithstanding its reconstitution of an African past.
2. The census category 'Church of God' subsumes both 'Holiness' churches and churches that are Pentecostal. Whilst subscribing to the 'born again' style of Christianity, holiness churches do not accept the doctrine of 'speaking in tongues'. In the United States, holiness churches were a further development on Methodism and preceded the emergence of Pentecostalism (Dayton 1980). Holiness missionaries first came to Jamaica in 1908 (see Austin-Broos in press).
3. For an account of the Salvation Army in Jamaica see Hobbs (1986). The date of entry into Jamaica for the Seventh Day Adventists was provided by the church's secretariat in Kingston. At the time of research on this material the church had no published accounts available.

SECTION III

Acquiring Gender Identities:
Socialisation and Schooling

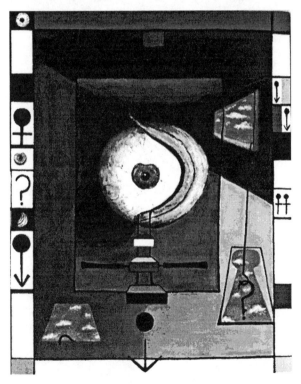

10

For Richer or Poorer:

How Western Psychology Does, Can and Should Contribute to a Caribbean Analysis of Gender Ideologies?

Monica A. Payne

Introduction

Psychology is one modern institution which has little to offer radicals. The institution needs to be opened up, deconstructed so that the conflicts within it become clear, so clear that it is too much to bear. This does not mean of course, that no elements of psychological theory are useful – there are always helpful spin-offs from harmful enterprises, like non-stick saucepans developed from military space research (and a psychology book which is as useful as a non-stick pan is a rare thing) (Parker 1992: 80).

In claiming (for example) that women "ask for it", that we have "self defeating" personalities, that we suffer from fear of success or cognitive deficits, psychology has colluded with and compounded our oppression . . . Psychology has infiltrated our everyday thought and speech with its individualized, depoliticized and victim-blaming accounts of human action, and that is why, as *feminist psychologists*, we must expose and challenge the oppressive values of our discipline and seek to transform them (Kitzinger 1991a: 50).

Psychology emerged as a discipline at a time when the Protestant view that individuals could communicate directly with God, and so had respon-sibility for their own salvation, was reaching its zenith, when political ideologies argued for a society in which individuals were ruled less coercively and took more responsibility for their own governance, when the industrial revolution was radically changing the nature of employ-ment and family life, when reformers agitated for universal primary education. These and other developments produced urgent demands for new kinds of knowledge about individual citizens: what causes people to behave in certain ways, and how can behaviour be systematically changed? How can those with particular talents, strengths, deficiencies or disabilities be quickly and definitively identified? In place of philosophical introspection, psychology offered a *science* of human behaviour whose meticulous collection of detailed information under controlled conditions promised to reveal, categorise, explain and ultimately predict individual differences.

It has been argued that prioritising development of a technology of testing over development of a body of critical theory as its inaugural rationale may partly explain why psychology has had so much difficulty relating to the complex debates occurring within philosophy, sociology and literature, or even taking seriously the need to examine the implicit metaphysical bases of its own theories and practices (Harré 1993; Parker 1992). Whatever the reason, western psychology has participated very significantly in the *construction* of twentieth- century discourses[1] of gender but, until recently, shamefully little in their critique. What are the implications of this for its future contribution to a Caribbean analysis of gender ideologies?

Any answer to this question must keep in mind that psychological theories, more than those of any other discipline, have been, and still are, ubiquitously (mis)used by others – politicians, policy makers, journalists, management consultants, teacher trainers, social commentators, religious leaders, television script writers, authors of self-help manuals and many more. Therefore, however much Caribbean psychologists may wish to avoid them, simplistic and/or outdated versions of Eurocentric theorising will continue to be 'thrust upon them'. The challenge, then, is two-fold: not only to inspire a regionally theorised literature but to provide an *accessible* intellectual critique of this virtually unstoppable penetration of western psychological discourse into everyday life.

The Present: Some Key Issues for Consideration

I begin by considering some aspects of the contemporary debate on gender and related issues within psychology. Although I have used subheadings to structure the discussion, all sections are closely interrelated.

Individualism: Who turns out good, who turns out bad, and who is responsible

The *raison d'etre* of psychology[2] is to discover why and how people behave as they do. It continues to focus on the individual because most psychologists believe that not to do so 'would be to do sociology, or political theory – and we are psychologists, and this is our particular area of expertise'

(Kitzinger 1991b: 113). To maintain this disciplinary distinctiveness, psychology constructed the individual as a unitary rational actor, the determinants of behaviour being seen as located primarily within the person, and the surrounding historical and cultural context accorded only secondary importance (Olssen 1991). Such a perspective has and still has, profound consequences for its theoretical intentions and research methodologies.

Unlike their sociological and anthropological colleagues who sought out working-class neighbourhoods and remote villages, psychologists saw no need to venture far from home.[3] In ignorance or in arrogance, it was assumed that studies of undergraduates, and children living close to university campuses, would provide a sufficient basis on which to build developmental models applicable to all human societies. Eventual venturing further afield, however, did not discourage belief in these 'universals': if data from other groups failed to conform, or suggested progress along common developmental pathways at a slower rate, the most readily prescribed 'remedy' was a western education. The ongoing 'export of ideal childhoods' (Boyden 1990) in documents such as the UN Convention on the Rights of the Child enables this prescription to continue to flourish despite the critiques of sociologists, the efforts of left-wing political activists, and the not inconsiderable worldwide evidence of its costs in both personal and economic terms.[4]

In addition to supporting the global modernist status quo, the very particular accounts of 'childhood' and 'family life' in psychological discourse privileged the nuclear family and a particular middle-class version of 'mothering' over other environments for the production of well adjusted citizens. Although these accounts have varied somewhat over the years (for example, post-war threats of 'maternal deprivation' if mothers worked gave way to some extent to notions of working mothers providing 'quality time'), mainstream theory still operates to sustain gendered discourses of parental responsibility and to stigmatise those who fail to conform to normative familial arrangements (Burman 1991). In the Caribbean, neither the well documented demographic normality of non-nuclear family forms nor the relative lack of psychological family research has prevented significant penetration of these discourses into the social science literature. Consider the following account from Brathwaite and Cole (1978: 86) for example:

There is general agreement in the literature that "disorganised" family structure characterised by high rates of desertion, illegitimacy, single parent and mother centred households, common law unions, transient and often unstable visiting relationships, extensive inter-family conflict, male dominance, authoritarian child rearing practices and over protection of children are the most common features of family life among the lower class in the Caribbean.

More recently, Dann (1987: 5) prefaced his study of male sexuality with the observation that:

it is estimated that over three quarters of Barbadian males are born to unwed parents. Moreover, even in those cases where a relationship has been consummated in marriage, there is approximately a one in three chance that it will terminate in divorce. Thus, allowing for a 10 per cent remarriage rate, less than one in five Barbadian males have the benefit of being raised in a legally sanctioned two-parent home.

Delving further into specific problems of male gender role socialisation, he notes:

Furthermore, roughly 25 per cent of young Barbadian boys are raised by teenage mothers. Such a situation exposes mother and child to a number of additional health hazards. At the same time there is also a more serious psychological problem associated with inadequate socialisation. The young Barbadian male is therefore typically introduced to society by a woman who may have one or more boyfriends, depending on her economic circumstances. In many cases there is no father figure to whom he can relate or on whom he can pattern his life. In such an environment of maternal dependency he learns that matriarchal households, male absenteeism and outside affairs, are normal. For him they constitute an anticipatory role model for the formation of the self and for future expected behaviour. (Dann 1987:5).

Of course, not all discourses invoked in these passages derive exclusively from psychological theorising. 'Illegitimacy' is, primarily at least, one of many legal constructs contributing over the years to the proscription of family and gender relations in West Indian societies (Lazarus-Black 1994); problematisation of the common law union is equally grounded in religious tenets. But it behoves psychologists to ask: on what grounds are single-parent and mother-centred households designated 'disorganised', why is it wrong for men to see matriarchal households (if indeed this is what they are) as 'normal', and why is having a teenage mother essentialised as a physical and psychological health hazard for a small child? Equally in need of exposure and deconstruction[5] in this sociological prose are psychological notions that early childhood experience moulds a virtually unchangeable sense of 'self', that the permanent presence of the biological father in the boyhood home is the only secure route to healthy masculinity, and a general privileging of the discourse of (preferably lifelong) monogamous heterosexuality.

The work of French historian Michel Foucault has been particularly influential in prompting psychologists to reflect on the way their theories operate. Foucault argued that when powerful social institutions wish to reduce control by external force, they must ensure that people become more *self*-controlled. One way to do this is through the operation of strong pressures on individuals to be certain kinds of 'selves'. Social sciences can be viewed as part of this regime of control by regulating the ways people can experience and talk about self (e.g. Foucault 1977). Psychology wields power by defining what is normal, habitual and to be expected as opposed to what is exceptional and deviant (Wetherell and Potter 1992). The associated tendency to interpret social ills as psychologically derived creates a psychological subject who is given the full burden of responsibility for correcting his or her troubles (Sampson 1989). A major challenge for Caribbean psychology then, is to expose existing individualistic discourses which problematise certain value systems and lifestyle arrangements and to respectfully explore alternative validities.[6]

Decontextualisation: Hiding and Denying Power in Psychological Discourses of Gender

Western psychology embraced the scientific world-view that 'good knowledge is derived from a process that removes the knower from the things to be known in order to know them better as *they*, the objects, really are' (Sampson, 1993: 1225). Psychologists sought to objectify their studies to avoid the risk of their own personal experiences inappropriately influencing the collection or interpretation of data. They employed a neutral and personally-distanced language on the assumption this permitted a superior account of social reality than the experientially limited and biased everyday language of their 'subjects'. It was assumed, for example, that infinitely more valid, reliable and serviceable information about the unobservable cognitive and emotional states underpinning people's social attitudes would be obtained by using standardised scales comprising statements with which subjects agreed or disagreed than by allowing subjects to say or write anything they wanted.

For more than two decades mainstream psychology successfully marginalised Foucauldian and other analyses exposing the way such presumptions of 'objectivity' and 'neutrality' function to keep issues of power hidden (Kitzinger 1991b). The debate is gradually moving to centre stage, however, and this is especially true in respect of theorising and researching on gender.

Feminist writers have, over many years, forcefully exposed the eclectic androcentrism of psychological theories of child and adolescent (and later also adult) development. On the one hand, theories of, for example, cognitive, moral and personality development were essentially 'womanless', focusing on *boys'* preparation for adult roles and *men's* working lives as the standard blueprints (Bird 1991, Crawford and Maracek 1989). Such standards were often so sufficiently implicit (and absent) they were taken to be a neutral description of the way the world really is (see e.g. Brittan 1989; Sampson 1993). Disciplinary androcentrism was in fact so powerful that even early feminist attempts to redress theoretical imbalances, such as Horner's proposal that women did not 'fit' McClelland's model of achievement motivation because (unlike men) their socialisation rendered them prone to 'fear of success', can now be seen as in fact perpetuating many of them (Crawford and Maracek 1989).

On the other hand, theories which set out to explain how and why men and women developed *differently* typically defined the feminine only in some relation to the masculine: opposite or complementary, usually inferior. Thus the 'masculine' qualities of individualism, autonomy and rationality are held in greater esteem than 'feminine' qualities of cooperation, dependence and emotional sensitivity (see e.g. Hare-Mustin and Maracek 1990; Wilkinson 1986). Once again, early attempts to set the record straight were not entirely emancipatory: for example, Sandra Bem's proposal that the 'androgynous' person (one possessing both masculine and feminine traits) was able to cope more flexibly and effectively with the varying social demands of contemporary western societies than the person who possessed only 'masculine' or 'feminine' qualities still upheld the notion of a dichotomy which privileged masculinity (Oliver 1991).

Bem acknowledged this in her more recent work in which she describes three 'lenses of gender' – androcentrism, gender polarization, and biological essentialism – which shape how individuals perceive social reality (Bem 1993). Nevertheless, some feminists continue to criticise her for continuing to talk about gender using a discourse which fails to include class, ethnicity and other socially constructed differences. Some practical attempts to 'empower' women, such as self-defence or assertiveness training, have been similarly accused of ignoring other features of social reality, creating an illusory sense of competence and freedom of choice while leaving oppressive structural conditions unchanged and unchallenged (Kitzinger 1991b).[7] Moreover, the problem is not limited to the ways in which masculinity and femininity have been defined and dichotomised, but how male and female identities or roles are presumed to be *acquired.* Many writers (to date, sociologists more so than psychologists) have come to reject the dominant 'sex-role socialisation' model of 'static, preexisting sex role containers' into which all biological males and females are forced to fit (Kimmel 1987: 12). Such a model, it is argued, is not only ill-equipped to inform an analysis of complex everyday social interaction, but by encouraging decontextualised thinking about gender in isolation from its own or any other set of power relations reproduces the very problems it seeks to understand (Griffin and Wetherell 1992; Kimmel 1987; Ramazanoglu 1992).

Rhoda Reddock (1993) has suggested that Caribbean theorising has 'only' been attempting to integrate issues of gender with those of race and class since the 1980s, but by the mid 1990s there have still been few contributions from psychology. Another challenge, then, is to redeem this state of affairs – particularly, perhaps, to offer new ways to examine hegemonic masculinity and dominant discourses of femininity while at the same time exploring discursive heterogeneity more successfully (see Lewis 1994).

Disciplining Human Difference: The Prioritising of Sex/Gender Difference

As noted earlier, psychology emerged at a particular historical time to deal with particular social problems; as such its procedures can be legitimately conceptualised as 'techniques for the disciplining of human difference' (Rose 1989: 123). From the beginning, the reporting of sex differences[8] has been central to this process of classification and calibration: in developmental and social psychology it is rare to find studies in which data fail to be analysed in terms of this variable. Hyde (1994) describes the study of sex differences as a 'growth industry' which shows no sign of declining, since there is insatiable public as well as scientific interest in 'how men and women differ'.

Historically, the search for sex differences was closely aligned with male theorists' desire to understand 'woman's nature', men serving as the unmarked reference group (Hare-Mustin and Maracek 1994). Women, for example, were assumed to envy men their penises, but men would not envy women their breasts; women were judged 'less assertive' rather than men being considered 'overly assertive'. Feminist psychologists agree, and have convincingly argued the case, that most early work was used to justify beliefs and practices which oppressed women, and that such prejudices are still not entirely absent, even though they tend to be couched in less explicitly derogatory language. What they are less agreed upon is whether feminist psychology should contribute to this literature, providing better research to help expose existing inadequacy and bias, or strive instead to divert psychology away from its traditional preoccupations.

In the 1970s, the former view prevailed. There was a massive increase in work on sex differences, as feminists sought to demonstrate that bias in research design, together with a publication bias which favoured the publishing of studies showing significant sex differences over those which did not, had exaggerated the extent to which men and women differ at the expense of examining *within* group differences (Hyde 1994; Riger 1992). The prevailing expectation was that empirical research, when properly analysed to remove artifacts, would typically yield null findings or, at least, differences that could be described as trivially small, and so help to dispel damaging stereotypes about women (Eagly 1994, 1995). However, recent examination of the literature using the technique of meta-analysis (which explores group differences in empirical data in terms of effect sizes rather than measures of central tendency) claims instead to validate the existence of many sex differences which could have substantial, educational or interpersonal consequences (Eagly 1994, 1995). Social constructionists would wish to argue that, of course, that meta-analysis has only 'proved' the existence of statistically robust sex differences within sets of data which are for the most part conceptually flawed and inherently unsound. Nevertheless, there is also an awareness that the consequences of trying to minimise sex differences may be as damaging to women as attempts to maximise them, in as much as assertions of 'no difference' can serve to deny women possibilities for equitable treatment in situations where they have traditionally been discriminated against (Hare-Mustin and Maracek 1994).

Where to now? One way to reduce the salience of sex and gender differences may be to conduct research which examines as many dimensions of difference as possible because 'multiple comparisons reduce perfidious distinctions' (Unger 1992: 236). Alternatively, some post-structuralists argue that we should move away from the study of sex differences, not so much because of a fear of the answers, but a 'resistance to the question': that is, a desire to move away from the view of gender implicit in questions about male-female difference which holds that the categories 'man' and 'woman' are natural, self-evident, and unequivocal (Maracek 1995: 162). Others take the view that, since other psychologists *will* continue to write on sex differences it is as well for feminists to help to ensure that empirical work meets high standards, and that the efforts of sociobiology and evolutionary psychology, which view behavioural sex differences as arising primarily from the differing roles of women and men in reproduction (e.g. Buss 1995) continue to be challenged (Eagly 1994; Hyde 1994).

Methodological Hegemony and other Eurocentricities

At this point it is worth returning to issues of race and class. Since the 1970s the field of cross-cultural psychology has claimed to be dedicated to forcing the mainstream discipline to be more cautious and less naive in its generalisations (Smith and Bond 1993). But, as previously noted, eurocentrism is reflected in method as well as theory: use of standardised instruments and procedures in research not only imposes assumptions about what kinds of information are important but effectively precludes all other perspectives, silences all other voices. In the influential *Journal of Cross-Cultural Psychology* it is clear that some old habits die hard. In 1995 it published papers which 'compared identity formation' in Turkish and American adolescents using the EOM-EIS (Extended Objective Measure of Ego Identity Status), the FDMS (Family Decision-Making Scale) and the Rosenberg Self-Esteem Scale (Taylor and Oskay 1995), and which un-problematically concluded from statistical analysis of TST (Twenty Statements Test) data from Indian and American university students that 'culture had a far greater effect on self-concept than did gender' (Dhawan *et. al.* 1995: 614). The Caribbean was represented by a study of the racial attitudes of pre-school children which used a slightly modified version of (1940s US) procedures measuring preferences for playing with black and white dolls. With no apparent mind to existing critique of this methodology, the author reported the majority of her sample preferred to play with a white doll and from this drew what she considered the highly generalisable conclusion (given that children came from Jamaica, Trinidad, Grenada and Barbados) that, ' . . . in spite of the fact that the West Indies is composed of a majority black population, the impact of colonialism has left a debilitating effect on West Indians' (Gopaul-McNichol 1995: 141).[9]

Such studies are probably enough to lead colleagues in other disciplines to dismiss the possibility of psychology contributing anything of value to an understanding of social behaviour, let alone to a critique of Eurocentric hegemony in western social science. However, growing numbers of psychologists are also distancing themselves from this kind of research. Some have examined ways of eliminating racism from western psychology without abandoning it altogether for alternative models (Howitt and Owusu-Bempah 1994). Others argue the need for more radical reform: preferring the designation cultural psychology, to deliberately de-emphasise the practice of comparing disparate social groups using measures developed in only one or even none of them, they challenge the mainstream to stop treating race and ethnicity merely as an 'add-on' to the study of white, Anglo-American culture (e.g. Henwood 1994, Moghaddam 1990), and reject current notions of methodological 'objectivity' as completely unacceptable:

The clear message is that current forms of . . . psychological practice deny certain groups any possibility of being heard in their own way, on their own terms, reflecting their own interests and specificities, and that this condition does not reflect mere chance but rather reflects the operation of the power of those in charge to dictate the terms by which psychological and social reality will be encountered. (Sampson 1993: 1220).

However, Amina Mama has recently pointed out that even within the growing body of literature in black psychology problematic, Eurocentric and androcentic features persist. Thus, a discourse of racial inferiority is replaced by one of pathology (as typified by the Gopaul-McNichol study mentioned above), and the black subject is still unitary and essentially male (Mama 1995).

The Dangerous Project of Discovering 'The Truth'

Finally, as well as inspiring a substantial body of critical writing deconstructing psychology's contributions to various socio-political hegemonies, post-structuralist perspectives from other disciplines have also provoked an even more radical attack on traditional assumptions about the fundamental nature of psychological knowledge. Post-structuralist writers reject the possibility of absolute truth and objectivity and argue instead that psychology is about the *creation* of inherently unstable and transient knowledge amenable to a plurality of interpretations: 'talk is constitutive of the realities within which we live, rather than expressive of an earlier, discourse-independent reality' (Sampson 1993: 1221). Such a hypothesis does not mean that prediction has to be abandoned, rather that it cannot be based on the inevitable principle of causality alone (Eckensberger 1995). It does not preclude the *possibility* of research, but rather challenges empiricist assumptions that research taps into 'the truth' and that the progressive accumulation of data will eventually lead to disclosure of 'the whole truth' (Gergen 1994; Parker 1992). Potter and Wetherell (1987: 45) explain the implications of this perspective for the study of attitudes, for example:

The crucial assumption of attitude researchers is that there is something enduring within people which the scale is measuring – the attitude. Discourse analysis points to many difficulties with this. We need to ask, for instance, whether people filling in an attitude scale are performing a neutral act of describing or expressing an internal mental state, their attitude or whether they are engaged in producing a specific linguistic formulation tuned to the context at hand. For the discourse analytic perspective, given different purposes or a different context a very different "attitude" may be espoused. Put another way, if a certain attitude is expressed on one occasion it should not necessarily lead us to expect that the same attitude will be expressed on another.

Likewise, such an approach dismisses notions of a permanent individual 'self' to which the person (or the psychological researcher) can have ongoing access: 'Subjectivity can be seen, not as integrated and static, a preformed self with strategies unfolding or realized within discourse, but as fragmented and fluctuating, slipping between, and produced by, competing and contrasting discourses' (Burman 1992: 50-51).

Edward Sampson (1989: 2) has described the resistance of (particularly North American) psychology to modify its assumptions in light of these challenges as 'truly amazing', but for many psychologists this threat to the enduring 'truth' of their own knowledge and its role as gradual discoverer of the route to a productive, self-fulfilling life within a progressive modern society remain too terrifying to contemplate. On the other hand, some who have taken up the gauntlet have voiced difficulties with deconstruction in that, despite its ability to analyse hidden assumptions, it is a potentially endless process, inasmuch as any deconstruction can itself be deconstructed. Furthermore, some argue that feminist postmodernism seems to be denying the validity of the category 'woman' just at a time when women were beginning to be heard (Kitzinger 1994; Riger 1992). Nevertheless, post-structuralist and postmodernist challenges can no longer be ignored with quite the arrogance of the previous two decades, and researching and theorising about gender, for all its limitations, is positioned at the vanguard of the campaign to drag psychology into the postpositivist age.

The Way Forward: Future Possibilities

Scholars in disciplines with a longer history of critical self-reflection may find it hard to credit just how recently the above debates have entered mainstream consciousness within psychology. On the other hand, this state of affairs is clearly reflected in the virtual absence to date of psychological contributions to Caribbean theorising on gender. What has to happen if this situation is to be remedied?

Some Implications for Theory and Research

Notwithstanding the growing fervour, and somewhat improving status of the anti-essentialist and anti-universalist lobby, most protagonists do not, for one reason or another, currently advocate throwing the baby out with the bathwater. Some feminists argue, for example, that much feminist post-structuralist scholarship has been a mimicking of prestigious male-centred theory, inaccessible and alienating to the majority of women it purports to support and obscuring the material realities of women's oppression (Kitzinger 1991b). Others suggest that taking post-structuralist approaches too seriously can foster a dangerous delusion that modernity is over. Ian Parker (1992: 80) reflects that 'one problem with the turn to discourse is that we could lose sight of how bad psychology actually is, and the oppressive ways in which it operates when it is not just theorising but also practising on people'. In similar vein, Erica Burman (1992: 50) suggests that:

Regardless of how distasteful most current developmental models and theories are, there must be a place for developmental psychology, that can theorize how we can create, and can become, the people who could bring about and inhabit a very different world from the one we live in now however much we deconstruct, comment on, take apart, we are still, unlike the deconstructionists, committed to putting something in its place.

Stephanie Riger (1992) identifies two contemporary feminist alternatives to post-structuralism which she calls 'feminist empiricism' and 'feminist standpoint epistemologies'. The empiricists operate from the position that the problem in science is not objectivity per se, but rather its traditional *lack* of objectivity which allowed male bias to contaminate the scientific process. Their goal is therefore to produce gender-fair research using traditional scientific methods, on the assumption that a truly neutral science will produce unbiased knowledge, which in turn will serve as a basis for a more just social policy. Feminist empiricism considers the characteristics of the knower are irrelevant if the norms of science are properly followed. In contrast, feminist standpoint epistemologies claim that feminist psychologists should centre their science on women because what we know and how we know will be influenced by the researcher's position in the social hierarchy. Riger (1992: 737) concludes that the most important thing to keep in mind is that 'gender is something we enact, not an inner core or constellation of traits that we express; it is a pattern of social organization that structures the relations, especially the power relations, between women and men'. If this is taken as the core conceptualisation of gender, all three epistemological positions, despite their contradictions, can contribute to our exploration of it:

What is critical is that we are aware of the epistemological commitments – and value assumptions – we make when we adopt a particular research strategy . To assume that the multiple voices of women are not shaped by domination is to ignore social context and legitimate the status quo. On the other hand, to assume that women have no voice other than an echo of prevailing discourses is to deny them agency and, simultaneously, to repudiate the possibility of social change. The challenge to psychology is to link a vision of women's agency with an understanding of the shaping power of social context. (Riger 1992: 737-738)

One of the major implications of accepting this challenge is to reform the historically superior positioning of the researcher vis-à-vis the re-searched. This requires a willingness to respect and explore participants' perspectives without straightjacketing them within preconceived 'scientific' models; it demands modification of the language used to describe what happens when research is conducted:

To speak of people as "males" and "females", to write of "running subjects" in an experiment and so on is morally troublesome. It denigrates the men and women who give up their time to assist one in one's studies. It displays a contempt for them as people that I find quite unacceptable. I find it deeply disturbing that students are encouraged to adopt this scientist rhetoric. One can only hope that with the end of the old social psychology there will be an end to its attitudes to people as well. (Harré 1993: 28)

To date, Caribbean theorising of issues such as the social construction of masculinity and femininity, and the complexity of relationships between gender, class and race has been undertaken almost exclusively by historians and sociologists (e.g. Lewis 1994; Reddock 1993). Due in no small part to the lack, until very recently, of a complete undergraduate and graduate programme of study within the University of the West Indies (UWI), the existing body of psychological literature is relatively small and almost entirely empirical. No coherent regional critique of the dominant developmental and social psychological discourse has been attempted. Although a few research studies have abandoned rigorously 'objective' methodologies, the bulk of existing work comprises student theses (mostly in education) and other projects conceptualised within mainstream western frameworks (and sometimes rather outdated versions of them).

It seems to me that to 'catch up' with other disciplines, and be in a position to participate meaningfully in future theorising, Caribbean psychology must break away from its almost exclusive reliance on positivism and embrace some of the possibilities of social constructionism. The erstwhile limited history of the discipline in the region may turn out to be advantageous in that there may not be too much epistemological baggage to jettison. To exemplify what I see as the benefits of such a shift let me compare two recent papers which address a gender-related issue of long-standing interest in the Caribbean – namely black role models in North American television programming.

Merritt and Stroman report a quantitative study of the evolution of the portrayal of black families in which randomly selected episodes of several prime-time situation comedies were coded for imagery relating to black characters' role significance, dress, occupational status, competence and wealth, and how characters interacted with one another. They concluded that,

> . . . a more positive portrayal of black families is emerging . . . Black families have both husband and wife present; these spouses interact frequently, equally, and lovingly with each other; and children are treated with respect and taught achievement-oriented values. All of this takes place in an atmosphere that harbors little conflictual behavior. (Merritt & Stroman 1993: 497-498)

My problem with this study is that its methodology does not prompt, let alone require, any reflection on the designation of this particular version of black family life as more 'positive' than its predecessors. While there is perhaps no need to argue the desirability of a reduction in earlier racist stereotyping, why blacks should want to uncritically endorse this quintessentially white, middle-class discourse on the ideal upwardly mobile family is surely more contentious, and demands further elaboration. I would contrast this level of analysis with the following extract from Squire's discussion of the *Oprah Winfrey Show*:

> In common with the rest of television, the *Oprah Winfrey Show* is heterosexist. Openly lesbian or gay guests appear rarely, the show carefully established the heterosexuality of well-known guests, and when it addresses homosexuality directly it either tends to problematize it or to mainstream it as a human issue, distanced from sex and politics . Sometimes *Oprah* gives screen time to camp men who function briefly and conventionally as jesters. More of a challenge to dominant assumptions about sexuality is the show's marking of differences within heterosexuality, for instance the line it draws between abusive and non-abusive heterosexual relationships. This acknowledgment of plural heterosexualities coexists with the show's more traditional representations of sexual relationships between women and men either as always involving the same desires and social patterns, as in episodes along the lines of "Save Your Marriage" and "Best Husband Contest" or as infinitely various, as in "Men Who Married Their Divorced Wives" and "Women Who Married Their Stepsons" (Squire 1994: 71-72)

I would argue that Squire's approach offers a much better model for those who wish establish a critical research base with which to explore not only the rhetoric of media colonialism but sites of gendered rhetoric more generally. Issues that immediately come to mind, for example, are male 'marginalisation' (Miller 1986; Payne and Newton 1990), the problematisation of teenage pregnancy, and the various male discourses of affection and possession used to justify domestic violence. What I am saying is that although other disciplines may feel ready to forge ahead beyond empirical data gathering into more sophisticated theorising, there is a very real sense in which psychology has to get its empirical house in order first. Until we think more carefully and critically about what data to go looking for, and what assumptions we bring to their analysis, there will be few possibilities for theoretical progress.

Implications for, and of, the Teaching of Psychology

With the advent of the psychology major at UWI, the mid 1990s may prove a pivotal time for psychology in the Caribbean, and it seems important to make a few comments about the way it is *taught* as well as the way it is practised. It may be unreasonable to expect the UWI programme to take a purely, or even primarily, post-structuralist stance. Indeed, for reasons noted above it is arguably very necessary to expose students to the body of mainstream positivist literature on gender as, even if they choose not to accept it themselves, they are likely to encounter its various manifestations in many areas of their everyday lives. Nevertheless, one cannot help but be a little anxious that the main introductory text selected for this new programme contains statements such as the following:

For social and sexual experiences to be gratifying in adult life, one needs to develop an appropriate *gender identity* – that is, males need to think of themselves as males, and females as females. This development is quite complex and begins in the womb (Atkinson *et. al.* 1990: 388).

The crucial issue, however, is not so much whether such material is read, but whether students are taught to read it *critically,* since so little of the mainstream literature automatically encourages such an attitude of mind. If psychology in the Caribbean is to avoid being too much at odds with, for example, sociology or gender studies, the best way forward may well be to incorporate psychology into programmes of teaching and research which are multidisciplinary (Young 1988), or possibly even more fundamentally amalgamated.

It is also worth reflecting on the 'increased demand' for psychology which underwrote the case for the new degree programme. What do

Caribbean people want psychology *for*? To promote their *self*-understanding? To become 'experts' (school counsellors, clinical psychologists, assorted therapists) so they can 'fix up' others to produce a healthier, happier society (Burman 1994a; Olssen 1991)? Is there any guarantee that current developments will not in fact increase rather than decrease the hegemony of Eurocentric theories of human nature within regional discourse?

Conclusion: For Richer or for Poorer?

For many so-called 'developing' regions, becoming 'westernised' is as much about internalising western notions of human nature as it is about adopting fiscal and economic policies. There is some evidence that willingness to embrace a critical stance can transform psychology into an effective agent for *challenging* such 'developments' (see, for example, Burman's (1994b) report on feminist psychology in South Africa). On the other hand, uncritical promotion of the positivist knowledge base of western psychology can function to *sustain,* even *enhance*, hegemonic discourses of gender. The expansion of psychology within the University of the West Indies must be closely monitored: which paradigms flourish will determine not only the possibilities for future critical input into regional theorising of gender ideologies but also whether or not it undermines the efforts of scholars in other disciplines. It is to be fervently hoped that developments will be for richer rather than for poorer as psychology establishes its place within Caribbean social science.

Notes

1. I use 'discourse' to mean 'a particular language or communicative pattern with its own underpinning assumptions, in which its taken for granted meanings are grounded in a particular logic and system of values, and what is meant is contained as much in what is not said as what is' (Grundy & Hatton 1995: 8).
2. For the sake of brevity the general term 'psychology' is used although the paper relates primarily to its developmental and social sub-disciplines.
3. Unlike sociologists and anthropologists who have been castigated by radicals in their midst for studying down – Connell (in Wetherell and Griffin 1992: 157) describes this as 'the powerless and oppressed and carrying reports about them to the powerful' – psychologists have, for the most part, studied their own middle – and upper-middle – class kind. One can argue, however, that the outcomes for the powerless and oppressed have been much the same.
4. Bacchus (1980) provides a seminal critique of this issue from a Caribbean perspective.
5. Oliver (1991: 350) describes deconstruction as a process of critique which forces us to self-examine, to uncover ideologies and challenge the basis of their imposition: ' . . . not so much a matter of pointing out that the emperor has no clothes on, as it is of

systematically stripping him of his outer garments so that we can see the real colour of his underpants and how well they fit . . . The goal . . . [of deconstruction] is not to resolve or replace, but simply to explore the effects of disrupting an ideology, to change the perspective from 'either/or' to 'both/and' and observe the shifts in meaning.'

6. For example, MacCormack and Draper (1987: 154) suggest it may be useful to explore the premise that within Caribbean society 'parenthood may be more important for the man and woman as individuals than as members of a partnership'; McKenzie (1993) draws attention to the fact that increasing numbers of well educated and/or high-status West Indian women are making the deliberate choice to have children but remain unmarried.

7. Kitzinger observes that when feminist psychologists write about their own experiences of power and powerlessness in the work environment, their accounts are remarkably free of reference to internalised feelings and almost entirely focused on structural and political constraints.

8. Within the psychological literature 'gender' has often been used not as a cultural category through which distinctions between various groups are developed and maintained but as an intrapsychic variable virtually synonymous with 'sex' (Unger 1992).

9. One could hope for the Caribbean to be served by richer ethnographic research tapping into children's spontaneous racial discourse: see e.g. Holmes 1995, which *inter alia*, suggests that notions of ethnic difference are much less salient than those of gender in young children's conceptions of self and others.

11

Meditation on
'The Subject':
Rethinking Caring Labour

Nan Peacocke

> *When the night has come*
> *And the land is dark*
> *And the moon is the only light we see*
> *Oh I won't be afraid*
> *No I won't be afraid*
> *Just as long as you stand*
> *Stand by me*
>
> STAND BY ME: By Jerry Leiber, Mike Stoller, Ben E. King
> © (Renewed) Jerry Leiber Music, Mike Stoller Music.
> All rights reserved. Used by permission.

A writer may be applauded for pondering the nature of love, even in an academic text, even under a title such as 'Rethinking Caring Labour'. But what does a son who is bathing his old dad, or an old woman who is feeding her husband with a spoon have to say about the actions of love's subjects? We are not likely to know. Such occupation is essential to the quality of human life, and, the world being as it is, of little interest. The following highly personal reflection exalts the occupation of caring and the passions that motivate it out of all proportion to the humdrum misogyny with which reproductive labour is relegated or mawkishly sentimentalised in Caribbean culture. Drawing on journal entries and dreams, the narrative records my family's experience of caring for my father, who had Alzheimer's disease, during the last five years of his life. Introduced into the story are observations and theoretical angles which attempt to contextualise the experience. Positioning myself as a kind of advocate of female subjectivity, I find identity and power there, urging that men too enter the relational space bequeathed by socialisation to women as the subjects (i.e. conscious, thinking agents) of caring labour. Though recognising that the work of caring is culturally imposed on women, I nonetheless disavow my earlier held assumption of caring labour as essentially a byproduct of women's subordination, attribute motive and agency to caring labour and suggest a feminist understanding of the labouring subject as a possible doorway into rebellious consciousness. This essay was written out of a family tragedy. It is based on the course of the Alzheimer's condition which afflicted Max Peacocke and changed the lives of those who love him. I am a witness and one who cared for him. I got the nerve to write of my family's intensely private experience as though it were about world change from Selma James who wrote that some people 'tend to see great social movements in terms of their most intimate personal relationships not really a bad thing for anybody'.[1]

The Lazarus Passage

In your dream you and your brother are sitting on aluminum garden chairs on an open patio surrounded by a red brick building. His head is down. You notice the grass between the concrete flagstones. Someone had imprinted the decorative patterns of breadfruit leaves and travellers palm into the cement. Your brother's tears splash on the flagstone but he makes no sound. You look up at white mesh curtains stirring in the open windows. The atmosphere is fresh and pleasant, yet there is a sterility about the place. It is an institution. You remember. Your father has died. Your brother has come for the funeral. But there is something else, you feel something hurting intensely but can't recall. This place was your father's home, but not yours. The nurse who cared for him appears in her white uniform. Then you remember why he had to be there. Your brother's emotion is acute. The nurse, smiling, beckons you into the building. The stairs are easy to climb, the place, after all, is designed for old people. You see his supine figure and bearded profile. But your father is not dead anymore. His beautiful head turns in recognition, he sits up and greets you. You feel an incredible joy. Your father can walk again and the four of you go back down the stairs to the patio where the old man plays with a number of cats, dogs and large birds who have appeared, apparently to mark his return. Your brother, the nurse and you discuss the matter. She explains that he still has the disease and will deteriorate. The joy you feel vanishes. Your brother will go away again and you will have to take care of your father. The weariness of years awaits you.

'A mother does not always get up in the middle of the night to tend a crying child out of altruism or affection; sometimes she gets up simply because she takes it to be her responsibility' (Julie Nelson).[2]

The area between domestic labour done for wages and caring labour is difficult to define. At the material level, the distinction can be made on the basis of whether the labour done is waged or unwaged. But this does not mean, for example, a poorly paid servant or dependent relative whose labour is exploited in the household, does not come to 'care' and begin to do caring labour. At the non-material level, the distinctive characteristic of caring labour is that it is done, or not done, *at will* and is therefore related to motive on the part of the doer. Again, a qualification must be made since caring labour is sometimes done out of a sense of obligation, and situations develop that test the will of the doer. Therefore, even when we attempt to define the distinction between domestic labour done for wages and caring labour we find ourselves in a paradox because the concepts neither match nor are mutually exclusive.

It could be that the standard we have at present for valuing either of these forms of labour necessarily undervalues that labour.[3] It could be that the revolutionary potential of efforts to value the economic weight of a woman's work is not that the status quo will some day bend to take her measure, but that the status quo will be brought down by the human longing to rebel against the confinement of cultures whose technologies produce concepts of labour as the work of beasts, slaves, machines and women. Perhaps the concept of caring labour, including the domestic work it requires, can only be fully understood through a metaphysical treatment: that is by knowing more of the human mind and its relations to the external world. For it is in this disregarded labour that the daily renewal of one's being for physical, intellectual and spiritual existence is done.

Recollection

Framed against the black interior of a doorway, a smiling man welcomes his newborn child. He is standing, fixed in time, on the wooden steps of a nursing home in Kitty.[4] Behind him a midwife with a worn smile, leans against the upright, still in her limp white uniform. The man, Max, holds the baby's head the way a woman holds a compact mirror when powdering her nose, cupped in his left hand. The baby's spine fits along the length of his left forearm over which cascades the infant's long lace hem. The child's eyes are closed, yet the inclination of the head toward its father suggests curiosity, engagement, anticipation.

This greeting, as it seems to be, was recorded for posterity by my mother, Nora, in a photograph album long since lost, and I had forgotten it. But one day, I recalled in detail that black and white image. It was perhaps two years ago, I was holding my father close so that my mouth would be near his ear. This way I could pour a verbal concoction of jingles, prayers and prattle down his uncomprehending but eager ear, and hope for a sound (a laugh was pure bliss) in reply. We posed an absurd Janus; he, facing a future he could not create or even witness, me, reciting the evidence of his past (his profession, the names of his grandchildren) as a kind of offering. Then the photograph appeared, held up beside us in my memory's hand. It were as though our figures, still fixed in their individual poses, had become separated by the action of the shutter and in the course of forty-five years had moved in spirit silence across black time, not meeting but in proximity. Now the figures were at the moment of passing, like the opposite and parallel motion of an Indian dancer's hands. In this protracted present a way of acknowledgement must once again be found along our separate traverse through eternity.

Perhaps the paraphernalia of human life, its sound, ceaseless motion and infinite arrangement is a collective design by the body of humanity, a kind of quantum distraction, intended to extend the present for as long as we can. How this could be I cannot say, but I've come to see even the lumpenness and gore of dying as the body's willing of the present to stay. Even when a person loses his memory, the body, determined as a woman who's changed her mind, follows the wanderer around the neighbourhood until someone finds the person and brings him home safely to his wife. Even when a sick person wants to go off with death, the body, mother of the mind, acts as if she knows what's best, holding the person back into life, expelling piss and puke just as she did for the person as a healthy baby. Even when an old, broken-up person, leaning over like a tree hit by a hurricane and held upright by straps, cries out 'I should be dead!' the body, housekeeper of the space where the spirit is housed, carries on, sweeping air into shattered lungs, thumping the heart's dough.

A body inhabits the present utterly, thinking, doing. Even when sleeping, a body is occupied in ceaseless labour. A man with Alzheimer's will say to his daughter, over and over again, 'I don't know what to do. It's horrible, horrible.' In the earlier stages, my father knew that he was losing his cognition. He just couldn't think how to do things and 'how' is the essence of occupation. He made this observation after an incident in which he was unable to set the table for breakfast. The simple actions of placing mats on a surface were beyond the ability of a man who had built houses, worked on a theory of prime numbers, and knew his way around the Orinoco basin with a compass. I found him crying with his mats askew.

My five-year journey as caretaker – next to wifedom and motherhood, the quintessence of socially approved womanhood – deepened my self-awareness. Once I thought myself to be politically progressive, historically conscious of my location in the colour, class and gender schema of the society I inhabit. Once I was more confident of the possibility of transforming social institutions. From where I stood (at some distance) it seemed, for example, that the historic recycling of poorly paid domestic work through generations of (in the Caribbean, black) women in poverty was an injustice which could be redressed through a political process demanding that women's work be valued. Now I think this is a simplification, indeed, a conceit, only someone who had never been a 'domesticant' would strut.

Paradoxically, I came to review the notions I had internalised about the nature of 'love's labour' which I once associated with female domestic servitude, or, worse, pure altruism. On reflection, by avoiding any self-identity with women's caring work, I was not only consciously protecting myself from exploitation but, aware that through socialisation women come to identify with an oppressed 'femininity', I was rejecting the pressure of my socialisation to find merit in the work done by the socially weaker gender. Yet I believed my politics to be feminist, never questioning the assumption that woman's work is imposed and that in holding that deeply gendered assumption I too undervalued my caring labour.

Now I see things differently. My labour, my mother's, my brother's, the labour and the products of labour of the many friends and relations who worked their time and material support into the management of Alzheimer's and, most astonishing, the labour done by Max himself was work of the most creative, political, artistic and spiritual nature: the making of human direction.

Why is M. using things for a purpose they weren't made for?
(Diary: August 20, 1983)

The cause of the malady, senile dementia of the Alzheimer type, is still unknown. For some reason pathological changes occur in the brain tissue. Nerve cells in the cerebral cortex having to do with memory, learning and judgement begin a progressive deterioration taking on physical changes. Dense groupings of hairlike fibrils and microscopic plaques composed of degenerated nerve extensions clustered around the protein substance, beta amyloid, appear in tissue samples. Associated with the formation of these 'senile plaques and fibrillary tangles'[5] is a massive decrease in levels of acetylchlorine, the chemical used by cells for neurotransmission. Earlier this century Alois Alzheimer, a German clinician interested in nervous and mental diseases (Nuland 1994: 111), published a paper on the case of a fifty-one year old woman who, having displayed symptoms of dementia (failure of memory, paranoia, loss of reasoning powers, incomprehension, stupor) was admitted to a psychiatric hospital where she died four years later, her legs drawn up in the foetal position often assumed by sufferers. The autopsy Alzheimer performed showed that: 'Between one quarter and one third of his patient's cortical cells either contained fibrils or had disappeared entirely' (Nuland 1994: 112). That was in 1907, four years before my father was born, he died on August 24, 1995. There has been progress on the care of patients in the last two decades (Nuland 1994: 115) and in the last two years the gene responsible for the early onset of Alzheimer's has been identified[6] yet: 'We know not a whit more about what might cure it than we do about what might cause it' (Nuland 1994: 91).

'I think, therefore I am' said Descartes to the pope. Well, even when a person can no longer think, as we understand thinking to be, s/he still *is* subject. Max too addressed the divine, on one of the (growing rarer) occasions when a sentence broke through: 'Mother Mary Oh God, if you're there, if you exist at all, I don't understand this!'

When the horror of what my father was going through was fully upon us, our family read everything we could find about Alzheimer's, and I can testify that information is power. On a metaphysical level I recall two statements which stayed with me like a mantra. One was, 'Few tragedies are more expensive' (Nuland 1994: 105) and another, 'If you look at love long enough you will become lovely.'[7] In contributing to this text I want to convey the meaning I found in labour consciously done by a female subject, hoping to demonstrate the female agency guiding the experience throughout and the value of feminine subjectivity to the interpretation of values. I also try to discern within these very personal boundaries (quite deliberately subjective) signs of the relational architecture underlying all human occupation, to look more deeply, to look beyond the gender coding which obscures women's social motives.

Nearly midnight. A hard one. Max eventually calmed down, gave us each 'a thousand kisses' and fell asleep. Nora and I had a stiff drink together and laughed at life before bed; we'd been on mopping up operations for two hours. We think Bush and the rest should be made to fight in the real 'mother of all wars', this one. (Diary November, 1991)

Caring for Max with Nora politicised me in a new way. I understand better that political consciousness comes profoundly during a process that moves the subject to the site of disempowered activity. I came to understand better, for example, how the present limitations of the women's movement in the Caribbean have to do with the failure to reproduce politically the purpose of feminist activism (women as subject) in a wider range of race and class locations.[8] This is true both in organisation and theory, as women working in multi-class collectives (in the Caribbean, Sistren Theatre Collective and Red Thread, for example) have shown.

My family's efforts to know more about Alzheimer's also informed us more about people's politics in the coming century: consumerism (of which politicised caring is a growing movement). While the physiology of the illness is not yet understood, there has been a minor revolution in the way people organise about it. In his candid, compassionate book, *How We Die*, Sherwin B. Nuland (1994) observes 'the way biomedical culture has evolved in the last third of the 20th century'. Here he refers to a combination of science, government involvement and consumer advocacy which is changing the politics of aging in the USA. He illustrates this confluence with the following example: A scientific consensus at a 1970 conference (Nuland 1994: 114) on Alzheimer's established that the distinction then being made between pre-senile and senile forms of the disease was 'not only erroneous but misleading'. *Alzheimer's pre-senile dementia* gave way to the more accurate discriptor, *senile dementia of the Alzheimer type* which has the same pathology irrespective of age. This change opened the door for a large lay population of older people with the disease and their families to make demands which in turn strengthened requests from the scientific community for research financing. 'In the United States this meant the involvement of the National Institutes of Health . . . The creation of the National Institute on Aging was the natural outgrowth of this process' (Nuland 1994: 114).

Perhaps the most profound change effected by the experience of Alzheimer's in industrialised countries is the awareness (even on the part of clinicians) of the necessity for support for those who do its caring labour: 'there is probably no disability of our time in which the presence of support groups can help so decisively to ensure the emotional survival of the closest witnesses to the disintegration' (Nuland 1994: 106). Given that the World Health Organisation (WHO) has identified Alzheimer-like disease as a leading cause of death, Caribbean people will be getting to know more of this illness. 'In terms of emotional damage, of neglect of personal goals and responsibilities, of disturbed relationships, and obviously of financial resources, the toll is unbearably high' (Nuland 1994: 105).

In the Caribbean, the global effect of political organising among elderly people is evident in some areas such as reduced bank charges and bus fares. Disabled people in the region are occasionally being shown some consideration in building codes mandating wheelchair access and elevators. Meanwhile the public is aware that the Cancer Society, Alcoholics Anonymous and many other voluntary organisations have quietly gone about caring work for decades. People with (and people caring for people with) disability and illness may find it necessary to become more vocal as public health standards are economically 'adjusted' to decline. Short of the wholesale extermination of the old, poor and ill by 'market forces', we can predict the political influence of elderly and disabled people in the Caribbean community will intensify in the coming century. Particularly when the link between ecological deterioration and the demographics of illness is asserted, the quality of life in this region will depend on how intelligently our aging population, and our young, mediate political innovation with the values of caring.

I use Nancy Folbre's definition of caring labour as 'labour undertaken out of affection or a sense of responsibility for other people, with no expectation of immediate pecuniary reward' (Folbre 1995: 75). This definition, like an inverted funnel, begins with the individual, raises the question of motive and then widens the concept of self-interest to a range of possibilities which appear to be arrayed outside of, but in reality are not separate from, the (caring) individual. Identity and self interest in the lived experience of caring are not traditionally represented in theory. A girl grows up learning to live with and to manoeuvre around her lot in the world as one of the 'less socially powerful sex' (James 1983: 15). Yet it is often the *self-positioning* of (notice I did not say *response* of) women, when life presents a crisis, to 'feel responsible' and to act in ways to influence the outcome. If '[c]aring seems to involve taking the concerns and needs of others as a basis for action' (Joan Tronto quoted in Folbre 1995: 74) the question is, why is it done mainly by women?

Too many damn women in the place.' Max, commenting on the over- representation of those carers.

Preliminary findings by Janet Brown and Barry Chevannes (1995) in their study on gender socialisation in the Caribbean[9] tell us that 'gender distinctions and assumptions were central to most child rearing practices. This was revealed in the way domestic chores were assigned, the types of leisure activities that were allowed, discipline meted out and physical affection shown'. The research is particularly telling 'because of its qualitative approach and community participation in looking at the input to children which shape the men and women of the future'. And what is that future? According to the findings, 'Men in the Caribbean measure their "manhood" in terms of proven and prolific sexual activity with women, their ability to provide financially for the family and the authority they wield over women and offspring.'

In the Caribbean, then, it seems that male socialisation tends to affirm men in controlling behaviour and alienate men from relational consciousness and practice. The socialisation of girls, while it prepares the evolving female person for domesticated (controlled) status, also provides her with a wider emotional reference and canniness in situations (such as family crisis and economic adjustment) in which both individual men and women have less control over depleting resources. To put it another way, Caribbean manhood, as it is conventionally defined, is coded as subject activity but renders men immobile or worse in a world where more and more they require, in Chodorow's words, 'a less bounded, less oppositional sense of self' (Folbre 1995: 81) in order to survive and participate in loving. 'Fluidity and discontinuity are central to the reality in which we live. Women have always lived discontinuous and contingent lives, but men today are newly vulnerable, which turns women's traditional adaptations into a resource.'[10]

D. is mad at his sister. She asked him to help her with something and, I think because he couldn't help, he felt badly. Instead of saying that, he got bitter. 'I work all day. And when I come home, I have no wife or woman to wash my clothes and cook for me. I haffe do it.' From what I can see he does really hard physical labour for not much money. But his pain seems to do with the humiliation of housework not the fact that he is exploited in the work place (Diary: October 18, 1995).

Women's work (whoever does it) is the work *not done by* those who have the social or, in the case of very wealthy women, the economic power to refuse it. History shows that women's participation in waged labour does not automatically bring with it any change in the sexual division of labour in the home. However, the revolution in technology is reshaping social organisation and that has implications for the concept of labour. For one thing there is now a fourth factor of production that must be added to the analysis of 'land, labour and capital'. This factor dislodges the conceptualisation of labour as 'object'.[11] When knowledge and intelligence are understood as the creation of common labour (the body's occupation), and that information is of the same fabric as re/production we will know that '[p]recisely because it focusses on motives, caring labour can apply to both men and women, the market and the family, production and reproduction' (Folbre 1995: 76).

Alzheimer's presented me with the irrevocable and forced me to confront the distinction between the subject and the ego. The guiding world myth of the past century has been the American dream of personal acquisition. It has got to the stage where we are buying the notion (and paying a lot for it too) that the self can be reshaped by acquiring the right products, lifestyles, mentors, and so on. The problem is that this approach reduces experience to its narcissistic dimension which may be innate but is only partial and in isolation cannot be an ethos for the survival of the self or the community. Preoccupied with finding identity in what we can get, we can't escape the corollary, an attachment to the fear of what we may lose. This is not a statement against the individualism of our culture. Creole culture is inherently individualist, its artistic forms celebrate the moments when a thousand influences become fused in the particular features or 'version'[12] of West Indian civilisation. It is a fact of our history that competitiveness, material acquisition, individuated self-interest, are part of the landscape of survival. But I think in our tendency to favour (for both sexes) characteristics which are coded as masculine, together with our tendency to sentimentalise hardship and the strong, silent, black mother, we are not politically conscious of 'the active role of women's agency'[13] or 'the importance of obligation as a moral category' (Sen quoted in Folbre 1995: 77) in building this civilisation.

I would rather be there when the Windies conquer Australia than scaling fish at the sink. These things are not comparable. But it's time for Caribbean social activism to think through how values created for the practice of caring differ from values created for the practice of acquisition. A people need both: to acquire (success, dignity, wealth) and we need to comprehend that our ambivalence about and sentimentalising of women's social role as caretaker generates antagonism. I refer to the economic cost of the devaluation of that role, to the human cost exacted from those whose labour props up a social design which discriminates against reproductive labour and rewards material production for acquisition and not for caring, and to the psychic anxiety associated with gender hierarchy. When the effects of this discrimination are contextualised in households, communities, and, in the case of the Caribbean, states, we begin to see the extent of the damage our civilisation is sustaining for lack of a broad politicising of caring by self-motivating agents.

'Blow down to the sea and die!' Max, his arms lifted, called out to a white bird he saw floating on the breeze beneath us toward Young Island. (Diary: March 1991)

I didn't really notice my parents aging. I suppose I didn't want to see. I had been away from the Caribbean for sixteen months. When, on what I'd intended to be a quick visit home (St Vincent) I saw my father's deterioration and my mother's determination not to see it, it wasn't just that I couldn't turn away and get on with my life – every force in my being flew to their side. But also, I somehow knew what to do, not all at once, but I knew I must create the circumstances in which we could be together. This was not out of altruism, duty, or my love, or theirs for me, it was what I had to do to continue being myself.

Y. once called me a 'dutiful daughter'. Oui, that hurt. Z. (dispensing pop psychology) says I'm 'acting like a wife'. To hell with that! H. says Nanny is Ni too!14 Ni will teach me to angle my bottom and bounce back the cliches. She tells me straight, 'You are fighting a private war against despair. Don't let those who do not understand what you are doing rattle your nerve.' Like P. says, 'You're doing the right thing.' Like W. says 'You're doing the thing right!' Like Christophine15 says, 'Have spunks!' Yea! (Diary: June, 1992)

I had to relearn myself as subject in this new place. A woman who was myself but, until then, obscured. One as old as the hills, but suddenly born to my recognition, capable of more than I knew myself to be. The hardest part for me was not learning this new occupation, after all I was socialised for that, it was learning to live with a new contradiction between the sense of defiance with which I was suddenly armed, the power of empathy to which I was joined in living, and what I deduced I saw in the eyes of the world when it looked at me: Cinderella without a prince, an aging daughter, the assumption of my role as unfortunate, a waste of my abilities, passive. Overwhelmed, I took the opposite position. It seemed at first that what I had fondly called my life up till then was rendered worthless by what was happening. All the time I was busy making plans, that disease, with a terrible, unrelenting logic, lived quietly aside. One day the implacable logic uncoiled in my path, poured fire over me and devoured me. The fact that no one knows why Alzheimer's happens does not reduce its impact. It is simply there, dispensing havoc. I chose then to begin my comprehension of the thing we do not speak of, the thing we do not see.

We must have death, but young, present, ferocious, fresh death, the death of the day, today's death. The one that comes right up to us so suddenly we don't have time to avoid it, I mean to avoid feeling its breath touching us. Ha! (Helene Cixous)[16]

At first I looked desperately for meaning in what was happening. Meaning would displace the anticipation of dread, the 'horrible, horrible' refrain, the appetite of the illness for my family. At this early stage, even awake, pictures flashed across my mind: pictures of a woman treading water in a vast ocean, pictures of raging rivers; and at night dreams of crumbling mountain chains. I tried by sheer will to 'hold things together'. But it was Nora, my mother who gave me the first clue of other possibilities. Recognising quickly (quickly was her way) that futility can't be stared down, she regrouped. Absorbing the changed reality, she changed her orientation toward Max from one who held her own in the battle of the sexes to one who must learn the emotion of pity for one's equal. Observing my mother learn I came to understand that it was not my father's annihilation I was witnessing, in time he gained in confidence and would make his own way through. The existing self of each of us, the subjects of experience, were being metamorphosed into consciousness. Over time the minute and particular features of this experience caused me somehow to imagine a future in which our society would be more acquainted with the dignity of our monsters: aging, disability, illness and indeed death.

She loves him and he responds. (Carolle Bourne, Nora's niece)

On Christmas day, 1991 a friend, known for his direct manner, helping Nora and Max across the street, expressed his admiration in the immortal words, 'Women are fucking heroes, man!' True. I saw Hercules, when I witnessed my mother's determined figure writing her newspaper column, but also when I saw her swept away by disappointment and the dread of a failed life. I saw Demeter when we walked together into Hades to fetch my father from chaos and bring him home. But this heroism is not remarkable because it leads to a particular destination – the golden fleece, the happy home, the conquest of fear – but because it has the quality of a continuing miracle. Making and remaking, redoing what has been undone – ingredients as common as bread and fish.

He's my friend. (Nora)

I am claiming a female quality to the orchestration of these events because the nature of Max's care involved repetitive domestic tasks, and women did them for the most part. The men, too, who cared for Max: my brother, the young male nurse in the nursing home, his men friends who came to visit, behaved in ways one associates with women: chatting, touching, kissing, spoon feeding, sometimes crying. The care of Alzheimer's requires routine. Routine is the maximum weapon against the disorientation the person feels ('I'm frightened, I'm frightened'). I believe we were all acting on a kind of interior knowledge that women possess based on the practice of millennia. Hundreds of thousands of caring acts were being drawn together under a single guiding motive: to have Max feel safe again. When the sum of all our actions were *intended* to serve this purpose the repetition of menial tasks took on another dimension.

Why do women think of safety in these terms? Some men will tell you they feel safer with a gun in the house. Women are more likely to argue that the children will get hold of it and be hurt. A woman's preoccupation with safety is so present, her acquaintance with fear so immediate, that she can empathise with someone else's need for safety without hesitation. Perhaps women's admission of their vulnerability to violence in its many manifestations creates cultural forms which have a value of their own. The situation with which Nora and I were faced could be countered with caring and with nothing else.

Hang on to the knowledge (that it was) possible for Max to feel loved right up to the end of his life in the same way that he and Nora made us feel loved. They will never really be gone from us because they did so much to make us what we are. (Alison Parchment, Nora's niece, fragment of a letter to Nan: August 28, 1995)

The tidal wave passage

In your dream you are at the seaside with your mother and younger brother. Life shimmers in this landscape for this is a dream and there is no garbage. Glinting blues and green volcanic peglegs, pastel sand hues and the reef's black crinolines discernable off the coast. Behind you in their hilly, familiar habitats, one hundred thousand species of incredible beauty keep 'nuff noise. To the east a stream arrives at the sea after a short, uneventful journey down the small shoulder of the island. You are standing back in the cool observing your mother and her boy child by the waterline. You hear your brother's childish shrieks of joy, his body is in constant motion. You feel your mother's contentment, as warm as the sun on their limbs. Something is unusual about your brother's body. It is not the type you know to be his, solid and chunky, the type that will grow into a man of six feet. Instead, your scrutiny reveals this is the body of a smaller, wiry boy. It is the body of your father when he was four. Your father has become your brother.

Strangely the argumentative landscape falls silent. You don't know why yet, but you have received a warning of harm. Even the rocks seem alert to something dated in their carbon recesses. Then on the horizon you see a wall of water. You, the woman, the child on the beach, all things bright and beautiful, are, like the rocks, transfixed with comprehension: the magnitude of the wave is as certain as our impending obliteration. Terror sweeps over you like a phantom wave. You rehearse your destruction in your dream's dream; the water's roaring weight, coralbone, wing, leaf and limb churn like the Red Sea scene in de Mille's classic. Somehow feeling returns to your legs and you can run down to the beach to get to them, to get to them, to get to them. Your mother has got her child. His legs and arms are wrapped around her waist and neck and she is running toward you. The phantom, fear has not killed you. The wave that's still coming can, but there is a chance. You are together, dreaming of safety, and you can run together and you do; up the river course trying to get higher, away from harm. You may, you may not; but you are together and you call to one another as you run, you run. You shout to one another. Its the same as shouting to yourself, but there are more of you, heading upland looking for a way. Bamboo leaves streak your wet faces as you make your way up the riverbank, away from here with the child, into another dream.

Notes

1. Selma James, *The Ladies and the Mammies: Jane Austen and Jean Rhys*, (Bristol: Falling Wall Press, 1983) p. 15.
2. Julie Nelson quoted in Nancy Folbre 'Holding Hands At Midnight: The Paradox of Caring Labour', *Feminist Economics* 1:1 (1995) p. 77.
3. *Woman Speak!* Nos. 26 & 27 (1990) 'Working Hands: Caribbean Women Organising' Andaiye (ed). The International Wages for Housework Campaign was founded in Britain in 1972. Mainly through the National Union of Domestic Employees in Trinidad and Tobago, the wages campaign has had an historic, if unrecognised, influence on women and development and feminist thinking in the Caribbean.
4. Georgetown, Guyana.
5. Sherwin B. Nuland, *How We Die: Reflections on Life's Final Chapter* (New York: Alfred Knopf, 1994) p. 113.
6. Charles Siebert, 'The DNA We've Been Dealt' *The Weekend Guardian* November 24, 1995
7. A quotation by Earnest Holmes, *Creative Thought* (Spokane: Religious Science International, 1995)
8. Joan French and Honor Ford Smith, Sistren Research 'Women, Work and Organisation in Jamaica 1900 to 1944' unpublished manuscript.
9. Caribbean News Agency (CANA) *Barbados Advocate*, October 29, 1995. News release on a Joint Research Project by the Caribbean Child Development Centre and the Department of Sociology, University of the West Indies funded by UNICEF. It appears that while our socialisation is effective we are not happy with it: 'The researchers found that man/woman relations across the region were characterised by a high degree of distrust and disillusionment and reflected the outcome of socialisation patterns common on raising the children who become the men and women in later relationships.'
10. Mary Catherine Bateson, *Composing A Life* (New York: Plume, 1990) p. 13.
11. In traditional Marxist theory 'commodity fetishism (O-S-O) causes us to perceive society as a system of objects and objective laws that prevail over and against all our intersubjective relations (S-O-S; S-S; S-s-S)' see Patricia Jagentowicz Mills 'Marx, Dialectics and The Question of Woman' in *Feminist Interpretations of Karl Marx*, Christine di Stefano (ed) The Pennsylvania State Press (forthcoming). As Adorno points out the subject is the object's agent, not its constituent see Theodor W. Adono *Subject and Object* in *The Essential Frankfurt School Reader*, A. Arato and E. Gebhardt eds (New York: Urizen Books, 1978) p. 506.
12. Evelyn O'Callaghan, *Woman Version: Theoretical Approaches to West Indian Fiction By Women*, Warwick University Caribbean Studies, (London: MacMillan, 1993) p. 10.
13. Amaryta Sen, 'Agency and Well-being: The Development Agenda' in *A Commitment to the World's Women: Perspectives on Development, Beijing and Beyond* Noeleen Heyzer (ed) with Sushma Kapoor and Joanne Sandler. (UNIFEM, 1995).
14. Sistren with Honor Ford Smith *Lionheart Gal: Life Stories of Jamaican Women* (1987), Sistren Introduction 'The stories explore two opposing images of the black woman, which coexist in the psyche of Caribbean women: the image of the warrior woman as typified by Ni (Nanny), the Maroon leader of the eighteenth century, and the image of the nanny, the domesticated servant woman.' p. 1.
15. Christophine is a character in Jean Rhys' novel, *Wide Sargasso Sea* (London: Andre Deutsch, 1966).
16. Helene Cixous, *Three Steps on the Ladder of Writing*, (New York, Chichester, West Sussex: Colombia University Press) p. 15.

12

Feminisms and Educational Research and Understandings:
The State of the Art in the Caribbean

Barbara Bailey

Introduction

Formal education has always been a central concern of all civilisations and cultures, playing an important role in the lives of people; and the school has been regarded as the social institution charged with the responsibility for this education through which the cultural heritage is transmitted and successive generations are prepared for life in the adult world of these societies. It is now recognised, however, that in the process of schooling a number of interrelated factors and mechanisms interact to produce asymmetrical outcomes for groups in the system which differ along social class, sex and ethnicity lines in ways which serve to protect the interests of the ruling classes and races, maintain dominant patriarchal ideology and so reproduce classed and gendered societies.

Over the past three to four decades, educational sociologists and feminist educators, mainly from North America, have attempted to situate education in a cultural and political context and have examined how these mechanisms operate to create unequal dynamics of power, control and influence. As a result of the research work of feminists who seek understanding of educational inequalities on the basis of principles associated with the three major strands of feminism – liberal, socialist and radical – three major sets of competing theories have evolved to explain this differential effect of schooling on students and particularly the negative impact on girls. The views of postmodernist and post-structuralist feminists on educational research and understanding are emergent and yet to be clearly defined. There is therefore limited literature on which to draw in relation to this group. Nonetheless, what is apparent, is that adherents to these 'camps' differ among themselves in terms of:

(a) their assumptions and therefore the tenets advanced to explain sexual inequalities in education;

(b) their research perspectives and methodological approaches;

(c) the concepts utilised in the research discourse; and,

(d) the solutions and strategies advocated to redress the situation.

Over the same period, individuals in the Caribbean, some of whom can be regarded as feminist, that is, they are 'aware of the oppression, exploitation and/or subordination of women within society' and see the need for 'conscious action to change and transform the situation' (Reddock 1988: 53), have also been involved in research on gender-based asymmetries in education. In most instances, however, no explicit link has been made between this educational research agenda, feminist theory and the feminist educational research paradigms emanating from North America.

The central concern of this paper will be to review literature in which these theories are enunciated and at the same time to locate the themes of regional research initiatives within the framework of these paradigms. Although other sources are included in the analysis, particular reference is made to papers presented at a 'Gender and Education' seminar held in 1989 under the auspices of the then Centre for Women and Development Studies of the University of the West Indies and the Faculty of Education, Mona. It is recognised and acknowledged that the quality and depth of the papers included in the review vary. The intention, however, is not to do a comprehensive critique of the papers but to identify the research theme that each addresses and to locate these themes within the framework of the feminist educational research paradigms. The major aim is to identify gaps in regional research efforts and therefore directions for further work in the area of feminist research and understandings in education in the Caribbean region.

Educational Feminisms

The basic assumption undergirding the position taken by *liberal feminists* is the notion that social systems are essentially just. Deviations from desirable conditions for women and the main cause of related social and sexual inequalities, in areas such as education, are therefore seen to be due to a lack of information and ignorance about the problems women face (Stromquist 1990; Weiner 1994). Feminists who subscribe to this position hold the view that the State is, in essence, a benevolent institution that will design and implement measures to correct these imbalances (Stromquist 1990).

The perspective of this group hinges on the sex-role socialisation paradigm where, according to Stromquist (1990), in relation to education, girls are socialised to have low levels of educational aspirations; where low levels of educational attainment by women are due to traditional socialisation messages and sexual discrimination practices in schools; and, where girls and women are socialised to 'fear success' in certain areas of educational and social endeavour.

In the opinion of liberal feminists, sexual inequalities in schooling result from a number of factors such as prejudice, traditional values, lack of proper role models and structural barriers (Weiner 1994). The major themes, therefore, that have dominated the research agenda of North American liberal feminist educators are access to educational opportunities, socialisation and sex-role stereotyping through schooling, sex discrimination practices in schooling, sex-stereotyping in optional subject areas and in career choice, achievement patterns and causes of differential attainment between the sexes in certain subject areas, biases in testing and sex differences in staffing (Weiner 1994; Acker 1994; Stromquist 1990). In keeping with this focus, the terminology and concepts used in the research discourse centre on access, choice, disadvantage, under-representation and underachievement (Weiner 1994).

The major goal of liberal feminists has been the securing of equal educational opportunities for women by working within the current system to achieve change quickly with minimum disruption and without making too many threatening demands on the educational status quo (Weiner 1994). The major solutions and strategies recommended by this group to redress imbalances, therefore, range from awareness raising, and the removal of the barriers (Weiner 1990); altering socialisation practices, changing attitudes and the use of legal processes, where necessary, to ensure equal access for women (Acker 1994).

In the opinion of Noddings (1992), in adopting these approaches, liberal feminist educators have accepted the existing patriarchal model of segregation of the sexes in the private and public spheres as one to be emulated and the concern is simply to provide equal access for women to this standard. She therefore sees the aim of this group as ensuring equity for women through an assimilation approach, that is, moving girls/women into areas regarded as the preserve of men and so preparing both sexes for adult roles traditionally reserved for men, for example in science related fields.

The sex-role socialisation paradigm of liberal feminist educators is therefore criticised by Stromquist (1990) as not fully treating the underlying causes of female discrimination and therefore failing to account for why women and men are given different socialisation messages in the first place; why socialisation practices persistently discriminate against women rather than men; or, why the State continues to tolerate discrimination.

Socialist feminist educators offer an alternative perspective, and insist that any explanation of social and sexual inequality has to take into account the interconnection between ideological and economic forces in which patriarchy and capitalism reinforce each other (Stromquist 1990). This group therefore draws heavily on the 'Reproduction Theory' of Marxist educators which claims that schooling, through a variety of overt and covert mechanisms reproduces the capitalist system (Bowles and Gintis 1976). In the view of socialist/Marxist feminist educators, selection procedures in schools allocate students in ways which ensure that the stratified class structure of capitalist societies is reproduced from one generation to the next. The school is also seen as the site for transmitting values that are necessary for the functioning of the capitalist system (Measor and Sikes 1992).

Socialist feminist educators draw attention to the fact that, in the process of schooling, not only class but also sexual inequalities are reproduced. In contrast to the micro-sociological classroom level focus of liberal feminist educators, this group has a more macro-sociological focus and views the school as the arena where patterns of social and sexual domination and subordination in the family and workplace are reproduced and sustained (Weiner, 1994). The net result is a sexual division of labour in both these spheres where women are prepared through the process of schooling to supply and maintain an inexpensive workforce and are indoctrinated to accept their circumscribed reproductive roles (Stromquist 1990).

Acker (1994) points to the fact that the main aim of socialist feminist educators has been to elucidate processes involved in oppression and which account for women's position within the family and the workplace. The research agenda of this group has therefore had a more complex orientation than that of liberal feminist educators and Weiner (1994) reports that researchers in this group have focused on how gender and power relations are continually reproduced through schooling; the formation of gendered class groupings in the context of schooling, that is, how working-class boys and girls become working- class women and men; and, the relationship between the family, schooling and the labour market in maintaining dominant class and gender relationships.

In contrast to the liberal feminists, the methodological approach of this group has been less empirical and more ethnographic with use of the 'apt illustration' and has focused more on theoretical arguments, historical research or policy analysis (Acker 1994) and makes use of a discourse which is Marxist in its origin and uses concepts and terminology such as capitalism, production, reproduction, class, gender, patriarchal relations and correspondence theory (Weiner 1994).

The long-term goal of educators in the socialist feminist camp is to remove barriers to sexual equality and thus to eliminate women's oppression. Weiner (1994) posits that this group, however, does not place much hope in the role of education to bring about this social change because of the structural nature of sexual inequality within capitalism. Weiner, therefore, argues that the discourse which has emerged from the research of socialist feminist educators has not been very instructive for practitioners at the classroom level. This view is supported by Acker (1994) who contends that the discourse emanating from this group is underdeveloped with respect to strategies for education action and is theoretical rather than classroom oriented; that is, the link between the macro-sociological nature of the theories and the micro-sociological level of school based research is somewhat obscure.

Transformational feminists, a strand within the socialist group, project a similar view and hold that existing social and political structures support the oppression of workers, women and various minorities. They, however, argue that the real problem is that women's experiences have been ignored in looking at these situations. The concern of this group is identifying practical initiatives to rectify the inequities but contend that solutions need to go beyond the equity and assimilation approach of liberal feminist educators. Their call is for a transformation of the male oriented standard curriculum to one which brings women into educational thought and includes female values, skills and ways of relating (Noddings 1992).

Measor and Sikes (1992) call attention to the fact that *radical feminism* is a more recent strand of the women's movement and in this sense is still emergent. They, however, note that there are two key ideas related to this perspective: firstly, patriarchy is of overarching importance and secondly, that the personal is political. With their emphasis on patriarchy, radical feminists contend that the main cause of women's subordination originates from power relations based on sexual differences and an ideology which defines men as superior to women and is maintained through a complex web of values, laws, norms and institutions (Stromquist 1990).

The research themes of radical feminist educators are, in some ways, more tied to the micro-sociological level of the school and the classroom than that of socialist feminists and, therefore more concerned with challenging the educational status quo. Their research focus has been on patriarchal processes of schooling and power relations between the sexes as well as the role played by sexuality in the oppression of girls in classrooms, females in staff rooms and therefore a concern for sexual harassment in schools (Weiner 1994); male monopolisation of culture and knowledge; teacher attention between the sexes; dominance of males over females in mixed school settings and the role of language in controlling ways in which women perceive themselves (Acker 1994).

With this focus, radical feminist educators have moved the debate away from the liberal and socialist-Marxist emphasis on issues of work, status and public life. Instead, like the transformationists, they concentrate on a concern for shifting the male baseline of knowledge and the male domination of the culture of the school, to a position where knowledge reflects the experiences of women and the female characteristics of empathy, caring and nurturing are brought to bear on the educational process (Measor and Sikes 1992; Noddings 1990).

Their methodological approach has therefore depended less on mainstream empirical approaches and more on feminist methodology and personal validation. The terminology that has dominated the research discourse of this group with their concern for patriarchal relations is similar, in some respects, to that of socialist feminist educators but goes beyond to a discourse on domination and subordination, oppression and empowerment and women and girl centeredness (Weiner 1994).

Acker (1994) identifies the major aim of radical feminist educators as wanting to see fundamental change in the social structure which will eliminate male domination and patriarchal structures. They, unlike socialist feminists, look to the school to re-educate society to non-sexist behaviours and practices as part of the overall challenge to patriarchal forces (Weiner 1994) and call for revision of curricula and texts, an extension of scholarship on gender and a pedagogical shift to more participatory approaches (Acker 1994).

In Weiner's (1994) opinion *postmodernist and post-structuralist feminists* have only recently engaged in the educational discourse on sexual inequalities in schooling. An interest of this group, the writer claims, is in the way in which discourse operates as a 'normalising' and 'naturalising' process in which knowledge and power are connected. The overriding concern of these groups of feminists is therefore on creating a counter-discourse and creating in students a critical awareness of their location within educational discourse.

Like radical educational researchers, the emphasis of these groups is on feminist methodologies with its concern for the practical and the inclusion of the voice of women as well as locating the researcher in the same critical plane as the subjects rather than in a hierarchical position. Weiner (1994: 70) contends that:

The terminology of this feminist research perspective is like that of Marxist feminism, sometimes highly complex and 'difficult' utilising terminology such as discourse, subjectivity, power-knowledge drawn from the mainstream post-modernist and post-structuralist writing.

The research discourse that emanates from the work of these researchers is, therefore, criticised as using highly complicated writing styles which negates the very openness and self-reflexivity that these writers invite (Weiner 1994). This discourse is, apparently, not very illuminative for practitioners at the classroom level.

The Caribbean Research Agenda

Much of the research conducted by educators in the Caribbean fits into the liberal feminist framework. Early research in the 1970s, however, focused on social rather than on sexual inequalities in education and therefore on an analysis of the development of the two-tiered system of education and the prominence of class and colour (race) as correlates of access and achievement, particularly at the secondary level. This theme is evidenced in work done by Gordon (1963), Miller (1971) and Lowenthal (1972) all of whom make reference to the 'high degree of correlation between the structure of the education system and the social stratification of the society'. (Miller 1971: 60)

It was not until some 15 years later that the importance of one's sex as a determinant of access to secondary education was addressed by Leo-Rhynie (1987) who showed that, in the Jamaican context, sex was in fact as critical as class and race as a determining factor. Although work by Miller (1971), Hamilton (1979) and Mair-Fisher (1983) established the link between socio-economic status (SES) and success in the Common Entrance Examination (CEE) in Jamaica, the selection examination for entry to the secondary level, it was Leo-Rhynie who first pointed to the fact that criteria used by the Ministry of Education in the selection process discriminated against girls generally and more so against girls in rural areas. She highlighted the fact that although steps had been taken to ensure social justice by implementing a 70/30 ratio to enable more children from the lower social classes attending primary schools to benefit from secondary education, steps had also been instituted to ensure an approximately equal number of places going to boys who would have gained fewer points than girls in the examination. She therefore observed that:

Birth and poverty were not to be barriers but gender and urban home location could be. Girls had a handicap of 10, and pupils in the Corporate Area had a handicap of 20. Thus, a girl in the urban area had to score 10 points more than a boy in the urban area to get a free place, this girl having to score 30 points more than a boy in the rural area who also got a free place. (Leo-Rhynie 1987: 6)

Interestingly, Miller (1987) views this situation from a male perspective and has argued that in Jamaican society, boys, and ultimately men, are at risk of being marginalised by the educational system and therefore ought to be given equal access as girls to a place in high schools. On the surface this appears to be a reasonable demand but has to be juxtaposed against the reality that boys consistently constitute the lower percentage of the entrants for this examination. In 1995, for example, 60 per cent of the entrants were girls, but they obtained 56 per cent of the awards (Sangster 1996). Awarding equal numbers of places to boys as to girls would therefore result in a disproportionate distribution of awards to boys and would, in fact, mean denying places to higher achieving girls. This view was strongly opposed by several persons, including Leo-Rhynie (1987), who argued that this would be blatantly discriminatory.

Layne (1989) has also examined the inequity existing between male and female access to secondary schooling in Barbados. His findings support that of Leo-Rhynie's where girls' superior performance was not reflected in their actual placement in secondary schools. Moreover, he noted that the unequal distribution of resources and rewards in education between males and females, as indicated by the dearth of women in top occupational positions in Barbados, was cause for concern.

In keeping with the liberal outlook of the benevolent State manifesting an 'ideology of citizenry' which applies equally to both men and women (Stromquist 1990), Leo-Rhynie (1989: 95) placed the responsibility for implementing corrective measures at the level of policy makers suggesting that:

Policy statements on education must not only reveal a sensitivity to factors within the system which overtly and/or covertly differentiate between male education and female education, and which result in a reduction of opportunity or stifling potential for either sex; they must also identify strategies for coping with these factors.

In addition to access to schooling, the major thrust of the research conducted in the region from a liberal perspective has been similar to that emanating from North America and has centered on the inequalities associated with the segregation model of education which typifies the education system. The basic assumption on which this model is predicated is that men and women are expected to perform different functions in life. Uncritical acceptance of this ideology is achieved through a process of socialisation by a number of agencies, the school being of paramount importance in this respect. This being the case, it is held that education of the two sexes should be separate and significantly different (Noddings 1992). This notion holds true for what obtains in both single-sex and co-educational settings.

The major themes identifiable in Caribbean research papers fit very readily into those identified by Wiener (1994) and Acker (1994) as being the focus of liberal feminist educators; namely, socialisation and sex-role stereotyping, sex discrimination practices, sex-stereotyping in optional subject areas and career choice, differential attainment in certain subject areas and sex differences in staffing.

As might be expected in a situation where the segregation model predominates, a large segment of the research coming out of the region has been concerned with sex-role stereotyping. Work done by Hamilton and Leo-Rhynie (1984) pulls together research conducted in Jamaica over the period 1974 to 1983 on sex role differences at the secondary level. The main finding that emerged from a review of some 30 studies done at that time indicated that in spite of both sexes showing similarities in areas such as motivation and achievement, school and home factors operated in traditional and expected ways to produce contrasting personality traits typically associated with the sexes. They therefore observe that:

Contrasting images persist of an active, responsible, analytically thinking, confident male, preparing himself to work in an age of science and technology, versus that of a girl who may be strongly motivated academically, but is also anxious and uncertain, and needs the support of home and school to achieve the educational goals which she sets herself. She is thus more likely to select a 'safe' course of study than a traditionally male-dominated one. (Hamilton and Leo-Rhynie 1984: 135)

Work done at a later time on sex-role socialisation calls attention to ways in which curriculum materials portray images that convey implicit messages that contribute to the acquisition of differentiated gender identities and the internalisation and acceptance of corresponding sex-linked behaviours and roles. One of the earlier efforts in this respect was work carried out by King and Morrissey (1988), who analysed 20 textbooks published in support of the History, Geography and Social Studies Caribbean Examinations Council (CXC) curricula, used at the secondary level in Commonwealth Caribbean States, to determine whether racist, sexist and Eurocentric biases were evident. Both racist and Eurocentric biases were identified but the authors observed that:

The textbooks reviewed are at their worst in terms of the portrayal of women. Women are invisible in most of the texts. Sexism appears through the use of language, masculine words frequently used to include women. When they do appear, women play subordinate or menial roles. The books also fail miserably in presenting the contributions of women to the development of the Caribbean. (King and Morrissey 1988: 43)

Work by Ayodike (1989) and Pollard (1989) focus exclusively on how women are portrayed in texts used in literature at the secondary level. Ayodike's work, based on six texts associated with the Caribbean Council Examinations English curriculum, revealed that damaging concepts of women were projected and there was little evidence of images which attempted to challenge the stereotypic image of females. Pollard, on the other hand, found that short stories authored by Olive Senior sought to convey the strength, wisdom and courage typically associated with Caribbean women, and could therefore provide positive images for young women to emulate.

Later work by Bailey (in press) and Whiteley (1996) established similar gender bias in language arts textbooks used at the primary level and science textbooks used at the secondary level in Jamaica, respectively. Bailey's findings corroborate patterns of gender stereotyping reported in studies from North America where, not only were girls/women under-represented in both the pictorial and word content of the books, as main characters and as directing and controlling speech, but males and females were also characterised as displaying traditional gender-appropriate behaviours. Whiteley's analysis of science textbooks published in Britain revealed that although there was a gender balance in illustrations of young people suggesting that students are expected to play an equal role in school science, there was an imbalance in the illustrations of adults, in favour of males, suggesting that, in the adult world of work, science is a province more appropriate for males. The intersection of race/ethnicity and gender was also noted by Whiteley who observed that in an attempt to use ethnically-appropriate illustrations, the absence of female exemplars further reduced the overall number of illustrations used in the science texts. In keeping with liberal feminist concerns, the implications of these findings for the formulation of traditional sex-linked attitudes and value systems and for reinforcing sex segregation of the curriculum and career choice are highlighted by these writers. Bailey, however, goes beyond a liberal focus and discusses the effect of gender biases in children's reading materials on the construction of gender-related conceptual schema and codes, echoing concerns identified with both socialist and radical feminist educators.

Drayton's work (in press) on images portrayed in Caribbean English textbooks, unlike those reported as having a liberal orientation, centres on the potential power of textbooks to perpetuate Eurocentric and patriarchal biases in contemporary Caribbean society. She therefore draws on Marxist theories of capitalism and the sexual division of labour to provide the frame for examining the intersection of race, class and gender in both the textual and non-textual elements of the texts. It is argued that, in spite of the demise of colonialism, Caribbean society is dominated by the few in powerful positions, mostly men, and that this domination is reproduced through social institutions like the school. Textbooks, she contends, are a universal vehicle and tool of this reproduction of dominant social values and ideologies and this is confirmed by the results of her analyses.

The other liberal feminist research emphasis which has been given fairly prominent attention by Caribbean educational researchers is the pattern of sex-stereotyping and differential attainment patterns between the sexes in various curriculum areas, particularly at the secondary level of the education system. A major portion of this work converges on the customarily male-dominated area of science and technology. Both Hamilton (1976) and Glasgow (1978) report on patterns of uptake of science subjects at the General Certificate Examination (GCE) Ordinary level and both found that while physics was overwhelmingly male-dominated, Biology was selected as the preferred science by girls. More recent work by Whiteley (1994, 1995) discloses a similar pattern for students pursuing science subjects in the CXC examinations in Jamaica, Barbados and Trinidad. Leo-Rhynie (1978) and Hamilton (1981) report on similar science subject bias at the higher GCE Advanced level for students in Jamaica.

Research conducted by Bailey (in press), Cuffie (1989) and Leo-Rhynie (1987) indicates that sex segregation is, however, not only confined to the area of science but in fact extends across both the academic and vocational areas of the curriculum offered in secondary level schools in

Trinidad and Tobago and Jamaica. Confirmation of the divide between the 'Arts' and the 'Sciences' has also been provided by King (1989) and Watts (1989). King found that in Trinidad and Tobago girls outperformed boys in Spanish but were not, however, necessarily convinced that a knowledge of Spanish would enhance their marketability.

The contributions of Watts and Cuffie, although fitting into the liberal framework, reflect concerns in keeping with the radical perspective. Watts' work focused on the study of literature at the secondary level which, she confirms, was regarded as belonging to the female domain and was therefore held in low esteem by boys. The writer is, however, not only concerned about the domination of literature by girls but contends that this is of particular significance given that literature can be used as an important vehicle for the development of self-perception, self-identification and for social and cultural understanding. Work done by Cuffie pointed to the influence of the single-sex/co-educational arrangement on choice, where, in the absence of the male presence, more girls in single-sex schools chose science than was the case in co-educational settings. Similar findings have been reported for Jamaica by Williams (1981) and McMillan (1982). Although not acknowledged by these authors, these findings reflect the interest of radical feminists in the patriarchal processes of schooling and the dominance of males over females in mixed school settings.

Research in the Caribbean has also centred on differential attainment patterns between the sexes. Early work by Leo-Rhynie (1978) pointed to a significant difference in success for male and female Jamaican students in the Advanced level examinations at that time and socio-economic-status (SES) proved to be a strong predictor of boys' success while the inverse relationship was found for girls. Hamilton (1985) included the single-sex/co-educational variable in her research design and reported that both girls and boys in single- sex institutions in Jamaica performed markedly better at 'O' level examinations overall than their counterparts in co-educational settings. Gender differences in the 1987 sitting of CXC examinations by candidates in Trinidad and Tobago are reported by Morris (1989). In that year boys demonstrated a small but significantly higher overall achievement in physics, chemistry, mathematics and agricultural science as well as in the traditionally female-dominated subject, biology, while girls showed superior performance in Integrated Science.

Parry (in press [a]) has also examined under-achievement of boys at the secondary level in Jamaica. She rejected the commonly held view that their failure is due to sexual rejection of their female peers and through the predominance of female teachers in schools. Instead, male sex/gender identity, as reflected in attitudes and behaviours which run contrary to the ethos of the school, is identified as playing a crucial role in male educational failure.

Liberal feminist educational philosophy holds that the pattern of participation and attainment in the curriculum by girls can be attributed to traditional socialisation messages and sexual discrimination practices in schools (Stromquist 1990). In keeping with this perspective the findings of the studies cited in this section attribute differences in curriculum participation and attainment to the socialising influence of both home and school in reinforcing notions of appropriate sex behaviours (Watts 1989); teaching styles which might cater more to one sex than to the other (Morris 1989); and, the covert influences of the hidden curriculum (Hamilton and Leo-Rhynie 1984). Additionally, Bailey and Leo-Rhynie (1994) have identified overt practices that create barriers to girls' participation in science.

In Parry's case, although the theoretical background to the paper makes reference to the fact that schools do not merely reflect the dominant gender ideology but actively produce gender divisions, a view of socialist feminist educators, her discussion centres on gender-linked attitudes and behaviours, presumably acquired through the socialisation process, as the main cause of male underachievement. This thesis therefore locates the work more within the liberal sex-role socialisation paradigm.

Another concern of liberal feminist educators which is closely linked to the sex segregation of the curriculum is the further segregation observed in career choice and occupational training programmes. Payne (1989a) examines the situation in Barbados and, in keeping with the liberal viewpoint, concludes that students' liking for certain jobs was clearly influenced by sex stereotyping. Salter (1989) studies how teachers, parents and socio-economic-status influence the career choices of girls. Her assumptions belong to both the liberal and socialist feminist camps as the educational system was seen to be supporting and reinforcing the traditional role of females, thus restricting them to choosing professions which were extensions of their traditional roles and which required traditional feminine skills.

Bailey's (in press) findings of patterns of participation of the sexes in a post-secondary skills training programme in Jamaica, parallel those of Payne and Salter. Bailey, however, goes beyond describing patterns and offering explanations for the observed differences to looking at the possible implications for girls' participation in the labour market. She uses the notion that labour market skills are socially constructed in such a way that women's work is considered to be low skilled and low status. She argues that the continued training of women to function predominately in feminised occupations is therefore self-defeating and can only serve to reinforce the subordinate position of women in society. Whereas this argument reflects somewhat of a socialist feminist position the interventions that she recommends are assimilatory in their approach and therefore locate the work more directly in a liberal framework.

Liberal feminist educators, with their general focus on discriminatory practices in schools, have also been concerned with sex differences in the pattern of staffing in schools. In the Caribbean, this area of research has been addressed by James-Reid and Jones (1989) and Taylor (in press) who examined patterns at the administrative level, and Miller (1989) who examined patterns at the classroom level.

James-Reid's and Jones' explanation of the observed disparity in the representation of women versus men in administrative positions in schools in Jamaica falls within the liberal feminist perspective. They suggest that one of the main causes of under-representation of women is a low level of motivation in seeking promotion, based on the perception that their chances for success are minimal. This, the writers claim, is the outcome of socialisation and sex-role stereotyping which promote the principle of men being more capable and therefore more suited for leadership roles. Taylor, on the other hand, argues that the sex-role socialisation paradigm is insufficient to fully explain the low organisational status of women in education. He therefore looks beyond this model and uses conceptions of male-oriented organisational behaviour and performance criteria which are used to judge women, to account for their 'exclusion' from administrative posts, and their 'isolation' from substantive decision making functions in comparison to men in similar positions. In this respect, Taylor's arguments are more in conformity with the view of radical educators who argue that sexual inequalities in schools are due to patriarchal forces and male-dominated power relations.

Miller, in his work, analyses shifts in male/female composition of the teaching force in primary level schools in four Caribbean territories from immediately after emancipation through to the 1980s. His analysis is placed in a socio-historical context and in relation to his 'place' theory where he postulates that society is organised and structured on the basis of multiple criteria, including race and gender, which determine the 'place' of individuals in society in terms of centrality or marginality. In relation to this thesis he concludes that:

In the Commonwealth Caribbean the predominance of women in private sector teaching is the result of marginalisation of women in the elite groups while the predominance of women in public sector teaching is the result of attempts to continue to marginalise the males of the subordinate groups in circumstances which would dictate advancement of the subordinate groups. (Miller 1989: 12)

In this analysis, Miller in fact goes beyond the liberal feminist sex-role socialisation paradigm as the basis for explaining numerical differences in participation of the sexes in the teaching force and draws on postmodernist ideology which moves away from the 'universals' of earlier feminisms to the plurality and diversity of the experiences of women and therefore of gender issues in any given arena. Barriteau-Foster (1992: 14, 24-25) points to the limitations of theories which emphasise the 'homogeneity of women's experiences' and advocates use of theory which 'dispels the victim syndrome and shows a multiplicity of ways women shift or influence positive and negative features of their environment'.

The Caribbean research highlighted to this point have, in a few instances, straddled at least two of the feminist educational perspectives identified in the literature, but most are predominately liberal in their orientation. Research which fits more directly into the socialist framework is that of Parry (in press [b]) where issues of equality and gender in Caribbean classrooms are the burden of the research. In this instance, she comments on gender differences in classroom behaviour and educational performance in relation to the Marxist educational theory on the acquisition of cultural capital and the impact of home/school congruence in the process. Parry concludes that although teachers are aware that gender socialisation affects classroom behaviour and performance, they locate sources of problems outside of the school and minimise their own role in the reproduction of gender habits inside the classroom.

There are few initiatives coming out of the region which fit directly into the radical perspective. A major concern of this group is with male monopolisation of knowledge and the need therefore for a reconstruction of knowledge and the extension of scholarship on gender. Acker (1994: 50) reports that a major proponent of this view is Spender who argues that 'what we know is dangerously deficient, for it is the record of decisions and activities of men, presented in the guise of human knowledge'. Noddings (1992) notes that an important initiative in changing mainstream curricula has been the introduction of Women's Studies courses to college curricula where topics draw on existing disciplines and represent significant modifications to those disciplines through feminist perspectives. This was achieved at the University of the West Indies by the initiation of a programme of Women and Development Studies on the three campuses in 1985, and the establishment of the Centre for Gender and Development Studies (CGDS) in 1993. The Centre's programmes 'question historically accepted theories and explanations about society and human behaviour; seek an understanding of the world by taking into account the achievements of women as well as men' (Mission Statement of the CGDS). This questioning and seeking has been carried out through the promotion of a series of interdisciplinary and disciplinary seminars aimed at generating research on gender issues and therefore shifting the male baseline of the traditional knowledge associated with these disciplines.

A major achievement in this respect has been the publication edited by Shepherd *et. al.* (1995), 'Engendering History', coming out of an international seminar hosted by the Department of History at Mona in collaboration with the CGDS (Mona Campus Unit) which focused on the history and experiences of Caribbean women. As a follow-up to this, teachers of history at the secondary level recognised the need to integrate data on women and history into the CXC history syllabus. The response has been a volume compiled by Shepherd (in press) on behalf of the Department of History, Mona, targeting teachers and students involved in the history curriculum offered by the CXC. This latter initiative addresses the concern articulated by radical feminist educators of applying and extending feminist theory at the pre-tertiary level (Noddings 1992).

The only other theme considered in this survey fits into a further emphasis of radical feminist educators, that is, the role of sexuality in schooling. Ottley (1989) addressed the issue of sexuality in the context of guidance and counselling programmes in Barbados and suggests that the development of gender identity and human sexuality were areas in which it was likely for counsellors to transmit bias. Payne (1989b), on the other hand, looked at sexuality within the context of student-student and student-teacher relations in co-educational settings in Barbados and examined the differential treatment of male and female students. The findings suggested that the sex of students had an influence on teachers' expectations and perceptions, which in turn determined teacher/student interactions. This, it was noted, had serious implications for issues such as reward and punishment, motivation and academic support.

Summary

This survey of much of the feminist educational research conducted in the Caribbean region indicates that the approach is fairly traditional fitting predominantly into the liberal feminist paradigm. A major concern has therefore been with sex-role socialisation as well as sexual inequalities in areas such as access to schooling, patterns of participation and attainment in various curriculum areas and in career choice and training. In keeping with the liberal feminist orientation the approach to these research initiatives has been very empirical and therefore mainstream and 'objective' in nature. The only obvious exceptions were those of Payne (1989 [b]) and Parry (1996a, 1996b) where a more ethnographic, participatory approach was used to tap subjective perceptions of participants.

Strategies for change emanating from liberal feminism include a focus on altering socialisation practices, changing attitudes and the removal of barriers which prevent the full participation of girls in any aspect of schooling. The solutions offered by Caribbean researchers to the educational inequalities, discriminatory practices and patterns of socialisation identified in much of the work reported in this paper are very much aligned with this liberal outlook. The concern has been with making recommendations aimed at getting a system which is viewed as being essentially 'good' to work better and be more responsive to the needs of girls rather than with making recommendations for changing the system in fundamental ways.

The literature reviewed suggests that what is required in the region is a more radical approach not only in terms of the research agenda but also in terms of the actions recommended to redress the inequities. Much more attention needs to be given to research themes that address issues such as patriarchal processes in schooling, the power relations between the sexes in classrooms, the role played by sexuality in the oppression of girls in school and the relationship of these factors to male/female differences in participation, attainment and the perpetuation of traditional sex stereotyping in all its forms.

Action needs to be directed more towards a transformational perspective which rejects both segregation and assimilation in education and occupational life. Transformationists instead call for new forms of education that incorporate significant aspects of female experience in the curriculum for all students and for a transformation of public and professional life in light of this experience. For this group of feminist educators the concern is for a dramatic transformation of social life and a need to: 'balance cognition with affect, thinking with intelligent doing, judging with receptive perception and control with harmony' (Noddings 1992: 677).

This, they see, as our only hope for survival both as feminist educators and as human beings.

13

Education of the Colonial Woman through the Eyes of the Novelist

Rhonda Ferreira Habersham

During our early years as British colonies, the educational, political and economic systems were adopted from the motherland. As a result, many of the prejudices and attitudes of Britain against women and their ability to learn were incorporated into daily living. This had a crippling effect on the girls being educated as they were reminded in ways – subtle and otherwise – that they were not capable of being as proficient in school as their male counterparts and in fact, never could or would be. History documents this cruel phenomenon quite adequately, but, we do not get the total picture of what it was like to be a female 'growing up under the Union Jack' until we read the novels of several modern West Indian authors.

History has so far failed to give a sensitive enough account of the educational system from 1930 until the present. It has also not adequately addressed that system's effects on the psyche of the woman. For this reason, novels may help towards a fuller understanding of the circumstances that women faced in their quest to better themselves. Novels generally give a good and even microcosmic representation of life, particularly, if they are inspired autobiographically or written from an autobiographical standpoint. Since they are so personal, they give an insider's view of the society and what it was really like to be part of the system. It is a subjective view because the writer is often conveying her own personal experiences.

This paper seeks to redress the balance by exploring the portrayal of the educational system and its effect on the colonial woman as is shown through several novels. Using the novels helps the reader to better understand the dilemma that the colonial woman faced in education. It is more possible to empathise with the protagonist as we are taken through the classroom and more importantly, through her mind as we read how she felt as a victim of the system. The novels that will be examined are Merle Hodge's *Crick Crack Monkey* and *For the Life of Laetitia; Beka Lamb* by Zee Edgell and *Angel* by Merle Collins.

The thread that seems to bind all the novels together is the common fate that the female protagonist suffers during her school years. At the beginning of their school year, the girls are excited about the new prospects and developments that they think school will bring. The reader, however, becomes acutely aware that the characters will not find happiness or acceptance in the school system, because like so many other aspects of colonial society, it works against the female. This society does not teach the individual to be proud of one's heritage and the children adopt these attitudes from an early age. At about the age of eight, Tee, the main character in *Crick Crack Monkey*, invents her double, whom she calls Helen. Her double transports her to wonderful exotic lands far removed from the reality of her life. All that she has learned in school of the British lifestyle is featured in her double life. There was 'a delightful orchard with apple and pear trees in which sang chaffinches and blue tits and where one could wander on terms of the closest familiarity with cowslips and honeysuckle' (Hodge 1970: 61). This character's low self-concept is reinforced when she passes the Exhibition Examination to a prestigious secondary school. There, she is in a largely middle-class environment in the school system and finds that she has great difficulty integrating herself into the system. The teacher looks down on her because of her rural background and skin colour and she finds herself alienated, not only in school, but, also in her home because she no longer seems to fit in with this environment. She notices for example, that in school, favoritism is extended to the fair-skinned girls and observes that 'it was more or less the same girls who were picked for the Dramatic Society and many of these same girls were also deemed to be the ones who were sufficiently sporting to be allowed onto the tennis courts' (Hodge 1970: 74). This experience in school has a dramatic effect on Tee. She cannot accept herself or this environment and also finds herself being ashamed of her own family and cultural background. The education that Tee receives, both formally and informally does not have a positive effect on her life. She comes to practically disown the lady who raised her and is ashamed of the so-called ordinary nature of the people in her former world. She does not want to belong to Aunt Bea's world either for it is filled with duplicity and deceit. She concludes that 'everything was changing, unrecognizable, pushing me out. This was as it should be, since I had moved up and no longer had any place to go' (Hodge 1970: 110).

The ambivalence that exists in Tee's mind as to where she belongs can be attributed in part to the education she received during her formative years. This education does not encourage her to be proud of either her cultural background or her racial background. Rather, she is made to feel like an outsider in her own land. An educational system that is removed from one's background is of no use to the individual or to the society. Tee is testimony to this. Dr Eric Williams (1951: 15) summed up this problem of colonial education by saying that 'education should proceed from the known to the unknown, from the village to the great wide world, from the indigenous plants, animals and insects to the flora and fauna of strange countries'.

In this climate of confusion and doubt, Tee cannot function properly and constantly seeks ways to affirm herself. This is true too of Laetitia Johnson, the protagonist in Merle Hodge's second novel *For the Life of Laetitia*. The reader enters into Laetitia's (or Lacey's) life when she has won a place in the secondary school of her choice. On her first day of school, she, like the rest of her classmates, is paired off with someone so that they can help each other get familiar with their new surroundings. Her partner turns out to be Anjanee Jugmohansingh, an East Indian girl from her village. Because of previous association, they are delighted to be together and from this moment, a friendship is born. During their first lunch time together, Anjanee becomes very furtive and the reason for this soon becomes clear. She is ashamed of her lunch and tells Lacey: 'Don't laugh at my lunch, you hear? Is not like what you have. Is only roti and talkerie'. (Hodge 1993: 44). This seemingly insignificant incident is relevant to an understanding of the cultural conflicts faced by students from different backgrounds who have to try and fit in with the already established school system.

Teachers too fall prey to the stereotypical roles allotted to the boys and girls and are sometimes exceedingly insensitive to differences in the students' background. An excellent example of this occurs during a social studies class when they are learning about 'Happy Families'. The children are informed that 'children who did not live in a house with their own exact mother and father were living in a Broken Home. Children living in such homes are Unhappy Children' (Hodge 1993: 50). They are then instructed to copy a picture of the Happy Family that is on the poster. This picture is of white people. To Laetitia's thinking, she is happy and so she will draw her concept of a happy family – her extended family which includes her aunts, uncles and five cousins. Her teacher does not appreciate this, nor, will she accept the fact that the 'perfect' nuclear family is the exception rather than the rule in the society in which she is teaching. To denigrate the child who comes from an extended family is in effect, to destabilise the child's world and aids in producing shame for her culture. Laetitia realises, however, that this teacher is foolish and comments that 'we did have some sensible ones' (Hodge 1993: 52).

The person who has to deal with the most tension from both school and family is not Laetitia, but her friend, Anjanee. Anjanee is often absent from school and is ashamed to say why until Lacey's pressuring forces her to admit her problems. Her father and family cannot see the relevance of a girl going to school. At every turn, she is faced with reprimands from her father concerning her education. It seems that the men are threatened in the presence of a female who knows more about any given subject than they do. The insecurity of her father and brother is detrimental to Anjanee's future as she has no support from her home and her father is powerless to do anything about it. The reality is that women in this East Indian culture are regarded as lesser beings.

On several occasions, her father keeps her at home so that she can fulfil her gender assigned duties. As a result of this, she falls ill and stays away from school for several days. She vehemently declares one day to Laetitia:

I don't want to end up like my mother! I *not* going to end up like my mother, I rather dead. If you see how much work my mother does have to do when the day come! And only me to help her . If it was me I would just walk away one day and leave them there in their mess. But when I tell her so, she does just shake her head and say 'Where will I leave them and go, *beti*? I ain't have schooling. You want me to go by the side of the road and beg?' (Hodge 1993: 65)

Without an education, her mother is forced into this position of being practically a slave to the family. Anjanee is shrewd enough to realise the importance of education to someone in a despairing situation like hers and wants with all her heart to succeed at what she does. However, the pressure of school and home combined lead Anjanee to commit the ultimate act of despair – suicide.

This news causes Lacey to have a nervous breakdown, the end result being that she returns to her grandparents' home until she is ready to deal with reality once again. Under the love and care of her family, she recovers and is better able to deal with the death of her friend. She says that: 'As the reopening of school drew closer, I felt as though I were taking up her life' (Hodge 1993: 213).

Like so many girls of her culture, Anjanee is a victim of her situation. She had to deal with racism and antagonism all at a very tender age. To her thinking, there was no hope and there never could be any hope. She would have to face the kind of life that her mother had to face and this to her is worse than death itself. It is a poignantly sad picture and the reader cannot help but feel that it is the responsibility of society to rescue such victims. The question remains as to who will rescue them if no one is sensitive enough to realise the hopelessness of the situation. Laetitia sees it but, try as she might, can do nothing about it. Ma Zelline (Laetitia's mother's godmother) sees it but is also in no position to do anything about it. The teachers appear to be unconcerned with what they see. Laetitia herself learns a valuable but hard lesson from this. She has learned what girls have to face and with the help and support of her family, she will be better able to deal with the trials and tribulations of this life in the future.

Another girl who learns hard lessons growing up is Beka Lamb. Beka grows up in Belize and is also subjected to the education of the colonial powers. Beka's mother helps her to understand the complexities of the society in which they live and it is important for the girl to understand this if she is even to begin to be successful in school.

For many of the girls, school is an escape from reality because it transported them out of the banalities into what they considered glamorous and exotic worlds. St Cecelia's, the Catholic School which Beka attends, 'was almost another world from the rest of Belize. The majority of students among whom were the poor, the rich, the brilliant and the mediocre acquired the art of suppressing segments of their personalities, shedding the lives they led at home the minute they reached the convent gates' (Edgell 1982: 112). It was a lifestyle of duplicity and denial that only made them miserable. A question that arises from this, is what were the girls taught that made them sink into a constant state of denial of their culture, their lifestyles? The school aimed to copy the ethics and aspirations of a different culture to which girls had to conform. Even their uniforms were not suited to a tropical climate but were instead almost totally British. This seems to symbolise one of the problems of the educational system. Nothing seemed to work quite as it should no matter what was tried. Beka Lamb, as young as she is, realises this.

She often feels that her world is falling apart and this is symbolised in the image of the watermelon. Colonial society is portrayed as very unstable and the changes that are ensuing in the colony parallel the changes that are taking place inside the young girl. 'It was all very confusing to Beka and as she scrambled around in her mind trying to fix on a way to prevent her own life from breaking down' (Edgell 1982: 82). She thinks that there is something radically wrong with her that she cannot accept what is being taught in schools and what her parents advise her to do. She sees it as 'the roar of seawater in her head' (Edgell (1982: 82) – a force more powerful than herself and over which she has no control. She declares to her teacher, 'sometimes I feel bruk down just like my own country, Sister' (Edgell 1982: 115).

Such a system is not improving in any way by the presence of teachers who contribute nothing towards the betterment of the girls. Father Nunez is such a man. He tells his class: 'As young ladies, you must walk always with an invisible veil about you so as not to unleash chaos upon the world. God in his infinite goodness, gave us the Blessed Virgin to erase the memory of Eve and to serve as an example to the women of the world' (Edgell 1982: 90). In these few statements, the sin of the world has become the woman's responsibility and Father Nunez has not even begun to indict the man as one of the contributing factors to the problem.

The effects of such a philosophy on the school girls is demonstrated graphically in the person of Toycie. Toycie becomes pregnant by her erstwhile boyfriend Emilio who subsequently deserts her and leaves her to cope with the stigma of an unwed mother on her own. She does have the love and support of her guardian and the Lamb family, but this does not prove enough for the weakened Toycie. The school system completely rejects Toycie and Sister Virgil states that 'they [the general public] would be shocked if I allowed Toycie to return to school after bearing a child' (Edgell 1982: 118). The effect on Toycie is tragic. She loses her baby, has a mental breakdown and is eventually relegated to a mental institution. In her demented state, she pretends to be in school and does all the actions of one studying. This is very ironic as it is the peculiarities of the educational system as administered by the ecclesiastical authorities which contributed to her present state. O'Callaghan (1990: 94) believes that this action 'is reminiscent of the psychotic trying to "acquire" the reality from which the "true self" is isolated by copying or imitating forms of behaviour which are perceived as real'. The denial of her native culture seems to have come to a climax by her reverting to the colonial masters' way which is symbolised in the educational system.

Beka has to deal with losing her best friend and continuing her academic life without her friend. Interestingly enough, school takes on the role of a healing balm in her life as all her energies are now concentrated on writing an essay for a national competition. She succeeds in winning, but can only think of her friend since she believes that, if Toycie had lived, she would have received the prize. In spite of her success at school, Beka feels stifled and suppressed in school and in the society as a whole. She longs to escape from it and believes that if she is in a different environment 'she could maybe pick up the pieces, glue them together and start all over again' (Edgell 1982: 147). She evidently does not feel this liberty in her world. In spite of all the trauma that she undergoes, the novel seems to imply that she will succeed, that she will not be destroyed by any person or attitude in society because all these experiences have made her strong.

Angel shares a similar experience with Beka and Tee. She too has to undergo schooling at the hands of the colonial masters. It is important to note that even the 'uneducated' people of the islands share the same views as those of the colonial powers and this affects the way in which their children are raised.

This is seen clearly in Angel's father's attitude towards educating his daughter as opposed to his son 'we mightn' be able to send both of them, and Angel is a girl. They grow up before you know it is confusion, they don' even finish school or they finish, get married, their name is not even your again and somebody else get the praise' (Collins 1987: 99). Fortunately, Doodsie (Angel's mother) is determined that her daughter will be educated. She almost nags Angel towards succeeding in the system telling her 'learn you lesson and don' grin grin wid nobody' (Collins 1987: 101). Her foray into secondary school proves a challenge as, in this environment, she is surrounded by people who are from a different religious persuasion from herself. Once again, in this world of colonial education, she is made to feel less than she really is and retreats into a make believe world where she herself is transformed into one of the ladies in some love story with 'long blonde hair flying in the unruly wind, blue eyes sparkling .' (Collins 1987: 113). This desire to be white is further aggravated by the nuns telling her to get her hair straightened so that it would 'look decent' (Collins 1987: 113). The implication given to the unsuspecting child is that she should be ashamed of her race.

The subjects taught in school are far removed from her cultural situation. She sings school songs about spring, a non-existent season in the tropics and enjoys operettas about gondoliers and fair maidens. A broad education involves learning about different cultures, but in this school, they learn little about their own culture and come to distance themselves from it completely. They do study West Indian history which Angel considers boring. Angel also becomes ashamed of her mother whom she considers 'unglamourous' as she did not 'go to the beach often for picnics as all the best mothers did in books and essays' (Collins 1987: 114).

In stark contrast to Angel is the figure of Janice who does not fall prey to denying her heritage in the convent experience. She does not forget what 'real life is all about' (Collins 1987: 120). An interesting change comes about when Angel is admitted to university. There, she experiences education of a different kind. Students are allowed to express their opinions and Angel undergoes a type of rediscovery. There is a complete rejection of the European way of thought even in the songs they list to:

Bring back Macabee version
It belong to – de black man
Give back King James version
Dat belong to – de white man (Collins 1987: 141)

She gets angry at what she was taught in school for she realises the gulf that separates her world from that of the colonisers. The young thinkers at the university preach revolution and Angel becomes fully involved with this movement which they call 'Search'. One change that is evident in their social circle is the equality of women in their discussions. Women are considered equal and Angel especially enjoys this particular liberation. They attend sessions on Rasta drumming, poetry readings and political discussions believing that the only way towards the liberation of the Caribbean is revolution. The novel does emphasise the political change that comes to Grenada. It is as if we are being prepared for the new emerging attitudes through the exposé of Angel's and her friends' experiences.

It is significant that the author, Merle Collins, would have her protagonist progress academically to the university level. This, in itself, demonstrates the progress of women in the field of education. It seems that the higher women go academically, the more freedom would be found for them as individuals and thinkers. Perhaps she is intimating that one way for women to be freed from the bondage that chains them is through higher education. At the end of the novel, Angel is a wiser individual for having gone through her educational experience at the University of the West Indies. Collins does show us, however, that most of her education has come through association with different intellectual individuals who are not afraid to express their opinions. It is significant that it has not come from the imported British system of education for this in itself is the beginning of independence and liberation. Angel is meant to serve as an encouragement for women to move forward academically and intellectually.

In all of these works, the novelists have set to show that the characters deliberately reject European culture as it pertains to education. The West Indian, especially the West Indian female has suffered long under the propagandist impact of European curriculum in which her culture and history have been downplayed, if not totally ignored. We see the development of the girls under this system behind in search of the life they have dreamt about and learnt about in school. Leaving for the mother country, however, indicates to the reader that they have been completely indoctrinated in European values and beliefs. The answer to their cultural dilemma is sought in a system that is completely alien to them and which has succeeded in alienating them from their own society. They have had to deal with under-representation in the schools, marginalisation in the classroom and the stereotypes of 'true womanhood' propagated by society.

Ambivalence pervades the lives of these girls who seek to find a sense of peace and fulfilment in the school system and in themselves. A clear manifestation of the psychological dilemma is seen in the characters' creation of other worlds. These imaginary worlds are dominated by blonde, smiling creatures that have nothing to do with the reality that they face at home and in school. Both Tee and Angel fall prey to this deception. This causes undue psychological stress for they begin to measure their lifestyles against what they have learned in their school books and all that they see is a yawning chasm that separates the two worlds. Toycie realises perhaps too late that the British society which those books glorify does not even begin to consider them citizens of the glorious British empire. O'Callaghan (1990: 97) believes that 'the harsh judgment of Toycie is also a judgment of traditional values, seen as backward and immoral by the modern foreign educators'.

These novels then, give us a much deeper understanding of what West Indian women had to face under the colonial system in their quest to be educated. The reader is left with a clearer idea of the struggles endured by females. Using the novels as a medium for change for women's education should not be underestimated. Teaching West Indian literature should be a priority to educators because it shows us the struggle that those who went before us had to endure. Hodge (1990:202- 208) summarises the importance of West Indian literature as it pertains to change in not only the educational system, but, in the society as a whole:

The potential of Caribbean literature for positively affecting the development of the Caribbean is an untapped resource. Caribbean fiction can help to strengthen our self-image, our resistance to foreign domination, our sense of the oneness of the Caribbean and our willingness to put our energies into building the Caribbean nation.

14

Socialisation and the Development of Gender Identity:
Theoretical Formulations and Caribbean Research[1]

Elsa A. Leo-Rhynie

To understand and address fully any individual's gender identity requires investigation of a unique confluence of personal and cultural meaning (Chodorow 1995: 24).

Gender refers to a range of perceptions, opinions, attitudes, values, behaviours, roles and positions which are socially, culturally and economically attributed to men and women, and which determine, to a large extent, the contexts and ways of life and work of these individuals. Definitions of gender such as the social organisation of sexual difference, point to a recognition of the extent to which the existence of a biological difference has organised thought and action in different cultures and the role of the social environment in shaping the 'masculine' and the 'feminine' in society. Roopnarine and Mounts (1987) have summarised many of the theories which have addressed the process by which this 'gendering' of individuals takes place and the way in which individuals acquire a gender identity. Gender identity can be defined as: 'a personal recognition and general acknowledgment of oneself as part of a socially defined group – male or female, which may or may not be derived from the basic sex difference from which the group originated' (Leo-Rhynie, 1995a).

The assumptions and the issues which have led to the formulation of these different theoretical positions and which have stimulated on-going debate, are neither clear-cut nor simple. Biological theories are mainly based on Freudian concepts, and are considered to be deterministic (Mitchell 1974; Rossi 1984), while a variety of other theories emphasise the major impact which a range of societal and cultural objects, events and institutions exert on children as they grow and develop (Bandura 1969, 1977; Walters 1963; Mischel 1966). A number of writers concede that while there are biological differences between the sexes, the similarities outweigh the differences, and non-biological explanations have to be sought to account for the gender distinctions evident in society (Bem 1981, 1993; Kohlberg 1966; Maccoby and Jacklin 1974; Martin and Halverson 1981; Lindsey 1994). In these instances, a biological factor is usually assumed, but its nature and influence are not assessed. More recently, Chodorow (1995) links the biological and the social, the personal and the cultural, and considers that these are so closely fused that gender identity is a subjective construct.

An interesting aspect of biological theorising is sociobiology, which considers the Darwinian concepts of the process of natural selection and survival of the fittest among human species as including adaptations which will ensure the passage of genes from one generation to the next and future generations. This instinctive desire for genetic continuity is considered to be the major motivational factor of almost all behaviour. Each sex therefore, has evolved characteristics which will enhance the realisation of its reproductive potential: so, for example, men are promiscuous to ensure that their genes are passed on, while women are more selective in terms of their choice of sexual partners (Barash 1982). Sociobiology is also used to explain the almost universal observance of male aggression, female care and nurturance of their children, as well as male dominance over women. Lindsey (1994: 41-42) notes two examples which provide support for this view – one is the 'cultural universal of an incest taboo' and the other is mother/child bonding which is universal, and is 'strong, invariable, necessary for the well being of the child, and precedes all other bonds in time'. Male bonding is to each other, originally to facilitate hunting and defence for the survival of the species. Thus, existing gender roles are seen as an outcome of the evolutionary history of the human species.

Theorists who stress the importance of the environment in the development of gender identity assume that gender is learned, can be changed, and differs in different cultures. Gender, therefore, can be considered to be a continuum of characteristics which individuals of either sex can demonstrate. The learning of gender roles occurs through a very complex socialisation process which can be defined as the process of shaping and/or modifying behaviour, through interaction with others, and it usually results in a certain degree of conformity to the behavioural expectations of gender, race and social class groups within the society.

The forces of socialisation exert their influence directly as well as indirectly. Direct instruction, as well as positive and negative reinforcement are expected to facilitate the development, among children, of attitudes, values and patterns of behaviour which will serve as guides to ensure that they conform to the norms of gender, social class and racial/ethnic groups. Indirect influence is achieved through the observation and imitation – modelling – of actions of significant others in the lives of children (Bandura and Walters 1963). Significant others initially include the primary caregivers, and family members, who will demonstrate behaviours which are representative of their sub-cultural group, and eventually extend to members of the peer group, media figures, fictional characters and famous personalities who are representative of the wider society.

Early theoretical ideas on gender acquisition were put forward by Lawrence Kohlberg (1966), who proposed a cognitive-developmental learning process to explain the acquisition of a number of concepts, one of which is gender. Gender appropriate behaviour, which may start out based on observation and imitation of those persons in the environment who serve as models, eventually becomes governed by generalised concepts which are formed, as the cognitive-developmental process continues, out of the experiences of the child. Cognitive-developmental theory has provided a basis from which several other theorists have proposed the development of gender identity. Maccoby and Jacklin (1974: 364), for example, acknowledging the inadequacy of reinforcement and imitation theories to explain the acquisition of sex-typed behaviour, speak of 'self socialisation', which is the learning of sex typed behaviour a process built upon biological foundations that are sex differentiated to some degree.

More recent information processing theorists have based their propositions on the concept of schema developed by Piaget (1970). These schema, Piaget contends, are constantly being built up as children grow, and serve as internal information organisers for concepts which are gradually developed as children accommodate and assimilate new information from the environment, and adapt to the changes which this new information can demand in their behaviour. Martin and Halverson (1981) propose that, as the child grows and develops, she/he gradually builds up more schema for behaviours which are considered to be relevant, appropriate and acceptable for their own than for the other sex group.

Bem's (1993) 'gender lens' represent a recent advance in her thinking which started out with ideas of androgyny, a term used to capture the concept of gender as a social construct. Her more recent work identifies three lenses of gender which she considers are passed from generation to generation through a process of 'enculturation' and which perpetuate gender differences. These lenses are: biological essentialism – the belief that all male/female differences arise logically from biological distinctions; androcentrism – in which the male situation is viewed as sexless and universal, and the female is seen as a departure from that norm; and gender polarisation which is an exaggeration of gender differences, and the organisation of social life around these differences. The bi-polar gender distinctions in society encourage the perception, accommodation, assimilation and classification of objects and behaviours into opposite poles of a single gender dimension, and this cultural emphasis and influence in respect of gender polarisation strongly influences peoples' lives. Bem posits that these 'gender lens' become central to individuals' perceptions of the environment and determine the extent to which they engage in sex stereotypical behaviour, as well as their gender-relevant functioning in social contexts.

Nancy Chodorow (1995) points to the inadequacy of psychoanalytic and socio-cultural explanations, on their own, to fully account for the development of gender identity. Chodorow's theoretical position is based on a clinical approach, and her assumptions are in opposition to many feminist assumptions. She emphasises that gender identity is 'an inextricable fusion or melding of personally created (emotionally and through unconscious fantasy) and cultural meaning' and cannot, therefore, 'be seen as entirely culturally, linguistically or politically constructed. Rather, there are individual psychological processes in addition to, and in a different register from culture, language and power relations that construct gender for the individual' (Chodorow 1995: 517).

Chodorow explains the individual's subjective use of past and present experiences, unconscious and conscious, to develop and create personal meaning, and argues that this psycho-dynamic process is an innate human capacity which is exercised throughout life. This process results in each individual developing a unique 'personal-cultural' gender, and the existence, therefore, of many different individual masculinities and femininities.

Chodorow does admit to the contribution of culture to the constructions and fantasies of gender, and uses Fast's (1984) distinction between 'objective' gender – characteristics which differentiate between the sexes, and 'subjective' gender – personal constructions of masculinity and femininity, and implies that the elements of objective gender can be identified through research and analysis of the cultural sphere, but that the ideographic nature of subjective gender is more difficult to access, and may only be accessible through the use of psychoanalytic tools. She points to her previous work on the reproduction of mothering which described how, as they develop 'boys and girls constructed their unconscious, inner self-object world, their unconscious sense of self boundaries (of connection or difference from others), and their sense of gender' (Chodorow 1995: 522).

She contends that work provides empirical evidence both of how psyches produce social/cultural forms and how social/cultural forms create gender ideologies which are internalised in psyches. All elements of existence and culture, in Chodorow's opinion, are used to develop psychological meaning for the individual, and so contribute to the development of gender identity. The particular recipe of elements which are important in the emotions, fantasies projections, introjections and personal understanding of gender by one person may be very different from that of another individual. The gender lens of Bem (1993), therefore, may have varying degrees of different components and so be differently constructed for different persons. Although the culture and culturally constructed institutions such as the family are vital sources of the perceptions, opinions, attitudes and values relating to gender, Chodorow considers that they are not used similarly by all persons, and different elements assume greater importance in the formation of gender identity for some than for others. As Hill-Collins (1990: 227) notes 'the same situation can look quite different depending on the consciousness one brings to interpret it.'

Recognition of the significance of the content and quality of infant interaction with objects, persons and ideas in the development of attitudes, values, psychological meaning, and a sense of personal identity, which includes recognition of self as part of a gender group, underscores the importance of exploring the experiences and interactions available to infants, children and young people in different cultural settings.

The unique and individual gender identities proposed by Chodorow are reminiscent of the postmodern feminist discourse which emphasises the varying experiences of women which differ widely across race, class and culture lines, and which observes that there may be as many theories of feminism as there are women. In recognition of what she describes as the 'tensions and contradictions in research on Caribbean women', Barriteau-Foster (1992) recommends the use of postmodern theoretical analysis in conceptualising concepts of sexual identity in this and other settings. This analysis reflects an attempt to understand the dynamic, constantly changing nature of social relations, and the ways in which individuals both shape and are shaped by their social interactions, which interactions are strongly influenced by, and also influence the expressions of gender, race, and class. The essence of this fluid subjectivity is expressed in post-structuralism which pulls together concepts from a number of postmodern theorists and assesses their implications for literary criticism. The meaning of many terms in common use is analysed by these theorists, and the question arises as to whether these meanings have objective reality or whether their use in the discourse and their relationship to other terms gives them their meaning. Gill Frith (1993: 162-163) identifies the most important point in the post-structuralist discourse as the view that 'meaning is neither fixed nor controlled by individual readers or writers; it is culturally defined, learned and plural subjectivity is seen as changing and contradictory: gendered identity is not static and natural, but formed within language and open to change'.

The effort to force the separate experiences and views of women into a unified whole is considered by postmodernists to be an attempt to conform to a patriarchal mode of thought, and they advocate departure from this to recognition and exploration of difference which is central to their theorising.

The Caribbean Cultural Milieu

Analysis of theories of development of female and male identity in Caribbean societies must be carried out in recognition of differences related to class, race and ethnicity, as well as other factors. Within the Caribbean, the history of slavery, indentureship and colonisation resulted in an hierarchical separation of the colonised from their colonisers. In the case of slavery, the traditional male-female relationships and family traditions of the homelands of the colonised could not be sustained, as different tribal groups with different cultural customs found themselves thrown together in an alien environment where use of their names and their language, and practice of their religion were forbidden. In this context, the gender relationships which became accepted and practised were those which met the needs of the historical place in which these persons found themselves; these were an amalgam of patterns from the African homeland, patterns observed among the slave masters and mistresses, and patterns which were imposed at various times by these individuals as well as by strategies of survival.

Slavery created, however, strong bonds between men and women who, along with their children, were considered to be the property of their white slave masters and mistresses. The diversity of women in the region, and the origins of this diversity must be recognised – the black woman under slavery was a field labourer like the male slaves; the brown women were often house slaves, and so were in positions to gain favours not available to black women. Indian women, who were indentured labourers, were usually able to retain their cultural heritage and practices, although they still experienced an oppressive system on the plantation. White women of different classes all suffered from oppressive practices, but they had different experiences, and these have to be considered in formulating explanations for these experiences. The female identity acquired by these women differed according to the cultural expectations and realities of their lives, and this diversity also pertained to men.

Chodorow insists that the acquisition of gender identity is the result of a process of individual and idiosyncratic interaction with culture. If this is so, it is important to know and understand those special cultural factors which play a role in this process. Ogbu (1981) stresses the importance of researching several aspects of the cultural milieu to identify those clues which can lead to a better understanding of the socialisation process and gender identity formation.

Research on the environments of children and youth in the Caribbean can reveal a great deal about the underlying beliefs of the persons who provide them with care, and the attitudes, values and behaviours to which they will be exposed. These may act, not only as sources of emotional or fantasised animations (Chodorow 1995), but also as mechanisms through which their gender lenses are developed (Bem 1993), thus having implications for the creation of the personal-cultural gender identities of individuals. Studies of these environments have been the subject of substantial research in the Caribbean, but in most instances, gender has not been a focus, and so the implications of this research for the development of gender identity have not been highlighted.

An exception is the most recent and comprehensive research project on socialisation in the Caribbean which was undertaken between 1993 and 1995, funded by United Nations Children's Fund (UNICEF) and designed, directed and administered by Janet Brown of the Caribbean Child Development Centre and Barry Chevannes of the Department of Sociology and Social Work of the University of the West Indies. Entitled The Gender Socialisation Project, it was mainly concerned with understanding the social behaviour of males in Caribbean societies, and exploring the processes relating to the origins and expressions of gender-related behaviour. The study focused on children and youth in the working classes of three Caribbean countries – Dominica, Guyana and Jamaica, and the methodology used provided a wealth of data, with detailed descriptions of opinions, attitudes and lifestyles of several individuals who inhabit the target communities. The ethnographic reports yielded vivid descriptions of the communities and the nature of the human relationships within them.

This major research investigation, together with other research investigations which have been carried out over the past two decades, provide insights into the 'elements of objective gender', those which Chodorow (1995) consider can be identified through research and analysis of the cultural environments in which children and youth develop. Although the unique nature of each individual's subjective gender would require more detailed, clinical analysis, exploration of the cultural context allows for an assessment of the extent to which factors in these environments have been, and have the potential to be, influential in the development and expression of gender lenses and gender identities among Caribbean children and youth. The data reveal complex processes at work in a variety of settings and point to continuing attitudinal trends as well as new responses and behaviours.

The theoretical review undertaken earlier suggests that gender identities are influenced in their development by:
(a) the cultural context, and belief systems which establish the parameters of gender behaviour in a particular setting;
(b) the extent and depth of interaction between children, their mothers and fathers;
(c) the role models available to children and youth, as well as the gender attitudes, values and behaviours expressed in the environments in which they grow and develop;
(d) the active role of children, youth and adults in the development of the personal-cultural link which results in a unique gender identity.

The findings of the various research investigations are examined within this framework in an attempt to determine the cultural influences which guide the learning of gender roles and the development of gender identities in the Caribbean.

(a) The cultural context, and belief systems which establish the parameters of gender behaviour in a particular setting

The division of socialisation and labour in the Caribbean along gender lines, is rooted in strong beliefs about masculinity and femininity, manhood and womanhood; based to some extent on religious teachings as well as on traditional cultural values. The work of Brown and Chevannes (1995: 130-131) reveals expressions about male/female roles in society, and the assertion of male supremacy and dominance which are suggestive almost of biological determinism: a man is tough, he is the provider, the head of the house, are supported by statements such as: 'God made us to control the world, animals, women, everybody'; 'no woman can brilliant like a man, because once you is a man you is a king – A woman is only a queen'; 'a woman no suppose to be the head a nutten as long as man involve in a it – a so the earth set up'.

These point to traditional values and concepts relating to manhood and womanhood, and reflect some of the tenets of sociobiology, as well as the biological essentialism, androcentrism and gender polarisation which comprise Bem's gender lenses.

Attainment of manhood is associated with heterosexual activity, and being financially capable of supporting the offspring which result, as well as the 'baby mother'. The woman is expected to be a good homemaker and domestic manager, and her competence in this area contributes to the man's status in the community. This attribution of status and respect according to the degree of material support provided for the household has not changed substantially from the findings of Brodber (1968) in Jamaica, and Rodman (1971) in Trinidad and Tobago.

Gender polarisation as described by Bem (1993) is evident and stereo-types of dominant, public, male; and accommodating, private, female persist; although definitions and presentations of masculinity and femi-ninity as opposing categories are more clear-cut in some settings than in others. The Brown and Chevannes data indicate that Jamaican women appear to be the most assertive of those in the three research settings examined, and the least likely to play the subordinate, passive role. One of the Jamaican women, Janice, for example, would not yield when she challenged a male player in the domino game and claimed that 'No man naa kip mi down or trample pon mi!' (Brown and Chevannes 1995: 36).

The data also support other research which reported long-standing value conflicts between men and women which result in the struggles and confrontation which typify male/female relationships. These struggles are generated through lack of trust, lack of financial and emotional support, as well as the sexual double standard. This tension between Caribbean men and women has been commented upon previously by Barrow (1986). Involvement of men with multiple sex partners is tacitly, though resentfully, allowed by women, as long as she is given the respect due to herself as the primary partner. Perpetuation of the expression of hetero-sexual behaviour with several partners as one of the markers of the attainment of manhood, would be explained by sociobiologists as the male ensuring the continuity of his genes.

The heterosexual prescription for sexual activity is very strong, and homosexuality is treated with scorn, derision and violence. The homopho-bia in Jamaica and the Caribbean is well known, and is vividly expressed in popular music. Very little is known about homosexuality and homo-sexuals in this setting, possibly because of the level of disapproval and animosity associated with this sexual orientation and lifestyle. Interest-ingly, however, in one of the communities studied by Brown and Chevan-nes, there was evidence of lesbian relationships among some of the women.

Gender polarisation is strongly evident in attitudes to sexual behaviour. Men are expected to take the initiative in sexual approaches, and women are still treated as victims and/or property – subject to rape, abuse, violence and abandonment. Brown and Chevannes (1995) report that both men and women consider that man/woman violence is deserved when a woman does not adequately fulfil her expected role in terms of domestic duties and sexual fidelity. There is the assertion, strongly sup-ported, that 'uman fi get lik' (women are to be beaten) (p. 42); Dali (14-years-old) boasts about his involvement in battery (gang rape) at age 13, and indicates that when it comes to sex, he has 'no mercy, pure agony' (p. 89); girls who are victims of battery rape are referred to in the community as 'mattresses' (p. 82); Nellie is offered to the researcher by her 'baby father' (p. 77), thus reflecting the view of the female as 'territory' over which her male partner exerts control. Abandonment is also common: Claudia's son, a successful doctor, does not remember her or does anything to assist her (p. 65).

Male/female roles in society are very often reflected in the lyrics of popular songs – calypso in Trinidad and Tobago and dancehall in Jamaica – and these reveal a contempt for women on the one hand, and admira-tion on the other. The powerful effect which the diverse and often contradictory messages, from a variety of sources, can have in the shaping of attitudes to women, and attitudes of women to themselves, could result in the development of a variety of 'subjective identities' (Chodorow 1995) among girls and women in the Caribbean. Barriteau-Foster (1992: 9), using a postmodern framework in her review of the results of the Women in the Caribbean Project (1979-82), referred to the diversity of women's reality, and views of themselves in relation to others, and concluded that the findings 'complement, contradict, compound and confound existing stereotypes of Caribbean women', illustrating the 'multiple interactions' of these women's lives.

(b) The extent and depth of interaction between children, their mothers and fathers.

Fulfiling the reproductive function is crucial to Caribbean women, who acquire status within their communities when they become mothers. Many have their first child early in life so as to establish the fact of their fertility. Powell (1986) reported that 50 per cent of Caribbean women have their first child while still an adolescent, and only about 25 per cent of the children in the Caribbean were born into a married union. The other 75 per cent grow up in family situations where there may be no resident male, or among adults who may not be actual relatives. In the Women in the Caribbean Project (1979-82), 1,600 homes in three Eastern Caribbean countries were surveyed, and it was found that more than 50 per cent of the children were reared by women other than their mothers, usually grandmothers. Roberts and Sinclair (1978) estimated that the figure for Jamaica was 15 per cent.

In most countries of the Caribbean, the number of female-headed households exceeds 30 per cent. These women assume the role of bread-winner for their families, and often delegate the child rearing function to another woman, usually a grandmother or other female relative. Children are often moved between a number of different households before they reach adulthood, and this phenomenon of child shifting, where children are transferred from one home to another throughout their childhood and adolescence, does not allow for any strong feeling of attachment to and/or identification with their parents, or any adult figure, and has implications for their ability to develop stable adult relationships. While some may be able to survive this deprivation of love, attention and stability in their lives without psychological damage, for many there is anger and hostility at being abandoned, and a lack of self-esteem resulting from their constant marginality in various household settings. These settings and processes, which differ markedly from those which form the basis of western theo-rising about gender, emphasise the importance of ongoing Caribbean analyses which address gender, its development and expression contex-tually.

Brown and Chevannes (1995) report the recognition, even theoreti-cally, of the importance of male involvement in the nurturance and upbringing of both male and female children, but very often this is expressed in terms of provision of material necessities rather than a process of interaction and emotional involvement. This has implications for the development of emotional bonds with a male adult during childhood. A distinction was made in the Jamaican sample between being a 'faada' and being a 'pa', the difference being explained by Brown and Chevannes (1995: 106) as follows: 'Being 'pa' simply means siring a child, whereas a 'faada' assumes responsibility for its upbringing'.

A number of instances of men acting as 'faadas' were described, and many fathers complained that their children were not told by their mothers of the demonstration of caring in the form of financial contributions which the fathers make to the household, and expressed the feeling of being sidelined by mothers in the rearing of their children. They were, for the most part, anxious to secure their children's love, which, in their view, was often reserved for the mother. It is not surprising that children develop strong bonds of love for their mothers, while in many instances this is not so with their fathers. Apart from the physical absence of fathers, their parental role in the home when present is often confined to disciplining the child. The father's punishment is usually harsh, and reserved for instances when the seriousness of an offence is to be emphasised. In the case of mothers, discipline is ongoing and there is often much love and affection shared between mother and child after a flogging has been administered. There are also gender distinctions in the frequency and severity of punishment – the harsher punishment meted out to boys is expected to toughen them, presumably to deal with the harsh realities of the street/public world, and this punishment is usually carried out with a strap or whip of some kind.

The male/female divide in terms of interaction with children reflects a situation of physical and psychological distance on the part of father and adult males, and reinforces the traditional roles of men and women as protectors and nurturers respectively. The desire on the part of many men to share in the nurture of their children, and the active involvement of several of them in this activity challenges the sociobiological view of this role being linked to the female of the species, while the varying expressions of these 'female' and 'male' roles in the society, and the many changes which are taking place in terms of these roles, raise questions as to the relevance of this theory in explaining gender behaviour.

(c) The role models available to children and youth, as well as the gender attitudes, values and behaviours expressed in the environments in which they grow and develop.

In the socialisation of children there is a public/private; street/yard; male/female divide which has persisted over the years. (Rodman 1971; Hodge 1977; Justus 1981; Moses 1981). These dichotomies reflect the bi-polarity of male/female socialisation and contribute to the gender polarising lens which Bem (1993) identifies. Interviews conducted in the Brown and Chevannes research reveal that girls and women are kept in the yard for their protection – it is assumed that if they are allowed too much freedom they will 'get into trouble'. In many instances, boys are also kept off the street, but there is a gender difference in terms of the danger against which they are being protected. In the case of girls, it is sexual assault, sexual involvement and the possibility of pregnancy; for boys it is crime, including drugs. There is , however, a symbiotic relationship between the yard and the street for boys – the street is expected to toughen and prepare boys for survival, which is an extension of the teaching being given in the yard. The street has nothing to offer girls besides danger and disgrace.

Various signs point to a contraction of the period of childhood among boys. In Jamaica the phenomenon of 'street children', who are almost exclusively boys between the ages of 8 and 17 years, and who live on the streets, fend for themselves and neither attend school nor return home at nights, is well documented (CVSS 1987; Rattray 1988; Leo-Rhynie 1994). Ennew and Young (1981: 59), examining child labour in Jamaica, commented that many children 'grow up before their time. They become proto-adults adept at surviving in the midst of poverty and unemployment'.

Boys learn adult male behaviours from watching and participating in the 'male culture'of their communities. Brown and Chevannes report that men spend a great deal of time outside of the home, and men's leisure time is catered for by other men. The local bars which are centres for meeting and which seem to be the training ground for young men are run by men in most communities, but also by women in Jamaica. These women establish a rapport with the men, joining in their discussions as equals, and having their opinions heard by these men. Drinking and drunkenness as a male activity was not stressed, except in one case in the Indo-Guyanese community. Gambling is, however, a predominantly male leisure activity – a mild form of the extreme risk taking found among males in some communities. It would almost appear that boys are socialised into this risk taking, which is expressed when they fight, hustle, beg, steal, peddle drugs and take other chances. These activities are, however, considered to be part of the survival strategies of the street.

The concept of male 'separateness' – the exclusion of women from male activity in both work and leisure, and the emphasis on difference, has been discussed by Patai (1984) who notes that this is taken to an extreme in some countries which promote military service and the involvement of young men in real or simulated war situations. The 'man as warrior' ideology is also strongly promoted in many cultures where manhood and masculinity are associated with street fighting, battles with police, bearing pain without flinching, violence, swearing and other aggressive behaviour. Brown and Chevannes noted that one of the lessons being taught to boys on the street in Jamaica is that conflict is to be settled through fighting – and a win-at-all-costs attitude prevails. Losers in a fight are ridiculed – even by their own parents, and the references to weaning the boys from their mothers, and 'toughening them up' seem designed to ensure their 'separateness' from things feminine, and firm placement in the category of males. Given the level of homophobia in the society, it is important for boys to avoid, at all costs, the label of 'sissy' or 'maama man' applied when they show emotion or behaviour considered inappropriate to the 'macho' male.

In the Brown and Chevannes study, young boys seem to learn their adult roles through observation and imitation; they participate in the adult male culture by running errands for adult males, and by watching activities, including gambling at the rum bar, from the sidelines. They then end up playing truant from school to gamble as they observe their role models doing. The ability to join in men's leisure activities appears to be one of the boy-to-man 'rites of passage'. They are forbidden by law to enter the rum shop when young, yet they are able to observe the activities taking place, and in the absence of a father or male presence in the home, they probably see the rum shop, and the conversations and activities they observe there, as a source of valuable information about men and how men behave in different situations. It is from these sources, therefore, and through these processes, that their gender lenses are constructed, and gender identities consolidated.

Children generally, but boys in particular, are exposed to explicit expressions of sexuality in the media (and there is little or no discouragement of this exposure by adult males), and this is resulting in an awareness of, and experimentation in adult sexual behaviour on the part of boys as young as four to six years (Brown and Chevannes 1995). Early expression of sexual behaviour by boys is accepted and even encouraged, with the expectation that this will definitely occur in the early teenage years. This preoccupation with sexuality and its expression among very young children can be partially attributed to their exposure to pornographic material on cable and satellite television which often portrays distorted views of sexual expression, such as women 'enjoying' violence during sex. These media images can have powerful influences on the development of sexuality among boys and girls, particularly in settings such as the Caribbean, where accurate information about human sexuality is often not readily available.

School is seen as being of little importance to boys' development into manhood. Brown and Chevannes note that the men who are regarded as successful by boys are those who have survived against the odds, who have not necessarily benefitted from education. The girls with all their education just do not experience success to the same extent. Sociobiologists may see this as an evolutionary trend, where the 'fittest' in terms of survival are no longer those who have attained the highest levels of education, and education is seen as important for the female parent who raises and nurtures the children, but as lacking relevance for men who are the providers.

Several parents subscribe to the concept of occupational multiplicity for male children, who are often kept from school to assist their parents in income generation, and also to develop their own entrepreneurial skills. The goal of education for boys seems to be vocational educational and having a 'skill', rather than mere 'book learning' which is all right for the girls. School also seems to be used as a means of extending the confinement of girls, keeping them off the 'street', and so deferring the inevitable pregnancy. The 'street experience' is seen, however, as an important part of the boy's education, so truancy, and dropping out of school seems almost to be expected of boys. One boy notes 'di school business is a fraud. A man have to learn to live from people who go through the rough and tough. Dat no teach inna school' (Brown and Chevannes 1995: 99).

(d) The active role of children, youth and adults in the development of the personal-cultural link which results in a unique gender identity.

The data presented by Brown and Chevannes (1995) provide evidence of differing individual responses to the same situation, personal interpretations which suggest the active involvement of individuals in the formation of the gender lenses used in the comprehension and application of attitudes and behaviours. In one example, three adolescent boys whose fathers were not providing either financial or emotional support to their households, reacted very differently to this paternal absence and near abandonment. One was resentful, hostile and angry, and was causing worry and distress in his mother; another, though obviously troubled by the situation, expressed a quiet contempt for the father, but no open hostility; while the third viewed any relationship he could have with his father as a purely financial one, which was upsetting when it broke down, but the emotional support provided by his mother offset his disappointment.

The evidence of change in gender roles over the past two decades challenges the essentialism of sociobiology, and supports the view that the acquisition of a gender identity is a dynamic process and that the individual is an active participant in this process. The changes taking place are not necessarily perceived positively by men; some complain about the entry of women to the labour market and what they see as the implications of this; some comment on the 'independence' which 'women's liberation' has brought to the women in the community; while the man who is not 'macho', and who may decide to share domestic duties with his female partner is not respected by his peers (Brown and Chevannes, 1995).

Changes in the economic situation in the Caribbean have resulted in many men being unable to support their families. This is counter to the cultural norm, and in the Indo-Guyanese community examined in the Socialisation Project, it is a source of great distress, as it has resulted in women seeking work outside the home, and in some instances earning more than their male partners. This has created embarrassment and frustration for the men, whose manhood/male identity is strongly linked to their ability to provide for their families. Many men will participate in criminal activity to fulfil this role. Frustration at having to depend on a female wage may be expressed in drunkenness and wife beating, as violence becomes a way for the man to reinforce his position as head of household and to compensate for his loss of economic power.

Women interviewed in the Brown and Chevannes study, who worked outside the home, felt that it was important to retain a personal savings account even though they did contribute to the household. This was their security in the face of their lack of trust in men. Women have been using their earnings, and education also, as tools of resistance; they allow women to have options, and to be able to challenge the authority of their mates. This is not appreciated by men, who bemoan the fact that women are refusing to suffer violence and abuse, and will try to fight back. Men also consider women to be mercenary, as being mainly concerned with the money the man can provide in a relationship, and although many women still view men as providers, in two communities, young women indicated that they want to know that the man's money is earned *honestly*.

There is also evidence of a number of emerging trends which the data of Brown and Chevannes reveal, and which have the potential to influence gender socialisation and gender relationships, as women seem to be changing the traditional roles associated with their involvement in sexual relationships. These include:

- Lesbian relationships in one community in Jamaica.
- Teen girls initiating sexual approaches and pressuring boys for sex.
- Independent women, shying away from men who may seek to dominate and/or abuse them, are financially supporting younger men and boys in exchange for sexual favours.

Sex is also increasingly seen as a commodity to be exchanged for a variety of material goods: the 'requirement' in some communities that the young men dress in 'brand name' clothes and shoes, and that young women be able to 'profile' in exotic hairdos and the latest dancehall fashions, is satisfied among many young people through 'barrels' sent by parents and relatives overseas. Much of this consumerism, however, as well as the payment of school fees, purchase of school books and educational supplies, is supported by 'payment in kind' for sexual favours. In the harsh economic conditions under which they live, parents often turn a blind eye to this, but some adults fear that boys may be enticed into homosexuality in this way.

Discussion

The research findings reveal certain constants: the relative freedom of male children, and the protectiveness applied to their female siblings/counterparts, the division of labour along gender lines from very early in life, the predominance of leisure time in the lives of men which is spent in activities which bond them to other men, the double standard relating to the expression of male and female sexuality, and the concept of male control and power in sexual relationships with women, extending to abuse and violence in some situations. The context of socialisation is the yard/home, the street/community environs, school and the wider society, as well as the media, chiefly television. It would seem that the gender polarising lenses of these societies are very clearly focused.

The very rich, 'textured' data emerging from these research investigations provide insights into the universe of experience, the 'elements of objective gender' (Chodorow 1995), from which children and youth develop their concepts of gender, construct their lenses of gender, and gradually acquire their subjective gender identities. Whether it is a process of identification through the relationships they share with their parents in early childhood, the role models which are available for their observation and imitation, the active interaction and learning of various aspects of the cultural belief systems (Bem's 'enculturation'), these experiences are all powerful social/cultural forces which influence the gender identities which Caribbean youth develop. Chodorow's contention that social/cultural forces create gender ideologies which are internalised in psyches, and that these psyches also produce social/cultural forces, suggests that the creation of gender identity is, as the postmodernists posit, a reciprocal and dynamic process between individuals and the environment, resulting in 'personal-cultural' constructs which are unique to individual persons. The Caribbean context obviously provides a range of experiences which have the potential to generate powerful gender related feelings and emotions which can be used in the process of continuously constructing and reconstructing personal gender.

The need to have a theory which is sufficiently flexible to take account of the 'objective' as well as the 'subjective' in this process of construction and reconstruction, makes Chodorow's perspective and postmodern approaches both attractive and relevant. The need to recognise difference, between as well as within male and female groups, as well as the way in which gendered relations differ in these groups, make the experiences of these individuals vitally important to the ongoing analysis of socialisation, gender identity, and gendered social relations in the Caribbean. Unfortunately, many of the socialisation experiences and gender meanings emerging from this context are not supportive of positive, equitable male/female relationships, community and nation building, and interventions are needed so that the process of construction and reconstruction of gender can bring about significant change in the development of gender identities in Caribbean societies.

Note

1. Acknowledgement: The analysis of research in this article incorporates several aspects of a review of the findings of The Socialisation Project of the University of the West Indies (UWI) which the author presented at a conference held in Jamaica in October, 1995. This conference was held to receive, review and discuss the major findings of the project, which was designed and directed by lead researchers, Janet Brown of the Caribbean Child Development Centre, and Barry Chevannes of the Department of Sociology and Social Work, UWI and funded by a grant from UNICEF.

SECTION IV

Representations of Femininity and Masculinity:
Embodiment, Sexuality and Family

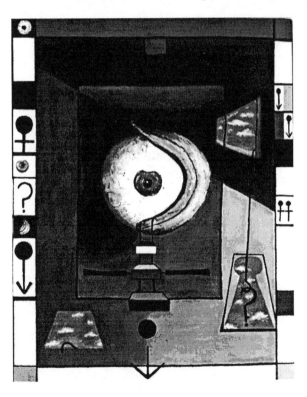

15

Body Talk:
Writing and Speaking the Body in the Texts of Caribbean Women Writers

Denise deCaires Narain

This chapter explores the ways in which a selection of Caribbean women writers have represented the female body in their texts. Making use of a range of feminist and post-colonial theorisations of the body, my discussion will focus on the way in which the body functions at the thematic *and* aesthetic levels in these literary texts, interrogating some of the connections between sexuality and textuality. I argue that the body of the woman functions in the body of these texts as a dramatic site of contestation resulting in a series of diverse – and often contradictory – inscriptions and strategies for recovery. Before addressing the literary texts, a few framing remarks are necessary to indicate the critical and literary contexts within which I wish to locate these texts.

The woman's body has always been the locus of attention in feminist discourse, often signifying the most intensely focused site – and source – of women's oppression. In response to this notion of woman's biology as (painful) destiny, women have represented the female body as cause for mourning – and for celebration. Theoretical perspectives on the female body have been similarly diverse but the perspective most relevant here is that associated with French feminists who insist that it is not enough to simply replace negative images of the woman with positive ones; instead they advocate a disruption of the very symbolic structures which produce gendered writings (and readings) and they argue for the mobilisation of a whole new economy of symbols. The writing practice, *ecriture feminine*, which these feminists promote is one which privileges the woman's body, and in particular the mother's body, as symbolic of plenitude and possibility – or *jouissance*. In this account, the messy corporeality traditionally associated with the female body is drawn upon so that the body of woman/the mother is used as a powerful source of strength and mobility, rather than as a sign of limitation and lack. Further, the perceived fluidity and boundarylessness of the relationship between mother and child before the child enters the symbolic order – and is *placed* in this symbolic order (or *dis-placed*, in the case of the girl child) – is utilised as a paradigm for a writing practice which seeks to undermine patriarchal discourse by a range of strategies: mimicry which slips into mockery of patriarchal discourse, irreverence of tone, polyphony, transgression of the rules of grammar, punning etc. The *voice* of the mother is often invoked as metonymic of the mother's body and pitted against the sterility of the Law of the Father. Toril Moi (1985: 114) argues in a discussion of Cixous' work that: 'Woman, in other words, is wholly and physically present in her voice – and writing is no more than the extension of this self-identical prolongation of the speech act.'

It is in this focus on the oral and the subversive potential of the spoken word that feminist and post-colonial agendas intersect most interestingly. Both perspectives characterise patriarchal/imperial discourses as sterile, oppressive and relentlessly categorising and there is a similar insistence in each of the need to subvert both the negative images as well as the symbolic structures which *produce* such distorted images. As a result, post-colonial writers (in a similar trajectory to women writers) have used literary texts to catalogue the violence done to the black body under colonial regimes and to celebrate the power of the black body to survive such violence. Fanon powerfully outlines the centrality of the body, because it is the *visible* marker of racial difference, in distorting the self-image of the black man:

I took myself far off from my own presence, far indeed, and made myself an object. What else could it be for me but an amputation, an excision, a haemorrhage that spattered my whole body with black blood? . My body was given back to me sprawled out, distorted, recolored, clad in mourning in that white winter day. (Fanon 1986: 112-113)

Contemporary post-colonial critics have attempted to recuperate this battered black body and, increasingly, to utilise it as the source of empowerment and agency rather than continuing to represent it as the site of pain and victimhood. In the Caribbean context, this has resulted in a privileging of *presence* – particularly the presence associated with *voice* – which has interesting gendered implications as well as connecting back to the metonymic use of the voice (as representative of the body) indicated above in relation to *ecriture feminine*. There is, then, a similar stress on 'orality' in both French feminist and post-colonial discourses. In the former, there is an imperative to 'write the body', to inflect the printed (patriarchal) Word with the physical presence associated with woman; in the latter, there is a similar emphasis on pitting the post-colonial body – with the spoken or performed word standing in for the body – against the hegemony of the printed word. This privileging of orality has often resulted in the elevation of Creole language to the status of *the* repository of authentic Caribbean identity. A figure such as Louise Bennett – who writes exclusively in Creole and pioneered the use of 'literary Creole' – is given enormous symbolic weight, captured succinctly in John Agard's description of her as 'mudder language giver (Agard 1985: 57). This equating of 'mother tongue' with the mother is given further symbolic weight by the structural link between Creole and *Mother* Africa (Creole having been forged out of a combination of West African languages and English). While standard English was (and continues to be) the dominant public discourse (used in all institutions of patriarchal power), Creole is perceived as the (discredited) language of the home with women ac-corded the role of culture/language keepers. A series of further associa-tions results in a motherland/mother tongue conflation in which woman/woman's language (here, Creole) is posited as a pure, 'untouch-able' symbolic space in direct contrast to the imposter language: standard English. A neat binary is then set up where Creole is associated with authentic Caribbeanness, with Africa, with the spoken/the lived, with the folk, with polyphony and open-endedness while standard English is associated with the printed text, with the elite, with institutions of power, with Europe and patriarchy.

Carolyn Cooper, in her text, *Noises in the Blood*, offers a reading of Jamaican popular culture which utilises this binary, privileging the 'slack', hybrid Creole text over the closure and 'uptightness' of the printed standard English text:

The subjects of this study are, for the most part, bastard oral texts – literary jackets. These vulgar products of illicit procreation may be conceived – in poor taste – as perverse invasions of the tightly-closed orifices of the Great Tradition. They require that the 'greatness' of tradition itself become subject to the vulgarizing redefinitions of *popular* 'good taste'. Though the promiscuous dilations of the critical text need to be contained within limits of respectability, the ordering imperative of academic propriety does not entirely silence the cunning language of subversive noises in the blood. (Cooper: 1993: 9)

Later in the text, the association of women with 'slackness' is made explicit: 'Transgressive Woman is Slackness personified, embodying the porous openings in the oral text'. (p. 10) Cooper's *re-cooperation* of Jamaican popular culture is motivated by the same kind of ideological imperative at work in many recent post-colonial interventions where the focus on the body seems to be driven by a desire to read the native body as a space somehow uncontaminated by colonialism, so that it functions as a reservoir of authentic nativeness. In this scenario, the speaking voice, especially the Creole speaking voice, is fetishised and given an inflated subversive potential, operating *automatically* as a radically destabilising discourse. There is, then, an ideologically-driven impulse in much post-colonial and in some feminist criticism to keep the oral/scribal binarism in place by overemphasising the closure of the written word and, concomitantly, overemphasising the open-ended playfulness of 'the oral'. Now, I'm aware of the violent conjunction of circumstances which resulted in the creation of Creole languages on Caribbean plantations and it is not my intention to diminish the history of this linguistic struggle, but it also seems timely to ask whether Creole has passed its 'sell-by' date as the *exclusive* symbol of the Caribbean people's ability to survive. It also seems timely to start unravelling the neat fit between Creole authenticity and Caribbean woman which is in danger of hardening into a prescriptive and limiting orthodoxy. Given that French feminism operates with a very culturally specific notion of 'the mother' in play and that much black cultural theory takes as its focus the black *male* subject, interventions such as Cooper's are timely and welcome, however problematic her conclusions are.

In terms of *literary* representations of the female body, the figure of the all-powerful mother has dominated the field. In the literary texts of male and female authors, the *maternal body* has loomed large, making other representations of the female body difficult. Dionne Brand (1994:45) argues convincingly in her essay, 'This Body For Itself', that ' these big mothers overwhelming our texts' have rendered the explicitly sexual female body invisible. Those writers who have dealt with sexuality, rather than soft-focus *sensuality*, have often focused on the trauma which adult female sexuality precipitates as in Jamaica Kincaid's *Annie John*, for example, where Annie's response to the unruly growth of her body at puberty is described:

But what could I do? I thought of begging my mother to ask my father if he could build for me a set of clamps into which I could screw myself before I went to sleep and which would surely cut back on my growing (1984: 27).

Rather than being the cause for celebration, as French feminists suggest, the burgeoning female body is the cause of alarm and fear. The three writers I will now focus on in detail all deal repeatedly – but in different ways – with the female body and female sexuality and allow me to explore some of the contradictions, tensions and possibilities of making connections between sexuality and textuality.

Swigging her breast in the face of history

Grace Nichols (a Guyanese now resident in Britain) is a poet who has consistently made the black female body the focus of attention in the body of her work. Her work thematises the black woman's body again and again to uncover this 'submerged' body and re-cover it in a more loving range of symbols so that, cumulatively, it signifies positively. In her first collection, *i is a long memoried woman*, Nichols catalogues the damage done to the black female body in plantation slavery and, in self-consciously filling in the gaps in Kamau Brathwaite's *The Arrivants*, she pits her word against his 'mastertext' of the dispersal of the African- Caribbean man (Nichols 1983). Where in Brathwaite's poem, the mother's body represents a 'safe haven' in a world where the black man is demonised, in Nichols's text, motherhood and mothering are represented as fraught and painful:

> she came
>   into the new world
> birth aching her pain
> from one continent/ to another
> moaning
>
> her belly cry sounding the wind
>
> and after fifty years
> she hasn't forgotten
> hasn't forgotten
> how she had lain there
> in her own blood
> lain there in her own shit
>
> bleeding memories in the darkness
> (p. 6)

Nichols capitalises on the imagery of the painful delivery of a child as a metaphor for the traumatic and violent birth of the Caribbean itself. In another poem, 'Ala', Nichols describes the punishment of a slave woman who has committed infanticide:

Face up
they hold her naked body
to the ground
arms and legs spread-eagle
each tie with rope to stake
then they coat her in sweet
molasses and call us out
to see . . . the rebel woman

who with a pin
stick the soft mould
of her own child's head
(p. 23)

Here, Nichols indicates the cultural specificity involved in notions of the 'good mother' and implies a redefinition which could encompass infanticide. In 'Sugar Cane', Nichols exploits the phallic shape of the sugar cane plant to capture the physical vulnerability of the slave woman who must look after this crop. In other poems, Nichols describes the black woman as using her body language to express in coded form what cannot be said openly. So, in 'Skin-teeth' (p. 50), the speaker outlines the menace which lurks behind the smile the master sees on her face. While, in 'Love Act', Nichols evocatively captures the ways in which the slave's body is 'the fuel/ that keep them all going' – the slave woman works the fields, is wet nurse to the master's children and must service the master sexually as well. If a smile can be treacherous in 'Skin-teeth', in this poem the sex act is described as having potentially fatal consequences as the speaker plots rebellion beneath the guise of succumbing to the 'love act'. In this collection, Nichols suggests that, in a repressive context where overt resistance is dangerous, the black woman's body be read as a coded surface where body language signifies what is forbidden to be stated openly. Many of the poems convey the poet's own sense of the inadequacy of words in the face of the violence and cruelty of the histories being dealt with, as in 'Eulogy' which, in its attempt to honour the memory of those slaves who died in the 'middle passage', repeatedly asks the question 'How can I eulogize their names? What dance of mourning can I make?' (p. 17) Nichols asserts the importance of the *presence* — or *thereness* — of the black woman, even if she is voiceless and she utilises this notion of a forceful but silent female presence in the epigraph:

From dih pout

of mih mouth
from dih
treacherous

calm of mih
smile
you can tell
I is a long memoried woman

While the epilogue hints at the *promise* of speech in the future:

I have crossed an ocean
I have lost my tongue
from the root of the old
one
a new one has sprung

i is a long memoried woman functions as a kind of catharsis for Nichols, preparing the way for the subsequent volumes where she activates the black woman's body with sexual power *and* with word power.

In *The Fat Black Woman's Poems*, Nichols (1984) organises this cycle of poems around challenging the image of the black woman as the 'big mother' – the 'every mother' or 'mammie' figure. Again, Nichols insists that the body is not as transparently readable as at first appears:

The fat black woman
remembers her Mama
and them days of *playing*
the Jovial Jemima

tossing pancakes
to heaven
in smokes of happy hearty
    murderous blue laughter
[My emphasis, p. 9]

Nichols then, offers a series of images of the black woman which harness her largeness to a quite different agenda — that of the beautiful, sexually active and assertive black woman. In 'Thoughts drifting through the fat black woman's head while having a full bubble bath' (p. 15), the speaker anarchically pits her naked – soapy – body against a series of figures representing patriarchy: 'O how I long to place my foot/ on the head of anthropology/ to swig my breasts/ in the face of history/ to scrub my back/ with the dogma of theology' (p. 15). In other poems, the speaker asserts her resistance to the constraints of fashion, refusing to be like 'the frozen thin mannequins' (p.11).

Where the battered body of the black woman is, perforce, silent in *i is a long memoried woman*, the fat black woman speaks directly *at* the reader empowering her voice with a subversive, sassy humour. So, in 'Invitation', having described her own powerful, large, fecund body, the fat black woman challenges a prospective suitor to 'Come up and see me some-time'; the poem concludes with the following: 'there's a mole that gets a ride/ each time I shift the heritage/ of my behind/ Come up and see me sometime'' (p. 13). The poem refers to history – 'heritage of my behind' – but is no longer silenced by the nightmarish violence of it.

In her third collection of poems, *Lazy Thoughts of a Lazy Woman*, Nichols (1989) continues to focus on the black woman's body but the body now is located more firmly within the metropolitan context of London. The concerns here are much less directly tied to Caribbean history and more readily readable as articulating a feminist agenda. So, there are poems which humorously challenge prevailing notions of ideal femininity which hinge upon slimming, elaborate beauty re-gimes, shaving 'unwanted bodily hair' etc. In 'The Body Reclining' (p. 4), the routine of domestic duties is rejected and the body is celebrated in its lazy repose – this is writing about the 'body for itself' which Dionne Brand advocates above. In poems such as 'Ode To My Bleed' (p.24) and 'My Black Triangle' (p.25), women's sexuality is associated with the power of nature and is presented as challenging the sterility of patriarchal power structures:

> And though
> it spares a thought for history
> my black triangle
> has spread beyond his story
> beyond the dry fears of parch-ri-archy

While, in 'Configurations', she dramatises the encounter between Europe and the 'New World' as a series of trade-offs between the black woman and the white man in the act of sex. The poem concludes with an ambivalent image of the woman asserting her control over him at precisely the moment when she should be *succumbing* to him:

> He does a Columbus –
> falling on the shores of her tangled nappy orchard.
>
> She delivers up the whole Indies again
> But this time her wide legs close in
>   slowly
> Making a golden stool of the empire
> of his head.
> (p. 31)

In 'On Poems and Crotches', female sexuality is mobilised at a more fundamental level as the inspirational force which produces the poetry itself:

For poems are born
in the bubbling soul of the crotch.
Poems rise to marry good old Consciousness.
Poems hug Visionary-Third-Eye.
Kiss Intellect.
Before hurrying on down
to burst their way through the crotch.
(p. 16)

The irreverence of tone in this poem, coupled with the insistence, at the level of theme, on the female erotic as a source of power is treated again in a different way in 'Wherever I Hang'. In this poem, a migrant in London explores some of the circumstances of her current displacement; the poem concludes:

To tell you de truth
I don't really know where I belaang
        Yes, divided to de ocean
        Divided to de bone
Wherever I hang me knickers – that's my home.
(p. 10)

In transposing the word 'knickers' for the word 'hat' in the line from a popular song, 'Wherever I lay my hat that's my home', Nichols inserts her speaker into the conventionally male role of the roving lover. But the poem also irreverently echoes the lines of a well known poem by Derek Walcott: 'I who am poisoned with the blood of both/ Where shall I turn, divided to the vein?' Nichols is not dismissing the anguish of 'the divided self' which haunts so many Caribbean-authored texts; rather, she is positing the possibility of dealing with this existential angst in a more whimsical, if not 'slack', manner.

There is in Grace Nichols' work a persistent attention to representing the black female body and, I have argued, her poetic project is concerned to recover – and re-cover – this body so that it is not read eternally as mutilated victim, as 'clad in mourning'. Certainly, Nichols provides images of the black female body as empowered – with sexuality being harnessed as a vehicle for this empowerment, rather than being the automatic signifier of black women's lack of agency. In terms of an aesthetics of the body, Nichols' texts do not foreground the kinds of textual game playing or multiplicity of voices associated with *ecriture feminine*; and, while she often makes use of a confrontational speaking voice in many of her poems, Nichols invariably signals the 'Creoleness' of the speaker with the *minimum* of linguistic codes – her poems are lean and contained, exhibiting none of the hyperbole or other verbal excesses associated with the Creole poetry of, say, Louise Bennett. I would argue, then, that while at the level of thematic focus, Nichols makes the black female body the subject of her work, hers is a writing *about* the body rather than a *writing* the body.

My people have been separated from themselves White Hen, by several means, one of them being the printed word and the ideas it carries

By comparison to Nichols, the textual strategies employed by Erna Brodber (a Jamaican novelist/sociologist) in her three novels (Brodber 1980, 1988, 1994) are much more easily associated with the writing practices advocated by French feminists as outlined above. These are 'open-ended' texts in which the reader must actively participate in constructing meaning out of a plethora of possibilities. While each of the novels has central female protagonists, these protagonists are so intimately and densely embedded in the contexts of their communities and the boundaries between the individual and community are so blurred that to use terms such as 'protagonist' or 'character' is, in some sense, misleading. These texts eschew the conventions of linear chronology and there is no authoritative discourse within the text to which the reader can look for guidance. Narrative attention seldom settles for sustained periods on any one moment or subject position; instead, Brodber circles back and forth over the same terrain, so that meanings proliferate and any understanding of the text can only work cumulatively. These are difficult but truly polyphonic texts – *noisy texts*, as it were.

One of the features of Brodber's texts which contributes to the 'difficulty factor' associated with reading her work is the way in which she privileges the speaking voice and attempts, generally, to inscribe 'the oral' into the written text. In *Jane and Louisa*, Brodber uses an oral form – a Jamaican children's ring game – to provide the novel's title and fragments of the refrain are used as headings for sections of the text. In each of the novels, the bulk of the narrative is provided in snatches of conversation, in internal monologues, in Anancy stories, in riddles and songs and in folk wisdom. These voices are presented in fragments, speakers are often not identified by name, speech marks are not used and no explanatory gloss is given to 'explain' Jamaican cultural codes. Via this cacophony of voices, Brodber positions the reader as *listener*. As one of the voices in *Jane and Louisa* puts it 'the voice belongs to the family group dead and alive. We walk by their leave, for planted in the soil, we must walk over them to get where we are going' (p.12). Brodber also experiments – most dramatically in *Jane and Louisa* and *Louisiana* – with a range of layouts and typography to resist the closure associated with the printed page. In terms of her textual strategies then, Brodber's texts are readily associable with *ecriture feminine*.

What interests me, for the purpose of this chapter, is the way in which, in tandem with this *writing* the body, there is also a relentless writing *about* the body and the results of each of these modes of representing or expressing the body suggests an interesting tension between the two. *Jane and Louisa* charts the breakdown and tentative steps towards recovery of Nellie who is damaged by a patriarchal colonial value system which negates her black Jamaican culture and by a patriarchal 'black brotherhood' which effectively silences her – she is reduced to a brittle 'cracked doll' (p. 61), mouthing an alienating ideological position. Nellie's recovery is made possible by the Rasta figure, Baba, who heals her by reconnecting her with the Creole language of her community (which her stay 'abroad' coupled with foreign education has alienated her from) – he 'rebirths' her into her own language: as Nellie puts it, 'I was willing to learn their ways but someone had to show me, *to born me*' (p. 70, my emphasis). Baba functions as the conduit for Nellie's reconnection with Creole and in doing so Brodber unsettles any easy fit between Creole culture and women. She also suggests the need for a further unsettling of gender roles by presenting Baba as the object of Nellie's gaze:

Baba was waiting for me. Straight and tall in a white gown. *He was the bride.* His hair was neatly plaited (as usual) and his beard obviously brushed . The man exuded the clean astringent atmosphere of lime. It was as if he had been cured, scrubbed, cleansed in lime. *What a beauty!* (p. 62, my emphasis).

When Nellie offers herself to him sexually, Baba refuses arguing, 'I fear that you offer yourself because you don't want you (p.71). Brodber presents an alternative to prevailing conventions of virile, West Indian masculinity, though implicit here in the pruning away of signifiers of sexual potency in the construction of a spiritual redeemer figure is the notion that a de-sexing – or textual neutering – may be a necessary economy.

Nellie's healing is also facilitated by her Aunt Alice but it is significant that this is her *spinster* aunt and that the experiences she introduces Nellie to are 'out of body' experiences where she learns how to transcend the limitations of the physical body and *see*. The novel is punctuated by references to female sexuality as the source of trauma and shame; the very first section refers to the way in which Nellie's mother's life is ruined by an early 'fall' into pregnancy: 'Yes now. The chile life spoil. Lord take the case!' The onset of menstruation, far from being the cause for celebration (as in Grace Nichols' 'Ode to my bleed'), is described as 'the hidey-hidey thing' and associated with the strangeness and decay of femaleness which signals the end of a 'gender-blind' childhood. This identification of female sexuality with disease and decay reaches its most intense expression in the penultimate section, 'The Pill':

Black sperms disintegrating black wombs, making hollow women and name-less pointless children . So the black womb is a maw . The black womb sucks grief and anger and shame but it does not spit. It absorbs them into the body. Take an antidote. Silence it. Best pretend it doesn't exist. Give it a cap of darkness, take a pill . What a life! What an abominable scrap heap thing is the womb. (pp. 142-143)

In this description, the black womb is configured as a 'scrap heap thing' precisely *because* of the multiplicity of signifieds associated with it in the Jamaican cultural context – it becomes the dumping ground for all of society's frustrations. *Jane and Louisa* ends with an image of pregnancy – Nellie dreams she is pregnant with a fish – but this image of fecundity is also rendered ambivalent by the fact that the fish is stuck and she is unable to deliver it, so that even though the novel ends with the hopeful words 'We are getting ready', the sense of Nellie suspended in a state of permanent pregnancy leaves the reader with an irresolute image which suggests she is in a kind of sexual limbo.

In Brodber's second novel, *Myal*, she returns again to the theme of alienation as a result of colonial education and links this version of 'zombification' or 'spirit thievery' to the effects of the various religious forms which are practised in the community of Grove Town – there are Baptists, Methodists, and Anglicans as well as those who practise Myal, Kumina and Obeah. Brodber puts these religious/spiritual discourses in battle with each other, using the bodies of two young women, Ella and Anita, as the theatrical spaces upon which this battle is staged. Ella, of mixed Irish/Jamaican parentage, hovers in a kind of racial limbo and because of her 'alabaster' difference, is set apart from the rest of the community who project a range of superstitions, jealousies and anxieties upon her. Early on in the novel, we are given a vivid image of Ella's zombification when she is seen solemnly reciting Kipling's 'White Man's Burden' – like Nellie, she has a voice but her words are not her own. Later in the text Ella marries an American, Selwyn Langley, who, attracted by her 'exotic mulatto' status, seeks to get from her as much information about the Grove Town community as he can. Ella succumbs to Selwyn's seductive attention and he manages to penetrate 'down' to the story of Grove Town and to drain her of it:

With her hymen and a couple of months marriage gone, there was a clean, clear passage from Ella's head through her middle and right down to outside . Selwyn's pushing had made a clean passage through which he had fallen into that group of Grove Town people (pp. 80-81).

The sexual imagery used in describing Selwyn's violent 'taking' of Ella's story becomes akin to rape when he mutilates her story into minstrelsy, calling it 'The Biggest Coon Show Ever'.

Having outlined the various forces at work in the zombification of Ella colonial education, Grove Town's prejudices, Selwyn's racism – Brodber dramatically stages the culmination of these 'force-feedings' when Ella's body bloats in a grotesque phantom pregnancy. Her return to Grove Town (from America) facilitates her healing and the whole of Grove Town is privy to the smell of the poisons which drain from her body: 'Cook say it was like twenty thousand dead bull frog, the scent that escape from that chile's body. That had to be the hand of man, Cook say to herself' (p. 94). Ella's reconnection with community had started, ironically, in the process of telling her story to Selwyn and her rehabilitation is completed with the cathartic draining of her body. When Ella decides to become a teacher in Grove Town it is, significantly, Reverend Simpson who points her in the direction of finding her own voice: 'Now listen, – he said to her. – You have a quarrel with the writer. He wrote, you think without an aware-ness of certain things. But does he force you to teach without this awareness? *Need your voice say what his says?*' (p. 107, my emphasis). Running in parallel with Ella's story is that of Anita, a *black* Jamaican, whose young body is possessed by the Obeah man, Mass Levi who is desperate for a cure for his impotence. His attempt to drain Anita of *her* vitality is ultimately thwarted by Miss Gatha (who practises Ku-mina), but not before her home is stoned regularly and her body, too, bears the imprint (she is bruised in one of the stonings) of his attempt to 'thieve her spirit'.

What Brodber dramatises in *Myal* with the use of Ella's and Anita's bodies is a playing out of the various ways in which cultural alienation is effected upon the whole community. Their bodies become the stage upon which a collective zombification is enacted and exorcised – and in both cases it is indigenous forms of spiritual healing which provide the cure. Specifically, the centrality given to Ella's phantom pregnancy suggests its function as a cathartic extension and playing out of the role of the womb as a terrible 'scrap heap thing' and of male/female sexual relationships as violently exploitative. But, unlike the image of deferred delivery with which *Jane and Louisa* ends, *Myal* ends with Ella about to make her debut as powerful *deliverer of the word* in her new role as teacher. In foreground-ing Ella's and Anita's bodies as being crucial to the construction of a healed/whole 'nation', Brodber is also signalling clearly the complexity and centrality of sexuality in narrating the nation.

It is the Voice I Hear

The body of the text in *Louisiana* is much more fragmented and fractured than *Myal*, equalling *Jane and Louisa* in the kinds of difficulties with which it confronts the reader. So, once more, the text is littered with a range of voices: snatches of conversations, sayings, proverbs, songs, jazz rhythms, 'spiritualisms' and so on, but, in this text, the constant traffic in voices includes an even more rapid shifting between 'real' voices, 'spirit voices' and the voices on the recording machine. Here, Brodber's canvas is much broader than in the earlier novels as her protagonist, also named Ella, is located as an anthropological researcher in the southern state of Louisi-ana in the 1930s. Mammy, Ella's primary informant, dies before Ella has finished her research project which involves using the new technology of the tape recorder to record her interviews. As Ella attempts to marshal her 'evidence' into systematic order, Mammy, and her spirit-friend Lowly/Louise, mysteriously communicate with Ella via the tape recorder.

Ella becomes increasingly receptive to these voices and, in the process, recuperates her own personal history and reconnects with her 'bitty old island' and her Jamaican heritage. Simultaneously, her role as conduit for the community's ancestral past is consolidated as Ella increasingly becomes the focal point for the community – operating as a spiritualist-cum-group-therapist. Her acceptance of her new role and her engagement with 'celestial ethnography' (p. 61) is most dramatically displayed when she's in Madam Marie's parlour (Madam is her 'tutor in spiritualism') where the community, which includes a large proportion of West Indian men, often meet to sing songs and engage in informal reconstructions of their past. One of the West Indian men starts to sing 'Sammy Dead' – the refrain of which has punctuated the whole text – and Ella is 'possessed' by the song; a possession which is described as an invasion of her body but one which, unlike the exploitative 'penetration'/possession perpe-trated on Ella and Anita in *Myal*, fills her with multiple possibilities for seeing and hearing her own, and their, stories: 'He/they didn't get far. I felt my head grow big, as if someone thought it was a balloon and was blowing air into it. And I spoke. I was seeing things as if on a rolling screen, a movie screen (p. 88). The balloon image here is inflated with possibilities, unlike the balloon in *Jane and Louisa* which stinks with shame. Here, too, men act as intermediary figures, facilitating the women's ability to find their own voices. So, in *Jane and Louisa*, Baba reconnects Nellie with the language of her people; in *Myal* Reverend Simpson points Ella towards a way of speaking against the grain of colonialist texts; in *Louisiana*, as one of Madam's visitors puts it: 'She wouldn't do it for us. It took some West Indian men to get her over' (p. 97). Brodber is careful, then, to suggest in her text that Ella 'qualifies' to represent the community because she has internalised not just Mammy's and Lowly's voices, but those of the West Indian *men* as well. Interestingly too, it is these men who represent the motherland/Jamaica for Ella.

As Ella internalises more and more of the voices of the community and of the community's ancestry, there is an interesting shift in terms of her physical presence in the text. Where at the start of the text she is presented as both the fastidiously (but mistakenly) 'correct' researcher and the 'little woman', pressing her hair, wearing slacks and fantasising/joking about her role with Reuben (her lover): "The beautiful lady inside and out, preparing her beautiful hearth for her beautiful lover, changes and powders the sheets. Southern fried chicken! Frying smells in a love nest!' (p. 27).

By the end of the text, Ella acknowledges the way her appearance has changed as her role has shifted:

Other changes have been taking place. They are relatively small things. My hair for instance. I no longer press. I don't know if this represents spiritual or intellectual movement or just plain convenience but there it is: my hair is natural and untouched. And I wrap it . I am also now very observable in the streets . With my headdress and my long dress, I know I present a dignity rather like hers [Madam Marie] and an aura which turns heads (pp. 98-99).

Ella also becomes a vegetarian and, throughout the remainder of the text, there are frequent images of her in her long flowing gowns as a 'vegetarian seer' (p. 10); this emphatically 'spiritual' identity is underscored by the fact that she is, despite being married to Reuben for several years, childless. It appears, then, that Ella's role as 'mother' of the community denies her the role of 'biological' mother. In a passage towards the end of the novel, Ella *becomes* the body politic:

I am the link between the shores washed by the Caribbean sea, a hole, yet I am what joins your left hand to your right. I join the world of the living and the word of the spirits . I am Louisiana. I wear a solid pendant with a hole through its centre. I look through this hole and I can see things . I wear long loose fitting white dresses in summer and long black robes over them in winter. I am Louisiana. I give people their history. I serve God and the venerable sisters (pp. 124-125).

In taking on her role as seer, Ella's sexual presence is de-emphasised and her body represented as the asexual vessel *through* which the community can find expression and healing.

In *Louisiana*, Brodber suggests that the woman's body operates as vessel or vehicle for the powerful *delivery* of the word which can *reborn* the black diasporic community. I would argue, then, that there is a shift in Brodber's texts away from the messy corporeality of the female body towards a more abstracted – or disembodied notion of the female body. This shift in the way the body of woman is represented in the body of her texts is central also to the moral focus of Brodber's oeuvre; a moral focus which, in terms of the thematics of her texts, suggests an eschewal of sexual pleasure in favour of 'the spiritual', even as the aesthetics of her novels assert powerfully the sexual pleasures of the text.

English is a foreign anguish

The black female body is also foregrounded in the work of Marlene Nourbese Philip, (a Trinidadian poet/novelist/essayist now resident in Toronto) becoming increasingly central in her two most recent collections of poetry (Nourbese Philip 1989, 1991). Indeed, in the essay which prefaces her third collection of poetry, she says, 'There was a profound eruption of the body into the text of *She Tries Her Tongue'*. She outlines the violent history of exploitation of the black female body and interrogates the ways in which the severe circumscription of the female body might impact upon the writing of poetry. In her early work – in a poem such as 'Don't Push Now' from *Salmon Courage* (Nourbese Philip 1983) – the poet dramatises the way in which patriarchy (in the particular institutional context of the hospital) seeks to control the woman's body in delivery:

But the boys in white were there,
the boys in white are always
there with the words
    'You can't push now
    Your doctor's not here
    You can't bleed now
    Your doctor's not here
    You can't be now
    Your doctor's not here
    You can't even die now.
(pp. 34-35)

This description of the power with which 'the men' frame the woman's experience of delivery is interrogated differently in *She Tries Her Tongue*, where the focus of attention is the delivery of the *word*. The poems in this collection map out the painful linguistic context in which the post-colonial woman poet finds herself, a situation in which she is reduced in status to a 'linguistic squatter'. In the title poem it is described as 'verbal crippling':

```
this this and this
                disfigurement this
                                    dis
        memberment
                    this
                        verbal crippling
                                        this
        absence of voice
                    that
        wouldnotcould not
    sing
    (p. 94).
```

The delivery of the poetic word becomes the subject of many of these poems and Philip frequently draws on sexual imagery to symbolise the drama of the struggle between patriarchal discourse – his Word – and the embattled woman poet seeking to find a 'mother tongue'. At both thematic and aesthetic levels, Philip seeks to convey the confrontation between the black woman speaker and white patriarchal institutions of power. Philip suggests that, because she is so physically and psychically circumscribed in the post-colonial context, one must look for the black woman's voice – and in Philip's work the voice often stands in for the body – in the interstices and gaps of male discourses. Concomitantly, this interstitial voicing operates to subvert and destabilise *his* word.

Many of the poems in this collection attempt to convey this sense of confrontation between the powerful and the powerless and the crucial role of language and representation in the playing out of this struggle. One of the textual strategies Philip uses is to throw examples of archetypally male discourses into relief by juxtaposing them with other kinds of discourse. So there are direct quotes from Ovid's 'Metamorphoses', etymological dictionaries, various texts on linguistics, fragments of a church service as well as the poet's own version of familiar, 'domestic discourses', such as cookery and gardening texts as well as children's stories. These intertextual links endorse Nourbese Philip's central point, that it is through language, through the specifics of imperial discourses, that the colonial subject has been so negatively inscribed. In these polyglot poems, the poet forfeits the fiction of speaking 'in her own voice' and, instead, foregrounds the ways in which the subaltern woman is always already spoken for and placed in language. For Philip, then, it is not simply a question of providing positive images of the black woman or of simply speaking in Creole; her poetic project seeks to interrogate the language itself that inscribes the black woman's body so negatively:' I want to write about kinky hair and flat noses – maybe I should be writing about the language that *kinked* the hair and *flattened* the noses, *made* jaws prognathous . . . (*She Tries Her Tongue*, p. 20).

Having diagnosed the problem, Nourbese Philip then exemplifies in her work the kind of textual strategies which might offer an alternative to the 'up-tight closure' of patriarchal discourse. In one of the most ambitious and interesting poems in this volume, 'Discourse on the Logic of Language', Nourbese Philip dramatises the battle over language using the imagery of delivery and birth. This poem is arranged in segments across the page with two of the segments placed so that the text must be held sideways to be legible; faced with this poem, the reader must first decide *how* to read it. Nourbese Philip attempts to give the reader enough of the linguistic history of the Caribbean to economically evoke the damaging hegemony of English – 'english/ is a foreign anguish'; she evokes this by juxtaposing a variety of arid, pseudo-legal, coldly categorising patriarchal discourses: edicts which dictate the destruction/disruption of the slaves' African mother tongues; pseudo-scientific accounts which seek to 'prove' the superiority of the 'caucasian's' brain; and a series of multiple choice questions and answers which seek to define the tongue as biological entity but in which many of the answers paradoxically subvert these neat 'biological' definitions. In the centre of the page, the poet dramatises her yearning for a 'true' mother tongue and attempts to deliver some 'untainted' speech from under the repressive weight of english; the tongue-twisting, stuttering nature of this language here invites parallels between the efforts involved in the delivery of a child and the halting, pushing out of the poetic word:

English
is my mother tongue
A mother tongue is not
not a foreign lan lan lang
language
l/anguish
– a foreign anguish
(p. 56)

The poem demands to be read aloud as the poet exploits the slippage in *sense* which a slight shift in *sound* can make, to foreground the elasticity and instability of the signifier and signified. Nourbese Philip insists that the reader engage sensually with the poem and invites a 'stumbling recognition' rather than offering an epiphanic moment of clear, 'poetic vision'. This section of the text offers a rewriting of the story of how the female, colonial subject enters the symbolic order, challenging the primacy of the phallus in Lacanian accounts of language acquisition and, instead, according this symbolic status to the mother:

THE MOTHER THEN PUT HER FINGERS INTO HER CHILD'S MOUTH – GENTLY FORCING IT OPEN; SHE TOUCHES HER TONGUE TO THE CHILD'S TONGUE, AND HOLDING THE TINY MOUTH OPEN, SHE BLOWS INTO – HARD. SHE WAS BLOWING WORDS - HER WORDS, HER MOTHER'S WORDS, THOSE OF HER MOTHER'S MOTHER, AND ALL THEIR MOTHER'S BEFORE - INTO HER DAUGHTER'S MOUTH.

(p. 58)

In this poem, then, Nourbese Philip foregrounds the sterility of patriarchal discourse by mimicking it – 'undoing by overdoing' – and highlights its obsessively categorising impulse and sets it alongside the evocative and sensuously corporeal language of the mother. In this scenario, the pre-verbal communication, between mother and child (Kristeva's 'semiotic') is valued highly – in one section the mother is described licking the baby clean after it is born. Nourbese Philip posits an imaginative, poetic possibility for the transmission of a 'mother tongue' to the child, one which would short-circuit the Law of the Father (defying Lacan's relentless pessimism and determinism) and which accords the mother a kind of *doubly* phallic power: the power of reproductive creativity and 'nurture-power' yoked to the power of the tongue acting here as a phallus to *penetrate* the baby with 'Her Word'. At the same time, in the same poem, the conventions of grammar and syntax associated with patriarchal discourses – His Word – are pulverised – and *parodied*, as when in one of the multiple-choice sections, she posits:

In man the tongue is
(a) the principle organ of taste.
(b) the principle organ of articulate speech.
(c) the principle organ of oppression and exploitation.
(d) all of the above.
(p. 59)

In her most recent text, *Looking For Livingstone*, Philip explores a different mother/daughter relationship, that of the black diasporic woman's relationship to 'Mother' Africa. Here, Philip ranges over the 'lost continent' of Africa to read the lost voice of that continent, attempting to read the silence 'worded over' by Livingstone's narrative of discovery and conquest of Africa. Having dramatised the difficulty of 'finding a voice 'in the post-colonial context in *She Tries Her Tongue*, she moves backwards in time on *Looking For Livingstone* to try to conceptualise and give shape to the violent encounter between Europe and its most 'Other' – the black woman. Nourbese Philip represents this encounter – via a dream sequence – in strikingly sexual terms:

HE – LIVINGSTONE – AND I COPULATE LIKE TWO BEASTS – HE RIDES ME – HIS WORD SLIPPING IN AND OUT OF THE WET MOIST SPACES OF MY SILENCE – I TAKE HIS WORD – STRONG AND THRUSTING - THAT WILL NOT REST, WILL NOT BE DENIED IN ITS SEARCH TO FILL EVERY CREVICE OF MY SILENCE – I TAKE IT INTO THE SILENCE OF MY MOUTH – AND IN A CLEARING IN A FOREST HE SITS AND WEEPS AS STANLEY COMFORTS HIM -

'I SAY, OLD CHAP, WHAT'S THE MATTER?'
MY WORD, MY WORD IS IMPOTENT –'
'FUCK THE WORD, LIVINGSTONE.'
'THAT'S WHAT I'M TRYING TO TELL YOU, OLD
CHAP–'

(p.25)

Here, Nourbese Philip utilises corporeal body language to convey the full force of the encounter between European patriarchy and a feminised Africa and to insist on the connections between sexuality and textuality and between sexuality and power.

In *Looking For Livingstone*, Nourbese Philip attempts a 'cartography of silence' (to use Adrienne Rich's evocative phrase) as she seeks to read the silences and gaps in the discursive terrain surrounding that over-inscribed 'dark continent' of Africa – the mysterious 'silent' Africa which Livingstone supposedly discovers and names into creation. Her text operates as a 'counter-narrative' to Livingstone's *discursive* appropriation of Africa, but her traveller is armed only with her *body*, a mirror and a crude map, unlike Livingstone, who travels with all the latest technology (including compass, sexton and gun) – and Bible. Travelling in vast loops of time and space, the woman traveller searches for Livingstone, encountering along the way several societies of women (the names of which are all anagrams of the word 'silence') who provide her with a range of 'native' ways of knowing and doing, so that, in imbibing this knowledge, she *becomes* a kind of *everyblackwoman* figure. The concept of silence is explored in a range of ways, stressing the sensuality of body language and contrasting the spareness of silence with the excessive proliferation of the word/ 'His Word', in what the poet characterises as a patriarchal marketplace of words. In one scene, for example, the traveller is forced to spend time in a sweat lodge to 'sweat away' and cleanse herself of the 'taint' of patriarchal language. Not only does Nourbese Philip, by the end of this 'odyssey of silence' encourage the reader to feel/think/imagine the word 'silence' differently. She also forces a rethinking of Livingstone's narrative by juxtaposing the woman's version of 'the quest' with his and by parodying and undermining Livingstone and Stanley's interactions. When the woman traveller finally meets Livingstone, for instance, she greets him with, 'You're new here aren't you?' (elsewhere, she'd imagined greeting him with a black handshake) while earlier in the text, she imagines Stanley and Livingstone squabbling like two school boys.

It is important to stress that Nourbese Philip does not simply reverse hierarchies, replacing patriarchal discourse (as exemplified by Livingstone's narrative) with some innately superior women's discourse. Rather, she dramatises the kinds of power relationships involved in any interaction between these two languages and epistemes and the ways in which they are mutually constitutive. She suggests ways in which a kind of feminine writing might be practised and how it might be used to destabilise and point up some of the excesses and gaps in male discourses. The dedication in *She Tries Her Tongue*, 'For all the mothers', mischievously makes clear – with its echo of 'mother-fuckers' – that she does not want to partake of any excessively romantic recuperation of 'the mother'. Nourbese Philip insists in her emphasis on charting the difficulties of *speaking* as a black woman and of *writing the body* of the black woman that to see and hear the body talk, the reader/listener must learn to read/listen *otherwise*.

It is with this challenge to the reader/critic that I would like to end for it reiterates a point made earlier in this chapter about the need for critical practice to attempt to be as multi-vocal and as flexible as the literature it seeks to interpret. So, rather than privileging any one of these writers for offering a better reading/writing/speaking of the black woman's body than the other, I suggest that the ambivalences and contradictions in their texts be held *together* as exemplifying the unsettling complexity – and infinite inscriptability – of the post-colonial woman's body.

16

Caribbean Bodies:
Representation and Practice

Caroline F. Allen

The 1960s feminist slogan, 'the personal is political', signalled a new focus on the embodiment of women's oppression. Feminists have developed the idea of 'sexual politics', emphasising the objectification and exploitation of womens' bodies, and attempting to develop alternative, woman-centred notions of sexuality and pleasure. A major concern is with the representation of the female body in popular culture, for example in the visual media, including pornographic magazines and films. Similarly, the Black Power slogan, 'black is beautiful', was a response to the realisation of 'the degree of fetishisation, objectification and negative figuration which are so much a feature of the representation of the black subject' (Hall 1992: 252). Both the feminist and anti-racist movements stress that oppression is not simply a structural question; material inequalities are underpinned by ideologies whereby women and black people are portrayed as intrinsically inferior to the hegemonic white male. The body is central to the discourses of superiority/inferiority on which sexism and racism are based.

However, despite the institutionalisation of gender studies in the Commonwealth Caribbean academy, surprisingly little attention has been paid to questions of embodiment. It is over forty years since Frantz Fanon first published his pathbreaking study, *Black Skin, White Masks*, which considered how racist discourses about the body engendered what he termed a 'dependency complex of colonised peoples', including the sexual fetishisation of 'racial'[2] characteristics. His examples were drawn largely from the experience of French Caribbean people in their relationships with those from the French metropole (Fanon 1982). In the English-speaking Caribbean, there have been numerous studies of the intersection of 'race' and class, yet few of these have explored the psychological dimension of racism, which is linked to sexuality and is inscribed in gender relations. The dynamics of reproduction of gendered and racialised body images should be placed within the context of economic and cultural relationships with other parts of the world, and the history of colonialism and imperialism.

The largest English-speaking Caribbean research project on gender to date, the Women in the Caribbean Project of 1979-82, was primarily concerned with structural questions, such as the extent and nature of women's work (Senior 1991). Though the vast majority of respondents were women of African descent, and thus were presumably subject to both sexist and racist discourse, questions of body image and sexuality were not examined. Caribbean social research has traditionally been dominated by positivist methodology and theoretical models which ignore or deny the validity of subjective experience (Arjoon et. al. 1996).

This paper reviews theoretical ideas on the body in society, and discusses their relevance to the Caribbean. Two major themes will be explored:

1. Representations of the body in Western culture and their implications for Caribbean people;
2. The role of bodily practices such as "keep fit" in reproducing discourses of gender and "race".

The aim is to stimulate analytical research on how relations of power affect representations of Caribbean bodies. Relations of power are understood in the Foucauldian sense, as 'means by which individuals try to conduct, to determine, the behaviour of others' (Foucault 1988: 18). This concept will be elaborated throughout the essay.

Western binarisms and representations of the body

Analysts of modernity note that ever since the philosopher Rene Descartes (1596-1650) uttered his famous phrase, 'I think, therefore I am', Western thought has been riven by the idea of dualism between mind and body. Reason, considered the basis of knowledge and thus progress, is thus fundamentally separate from emotion, with the latter influenced by bodily experience (Williams and Bendelow 1995). This laid the foundation for positivist science, whereby the pursuit of pure reason enables the discovery of facts.

In effect, universities are temples of the rationalist, modern project, and the distinction between 'town and gown' reflects that between body and mind, with 'town' providing the bodies which cultivated minds will analyse. For Morgan and Scott (1993), the Cartesian legacy provides an important explanation for the neglect of the body in sociology. Sociology has, since its inception, argued against biological essentialism; human behaviour is thought to be shaped by social and economic forces which cannot be reduced to instincts. Thus sociology is associated with culture rather than nature, with the abstract rather than the concrete.

Rationalities have tended to open up distinctions between the ordered, the controlled and the abstract on the one hand, and the disordered, the uncontrolled and the concrete on the other, with the relegation of the body and bodily matters to the latter, implicitly discredited, set of categories. (Morgan and Scott 1993: 2)

Christianity lent moral weight to this process. Particularly since the advent of puritanism, Christianity has stressed the virtues of abstinence, asceticism and control over and denial of bodily pleasures. For Max Weber, who analysed *The Protestant Ethic and the Spirit of Capitalism*, rationality was associated with a deep loathing of the body and community (Morgan and Scott 1993).

Further, the moral ascendancy of mind over matter contributed to ideas of superiority of mental over physical work, of capital over labour, of salaries over wages, of white-collar over blue-collar, of urban over rural, of master over slave. All these permeate the construction of the 'First World' in relation to the 'Third World'. Thus Western binarisms are imbued with class and 'race' prejudice. The dominator is seen as superior to the dominated, with domination grounded in control over the body. The body becomes the West's 'other', somehow separate from self. Christian imagery compounded racism via the association of white and black with good and evil, light and dark, purity and corruption (Dyer 1988; Fanon 1982; hooks 1992). The implications for the construction of Caribbean identity are severe, given the history of colonialism, slavery, indentureship and Western religious teaching. Fanon argues that the black man is so objectified that it is impossible to understand what he is except through the constructions of the white man, while the reverse is not true:

For not only must the black man be black; he must be black in relation to the white man. Some critics will take it upon themselves to remind us that this proposition has a converse. I say that this is false. The black man has no ontological resistance in the eyes of the white man (Fanon 1982: 110).

While Fanon did not consider black women in detail, it is clear that they are objectified by discourses of both 'race' and gender. Hooks describes their image in the USA thus:

In general, in this culture, black women are seen and depicted as down to earth, practical, creatures of the mundane. Within sexist racist iconography, black females are most often represented as mammies, whores or sluts. Caretakers whose bodies and beings are empty vessels to be filled with the needs of others (hooks 1995a :97).

Crucially, these binarisms were constructed to the benefit of the hegemonic class of white males in the West. This construction is not the product of a homogeneous Western culture, but of a culture internally differentiated by numerous binarisms which contribute to this hegemony. Differences are projected onto the bodies of people both inside and outside Western countries. Kimmel (1996) describes an individual who would fit the hegemonic norm in the USA; a white, Anglo-Saxon male, physically fit executive, who is university educated, heterosexual, married with a nuclear family, owns a four-wheel drive and lives in his own house in middle America. Far from being the statistical norm, such a complex of attributes applies only to a minority of people, yet it is the standard according to which others are measured, and may come to measure themselves. Any person who does not possess one or more of these attributes is regarded as deficient and inferior.

Such a hegemony persists because of its construction as myth. Barthes (1972) sees myth as a message which seems entirely natural – the 'historical intention' behind it is hidden. Mythology does not operate through silence, but by telling stories, by organising perception. It relies heavily on essentialism, which serves to de-politicise situations of domination:

A conjuring trick has taken place; it has turned reality inside out, it has emptied it of history and has filled it with nature . In passing from history to nature, myth acts economically: it abolishes the complexity of human acts, it gives them the simplicity of essences, it does away with all dialectics, it organises a world which is without contradictions because it is without depth, a world wide open and wallowing in the evident (Barthes 1972: 142-143).

The order of things is given universal and 'eternal justification' by constructing stories in which the dominant are portrayed as naturally superior.

Derrida (1976) challenges the very notion of fixed, stable identity, showing that this relies on a process of 'difference', which has two components. First, difference, involving the comparisons (including binarisms) of language and communication and thus the establishment of meaning via distinction rather than essence. Second, deferral, meaning that there is a time lag between presence and what constitutes that presence; the past is always reflected in identity. Thus in talking about identity we are describing what we were rather than what we are. Identities are therefore fragile and historically contingent. Thus Kimmel's hegemonic American man may not share the same attributes as a hegemonic Caribbean man (there may, for example, be less emphasis on marriage). The configuration of valued attributes is historically constructed; there may be a wide variety of ideal configurations in the Caribbean, reflecting the varied cultural influences and histories of colonialism and imperialism (Mohammed 1994; Barriteau-Foster 1992). These ideals may sometimes contradict each other and clash, bringing normative confusion.

Kimmel (1996) and Rutherford (1988) note that Western, white, heterosexual masculinity relies on elaborate myths about 'others'; stereotypes which justify racism, sexism and homophobia. At the same time it remains silent about its own characteristics. Dyer (1988) focuses on the representational use of 'whiteness', as signifying 'everything and nothing'; goodness and purity at the same time as neutrality and absence. The process of unmasking masculinity, of deconstructing it by demonstrating how it defines itself through 'difference' has largely been undertaken by 'others' rather than the dominant group. What interest would they have in dismantling these stories? For Foucault, the success of power is proportional to its ability to hide its own mechanisms (Foucault 1979).

Thus, the white, heterosexual man becomes centred at the apex of society, positioned as mind, defining and classifying the bodies around and below him. As long as the others remain as passive bodies, his position is assured. An example of the role of mythology in establishing such a position can be found in the writings of one of the 'founding fathers' of sociology, Emile Durkheim (apparently, there are no 'founding mothers'), whose ideas are taught in basic sociology courses in schools including the University of the West Indies. Durkheim sees man as 'almost entirely the product of society', while woman is 'to a far greater extent the product of nature'. He says of man, 'his tastes, aspirations and humour have in large part a collective origin, while his companion's are more directly influenced by her organism. His needs, therefore, are quite different from hers. (Durkheim 1952: 385). Thus men are placed at the centre of sociological enquiry. Such a positioning pervades positivist social science, with 'economic man' being perhaps the most extreme model of the Western rational actor (Arjoon et. al. 1996).

However, the cleft between mind and body creates huge psychological tension, since it is extremely difficult to deny corporeal feeling. Sexuality assumes a central importance, as the hidden underside of the discourse of bodily control (Foucault 1979). For Jeffrey Weeks (1986: 26):

The Christian West has seen in sex a terrain of moral anguish and conflict, setting up an enduring dualism between the spirit and the flesh, the mind and the body. It has had the inevitable result of creating a cultural configuration which simultaneously disavows the body while being obsessively preoccupied with it.

This configuration involves a sexual fascination and fear of others, seen as intrinsically more embodied (Fanon 1982). Various strategies of separation are used to preserve the man's emotional and sexual composure, including confining women to the private, domestic space while men demonstrate their rationality in public.

Morgan (1993) notes that the discourse is reflected in the clothing of Western men, particularly formal wear. Uniform and the business suit 'tend away from the physical body and very much toward the social body' (Morgan 1993: 79). An interesting Caribbean reworking of this set of meanings is the 'shirt-jac', a work tunic worn by many men. As Cozier (1996) notes, the shirt-jac has short sleeves, suitable for the tropical climate, and is symbolically different from the formal dress of British colonialists, having come into fashion during the decolonisation period of the late 60s and early 70s. However, ironically, it combines the colonial styles of the suit and the bush jacket, often being made of the same heavy material as business suits and decorated with military-style epaulettes and pockets. In contrast, Caribbean women at work are allowed or even encouraged to wear colourful clothes which place more emphasis on bodily contours, though the geometric cut of female business suits conforms to the austerity of the masculine work environment.

However, the way that African-Caribbean youth dress outside the work environment is challenging gender dichotomies. Both sexes often wear bright colours, baggy T-shirts and pants, jewellery and braided hair. They face criticism for this from more conservative quarters. For example, the Barbadian singer, Edwin Yearwood, who won the three awards of Soca Monarch, Calypso Monarch and Road March Monarch at the Barbados Cropover Festival in 1995, was widely criticised for wearing four earrings and a 'ragamuffin' hair style; some tried to prevent him visiting and performing at schools because of what they saw as a 'bad boy' image (*Daily Nation*, November 8, 1995; *Sun on Saturday*, November 12, 1995; *Trinidad Guardian*, January 19, 1996). Thus breaking Western norms of dress is taken to signify social deviance. Correspondence with the Barbadian press debated whether earrings look better on men or women, indicating the persistence of dichotomous thinking about gender, and a strong difficulty in accepting that the styles include an element of cross-dressing (*Daily Nation*, October 12, 1995; *Sun on Saturday*, November 4, 1995).

The same Western cultural configuration classifies women as madonna or whore according to their relationship to their bodies. Both throw the contradictions of masculinity into sharp relief (Rutherford 1988). In her chastity, the madonna reflects the masculine portrayal of self as more spirit than flesh. Thus she is not quite a woman. On the other hand, the sexual appetite of the whore challenges the construction of woman as passive and defined by man. This masculinity demands mastery of others as well as self, and thus violence against women becomes 'the ritualistic enactment of cultural meaning about sex' (Coward 1984: 239).

Such a complex can be seen at work in the portrayal of women in Carnival in Trinidad and Tobago and the Eastern Caribbean. In the Carnival season, there is a regular public outcry, particularly from relig-ious representatives, about the 'immorality' of scantily-clad women who dance suggestively in public, thus violating the stipulations of the 'ma-donna' construct. At the same time, sexually suggestive photographs of women are used to sell magazines and newspapers and market the tourist product overseas (O'Callaghan 1994), suggesting the trade in bodies underlying the 'whore' construct. The transgressive nature of Carnival lies precisely in the challenging display of the bodily agency of 'others' (black people, women) in public spaces from which they have been excluded (Pearse 1988; Lawlor 1993). It is such a disturbance of modes of repre-sentation which Lord Kitchener celebrates in his 1996 calypso, *The Doctor's Daughter*. Kitchener describes a scene where a young, middle-class woman displays her highly developed 'wining' skills while playing mas on the streets of Port of Spain, to the excitement and consternation of a gathering crowd of people. The middle-class female body is one which is normally hidden from view, particularly that of working-class people. 'Race' may also be at issue here, as so many doctors' daughters are of white or high brown complexion, or of Indian descent.

Kaufman (1996) and Kimmel (1996) stress the anxiety created by the tension in the construction of masculinity; the fear that the 'other side' will be unmasked to reveal the self as unmanly. Men have a contradictory experience of power, frequently feeling powerless because they fear such a revelation. Kimmel asserts that men seek approval from other men, via their control of self and other. Masculinity is thus primarily a homosocial enactment, with other men having the most power to undo the image. Kaufman uses the imagery of men clothed in suits of armour to hide their emotions. The following section includes an examination of how the development of muscles serves as a representation of the armour-plated self.

While binarisms are vital to traditional Western constructions of femininity and masculinity, it is important to recognise that it is possible to avoid binary thinking. Derrida's notion of 'difference' stresses that language is based on distinction, on concepts of presence and absence, rather than simply opposition. Thus, while black and white are conceived as opposites, what is the opposite of brown, or pink? Moving beyond essentialist, binary thinking allows for concepts, for example of masculinity and femininity, which are multifaceted, consisting of areas of overlap as well as areas of difference. Going beyond opposites is particularly important in the Caribbean multicultural context (Mohammed 1994 and 1995; Barriteau-Foster 1993). For example, as Modood (1988) argues, the term 'black', as used in anti-racist discourse, is frequently taken to denote people of African descent, thus excluding the experience of people of Asian descent, such as the East Indians in the Caribbean, who have their own particular and different experience of racism.

Discipline, reflexivity, capitalism and the production of gendered bodies

This section discusses how power relations, particularly as they relate to gender, may be reflected or resisted in the ways in which Caribbean people care for and control their bodies. Before contemplating Caribbean examples, I provide a theoretical and historical background to assist in understanding the importance of control of the body in contemporary society.

Michel Foucault argues that Cartesian rationalism was among the Enlightenment theories which led Western thought to be dominated by the question of the subject, or, in other words, the question, 'Who am I?' (Rabinow 1984). He analyses the implications of this for the care and control of bodies. He offers the insight that people are active participants in the production and reproduction of social definitions of self and other. Thus they exert discipline on their bodies to achieve or affirm a certain concept of self. Foucault argues that an elaborate 'disciplinary technology', combining knowledge and power, has developed which, increasingly, involves people in producing bodies and subjectivities which are useful to others. Self-discipline thus becomes social discipline. The modern state is particularly important in this, in the sense that it aims to achieve policy goals through the discipline of bodies (Foucault 1984a). However, bodies are also manipulated in the interest of making profits, a point which was not adequately explored by Foucault and which will be explored below.

Foucault shows that the modern state operates an 'individualising and totalising' system of surveillance and control over bodies (Foucault 1982: 213). 'Globalising and quantitative' information is collected about the population and the distribution of its pre-defined, 'objective' characteristics. Analytical information is collected about individuals (Foucault 1982: 215) and their performance according to scientific criteria. Through these means people are classified and measured according to particular categories and criteria (e.g. sex, 'race', age, weight, sexual orientation, intelligence quotient) which are thought relevant to the rational operation of the society. This categorisation and quantification describes bodies and attaches identities to them, dividing them from each other.

The process of attaching identities is deepened by the institutionalisation and professionalisation of 'pastoral power'. This 'very special form of power' draws on the Christian notion of individual salvation. But it is,

no longer a question of leading people to their salvation in the next world, but rather ensuring it in this world. And in this context, the word *salvation* takes on different meanings: health, well-being (that is, sufficient wealth, standard of living), security, protection against accidents. (Foucault 1982: 215)

This form of power, therefore, relies on the idea that 'It's for your own good'. Schools, the health service and fitness clubs are examples of institutions dedicated to the exercise of pastoral power. They seem to operate a benign form of imperialism, which works,

to incite, reinforce, control, monitor, optimise and organise the forces under it; a power bent on generating forces, making then grow, and ordering them, rather than one dedicated to impeding them, making them submit, or destroying them (Foucault 1984b: 259).

These institutions, through the rigid way in which they allocate different 'types' of body in space and time, express and establish hierarchies and territorialities in the minds of subjects. They produce bodies that are 'docile' in the sense that they 'may be subjected, used, transformed and improved' (Foucault 1984a: 180). Modern life has seen the associated proliferation of pastoral professionals, such as doctors, psychoanalysts and sports coaches, who control analytical information and assist the individual in understanding him or herself. Thus the person develops a concept of self through the interaction of these forces and a process of active, *subjective* interpretation. As Foucault explains:

There are two meanings of the word *subject*: subject to someone else by control and dependence, and tied to his own identity by a conscience and self-knowledge. Both meanings suggest a form of power which subjugates and makes subject to (Foucault 1982: 212).

Giddens (1991) suggests that in what he terms the late modern era there is a move towards,

greater *reflexivity* in subjectivity – the idea that more and more aspects of social life can be subject to strategic transformation and modification on the basis of new knowledge and the capacity to discursively interpret conduct (Bunton and Burrows 1995: 208).

This is an era of globalisation, where social relations are 'disembedded', i.e. lifted out of their local context and restructured across time and space (Giddens 1990). As local (national or ethnic) systems of meaning are thrown into question by this process, there is increasing recourse to 'expert systems' to make sense of experience. These systems 'consist of repositories of technical knowledge that can be deployed across a wide range of actual contexts. An expert system gives guarantee what to expect across all of these contexts' (Waters 1995: 49). The ever-increasing flows of information across national borders add to the sources through which identity can be interpreted. Pastoral power is now exerted through an increasing range of advisory sources such as magazine columns, books, television programmes, the internet and professional experts on practically every subject. Identities are constantly reworked as people reflect on new information and images and reinterpret themselves in the light of them. Knowledge changes constantly, so that modern life seems to be uncontrolled; Giddens (1991) likens it to being aboard a 'careering juggernaut'.

Lash and Urry (1994) assert that information has both a cognitive and aesthetic element. Thus subjectivities are reworked not only through a process of rational action in response to cognitive information, but as a result of emotional responses to the aesthetic and expressive elements of the signs that are transmitted. Bordo (1989) observes that ideals of conduct are being transmitted increasingly by the use of standardised visual images in movies and on television. Thus emotional and sexual responses to images of the body are increasingly important instruments of social control.

The dynamic driving Giddens' 'careering juggernaut' is capitalism. Haug (1986) argues that capitalists employ a number of techniques to stimulate higher rates of consumption, including built-in obsolescence with reductions in quality and quantity so that items must be frequently replaced. More important than these, however, is the stimulation of demand by appealing to the consumer, and particularly to his or her aesthetic and sexual sensibilities. 'For the ideal of commodity aesthetics is to deliver the absolute minimum of use-value, disguised and staged by a maximum of seductive illusion, a highly effective strategy because it is attuned to the yearnings, and desires, of the people (Haug 1986: 54).

'Aesthetic innovation' (Haug 1986) is used, particularly in advertising and fashion, playing on desires and fears and offering constantly changing ideas for the re-fashioning of self. Thus the increasing 'reflexivity' of modern life corresponds to the constant expansion in the ways in which capitalism attempts to manipulate consumers. To do this it uses the technology of power which Foucault describes: the collection of information about consumers (market research) and the mobilisation of pastoral discourse using slogans such as 'the company that cares'.

Thus, as Bordo (1989: 14) writes, 'through the organisation and regulation of the time, space and movements of our daily lives, our bodies are trained, shaped and impressed with the stamp of prevailing historical forms of selfhood, desire, masculinity, femininity'. In the historical situation of Western, white, male, heterosexual hegemony, the bodies and emotions of 'others' become major objects of knowledge, control and thus are particularly subject to disciplinary regimes. At the same time the capitalist dynamic requires that gendered identities are constantly in flux and modifiable: 'there is always the promise of improvement' (Coward 1984: 13).

Caribbean people are no strangers to the globalisation process, where social relations are lifted out of their local context and restructured across time and space. Mintz (1993: 10) asserts that:

Caribbean peoples are the first *modernised* peoples in world history. They were modernised by enslavement and forced transportation; by 'seasoning' and coercion on time-conscious, export-oriented enterprises; by the reshuffling, redefinition and reduction of gender-based roles; by racial and status-based oppression; and by the need to reconstitute and maintain cultural forms under implacable pressure.

These diverse processes mean that Caribbean people have a very long history of renegotiating identity, resisting or reflecting the discourse of colonialists, and drawing on numerous cultural traditions (Hall 1991). Furthermore, Caribbean countries are small with highly open economies; the high proportion of imported products and media multiply the sources for negotiating identity. The extreme 'reflexivity' of contemporary life is, for Caribbean people, not merely a *late* modern phenomenon, but has infused their experience of modernity from the start.

It is clear that Caribbean culture is imbued with the latest rhetoric about care and control of the body, which stimulates ever higher levels of reflexivity. The words 'health', 'fitness' and 'beauty' figure prominently in this, and are often used interchangeably (Glassner 1995). Armstrong (1993) observes that the contemporary discourse of health promotion increasingly encourages people to see themselves as lay health practitioners rather than simply objects of medicine. Thus Caribbean newspapers run regular features encouraging people to adopt health promoting behaviours, such as the *Trinidad Guardian's* weekly feature, entitled 'Work that Body: Get in Shape for Life', sponsored by the 'Good N' Natural' line of products from National Flour Mills. The importance of harnessing individual bodily practices to social goals is made clear in the following quote from Trinidad and Tobago's report on *Restructuring for Economic Independence*:

In the first instance, efforts will be made to achieve the heightening of consciousness within the individual of his personal responsibility for good health. This will serve as the foundation for preventive health care which will be accorded high priority since success in this area will assist in reducing the burden on the health care system. (National Planning Commission 1990: 123)

This cultural trend is fed by foreign sources including US television programmes and advertisements, on network, cable and satellite channels, which offer advice on how to manage stress, your diet, your waistline, your wardrobe, your relationships, your children, your home, your sex life – indeed, any number of intimate aspects of everyday life. The highly popular *Oprah Winfrey Show* is such a source. Women are particular targets of these presentations. 'Everywhere women are offered pleasure. Pleasure if we lose weight, pleasure if we prepare a beautiful meal, pleasure if we follow a natural instinct, pleasure if we acquire something new – a new body, a new house, a new outfit, a new relationship' (Coward 1984: 13). The flip side of this is guilt. Guilt if we do not lose weight, etc. (Coward 1984). Pleasure and guilt are partners in sustaining the 'desiring machine' (Young 1995) of capitalism.

However, Caribbean men and women differ in the ways they care for and control their bodies: self-discipline is gendered. Bordo (1989) observes that in the West, power differentials between men and women are projected into norms concerning the size of their bodies. Male bodies should occupy more space than women's bodies. We see this exemplified in fitness clubs which are an increasingly common feature of the Caribbean landscape. Women predominate in aerobics classes, where one of the objectives is to lose weight, i.e. reduce the size of the body. Men are more likely to be found in gyms, pumping weights in order to increase the size of the body.

The spatial distribution of power is also reflected in the locations where men and women take exercise. Men are far more likely to exercise outdoors than women, reflecting the public/private dichotomy mentioned above. From the earliest age, boys are visible outside playing sports, whereas girls are rarely seen outdoors unless they are going to another home, to school or to church. This territoriality is jealously guarded by men. Women who attempt to exercise outside are likely to run the gamut of sexual remarks and may even risk sexual assault. These have the effect of keeping women in their place.

Exercise and competition are major aspects of Caribbean boys' play, whereas girls' play is more sedentary and orients the girls towards caring for others, for example by playing with dolls. In adulthood, women who take exercise tend to be involved in non-competitive forms such as aerobics, jogging and dance whereas men often continue competitive hobbies like cricket, basketball and football. Dance, especially, incorporates an element of sexual display. Thus a woman is encouraged 'to experience her body as an object-for-others, whereas men have learned to experience themselves in active, forceful ways : to act, instead of being looked at and acted upon' (Whitson 1994: 355). Whitson argues that this experience leads women, when operating in a competitive environment, to exhibit 'inhibited intentionality' in their bodily movements, which are characterised by their partiality, by their tentative use of space. Therefore,

[n]ot only is there a typical style of throwing like a girl, but there is a more or less typical style of running like a girl, climbing like a girl, swinging like a girl, hitting like a girl. They have in common, first, that the whole body is not put into fluid and directed motion, but rather, in swinging and hitting, for example, the motion is concentrated in one body part; and second, that the woman's motion tends not to reach, extend, lean, stretch and follow through in the direction of her intention (Oriard 1982 quoted in Whitson 1994: 355).

Females who succeed in competitive sport, such as the athlete Merlene Ottey from Jamaica, are exceptional, and it would be interesting to analyse the social experiences which contributed to their success.

In the Caribbean, body-building is enjoying immense and growing popularity. Body-building magazines, pills and food supplements sell in large numbers. Most are imported from the USA; the General Nutrition Company is a USA multinational with retail outlets selling body-building dietary supplements in Trinidad. According to a recent tourist brochure, Barbados boasts more champion body-builders than any other place on earth 'Barbados 1995 Ins and Outs'. Muscularity is particularly expressive of gender discourse. Bordo (1993) views it as a symbol of mythical phallic power; the embodiment of purposeful, active, rational masculinity. Like the phallus, the hard body projects the man as penetrator, coloniser, dominator. It serves 'to muzzle his inner feeling and his dread of emotional engagement and vulnerability' (Wacquant 1994: 81). Thus body-building can be seen as an extreme manifestation of the cultural value placed on 'hardness'. This is evident in popular discourse such as the Barbadian calypso by Mac Fingall, *Big Belly Man* (1996). Here a 'sexy' young woman asserts that she 'ain't dancing with no big belly man' and that 'she want a bony man'. The double entendre makes the connection between the hard body, the phallus and sexual attractiveness.

Ironically, however, the hyper-masculine body-builder's torso is achieved at considerable expense to the social enactment of masculinity. The 'dedication, determination and discipline' (Wacquant 1994) required absorb huge amounts of time, and rigorous adherence to routine and diet, interfering with work and sexual relationships (Connell 1990). The use of anabolic steroids and growth hormones have side effects which in fact serve to counteract many traditional physical indicators of masculinity. Side effects include,

premature baldness, bouts of diarrhoea, increased body hair, spells of dizziness, epidemics of acute acne, and chronic rectal bleeding (necessitating the wearing of Huggies), not to mention the less visible but no less consequential lowered sperm count, thyroid, liver and kidney malfunction, hepatitis, gallstones and cancer. (Wacquant 1994: 81)

While the use of steroids in body-building in the Caribbean is likely to remain undocumented, there is surely a need to examine the effects of dietary products and body-building practices on health, as the recent problems, at age 43, of a former champion Trinidadian body-builder made clear. This demonstrates the dangers in taking at face value advertising which associates narcissistic practices such as body-building with health.

Body-building, far from affirming the body, is about *denial* of bodily pleasure (Gillett and White 1992). Body-builders adhere to a strict moral code, enshrined in sayings such as 'there is no such thing as overtraining, only weak minds' (quoted in Wacquant 1994: 79). Young *et. al.* (1994) argue that violent sports and disregard for health help reinforce notions of masculinity. Injury is reframed as a masculinising experience, and '[b]ecause a hegemonic ideal of masculinity is the suppression of affect, continuing to play with pain is viewed as appropriate male behaviour'

(Young *et. al.* 1994: 182). This fits into the Western masculine construct of the superiority of mind over matter, of spirit over flesh.

What, then, do we make of females who pump iron, whose numbers appear to be growing in the Caribbean? In some ways, their practice is deconstructive, showing that women too can be hard and disciplined. On the other hand, they affirm the hegemonic masculine notions of what is valued in society; rationality, domination, will-power, control over desire. As Bordo (1993: 23) notes, 'So far, the transformation has chiefly gone in the direction of permitting (and even eroticising) *hardness* in women, but never softness in men'. Furthermore, the appropriation of male attributes by women is only likely to be permitted up to a point. Holmlund (1994), in her analysis of the movies *Pumping Iron* and *Pumping Iron II: The Women* shows how the women were often filmed in soft focus, and were portrayed accompanied by steady boyfriends, whereas male body-builders were seen surrounded by adoring female fans but had no apparent emotional connection with any of them.

Bordo describes how she turned to weight-training to deal with the pain following the break-up of a long-standing relationship:

I remember the way having definition in my upper body made me feel when I walked by men – not just more attractive, but powerful. For the first time, I felt their eyes did not penetrate me and reduce me, but glanced over me with admiration, as though I were an equal . I no longer felt that my body coded my soft and bruised feelings; instead, it coded independence, toughness, emotional imperviousness. (Bordo 1993: 725)

Thus the growing popularity among women of practices which harden the body is a response to the pain resulting from the psychic damage inflicted by men on both themselves and others. Gillett and White (1992) suggest that involvement in activities demanding high levels of bodily discipline stems from felt unmet needs and personal deficiencies. These anxieties are increasingly projected onto the body in the current visually oriented consumer culture. For women 'Over the mirror always hangs the image of the socially approved, massively consumed, widely circulated generic woman. She alone it seems is guaranteed an easy ride through life, guaranteed the approval of all and safe in expecting uncritical love' (Coward 1984: 80).

For the Caribbean person the image gazing critically from above the mirror is likely to be that of a white person. Above, I described racist discourses which classify 'others' in terms of difference from ideals attributed to white people. In the media, white people are portrayed as more successful in practically all areas of life. In local advertising, white people tend to be portrayed in roles of expert, manager or tourist while others appear to be graduated in terms of rank as producers or consumers according to the paleness of their complexions. Imported television programmes idealise white, firm, athletic bodies. In *Baywatch*, for example, the only black person is the policeman, whose relationship with the other characters is strictly professional and thus stripped of emotional or sexual content. Popular soap operas from the USA, such as *The Bold and the Beautiful* and *The Young and the Restless*, are dominated by rich, white characters, and encapsulate, in their titles, hegemonic and gendered ideals relating to the body. Condoms sold in the Caribbean, with names such as *Erotica*, *Rough Rider* and *Wet n' Wild*, are packaged with pictures of white women.

Young (1995) sees *ambivalence* at the heart of colonial discursive productions, indicating simultaneous attraction toward and repulsion from the body of 'the other'. Thus, despite ample evidence, particularly in the form of 'miscegenation', that colonialists constitute black people as sexual objects, the latter are also taught to see themselves as sexually unattractive. This 'ideological dissimulation' (Young 1995:152) leads to the association of blackness with victimisation and helps sustain bodily practices such as the use of skin-lightening creams and hair-straightening lotions through which signs of blackness are reduced (hooks 1993).

Discussion: Resistance and practices of the body

On one level, such practices of bodily modification are experienced as liberating and transforming, as they seem to offer a way out of victimhood and lack of control. They are used by both women and men as ways of gaining power within the current configuration of gender and 'race' relations. On another level, however, the inward gaze diverts attention from broader political questions, such as 'Who produces these ideal body images, and what are their motives?' Bordo (1989) argues that exacting and normalising disciplines of the body, which are becoming increasingly central ordering principles of time and space in everyday life, serve to render us less socially oriented and more centripetally focused on self-modification. The fetishism and voyeurism which dominate visually oriented consumer culture serve to muffle other forms of desire – for public power, for independence, for emotional intimacy (Bordo 1989; Haug 1986). They are instruments of an insidious form of colonialism. The disciplines serve to individualise us, and are central to a process of 'divide and rule'.

Resistance must be continuously reassessed. Capitalism is an extremely flexible system, and seems able to absorb and co-opt much resistant practice by projecting it as just another style, just an alternative lifestyle, erasing questions of hierarchy and power. Mattson (1990) for example, considers the group, Public Enemy, which uses rap to explore black identity, politics and racism. He argues that the group's choice of expression – the culture industry and 'style' – shows a distinct shift in the way black identity is forged.

Whereas Malcolm X constituted his identity through everyday struggles, and the Black Panthers devoted much of their time to community programs, Public Enemy's self-constitution as a group comes *solely* from the culture industry . [T]hey take up the tradition of black protest not as politics but as style. (Mattson 1990: 178)

Marable (1993) and hooks (1995b) criticise the use by the media of role models, such as Michael Jordan, in attempting to instil in black people (particularly men) a spirit of competitive individualism, expressed through control over commodities. This transformation of politics into style is reflected in the popularity among Caribbean youth of dress styles reflecting rap and basketball influences, blended with Rastafarian symbols such as the red, gold and green colour combination, along with an element of 'gender bending' discussed above. Such cultural statements are important and powerful, as evidenced by the degree of protest they evoke from conservative quarters. However, they are also commodified, and thus may serve to stifle other forms of resistance.

A major theme of this paper has been Western constructions of the body, and practices which reproduce or resist these colonial constructions, particularly as they relate to gender. Caribbean resistance, however, cannot merely be a question of opposing these constructions, throwing them off and replacing them with signifiers of a subaltern heritage, from Africa, India, pre-Columbus America, China etc. Fighting Western taboos and stereotypes is not sufficient of itself to guarantee freedom. Foucault (1988: 4) insists that 'liberation opens up new relationships of power, which have to be controlled by practices of liberty'. Traditions from 'lands of origin' will carry their own discourses regarding the body and gender. A major challenge is to analyse these traditions and reflect on what they can offer in terms of discourse which affirms and celebrates the bodily subjectivity of both men and women rather than oppressing either of them. This is an area which is ill-explored, largely because of the domination of the West in academia.

Furthermore, the search for origins is futile. As Foucault (1984: 78) points out, if we listen to history, we do not find the essence of things but rather that 'their essence was fabricated in a piecemeal fashion from alien forms'. This is especially relevant to Caribbean people whose subjectivity results from the interpretation of numerous cultural traditions, including those of various European countries (Hall 1991). It is perhaps this hybridity which gives Caribbean people their unique strength.

Nowhere is it more evident than in Carnival. The practices of masquerade 'destabilise hitherto stable categorisations of who is negated on racial, ethnic, sexual or class terms' (Ampka 1993: 5). They arise from the popular culture of parodic and unofficial folk humour that attacks the authority of the ruling classes. Thus, for the duration of the Carnival, the lowest person in the social hierarchy can become monarch, gender roles can be switched, masqueraders can wear or combine the apparel of numerous 'others' (Lawlor 1993). Objectifying and constraining bodily identities are challenged: 'at Carnival the deaf child dances; and the blind child wears a costume. [and] age is no barrier' (Bishop 1991: 3). Contesting individualising and totalising power, Carnival stresses community, interdependence and fusion. The costume designer depends on the musician and the masquerader to bring the costume to 'a dimension which, as a still, unmoving thing, it will never have' (Bishop 1991: 6). 'In Carnival the body is exploded into a mobile, erotic, desiring, entity that seeks connection with other bodies, things beyond the boundaries of its own skin' (Lawlor 1993: 4).

Of course, Carnival lasts for only a few days each year, but nevertheless hints of resistant practices which are carried over into everyday life. The everyday use of parody in 'picong' humour in Trinidad is an example of such resistant practice. However, Carnival itself is becoming increasingly commercialised and commodified. The marketing of costumes, music and associated products such as soft drinks is increasingly controlled by big business, placing the masquerader increasingly in the position of consumer rather than producer of image. Vigilance is necessary to prevent style from subsuming content and the revolutionary implications of the message.

Notes

1. Acknowledgements: To Heike Baumlisberger, Edgar Hassan, Robert Leyshon, Keith Nurse, and Evelyn O'Callaghan. Thank you for your support and inspiration.
2. Throughout this paper, the words 'race' and 'racial' are placed in inverted commas to emphasise, not only that they are social constructions rather than biological essences, but that they involve ideologies supporting domination and subordination, This is a convention used by, among others, Donald and Ratansi in their book, 'Race', Culture and Difference (1992).

17

'Compulsory Heterosexuality' and Textual/Sexual Alternatives in Selected Texts by West Indian Women Writers

Evelyn O'Callaghan

Sex and the West Indian Woman Writer

At the Second International Conference of Caribbean Women Writers held in April, 1990 at the University of the West Indies, St Augustine, Jamaica Kincaid introduced her presentation one evening by informing the delighted audience that she was going to read a passage about sex. This, she noted, was a subject on which most West Indian women's texts are reticent. And indeed this seems to be the case. Kincaid herself, in *Lucy*,[1] is frank in describing her protagonist's delight in erotic play:

He kissed me on my face and ears and neck and in my mouth. If I enjoyed myself beyond anything I had known so far, it must have been because such a long time had passed since I had been touched in that way by anyone . He buried his face in the hair under my arms; he took first one breast, then the other into his mouth as if he meant to swallow them whole. (pp. 66-67)

Yet in the midst of this pleasure, Lucy remembers she has not used contraception and a series of negative fears – of unwanted pregnancy, of social censure, of dependency on a man – cloud her enjoyment and fill her with 'confusion and dread'. Later, as she and Hugh make love for (unknown to him) the last time, Lucy thinks back over previous sexual experiences. There was 'the boy I used to kiss in the library and continued to kiss long after I had ceased to care about him one way or the other, just to see how undone he could become by my kisses' (p. 83). She loses her virginity to Tanner, but will not give him the satisfaction of this knowledge since 'I could not give him such a hold over me' (p. 83). And her kissing session with Peggy appears to have been a poor substitute for the failure of a pick-up, 'a boy in a record store' whose promising good looks are belied by his limited conversational repertoire:

We were so disappointed that we went back to my room and smoked marijuana and kissed each other until we were exhausted and fell asleep. Her tongue was narrow and pointed and soft. And that was how I said goodbye to Hugh, my arms and legs wrapped tightly around him, my tongue in his mouth, thinking of all the people I had held in this way (p. 83).

After Hugh, Lucy has an affair for some time with a painter, Paul, an affair that is strictly sexual: 'except for eating, all the time we spent together was devoted to sex' (p. 113). During this affair, she has a one-off liaison with a salesman she has just met, again only for sexual excitement and with no further contact: 'We did not exchange telephone numbers' (p. 117). Significantly, all these experiences are depicted as Lucy's sexual *conquests*, for issues of power and control predominate in every 'relationship'. All are described in the section of the novel entitled 'Cold Heart' which is appropriate given that no matter how many times Lucy has sex, she refuses emotional commitment. Ultimately, her sex life involves as much withdrawal as intercourse: the refrain, 'I did not fall in love' (p. 100), is reiterated at any threat of intimacy and as soon as Paul 'got the idea he possessed me in a certain way, that was the moment I grew tired of him' (p. 155).

It has been argued, and I believe legitimately, that Lucy can be read as an older development of Kincaid's protagonist in her earlier novel, *Annie John*.[2] In light of this, Lucy's acknowledgment that she 'had spent so much time saying I did not want to be like my mother' (p. 90) sheds light on her casual and manipulative attitude to sexual relationships. This mother, as described in *Annie John*, valorises an entirely *opposite* attitude to Lucy's views on female sexual morality. Best encapsulated in the much quoted vignette 'Girl' (from Kincaid's first collection of prose, *At The Bottom Of The River*[3]), this attitude corresponds to the Victorian idealisation of the 'Angel in the House': a proper young lady is domestically adept, values cleanliness, manners, decorum, service to males and, above all, chastity. Thus, in *Annie John* (p. 102), when her mother observes Annie conversing – quite innocently, as the reader is aware – with a group of older schoolboys on the street, her response is outrage:

She observed me making a spectacle of myself in front of four boys. She went on to say that, after all the years she had spent drumming into me the proper way to conduct myself when speaking to young men, it had pained her to see me behave in the manner of a slut in the street and that just to see me had caused her to feel shame.

For Annie, heterosexual relations are a minefield to be traversed with care, bounded as they are with her mother's rules and regulations about the way a decent 'young lady' must behave; Lucy reacts to these strictures by becoming precisely the kind of slut her mother most despises. For Nellie in Erna Brodber's *Jane and Louisa Will Soon Come Home*,[4] the voices of mother, aunt, and granny chorus a similar warning: 'save yourself lest you turn woman before your time' (p. 17). To become a woman is to be vulnerable. Thus the approach of puberty is viewed as something frightening: 'you are eleven now and soon something strange will happen to you' (p. 23). Physical maturation is seen as shameful, involving changed attitudes to the *person* by virtue of her developing *body*: 'But Papa looks at me from head to toe, focuses on my middle and says with strange solemnity: – My. But you have shot up – and my balloon stinks with shame. Something breaks and there is no warmth no more. So I am different. Something is wrong with me' (p. 23).

However, like Lucy, Nellie also internalises an alternative view of female sexuality, this time one propounded by her peers at university. Such a view holds that '[y]ou want to be a woman; now you have a man, you'll be like everybody else. You're normal now!' (p. 28). As in *Lucy*, the depiction of Nellie's sexual initiation with a man is dominated by a feeling of distance from the experience. She is 'going through with it' to conform to a socially constructed norm of womanhood, much as this conflicts with that of the 'young lady' touted by conventional morality (the very norm that Lucy rejects): 'You ought you ought to have torn up the script and backed out. But he paid the taximan what you knew must have been his weeks' food, so you let him touch you' (p. 28).

But unlike Lucy, Nellie cannot shake the internalised ideal of the 'Angel in the House' and her experience is, as a result, sordid and revolting: 'One long nasty snail, curling up, straightening out to show its white underside that the sun never touches. Popped it out of its roots, stripped off its clothes and jammed my teeth into it sucking' (p. 28). Frank as this evocation of fellatio may be, there is no pleasure on the woman's side, and Nellie is left with a renewed sense of the shameful nature of her sexuality: 'I need to be cleansed I need cleansing' (p. 119), reinforcing the lessons taught by the older women of her community.

Alecia McKenzie, born in 1960, represents a new generation of women writers from the West Indies and it might be supposed that her collection of stories set in the Jamaica of the 1970s and 1980s, *Satellite City*,[5] would be free of the kind of taboos on female sexuality described by Kincaid and Brodber. To some extent this is the case. Working-class women openly live with men out of wedlock, although for many – Pinkie and Delsha, for example – such unions are stressful and abusive, with little mention of sexual pleasure. For middle-class, educated young women heterosexual experience is matter of course, casually referred to in passing. In 'Natasha', university student Andrea 'slept late after a dorm party the night before. Errol was with her' (p. 33). Journalist Marci ('Stuck in the Maid's Room'), visits Ray at home after a few dates and what ensues is described in a matter of fact, if somewhat clinical fashion: 'Ray got up and lit a candle. Then he turned off the television. He pushed her back on the bed, took off her clothes, took off his own. They made love. He came and she didn't. He felt her disappointment. They lay together for a while. Then she got up and put on her clothes' (p. 22).

Shortly after, Marci announces that she will be leaving to pursue a scholarship in communications in the USA. The ironic lack/failure of communication in this encounter is echoed in nearly all depictions of male/female sexual relationships in McKenzie's collection. And while acknowledgement of female heterosexual activities in this text suggests increasing social tolerance of women's carnality, society turns a blind eye to more murky sexual waters: for example, incest (Marci has been abused by her stepfather), sexual abuse (Maisie in 'Bella Vista' is the victim of statuary rape at 15 by a powerful lawyer/political thug, who leaves her pregnant and poor) and the predatory nature of male sexuality (12-year-old Natasha in the eponymous story is leered at and harassed by ghetto youths who intend to use her as soon as she is physically mature). As in *Jane and Louisa*, women are vulnerable: a girl who yields to sexual temptation generally ends up pregnant, abandoned, destitute and 'fallen,' with dreams of education and 'betterment' shattered.

As this partial survey indicates, female sexuality in the work of West Indian women prose writers is either shrouded in secrecy and shame, or a matter of casual and unfeeling acquiescence to male pressure. In most cases, it has negative consequences for the woman's economic, social and psychological well being. Apart from Kincaid's fiction, sex is rarely described with any degree of explicitness and certainly without the joyful eroticism that characterises much hispanophone and francophone Caribbean writing by women: a sample of such writing in Pamela Mordecai and Betty Wilson's anthology, *Her True-True Name*,[6] seems to me to bear out this claim. Could the problem be *heterosexuality* itself? Is the alternative represented as less problematic for women in the literary texts? I attempt to investigate such queries in the following section.

Alternatives to 'Compulsory Heterosexuality'[7]

Adrienne Rich argues that in the 1980s the current climate of Western society became increasingly conservative:

The New Right's messages to women have been precisely, that we are the emotional and sexual property of men, and that the autonomy and equality of women threaten family, religion and state. The institutions by which women have been traditionally controlled – patriarchal motherhood, economic exploitation, the nuclear family, compulsory heterosexuality – are being strengthened by legislation, religious fiat, media imagery, and efforts at censorship (p. 228).

Lest Rich's assessment be seen as culture specific, one can look closer to home: consider the current debate about 'Caribbean men in crisis' and the citing of women's increased access to education and economic independence as the cause of such crisis. Certainly the widespread media condemnation a few years ago of Barbadian women who attended a male strip-show and *enjoyed themselves*, speaks to the kind of conservatism Rich depicts. In a climate that seeks to strengthen *control* of women, feminism is crucial; but even within feminist scholarship, Rich considers, there is an almost blanket assumption that heterosexuality is the norm for women, and lesbianism is a marginal or less 'natural' phenomenon, a matter of 'sexual preference' (p. 229). Rich calls for a rejection of the 'bias of compulsory heterosexuality, through which lesbian experience is perceived on a scale ranging from deviant to abhorrent or simply rendered invisible' (p. 229). In addition, she considers that 'heterosexual feminists will draw political strength for change from taking a critical stance toward the ideology which *demands* heterosexuality' (p. 228).

Summing up, Rich (p. 248) explains her motive for writing on this topic: 'I was urging that lesbian *existence* has been an unrecognized and unaffirmed claiming by women of their sexuality, thus a pattern of resistance, thus also a kind of borderline position from which to analyse and challenge the relationship of heterosexuality to male supremacy.'

Are West Indian women writers party to an unthinking naturalisation of 'compulsory homosexuality'? *Do* they partake in the silencing of lesbian existence or are there texts which demonstrate such existence as resistance to male supremacy? By and large, I would answer the first question in the affirmative with the proviso that, as noted above, heterosexuality for West Indian women is rarely unproblematised in the fictions. With regard to the second enquiry, there seems to me a clear distinction between 'older' writers such as Rhys, Allfrey and Gilroy and regional-based writers (Hodge, Brodber, Senior, Pollard, Goodison, Collins and Edgell, for example) in whose works the lesbian experience is hardly acknowledged, and 'newer', usually foreign-based writers like Michelle Cliff, Dionne Brand, Marlene Nourbese Philip, Patricia Powell and Shani Mootoo, whose texts openly confront such experience.

Kincaid occupies an anomalous position in my crude dichotomy. While there is a possible homoerotic subtext in several of the impressionistic pieces that make up *At the Bottom of the River* ('one day I will marry a woman – a red-skin woman with black bramblebush hair and brown eyes, who wears skirts that are so big I can easily bury my head in them' (p. 11); 'That woman over there, that large-bottomed woman, is important to me. It's for her I save up my sixpences instead of spending for sweets. Is this a love like no other?' (p. 21)), this evocation of 'the woman I love' is invariably bound up with the mother figure. In *Annie John*, Kincaid's subsequent work, the daughter's close physical and emotional bond with her mother is sensuously and movingly depicted; the two female bodies are frequently described in such close proximity, delighted in their resemblance, mutually admiring and almost fitting together as one:

As she told me the stories, I sometimes sat at her side, leaning against her, or I would crouch on my knees behind her back and lean over her shoulders. As I did this, I would occasionally sniff at her neck, or behind her ears, or at her hair . At times I would no longer hear what it was she was saying; I just liked to look at her mouth as it opened and closed over words, or as she laughed. How terrible it must be for all the people who had no one to love them so and no one whom they loved so, I thought. (pp. 22-23)

By contrast, Annie's pubescent love for Gwen and the Red Girl, expressed via kisses, caresses and mutual admiration, are but substitutes for this early, intense bonding and appear to be ways of filling the gap left by the mother's withdrawal of affection, or a means of punishing her for withholding that love. In *Lucy*, such schoolgirl affairs are remembered but are relegated to a phase en route to heterosexuality: 'there was a girl from school I used to kiss, but we were best friends and only using each other for practice' (p. 83). Similarly, while her friendship with Peggy involves the odd kissing episode, this too is clearly practice for 'the real thing' with a man, and eventually Lucy chooses 'the company of a man over hers' (p. 101) and the women drift apart.

While Kincaid's characters move from female bonding to 'compulsory heterosexuality', there is still an openness in the evocation of physical affection between women which is missing in the work of other West

Indian women writers. An exception is Marlene Nourbese Philip's *Looking For Livingstone*,[8] in which a departure from heterosexual relations is represented. In the novel, the narrator's travels within an allegorical Africa, an area of timelessness and silence, bring her to the land of the NEECLIS where she has a love relationship with the weaver/needlewoman Arwhal. The carnality of the relationship is acknowledged,

reading to each other as we lay naked at the water's edge watching the noon-day sun play hide-and-go-seek with water-damp bodies – first a flank then a nipple, challenging finger or tongue to follow – now a buttock, next the soft surround of navel, soon the long, swift curve of back tufted, secret triangles of crinkly pleasure (p. 53).

For Kincaid and Philip, among others, it is perhaps only in the wider and more sexually tolerant world of the metropole, and the availability of presses seeking to publish 'minority women', that such frank, erotic language can be spoken. Here too, some writers of West Indian origin have explicitly espoused lesbianism. Dionne Brand is one who has found in voluntary exile the freedom to challenge 'compulsory heterosexuality.' In an interview with Frank Birbalsingh,[9] Brand confides that 'the long sojourn [in Canada], which has turned out to be more than a sojourn, has shaped the issues' for her (p. 130). Her Marxist politics, her feminism, her black and lesbian identity have gelled and matured in exile. Her sequence of prose poems, 'Hard Against the Soul', explicitly affirms the importance and validity of loving another woman; her work according to Carol Morrell,[10] 'is a moving testimony on behalf of all outsiders – blacks, immigrants, women and lesbians'. Interestingly, as she writes about the making of her film *Older Stronger Wiser* (1989), Brand looks to a vision of older black women of her community as free of the tyranny of received femininity and 'the prisoned gaze of men'. Such women serve as a source of strength to affirm her sexual *difference* too, despite the hostility of men or women (black as well as white) directed at black lesbians. Birbalsingh notes the novelty in Brand's texts with regard to the ways in which Caribbean women are portrayed: 'That's new; it doesn't exist in previous West Indian writing: the kind of women who drink, socialise openly and are completely frank about their sexuality.' Brand replies: 'But I grew up with those women; my aunts were those women. My aunts had big loud laughs. I'm not saying that they conquered life, or that life was beautiful for them or anything; but I saw them wrestle with it, and I wanted to describe that wrestling' (p. 134).

In *Sans Souci*,[11] Brand details such women wrestling with life, with poverty, unwanted pregnancies and most of all with violent and uncaring men. The men in this collection of stories are largely predators on women and girls. In the first (and title) story, Claudine relives her rape:

That is how her first child was born. He grabbed her and forced her into his little room and covered her mouth so his mother would not hear her screaming. She had bitten the flesh on his hand and still he had exploded her insides, broken her . She was thirteen. She felt like the hogs that were strung on the limbs of trees and slit from the genitals to the throat. That is how her first child was born (p. 12).

The final story, 'Sketches in transit going home', caricatures men in bestial terms: Jasmine, going home to Trinidad for Carnival, shudders at the memory of her office cleaning job with 'the white security guard trying to feel her breasts as she left the building' (p. 132); the narrator describes with loathing a fellow Trinidadian passenger who,

was confiding stories about how many women he had fucked and how many more he could fuck to a friend whom he met on the plane. His breath wheezing between his teeth. He was anticipating the feting and the drinking and the bacchanal. His cock was like a weapon, he said, like a hungry animal (p. 138).

While some of the female characters are victimised by men, a few – like the indomitable Blossom, in the story of the same name – fight back physically ('Next thing Blosom [sic] know, she running Victor down Vaughan Road screaming and waving the bread knife' p. 38) and by taking control of their own lives. In contrast to such confrontational and dysfunctional unions, women's relations with other women tend to be supportive and pleasurable: aunts and grandmothers care for and nurture young girls, women go out to dance and drink and talk with girlfriends. Potentially lesbian relationships are only hinted at, for example in the sensual pleasure of schoolgirls worshipping a French teacher's bosom in 'Madame Alaird's Breasts'. Perceiving in the womanly figure 'a vision, a promise of the dark-red fleshiness of real life' (p. 82), 13-year-old girls discuss in awe.

Madame Alaird's breasts [which] were like pillows, deep purple ones, just like Madame Alaird's full lips as she expressed the personal pronouns. Madame Alaird's breasts gave us imagination beyond our years or possibilities, of burgundy velvet rooms with big-legged women and rum and calypso music. Next to Madame Alaird's breasts, we loved Madame Alaird's lips. They made water spring to our mouths. (p. 80)

Lesbian experience is explicitly mentioned as a possibility only once, in 'At the Lisbon Plate'. Significantly, lesbianism is linked with the choice of specifically *feminist* politics,

a rumour went around that Elaine and I were lovers. It wouldn't have bothered either of us if it were true at the time or if it wasn't said in such a malicious way. But it was because of how we acted. Simply, we didn't defer to the men around and we didn't sleep with them, or else when we did we weren't their slaves forever or even for a while.

So both factions, those we slept with and those we didn't, started the rumour that we were lovers. (p. 103)

Even the free-spirited and consciously feminist narrator here, like the women of Trinidad that Brand speaks of, must wrestle with sexism, racism and cultural marginalisation; it seems easier to do so with the support of a female, rather than a male companion.

I suggested earlier that challenges to 'compulsory heterosexuality', particularly the foregrounding of lesbian experience, are more prevalent in West Indian fiction by women who are resident in the metropole, largely because of a more tolerant attitude toward gays as well as the presence of feminist and lesbian publishing outlets. This seems to be supported in Shani Mootoo's collection of stories, appropriately entitled *Out On Main Street*.[12] Described as an Indo-Trinidadian-Canadian, Mootoo's fictions, like Brand's, are set in both Trinidad and Canada although while Brand focuses on African-Caribbean women, one of Mootoo's themes is the cultural distance between Indians from the subcontinent and those who have been creolised in the West Indies. In the title story and in 'Lemon Scent', a clear distinction is made between attitudes to lesbians in Canada and at home in Trinidad. In the latter, the most intense and erotic of the collection, two Indo-Trinidadian women pursue a passionate love affair under the jealous eye of Kamini's husband. Worried about his wife's depression, the husband asks Anita to come and visit her, having noticed that Kamini 'seems to sizzle with life in Anita's presence' (p. 26). But her sensual preparations for Anita infuriate him, and he warns his wife, 'You know, she might be one of those types who likes only women. With his lips almost against hers he whispers, "If I ever find out that you two have slept together I will kill you both" ' (p. 28).

Despite the threat, Kamini makes love with Anita in a landscape described as paradisal:

Anita reaches out and touches Kamini's lips with hers, taking in the smell of skin, lips, mouth. She slides her lips around to Kamini's cheek and leaves them lightly resting there, her tongue anxious but holding back. The earthy smell of the forest, alive with decaying fruit, subsides for a moment as Anita feels herself suddenly awakening again to the familiar warm lemon scent Kamini feels Anita responding to her smell. She lies back onto the blanket as her lover's mouth follows hers. Her fingers take time curling over Anita's shoulders, drawing her down closer as she curves her pelvis up towards Anita's. She lets Anita nestle her body between her thighs. (p. 32)

But immediately '[a]fter making love, she always parts the branches and pensively looks over to the house' (p. 29). For all her passion for Anita, Kamini is trapped by fear in the sham of her heterosexual marriage.

By contrast, the lesbians of the title story, strolling together along a Canadian 'Main Street', are very much 'out':

Yuh see, Janet pretty fuh so! And I doh like de way men does look at she, as if because she wearing jeans and T-shirt and high-heel shoe and make-up and have long hair loose dat she easy .Dat kind a thing always make me want to put mih arm around she waist like, she is my woman, take yuh eyes off she! .And den is a whole other story when dey see me with mih crew cut and mih blue jeans tuck inside mih jim-boots. Walking next to Janet, who is so femme dat she redundant, tend to make me look like a gender dey forget to classify. But if I ain't walking like a strong-man monkey I doh exactly feel right and I always revert back to mih true colours. De men dem does look at me as if dey is exactly what I need a taste of to cure me good and proper. I could see dey eyes watching Janet and me, dey face growing dark as dey imagining all kind a situation and position. And de women dem embarrass fuh so to watch me in mih eye, like dey fraid I will jump up and try to kiss dem, or make pass at dem. Yuh know, sometimes I wonder if I ain't mad enough to do it just for a little bacchanal, nah! (p. 48)

In spite of suspicion and prejudice, the women seem unashamed of their sexuality and indeed have the benefit of solidarity with a community of lesbians who are instantly recognisable:

Well, with Sandy and Lise is a dead giveaway dat dey not dressing fuh any man, it have no place in dey life fuh man-vibes, and dat in fact dey have a blatant penchant fuh women dey call out to us, shameless, loud and affectionate. Dey leap over to us, eager to hug up and kiss us like if dey hadn't seen us for years. (p. 56)

Humorously, Mootoo identifies the specific dress code of the 'public' lesbian[13] in her final story: 'I recognised the shortness of the hair, the breastlessness of shirt, the Birkenstocks and grey socks' that constitute 'family' (p. 113).

Acceptance within such a community, the text suggests, is one of the benefits of a large cosmopolitan city. And the lack of acceptance in the West Indies, the silencing, prohibiting and censuring of lesbian experience, is the main reason that Janet in the (title) story flees Trinidad as soon as her schooling is complete,

she pack up and take off like a jet plane so she could live without people only shoo-shooing behind she bac k . . .'But A A! Yuh ain't hear de goods 'bout John Mahase daughter, gyurl? Everybody talking 'bout she. Hear dis, nah! Yuh ever see she wear a dress? Yes! Doh look at mih so. Yuh reading mih right!' (p. 47)

Wanting (to be) Mother?

Mootoo's fiction deals not only with lesbian experience among West Indian women at home and abroad, but with heterosexual women trapped in the restrictive prison of married servitude. Further, the misery of such women is compounded by their internalisation – as in the case of Brodber's Nellie and Kincaid's Annie – of their own mothers' insistence that this indeed is women's place. 'A Garden of Her Own' details the long-suffering Vijai, virtually embalmed in an urban Canadian 'bachelor apartment', where she ekes out her days cooking and ironing and cleaning and, above all, *waiting* for her husband, an insensitive and boorish man whose idea of affection is to give her shopping money or have a quick bout of wordless, selfish sex before returning to his armchair and newspaper. Desperately homesick, her memories of her family nonetheless reconstruct carefully gendered roles:

Sometimes Papa didn't come home til long after suppertime. Mama would make us eat but she would wait for him. Sometimes he wouldn't come for days, and she would wait for him then too . Mama, why did you wait to eat? If I were to eat now would you, Papa, he think I am a bad wife? Why did you show me this, Mama? I must not nag (p. 15).

In 'Wake Up,' a daughter learns first-hand the similar lesson: that a good wife waits submissively, serves attentively, always blames herself, never complains at bad treatment, and represses all her own desires in self-sacrificing martyrdom. The role fills the daughter with horror: 'Being female, my future looks grim, claustrophobic. I worry that I am expected, as a girl, to grow up to be just like her. The alternative to being just like her is to be just like him. And as much as I cry inside at his rejection of her and so of us, his freedom looks more exciting, interesting' (p. 42).

In so many texts by West Indian women writers, this theme recurs: mothers or other older women socialise girl children into a life of renunciation, denial, repression and guilt at their own sexual needs, with terrible psychic results – including failed heterosexual partnerships – for the adult female. Much of this 'package' (ideal womanhood) is tied up with 'compulsory heterosexuality' and the power relations encoded therein; again, the mother is the instrument of its naturalisation.

Feminist theory has made the point, to use the title of Monique Wittig's essay, that 'One Is Not Born A Woman',[14] but *constructed* as such. In this article, Wittig disputes the naturalness of 'woman' as a social category as well as the biological origins of both gender difference and the related inequality of female to male. Women, she argues, are culturally imagined and within heterosexuality's rigid two-gender system, are imagined as belonging to/serving men, in the way Mootoo describes above. Lesbians then, are *not women* given that they evade heterosexuality's insistence on a firm connection between gender, sexual practice and economic and political power.

Leaving aside for the moment this last radical claim, *how* precisely are women constructed and 'socially imagined'? What is the mother's role in this construction, and why does it lead to the kind of problematic mother/daughter relations that have been a feature of West Indian fictions by women? And how is the mother implicated in the socialisation into 'compulsory heterosexuality'?

In her important essay, 'The Traffic in Women',[15] Gayle Rubin examines some of the theories which seek to explain 'the question of the nature and genesis of women's oppression and social subordination' (p. 157), and makes the now familiar observation that '[s]ex as we know it – gender identity, sexual desire and fantasy, concepts of childhood – is itself a social product' (p. 166). Now a sex/gender system *per se* is value neutral, she claims; but the specific *social relations* which organise certain systems have made them oppressive of women (p. 168). In seeking 'observable and empirical forms of sex/gender systems' for study, Rubin determines upon kinship systems since they 'are made up of, and reproduce, concrete forms of socially organised sexuality' (p. 169). It is kinship systems which impose cultural organisation on the facts of biological procreation and, in Lévi Strauss' formulation, the essence of kinship structures lies in the *exchange of women* between men, with marriage being the most basic form of gift exchange. 'The result of a gift of women is more profound than the result of other gift transactions', Rubin explains, 'because the relationship thus established is not just one of reciprocity, but one of kinship' (p. 173).

Focusing on kinship systems and the 'gift of women' clearly places the oppression of women within social constructs, rather than ascribing it to biological difference (p. 178). The maintenance of difference is indeed *crucial* to the maintenance of the system: the division of labour by sex, for example, 'can therefore be seen as a "taboo": a taboo against the sameness of men and women' and also 'as a taboo against sexual arrangements other than those containing at least one man and one woman, thereby enjoining heterosexual marriage' (p. 178). At the most basic level then, Rubin finds (as does Adrienne Rich) that 'the social organization of sex rests upon gender, obligatory heterosexuality, and the constraint of female sexuality' (p. 179). This certainly appears to be both explanation for and source of the homophobic prejudices, and the difficult male/female relationships depicted in the fictions discussed.

Since kinship systems rest upon marriage, they 'therefore transform males and females into "men" and "women", each an incomplete half which can only find wholeness when united with the other' (p. 179). Accordingly, exclusive gender identity requires the suppression of whatever traits are supposedly 'natural' to the other sex; Mootoo's lesbians, 'out' on Main Street, clearly challenge this taboo. Indeed, the narrator sees herself through heterosexual eyes as belonging to 'a gender dey forget to classify'. In light of this, Wittig's claim that lesbians are not women achieves credence. One is not a woman born, but made; and a woman – whose 'natural' traits are the opposite of a man's – is a gift exchanged between men; so a lesbian, who fits neither of these womanly categories, is not a woman. Rubin points out that gender is not simply identification with one sex, but involves the direction of sexual desire at the *other* sex, hence the taboo on same-sex love. Thus, she continues, '[t]he suppression of the homosexual component of human sexuality, and by corollary, the oppression of homosexuals, is therefore a product of the same system whose rules and relations oppress women' (p. 180). For clearly, 'as long as men have rights in women which women do not have in themselves', suppression of female homosexuality would seem to be intrinsic to the system.

Now kinship systems, as developed by Lévi Strauss, may account for 'the asymmetry of gender – the difference between the exchanger and the exchanged – [which] entails the constraint of female sexuality' (p. 183), but to 'explain the mechanisms by which children are engraved with the conventions of sex and gender' we must turn to psychoanalysis. For, as Rubin points out, 'psychoanalysis provides a description of the mechanisms by which the sexes are divided and deformed, of how bisexual, androgynous infants are transformed into boys and girls' (p. 185). And here, as we know from Freud and the development of his ideas by Lacan, is where the mother comes in: more specifically, here is where the *separation from* the mother, the crisis at the heart of *Annie John*, is crucial. For in the pre-Oedipal phase children are not differentiated into masculine and feminine, but are bisexual; 'and for children of both sexes, the mother was the object of desire' (p. 186). How then does the girl-child acquire 'normal' adult heterosexuality? Well, in Lacan's scheme, 'the Oedipal crisis occurs when a child learns of the sexual rules embedded in the terms for family and relatives' (p. 189), and ends when the child understands and accepts his or her place in the system, gendered according to the rules of the particular culture which is 'domesticating' it.

In most kinship systems, the basic rules include: each child must become one or the other gender; the genders do not have the same sexual rights or futures – the possession or the phallus confers certain rights for men, including the right to a woman; the incest taboo prohibits some sexuality – the mother is unavailable to either child, because she 'belongs' to the father (pp. 192-193). The usual pattern has the boy exchanging 'his mother for the phallus, the symbolic token which can later be exchanged for a woman' of his own (p. 193); for the girl, things are more complex:

For the boy, the taboo on incest is a taboo on certain women. For the girl, it is a taboo on all women. Since she is in a homosexual position vis-à-vis the mother, the rule of heterosexuality which dominates the scenario makes her position excruciatingly untenable. The mother, and all women by extension, can only be loved by someone 'with a penis' (phallus). Since the girl has no 'phallus', she has no 'right' to love her mother or any other woman, since she herself is destined to some man (pp. 193-194).

Thus she turns away from the mother in anger and disappointment, to the father who has the phallus which she can only 'get' via intercourse or having a child, as a gift from a man (p. 195). In this scheme, as Karen Horney has pointed out, the creation of 'femininity' in women is an act of psychic brutality and leaves women bitterly resentful of the suppression to which they have been subjected (p. 196). Rubin considers that since the 'psychoanalytic theory of femininity is one that sees female development based largely on pain and humiliation' (p. 197), there is a clear need for a revolution in kinship so that the sexual property system can be 'reorganized in such a way that men did not have overriding rights in women' (no exchange of women), and there will be no gender as we know it (p. 199). Instead she dreams of 'an androgynous and genderless (though not sexless) society, in which one's sexual anatomy is irrelevant to who one is, what one does, and with whom one makes love' (p. 204).

I have rehearsed Rubin's essay at some length because it conveniently summarises a great deal of anthropological and psychoanalytic theorising on the reasons for the imposition of obligatory heterosexuality, and the methods by which individuals are compelled to assume their gender places within it. The essay also raises the importance for the girl of the pre-Oedipal bond with the mother's body, an initial homosexuality that she is forced to renounce. But as some of the fictions mentioned above demonstrate, this renunciation is *not* always complete. While the mothers in *Annie John* and *Jane and Louisa* negatively influence their daughters by imparting a legacy of feminine submission and sexual denial they impart, the 'female imaginary' in which access to the mother's body is never denied remains a paradisal memory. I mentioned earlier Nourbese Philip's depiction of lesbian love in *Looking For Livingstone*; but it is interesting to note that Carol Morrell, in her editorial comments on the writing collected in *Grammar of Dissent* (p. 20), considers that such a departure from heterosexuality 'is also a continuation of the spiritual and physical bond between mother and daughter' prevalent in Philip's work. And one can argue of Kincaid's fiction that the intensity of this bond, and the traumatic – and *incomplete* – nature of its rupture, is what drives all her protagonists to seek alternative female love objects and then, even after acceding to the heterosexual 'norm', to retain sexual and emotional control in a manner reminiscent of the all-powerful mother.

Similarly, in Michelle Cliff's *Abeng*[16] the mother's lack of physical and emotional intimacy with her light-skinned daughter (pp. 51-54), leaves Clare forever longing for that taboo union:

'Cry-cry baby, suck your mama's titty', children used to taunt one another. At twelve Clare wanted to suck her mother's breasts again and again – to close her eyes in the sunlight and have Kitty close her eyes also and together they would enter some dream Clare imagined mothers and children shared (p. 54).

Thus the longed-for intimacy with another woman is evoked as either implicitly or explicitly lesbian in Clare's historical memory of the old slave woman Mama Ali who 'loved only women in that way' (p. 35), or in her love for the black girl Zoe with whom she swims naked and for whom she feels desire – 'she had wanted to lean across Zoe's breasts and kiss her' (p. 124) – even though '[i]n her love for Zoe, Clare knew that there was something of her need for her mother' (p. 131). An older Clare is the protagonist of Cliff's later novel, *No Telephone to Heaven*,[17] and demonstrates the same problem; explaining how her mother's abandonment and lack of love has affected her, Clare confesses that, like Lucy, 'love, affection does not come easy to me' (p. 154).

Adrienne Rich, in 'Compulsory Heterosexuality', goes over the psychoanalytic ground covered by Rubin regarding the acquisition of gender for women. She cites the work of Nancy Chodorow, who has investigated 'how mothering by women affects the psychological development of girl and boy children' and who concludes (in Rich's paraphrase) 'that because women have women as mothers, "the mother remains a primary internal object [sic] to the girl, so that heterosexual relationships are on the model of a nonexclusive, second relationship for her, whereas for the boy they re-create an exclusive, primary relationship" '(p. 231). The daughter never totally lets go of the mother's body, and indeed Chodorow acknowledges that lesbian relationships tend to *recreate* mother-daughter emotional connections. In summarising this section of her essay, Rich asks:

If women are the earliest sources of emotional caring and physical nurture for both female and male children, it would seem logical, from a feminist perspective at least, to pose the following questions: whether the search for love and tenderness in both sexes does not originally lead toward women; *why in fact women would ever redirect that search*; and why such violent strictures should be found necessary to enforce women's total emotional, erotic loyalty and subservience to men (p. 232).

Rich goes on to suggest answers to these questions in an effort to challenge the assumption that most women are *innately* heterosexual. Fascinating as this is, what interests me here is the italicised query, as well as a paradigm postulated elsewhere in the essay which Rich calls the 'lesbian continuum' (p. 239). This continuum includes a range 'of woman-identified experience' from sexual experience with another woman to 'other forms of primary intensity between and among women' (p. 239). I would like to adapt this continuum to describe the range of 'lesbian experience' depicted in the West Indian texts mentioned above, as varying responses to Rich's italicised question. That is, given the pervasive and frequently problematic treatment of the mother/daughter relationship in West Indian writing by women, responses to the initial bonding with and desire for the mother's body range from an eroticised evocation of a paradisal unity with the mother's female body (*Annie John*, parts of Nourbese Philip's *She Tries Her Tongue: Her Silence Softly Breaks* [18]); through an attempt to substitute for its loss other primary relationships with girls/women (*Lucy, Abeng, No Telephone to Heaven*, parts of *Looking For Livingstone*); to an outright embracing of lesbian sexuality in the work of Brand and Mootoo. Of course this is only a bald sketch of such a continuum, and needs assessment in terms of applicability to a wider range of texts; and it does not take into account other important aspects of the fictional treatment of mother/daughter relationships, such as the post-colonial links between mother and imperial 'Mother Country'. Nonetheless, in texts where female induction into 'compulsory heterosexuality' is portrayed as deeply painful, and involving some sense of betrayal by mothers who are complicit in the process, the only *partial* redirection of the search for love and nurture away from the mother/female body seems to me to be a useful focus in discussing alternatives to heterosexuality in these texts.

Maternal Loss/Abandonment and the Ventriloquising of Male Homosexuality

In the last section of my paper, I want to continue to explore the relationship between homosexuality and absent or dysfunctional mothering, in the work of two openly lesbian West Indian women writers, Patricia Powell and Michelle Cliff. A striking feature of their texts is that while homosexuality is dealt with frankly and with varying degrees of explicitness, it is *male* homosexuality. There may be any number of reasons for this; perhaps the most obvious reason is that both writers, though resident in the United States, are originally from Jamaica and the virulent homophobia in that island is almost exclusively directed in its most violent form at gay men. In fellow-Jamaican Alecia Mckenzie's *Satellite City*, this deep prejudice is mentioned in the story, 'Grandma's House'. A new neighbor moves in, and the young narrator reports: 'All the people in the neighborhood said he was a battyman, "batty" being our word for buttocks. That meant Mr Matthews was a homosexual' (p. 106). Mr Matthews likes the little girl, and gives her gifts of handkerchiefs which her mother burns; 'She'd pour kerosene on them and set them afire, telling me all the time to "stop taking things from that dirty man" ' (p. 107). In another story, 'Jakes Makes', Carmen's brother Richie confides in her that '[h]e wasn't like the other boys in our neighborhood' (p. 64), and even though his sister and their friend, the titular carpenter Jakes, accept and urge him to be proud of his difference, at university he is isolated, even bullied, and whispered about for his aloofness to women (p. 72). Carmen accounts for this to her friends by lying: 'I told them he was thinking of becoming a priest' (p. 72). Lesbianism may be silenced, but acknowledgement of male homosexuality is incitement to violent hatred. Those who heard Pat Powell's moving account[19] (during a Caribbean Women Writer's Conference at Wellesley College) of the cutlass-wielding crowd who came out to attack a planned gay protest march, will understand the depth of this intolerance in Jamaica.

In *No Telephone to Heaven*, Cliff's homosexual character identifies himself to Clare as a 'battyman' (p. 121), enquiring whether she has ever been tempted by '[p]ussy, sweetness loving your own kind' (p. 122), and offering to set her up with a voluptuous older woman should she feel inclined. More precisely, the 'battyman' is a transsexual, for Harry/Harriet eventually chooses to dress and live as a woman. The barely tolerated product of a maid and her employer's son, raised by the employer's family while his mother the maid is sent packing, Harry/Harriet tells Clare: 'my asshole was split when I was a boy by an officer at Up Park Camp . Ten years old and guilty that a big man in a khaki uniform, braided and bemedaled, in the garden of Her Majesty, did to me what he did. What else to expect but guilt or shame whiteman, Black bwai.' (p. 128)

At the same time, Harry/Harriet assures Clare that the rape – symbolic of the violation of the Caribbean at the hands of European colonisers, and indeed paralleling the 'seduction' of his mother – was not the cause of his 'difference': 'No, darling, I was born this way, that I know. Not just sun, but sun and moon' (p. 128). At the same time, the account stresses the abandoned state of the child who remembers always 'following after the maid, the one they hired to replace my mother – Hyacinth, her name – forever after the poor woman, "Beg you loan me fe you lipstick," '(p. 128). Loss of the mother, and a desire to recapture the female body, perhaps through imitation, goes a long way to explaining Harry/Harriet's deliberate and confrontational assumption of a 'camp', '[b]attyman trash' persona, until the final decision to live as a woman. Even then, as a nurse who works for free in the poorest ghettos, Clare knows that should these people find out that 'a male organ swung gently under her [Harry/Harriet's] bleached and starched skirt they would have indulged in elaborate name-calling, possibly stoning, in the end harrying her to the harbor [f]or her people did not suffer freaks gladly' (p. 171).

Of course, this is what Clare has in common with Harry/Harriet: she too is a freak, a mixed-race Jamaican woman forced to 'pass' for white in the USA, unsure of her racial, cultural or political place, and deeply damaged by her mother's abandonment. In the end, Clare seeks a kind of homecoming, recovery of the mother in recovery of place, by literally burning her outline into her grandmother's ruinate land, along with a group of guerrillas determined to change the course of Jamaican history. Clare's relationship with Harry/Harriet is the nearest she can get to love, because she can recognise in him her own 'in-betweeness', her ambivalent positioning in relation to racial, class, or even gender identity: 'They could swim together as girlfriends . Touching gently, kissing, tongues entwined, coming to, laughing' (p. 130). The link between loss of the mother's body for Clare and for Harry/Harriet, and their tortured path to recovery of the *motherland* via different sexual and political choices, is clearly made in Cliff's disturbing novel.

In Patricia Powell's two novels, the connection between maternal abandonment or loss and homosexuality, is once again explored. West Indian literature has long recorded the phenomenon of absentee parents due to economic circumstances: since the turn of the century, the allure of job prospects abroad have resulted in children being left behind. McKenzie's character Carmen in 'Jakes Makes' observes of Jakes that 'like us, his parents had dumped him with his grandmother and gone off to England. And like ours, they never came back for him. But that wasn't unusual on the island; people always planned to come back but they never did (pp. 60-61).

In Powell's first novel, *Me Dying Trial*,[20] her husband's abusive behaviour and the prospect of earning independence and a decent living

abroad, prompts Gwennie to leave Jamaica for the USA, distributing one
child to an aunt, two to her grandmother and leaving three others with
their father. The eldest boy, Rudi, has been forced from a young age to
assume the care of the younger children and it is he who bears the brunt
of their father's drunken rages and abuse, as well as his domestic and
financial neglect, during the long years of his mother's absence.

While Gwennie lived with the family, her constant friend and source
of relief from her husband's jealousy and violence was a fellow teacher,
Percy. Percy is a divorcee, but,

somewhere deep inside, she know him gone the other way. It wasn't judgement she
passing, but she can't just close her eyes to the way him always dress neat, or how his
hair and face always tidy, how shirts always match pants, ties always large and
flamboyant . She can't quite put her fingers on it, but she can tell, even by the way him
walk, sorta dainty-like, like him stepping on hot bricks. (p. 65)

So far, Percy's homosexuality is signalled textually via stereotypes: gays
dress well and walk funny. But in other ways too, Percy is different to the
men Gwennie encounters. For one thing, he is gentle and considerate, and
socially committed: indeed, it is these qualities that draw Gwennie to him.
And it is Percy, with his lover Martel, who proves to be a friend to Rudi in
Gwennie's absence and his home, with its calm atmosphere and cultured
domestic pleasures, that serves as a haven from the misery of his father's
house and the dreadful responsibilities forced upon Rudi: 'The only thing
that seem to liven him up though, is the weekend visits to Percy Clock's
house' (p. 81).

For all her pretence at not 'passing judgement', Gwennie views homosexuality as 'unnaturalness', forbidden by the Bible and thus indubitably
wrong (p. 65). So too does Clive, the Trinidadian lover she grows close to
after living some years in Connecticut. For Clive, gays are 'batty-man', 'an
abomination before God and man' (p. 147). Throughout the novel, the
intolerance of organised religion to any sexual choice besides 'compulsory
heterosexuality' is bitterly exposed. By contrast, Peppy, the daughter with
whom the story is most concerned, has been raised by an unconventional
aunt and although she initially considers the relationship between Percy
and Martel 'funny' and 'peculiar' (p. 82), by the time Rudi confesses his
own homosexuality to her, Peppy echoes Aunt Cora's views on 'batty-
men',

she tell me that's what them call men who love other men. And she say nothing wrong
with it, but plenty people don't like hear about it. But as far as she concern, people can
do whatever them damn well please with whichever part of them body them damn
well want. For them not paying taxes for it. (p. 96)

Peppy has had contact with lesbians in the community previously, which also accounts for her sympathy with Rudi in the face of Pastor's condemnation of all 'sodomites'. There is Miss Clementine (p. 96), a friend of Jasmine's mother; indeed, Jasmine is raised by her mother and her lesbian lover, Miss Pearl, and is happy about the arrangement, given her father's 'part-time' parenting (p. 98).

Indeed, compared to the dysfunctional heterosexual couples in the text, Jasmine's family is the most 'normal' and seems to provide the best environment for the child. Even as Martel and Percy bicker about Percy's possessiveness, Jasmine's mother and Miss Pearl achieve a relationship based on mutual commitment (they wear wedding rings) and *equality*: the butch/femme role-playing that Peppy expects is not forthcoming (p. 177). 'And them loving to one another, too. Jasmine say them have quarrels, but nothing compared to what used to go on when the father was there' (p. 177). Significantly, after Peppy has been brought to America, but cannot achieve closeness with the mother who abandoned her as an infant, she finds her mother's house less and less of a home. Instead, she spends more and more time with her girlfriend Merle, and thinks of home as 'back at Merle's little one-bedroom apartment, wrap up safe underneath her heavy quilt' (p. 191); the suggestion here, is that in the lesbian relationship Peppy finds the tenderness and love absent from her relationship with her mother.

Gwennie has been a stranger to her daughter since infancy (p. 66), and her abandonment leaves scars: 'it cause Peppy to wonder why the mother leave them and gone for such a long time, if she didn't miss them and was just as unhappy' (p. 78). Of course Gwennie *does* miss them, *is* unhappy, and her 'abandonment' is in fact a means to bring her children to her. But the attempt at mothering comes too late, and Peppy rejects her: 'You only give me away. Couldn't even wait til me crawl out the womb properly, you hand me over' (p. 63). Love comes from other women, first Aunt Cora and then Merle. One is reminded here of Catharine Stimpson's claim in 'Zero Degree Deviancy',[21] that lesbian novels, in mapping out the boundaries of female worlds,

seek the mother as well. A mother waits at the heart of the labyrinth of some lesbian texts. There she unites past, present, and future. Finding her, in herself and through a surrogate, the lesbian reenacts a daughter's desire for the woman to whom she was once so linked, from whom she was then so severed. (p. 256)

While I doubt Powell's novel can be easily termed 'a lesbian novel', there is an abiding concern here, as in the other texts mentioned, with the search for that primal bond, that primary love relationship with the mother, that has been so traumatically lost.

For the homosexual son, maternal abandonment and perceived rejection are even worse. Rudi has no surrogate parent, indeed *he* is forced to take on that role for his siblings. He finds comfort in the company of other gay men, and eventually in that of a lover (p. 98); when finally reunited with his mother, he finds in America the confidence to assert his sexuality and the self-acceptance to openly love another man (p. 176). But the final rejection comes, once more, from his mother for Gwennie refuses to condone his choice, terming his homosexuality 'sin and nastiness' (p. 182), his love 'nasty living' (p. 188), and turns him out of her home. Ironically, while she blames herself for her son's sexual 'abnormality', it is not *her* abandonment that she sees as the primary cause, but the lack of a proper father figure: 'These days in the newspaper she see it print up often, children growing up in households without fathers can't form good relationships with people. Plenty of them grow up without proper direction and sometimes the boys don't turn out manly enough' (p. 162).

In *Me Dying Trial*, loss or rejection by mothers, no matter how well intended the separation, leads to reciprocal rejection of mothers by their children: Peppy turns to another woman for love, and, faced with his 'manly' father's abuse and the dysfunctional heterosexual union of his parents marriage that causes the loss of his mother, Rudi looks to same-sex relationships for love and tenderness.

Maternal rejection of a homosexual son figures even more strongly in Powell's second novel, *A Small Gathering of Bones*.[22] The plot concerns a contemporary Jamaican middle-class homosexual love triangle. Dale, a university student, and Nevin, who owns his own business, are lovers who share a home and continue to do so during and after Nevin's brief affair with Ian, who works in finance. In fact, even as Dale and Nevin's relationship deteriorates and both explore other partners, Dale becomes close friends with Ian, who contracts and eventually dies from a mysterious and terrible disease. Like Percy in *Me Dying Trial*, Ian is distinguished by his sartorial sense, his effeminate walk, manicured fingernails; more, he wears face powder! Nevin, by contrast, is 'macho' in clothing and conduct, while Dale, pretty nondescript in terms of dress, is happiest homemaking, weaving and crocheting, and teaching bible classes – this last despite a consistent sense of the established church's abomination of 'sodomites'. In the spread of characters and 'types' of gay men, Powell refuses to rehearse the socially sanctioned homosexual stereotyping represented in her first book.

Mothers are crucial to these men. Nevin lives next door to his, and Dale finds in her a source of counsel and, initially, tolerance; indeed, she encourages him to bear with Nevin's infidelity. Dale loved his now-deceased mother passionately, and remembers his life with her as a source of joy and creative stimulus (p. 11), although he bears a sense of guilt for the seizure she suffers when he 'comes out' to her (p. 40). But the most intense maternal affection is seen in Ian, who 'love his mother to distraction' (p. 19), and showers her with gifts, money and gestures of affection. By contrast, fathers are absent. Nevin's father, crippled after his wife pushes him down the stairs when he attempts to beat her, is 'mean and bad-tempered' with not a word to say to his son (p. 13); Ian's father meant little to him when alive, and is never mentioned; Dale's father is remembered as authoritarian and cold (p. 27) or absent – he left his wife, and has a new family in England. What attracts Dale to another (married) man is 'his sweet gentleness with his children that reminded Dale so much of what him couldn't get from his father' (p. 44). In no case is a happy heterosexual union between mother and father recalled; in fact, the 'talking head' psychiatrist whom Dale consults, picks up on the similarities between his unhappy relationship with Nevin, and his mother's equally miserable life with the husband who left her for younger conquests (p. 64). For all three men, the primary emotional relationships in their lives are with their mothers.

But in this text too, the loss of/abandonment by the mother is traumatic. Dale's anguish at Nevin's philandering evokes a violent response that is explicitly connected with his sense of maternal abandonment: 'Somebody new was taking over. Nevin was dashing him aside. Like his mother had left him' (p. 57). In the light of this, Ian's implication (pp. 102-103) that Dale's fear of rejection leads *him* to withdraw from commitment before he can be abandoned again, rings true. Nevin's relationship with his mother is less clearly drawn, although despite their surface implacability, each is clearly concerned about the other and they retain almost daily contact. The most heart-rending instance of maternal rejection is Mrs Kayson's denial of her son, Ian.

For all his showering her with gifts, the mother remains a hard, cold and self-righteously doctrinaire moralist with little human compassion. An occasional attendee at his church, Dale hears her described: 'Them say she love to find fault and keep malice. Can hold grudge longer than anybody them know. Love to cause contention. That she never have a welcoming smile to offer anyone, only several hard lines that crease her mouth corners and a hard gleam in her eyes' (p. 19).

Delighted with his new lawyer lover, Ian shares the news with his beloved mother. Her response is simple, categorical and unwavering:

I am not your mother. I don't know who you are. So please go . I never did like you from the beginning. Miss Iris couldn't get you out. Twist up yourself inside me womb like you plan was to stay. Them did have to force cow-itch tea down me throat to get you to budge. Even then you were no damn good. Should've followed me heart and put a blasted end to you, then. (pp. 21-22).

And indeed, she does. Her cold, sanctimonious judgement of her son to Dale, who brings the news of Ian's dreadful illness, once more indicts the very Christianity she professes: 'When your child choose a course God didn't cut out for him, you dish him dirt . You wash your hands clean. You banish him from your life' (p. 37).

Despite Ian's pathetic attempts to keep up the fantasy of continued contact with his mother, and his last-minute conversion to religion to win her approval, her cruel rejection is as much a factor in his psychic degeneration as AIDS is in his physical deterioration. Both are described with unsparing horror. Dying, Ian goes to his mother's house on his birthday and begs her, weeping, for some reassurance of her love. Dale reconstructs the final encounter described by a witness:

"Mama". And maybe him would start to cry, silent, salty tears of relief and love that temporarily blind his vision and fill his heart.

"Get out". And the hardness of her voice would stop him dead in his tracks, and his outstretched arms ready to pull her to his chest, would waver uncertainly . And maybe she took one step forward and chucked him in the chest with both of her hands clamp shut into fists, and maybe the wind flew out of Ian's chest, and his heels forgetting altogether that they'd reached the tip of the step, tilted backwards, off balance, for it'd been so long since he'd set foot in that house (p. 136).

'But Dale, she push him', says Ian's sister of her mother, as Ian's broken body lies at the foot of the stairs. The prenatal urge to 'put a blasted end' to the son she never loved is finally carried out. The failure of maternal love and commitment helps to push Ian into the arms of multiple, anonymous lovers and thus into the hell of incurable disease; the mother herself kills her son for not being the obligatory heterosexual.

In 'Zero Degree Deviancy', Catharine Stimpson notes the pervasive yoking together of homosexuality and deviancy in the modern period, a claim Rich's essay insists is still valid. Stimpson considers that few texts dealing with the subject can ignore this conjunction; writers may acknowledge the link, ruefully or angrily, but they must always deal with it. She posits two main responses in the lesbian novel in English. One is the 'narrative of damnation' (p. 244), depicting the lesbian's suffering as a lonely outcast, the paradigm for which is Radclyff Hall's *The Well of Loneliness*. In this text, homosexuality is imaged as a sickness, a congenital abnormality, 'sexual inversion': Steven is a 'woman-who-is-man' desiring to prove her 'masculinity' by taking as lover a feminine 'woman-who-is-woman'. This abnormality is the source of withdrawal of mother love from Steven, the child who is not what the mother expects or wants from a girlchild: femininity. Stimpson's other model is 'the enabling escape, a narrative of the reversal of such descending trajectories, of the lesbian's rebellion against social stigma and self-contempt' (p. 244). The latter narratives, she clarifies, 'invert the application of the label of deviant: the lesbian calls those who call her sinful or sick themselves sinful or sick; she claims for herself the language of respectability' (pp. 254-255). The 'escape' in question can be textually represented as some kind of alternative space, as in a pastoral idyll, or as an alternative epistemology of the type Gayle Rubin describes, where gender no longer carries the social markers and behavioral rules imposed by 'compulsory heterosexuality'. Powell's novels, it seems to me, locate the reader in the 'narrative of damnation' by foregrounding mothers who insist that homosexuality is synonymous with deviancy, sickness and sin. But by indicting mothers who abandon or reject their children for failing to conform to an inflexible moral hierarchy, Powell points the way to an alternative way for thinking about gender and sex in the West Indies.

Episodes in these novels/works of fictions grimly define the terrible consequences of judgmental parenting. In *A Small Collection of Bones*, Powell has Nevin's mother relate the tale of a '[l]ovely lady. College teacher. Well respected and successful in her vocation. Church going. Choir singing. All in all decent. She never marry. Did share a flat with another lady' (p. 50). This paragon of virtue, perhaps because of her failure to conform to obligatory heterosexuality, was hounded by the father she dutifully supported, who 'used to bother her about her ways. Write her letters, send telegram to her school. Next thing you know, she meagre down to nothing end up inside alms house, poor as church mouse' (p. 51). Father persecutes daughter for not conforming to his version of morality; mother persecutes son for the same reason, in the instance of Ian and Mrs Kayson. Alecia McKenzie, in her story 'Grandma's House', mentions Miss Evelyn who loved to dance and laugh, but whose Christian mother ('a fierce-looking woman who wore a white dress and matching turban that screamed against her very dark skin and knew how to speak in tongues'), considers such activities sinful. The mother persecutes her daughter, 'nagging her to join the church', until Miss Evelyn gets fed up and swims out to sea. 'Miss Evelyn's mother also came to the funeral but she wouldn't enter the church. Suicide was a sin' (p. 108).

It is tempting to read such texts as indictment of the dogmatic school of West Indian parenting that holds to the gospel of 'a rod spared is a child spoilt', particularly in matters of sexual morality. Clearly, the trope of absent/abandoning/rejecting mother that recurs in the work of several West Indian women writers, its relation to the problematic development of female sexuality, and its link to depictions of homosexuality in the writing, needs further and more thorough study. Finally, let me end by suggesting that the rejecting/rejected mother may also be read as a figure for the motherland: so mother/motherland is rejected in *Annie John* for 'her' indoctrination in colonial discourse. The lost motherland is sought repeatedly in Cliff's novels, even if the quest brings death for the abandoned, alienated daughter. In the rawer and more contemporary fiction of Cliff, Powell and McKenzie, Jamaican society has been so dehumanised by political violence and economic parasitism that the motherland now devours 'her' children, callously abandoning or rejecting the vulnerable, the weak, the needy, the different. It is an apocalyptic vision, and one that needs to be attended to.

Notes

1. Jamaica Kincaid, *Lucy* (New York: Farrar Straus Giroux, 1990).
2. Jamaica Kincaid, *Annie John* (New York: Farrar Straus Giroux, 1983).
3. Jamaica Kincaid, *At The Bottom Of The River* (London: Pan, 1984).
4. Erna Brodber, *Jane and Louisa Will Soon Come Home* (London: New Beacon, 1980).
5. Alecia McKenzie, *Satellite City and Other Stories* (Essex: Longman, 1992).
6. Pamela Mordecai and Betty Wilson, *Her True-True Name: An Anthology of Women's Writing from the Caribbean* (London: Heinemann, 1989).
7. Adrienne Rich, 'Compulsory Heterosexuality and Lesbian Existence', in Henry Abelove, Michele Aina Barale and David Halperin e's, *The Gay and Lesbian Studies Reader* (London and New York: Routledge, 1993)pp. 227-254.
8. Marlene Nourbese Philip, *Looking For Livingstone: An Odyssey of Silence* (Toronto: Mercury Press, 1991).
9. Dionne Brand, 'No Language is Neutral,' in Frank Birbalsingh ed. *Frontiers of Caribbean Literature in English* (London: Macmillan, Warwick University Caribbean Studies, 1996)pp. 130-137.
10. Carol Marrell, Introduction to *Grammar of Dissent: Poetry and Prose by Claire Harris, M. Nourbese Philip, Dionne Brand* (Fredericton: Goose Lane Editions, 1994)p. 23.
11. Dionne Brand, *Sans Souci and Other Stories* (New York: Firebrand Books, 1989).
12. Shani Mookoo, *Out On Main Street and Other Stories* (Vancouver: Press Gang Publishers, 1993).
13. In this context, well might we heed Biddy Martin's stricture about promoting *any* view of lesbian identity as uniform and monolithic! Identity, Martin argues in 'Lesbian Identity and Autobiographical Difference[s]' (in Henry Abelove *et. al.* eds. *The Lesbian and Gay Studies Reader*, (London and New York: Routledge, 1993) pp. 274-293, is rather

the site of the complex interactions of many variables including race, class, gender and sexual practice. While all the texts mentioned in this paper need to be examined in light of such interactions, it is beyond the scope of the present exercise to do more than touch upon them.

14. Marique Wittig, in Henry Abelove *et. al.*, eds *The Gay and Lesbian Studies Reader* (London and New York: Routledge, 1993)pp. 103-109.

15. Gayle Rubin, 'The Traffic in Women: Notes on the "Political Economy" of Sex,' in Rayna Reiter ed., *Toward an Anthropology of Women* (New York: Monthly Review, 1975) pp. 157-210.

16. Michelle Cliff, *Abeng* (New York: The Crossing Press, 1984).

17. Michelle Cliff, *She Tries Her Tongue: Her Silence Softly Breaks* (Charlottetown: Ragweed Press, 1989).

18. Marlene Nourbese Philip, *She Tries Her Tongue: Her Silence Softly Breaks* (Charlottetown: Ragweed Press, 1989).

19. Patricia Powell, 'Voicing Gay Sexuality: A Caribbean Experience'. Address to Fourth International Caribbean Women Writers Conference, Wellesley College, April 20-23, 1995.

20. Patricia Powell, *Me Dying Trial* (Oxford: Heinemann Caribbean Writers Series, 1993).

21. Catharine Stripson, 'Zero Degree Deviancy: The Lesbian Novel in English', in Elizabeth Abel ed. *Writing and Sexual Difference* (Sussex; Harvester Press, 1982), 243-259.

22. Patricia Powell, *A Small Gathering of Bones* (Oxford: Heinemann Caribbean Writers Series, 1994).

18

'Young t'ing is the name of the game':

Sexual Dynamics in a Caribbean Romantic Fiction Series

Jane Bryce

In 1993 a new romantic fiction series appeared in the Caribbean, modelled on the British series Mills and Boon but specifically aimed at readers in the region. The English publisher, Heinemann, had spotted the potential for a local version of mass market romance, and invited writers in the English-speaking Caribbean to try their hand. Caribbean Caresses were the result. Identical in format to Mills and Boon, the titles of the six-volume series apparently challenge nothing in their bland invocation of stereotype (*Fantasy of Love, Love in Hiding, Merchant of Dreams, Heartaches and Roses, Sun Valley Romance* and *Hand in Hand*). The crucial difference is the covers. Where regular romance readers are accustomed to seeing white heroines, all the couples depicted on the front of the Caribbean Caresses are dark-skinned: of the six, four are obviously African, one obviously East Indian, and one of the couples shows the influence of the different racial groups which have historically occupied Trinidad. This simple difference alone signals innovation. But it is when we proceed beyond the covers that really interesting deviations begin to emerge.

Romantic fiction is the most conservative and stereotypical of literature forms, and at the same time one of the most potentially subversive. It is bound by rules which derive from the medieval European chivalric code, with its highly conventional and idealised concept of the relationship between the sexes, known as Courtly Love. Central to the convention is the idea of the Lady, who represents an ideal version of femininity which, filtered through a repressive Victorian morality became in turn the Angel in the House – restricted to the domestic sphere, virginal or maternal, nurturing, forebearing, submissive and pure. This myth of desirable femininity still, against all the odds, exerts its influence today, even in unlikely contexts. The Jamaican writer Erna Brodber, documenting stereo-types in the Caribbean, describes the appearance of 'Excellent Ellen' in the Jamaican *Daily Gleaner* of 1834, whose characteristics – of delicacy, paleness, tact, diffidence and submissive suffering – were even then far from the norm for Jamaican women, whether white or black (Brodber 1982: 22). The Barbados *Advocate* in 1950 reprinted a report entitled 'A Husband's Dream', on the selection by a French club for the introduction of 'bachelors to prospective brides', of their 'Household Pearl of 1950' (p. 15). Brodber, having detailed the ways in which Barbadian women did not conform to this domestic ideal, goes on to show how, by the 1970s, 'Upwardly mobile women have become willing to design their lives to fit the stereotypes which, with economic progress, [have] entered creole culture as an alternative course of behaviour for women and which they have obviously internalised' (p. 21). This image, which – in its various guises of Lady, Excellent Ellen or Household Pearl – is fundamentally a European cultural icon, becomes, in the Caribbean setting, at best a travesty, at worst a repressive mechanism for the devaluing of other, more realistic, attributes of women. The Lady, above all, is white. In her guise of romantic heroine she may be found on Caribbean beaches, attracting the gaze of the white hero, while a black waiter offers them exotic cocktails. How is she transformed into the dark-skinned, Caribbean hero-ines of the Caribbean Caresses? Is it just a matter of internalising the stereotype, a process which could perhaps be seen as the literary equiva-lent of hair-straightening or skin-lightening? Or do these novels attempt something more subversive?

Lorna Skeete, the heroine of *Merchant of Dreams*, is a hard-working advertising executive. Her search for a male model for an Atlas Stout commercial brings her face to face with a picture of Damien Bradshaw, 'a gorgeous hunk' she briefly fantasises over, before reminding herself severely that 'great-looking guys like Mr Damien Bradshaw didn't usually have much time for girls who looked like Lorna Skeete. 'Young t'ing' was the name of the game' (p. 12). Lorna's description is uncompromising: 'Her round, dark brown face looked back at her. She wore no make-up or jewellery except for a pair of plain pearl studs in her ears Oh, dear, she really ought to lose some weight again, she thought and went out of the door' (p. 3).

Lorna, it turns out, is a contradictory character. Ambitious, talented and confident at work (though underpaid and exploited), she is prey to insecurity when it comes to men. Having successfully dodged the cultural expectations that dictate particular professions (nursing and teaching, for example) as being appropriately 'feminine', Lorna retains a surprising level of vulnerability in her emotional life. This shows up in her now ended relationship with Colin, in which 'she was so happy that this big, beautiful, sexy man was all hers, when he could have had any number of pretty young chicks just by looking at them' (p. 13), that she doesn't notice he's using her until it hits her in the face. Needless to say, this lack of self-esteem is the major factor in her failure to realise the Hero is serious about her. How could he be, when pretty 'slim t'ing' Gillian is all over him in her tiny pink bikini? How is she to know that here is one man who likes women to have a brain, and appreciates a full bosom and muscular legs? Lorna's blind spot is, moreover, very convenient in terms of the romantic formula, which decrees that there must always be an Obstacle in the way of true love. *Merchant of Dreams* quite consciously (perhaps the title is less innocent than it appears) plays with the romantic formula, exposing the gap between Real and Ideal, turning stereotypes upside down and in the process, pointing towards the possibility of a different way of doing things.

The gap between the Real and the Ideal has been noted by researchers in other contexts than romantic fiction. Merle Hodge, introducing Brodber's study of stereotypes, extends her findings, drawn from the church and the press, to literature. The Caribbean novel, she suggests, is marked by 'the tension between official and real culture', which she sees as 'a permanent feature of Caribbean culture, and the discrepancy between Ideal Woman and Real Woman documented by Brodber is but one aspect of this phenomenon' (Brodber 1982: viii). In a similar vein, Olive Senior, another Jamaican writer and researcher, observes that,

the vacillation in women's behaviour might be seen as expressing the dichotomy of their cultural inheritance, where the stereotypes are European (protected/dominated female) but the role models and role performance are West African (woman as independent actor). Thus part of the vacillation arises from contradictions within the society itself (Senior 1991: 180).

In this sense, then, the heroine of *Merchant of Dreams* is 'realistic', since her behaviour reproduces this vacillation between European stereotype (slim, dependent) and West African role model (pragmatic, independent). Yet there is a danger in seeking to demonstrate the Real in what is, after all, a fantasy form. If the gap between Real and Ideal exerts an alienating effect in the lives of actual "real') women, the fictional heroines of Caribbean Caresses are inevitably at one further remove. The extent to which they can claim to be more 'real' than western romance heroines is therefore a function of reader response and identification, and of the genre itself. Possibly the most that can be said is that the series, by envisaging a *new* Ideal, is closer to the Real than most Western mass market romance, at least as far as Caribbean readers are concerned. Yet most 'real' of all, as Brodber and Senior indicate, is, not the resolution, but the tension between the two. The difference between the female protagonists of 'serious' contemporary West Indian fiction (by writers who include the researchers from whom I quote in this article), and Caribbean Caresses heroines, is that, while the former negotiate this tension in a variety of ways, including leaving the Caribbean, the latter do, ultimately, resolve it in marriage. This resolution, however, is by no means a wholesale capitulation to the romantic stereotype, but part of a larger utopian vision, of which gender equality is metonymic. This revisioning of social reality, with all its attendant tensions and contradictions, is a partial answer to Olive Senior when she posits: 'A fundamental question is: what is the ideal of womanhood that is being projected and absorbed in the Caribbean today?'

To answer this question more fully, I intend to examine the representations of women and men in the Caribbean Caresses series – particularly the heroines and heroes – to see how far they are determined by prevailing stereotypes and to what extent they rework them and thus subvert the formula. This exercise would be quite pointless if I did not share the view, put forward by Karin Barber, that popular culture does more than merely reflect social norms; it also contributes to shaping them (Barber 1987). The fundamental characteristic of popular formulaic genres, whether horror movies, love lyrics or romantic fiction, is their predictability, and much of the pleasure of these forms of entertainment is derived precisely from the fact that their devotees know what to expect and get it, with the resulting sense of fulfilment and resolution. Caribbean Caresses would fail as romantic fiction if they did not overtly adhere to the formula, including obstacles in the way of love, and a happy ending. What is interesting about them, however, is the way their attempt to transplant the formula to the Caribbean context works against the straightforward reproduction of stereotypes, and results in significant deviations which, in turn, point to a changing social consciousness.

Real and Ideal: Exploring the tension

The relocation of romantic fiction from a Western to a West Indian frame necessitates an ontological, as well as a geographical shift. The Caribbean, along with numerous other non-Western locations, from 'the jungles of Borneo' to 'the deserts of North Africa', features in conventional romantic fiction as a site of the exotic. However diverse these settings, they are all marked by the same characteristics of sensuousness and latent danger, which typify the 'non-civilised world'. The logic of the series of oppositions implicit in conventional romance – Western/other, familiar/exotic, civilised/wild, home/away – disintegrates the moment the focus of subjectivity shifts from white Western outsider to native of the exotic territory: suddenly 'other' becomes self, exotic becomes familiar, and 'away' becomes the site of 'home' itself. And yet, since it is part of the formula and therefore a source of pleasure for the reader, some of the old logic must be retained – a sense of escape from the everyday, of lurking danger, of the otherness which is an essential part of the experience of being in love. How is this simultaneous conformity and deviation accomplished by Caribbean Caresses? What sort of world do the protagonists of these novels inhabit, and to what extent does it participate in the dichotomy of Real and Ideal?

Olive Senior, summing up aspects of 'woman's "true" situation' in the Caribbean, points to the progress of younger women in particular:

There are in some of our larger cities and towns numbers of highly visible, well-dressed, apparently self-confident women, who in their lifestyles and manner appear to have gained equality with their male counterparts the majority of these women are young, well educated and largely from the middle class or have adopted a middle class lifestyle. (Senior 1991: 187)

This is without doubt the group to which the Caribbean Caresses heroines belong – professional, independent, educated, and highly motivated to succeed. Their occupations include dress designer, advertising executive, adult education project worker, flower shop owner (businesswoman), linguistics researcher and personal assistant. None of them, however, comes from a particularly privileged background. Typically, they are from 'ordinary' families, and fully aware of the interrelationship of class and poverty, as anyone in the Caribbean must be. Giselle of *Sun Valley Romance*, for instance, the dress designer, is forced to give up her university career when her family can no longer support her, and, though she falls back on her own artistic talent, dressmaking is also a traditional feminine skill inherited from her mother. Lorna of *Merchant of Dreams*, the advertising executive, far from finding her profession glamorous, is exploited by her boss, underpaid and subjected to large amounts of routine drudgery. John Gilmore, alias Lucille Colleton, her creator, is explicit about the extent to which he sought to invoke the Real over the Ideal in his representation of Lorna and her working life. He wanted, he says,

to present a somewhat more realistic view of the Caribbean [as] a place where people are getting on with things in an ordinary manner the heroine is the creative director in an advertising agency and there's a lot of routine work which has to be done to deadlines, a lot of pressure and very little glamour.

Similarly, asked about the role reversal whereby the heroine of his novel hires the hero as a model, Gilmore/Colleton claims this is a deliberate reference to the fact that 'in Caribbean society you get a lot of professional women who make their way in the world because they have to and I wanted to use this for my heroine'. What Gilmore is pointing to here is both the fact that West Indian women have been traditionally self-supporting, and to the ongoing reality that reliance on a man is for most of them simply not an option, romantic fantasy notwithstanding. The implication of this for the relationships which drive the narratives is that, implicit in the heroine's choice of a man, marriage and romantic resolution, is an insistence on gender equality, rather than swooning submission. Valerie Belgrave, author of *Sun Valley Romance*, maintains that while 'you can hardly have a romance in a setting of great poverty and suffering', there is still the potential for subversion of what she sees as an essentially middle-class form:

One of the things is to subvert the conflict of dominance and subservience by the woman I try to strengthen the harmonising of the sexes, to lessen the antagonism between the hero and the heroine to make the heroine have a career, to have her family and the socio-political situation be of importance, and to do all this while maintaining the romantic canon [sic] to a large extent.

It would seem, then, that these authors' self-conscious use of the romance form is partly an effect of their positioning as West Indians, for whom representation is not only a matter of 'reflecting reality' but also an act of reclamation. In their context, the formula cannot be employed innocently, for it invites interrogation every step of the way. An attempt to insert the Real into the artificial conventions of the romance form is part of that interrogation.

Apart from work and the construction of a specific notion of femininity, other aspects of the Real may be traced in such factors as the attention given in the series as a whole to family, community, local cultural manifestations such as Carnival, and the importance of all these in creating a sense of place, and ultimately a sense of identity. Nor is this is a question of isolated individualism, as is so often the case with formula romances in exotic settings, where the couple are divorced from their familiar environments, including family ties. A distinct sense of national pride emerges from the specificity of place, custom and language – the subdued but nonetheless assertive use of creole inflexions within a largely standard English narrative. Beyond these manifestations of cultural specificity, how far does the Real inform the driving narrative force of Caribbean Caresses: love between a man and a woman?

'Rip, torn, stretch and kick apart'

Romantic fiction is quintessentially about love: love realised, love triumphant, mutual, monogamous, faithful, till death us do part. This construction of love is idealistic in any context, and the Caribbean is no exception. Love as an aspiration is, however, given a different inflexion in a context where, according to social science studies of West Indian gender relations, the attitudes of the sexes to each other are predominantly negative. In her study 'Male images of women in Barbados', Christine Barrow finds, 'the Barbadian male image of today's women is almost totally negative' (Barrow 1986: 61). 'Young women of today', in contrast to an 'idealised view of how women were in the past', are seen as no longer subservient or submissive. Rather, they are 'out fulfilling their own ambitions and desires', as a result of which they have become 'aggressive, ugly and "flashy", no longer deserving of the respect (men) allege was traditionally accorded to women' (p. 60). At the same time, the men participating in the survey 'argued that Caribbean man perceives women as existing for his sexual pleasure'; they also claimed that women are avaricious, and see men primarily in terms of financial gain (p. 58). This means that to love a woman 'is to be "foolish" and vulnerable', since "if a woman say she love you, it is something you have that she want" (p. 59). In these circumstances, love will inevitably be' "rip, torn, stretch and kick apart"' (p. 60).

On the other side, Olive Senior (1991), examining 'general views of male/female behaviour' in her chapter 'Women and Men', finds 'women citing certain negative behaviours on the part of men which our informants almost seem to take for granted as part of the male repertoire unreliability, infidelities, and a wide range of oppressions including physical violence, humiliation, mental cruelty, drunkenness, desertion, financial irresponsibility, etc' (p. 166). Senior also cites Merle Hodge's view that 'the whole range of mental cruelty [from men] is part and parcel of women's experience in the Caribbean' (p. 167), and ponders that, in the light of these complaints, 'the Caribbean woman seems to "put up with a lot" from her man' (p. 170). Senior's examination of women in the whole range of available relationships – as 'outside women' of married men, in sharing partnerships, often with parallel families, as well as, less commonly, as wives – reveals a contradictory tendency on the part of women to pursue an Ideal which is all too rarely realised. She concludes that women are in quest of 'warmth. love and tenderness', and their 'emotional vulnerability lies precisely in this desire for satisfactory "relationships" and a susceptibility to male charms, despite everything' (p. 179).

What is striking is the extent to which the heroes and heroines of Caribbean Caresses, the very 'young women of today' of whom the men in Barrow's study speak so disparagingly, and their love objects, fail to conform to these prevailing norms or stereotypes. In the 'world of Caribbean romance' created by the novels, such features of Caribbean society as male violence, unfaithfulness and the 'outside woman' phenomenon are absent, as are teenage pregnancies, conflict with parents, and, to a large extent, sex. Using these parameters, the novels could be deemed to be quite unrealistic. Reading them another way, however, it's possible that the very way the romantic formula translates into the Caribbean context, is informed and shaped by the kind of presuppositions about gender roles and behaviour pointed to by Barrow, Senior, Brodber and Hodge. Citing Hermione McKenzie, Senior suggests that the dissatisfaction shown by both sexes towards the prevailing status quo is driven by a need for an elusive Something Other: 'In a social structure which so often defeats fidelity and tenderness, the shift from partner to partner by both men and women may still be seen as a persistent quest for exactly these qualities in a relationship' (p. 179). Caribbean Caresses' lovers, then, are only removed from the Real in that they actually *attain* fidelity and tenderness. The obstacles in the way of their doing so may arise in part from the generalised distrust already noted, negative previous experiences, contradictions between appearances and reality, and the failure to credit behaviour which deviates from the stereotype as real.

The obstacles which, according to formulaic convention, create difficulties for the lovers, often consist in a misunderstanding, such as the hero being seen with another woman he seems to be involved with, or his suppressed desire for the heroine coming out in brutish behaviour. Caribbean Caresses follow this convention fairly closely, with a narrative pattern emerging as follows: the heroine's experience with another man has put her on her guard towards the hero, who is, nonetheless, quite recognisable to the reader. This other man is, therefore, not-the-hero. Because of this experience, when the hero is seen with another woman, she instantly constitutes the Obstacle. The heroine's refusal to be used or strung along by the hero is one of the ways Caribbean Caresses work against the social stereotype, which decrees that men are intrinsically unfaithful and women must take what they get. In this way, the novels not only conform to, but also manipulate the formula so as to speak to a specifically Caribbean context.

To take one example, Erica, the heroine of *Fantasy of Love,* is first seen in the company of Mark, her escort at a party where he is ignoring her. Erica longs to dance, but can only tug gently at his arm, 'knowing if his friends noticed they'd laugh and tease him, saying that she was trying to control him' (p. 1). Mark, a 'typical' Caribbean man in his need for control and his sensitivity to peer group opinion, is instantly signalled as not-the-hero. His subsequent behaviour bears this out – his annoyance when Erica shows him up by lying down at the party, his casual ordering of her to collect him a plate of food, his duplicity and two-timing of Erica, which finally makes her retort, 'Men [are] something else again. All of them' (p. 69). Meanwhile, although she misrecognises him, the tall, dark stranger who watches Erica at the party definitely *is* the hero. We know this by his sensitivity, the way he takes care of Erica when Mark is neglecting her, his teasing of her which she takes for arrogance ('all men were the same unreliable spoilt' [p. 5]), and above all his effect on the heroine. Apart from noticing his 'beautiful warm brown eyes a clear contrast to his ebony skin . . . the strength of his arms and shoulders . . .' (p. 12), 'she didn't feel intimidated by him. He didn't make her feel small and insecure she was spurred on, her mind racing ahead to match wits with him' (p. 14). In other words, he is *not* the typical West Indian man, and this is borne out at a further meeting, where Erica discovers he is in fact Dr Julian Baird, her project consultant, and that he is black British.

A not uncommon feature of the Caribbean Caresses hero is that he has been in some way removed from the Caribbean, so that he is simultaneously a part of the heroine's society, and also different, marked by his experience abroad. Gary, hero of *Sun Valley Romance,* has been educated in England, with the result, he claims, that he is 'more of a free thinker than a capitalist leader' (p. 69), a trained architect with 'finesse and sensitivity and who loved art and beautiful things' (p. 86). In the house he designed himself, he appears 'wiping his hands on a kitchen towel.

The little domestic gesture pulled at her heart' (p. 67). Like Erica, Giselle, heroine of *Sun Valley Romance*, is taken by 'the lack of mockery, the absence of the desire to master her that she had known in other men' (p. 74). Ironically, it is Gary's idealism and sheltered class position which conspire to blind him to the depredations being wrought on Giselle's village by one of the companies in his conglomerate. It is through his association with Giselle that he is awoken to the reality of class conflict, poverty and powerlessness, and their effects on people's lives. More down-to-earth, Damien of *Merchant of Dreams*, impresses Lorna, apart from being a 'hunk', by the fact that he sells for a living, forcing her to acknowledge 'this guy's got more than good looks – you've got to have drive and initiative for a job like that' (p. 63). Like Julian and Gary, his winning card is his lack of machismo and his ability to put the heroine at her ease: 'It made such a change to find a man who talked about his failures as well as his successes' (p. 64).

The profile of the Ideal Man that begins to emerge is one which deviates sharply from the stereotypical West Indian man. He is sensitive, caring, domesticated, trustworthy, straightforward and easy to talk to, and accepts the heroine as she is. The heroine's inability to believe he is all these things, and her readiness to see him as a user and manipulator, is perhaps testimony to the power of the very stereotype to which he does not conform. This has a great deal to do with the socialisation of Caribbean men, and a construction of masculinity which almost requires men to adopt a hard-bitten and exploitative attitude to women. Social science studies suggest that the relative absence of fathers as role models for boys growing up is a defining factor in male behaviour. Senior posits: 'The paradigm of absent father, omniscient mother, is central to the ordering and psyche of the Caribbean family', the mother's power resulting in an ambivalent relationship with women, both fearful and resentful (Senior 1991: 8). Julian of *Fantasy of Love* exemplifies this attitude when he comments drily: 'Ah, the indomitable West Indian woman again, I have no doubt' (p. 42). This sore point is explained at the end of the novel by an elderly relation describing his parents' relationship: 'Julian feels that she dominated his father too much, she controlled him. The marriage eventually broke up and Julian hasn't seen much of him over the years. He has always seen his mother as the typical strong, controlling West Indian woman' (p. 135). Again the stereotype interposes itself between hero and heroine, exerting a negative effect.

The 'paradigmatic ordering' pointed to by Senior is reproduced in the typical Caribbean Caresses family. Two of the heroines have lost both parents, one being brought up by her grandmother; two have lost their fathers but live with their mothers, one with a stepfather; Erica's mother features but her father is asthmatic and plays no role, and Lorna regularly goes to her mother's for Sunday lunch, but her father is absent. In *Sun Valley Romance,* Gary's father is dead and his stepfather is 'presently unwell' and does not appear. His mother, however, is formidable: 'Gloria Henshaw was one of the wealthiest women on the island of Trinidad as clever at keeping her glamorous image as she was in her business ventures', one of the first black beauty queens, a poor girl who married two rich husbands and now requires that her son, Gary, run her business empire (p. 11). Part of the drama of the novel lies in her attempt to dictate to Gary, and his eventual standing up to her. The heroine Giselle's stepfather is an example of a 'bad' West Indian man, shiftless and bullying, always at loggerheads with her brother, Garnet, but who reforms through participation in the community's resistance to the mining conglomerate which threatens the village. Probably the most deliberately negative masculine characterisation is that of Randy (not-the-hero) of *Heartaches and Roses,* who controls and exploits all three of the women in his life – Betty, his fiancée, his ageing mother and his secretary, Susan, who is also his 'outside woman'. Having convinced Betty that, having had a hysterectomy, no one else will want to marry her, he then persuades his mother to move into Betty's house, ostensibly for her greater comfort and safety, but actually so that so he can use the rent from her own house to pay for his mistress. All this becomes apparent when Betty visits his office and overhears Randy and Susan in conversation about his mother. Susan wants her sent to a home, to which Randy replies: 'My mother worked very hard for many years to support me, and I would like to be able to take care of her when she's old' (p. 98). He explains to Susan that since she (Susan) refuses to take care of mother, he is prepared to marry Betty, who 'really loved and cared for her own mother, and that's one thing I've always admired about her' (p. 99). When Susan points out that what the old lady really wants is grandchildren, Randy responds: 'I'm certainly planning to have a few. I can assure you, before mother gets much older, she'll see her first grandchild' (p. 99). Randy's breathtaking selfishness and casual sexual exploitativeness epitomise stereotypical West Indian male behaviour, behaviour which must also be partly attributable to his mother's over-indulgence of her precious son. All three women are represented as being in competition for his economic and/or sexual favours, and the mother, at least, endorses this power relationship when she comments: 'I hope my son will be able to control his wife' (p. 100). How closely this approximates the Real may once more be assessed by comparison with the evidence from social science, as for example this statement from one of Graham Dann's respondents in *The Barbadian Male: Sexual Attitudes and Practices*: 'I think a woman should always be under the man. A man should always be over she' (Dann 1987: 52), or the following comment from pastoral counsellor Neilson Waithe's study, *Caribbean Sexuality*: 'The belief that men must satisfy their sexual urges, and women want men to be in control of them, are motivating factors in the approach to sexuality of the Caribbean male' (Waithe 1993: 53).

It is highly significant of course that the masculine representation which approximates most closely to the Real is, not the hero but quite the reverse, the monitory image of an exploiter from whom the heroine is rescued by her alliance with the true hero. Yet even among the hero-figures, elements of the stereotype may be found, which quite naturally contribute to the heroine's confusion over whether he is, in fact, a hero. In *Love in Hiding*, the heroine, Rena, is an orphan brought up by her grandmother. Thierry is the boy next door, whom she idolised as a big brother until he was sent away to Canada to become an engineer, returning years later intent on marrying her. Unfortunately, as she is already involved with the gentlemanly Raj, he feels unable to reveal this to her, and concentrates instead on interfering in her life, telling her what to do and demonstrating his sexual power over her, in a way which borders on the sadistic. The fact that he is able to do so speaks to the vacillation between Real and Ideal noted by Brodber *et. al.*, for it evidently reforms Rena's behaviour and self-concept. Most notably, she is obsessively afraid of being thought a 'tramp', and construes her sexual response to Thierry as coming dangerously close to this undesirable feminine stereotype. At his 21st birthday party, when she is 15, Thierry rescues Rena from a drunken older boy, but promptly turns the blame on her: 'What the hell are you trying to do? Incite rape? My god! You're going to stop behaving like a tramp', whereupon he proceeds to 'administer four hard slaps to her rear' (p. 8). This scene is described in language implicitly suggestive of rape, with Thierry 'making her look at him by holding her chin while the fingers of his other hand tangled in her hair to keep her head just where he wanted it', while she listens to him with 'streaming eyes, bitten lips, torn dress and misery she couldn't conceal' (p. 9). This relationship of dominance and submission continues at work, where she finds he is now her boss, insists on driving her to work, carries her into the house, undresses her, and generally acts the role of protective elder brother/jealous lover. Thierry is characterised by his 'raw animal magnetism' (p. 32) and his 'tiger's eyes' (repeatedly). Rena is alternately helpless victim and rebellious convent schoolgirl (her last resort is in fact to run away back to her convent in Barbados with the intention of joining the order, from which she is saved at the last minute by Thierry's arrival). In this novel, sex is both a woman's most precious gift to a man, and the source of her vulnerability, used as a weapon against Rena by Thierry, whose 'response' opens her up to male power and the possibility of abuse:

Then he kissed her angrily. She fought him silently. Her teeth ground together to prevent his entry. His teeth savaged her lips and she was forced to open her mouth. She would have bruises tomorrow . Then he was plundering the sweetness of her mouth. His kiss had changed. He no longer sought to punish and she felt the heat shooting through her. At her total response he went wild . Then he suddenly seized her wrists in a grasp that hurt and pushed her away (p. 84).

Again, the language here is suggestive of rape, but when she starts to submit, he withdraws, leaving her dishevelled and panting. The extent of his power over her may be seen when Rena announces her engagement to Raj. Thierry reacts furiously, ordering her to come and stand in front of him with a mixture of suppressed sexual arousal and latent violence, to which she responds with absolute submission: 'She walked slowly towards him in the manner of a sacrificial maiden aware that he willed her to come to him. Those few steps were the hardest she had ever had to take, but she made it, and stood before him with bowed head' (p. 65). Given the reality of male violence, and in the context of the earlier scene where he actually beat her, this passage carries a very uneasy sub-textual message.

The construction of the hero in this novel is a long way from the gentle, sensitive, caring men of most of the others, or indeed from Raj, Rena's fiancé, who plays Edgar to Thierry's Heathcliff. Like Heathcliff, Thierry is, significantly, also a brother figure, as is Andel, hero of *Hand in Hand,* who has, like Thierry, known the heroine as a child, gone abroad and returned years later. Experience overseas marks the hero as older and more worldly than the heroine, and Andel too is in possession of a secret to which he alone holds the key. Unlike Thierry, however, he is a revisionary hero – gentle, protective, responsible, patient and faithful. What most obviously links the hero figures though, beyond coincidences of plot, is of course their single-minded attraction to the heroine, their ability to discriminate even when surrounded by beautiful women, and their steadfastness, which wins them the prize in the end. In a context, as already described by Hermione McKenzie, 'which so often defeats fidelity and tenderness', and makes multiple relationships almost inevitable, this must be read as a quite deliberate reconstruction of the stereotypical philandering male. Who then are the women fortunate enough to attract these unrepresentative men?

As already mentioned, while all the heroines are West Indian women, four are African, one East Indian and one deliberately unspecified. It is expected of a romantic heroine that she will be beautiful, but the question of what actually constitutes beauty is not so easily answered. In a context where the Western stereotype – slim, delicate, blonde, white skinned – exerts its sway via the media, beauty contests, Barbie, even the dark-skinned Pocahontas, romance authors are faced once again with the necessity of deliberate reconstruction, although they have chosen different strategies to accomplish this. Betty of *Heartaches and Roses,* for example, answers most closely to a conventionally held notion of attractiveness, even while her blackness is emphasised: 'long, dark lashes enhancing a pair of sleepy, slanting brown eyes a small, round nose and lips as rosy as a ripe mango in a round, smooth face black hair braided into a bundle of small plaits her body was slim and lithe' (p. 24). The physical characteristics of Khadija of *Hand in Hand,* are given to us in the context of her morning run along the beach, 'her waist length black hair streaming behind her as she pounded down the edge of the surf, practising her Spanish grammar as she ran' (p. 1). Dressing for a date with the hero, she laughs at herself for going to so much trouble – the implication being that she usually has more important things on her mind: 'Her outfit was a shalawar in royal blue silk which brought out her well-defined brows and deep sparkling brown eyes (she) swept her silky black hair up and coiled it around in a neat roll. She secured it with a brass comb and two black laquered chopsticks' (p. 21). Again, the details emphasise a specific cultural background, here East Indian, and while she is undoubtedly alluring, the author takes pains not to objectify or exoticise her, by giving her sister a comic reaction: 'Ay, ay, girl! You going to kill the man!' (p. 21). This is a difficult line to tread, when romance fiction has traditionally characterised dark-skinned, dark-haired beauty as the exotic Other of fair, pale-skinned, golden-haired, etc. Giselle, of *Sun Valley Romance,* has to contend with a white-skinned rival referred to as Gary's 'Carnival blonde': 'an exceptional beauty the exotic look of a perfectly tanned skin contrasted with the long blonde hair that framed her face and fell down her back like a golden waterfall' (p. 80). Giselle herself is constructed as a quintessentially Caribbean beauty, most notably at Carnival, jumping with a band called, emblematically, the Barbaric Warriors; 'The choice of costume with its heavily "ethnic" look suited her exotic beauty made her appear regal and distant and added to the effect of sensuous, savage beauty' (p. 41). The problem of revisioning physical attractiveness in a specific cultural context is demonstrated here by the way the description, while consciously invoking a Carib past, teeters dangerously on the brink of exotic stereotype.

Apart from the somewhat ambivalent question of physical appearance, the heroine is characterised in all these novels as deviating conspicuously from the Sexual and Economic Exploiter stereotype. She is, typically, a self-supporting, professional woman who need not rely on a man financially, even though a number of the heroes are richer and can offer her social and material elevation. Her need for a man is therefore primarily emotional and, to a lesser extent, sexual, but the true heroine, though beautiful, never flaunts herself, and, though passionate, never loses control. In this she conforms fairly closely to the Ideal, or, to put it another way, to the Western-inspired Lady stereotype. Other women may use their bodies to try and attract the hero, but the true hero remains impervious, preferring the innocence, the unspoilt charm of the heroine.

We have already looked at the way Lorna of *Merchant of Dreams* makes few concessions to stereotypical femininity, while still being insecure about her power to attract. Along the continuum the heroines represent, Lorna is the most deliberately non-conformist, as we see in relation to her celebration of her blackness. Out on a shoot in the hot sun, Damien offers her lotion, which she refuses bluntly, all too conscious of Gillian, the model, with her 'flawless golden brown skin': 'Look, I'm not one of those people who are afraid of the sun making them too black, you know' (p. 23). There is an obvious ironic inversion here, since what they are shooting is an ad for Atlas Stout, and the ubiquitous beer posters which adorn the walls of rum shops in the Caribbean invariably favour fair-skinned models, or dark-skinned women lit in such a way as to *appear* fair. Lorna moreover is shown tucking into her mother's lunch of 'pork chops, fried plantain and sweet potato pie', classic West Indian cooking, even while she worries about its effect on her figure (p. 34). The novel incorporates and plays with the tension between Real and Ideal, both in its construction of the heroine's subjectivity, and in relation to her professional function as a 'merchant of dreams' as analogous with the romance form itself. The author deliberately exposes the mechanisms underlying fantasy, whether that of advertising or of romantic fiction, by realistic descriptions of the techniques used to create the illusion. At work, for example, Lorna and others are shown to be at the mercy of unscrupulous employers, with no recourse to outside arbitration:

Being an executive meant working all hours on evenings, plus weekends and bank holidays . She'd never actually worked on Christmas Day, but two years running she'd had to come into the office on Boxing Day .The junior artists got paid overtime, though it always seemed to be next to nothing, but executives didn't (p. 49).

Lorna recalls the annual Christmas party, where everyone receives a bottle of rum which she suspects comes free from a client of the agency, and the time an account executive asked the boss for 'some of the twelve-year-old Scotch whisky he was drinking', and promptly got the sack (p. 50).

What the heroines *do* is integral to their characterisation, though, in accordance with the Real, their jobs are far from being glamourised. As Olive Senior testifies: 'Many women in high executive and administrative positions have got the opportunity to be there because they are willing to accept far less in salaries and perquisites and operate under conditions that men of much lesser qualifications and capabilities would consider insulting' (Senior 1991: 191). Erica of *Fantasy of Love* works on an adult education project aimed at three groups of women: rural women, women in prison and higglers. Though these women barely appear, apart from as supporting extras in a scene where Erica takes Julian to a market, the fact that they are visible at all points to the relatively privileged position of the project workers, and to the social and economic hierarchy to which they too are subject. At a meeting with the board Erica observes: 'They were all men, all grey-haired, all wearing glasses men in charge on one side of the table, women implementing on the other' (p. 19). Compounding this imbalance is the fact that the consultant is a foreigner, so that, when challenged by him, Erica defends herself and her project with nationalistic fervour: 'The nature of Jamaicans is such, Dr Baird, that they are always willing to surpass their wildest dreams' (p. 80). Betty of *Heartaches and Roses* is attracted to the hero, who runs a hotel in Tobago, partly because, like her, he is a businessperson. His proposal of marriage is entwined with a discussion of how much money Betty would lose if she didn't go back to her flower shop, and part of what brings them together finally is her skill as an accountant, which enables her to keep the hotel going when he is in hospital after an accident. Giselle of *Sun Valley Romance* also ends up with her own business, and learns very quickly how to defend herself against exploitation by the formidable Gloria Henshaw, whose guise of fairy godmother conceals pragmatic self-interest: 'It was all so miraculous, like a fairy tale. How lucky she was! But, just as she was starting to express her appreciation and gratitude, Mrs Henshaw, "the patron", turned into Mrs Henshaw "the shrewd businesswoman" '(p. 76).

These examples demonstrate one of the most significant features of the construction of femininity in the Caribbean Caresses series, and one which is closer to Real than Ideal. As always, though, Real and Ideal are in tension, and nowhere more so than in the heroines' relationship to sexuality.

The Heinemann authors' guidelines for the series are quite specific on this score, and bring into focus questions of marketing, target audience and preconceptions as to what is or is not appropriate for young, mainly feminine readers in the Caribbean: 'As we would hope to sell to the upper level of the school market, please treat any sex scenes carefully – you can lead your couple into the bedroom, and even into bed but suggestion, rather than explicit detail, says the rest.' At least three of the authors agreed with this circumspection. Asked to comment, Annette Charles (*Love in Hiding*) responded that most family groups in Trinidad 'still prefer girls to be innocent until they get married'. Dorothy Jolly (*Heartaches and Roses*) agreed: 'The way I was brought up, you get married and *then* you have sex, especially in a small country like Dominica.' Annette Charles *Love in Hiding*, whose heroine Rena is engaged to Raj, an East Indian, pointed out that in the Trinidadian Indian community it is still common for 'a fellow to go to a dance and see a girl, and the next thing, he goes to the father and they arrange a marriage'. Valerie Belgrave (*Sun Valley Romance*) declared: 'I myself am a good convent girl. I think one of the things about this book is that it's a wholesome book, and the characters are both wholesome so sex didn't come into the story.' Of the six heroines, three – Erica, Lorna and Khadija do have sex by the end of the novel. Rena and Thierry end up in bed, but apparently confine themselves to passionate caresses. Betty could be assumed to be sexually experienced since she has been in out of an engagement, but to what extent is never specified. Nonetheless, this sexual reticence is possibly the least realistic aspect of the novels, and certainly the one most complained about by readers I have canvassed. Myra Murby, commissioning editor for the series, asked whether it could not have been a little more daring, responded: 'We had to be very careful because the Caribbean is quite a moral place and certain things are definitely frowned upon things that happen in Europe are not considered the thing in the Caribbean.' Though this may be true at the level of the Ideal, the evidence of social science research, popular culture, from calypso to dancehall, and the popularity of imported television serials and upper school-age fiction like the American series Sweet Valley High, is that, once again, Real and Ideal diverge quite sharply on the issue.

It appears that the Caribbean Caress series can best be characterised as an experiment in negotiating the tension between Real and Ideal which plays so conspicuous a part in Caribbean life and fiction. In attempting to indigenise a Western formulaic genre, these little novels confront fundamental issues of identity, gender and sexuality, as well as the way these intersect with economic and social factors – access to education, types of work, status and independence. Implicit in their revisioning of gender relationships is a critique of both Real and Ideal, and the negative effects of these on the lives of women and men in the Caribbean. The fact that they answer to a felt need of many people is testified to here in a quotation from one of Olive Senior's respondents, described as 'an Antiguan in her forties': 'I don't think a woman can live without love women need to be loved . I mean, when you're loved you feel wanted, you feel appreciated you have somebody that you can talk to, you can exchange ideas with, you need a companion you know' (Senior 1991: 166).

Notes

1. These remarks and those of Valerie Belgrave which follow, are taken from an interview with John Gilmore for the BBC Radio 3 programme, 'Books Abroad', broadcast June 15, 1996.

2. In the Content and Methodology section of this paper, Barrow explains that it deals with 'the images that two groups of Barbadian men have of women' and, 'while it is likely that these images have crystallised into more widely held stereotypes . . . we were unable to investigate this in much detail. Neither were we able to examine the effect they have on women's self-image and performance, though we cannot deny that this occurs. These limitations result largely from the Focus Group Research Methodology which was considered the most appropriate within the severe time and resource constraints of the Women in the Caribbean Project' (Barrow 1986: 54). In other words, it is a very partial survey, but may be taken as part of a collective testimony, which would also include the group discussions drawn on by Earl Warner for his dramatisation 'Mantalk', shown in Barbados and Trinidad in 1995 and 1996 respectively, and reviewed by Jane Bryce in Caribbean Week, December 1995.

3. For this insight and others, I am grateful to my student, Armel Drayton, whose paper, 'Representations of Women in Selected Caribbean Romance', was submitted as part of her degree in English at the University of the West Indies, Cave Hill, in 1995.

4. The remarks quoted here by Dorothy Jolly and Annette Charles are taken from a joint interview with Jane Bryce, in the home of Dorothy Jolly in Valsayn, Port of Spain, Trinidad, August 6, 1996.

5. BBC Radio 3 interview.

6. Without claiming to have done a systematic reader survey, I have had reactions from students on the MA course at Cave Hill, Women Writing and Feminist Theory (co-taught by Evelyn O'Callaghan and Jane Bryce) who read the whole series for the module on

romance, also from students on the Creative Writing course (taught by Jane Bryce), some of whom participated in the BBC Radio 3 programme, 'Books Abroad'.

7. Interviewed on the BBC Radio 3 programme, 'Books Abroad'.

19

Caribbean Masculinity and Family:
Revisiting 'Marginality' and 'Reputation'

Christine Barrow

Caribbean gender theorising has expanded to encompass masculinity. A burgeoning intellectual discourse along with public concern and outcry have directed attention to the black man as 'marginalised', 'at risk' and 'in crisis'. More often than not, the problem is attributed to 'family breakdown'. The father/'husband' is 'irresponsible', the mother overburdened and the boychild inadequately socialised. The pattern repeats itself in the next generation as the family fails to function as the cornerstone of mature adulthood and stable society. 'Male marginality' emerged in the structural functional studies of the 'matrifocal family' among the 'lower-class, Negroes'. Accordingly, the familial roles of men, defined as father and conjugal partner, are perceived as limited to providing economic support and occasional discipline and as woefully inadequately performed. Men are peripheral to the family – their place is elsewhere. Derived from an alien construct of family and gender, the model problematises more than it seeks to understand Caribbean family and has generated five decades of bias and disparagement. By challenging the thesis of 'male marginality' in family life, the intention of this paper is to contribute, albeit only in part, to the current debate on Caribbean masculinity.

As a preliminary step in this endeavour, functionalist presumptions of Caribbean family are briefly reviewed. The major task which follows is to revisit the family and man's place by focusing on extended family roles, by reassessing performances as fathers and conjugal partners and by relocating the social identities of Caribbean men, at least in part, within a reconstructed family domain. Ethnographic support is provided by in-depth interviews with Barbadian men.

Functionalism, Family and Gender

As social scientists, the anthropologists who arrived in the Caribbean from the 1950s were 'objective', resolutely separating themselves from their predecessors' portrayals of family life as 'pathological', 'immoral' and 'deviant' and from historical 'speculation' in terms of African origin and slave plantation heritage (Barrow 1996: 2-8). They were, nonetheless, unable to see beyond their own model and remained trapped within Parsonian structural functionalism and a measure of persistent ethnocentrism.

For them, the natural and efficient performance of the family's major function, *viz.* the socialisation of children for responsible adulthood (Greenfield 1961: 74, 1966: 110; Smith 1956: 108), required nuclear, co-resident, patriarchal, stable structures, consisting of an adult heterosexual couple, preferably married, and their young children (Clarke 1957: 141). They insisted that this was the ideal, not just among themselves, but also for Caribbean people, and were often at pains to find enough cases to identify this form as the norm (Greenfield 1966: 139), even if only at the early stage of the family life cycle (Smith 1956: 228, 257). But, no matter how thorough the search, even they could not ignore the anomalies that stared them in the face. More often than not, in their Caribbean research villages nuclear family structure and co-residence just did not coincide. True to their model, they resolved the dilemma by privileging the corporate bonded unit, the household or 'domestic group' (Smith 1956: 51-52, 108-110), and, given their agreement that 'the main functioning family unit in the Caribbean is the household group' (Greenfield 1961: 72), assumed the two to be identical. Their complex typologies, based on statistical household surveys, distinguished household groups that were nuclear from those that were not properly constituted and variously labelled 'denuded', 'sub-nuclear' or 'incomplete' (Clarke 1957: 117; Greenfield 1966: 142-143). Only co-residential common law and marital unions were recognised; visiting unions were not 'real', merely 'semi-conjugal' (Smith 1956: 109-110, 185), however long they had been in existence and whether or not children had been born to the couple. Extra-residential kin ties extending vertically or laterally beyond the nuclear family remained invisible.

In a seminal article, Nancie Solien insisted that Afro-American family and household were not necessarily co-terminous. Shifting attention from domestic structure to 'personal interrelationships' between family members, she introduced the notion of a 'non-localised family', 'scattered in several different households' (Solien 1960: 104-105; see also Smith 1957: xvi). However, she remained firmly committed to the functionalist definition of family as nuclear, that is as 'a group of people bound together by that complex set of relationships known as kinship ties, between at least two of whom there exists a conjugal relationship. The conjugal pair, plus their offspring, forms the nuclear family' (Solien 1960: 106).

The unit of a single parent, usually the mother, and her children was 'on a lower level of organisation than a family' and larger kinship units were defined as families only by virtue of their nuclear core (Solien 1960: 105, 106). In sum, Solien made an important early breakthrough, but did not go far enough. In her reconstruction of Afro-Caribbean family, she eliminated one functionalist bias, that of co-residence, but retained another, that of family structure as nuclear.

The functionalists also identified two distinct families to which all individuals were presumed to belong during their life cycles, the family of orientation followed by the family of procreation. Given the assumed common identity of family and domestic group, a man's initiation to adulthood completely restructured both his family unit and his familial roles – from son and brother to 'husband' and father. 'The establishment of the new family unit *marks the end of the young man's duties as son* in his family of orientation. He has now become the head of a family of procreation' (Greenfield 1966: 115) (emphasis added).

Within this paradigm, enduring ties to his family of birth, especially as a son to his mother, were devalued or, on occasions, rendered invisible.

As regards descent, kinship systems were identified as bilateral (Greenfield 1966: 154; Henriques 1953: 139; Rodman 1971: 135; Smith 1956: 152), but with a difference. The family core was portrayed as female, consisting of grandmother, mother(s) and child(ren), and maternal kin solidarity (Greenfield 1966: 154; Clarke 1957: 173) and 'family land descended in the female line' (Clarke 1957: 180) were acknowledged. But, perhaps in their anxiety to disassociate themselves from the theme of matrilineal African origin, functionalists searched for men as fathers and husbands and ignored their insertion into the kinship system as brothers and uncles.

The model also prescribed gender roles as separate, mutually exclusive (though complementary) and hierarchically ordered. Thus, the 'division of labour between mother and father is ideally sharp and clean' (Rodman 1971: 81). She remains at home preoccupied with housework and child care, protected, supported and submitting to her husband's authority (Greenfield 1966: 115). He, meanwhile, takes responsibility for economic support as a productive worker in the public domain. According to Smith (1956: 79), 'the role of husband-father as head of the household, responsible for the group and being the chief provider of cash and economic resources is well established in the system.'

In reality, however, the majority of Caribbean men constituted a glaring 'abnormality', demanding explanation in anthropological family studies. This was proffered in terms of 'male marginality'. As a member of a lower-class community, a man's familial role lacked managerial or status defining functions and depended on his performance as breadwinner (Smith 1957: 68, 73). 'There are no tasks allotted to a man in his role as husband-father beyond seeing that the house is kept in good repair and providing food and clothing for his spouse and the children' (Smith 1956: 113). But, within the conditions of job insecurity, high unemployment and migration along with low social and racial status, he could not fulfil this obligation. He was therefore deemed 'marginal' to the family on two counts – first by the circumscribed male role definition and second by his inability to fulfil even this narrow prescription. Furthermore, with patriarchy assumed to be the very foundation of family life, its Caribbean antithesis constituted a disturbing find. Male marginality 'is so all-pervasive that it has ramifications for the entire system of family and kinship organisation' (Rodman 1971: 177-178). It is 'the major source of family break up' (Greenfield 1966: 141) and reduces families to mother-centred or 'matrifocal' units (Smith 1973). Consolidating the model to reflect social gender duality, Peter Wilson (1968, 1971) added a 'modest and obedient' female versus an 'aggressive', 'virile' male psyche to come up with two value complexes. Masculinity is represented by 'Reputation', defined as 'a complex of values which reflects the congruence of the way a man views himself and the way he is viewed by others' (Wilson 1969: 80). The feminine corollary of 'Respectability' has been reviewed and, for the most part, emphatically rejected in subsequent literature (Barrow 1976, 1988: 162; Besson 1993; Bush 1985; Sutton 1974) while 'Reputation' remains intact, if anything reaffirmed (Dann 1987; Miller 1991: 93-97).

These gender discourses also inform State ideology and policy. Remoulding black men and women according to these received images was integral to the colonial government's vision of a civilised social order in the post-emancipation Caribbean. The master plan for social gender reconstruction harnessed the combined forces of government, education and religion to domesticate women and to recast men as responsible, productive workers and household heads. Pockets of success were evident along the way as individuals internalised the dominant gender model en route to respectability and upward mobility, but the overall effect was a reaffirmation of the social hierarchy of multiple identities of gender, as well as race and class. Alternative gender discourses are common among oppressed groups. Caribbean masculinities, for example, shaped by a history of emasculation and powerlessness, often work in 'deviant', sub-legal zones in opposition to dominant ideals.

The Caribbean experience therefore, exposes the inadequacies of structural functional discourse. These essentialist, patriarchal stereotypes of masculinity (and femininity) depend and thrive on notions of difference: female is what male is not. Male is to female as provider/protector is to homemaker/nurturer and as superior/dominant is to inferior/subordinate. Such categorical grouping has little to do with social reality and cannot capture the processes of gender construction, identification and differentiation. Gendered identities are not individual and innate, but social, relational and acquired. And, as the theoretical shift to post-modernist and post-structuralist perspectives reveals, they are also multiple and mutable (Moore 1994).

Male Marginality Revisited

Rooted in the functionalist literature on the Caribbean family are three dominant premises: first, that kinship relations which fall beyond the boundaries of nuclear unit and household boundary are of no consequence; second, that the significant male family roles are those of co-resident conjugal partner and father and that, as such, Caribbean men are 'irresponsible'; and third, that men have no real place within the home and family – they are 'marginal'. Paradoxically, as we proceed to test these against the narratives of Barbadian men, it becomes clear that functionalism blocked a full exploration of its own ethnography. These early interpretations were often at odds with the meticulous fieldwork on which they were based and which, indeed, is echoed on several occasions in the contemporary voices of Barbadian men.

A sample of 92 black Barbadian men, selected to cover variations in age (from 22 to 96 years) and occupational status, freely expressed their views and recalled their experiences of family life. Responses to simple, open questions such as 'What is it like to be a father?' and 'Tell me about your mother' were tape recorded and transcribed verbatim. Pioneered for the Caribbean by Jack Alexander (1977) and by Raymond Smith (1988) in a thorough revision of his earlier work, this methodological approach clears away theoretical hegemony and premature closure. It restores Caribbean kinship ideology, history and culture by privileging the images and meanings given to family life by social actors as they construct their worldview and understand themselves as gendered individuals. In the process, the narratives of the Barbadian men challenge the functionalist synchronic premise of a distinct socio-economically determined black family structure of 'male marginality' and monolithic masculinity.

Sons, Brothers and Uncles

The functionalists' denial of a man's continuing responsibilities to his family of orientation are refuted by their own pervasive evidence of strong, persistent mother-son bonds. 'Consciously or unconsciously he learns that it is to his mother he must look for any security or permanence in human relationships' (Clarke 1957: 107). They claim that it is common for a son to continue to live with and assume responsibility for his mother well into adulthood (Smith 1956: 137; Henriques 1953: 137), building and repairing her home (Smith 1956: 111), supporting her financially (Davenport 1961: 444; Greenfield 1966: 107-108; Smith 1956: 71-72) and postponing marriage or common law co-residence until she dies (Greenfield 1966: 136, Smith 1956: 72). He may even become a 'husband substitute'! (Clarke 1957: 158). However, the bond is deemed irregular, as the source of social and psychological problems and as interfering with a man's 'normal' progress to his own home and family of procreation. Clarke identifies 'the persistence of the son's dependence upon her into adolescence and beyond', describing the relationship as 'exclusive and often obsessive' and holding it to blame for his 'failure to develop satisfactory relationships with other people or achieve personal independence' (Clarke 1957: 164). Henriques (1953: 130) also speaks of the 'profound psychological dependence of the adult Jamaican on his mother'. Mothers, in turn, compound the problem by reminding sons of their responsibilities and jealously holding on, even using obeah, in an effort to disrupt any conjugal relationships they might form (Clarke 1957: 162-163; Greenfield 1966: 114; Smith 1956: 120).

Virtually all (85 per cent) of the sample of Barbadian men were raised by their mothers, in six cases jointly with maternal grandmothers. The remaining men, whose mothers had died or migrated or moved to live with a new partner, identified a substitute, generally the maternal grand-mother or aunt. Only five men were critical of their mothers (of these, two had migrated, 'deserting' their sons and one was an alcoholic) while four were noncommittal, leaving the great majority (89 percent) who spoke positively. Indeed, despite living apart in the majority of cases, they described their mothers and close, enduring relationships with intense emotion.

Repeated mention was made of 'caring', 'loving' and 'hardworking' mothers who made endless sacrifices for their children and who were strict disciplinarians, prime motivators in their children's development and respected members of the community.

My mother was a plantation worker and worked very hard. She made sure we had beds to sleep in at night and that we did our school work and on returning home that we did our chores. She would chastise us and then be loving afterwards. She did not favour one child over the others, treated us all the same. If there was not enough food to feed us she would divide hers and not get for herself. She was a friend, advisor, and really involved in my life. She would talk to me and give me the opportunity to share my ideas with her. She had a good character, really a nice lady, really a nice lady (Carpenter, age 42).

She was very pretty, at least to me. Nice woman, always did her best. Christian-like, we had Sabbath days. We had to go to church every Saturday when I was young. That was a pain, man! But because of a lot of things she taught me, is why I am the way I am now. She tried her best to get things to go good for us. She used to make our clothing and did a lot of baking. When other people had to be buying bread to take to school she would bake our bread. When I think of her I think of a calm, nice, cool person, loving. She believed in being honest. You know another thing too, there was a thing she would say: "speak the truth and speak it ever, call it what it will; he who hides the wrong he did, does the wrong thing still". I live by that, I live by that. That is one of main things I remember her for (Quality Control Supervisor, age 31).

My mother was very simple in her ways and was very kind and caring. She was quite poor, but she would try to help the people in the village. She would cook for people and give to the children as well. Everyone loved and respected her (Unemployed, age 38).

She was the one to lay the spiritual foundation. And she saw the value of education, even though she finished her education at thirteen years old. And she was always there for us. In sickness it was mother, getting married – mother, keeping us together – mother, remembering birthdays – mother, encouraging and praying – mother, disci-pline – mother. Even though we may be out of the district, we would find ourselves coming back to her (Teacher, age 38).

The men spoke of their responsibilities to their mothers through old age as a natural reciprocity, not as functionalists would have us believe, as an imposition interfering with responsibilities to a family of procreation.

As my mother's favourite child, up to today I feel I must be there for her always, especially though hard times and provide for her things to make her life more comfortable. Even though I'm married, I still live close to home. As a matter of fact she would not want me to move any further away. Simple little things she does for me. She cooks for me and brings food over when my wife is not in the island. She comes over by me every day to make sure I am fine and when I am sick she comes over ready and willing to rub me down. I wish I could do more for her, like provide certain things for her. If I had the finances, I would have a nice home somewhere in the hills for her where she could go and relax (Company Manager, age 34).

Sons also reported their mothers' concern at 'losing' them to other women.

Though my mother and I have a great relationship, it started to change when I got married. She couldn't handle it. Looking back, I think it was because she felt she was losing me. She knew that before I was married, any time she called me, I would be there without question. These days, life has changed and I cannot always just get up and go. So that put a strain on our relationship, for about two years and then things started to settle down again. And she and my wife are closer than you would think (Company Manager, age 34).

When I tell she I did getting married, she feel that she would get replace' by another lady. And she did quote from the Bible: "The Bible say ya mother come first" (Office Assistant, age 38).

A mother's death was described as traumatic:

When she died, I was lost. I didn't know who or where to turn. Gran had already gone I was alone (Retired Chauffeur, age 89).

Any loving son who loves his mother, when she gets older and sick, you feel that you are going to lose something that is important to you. You must remember there is only one mother and especially since I was a single parent child. I loved my mother a lot more, I think, than who had a mother and a father. It was two years ago she died and up to today I still miss my mother. I know it is a debt we all have to pay, but I still miss her. Recently one night I was sleeping and I woke up believing she was still alive before I realised (Lumber Yard Porter, age 50).

Functionalists also underestimated Caribbean sibling relations, confining their remarks, as their model directs, to young children in a nuclear family. Noting the importance of co-residence for sibling solidarity, they bemoaned the frequent separation of brothers and sisters into different households (Clarke 1957: 108,174; Rodman 1971: 98; Smith 1956: 156). More often than not, it was sibling rivalry and jealousy in response to parental favouritism that was reported (Henriques 1953: 129; Rodman 1971: 93). Of particular significance, is Smith's contrast between lower-class Guyanese family structure and the matrilineal system. He claimed that, in the former, men 'do not exercise responsibility in relation to their sisters and their sister's children' and proceeded to note 'the complete

absence of any well defined pattern of mutual rights, duties and obligations between uncles and aunts, on the one hand, and nephews and nieces
on the other' (Smith 1956: 143-144).

Again, there is some contradictory, though more scattered, ethnographic evidence in their writings. Case-studies, for example, make reference to the predicament of a sister with no brother to defend her
(Henriques 1953: 198) and to a woman who raised her dead sister's three
children as her own (Smith 1956: 127). Davenport (1961: 423-424), in
fact, describes 'positive and strong', affective relationships between siblings which are carried over into adulthood, as are close bonds maintained with elder sisters who functioned as 'mother substitutes' (Clarke
1957: 142-143). And Rodman (1971: 94) identifies specific mutual responsibilities, though he belittles them – 'the obligations between siblings
are vague in nature and involve little more than a general expectation to
help each other in time of need'.

Of the 80 men in the sample with sisters and the 76 with brothers, only
11 (14 per cent) and 12 (16 per cent) respectively described the relationships as 'not close'. Several recalled incidents of sibling solidarity in which
they cooperated during daily chores and protected each other from
outsiders, even from parental wrath. Their narratives expressed a special
closeness and responsibility to protect and provide for their sisters, to keep
them on the right path, especially if there was no father or conjugal
partner there to do so. Elder sisters who helped to raise them got special
mention:

I remember once my mother called me and said that Joan (sister) had a black eye. It
was she boyfriend that did it. Peter (brother) and me, we went and tek he. We brek
he up, man. Hit my sister? You a madman? True, Joan wasn't really cleaning the house,
coming home late and he wasn't getting he food one time. But you don't hit my sister
(Unemployed, age 22).

My eldest sister, she was the one I didn't feel was going too right with guys. I felt sorry
for her. Of the five of us, she is the only one who doesn't have a secondary education.
The unfortunate thing about it is that I always figured that she was an unfortunate
child in several ways. She was sickly and would have to remain at home from school
and I felt that it affected her education early. I felt sorry about that. And there were
quite a few times when I did not approve of how she was operating. I reckon that she
ought to have been more settled. I did not like it and I tried to talk to her about it
(Reporter, age 38).

My eldest sister, Grace, we are very close. She was very influential in my upbringing.
I could describe her to some extent like a second mother to all of us. She used to be a
primary school teacher and she used to give me lessons for the Common Entrance
Examination. I give her the credit for passing that exam and going to secondary school.

And she was the one to take me to church to be christened. And she bought my school clothes and provided money for entertainment (Insurance Agent, age 26).

When men form conjugal unions and move away from home, the feelings of a sister may echo those of a mother:

As a Barbadian male, when you get married, the females in your family change towards you. For example, my sister that I grew up with, when I told her I was thinking of getting married, she told me, "I won't see or hear you any more". I said, "But why should you think so?" She said, "You're going to be married." And don't you know that over time our relationship has changed to some extent. It has. At first, she stopped calling as much as she used to, and did not come over as much. She tells me that I am still her favourite, but I often point out to her that she does not show it as much. And she says, "But you have a wife now". And I tell her, "Yes she is my wife now, but you were my sister from the time I was born" (Company Manager, age 34).

Informants described relationships with brothers less affectively, though elder brothers are expected to 'look out for' the younger ones, to protect them at school and in male peer group activities, and also to encourage their education, financially and otherwise. One man reported a promise to his dying mother that he would care for his mentally retarded brother.

Responsibility for siblings may also extend to their children, that is to nieces and nephews. One informant, for example, recounted that, while he was abroad as a seaman, his sister took one of his two children, reportedly suffering from malnutrition, to their mother to nurse back to good health. This meant taking the child away from its mother, a woman with whom he had a visiting relationship.

For those who were not as close to their siblings as they would wish, this was attributed, more often than not, to an age gap or to being raised in different households, rather than to parental favouritism. Some were separated by migration and described emotional reunions. Others, whose fathers had migrated, mentioned half siblings whom they had never met or of whose existence they were unsure.

As a boy growing up, one of my brothers was already a man. In fact, by the time I was ten it was only me and another brother and he was six years older than me. The other brother and sisters had already moved into their own homes. My oldest sister emigrated to the United States as well as my oldest brother. We're not as close as we could be, but this is not just the emigration, but also the wide age difference. But they call occasionally and they write. Sometimes they would send items by persons who are coming to Barbados, but they don't really visit regularly (Lumber Yard Porter, age 50).

I went to the States for the very first time and met both of my brothers at the airport. That is something I always remember. To me it was very sentimental and touching as I didn't see my brothers for many years. To see them again for the first time was quite overwhelming (Retired Cruise Ship Steward, age 80).

To summarise, Caribbean family studies have identified matrilateral links only in passing and then generally only with reference to mother and son if the man in question remained in his mother's house. But even these bonds were dismissed as 'abnormal' and 'obsessive', delaying the transition to his own family of procreation. In contrast, for Barbadian men responsibilities to mothers, grandmothers and siblings endure. A change of residence and the responsibility for a spouse and children clearly affect these relationships, but do not determine their existence.

Fathers and Conjugal Partners

Defining family as nuclear, functionalists identified only two male roles as significant, those of father and conjugal partner. As fathers, men were consistently 'marginal'. 'Children derive practically nothing that is of importance from their fathers they do not suffer if they never even see their father' (Smith 1956: 147).

The occasional mention of paternal care and devotion is obscured by images of harsh discipline or neglect (Clarke 1957: 107). A father's presence at home demands silence and restraint; misbehaviour is punished with 'beatings' much more severe than those meted out by the mother (Smith 1956: 134; Clarke 1957: 159). Other than this, fathers take little notice of their children (Henriques 1953: 131). Those who live elsewhere are very remote in the lives of their children. They are, nonetheless, psychological role models for their sons (Rodman 1971: 81) and the idea of 'having a father' is culturally significant. As Smith (1956: 133) states, 'it is inconceivable that a child should be fatherless, no matter how vague the father-figure may be'. Rodman (1971: 75), however, refers to cases of disputed or unknown paternity, for 'a mother is always certain a child is hers while a father is never absolutely certain'.

All but two of the Barbadian informants were fathers, the two exceptions being in their early twenties and single. The majority, 69 (75 per cent) had between one and three children. Only eight men indicated that they had six or more children, six of them aged 60 and above. One 96-year-old man boasted 13 children, though three had died. Several young fathers were present at the birth of their children and their descriptions of younger children especially and of their responsibilities as fathers, extending far beyond financial support and occasional discipline, were particularly positive.

Man, that boy is the sweetest thing on earth. He is thirteen months . He is something else, a smart little radical. I like him bad, I never felt this way about anything or anybody. He sweet, man (Quality Control Supervisor, age 31).

People tell you about having children and how wonderful it is. Well it's more than that. To see my daughter develop . And you always hear about children and their mothers and when the mother is not around they cry. Well, I remember one time the two of us left home early in the morning and came back home at 8.30 at night and not once did she ask for her mother. But whenever I'm not there, she's always, "Where's my Daddy?" (Company Manager, age 34)

My duties as a father are to care for and take care of the children. I have two boys, one is 16 and the other one is 12 and I don't have any regrets about not having a daughter. As father I clothe them, feed, guide and train them and be there for them. I was the one who was there to take them to the baby sitter and to bathe them and feed them and later to take them to school. During the vacation I was the one who watched them and spent a lot of time with them, driving about, going on sight seeing tours of Barbados, to the park and picnics and to church . I was a strong believer in discipline and I was probably too hard on the boys. But I never used to lash them just so. I would rather organise a beating, a special place and time . Once when they were away with their mother, I couldn't help feeling that something would go wrong. When I'm in charge I feel nothing can go wrong (Teacher, age 45).

Not all, however, expressed such confidence in themselves, especially the 32 men (35 per cent) who had fathered children living elsewhere, including 'outside children'.

I became a father for the first time under a strange circumstance. My first son was born when I was 33-years-old. So I was not a youngster. The relationship then was little more than a casual relationship. I call him my weekend baby, my weekend child. It's such that I can go for him any time I want, but it is not convenient. So I just go on weekends. And I compare that to what I do for my other two and that is because I was there to change them, bathe them, feed them. That I feel I never did for him. Not that I wasn't willing, but because I wasn't there (Pharmaceutical Representative, age 40).

As babies and then as boys we were quite close, especially the older one. But not as much as it could have been. When they were growing up, I was so much engrossed in playing cricket, that I never really took time out to do things that fathers would generally do, like take them to the beach. I regret that now. We went a few places, but not as much as could have been. I perhaps was thinking that those sort of things would be done by their mother. That changed after I separated from the mother. The boys went to live with her. Deep down in my heart, I guess I was a bit hurt about the whole affair. I didn't really see them much. It's just that I didn't really want to go around their mother and as a result I avoided them. There is a slight change in that me and the last boy are better friends, but it may be because he is more talkative. The older one, if he wants something and he can't get it from someone else, then he would come to me. I am not the first person he would come to. The second one, he would come to me. It seems that his mother usually tells him when he wants anything to come to me. But if they have personal problems, they don't come to me. I accept that, I don't question them (Public Utility Manager, age 47).

Despite these inadequacies, most contrasted their own performance with that of their fathers. Only 13 (14 per cent) of the informants reported a positive relationship with their fathers. A further 17 described it as reasonable, while three indicated that it was limited to sporadic financial support. This left a total of 58 (63 per cent) who had no contact with their fathers (five died and four are known to have migrated) or who described them in strongly negative terms. Comments included, 'I never knew him', 'My father never gave me nothing' and 'My mother was mother and father to me' and reference was made to their fathers' drunkenness, violence and 'womanising'. It is interesting to note that in only four cases was a substitute father mentioned (three uncles [mother's brothers] and one stepfather). Several informants went to great lengths to explain a deliberate policy on their part not to repeat the mistakes of the last generation.

I knew that my experiences with my father was not going to happen to my children. I was going to show them affection. I was going to give them better than I got when I was growing up (Office Assistant, age 38).

In the functionalist literature, men are also described as 'marginal' in their roles as conjugal partners. Even the co-resident marital and common law relationships are characterised by 'casual attitudes', 'weakness', 'individualism' and frequent 'marital-shifting' (Rodman 1971: 71,161). Property is rarely owned jointly, money is earned and saved separately (Henriques 1953: 120; Rodman 1971: 62, 160) and leisure activities segregated (Greenfield 1966: 104). Male infidelity is common and tolerated by 'wives' unless it becomes an embarrassment or a significant drain on family finances (Clarke 1957: 105; Greenfield 1966: 104; Otterbein 1966: 292; Rodman 1971: 129; Smith 1956: 114). All in all, conjugality is perceived as a troubled relationship of suspicion and stress (Greenfield 1961: 81). Rodman (1971: 115) noted a 'low degree of trust between males and females which pervades all stages of the marital relationship in lower class Trinidad'.

Male conjugal marginality is seen to vary with time and circumstances. Joint activity diminishes as a woman becomes a mother (Smith 1956: 147-148) and later, supported financially by her adult children and her own income-generating activity, she might become completely independent of her partner. At this stage: 'Men, in their role of husband-father, are placed in a position where neither their social status nor their access to, and command of economic resources are of major importance in the functioning of the household group' (Smith 1956: 221).

Most writers also note variations with socio-economic status. Thus, men who do not reside with their conjugal partners and children, who 'drink the greater part of their earnings' (Henriques 1953: 120) and who do not contribute financially are held in low esteem. They have very little authority and very few rights (Rodman 1971: 178; Smith 1956: 158). Most marginalised of all, are men who live in houses owned by their partners; their position described as 'tenuous, embarrassing and unauthoritative' (Greenfield 1966: 119).

Barbadian informants confirmed much of this. They described women as intrinsically different, unpredictable and a challenge to manage (see also Barrow 1986) and the conjugal union as the most problematic and uncertain of all family relationships. 'That is an extremely hard task. Some women are so hard to please, you never know what they want from you' (Assistant Baker, age 26).

Nevertheless, as indicated below, the majority were involved in some kind of union.

Single	6
Visiting	9
Common Law	19
Married	54
Separated/Divorced	2
Widower	2
Total	92

Virtually all mentioned at least one previous relationship and several claimed more than one simultaneously.

Responses clearly reflected what they felt was expected of them. Their ideal of the male conjugal role emphasised qualities of romance, contribution to domestic chores, negotiation through conflicts and the acknowledgment of gender equality.

I did the right things. I would get top marks. I was very attentive, very attentive, always very alert and mindful of the requirements. I had no problems remembering what she wore. When it came to birthdays and special occasions, I was always there. In terms of the sentimental, emotional aspect, I have done well (Teacher, age 25).

Being a husband has changed from when I was a boy. Husbands should not just see themselves as providers, but should take an active part in all the activities in the household, and should be able to do all the things, cleaning and cooking, all that, that the wives do. The women of today are working, no nonsense women with a great sense of independence and no longer hold the view held long ago that the man is the boss. I am not a macho man. I can learn from experience and I am not too proud to say that I am sorry. Men still feel that they will be less of a man if they say they sorry (Office Assistant, age 38).

Most critical of all is fidelity. While informants recognised the ideal of conjugal faithfulness, statements reflected the double standards of sexual morality and considerable ambiguity concerning their own behaviour.

Several were involved in 'outside' affairs, the majority insisting that these were entirely separate and not a threat to their principal unions. Indeed, some attributed their infidelity, at least partially, to their wives, contrasting the fun outside to life with the woman at home who had nothing new to offer or who was neglecting them for the children.

Women tend to become complacent in marriage. They place sex and so on at the bottom of their list and men are forced to look elsewhere. Yes it happened with me, but not deep; short, more for physical gratification. They did not stop me from being a husband and I did not feel any different about my wife (Teacher, age 41).

Having children changes a relationship. When there were no children our sex life was more carefree, more spontaneous. Setimes one pays so much attention to children that the other partner feels neglected and, well, you know when the man gets left out what would happen (Reporter, age 38).

The reason I used to go out with Joan is I can't have fun with Sharon. People don't understand why you find that men have to have an outside woman. You can have fun with an outside woman more so than with an inside woman. The person home, you with them all the time. You don't have anything new to learn about the person. You know everything (Quality Control Supervisor, age 31).

In order for me to change, I would have to go to church. There is just this craving in me for women. I must be want to be a "wutless" man like my father. I always say it is something in my body. I don't know if it is heat, or emotions. All I know is that I operate how I see my father operate (Retired Plantation Labourer, age 67).

No I don't like this running around thing. I had one or two girls on the side, but I never got into a serious relationship outside of my marriage. But she (wife) is too quiet. After being out with the boys sometimes when I get home late and expect her to challenge me, she says nothing. A man needs some confrontation sometimes you know. So I have been tempted to have an extra relationship. But these days I am even more particular because I don't want any AIDS. But I must admit, why can't we be like the Africans where a man could have more than one woman. It is true that some Bajan men head more than one household, but I respect my family. It would be better if more than one wife was allowed (Customs Clerk, age 52).

Sherry is one fine chick with a bubbly personality, but it has been a long hard struggle. There have been temptations, and what temptations, but I've resisted each and every one of them (Mason, age 29).

Suspicion and jealousy are endemic to many unions.

'Once when I come home late she ask where I now come from. So I ask she if she want me to go back and she keep quiet' (Policeman, age 38).

Men expressed extreme wariness about being 'trapped' into marriage, commitment and responsibility.

Lisa and I had something real going, you know the perfect match. We had been together for a long time. Then she started pushing the M word – marriage. Well, I was only 20 and she was 19 and I did want more time to get to know her before jumping into such a big decision. It ain't that I did afraid of making a commitment, despite what happened to my mother. I actually looking forward to the day I get hitched. I actually want to experience that. Well, things change. For starters she gone and get sheself pregnant. She stopped taking the pill so she could get pregnant and I would be forced to marry her. Well, she got a surprise, because it didn't work that way. I love the baby from the day it born, but I could never forget how she try to trap me (Assistant Baker, age 26).

In general, the majority agreed that conjugal relationships should be approached with extreme caution, were difficult to manage and required constant monitoring. But, once a man is ready to 'settle down' and has found the right woman, especially one like his mother, conjugal commitment could be made to work well.

I was looking for someone like my mother and she reminds me of her in a way. But my wife is stubborn. She has her own strong personality. She stops me from being on the run. One of the joys of marriage is having someone to look out for you, stop you from being wild. It gives you a better sense of direction and purpose and the warmth of having someone to treasure and cherish (Accountant, age 37).

In summary, these narratives imply that the informants were more comfortable and committed as fathers than as conjugal partners and that fatherhood is defined more holistically and with more meaning in their lives than for men of the previous generation. The dilemma as they see it is that, in practice, effective fathering depends largely on co-residence and, in turn therefore, on the union with the children's mother; that is, on maintaining what is the most intractable and potentially unstable family relationship of all.

Masculinity and Family

If men are considered 'marginal' to the family then where are they, what are they doing and with whom? Most of the functionalists confined their attention to the domestic group and left these questions unanswered. Apart from scattered ethnographic mention, men remained invisible, that is until Wilson's male construct of 'Reputation' placed them firmly within peer groups or 'crews' (Wilson 1971). These 'loafing groups' of men (Davenport 1956) constituted 'the focus of solidarity and joint activities' (Smith 1988: 38) within which a man's status was derived from his performance as a 'man of words' as he recounted tales of his exploits, especially abroad as a migrant worker and 'professional seducer' (Clarke 1957: 69); in lavish expenditure, drinking fighting and aggressive behaviour; in playing cards, dominoes and draughts; and in hustling, smuggling and gambling (Clarke 1957: 73; Greenfield 1966: 5, 104; Rodman 1971:

180; Smith 1956: 137, 209; Wilson 1969: 74-76, 1971: 21-28). Not surprising is the report that 'domestic chores diminish masculinity' (Smith 1988: 148). As Graham Dann (1987: 171) summed it up, 'stepping outside, moving around, liming with the fellas, firing a drink and slamming a dom, is the real world and worldview of the Barbadian male'. At the core of masculinity is virility,

the most highly valued quality that a man can possess as often as it is mentioned that males are permitted and expected to be sexually active it is also mentioned that men must be virile, and that their virility is especially manifested by their sexual activities and their fathering of children (Wilson 1969: 71; see also Clarke 1957: 91, 96; Smith 1956: 141; Smith 1988: 137; Wilson 1969: 71).

Male sexual prowess is a lifelong preoccupation. The sex play of a young boy, 'the force ripe little man', is 'regarded with amused indifference, if not admiration' (Clarke 1957:98, 169) and the concern continues throughout his life.

Men do not look forward to old age . Their interest in sexual intercourse continues and the fear of impotence is strongly felt. This cannot be regarded merely as a "biological drive", but must be seen as a means of expression of the desire to assert masculinity. From puberty to death, men are preoccupied with proving their potency (Smith 1956: 141).

It is biological, not social fathering that enhances masculinity. 'The man is satisfied by the proof of his virility and does not necessarily accept any of the obligations and duties of parenthood there is no public censure if he does not acknowledge or fulfil them' (Clarke 1957: 96). It follows that unemployment and lack of economic support has less effect on one's status as a man. 'Masculinity does not depend on work performance; it is demonstrated by 'manly activities with other men, by sexual conquest of many 'girl friends', and by 'having children all about' (Smith 1988: 147).

As these images converge in the construction of Caribbean masculinity, three points emerge. Firstly, masculinity is validated in the company of other men and, secondly, in behaviour not merely 'outside', but antithetical to what the domains of home and family stand for. Men give priority to friendship over family relationships (Wilson 1971: 22-23); ostentatious spending in peer group activity reduces family income; 'irresponsible', 'uncivilised' sexual indulgence (Alexander 1977: 377) threatens marital stability; mobility and migration take men away from home; and the reproduction of 'children all about' detracts from the social role of fathering. In other words, men are not merely marginal to the family, they are anti-family. Thirdly, by extension, men invest in a discourse of masculinity which is both submerged and intent on 'undermining, disobeying or circumventing the legal system of society' (Wilson 1969: 81), that is in opposition to dominant national ideals.

All of this may be ethnographically valid and conceptually attractive. But the voices of Barbadian men compel a review of the dichotomy of masculinity versus the ideologies of state, family and femininity. Their testimonies do not place men beyond the domain and jurisdiction of dominant culture and their masculinity, though validated 'outside' as 'one of the boys', is also located within the family. Virility is central, but they also spoke of 'resisting temptation' and of the period in a man's life cycle when he 'settles down' by renouncing youthful, sexual indulgence for the serious covenant of marriage and family. Not all men transform their lifestyles and some do only temporarily before moving on to 'outside' relationships. Additionally, although the proof of masculinity is biological, informants also practised and enjoyed fathering children, contrasting themselves with their own negligent or abusive fathers. The problem of marginal fathers and 'outside' children clearly persists (Brown et. al. 1993: 163-168), but their testimonies suggest a generational change in imaging and defining fatherhood into their lives. The social fathering of a few emerges at least as importantly as the biological fathering of many. Responsibilities to the family of origin persist, especially as sons to mothers, and not as an unfair burden.

The key to a successful performance 'as man' lies not in 'Reputation' and 'marginality', not in escaping family and acting out in the public domain of work place and rum shop. Even in the licentious atmosphere of the drinking group, family identities are not forgotten, for derogatory jokes about mothers and sisters are taboo (Wilson 1969: 73). The least 'settled' of young men maintains close ties with his grandmother, mother and sister(s), women who, in turn, are not immune to any 'irresponsibility' on the part of their menfolk.

I get a lot of pressure from my brothers and sisters. If I was to lost my job under any kind of fishy circumstances, they would take it more sorely than I would because they look up to me . You have to look at all your actions in your personal and public life to see how it affect your family. As a man in a family, it is very demanding. A lot is expected of you; you are not expected to fail in areas of providing for your family, or if someone gets into trouble and they need someone to depend on, you are always expected to be there, always (Company Manager, age 34).

In sum, a 'regular fellow' balances the identities of 'family man' and 'one of the boys' – 'he would come and fire one with the fellas 'pon on a Friday night, but he wouldn't leave out he family'.

Within his family, the extended family that is, the 'real man' strikes a balance between potentially conflicting identities, roles and relationships.

He must show that he is 'in control' by maintaining an equilibrium within a dispersed kinship network that incorporates legitimate, respectable relationships at home as well as those which are 'outside' and 'irresponsible'. He must manage the competing and often contradictory demands of mother (occasionally sisters) and wife, wife and 'outside woman' ('deputy'), children at home and those 'outside'. The dynamics of male family life pull in different, often opposing directions. Most 'tricky' of all, are 'handling himself with women', especially with more than one conjugal partner simultaneously, and maintaining a role as father after a conjugal break, for children ultimately 'belong to the mother'. Even the mother-wife duo can become problematic if a man is seen to allow one or other woman to dictate and dominate.

After we married we lived at my mother for about a year while our house was being built. And then we moved to the same gap as my wife's family. After about nine years, after me and my mother had bought some land together, then we moved again. So my house was next door to my mother and I hold this responsible for the final break up . She [wife] liked living in the area where we lived before, although when I purchased the land, I took her to see it and explained to her about the land, how I got it and who would be living next door. She never said anything. She seemed to accept it and then on the day that we were moving the house (a chattel house), it appeared that she didn't like the idea. She didn't like the idea of living close to my mother because she saw my family as dominating her life, that they would come at me and do whatever they wanted and I wouldn't stop them. She used to say that she didn't have a say and that my family was dictating to me what I should and shouldn't do (Public Utility Manager, age 47).

Contrast this with the experience of the informant, quoted earlier, who boasted success as his wife and mother had grown 'closer than you would think'.

Conclusion

Structural functionalists were transfixed on the 'abnormal' Caribbean family. They 'asked questions about it and received the answers they were looking for'; male marginality was their preoccupation, not that of the people they were studying (Alexander 1977: 372). 'Marginal' as husbands and fathers, invisible as sons, brothers and uncles, Caribbean men, in so far as they appeared at all, were located elsewhere and in opposition to family and to women. A revised approach which listens to people's images and experiences of family and restores culture and history, clears the way for the re-entry of men and the reconstruction of Caribbean masculinity. The discourse of multiple and mutable masculinities transcends the limitations of binary theorising inherent in the models of 'marginality' and 'Reputation'. Varieties, changes and contradictions of masculinity are linked to biography, life cycle, generation and history. Although this study confines attention primarily to family to challenge the 'marginality' thesis, it should, hopefully, enhance a more holistic treatment of Caribbean masculinity.

Caribbean men, women, family and the State inhabit the same world, with all its ambivalence and contradiction. Male symbolically structured space may be 'outside' the household, but it is not separate from nor opposed to family. Only if household and family are defined as one, as functionalism assumed, does this follow. Informants spoke of taking children *out*, but they did so as fathers. As brothers, they protected their sisters from *outsiders*, especially other men, and, as kinsmen, they mediated between family and the *outside* world. Masculinity is not an exclusive discourse; it is negotiated in gender relations and also expressed and confirmed in male only performances. Male social identities are constructed in compliance with as well as resistance to dominant culture and ideology. Men are not perfect, but to successfully manage gender identities, they must present to the world an image of skillful, strategic navigation through potentially conflicting masculinities. Paradoxically, it appears that 'marginality' is only now becoming a preoccupation for black Caribbean men themselves, that is as they contrast themselves with their own fathers and begin to define 'sensitivity', fatherhood and housework into their lives.

Women's Power in a Man's World:
Contestations of Gender, Race and Culture

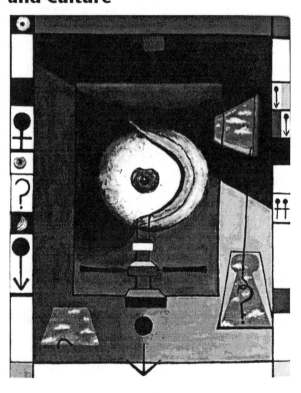

20

Siren/Hyphen; or, the Maid Beguiled

Marina Warner

'This female savage', noted the missionary Jean-Baptiste Labat, in his *Nouveau Voyage aux îles de l'Amérique*[1] 'was, I believe, one of the oldest creatures in the world. It is said she was very beautiful at one time . . . ' He was describing a Carib known as Madame Ouvernard, who, when he met her in Dominica in 1700, 'was more than a hundred years old'. She was held in great esteem on account of her great age, rather than her past, he writes, though she was also remembered as the wife of the late Sir Thomas Warner, English governor of St Christopher's and Nevis. 'She had a lot of children by this Warner', wrote Pere Labat, 'so that her Carbet, which is very large, was peopled with a marvellous number of sons, grandsons, and great-grandsons.' Among them, one son only has left a strong trace in the records: the former Governor of Dominica, known as 'Indian' Warner, who had died in 1676. During the protracted conflicts between the French and the English, 'Indian' was killed, in complicated and mysterious circumstances; his half-brother Philip, son of Thomas Warner and his second, English wife, was charged with treasonable murder and brought to London to be tried at the Tower of London. Unsurprisingly, he was acquitted, after the settlers of Barbados issued frantic pleas on his behalf, but he did not regain his position as a local Governor. Labat met 'Indian's mother a quarter of a century later. Other offspring or their descendants are not recorded, as far as I can tell, in official genealogies, documents or gravestones, in contrast to the issue of that branch of the family descending from Thomas Warner's first two English wives, Sarah and Rebecca'.[2]

Pere Labat and his company were on their way to Guadeloupe, but they interrupted their journey for a few days' visit to Mrs Warner's Carbet, though the missionary hung up his own hammock rather than lie in one of hers and risk a dusting of roucou powder. He tells us little more about his time there, but he does describe his hostess: 'This good woman was completely nude, and so naked that she had not two dozen hairs on her head; her skin was parchment, wrinkled and dried in the fire. She was so bent that I could not see her face except when she leant back to drink. However she had plenty of teeth, and still lively eyes.'[3]

Labat does not connect this Madame Ouvernard with a story a compatriot had told earlier in his history of the conflicts and massacres which led to the establishment of French and English power in the area. Jean-Baptiste du Tertre, in his *Histoire Générale des Antilles of 1667-71* shows a more full-blooded commitment to the 'pictured page' and rather less discretion about the ethics of pioneering empire-builders when he describes the complex struggles that took place between indigenous peoples and the colonists. Describing the settlement of St Christopher's by the French (under Pierre Belain, Sieur D'Esnambuc) in collaboration with the English (under Thomas Warner), he relates how the settlers had been welcomed at first and helped 'libéralement', by 'les Sauvages'.[4] But relations soon changed – he does not dwell on the causes.

Du Tertre gives his account of a founding act of conquest. He writes how in 1625 or 1626, a Kalinago (Carib) woman named 'Barbe' learned that the indigenous inhabitants of several neighbouring islands were planning an ambush on the night of the full moon.[5] She passed on the information to the English, because she held them in affection and esteem – she was Warner's mistress. On learning of the danger they were running into and in order to forestall a massacre, the incomers decided to commit one themselves instead, and that night they fell on the savages in their beds, and stabbed them, leaving a hundred or two hundred dead. But they kept, du Tertre continues, 'their most beautiful women'.[6]

Through the treachery of a woman, more women are obtained, and authority over their people; or, to express it differently, the changed allegiance of one islander inaugurated the transfer of her compatriots' obedience as well; as in founding myths like the 'Rape of the Sabine Women', the acquisition of females and the settlement of new territories are inextricably intertwined.

Du Tertre gives her the name Barbe,[7] but this seems so punningly close to the idea of Barbarian, and the tale itself echoes another crucial legend of encounter and empire, of Pocahontas who saved John Smith out of love.

As a figure of mediation between coloniser and indigenous peoples, Pocahontas or 'Barbe' has another, notorious precursor: Malinche, interpreter and consort of Cortez, about whom a great deal has been written.[8] Malinche provides the hyphen of language between Aztec and Spaniard, and that small cipher of union translates into a sexual bond, which then translates her name, too, and commutes her identity. This triple exchange – of land, of body, of name – institutes a new order of power, in the case of the Spanish conquest of Mexico, the settlement of the Algonquin territories of Virginia, and, in alignment with historical precedent, in the newly annexed islands of the British Caribbean in the early seventeenth century.

But this kind of tale is the irresistible stuff of legend, cartoon historical romance, boldly drawn and highly coloured as a Hollywood costume drama. The love of Pocahontas for Smith is an originary myth of the New World, sensitively analysed by Peter Hulme in his book *Colonial Encounters*.[9] (In spite of the alertness Disney production teams show towards current research, they chose shamelessly to ignore this skeptical, historical reading and to press romance to the service of legitimising propaganda in *Pocahontas*, the new animation feature about another 'female savage', another Indian princess.)

'Barbe' may have been altogether legendary, and her warning invented to excuse an assault in cold blood, but she merges with the historical Madame Ouvernard in the folklore of empire: her act of heroic treachery becomes attached to the Indian wife of the first governor of the West Indies for the British Crown. Or so the story came down to me, and was preserved in my memory (or was it my fantasy?)[10] and found its way into one of the tales Serafine tells Miranda in my novel *Indigo*.[11]

Serafine is a *conteuse*, and she has many ancestors and precursors: like the figure in Simone Schwartz-Bart's *Pluie et Vent sur Télumée Miracle*, Christophene in Jean Rhys's *Wide Sargasso Sea*. In real life, Derek Walcott has paid tribute to his Aunt Sidone, whom he remembers telling him and his twin brother stories after school as darkness fell in St Lucia; Gisèle Pineau has described her grandmother Man Ya, passing on, in France, memories from the narrative store of her native Guadeloupe:

Pour nous, enfants, elle mettait des soies colorées à ses paroles et accrochait des étoiles à sa vie des Antilles. Elle racontait – en créole – sa langue unique – les soucougnans et les esprits, les hommes tournés en chien et les chevaux à trois pattes, les sorcières et les envoûteurs, les démons, les bons anges'.[12] (For us, as children, she added coloured silks to her words and hung stars on her life in the Caribbean. In Creole – her only language – she told of vampires and spirits, of men turned into dogs and three-legged horses, of witches and enchanters, of demons and good angels.)

The writers Jean Bernabé, Patrick Chamoiseau and Raphaël Confiant have reclaimed the *conteur* (male) as a spiritual forebear, and through him, have mounted a controversial attempt to reaffirm the Uncle Tom figure, who does not run away from the plantation to the forest or the *morne,* but stays at home, obedient and docile.[13] The chattering, genial servant in the big house becomes the polar opposite of the incendiary Maroon, that ultimate male hero figure of the Caribbean. These French Caribbean writers offer another view of language's possibilities as an expression of resistance – from within:

Ainsi il [le conteur] se protège, protège sa fonction, protège le message de la résistance détournée qu'il propage. La parole d'un si bon esclave, se dit le Béké, ne peut pas se révéler dangereuse.'[14] (So he (the storyteller) protects himself, protects his role, protects the message of devious resistance that he propagates. The words of such a good slave, so the Boss says to himself, cannot turn out dangerous.)

Quiet storytelling works as a fifth columnist, while rebel sloganeering burns itself up in its own heat.[15] A. James Arnold is right to point out how odd and how misleading it is that Bernabé, Chamoiseau and Confiant leave women and women's voices out of their discussion of the Maroon and the storyteller as opposing models in history.[16] But at the same time, women cannot be smoothly allotted their place in the same division of roles; the historical – and mythical – part they play in the inauguration of new histories, new societies, new families demands a fresh taxonomy. Women, through their bodies, become the hyphen between the forest/*morne* and the *habitation*/house/plantation, either by force, or by choice. Madame Ouvernard, in her Carbet in Dominica, is neither Maroon nor docile house slave; she figures as the connection between the two societies, a connection that has been effaced from memory just as her own name has been lost under 'Barbe', under her married title.

The English phrase 'natural' son, which is how 'Indian' Warner is described in contemporary documents, catches the way the fertility of a native woman produces offspring who *naturalise* – or can be perceived to *naturalise* – the new social and historical power, who can cancel – or, again, can be seen to cancel – the denaturing character of the process by which that power is established.

But the documents of the time reveal a rather different sequence of events from the highly coloured adventure of love and betrayal in the legend – it would be surprising if they didn't. The material emerges from the confused story of 'Indian' Warner, his political allegiances and changes of policy as a Kalinago leader, involved in the resistance the local inhabitants put up to British and French ambitions in the Windward

Islands. This resistance took both military and political forms, as Hilary Beckles has shown; by playing the Europeans against one another, in a variety of divide-and-rule, the Kalinago were able to stall the settlement of St Vincent and to retain some authority over Dominica.[17] 'Indian' Warner was deeply involved in this shifting strategy.[18]

Interpretations of his moves were complicated in the view of contemporaries, by his birth. However, in the depositions at the subsequent trial of his half-brother and murderer Philip Warner, 'Indian' Warner's mother never comes into focus in the foreground: as Hulme and Whitehead remark, 'Indian' Warner's 'legitimacy' as the son of Sir Thomas Warner is ceaselessly disputed, but the one person who could have testified as to his birth – his mother – was never asked.[19] Some fragments in the record do however concern her, a few subordinate phrases relate to her, and they reveal how crucially women's bodies and identity mirrored the conquest of land and the renaming of territory.

Hulme and Whitehead, in their annotated edition of documents from the Public Record Office, began investigating this tangled episode of collaboration, treaties, and treachery, and they give rich source material for 'The Case of 'Indian' Warner'.[20] But there is more material; it is difficult, some of it written in a particularly rebarbative script of the seventeenth century, and the remarks which follow merely attempt to scratch the surface of the story.[21]

When Philip Warner was being tried for the murder, several of his colleagues and acquaintances among the English in Barbados and other islands wrote to the court to plead in high dudgeon on his behalf; they defended the killing on two principal grounds, that 'Indian' was not the son of Sir Thomas, but a slave, and Philip was therefore no Cain who had slain his brother; and that secondly (and consequently) 'Indian' was just that, an undifferentiated Other, not an Englishman, who had been moreover seditious, treacherous, and predatory. These complainants did not deny, however, that the boy had been brought up in the Warner household, but to determine his exact relation – or rather insist upon his lack of relation – to Sir Thomas, they tried to distinguish between two kinds of chattel: a slave and a child. Both were family, in the seventeenth-century usage of family as household, still saturated with the Latin meaning of *famuli*, servants.

Colonel Randall Russell testified, in Nevis, in the presence of Colonel William Stapleton, then Captain-General and Governor-in-Chief of the Leeward Islands, that 'in the month of July in the year 1637' he arrived from England at St Christophers (St Kitts) and 'was recommended unto the House of Sir Thomas Warner (then Governor-General) and there Lived in his Imploy several Years and by his Command to mind, and to keep account of his *family, both of Indian Slaves (and others)'* (emphasis added).[22] Russell then describes how 'several [of the slaves] had run away from St Xtophers to Dominicoe *sic* and one of them was the Mother of (Warner) so named, being the first borne Slave on St Xtopher's in the aforesaid Governor-General's family, and Carried with her Son in his Infancie.'[23]

This reference to the naming of a first-born slave was remembered in more vivid detail by two more witnesses who came forward to clear Philip Warner of fratricide. Lieutenant Robert Choppin, who had worked as a servant in the household forty plus years before, described how within a short time after Sir Thomas' return to St Kitt's from one of his voyages back to London, 'Thomas Warner Called All his Slaves before him, being All Indians, to the Number of About Twenty-four, and One Indian boy, or Male Child, the first Born in his family of Slaves, being about Six Months old, how the Said Sir Thomas, Named him Warner.'[24] This witness, like others, went on to make it clear that this public ceremony of naming, this custom of installing the child in the family or household by giving him the same surname, had not been a christening.

Whether this ceremony of inclusion was widespread in colonial households in the Americas is debatable, but certainly the first witness, Colonel Russell, thought the reason that Indian was given the surname Warner as 'the first borne slave' might suffice to persuade his listeners (who would by the 1670s be accustomed to the slave trade's habit of naming slaves after their owner). Yet the image of the Governor, returning from the 'mother country', gathering his household around him to greet the arrival of an infant son, points to an idea of community in which relations were not as regular as the law (or the church) might have wished. The witnesses' testimony, to modern ears, achieves the opposite of their intention, and rather confirms that 'Indian' was publicly acknowledged as Thomas's son, and welcomed. If he were indeed the first child born in the house, it would mean that 14 years had elapsed between Thomas Warner's first landing, in 1623, and the new arrival of the son in 1637 – a prolonged (and unlikely) period of time, but certainly a cause for rejoicing. 'Family' had not yet acquired its modern implication of blood tie, but it was about to be narrowed in order to do so, as 'Indian's' case illustrates.

Imputations of barbarism move in two directions; and in family arrangements as well as the conduct of war, the English colonists were very quick to anticipate the savagery they ascribed to their opponents, and to make a preemptive strike. Every one interprets barbarism according to their own lights (Montaigne's axiom could be reversed: not that 'Men think barbarism that which is not common to them' but 'Men think barbarism that which is common to them (but understand to be shameful)'). Empire-builders could render unto the savage what the savage of their own *imaginaire* desired. A letter from the King – Charles II – written by Sir Henry Coventry to Sir Jonathan Atkins, Governor of the Windward Islands, offers a most notable example of imperialist projection at work – more notable than the massacre that took place in order to prevent a massacre. His Majesty has heard of the death of 'Indian' Warner, and he expresses his very great displeasure: the murder has damaged the delicate and complex diplomacy of the English in the area and given the indigenous peoples cause to love the French more. 'Since there is reason to believe that the Windward Islands may have been much alienated from the English by this action,' writes Sir Henry, 'His Majesty leaves it to the Governor to give that people some signal and public demonstration of his justice upon the authors *by sending them some heads.*' (emphasis added) The letter continues, 'and by some other proper way which he shall think fit that they may be satisfied of the detestation His Majesty and the whole nation has of this proceeding of Colonel Warner's.' [25]

A propitiatory offering of 'some heads' does not suggest policy based on Christian principles. It is difficult to know how Christian early life in the settlements would have been, and whether religion would have marked a strong difference between the Caribs and other Indians and the English; but it does not seem very likely in this atmosphere of concubinage/polygamy, piracy and pillage that the lack of a christening would matter very much when it came to owning or disowning a child.

After describing the naming and presence of the baby in the household, the testimony of Colonel Russell then went on, as we saw, to relate how several members of the household ran away, 'Indian's mother with them. So, 'Madame Ouvernard' was a runaway as early as the 1640s, and her son was not brought up in the household, but in Dominica, among the Kalinagos of his mother's Carbet.

Russell then went on to tell another most interesting episode in the life of 'Indian' Warner, about his reunion with his father 'Many years after'. He reports that a captain of a Scottish ship, one Fletcher, calling at Dominica met 'Indian' Warner' and ('Inveigled by the Aforesaid Slave', says Russell) took him on board after he identified himself as the son of Sir Thomas. Then, 'It came to the knowledge of Sir Thomas Warner that he had on board the same Scotch ship one Indian slave which slave (was by) Sir Thomas Warner ' who immediately asked that he be 'delivered' to him, which he was 'upon Satisfaction given to the aforesaid Fletcher'. 'And as a Slave,' concluded Russell, 'So Lived in the aforesaid Sir Thomas Warner his family *sic* until the day of his death.'[26] Recalling events of forty years before, the Colonel appears to me to be trying to impose on the story the more recently developed market structures of the slave trade, and turn a family drama into a typical transaction in the history of slavery, of a runaway restored to his owner with due payment of a fee to a middle man. But the feelings expressed, the interest implied in 'Indian's' actions at the time, do not altogether bear out this construction.[27] The first impulse towards inclusion – Thomas Warner's ceremony of naming the native-born child – is replaced, within that child's lifetime, by the contraflowing impulse, to exclude him. The mother's part, while obscured in the background, is crucial: she moves from the plantation house ('runs away') to another island, where the Kalinagos historically sustained some degree of autonomy alongside colonial arrangements; raised for a time in this atmosphere, the child returns to reopen the relationship. The history of 'Indian' Warner's activities as a Kalinago leader, summarised and analysed in Hulme and Whitehead, reveal the complications of his negotiations.[28]

Du Tertre gives the later part of 'Indian's' life the colour and the cruelty of a fairy tale. After her husband's death in 1648, Lady Ann (the last of Sir Thomas' three English wives, and herself childless), tormented the love child of his illicit Kalinago wife, and out of jealousy, 'made him work in the fields with the slaves of the household'.[29] 'Indian', who had been taken back into the household apparently at the mutual wish of himself and his Master/Father, continued to live there afterwards 'some years with his Lady Ann Warner, till he ran away again to the Island of Dominicoe'. Colonel Russell in his evidence also related that after Thomas Warner's death, 'Indian' ran away to Dominica, 'Carrying Several Other Indians with him.' [30] And rejoined his mother there, perhaps conducting from her Carbet the diplomacy with contending French, English and indigenous inhabitants of the islands which eventually led to his death in 1676 at the age of 38. His mother, who survived him, might not have been quite as old as Pere Labat thought: if she had been in her twenties when she was Thomas Warner's consort, she would have been in her eighties in 1700.

The figure of the native wife haunts colonial memory, as Bertha haunts Thornfield, and took possession of Jean Rhys' great novel. She lives in the shadows, or disappears altogether from view in the towers of narrative, just as Bernabé, Chamoiseau and Confiant forgot to include her case in their account of the *conteur* in the plantation household, but she does make a powerful appearance in Robert Louis Stevenson's short story, 'The Beach of Falesá', and though it may seem a big leap, from the Caribbean to the South Seas, from the seventeenth century to the late nineteenth, there are some telling points of comparison for any inquiry into the meaning of such marriages as Thomas Warner's and Madame Ouvernard.

In 1989 towards the end of his life, R. L. Stevenson sent the story to Clement Shorter in 1892, the editor of *The Illustrated London News*, whom it shocked deeply, so deeply, that to the fury of Stevenson, who did not know until after the fact, he censored it.[31] The story was not published in Britain in its complete form until 1979 in the Penguin Classic collection edited by Jenni Calder, though it had appeared unexpurgated in the USA in 1956.

Censorship can often touch those tender, distempered parts of a society, and it was the opening scene, in the chapter called 'A South Sea Island Bridal' that upset the earliest readers. Stevenson describes the arrival of a new white copra trader – Wiltshire – on the imaginary Polynesian island of Falesá, who is met by one of the veterans, a man named Case, one of Stevenson's most brilliantly realised villains. Case offers to fix Wiltshire with a native wife, and Wiltshire chooses Uma, while his pander comments, '*That*'s pretty' (emphasis added).[32] Case promises to arrange the 'marriage' and when Wiltshire demurs at this, assures him: 'Oh, there's nothing to hurt in the marriage Black Jack's the chaplin.'[33]

Uma arrives for the ceremony, which is to be performed in the house of the 'Captain', another of the scoundrels Stevenson records with such familiarity, and 'she was dressed and scented; her kilt was of fine tapa, looking richer in the folds than any silk; her bust, which was of the colour of dark honey, she wore bare, only for some half a dozen necklaces of seeds and flowers; and behind her ears and in her hair she had the scarlet flowers of the hibiscus.'[34] This picture, for all its Gauguin-like accessories, is quiet, recollected, and it leads without break in tone to the narrator's first glimmer of self-knowledge: 'She showed the best bearing for a bride conceivable, serious and still; and I thought shame to stand up with her in that mean house.'[35]

Black Jack is dressed up as a priest, and performs the service in English. Uma is given her wedding certificate:

This is to certify that Uma, the daughter of *Faavao*, of Falesá, island of –, is illegally married to *Mr. John Wiltshire* for one night, and Mr. John Wiltshire is at liberty to send her to hell next morning.[36]

The Illustrated London News removed this paragraph altogether. Later editions changed 'one night' to 'one week' (as if that showed willing at least). The barefaced breach of promise of 'The South Sea Bridal' stuck in the craw of a London editor in the 1890s and the tenor of the 'unwholesome' story disappointed a public expectant of Stevenson's more rollicking and heroic yarns. Yet it is another of his studies in gentlemanly hypocrisy, more nuanced and more poignant than the famous *Dr Jekyll and Mr Hyde*.

'The Beach of Falesá' then chronicles Wiltshire's gradual attachment to Uma, whose own sincerity and true affections and generosity of spirit contrast sharply with her husband's. Stevenson is too subtle a portraitist of human character to show Wiltshire's wholehearted redemption. He rather exposes through him the sexual exploitation that he had observed in the islands, and unravels its connections with trading and other forms of power.

Wiltshire says at a later point in the story that his name is pronounced Welsher [37] – but he does not in this instance 'welsh' on his promise, but decides to come square and marry Uma for real. When Mr Tarleton, a missionary, opportunely arrives on the island, Wiltshire commandeers him to perform a true wedding – tearing up the bogus and insulting contract; Uma first turns pale, crying 'Aué!' She thinks herself, at that moment, what Wiltshire knows he has already made of her – 'a maid beguiled'.[38]

Stevenson resists moral sentimentality and shows the trader hoping to profiteer to the end, and only restrained from cheating his customers by his bargain with the same preacher who married him and Uma truly in the sight of God. The pair remain married; Stevenson's impersonation of Wiltshire grows ever more the jocular Englishman abroad (he praises her as his 'A1 wife'), and ends with Wiltshire sending his 'eldest' – a boy – to Auckland to be educated, and worrying about his daughters:' the girls. They're only half-castes, of course; I know that as well as you do, and there's nobody thinks less of half-castes than I do; but they're mine, and about all I've got; I can't reconcile my mind to their taking up with Kanakas, and I'd like to know where I'm to find them whites?' [39]

Kanaka is the slang word in Stevenson's South Sea stories for islander: Uma is a Kanaka. 'The Beach of Falesá' would not hold the interest it does today as a clear-eyed setting forth of colonial bad behaviour if the ambivalence of traders' consciences ended with Welsher/Wiltshire's frustrated thieving and muddled prejudices. Stevenson develops Uma in the background – she speaks in pidgin throughout. This speech mimesis, at once childish and inaccessible, effectively muffles her for a reader unfamiliar with the dialect and the literary convention (which must have held true for Stevenson's contemporaries too). Since Stevenson names his characters meaningfully (Welsher/Wiltshire; Hyde hiding inside Jekyll) there may resonate in her very name the idea of Mother – You-Ma, or even, Ur-Ma, and her name gave the story its original title. Less fancifully, the genealogy Stevenson sets up polarises boys and girls in the same manner different gateways, inscribed 'Boys' and 'Girls' gave entrance to the same Victorian schoolyard. Uma appears in the story with her mother, Faavao, who is depicted as strange, almost bewitched; it emerges that she arrived on the island with Uma, trailing after a white trader: Uma's father is not mentioned. The last paragraph of the story implies that the boy who has gone to Auckland to be brought up an Englishman (it is implied) has escaped the condition of the half-caste, for whom Stevenson has Wiltshire so frankly declaring his distaste.

This contrast between the mothers, wives, daughters who remain of their race – or are named as mongrel – and the men who can be taught to belong reflects the polarity nature/culture which occupation of the newfoundland, or marriage to the native wife attempts to ease – by hyphenation. Stevenson's story also reverberates with another, interesting comment on South Sea Island arrangements in the story: when Wiltshire approaches the Captain's house for the mock wedding he tells us 'we had come into view of the house of these three white men: for a Negro is counted a white man, and so is a Chinese!' The narrator comments: 'A strange idea, but common in the islands.' [40] The category 'white man' does not denote complexion, or race (as do 'Negro' and 'Chinese' in the same sentence) but a social group, a perception of alliance, founded, the story will unfold, principally in economic interests and alliances. Stevenson in passing widens the standing metaphor of 'whiteness' to describe hierarchical arrangements – what would now be called 'the construction of race', just as the deponents in Philip Warner's trial were attempting to exclude 'Indian' Warner from the 'family' to which he had once been publicly admitted.

However, relative as Stevenson's perception of 'white' is in the story, and open as the category becomes in consequence to realignment, it implicitly excludes women. Indeed, when the villainous Case dies, his widow, to whom he has, against all expectations, left all his worldly goods, leaves to return to Samoa, to her own people: 'she was in a hurry to get home'. [41]

The female characters in the story are sexually moveable goods, commonly exchanged, lightly and callously without thought for their feelings, as the travesty of the original 'South Sea Island Bridal' shows. But their nativeness remains rooted in homeland, with all its associations with nature, and remains outside the embrace of the construction of 'white man'. The very name of the imaginary island, Falesá, means 'sacred house', and though it was used by Samoans for 'church', it may have reverberated, for Stevenson, with the idea of newly inaugurated home itself, to which women are the magical door, the enchanted means of access.

Uma's own mother, Faavao, for example, is marked out as uncanny, potent, an irrational force of nature and her entrance to the story is marked by her witchcraft and magic: 'a strange old native woman crawled into the house almost on her belly. She said no plain word, but smacked and mumbled her lips'. [42] Uma herself enjoys superior intimacy with the supernatural in her husband's eyes, even though her sweetness of character dilutes its dangerousness. Immediately after the false marriage, Wiltshire opens his new store, and finds that nobody comes to trade copra in exchange for his goods. The islanders stand away from him, staring, giving him the creeps, as Uma's mother did. He finds, from Case, that he is tabooed, or as good as, and that Uma is the culprit: alliance with her has, at this stage in the story, embroiled him in the native and alien world of magic and witchcraft.

The plot pivots on Case's manipulation of the islanders' beliefs: he is exploiting local legends about hauntings and enchantresses for his own ends and Stevenson's racy yarn focuses on Wiltshire's unmasking of Case. Stevenson has been criticised for portraying South Sea Islanders as vulnerable to colonial magic, gullible when a mockery is made of their own religious system, but again, 'The Beach of Falesá' contains, in this respect, another assumption regarding the place of women, all the more interesting because it appears to be unconscious. For the villainous Case has appropriated a local legend about women's powers of enchantment for his own ends. It is Uma, however, whom Stevenson chooses to pass it to Wiltshire, who protests at her credulity, and her people's.

The story tells how six youths had been shipwrecked on the coast of the island about six miles away: 'They were scarce set, when there came out of the mouth of one of the black caves six of the most beautiful ladies ever seen; and began to jest with these young gentlemen.' Only one of them refuses to join in the revels, and he alone is saved. For when the others return from the cave, 'they were all like drunken men, and sang and laughed in the boat and skylarked and the same night the five young gentlemen sickened, and spoke never a reasonable word until they died.' [43]

The enchantress who lives with her handmaidens in a lonely place, in a cave, on an island, has different names, and the South Seas is by no means the only place she is found. Demonesses with lovely faces, nymphs who turn into foxes, Circe in the *Odyssey*, Alcina in the Gerusalemme Liberata, the Sibyl of the Sibylline Mountains in Umbria in Italy, Venus of the Venusberg who tempts the knight Tannhaüser, all display their cloven hoof and much worse in the morning, after the first night of love, or in the aftermath of a thousand years of heedless bliss.[44]

It is as they say, an old story; a story as old as the hills. Was it a South Sea Island tale Stevenson had heard, or was he drawing on his own Scottish home lore about Tam O'Shanter and the nightroaming beauty who heartlessly consumes a mortal with her love? It does not matter, but it is significant that when Wiltshire is lying in the undergrowth waiting to ambush Case, his mind turns to the island folklore:

Little noises they were, and nothing to hurt; a bit of a crackle, a bit of a brush; but the breath jumped right out of me . It wasn't Case I was afraid of, which would have been common-sense; I never thought of Case; what took me, as sharp as the cholic, was the old wives' tales – the devil-women and the man-pigs. [45]

Then, he sees: 'There, coming right up out of the desert and the bad bush – there, sure enough, was a devil-woman, just the way I had figured she should look.' [46]

But it is (only) Uma, coming to find her husband and help him, whom he has mistaken for a sorceress of local legend (those overtones of 'the bad bush!'). The fear needs to be experienced by Wiltshire in the story because it is part of Uma's enchantment for him – it's part of sexual charm, part of 'nature' ipso facto, according to the construction of woman in such a narrative.

The legend is presented as local, but the migrations and metamorphoses of fairy motifs and tales of enchantment have charmed me for a long time, and when I was in the Museum Of Contemporary Art in Port of Spain in February 1995, I saw a group of sculptures by Louise Kimmé. Kimmé is German-born but now lives in Tobago, and she draws on Caribbean legends of soucouyants and sorcerers. Among the carvings was 'La Diablesse', the irresistible haunting enchantress of the night who wears flouncy clothes and a picture hat and charms her victims who do not realise that she is a devil-woman in disguise until it is too late. Kimmé's La Diablesse was appropriately dressed to the nines, with her cloven hoof peeping from under the frilly hem of her dress.[47]

Carlo Ginzburg, in *Ecstasise*, his study of witchcraft, analyses the recurrent motif of the limping shaman, or the sorceress with one hoof, or even Cinderella and her single glass slipper.[48] He sees such lopsidedness as the symbol of belonging in two worlds, of being able to gain access or give entrance to another sphere. Uma, once a 'maid beguiled', is mistaken for a devil-woman with magic powers; marriage to her and children with her have indeed opened the door to a new world for Wiltshire at many levels – emotional, social, familial, national.

Barbe/Madame Ouvenard created a connection between the native inhabitants and the English which 'Indian' Warner embodied; the conflicts around his identity, his place of belonging, reveal the way anxiety around the issues of nationality and race grew between the first encounter and the establishment of imperial power. In the struggle to define ever more tightly zones of inclusion and exclusion, women constantly disrupted the boundaries, offering different ways of belonging, giving a symbolic entrance to the enchanted cave of native land, offering alternative nativity stories.

Notes

1. Jean-Baptiste Labat, *Nouveau Voyage aux iles de l'Amérique*, 2 vols. (P. Husson *et. al.*: The Hague, 1624) quoted in Peter Hulme and Neil L. Whitehead, *Wild Majesty Encounters with Caribs from Columbus to the Present Day* (Oxford University Press, 1992) pp. 105-106.
2. See Aucher Warner, *Sir Thomas Warner Pioneer of the West Indies A Chronicle of His Family* (London, 1933); I am also grateful to Desmond Nicholson, of the Museum of Antigua and Barbuda's Historical & Archaeological Society, for his database of epitaphs and other documents related to the Warner family in Antigua.
3. Labat, op. cit., quoted in Hulme and Whitehead, op. cit., pp. 106-107.
4. Jean-Baptiste du Tertre, *Histoire Générale des Antilles Habitées Par les François*, 4 vols. (Paris: Thomas Jolly, 1667-71), 1: 128-129 (ck.).
5. I am adopting Hilary Beckles' usage here. See Hilary McD Beckles, 'Kalinago (Carib) Resistance to European Colonisation of the Caribbean', *Caribbean Quarterly* 38:2-3 (1992) pp. 1-124.
6. Ibid.; Aucher Warner, op. cit., pp. 35-36.
7. Du Tertre, op. cit., p. 1.
8. See for example Tzvetan Todorov, *La Conquête de l'Amérique La Question de l'autre*, (Paris: Seuil, 1982) pp. 131-134.
9. Peter Hulme, *Colonial Encounters: Europe and the Native Caribbean 1492-1797* (London: Routledge, 1986) pp. 137-173.
10. Aucher Warner, op. cit., p. 37 tells the story of Barbe, but discreetly, without connecting her to Thomas Warner in any special way.
11. Marina Warner, *Indigo* (London:Chatto & Windus, 1993). When Serafine passes on this interpretation of Ariel/Barbe's actions, she becomes the conduit of a false narrative, her own storytelling voice taken over, overwritten, as the names of Madame Ouvernard and her son 'Indian' Warner have also been written over by history. Serafine could not be otherwise than an unreliable narrator, because traditions change stories and individuals

on their own can't shape them outside of the frame of those traditions; but this moment, when she tells Miranda about Ariel's treachery, is intended to create one of the sharpest ironies in the book.

12. Giséle Pineau, 'Ecrire en tant que noire', in Maryse Condé and Madeleine Cottenet-Hage, eds *Penser la Créolité*, (Paris: Karthala, 1995) pp, 289-295.

13. Jean Bernarbé, Patrick Chamoiseau and Raphaél Confiant, *L'Eloge de la Créolité* (Paris 1989); discussed in A. James Arnold, in 'The gendering of *créolité* The erotics of colonialism', Conde and Cottenet-Hage, op. cit., pp. 21-40.

14. ibid., 61; p. 30.

15. In *Indigo*, Serafine as nurse, fulfils a similar role, because while she unwittingly colludes with the master narrative of empire, she also passes on to her charges – especially to Miranda – the strategies and the knowledge she needs to survive.

16. Ibid.

17. See Beckles, op. cit., p. 11.

18. Hulme and Whitehead, op. cit., pp. 104-105.

19. Ibid. p. 105.

20. Op. cit., pp. 89-106.

21. Public Record Office, Kew, papers: CO 1/22; CO 1/31, CO 1/34, CO 324/2, CO 1/35, CO 1/37. I am very grateful indeed to Rosemary Hall for her help in locating the documents, ordering copies and helping me to decipher them.

22. Russell, December 20, 1675, CO 1/35.

23. Ibid.

24. CO 1/35.

25. W. Noel Sainsbury, Preface, *Calendar of State Papers* Vol 9 (America and West Indies 1675-76) December 1893, p. li.

26. Russell, 20 December 1675, CO 1/35.

27. Lieutenant Choppin corroborates this story, but places Capt. Fletcher's meeting with 'Indian' in Antigua, and adds that he was 'employed, at fishing, & fowling .' Choppin, December 18, 1675, CO 1/35.

28. Hulme and Whitehead, op. cit., pp. 89-106.

29. Jenni Calder, ed., Robert Louis Stevenson: *The Strange Case of Dr Jeckyll and Mr Hyde and Other Stories* (London: Penguin, 1979), 'A Note on the Texts': 25: see also a richly detailed analysis of the bowdlerization in Barry Menikoff, *Robert Louis Stevenson and 'The Beach of Falesá': A study in Victorian Publishing* (Standford University Press, 1984) pp. 3-31.

30. Russell, CO op. cit.

31. Jenni Calder, ed., Robert Louis Stevenson, *The Strange Case of Dr Jeckyll and Mr Hyde and Other Stories* (London: Penguin, 1979), 'A Note on the Texts', p. 25.

32. Ibid. 'The Beach of Falesá', p. 104.

33. Ibid., p. 105.

34. Ibid., pp. 108-109.

35. Ibid., p. 109.

36. Ibid.

37. Ibid., p. 133.

38. Ibid., p. 131

39. Ibid., p. 169.

40. Ibid., p. 105.

41. Ibid., p. 168.

42. Ibid., p. 107.

43. Ibid., pp. 147-148.

44. See Marina Warner, *From the Beast to the Blonde: On Fairy Tales and Their Tellers* (London 1994) pp. 3-11.

45. Stevenson, op. cit., p. 161.
46. Ibid.
47. Christiane François took me to see the Collection – many thanks to her for her inspiring guidance; see also the children's book, Richardo Keens-Douglas, *La Diablesse and the Baby* (Buffalo: Firefly Books).
48. Carlo Ginzburg, *Ecstasies Deciphering the Witches' Sabbath* Trans. Raymond Rosenthal, ed. Gregory Elliott, (London: Hutchinson, 1989) pp. 122, 243-249, 305-307.

21

Sometimes You have to Drink Vinegar and Pretend You Think is Honey:

Race, Gender and Man-Woman Talk

Merle Collins

At a conference on the Caribbean short story held in Angers, France in January 1996, one presenter introduced some quotations from my short stories as examples of what she referred to as 'woman talk.' Among them were the following:

That one wasn't husband, was waste-band (Collins 1990: 77).

Tisane's mother always said, 'Don't wait on nobody to make you happy; especially not no man. Man, them is the most mix-up set of people the good Lord ever created! Dem does only think bout theyself. (Collins 1990: 25)

Tisane had said that you couldn't depend on fathers; usually they weren't there and visited only to shout and beat sometimes; Tisane had warned that on the whole children were better off without them. (Collins 1990: 16)

When man smiling for you is time to run, chile. Dat not nothing good. (Collins 1990)

And when Uncle Roy try to carry her on his back, Miss Doris say that Grannie say she rather sit down and make her peace with the Lord on the side of the road. Because is not only one home she have to reach, and if she could only reach one by riding on the back of some worthless man, she rather sit down and make her peace with the Lord by the side of the road (Collins 1990: 52).

It was a peculiarly unsettling experience sitting in that audience listening to the quotations being read. Many of the conference participants had not read my work, had not met the characters in the stories. As the only representative from that story-book world in the room, I took on the form of all my characters, or at least of that aspect of the characters that was being presented to them and I felt uncomfortable about the curious glances that were being turned my way. The chairman appeared to confirm my summary of the situation by his facial expressions, and, in his summary, by suggesting that discussion might be more easily directed towards the orality than towards the man-woman talk.

Afterwards, I tried to assess the reasons for my discomfort, I suppose that (1) I felt that the stories were about much more than these perceptions of gender relations and I wanted members of the audience to be interested enough to read them; (2) I wondered if in this environment people were less likely to recognise the Caribbean woman-man wisdom talk and so, without the stories, would have less on context within which to understand it; (3) knowing these characters, in the fictitious stories and the real-life stories that had created them, I understood completely how they had come to their philosophies, shared some of their opinions and was troubled by responses which seemed to suggest an inability to accept them for who they were. More than anything, I suppose, I was troubled by the possibility of having people judged on some slight knowledge of their existence.

From a very early age, man-woman talk shaped many of my perceptions of existence. The women in my family, who were the ones who did most of the talking and instruction that directed my early socialisation, taught me from the memories of their own experiences and by analyses of ongoing experiences. It was woman's talk about man, about relationships, about friendships, about race, class, gender, politics and society – about all of the things that had shaped and were continuing to shape their existence. For many things, they counselled assessing the situation and deciding accordingly.

Many a story began, ended or was punctuated by saying such as 'Child, sometimes you have to drink vinegar and pretend you think is honey' or 'Don't live on nobody eyelash so that when they wink you fall.' I want now to take a look at some of what I will call these 'vinegar stories' which have contributed, for me, to examining truth in fiction. These stories, of course, are inevitably dated, told in my own childhood, but rooted in the life experiences of my parents, some in the period of the 1940s and 50s. Dated, but reflecting the experiences of the storytellers, informing their worldview and mine, helping me to put the work around me into historical perspective and to understand how much the new carries within it essences of the old. One such story, a version of which I heard years ago, later created by the characters Doodsie and then Angel in my novel *Angel* (1987:203) and further recreated here, as stories always are when the space and the teller change, went roughly as follows: (The 'I' is the narrative voice of the storyteller of the time).

Vinegar-Honey Talk I

One time, I was working with a Scottish lady in Trinidad in Point Fortin. That lady was something. In those days, when you working in people house, is like they think you nothing, nothing at all. Some of them not too bad when you get to know them but I tell you, that one was a devil. She was disagreeable. When she see you working for her there, she sure, sure you is a thief. Because all who working is thief. She would pounce on you like a wasp. All those girls tell me that even the short time I work for her, I stay well long. Any time I open the fridge for a drink of water, she appear immediately and ask 'What do you want?' And some times I just hand her the glass and say 'a drink of water'. Let her get it for me. And then, you know, she handing you the water and watching you as if she sure is not that you really want. And the way she used to appear for the least little thing, is like she behind the door watching you. Fancy I working in the kitchen and I can't open the fridge. It come so I used to be looking over me shoulder before I do any little thing. After a time, I say, well, no. I want the work, is true, but people can't live like that. Look, eh, I couldn't even wash my clothes because I had to give account of every minute in every day. And you dare not rinse a dress in her house on her time. And the time I leaving the kitchen, no time to do anything for meself. And, you know, is only one weekend a month off. One time, you godmother, you musn't forget her, non, chile, the things she do for me in this life already! She come one time to take some clothes to wash for me. The lady see her going with the parcel and she call out to ask, 'Who is that? What is this she's taking away?' You know I had to call back H – to open the parcel so the lady could see? Is H – self that say after that, 'Non; you want the work is true, but we will have to find something else for you. You can't stay here.' So we look around, she help me, we talk to those other girls and is you see eventually I come and leave this place. The lady I work with after that was a good one, and the children was respectful and everything. A different kind of person entirely. But child, you see what I telling you? I just stay here and play dotish until I could settle meself better. All-you children don't known trouble, non. Sometimes you have to drink vinegar and pretend you think is honey.

The Theory

In the above story, I was taught, by listening, much of what the teller felt she had come to learn from her experiences were the truths of existence: White women for whom one worked often had little regard for black workers. Black people usually worked for whites and not the other way around. Race was often a major determining factor in social class. Sometimes, black workers accepted poor conditions not because they were unaware of the existence of better conditions, or even of the possibility of struggling to attain these, but because, especially when they were far from home, they had to adopt strategies which allowed them to plan for future advancement and at the same time earn a living, however meagre. I had learnt that solidarity between black women workers was important to improvement of their individual and collective circumstances. And the recurrence of certain factors in many of these stories taught me that white women often remained at home to administer the household while the white men of the household were out working elsewhere, so that racial and other contradictions were often manifested in the (white) household between the women of the different races. There was mutual suspicion and dislike between these two groups. The race and class contradictions between them did not allow for discussion of gender similarities. Both sets of women occupied the household space, but one worked in a role subordinate to the other and there was little room in this relationship for discussion of issues regarding gender. Perhaps there would be little honesty if the situation for such discussion presented itself. The class barriers prevented effective communication. The white woman was conscious of occupying a superior socio-economic position. The black woman recognised in the white woman one of the people responsible for her position of subordination. The white woman employer was a representative of her class and her race. She considered herself superior and there seemed to be no room in this relationship for exchanges about shared gender strategies. Race and class differences were the important determining factors in these social relations. The struggle the black woman saw for herself in her relationship with the white household was a long-term one. For the moment her apparent meekness would be a strength; she would use the space this gave her to develop the means to allow her to prepare her children for the type of education which would keep them away from domestic work and from subservience to white women in their household. The story that was presented to me here came not only from a particular race perspective but perhaps more specifically from the perspective of a class. My own early assessment about correspondence between race and class came from these stories and from noticing who were the people in positions of authority, what were their attitudes, what were their 'skin-tones' and what was the attitude of those closest to me when authority was around.

Vinegar-Honey Talk II

Where you come from this hour? Lessons? Child, speak the truth before you make me throw you to thy kingdom come, eh! I hear that sometimes when Mr T – don't have lessons, you and those other little devils does stay and play. So when you reaching here late, late telling me is lessons, is not lessons at all. You hanging you head? So is true! Eh? Well, child, you want to kill me? You know we living so far from the road that when you late I have to finish all me work and then walk all that distance to meet you! Eh? And look, I was even ironing tonight. You father not taking on. When he vex with you, he just sit down and don't bother and me, when I vex or not, he know I will come out, because I can't think of you, a little girl, in the road alone this time of night. Look at me! Inside there, I drinking vinegar and I playing is honey because I trying to make sure you put something in you head so you won't have to drink vinegar too. Eh? What happen to you at all? I tell you already this is man world, and you have to put something in you head to take care of youself. Look at you father! He working, is true, for those white people and they paying him next to nothing. But he working. At the end of the month, he stretch out his hand and they put a salary in it. Little as it is. And every day he come home and sit down and stretch out his foot and clear his throat and say how he tired and wait for meself that not tired to put his food on the table. At the end of the month, where me salary? None. I not working, you know. Is me planting peas around the house, is me planting tomato, is me watching the cocoa he put out to dry and pulling it in if rain come. But if anything sell is his, you know. The man own. And he might give me a dollar if he feel like it. The work I doing in the house self, that not work at all. Is so it is for woman. Always less. You never see those woman work in the field? They carrying heavy, heavy basket of cocoa and come end of the week, their salary less than the man own. And I could never done thinking that really unfair, especially when is cocoa-picking time. Those man stand up there with a cocoa-knife juking down the cocoa. And then later on when the cocoa basket full now, the man self helping the woman to lift it put on her head and carry it down in the yard. Come time for pay, the woman pay less than the man own. Why? Because she is woman. You hear what I telling you? She banning she belly to carry the load on her head but the bigger pay is his just because he is man. Under the cocoa, those woman don't work less than man. But you see? You hear what I telling you? Unless you put something in you head, you worth nothing as woman. So I warning you, I don't want that for you. But you have to want something for youself, too. I telling you so you know what to expect. Well look at trouble here, non! You stay and play? I tell you already man is boss, you know. They having two, three woman and all working for them. Sit down there and play stupid. I drinking vinegar, child, and I only playing I think is honey because I see a future for you. So I tell you!

The Theory

All workers are in a subordinate socio-economic situation and heavily exploited but women are additionally exploited on the grounds of gender. In the everyday existence of the black working woman, there is no 'weak feminine' stereotype, but the monetary reward suggests that women are considered weaker and less valuable as workers. Women are exploited by both the dominant socio-economic group and by their own men, i.e., men who are in a socio-economic situation similar to theirs. This usually means men of their race. Women are considered inferior because of their gender and unless they can find ways of breaking out of the mould, service to men is their destiny. Education, which provides preparation for the working world, is one sure way of breaking out of the mould. The better prepared one is educationally, the more likely it is that one would be able to escape the particular forms of oppression against one's class, one's race and one's gender. Because women have experienced gender oppression, they are more sensitive than men are to this particular form of exploitation and more likely to be supportive of other women and concerned about the socialisation of girls, whom they recognise to be vulnerable of their gender.

In the telling of these stories, one also learnt about organisational strategies. Talk about men and their attitudes to women were usually in all-female groups, or one to one female discussion. In such groups, one heard that men were often indisciplined in relationships; women shouldn't be. The woman who was, acquired a damaging reputation. The man acquired a reputation which might be a source of pain to the particular woman who was married to him or was 'in house with him'. Other women, and the society at large, might speak in terms of reprimand, but his indiscipline did not seriously damage his reputation or make him unattractive to women. It could even make him more attractive, since this notoriety, was also deemed to be a sign of the virility expected in men. In stories about such men, one often heard the resigned comment, 'is so man is already'. And so men (and women) learnt that indiscipline in sexual relationships was a sign of manliness, a proof of virility. In spite of the apparent analysis that these were man's natural instincts, however, these stories were always told in a tone which suggested to me that there was resentment of these male instincts.

This type of story/talk helped to shape my perspectives of existence and continue to influence my approach to theory. Because of that early introduction to theory and its relation to practice, I am sometimes suspicious of theorising words (political, sociological, etc.) for which I cannot think up a story. When, in my real-life stories, I heard of a white woman's distaste for and cruelty towards the mixed-race child who worked in her kitchen because she was the offspring of her husband or her husband's relative, I shared in the teller's hurt that this woman was 'like a devil', but wondered too about the white woman's feelings in this situation. But stories always change with the re-telling. Perhaps I did not wonder then; perhaps that wondering comes with the benefit of my distance now from the story. Distance, that is, time and experience. The efforts of my forebears have ensured that I do not have to work in the white woman's household and so am not exposed on an intimate, in-house basis to the race and class antagonisms which made discussion and identification on the basis of gender a near impossibility. Perhaps that is why I am even considering the white woman's perspective on this. I say 'near' and not 'total' impossibility, because there were stories, too, of those white women who were not too bad to deal with and whose husbands 'make them so shame' by going with 'any and everybody'. The fact that these white women displayed some humanity made sympathy and understanding that 'man is man' possible. Race and class differences, however, made it difficult to share these experiences based on gender.

'When I heard that the bossman was nicer than the lady to deal with but that his 'hand was too fast for his own good', I learnt about the complexities of gender relations in what might be called a colonial situation. When I heard that white women employers gave gifts of old cards and old pictures which workers accepted with smiles because 'you have to know where you bread butter', I learnt about pragmatism in these apparently untenable situations.

What all of this says to me, therefore, is that it is easier to discuss commonalities that exist because of gender when you are no longer in an intimate subordinate situation that forces a focus on the race and class contradictions. In other words, sitting in an international forum discussing gender, I am conscious that race and class are not factors to be forgotten, that as a black woman who has had access to formal education, I am discussing questions of gender with people whose interests would otherwise be far removed from time. That if I were working as a domestic in their homes, or as a shop-floor worker in their business places, I would be less likely to be concerned about our commonalities based on gender. Class differences can make gender identification difficult. I have heard vinegar-honey stories by white women shaped on class experiences similar to mine. These stories of female relatives working as domestics, how they were treated and how they socialised their offspring are remarkably similar. In one case, the complicating factor was nationality – Irish/English, a distinction which is important in Britain, but would have had little significance to me growing up in the Caribbean. Even in Britain, now, these stories told on a one-to-one basis create quite an impression, because in a more open public space, race would generally separate me from working-class white people who may have been shaped by vinegar-honey stories focusing on class and gender.

Variations on my particular vinegar-honey stories doubtless inform the attitudes of all Caribbean people, women and men. The emphases – on race, class or gender would vary depending on the race and class of the teller. Those (white, black, African, Indian, Portuguese, etc.) who employed servants would doubtless have different stories to tell. The white Caribbean woman's talk about men, gender and race would also be a different one. And there were black people who did not have the experience of work on the plantations and who employed servants. There were, too, those who started off working in the homes of others and later employed people in their own homes. The experience is rarely one-dimensional.

So what does all of this teach us? How does it/should it inform our thinking on issues of race, class and gender in the Caribbean? Whether or not we state it explicitly in our analyses, these private stories shape our discourse and our (Caribbean) responses to international discourses. Every forum I attend, I carry with me the legacy and lessons of my particular set of historical perspectives. When I hear talk of solidarity among women, the images that flash across the screen of my imagination are those of employers and workers, women with formal education and women without, white women, black women, three young Polish girls who seemed to appear from nowhere to startle my schooldays to an awareness of poverty among whites. And I know that the talk in a 'learned forum' is infinitely different to the vinegar-honey talk of the streets and the houses wherever those streets and houses may be.

I am constantly conscious, too, that the vinegar-honey experience is still with us, the world over; complicated by issues of race, class and gender. Some Caribbean women who, because of their socio-economic status, would not be domestics in their own countries, often work as domestics in places such as the USA and Canada. Issues which these women would generally not discuss with women workers in their own homes, their (usually white) women employers would generally not discuss with them. These race and class issues, nationally and internationally, make it impossible to attain easy globalisation of women's issues. In whatever forum women are organising, or discussing the possibility of cooperation, specificities have to be given room for expression. If even there is no one present or willing to express them, it is useful to take them into consideration when examining gender ideologies.

The time spent in various countries and with various experiences has transformed and re-shaped, but not changed the essence of my early influences. To some extent there is always a return for contextualisation of the present. It is a bit unnerving, therefore, when I can sense that characters speaking from the world of my fiction are being measured against the various labels that inform the race and gender discourses of the 1980s and 1990s. It is understandable, of course, and perhaps even necessary, but unnerving, nonetheless.

When, in the aftermath of the 1983 collapse of the Grenada experiment with revolutionary politics, I came to write my first novel *Angel*, I realised that a great deal of the formal political interaction in this fictitious recreation was among the males; a lot of the informal political interaction and psychoanalytical assessment was centered around the women. This reflects not only much of modern formal political realities but also my experience as a young woman growing up and observing the overt and covert leaders. After passing on all of the strong discipline and socialising influences of their stories, women often made comments like, 'I don't have the strength to handle you; when you father come, he will deal with you.' And so the overt expression of physical authority, superiority by virtue of physical strength and gender, was left to the 'dominant' male. And the man-woman attitudes in the home translate to man-woman talk and man-woman attitudes in the wider arena of the society.

Man, ruler by virtue of his gender, shaped the formal political pro-
nouncements of the time and continues, largely, to shape them today.
The political leaders, formally educated or not, were male. The mantle of
political leadership passed from white males to black males. Our (Caribbean) formally educated writers of political and other treatises were first
of all largely male. And naturally what fed into perspectives presented to
the nation were their (male) experiences. But there were several places
in which their experiences coincided with those of the women. Everyone,
whatever their opinions might be, could relate to discussions about race
and class and how those were expressed in the colonial condition. People
might have varying class perspectives, but there was a framework for
analysis. But gender was a different issue.

Because women were not in these leadership positions, their perspectives on gender were generally not part of the equation; and male leaders
were not particularly interested in gender because they had little cause
for complaint about their position – 'who feels it knows it', a well-worn
and well-applicable cliche. The men, while perhaps not necessarily plot-
ting to keep the question of women's subjugation out of the equation
where socio-economic and political change was concerned, were just not
touched by these concerns. Therefore, when the women of my early
socialisation were declaring the importance of formal education to escape
from subjugation, they were also, perhaps inadvertently, declaring the
importance of women utilising the opportunities provided them by their
formal education to write themselves into the equation of existence. Given
women's knowledge of their experiences, it might be expected that those
who eventually had the opportunity to do so would promote the importance of equal pay for equal work, would be interested in issues of property
rights for women, would be concerned about how women and their male
partners were interacting in relationships. So that those who insisted on
formal education for women against the prevailing notions of the day
were contributing directly and indirectly to the empowering of women.
Those women who told their vinegar-honey stories were also doing that.

The vinegar-honey stories helped to put certain organisational strategies into perspective. Stories about the nature of men and advice about
what might be expected of men in relationships would be told when only
women and girls were present. It was always made clear that the boys
who were in the family were important too, but 'they start off as boss
already' and so, it was felt, (perhaps wrongly) didn't need the kind of
stories that the girls needed. In any event, it was woman-story about man
and so men, it was felt, should not be present. These things were not

verbalised, but spoke themselves in the silences when men and boys approached.

Stories about employers, on the other hand, were everybody's. Even if the women began these stories, men participated with their versions if they were there or if they arrived during the telling. Men spoke of their experiences as yard-boys, drivers, (both heads of field gangs and chauffeurs), field workers. They spoke, too, of how women helped by giving them a little extra from the kitchen to eat sometimes; women spoke of how men would at times provide them with a little extra from the fields or the yard. Both talked about details of their employers' lives gleaned from the house and the field. In these interchanges, there might be open comment about the fact that 'so-and-so who used to work in the kitchen' was actually the child of the boss's brother. There might be comments, too, about the Madam's dislikes of this worker/niece. But while this kind of comment might be made in the presence of everyone, only women's ears would hear a subsequent comment such as, 'this man you see I have there, he have all the boss habits. Is so he running after every woman that working under him in this little position they give him'. These women story-tellers knew what experiences they shared in common and unless confronting the men, were silent in their presence about perceptions which they didn't share. Discussions on gender were women's business. Discussions about race and class were everybody's business. It is not surprising, given that it operated this way in private spaces that it translated similarly into public spaces.

During the period 1979 to 1983, when Grenadian political leaders were trying to pursue a revolutionary ideal, the anti-colonial ethos, incorporating race and class in their various manifestations, was every leader's concern. The male revolutionary leadership also gave broad support to women's rights. As time moved on, however, it became clearer that the women were the ones who would have to struggle to ensure that gender was, in practice, not an important sideline, but equal with race and class in the anti-colonial agenda as part of the push towards changes that might be considered revolutionary. Male revolutionary leaders seemed to have no trouble giving broad theoretical support to the idea of women's rights. Increasingly, however, women perceived that it was more difficult when it came to inter-personal relationships and the practical application of ideas. Public shows of support were easier to come by; equal pay for equal work, certainly. Promotion and adoption of a maternity leave law, yes. There were more problems regarding how all of this translated into the domestic arena. Were children more the woman's responsibility? If both had to attend meetings but care for the children was also necessary, was it more important that the man went? Were several simultaneous relationships on the part of men a sign of sexism? Did it imply disrespect for women?

A once private 1982 letter from the Women's Committee of the New Jewel Movement(NJM) to the Political Bureau is now in the public domain and so can be quoted freely, hopefully contributing to our understanding of the socialisation which can prevent/has prevented male political leaders from taking gender issues seriously. Some extracts from the letter (1982) read as follows:

When some women party members raise the problems of having no one to leave their babies with at 5:00 a.m. or no one to get the children breakfast or ready for school, the attitude of many heads of PCB's (Parish Council Boards), Committee and study groups has frequently been that 'you just have to solve that problem'. As a result, some women members have been deemed 'indisciplined' as a result of missing meetings, others have taken serious risks with their children, like leaving babies in the care of young children of 10 to 12 years, some have faced the criticisms of the masses for 'neglecting' their children. Recently, an incident occurred when a sister from St Andre's was kept at a meeting in town till 6:30 p.m. On returning to St Andrew's she found the Day Nursery shut and spent 2 hours searching frantically to find out where the nurses lived to recover her child.

Where, one might ask, are the children's fathers? The letter subsequently goes some way towards answering this by expressing concern about fathers, even when they share the home, do not take equal responsibility for children and when they do, pay little attention to making the financial contributions necessary for daily care of the children. The fathers thus criticised were the 'revolutionary' fathers who were working actively in other areas to further the anti-colonial goals of the Party.

The letter also urges these politically aware men to change their attitudes towards women in interpersonal relationships and to avoid displays of their sexuality designed to intimidate women into accepting their point of view.

None of this is surprising or unexpected, given what the vinegar-honey stories suggest. Additionally, the letter acknowledges that 'Party members will not all change overnight' and recognises 'the real effort and progress made by our senior Party members in overcoming male chauvinist attitudes'. It recognises, then, that the men referred to here are the products of the society which socialised them. The vinegar/honey stories heard by these men from women focused on race and class, not on gender.

The letter from the Women's Committee came from people who, now operating also in the public domain, may not have felt they could achieve much on the question by pretending that the vinegar given to them was honey. Perhaps once it had been necessary to keep up this pretence to make one's way towards the places and times that would allow for open expression of views. But the time, it must have been assessed, had come for woman-man talk to say, this vinegar not really honey, you know. And is honey we want.

Perhaps official reticence about confronting gender issues reflected not only male leadership strategies to avoid certain forms of accountability but also a society's reticence about discussing 'private' matters. The very idea of including gender issues in public discussions violates the secret codes that were used for these discussions in early socialisation. But strategies have to be different. In those years of my early socialisation, few people operated in the public domain or in public life generally. Now that they do, they bring with them the 'secrets' from their private spaces. It is understandable, therefore, that gender discussions will become public, that attitudes based on perceptions of gender will be challenged. That woman from different classes, having had very divergent experiences, will have various things to say and widely differing perceptions about issues.

In recognising the commonalities among women, women's movements and those concerned with women's issues, have also to recognise the wide divergencies. There cannot be and there need not be an easy globalisation. As a black woman in London, I found it easier to speak about my experiences of race and class there with black men than I did with white women. Where women's issues were concerned, I was conscious when I spoke to Caribbean women, whether they shared my views or not, that they understood better the context in which they developed.

For me, an important dimension to all of this discussion about gender is finding the practical framework to work out ideas about this issue. In my novel *Angel*, the character Angel eventually finds a framework for grappling with her ideas about race and class. Her ideas about gender remain essentially internalised, finding no open space for fruitful growth. Throughout the novel, both Angel's sexuality and her opinions about gender remain generally subjects for the private spaces. She is uneasy in her reaction with men because the vinegar-honey stories of her socialisation have made them suspect. Since no public space is created in the novel for engagement with these suspicions, they remain largely unexplored, affecting Angel's response but, true to her socialisation, not usually being confronted in her association with me. In the novel, Angel seems to have succumbed to the opinion that 'is so man is already', and, perhaps having decided that she is uncomfortable with what is, chooses not to challenge or engage with the woman-man dichotomy in the same way that she does with the race and class issues. Hopefully this is not a reflection of how race, class and gender will be handled outside of the world of the novel. It is still largely not there as part of the race/class issues in the public political spaces; hopefully it will be.

 When I come to engage with theory, I find it useful to bring it all back to the practice, to contextualise it by remembering the stories that shaped me. I guess this is socialisation again. I often think of another favorite saying among relatives who wanted to ensure that formal education, while necessary to keep pace with the tenor of the timess, did not make one too cocksure: sense make before book.

22

Ram and Sita:

The Reconstitution of Gender Identities among Indians in Trinidad through Mythology

Patricia Mohammed

Indian Mythology and Gender Imagery

There is no agreement between Eastern and Western scholars on the date of the Sanskrit sacred literature which informs both Indian mythology and Hindu philosophy and religion. The body of sacred and secular literature which contains among other works the songs of the *Vedas*, the *Upanishads*, the *Bhagavad Gita*, the *Mahabharata* and the *Ramayana*, are believed to have been written before 300 BC, during 3000 years of uninterrupted Sanskrit culture in India. This literature in its many forms of verse and prose, are metaphorical depictions of the history of a society. While they are presented as allegory, the stories retold in these books are believed to have been based on historical fact, telling as it were of great wars between one ruler and the next, the conflicts within kinship groupings of men and women, and the battleground on which contemporary India was constructed. The action in the stories is interwoven with symbolic meaning and they have provided the sources through which Indian culture has been interpreted and reinterpreted with continuity and change over the centuries.

India is a vast continent and the references to India in this study invariably bring to mind the complexity of any sphere of culture in India. For the kind of research and analysis being carried out in this brief essay, largely dealing with the *longue duree* interpretation of gender ideology, I have had to be selective in my treatment of India. There was undoubtedly great regional variations in the ideology of gender and the practices within India itself, as interpreted by different caste groupings and the different sexes in India. In addition to geographical variation between regions within India, there were also even larger variations between rural and urban India. Nor were attitudes and rules regarding gender ideology static in the history of Indian society. Meera Kosambi points out that in Maharashtra, subjugated by English political supremacy in the early nineteenth century, by 1829 the custom of *sati* or widow burning was abolished, the legal sanction regarding the remarriage of Brahmin widows was removed and the practice of female infanticide was abolished, raising the minimum age for consummation of marriage by 1891. Kosambi observes that these shifts were major ones in the eyes of the law, but relatively minor in practice and in the status of women in general in India. Few women actually challenged these patriarchal ideas established over centuries. Few had the means to challenge these practices.[1] To establish a schematic idea of the gender system from which Indian migrants came, and to depict the actual shifts which were taking place within the period 1917 to 1947, I have focused on a framework which emerges as the dominant ideas of the gender system in India, those which in my view superseded regional variations and which influenced the basis for the continuation of patriarchy.

This treatment of India as regards Hinduism and a system of gender relations appears supported by Nirad Chaudhuri's consideration of the significance of geographical diversities. He comments that there is a great temptation in writing on Hinduism to avoid problems by representing one form as the sole or complete expression of the entire religious complex. 'Nonetheless' he notes, 'the geographical diversities should not be over-emphasised. They have not created any exclusive loyalty to a particular regional form. No south Indian will think that the Benares or the Ganges is less sacred to him than Madura or Cauveri, and in exactly the same way no north Indian will undervalue the sacred places or rivers in the south. Hindus, wherever they might live, have a uniform and coherent outlook on religion'.[2] I am persuaded to follow this line of analysis in Trinidad not only by Chaudhuri's more familiar knowledge of the religious culture of India, but also by relating this reading to my own understanding of the practices and rituals associated with Hinduism in this society. The major differences among Hindus which emerged in Trinidad were in the third decade of the twentieth century when the Arya Samaj sect began to enjoin Hindus to challenge ideas of caste and the subordinate status of women.[3]

Hindu mythology has influenced all peoples who lived in India. Hindu religion and mythology are closely intertwined and in conflating the two, it can be argued that I am too easily dispensing with characteristics specific to the other religious groupings. Nirad Chaudhuri argues that Hindu mythology has been the most serious obstacle in the way of understanding Hinduism as a religion' and that the relationship between Hindu mythology, cults and devotion are complex, sometimes coinciding, often independent of one another. Chaudhuri observes that this inability to separate religion from mythology is not at all confined to Hinduism, but can be found in all Indo-European religions, especially those of the Greeks and Romans.[4] He points out that there is a fusion between Hinduism as a religion as well as a cultural source of inspiration which fed directly into the national identity of Indians in India. During the first half of the twentieth century, Hindu mythology was equally resilient as a cultural and political force in Trinidad, despite the differences which emerged later on in the new society among the different religious groups. To be Indian, whether one was Hindu, Muslim or Christian, was still to identify with symbolic aspects of Indian culture which predated the development of contemporary Hinduism in India.

Myths have a tenacious hold on the reproduction of a culture and they provide a fundamental framework for gender identities as they are being beaten into shape by each passing generation. The reasons for their tenacity must be sought in an understanding of the origins and use of myths by human society and the symbols they generate, 'the purpose of the myth being to provide a foundation for the rite'.[5] The influence of the myth and symbol on the human mind is that it does not only function at the conscious level, but is absorbed into our unconscious acceptance of reality. Among the many facets of culture which are passed on through myth, religion, symbol and ritual is the lexicon of gender. What each culture perceives as the paradigm for masculinity, femininity and gender relations has been derived from its mythology and reinforced in each new historical phase through religion and ideology. Mythology provides a blue print for gender identities in each culture.[6] This transmission of gender ideology is also carried over in other religions as for instance through Christianity in its written texts the Old and New Testaments. Similarly, for other groups, it may be transmitted through folk tales, traditional rituals and religion which are carried over to new societies not as written texts but in custom and practices. This was perhaps the way in which African mythologies and ideas regarding gender were transferred into the new setting of the Caribbean and persisted despite the debilitating experience of slavery. There is need for more research to be developed in this area.

The sacred and romantic Sanskrit literature interwoven with idealism and practical wisdom, was an expression of the spiritual vision of Indian culture. Thus we find the derivative of 'Sanskritisation', a process which brings groups outside of Hinduism into the fold and raises the cultural status of groups already within it. The notion of Sanskritisation ensured the continuity and unity of Indian culture, despite movements away from India. This continuity and unity also provides another reason for the transposition of strong gender identities within the culture. The mythological ideas and symbols which had shaped masculinity and femininity in Indian society continued to inform the construction of gender identities in new societies where Indians migrated. For the Indians who settled in Trinidad from the middle of the nineteenth century onwards, what were regarded as the holy texts were derived from both a classical and contextual mode, the classical based on the original literary sources, and the contextual offering variations depending on the areas from which the migrants had come. The variations in myth, symbol and ritual, like that of language as well, moved to standardisation and selective adaptation by those who conveyed them. The migrants in Trinidad, drew on their collective history to reconstruct their lives away from India. The collective ways in which migrant groups reconstruct their ideologies mediates differences which are derived from regional variations. In Trinidad, a relatively small number of migrants had been brought to Trinidad from India and drawn largely from the United Provinces of central India, and despite differences, the levelling nature of the indentureship system forced onto this group of migrants a need to consolidate a language[7] and tradition which superseded regional differences of practices and rituals. To a large extent these were retold by oral scribes, the few who were learned or literate. Here, as with all oral forms of transmission, they were selectively shaped and molded by the tellers of these myths, both consciously and unconsciously, in their own patriarchal interests. Thus was replicated the dominant ideas regarding gender among Indians: the superiority of Ram and the subservience of Sita.

The *Bhagavad Gita*, the *Ramayana* and the *Mahabharata* in their present forms make up a compendium of mythological narratives and religious information which embodies the spirit of the first few centuries of Aryan settlement in India. The *Mahabharata*, for example, a vast epic of over 100,000 couplets, is the longest poem in the world, about 30 times as long as Milton's *Paradise Lost*. The main story of the *Mahabharata* centres around forces of good and evil represented as the Pandavas and the Kuravas, two dynasties of Indian kings. Nirad Chaudhuri writes of the compendium that although it has undergone several interpretations, it remains a most dependable source of legends of the Indo-Aryans.[8]

The Persian version of the *Mahabharata* is dated ad 1761-63. The *Ramayana*, in the rendition incorporated into the *Mahabharata* relates the story of Rama, the eldest son of King Ayodhya. An envious stepmother, who covets the throne for her own son, causes Ram to spend 14 years in exile in the forest accompanied only by his loyal brother Laksmana and his devoted wife Sita who was married to him when she was six-years-of-age. During this period Sita is kidnapped by Ravana (Rawan), the demonic king of Sri Lanka. With the help of allies Rama eventually defeats Ravana and rescues Sita. Though Sita has remained faithful to Rama throughout her long captivity, Rama does not accept her back before she had proved her chastity through a fire ordeal. Sita, ever obedient to her husband, enters the fire 'in the presence of gods and men' and Agni, the god of fire himself, returns her, unharmed, to Rama. Rama is crowned and embarks on a glorious reign, with Sita as his queen. Yet, after some time, a washerman in the city whose wife had been absent from home for one night refuses to take her back, saying, he was not like the king who took his wife back after she had spent years in another man's house. With this gossip starts and though the gods themselves have vouched for Sita's honour, and she is by then carrying Rama's child, he banishes her to the forest.[9]

The story of Sita and Rama enjoys enormous popularity all over India and elsewhere Indians have migrated, to this day. Rama provides the model on which Indian masculinity is constructed through mythology, Sita embodies femininity, the ideal of female love and devotion and a lesson to all women on how they should behave in their daily lives. This obsession with female chastity which condemns a woman even on the basis of the most unfounded gossip, permeates the whole concept of Hindu marriage and Hindu religion. It is the wife's chastity which protects her husband and thereby his honour. This provides the most compelling argument for the retention of child marriage in India, as an unmarried girl who had entered puberty was considered at risk of sexual involve-ment, and a disgrace to the family if she got pregnant. Thus the male patriarchal order is configured as contingent on women's acceptance and collusion with the control of female sexuality.

The narratives of the *Ramayana* were ever present in the oral and written culture of the Indians who migrated from India to Trinidad as labourers under the system of indentureship. This system lasted from 1845 to 1917, and over 143,000 Indians were brought to Trinidad. During the period of indentureship the majority of Indians under contract lived in barracks on the estates. In the early post-indentureship period there was a rapid acceleration in the reconstitution of villages and communities, and with this the re-emergence or consolidation of many of the customs and traditions which were brought from India. In this period the unbalanced sex ratio which characterised the system of indentureship had not evened out. Women were still in shorter supply and very important both to the physical reproduction of this group as well as the reproduction of ritual. This shortage of women and the general disruption of cultural norms and traditions, of family and kinship networks and of institutions which jealously guarded structured identities like caste and gender, allowed femininity to define itself outside of boundaries which confined it in India. Some women challenged the idea of monogamy and went about choosing their own husbands and leaving one for another if it suited them. This challenge obviously affected the capacity of the patriarchal contract received from India to be reinstated in Trinidad society in its entirety.

What was the patriarchal contract in Trinidad in 1917? There co-existed three patriarchal systems simultaneously in Trinidad at this time, all competing with each other. These were the dominant white patriarchy which also controlled state power as it existed then, the 'creole' patriarchy or that functioning (and also emerging) in the other dominant group - the Africans – and, by now, a mixed [10] group significant in the population of Trinidad, and finally that found among the Indian population which had brought its cultural baggage from India. What were the interactions of these systems and why did they affect the consolidation of an Indian community? I am proposing the existence of a hierarchy among these three co-existing patriarchal systems, and that Indian men found themselves at the lowest end of this ladder. They were still largely agricultural labourers, even though in this area they had already begun to establish themselves as landowners and peasant farmers. They had only just entered the arena of national political struggles, and they had not yet produced a significant crop of educated or professional men who could compete evenly with other men for other resources on the wider social scale. Thus the patriarchal contract as it existed in Trinidad in 1917 was that of a competition between males of different racial groups, each jostling for power of one sort or the other - economic, political, social status and so on. In the face of a hegemonic control by the white group and another kind of dominance by the 'creole' population, the contestation was both a definition of masculinity between men of different races, and for Indian men to retrieve a ruptured patriarchy from the ravages of indentureship and thus be better placed to compete in this patriarchal race. This required a consolidation of the traditional patriarchal system brought from India. The question is, why was a consolidation of the latter so important to the Indian community as a whole?

The answer can again be sought in the conditions which affected all Indians – male and female – despite their internal divisions by language, religion, caste, and area of origin. It was important for the Indian community to constitute itself in Trinidad, only now emerging from the derided positions they found themselves in during the system of indentureship. The symbolic boundaries which comprise community among migrants can very rarely be articulated in discrete categories as they emerge alongside and in conjunction with other struggles in the same society. In Trinidad, I am proposing that the boundaries of a gender system based on the 'classic' patriarchy from which Indians had emerged, became one of the significant markers which identified the difference of the Indian community from others in the society. Thus it was important for the Indian male, emasculated in part by the demeaning conditions of indentureship, to re-establish in the new society a system of power relations between the sexes which clearly reinforced the old patriarchal order – male dominance and female subservience.

Our needs as human beings, whether male or female are not determined by our gender alone. Indian women were not indifferent to the re-establishment of their familiar culture and they colluded with men to a large extent, building institutions and re-establishing norms which appeared to other groups in the society to be particularly oppressive to themselves. For instance, child marriages were arranged by both parents, mothers-in-law controlled their daughters-in-law, and sons were still given the best opportunities for advancement in the family. The use of the word 'colluded' here conveys the impression that this was a conscious and rational choice on the part of women and a calculated and deliberate policy on the part of men. We cannot always read into these actions in human history a consciousness raised by contemporary definitions and practice but see them as a calculated response to material and emotional circumstances in which people find themselves through the accidents of history. Realistically, Indian culture as it was being reconstituted in Trinidad, was never purely reconstructed from the original blueprint derived from India. The influences of gender ideology and practices from the other groups, especially that of the dominant African group, posed a major threat to the Indian patriarchy and provided one other source of disaffection between these groups in the society. Indian women had during the period of indentureship challenged the fundaments of patriarchy by flouting the ideals of monogamy required for women, and even more troubling were the incidents of women who married or mated with non-Indian men, particularly men of African descent. Nonetheless, this hybridisation of East and West, the latter which includes African forms carried over to Trinidad, did not fully tamper with the reconstitution of an Indian gender system. This is supported by evidence from historians who remarked on the absence of any reported liaisons between Indians and Africans before 1900,[11] and later, into the twentieth century, by Colin Clarke who points out that as late as 1960 'the evidence shows small increases in urban exogamy by race, yet Indian rural endogamy has scarcely altered over the years'. [12]

Reconstitution as a community required for both Indian men and women in the first half of the twentieth century a consolidation of the classic patriarchal system brought from India. In Trinidad, the boundaries of a gender system based on the 'classic' patriarchy from which Indians had emerged, became one of the significant markers which identified the difference of the Indian community from others in the society. The way in which this was done was through a masculine assertion of power in Indian gender relations, and for a masculine definition of the Indian community to emerge in the contestation of patriarchy in the wider society of Trinidad. The mythology, which informed religion was one of the main sources through which a framework for gender relations between Indian men and women was reintroduced into the new setting.[13]

Conveyors of Myth and Symbols

The most important venues for transmission were the prayer meetings and religious festivals where the Hindu *pundits* (and later Muslim *imams*) would have before them a captive audience. The system of indentureship made little distinction between caste of Indians, other than to attract primarily those of the lower castes who were thought to be more suited to agricultural labour. On the estates and villages, those who claimed to be *Brahmin*, and were learned, were automatically adopted by the indentured, and later free population, as religious leaders of the Hindu population. As the *pundits* and *imams* were the transmitters of these myths and the purveyors of ritual knowledge, it was no coincidence that the symbols and images of women which were focused on are those which ensured a patriarchal stronghold.[14] The conveyors of these sacred texts had the opportunity to profoundly influence the construction of gender. It is instructive to examine the effects of one such festival.

By the second decade of the twentieth century festivals conveying the messages of the religion in a more accessible form, were of tremendous importance to the Indian community and attracted entire villages. 'People in this village know more about the *Ramayana* not from what they read but from going to the Ramleela' (Majaraj 1987:12). The *Ramleela* was an open air festival which lasted for several days.[15]

The drama which unfold from day to day enacts Book VI of the *Ramayana*, the section in which Sita is lost, and wooed by Rawan disguised as a hermit. It tells of her kidnap and subsequent discovery by Rama. The part which this section emphasises to the mixed audience of men and women, boys and girls, is that Sita maintains her fidelity to Rama despite all the clever advances of Rawan. The lesson to women is one of monogamy, chastity and devotion to the husbands chosen for them by their parents and elders. By 1934, the festival of *Ramleela* was an entrenched part of Indian culture in Trinidad. The *Sunday Guardian*, 21 October, 1934 reports on the end of the Ramleela festival held at Waterloo Estate Savannah 'her gaiety and enthusiasm ran free among thousands who took part in this ancient and sacred drama'. In addition it was reported that the festival was simultaneously being held at Dow Village, California, that it had begun on Tuesday October 9th, at the Tacarigua savannah and came to an end on Thursday last and that 'The Hindu festival of Ramlilla [16] has it final celebration at Cedar Hill Estate Savannah on Wednesday last, and in spite of the inclement weather there was a large gathering. The scene was reminiscent of on Oriental Pageant.'

This excursion into mythology is not to be taken merely as a speculative digression for we must appreciate the significance of mythological imagery in the reconstruction of masculinity and femininity. Indian culture was influenced by its mythological base, as Western civilisation has relied on the retelling of its Greek myths with its scores of gods and goddesses, and later the influence of Christianity. The ongoing construction of gender in India itself through the ages was continuously built and rebuilt on the philosophical debates carried out by the learned male Brahmins and on their retelling and elaboration of these myths to ensure the power of the male. When the migrants left the shores of India these myths and symbols became part of the cultural baggage they took to the new society. 'The *Ramayana* sustained our forefathers in Trinidad. This journey they have taken was comparable to that of the temporary exile of Ram and thus women here were to belike Sita, self suffering wives, faithful to the end'.[17] The importance of idealising characters of the *Ramayana* which persons must emulate in their lives was crucial for another reason. Placed in the lowest class in the new society, and deprived of the cultural sustenance to which they would have been accustomed, these myths and rituals helped to transform the mundane of everyday to epic quality, and persisted as a reference point around which gender and ethnicity were demarcated.

The Gender Imagery Transmitted through Myth

It is only possible here to demonstrate briefly how the telling and retelling of these myths and the transmission of symbols insidiously constructed notions of masculinity and femininity in the minds of the listeners. 'How a young lady ought to conduct herself was made clear to me in this story my mother told me – the story of Draupadi from the *Mahabharata*' says the protagonist Kamla in the novel *Butterfly in the Wind*, an autobiographical novel of the author's childhood days in Tunapuna, Trinidad in the late 1930s and 1940s.[18]

The *Mahabharata* tells, with innumerable interpolations, the story of the great war between the Kauravas and the Pandavas, two rival factions of one royal family. At one point in the story the Pandavas learned that the King of Panchala had proclaimed a svayamvara at which his daughter Draupadi was to select a husband from among the suitors. Disguised as Brahmins the Pandavas attended the svayamvara and Arjuna, a mighty bowman and warrior defeated everybody, including the hundred Kaurava brothers who were among the competitors. On their return home Arjuna's mother, when told he had won a great treasure unwittingly advised him to share it with his brothers. Thus Draupadi became the common wife of all Pandava brothers and to avoid jealousy it was decided that she would dwell for two days with each of them in turn.[19]

Basham notes that 'The locus classicus of ancient Indian polyandry is the *Mahabharata*, where the heroes, the five Pandava brothers, share their wife Draupadi in common'.[20] It is interesting, however, that in the retelling of this tale by pundits and others, the practice of polyandry was never promoted as a virtue for women yet the second part of the myth is constantly invoked as another ideal of chastity, like that of Sita's virtue, to which women should aspire. This part tells of the attempted rape of Draupadi by Duhsasana, the most wicked of the Kaurava brothers, after the eldest Pandava brother has lost everything, including Draupadi, in a dice game, to Sakuni, the uncle of the Kaurava princes. Draupadi is dragged into the assembly and Duhsasana begins to peel off the layers of her sari. But Krishna (the god) intervenes and although the king pulls and pulls at her sari, Draupaudi remains clothed and cannot be publicly stripped. This tale is related to Kamla to stress the chastity and virtuous behaviour expected of a young girl and woman under any circumstances.

The other side of the story is not even contemplated as a violent invasion of a woman's privacy. It is accepted behaviour for a man to attempt to rape a woman, especially if the man is a powerful one.

The assembly is a company of men. Draupadi's body is private property, the property of men. Like all property, she can be bought, sold, exchanged. In the *Mahabharata* the woman is property, to be exchanged between men, she is held captured by the male gaze; the nakedness would be her shame; Shame is man's threat against women: a woman without shame is a woman without worth.[21]

Women are viewed through male eyes and defined as property of the male. Man's honour remains vested in woman's virtue. The double paradox keeps patriarchy intact and contingent o the woman's collusion, hence Kamla's mother also reinforces for her daughter the ideals of femininity and masculinity which she had inherited from her own mother.

An Indian historian, Uma Chakravarti, observes from her examination of various sources of the Ramayana story that as the Sita legend develops in the historical context of India, 'the emphasis on chastity and the assumption that ideal marriage is based on female devotion are aspects grafted on to an originally simple story. Over the centuries important details added to the story have had a crucial influence on the shaping of the feminine identity'.[22] While poetic licence is often taken in the retelling of these tales over time, there is no doubt that they continued to serve as moral fodder for the Indian migrants in Trinidad. In her reminiscences of childhood in Tunapuna during the 1940s, Kamla again summons up memories which are very revealing for our purposes.

In Tulsidas retelling of Valmiki's *Ramayana*, there is an episode where Sita, wife of Rama, has just been freed by the capture of Lanka, and the death of the powerful king Ravana who has kept her captive. It has to be proved publicly that the Sita has been faithful to her husband in both thought and deed. So she is put through what my mother described as her 'trial by fire', 'the proving of her purity' by the cleansing ritual of fire which consumes all human ugliness including woman's unfaithfulness . . . It was only when Sita stepped out of the fire, without a hair on her body singed, that she was able to return to her husband Rama. Young Hindu girls like myself, aged eight when I heard this story, enjoyed the rich imagery and poetry of these epic adventures, without being aware that we were unconsciously absorbing the sentiments and values of Valmiki.[23]

When she was older, Kamla questioned the ordeal through which Sita had been placed asking her mother: 'If Rama was God, shouldn't he have known that Sita was faithful? Didn't he trust her word?' While it seems that Lord rama has complete faith in his wife, he needed to allay the fears of his subjects that Sita had remained a completely chaste woman during the period she was captured by Ravana, and that she was fit to be queen. Kamla was still unhappy with this response so her mother explained further: 'You must remember Kamla, that as queen she held a position of responsibility and of trust. All wives hold positions of great trust' but Lakshmi who was a generation removed from her mother was unsatisfied with this explanation and persisted: 'Do husbands hold position of trust? I provoked.[24]

Kim Johnson arrives at similar point of view in his examination of this myth which recreated ideals form femininity and masculinity in Trinidad. He draws our attention to another useful fictional source, one derived from Trinidad itself – a passage form Seepersad Naipaul's short story 'The Adventures of Gurudeva':

And thus they felt because they knew that such was their lot as well, and they wondered in a vague, resigned sort of way why the Deity had allowed them to be born at all. For they had heard it taught by their fathers , by the elders of the village, as well as by the pundits who often read the Ramayana on evenings, that the husband was to the wife God, lord and master – all in one – and that a woman's highest virtue lay in her absolute submission to her husband's will. 'But you see', Dhira told Mira in Hindu, 'it is all a very one sided operation. They want us all to be like Sita but on the other hand, they are far from being like Rama, the incarnation of the great God Vishnu himself, it is not fair.

Seepersad Naipaul retold stories with an Indian mythical flavour for a Trinidad audience, relating it to the context of the new society in the 1930s. Johnson observes of the recreation of the story of Sita's ordeal that 'This didactic tale of good triumphing over evil, virtue over immorality, is told in drama in Trinidad as a lesson in morality especially aimed at women'.[26] It seems a bit one-sided in the interpretation of the myths and tales which have emerged that masculinity is invariably allocated the dominant and active role while women are posited in a submissive and virtuous one. In both instances related here, nonetheless, the younger women have challenged the lack of reciprocity in the relations between men and women. Clearly between myth and reality some changes had taken place and these were surreptitiously shifting gender ideology in the new society.

The Birth of the Western Eye

An interesting development seems to have occurred in the evolution of Indian folktales indigenous to Trinidad. While admittedly I have moved from grand mythology to folktales, the construction of folktales served a fairly similar function in Trinidad. Especially prior to the advent of the cinema, radio and television, they were important sources of evening entertainment derived from local experiences but placed in the category of 'folk wisdom', the latter which claims to distill the collective experiences of people into moral statements. Introducing a sample of Indo-Trinidadian folktales Kenneth Ramchand suggests that 'consciously or unconsciously . . . these tales register the new environment of the indentured Indian.'[27]

The tale entitled 'Dishonest World' begins as follows

It had this man who had a pretty wife, when he go to wuk the wife saga boy[28] used to come and make joke and thing. When the wife see 4.00 o'clock she used to take she datwan[29] and sit down by the door to scrub she mouth. The husban say, 'Hear nah you go dead you know, you now scrubbing you mouth'. The wife replied, 'When ah doh see you ah does can't eat or do anything, ah can't live without you'.[30]

The gist of the story as it continues, is that the husband suspects his wife of having another lover, and confirms it by spying on her one day. He tells the raja of king that he wants a week off, and proceeds to traverse the country to see if he could find an honest person, unfortunately coming to the conclusion at the end of the week that no one was honest, finding that the sadhu or wise man he first met was dishonest, the rani or king's wife was cuckolding the king with his groomsman, and he concludes 'even god is worse'. There is a disillusioned ending for him as he decides he might as well stay with the dishonesty he knows as he could encounter no honesty. The story has a profundity which one must draw attention to, the displacement of the individual trying to recreate his world in a culture which has been uprooted and transplanted. This man's journey to discover honesty and truth, is in keeping with that described int he brahminical thought of the four life stages of man, one of which is that of the search for knowledge which could only be found through abstinence and self-abnegation. In another sense it also relived the episode in the *Ramayana* of Ram's banishment into the wilderness. What is clearly a major disruption here is that is initially premised on the sure knowledge of his wife's infidelity. In several of the stories in this small collection of folk tales, quite a few wives are depicted as cheating on their husbands, a feature which is extremely inconsistent with the imagery of fidelity of women in Sanskrit mythology.

Heroes and Heroines of the Silver Screen

It was at this time an unhappy marriage of the East and West. Which religious symbols should Indians ascribe to? What values should they uphold? This confusion would persist for many decades to come but as if to add to their growing consternation, a new Indian influence was to prove both regenerative of the old flavours and at the same time presenting new ones. The introduction of Indian films into Trinidad from 1935 was more than just another form of entertainment.

Aged Indian people who recall the films of yester-age often feel it was as a kind of ethnic ritual, an attempt to keep one's forefather's love and yore. Ramdaye, an aged woman from what used to be called the 'coolie block' up in Diego Martin, is illustration of this. Her father came from India, while her mother was born in Trinidad of parents there. To her, Indian films are more frivolous entertainment. These films are an act of piety, a feeling of veneration towards her background almost a spiritual experience like a pilgrimage.[31]

Almost every Indian man or woman in Trinidad over the age of sixty remembers clearly the first Indian film which was shown on the cinema screens in Trinidad in 1935. The film as titled *Bala Jobhan* and this and the continuous stream of films which were brought in after 1935 had a remarkable influence on nurturing ideas of Indianess and Indian culture among Indian men and women in Trinidad. Until 1935 only English-language films were available in Trinidad. Films like *The Scarlet Empress* starring Marlene Dietrich which was advertised at the Empire Theatre in Port of Spain on 9 December 1934, clearly has an appeal to the local audience which would have included more Indian men than women, for women were not generally allowed to go to the cinema. But films such as these could not bridge the gap between fantasy and reality for the generations of migrants who were still emotionally linked to India. For the children of these migrants who were born in Trinidad, this represented the India they had never sen. By the mid-1930s the majority of the Indian population in Trinidad, though these were second and third generation Trinidadians, would have lost the first-hand contact with the motherland as the last group of migrants were brought in 1917. With the advent of Indian films, the epic grandeur of an India left behind was now being transmitted into the new land of their adoption. They saw India in the landscape, the clothing, the practices of religion which were transmitted on the screen, the fictional characters who lived out the morals which their priests preached they should replicate in their own lives. It gave greater credence to their own practices, when a wedding ceremony carried out on the screen mirrored what the *pundits* and *imams* in their own society were doing.

Thus from 1935 when Mr. Ramjit Kumar , a London-trained engineer originally from Lahore, India, introduced *Bala Jobhan*, followed by others such as *Afzal, Chabukwali, Jungle Ka Chavan, Andaz,* and *Midnight Mail*, these were shown to packed houses in Trinidad. Already by 1936, the Yogi, a writer in the 'Indian News and Views Column' was requesting the appointment of two Indians on the Film Censor Board of the colony, one for the Hindi language and one for the Urdu language. He justified his request on the basis that 'There are many Indians who are interested in the importation of these films which have undoubtedly won the fancy and admiration of the entire Indian community' (Trinidad Guardian, 6 August 1936). While the Indian 'talkies' were responsible for a general cultural rejuvenation among Indians in Trinidad, our primary concern here is their impact on gender imagery.

In its attempt to appeal to film-goers situated in a Western setting the advertisements for the films were often a mixed bag even if the stories which they relayed retained the original flavour. One film is selected here for illustration. When the matinee of the film *Madhuri* for instance was advertised, the caption under a photo of the leading actress stated 'Sulochana, popularly known as the "Greta Garbo of India", who appears in *Madhuri* now showing at the Roxy Theatre". Despite the glamorous allurements of Sulochana, there character Madhuri which she portrays on screen is not unlike that of Sita who maintains her loyalty and fidelity to her husband Rama. Madhuri also remains faithful to Amber, the male protagonist of the film, in the face of many misadventures, which involves resisting the advances of traitors and kings to save Amber from the gallows, still to be greeted with disbelief form him until she has proved her virtue again and again. The actions of both male and female protagonists are interpreted by the audience as the moral point of film, and invariably replay the major themes of mythology, goodness over evil, and the trials and tribulations which a woman must endure to live a virtuous life and preserve her husband's honour.

Indian Womanhood and Manhood in Trinidad

The avenues of prayer meetings, festivals, storytelling and the cinema were crucial ones in transmitting gender ideology, but men were also the conveyors of myth and symbol in the more public sense. While pundits interpreted the texts for the population, and visiting male missionaries from India lectured to audiences on the ancient culture of India, there were many Trinidadian-born men who were carriers of myth and symbols through their own work, men like Seeperesad Naipaul who contributed a two-page section of the *Guardian* newspaper on Thursday and Friday during the years of 1926 to 1934, and C.B. Mathura who edited a news paper called the *East Indian Weekly*, from 1928 to 1931.[32]

The reports in both these sources served to entrench notions of Indian womanhood which were conveyed through mythology. In 1935, Asshia, an Indian man, was accused of the murder of his wife Poptee and her lover, Rampersad. The newspaper reports that 'when Asshia arrived at Ramperdas's house, Poptee knew that he would have seen her and why did she not open the back door of the house and run out'. The reporter continues, 'she did not do that but with the characteristics of an Indian woman went to make peace between the two men' (*Trinidad Guardian, 11 July 1935*). What were the 'characteristics of an Indian woman' as perceived by this reporter? Throughout an article entitled 'Indian womanhood' reprinted by Seepersad Naipaul in his Thursday edition of "Indian News and Views" in the *Trinidad Guardian,* Mrs. K. Shivpuri, B. A. B. T. (Alwar) of India cites what is considered in the Brahminic tradition, the ideals expected of Indian womanhood.

Man has always been, so to say, incomplete without woman. He cannot perform any religious rites (Yagna) without his wife taking part in it . . . People think that because an Indian wife sacrifices so much for her husband she is like a slave to him. This is of course far from the truth. The ideal Indian woman has always done her best to keep her husband very happy and comfortable, even at the risk of her happiness. If she makes any sacrifice it is because of her love and devotion to her husband. She sacrifices because she gets pleasure in making her companion comfortable. (*Trinidad Guardian,* 6 August 1936).

Mrs. Shivpuri goes on to elaborate on the sacrifices required of Indian women in relation to their male partners.

If a modern girl . . . wants real happiness, lasting love, she would not go after equality, nor crave for it but should behave in a better manner in the old Indian way, look after her husband's welfare and when that educated man of today finds that his wife has the goodness and qualities of the ancient loving wife, he himself will come round and respect and love her more that she could ever expect. (*Trinidad Guardian,* 6 August 1936).

Indian womanhood is depicted here through the eyes of the male and defined only in terms of her relationship to the male. 'It was their unbounded love and sacrifice for their husband that they were known for so far.' The notion of a collective Indian identity with its traditional masculine and feminine identities were being reconstructed at this time in Trinidad. Thus Indian women in Trinidad were expected to live up to the ideals interpreted from sacred texts and to also be like their sisters in India, itself an invented norm which did not fit the reality of all Indian women in India. Mrs. Shivpuri's article, among many others, were being printed in the newspapers to appeal to women to retina traditional roles which were fast changing both in India and Trinidad itself.[33] According to Mrs. Shivpuri and others writing at this time, the ideal Indian woman does not attempt to challenge this balance in gender relations which requires that women always sublimate their needs to those of their husbands.

How many of these ideas were still part of the belief and practices of second and third generation Indo-Trinidadian men and women? Mrs. Dropatie Naipaul, wife of Seepersad Naipaul was sorely offended by those Indian women in Trinidad who failed to match the ideal expressed above. These were clearly also the rules which governed her own (Brahminic) childhood socialisation.

You see a woman has a place in this world and when she abuses that place, she has lost the thing they call womanhood because she is no more that woman. I decide I would never fail in my duty. That is something very important and not every woman has that in them. I could afford to tell you – if they have it they wouldn't be as slack. I am talking about Indian people, forget about the others. My sisters all felt the same way about their duty as wife and mother. It was an honour to me – everyday practice meant that I have a duty to do everyday and I must fulfil my duty everyday and that is a duty everyday and that is a duty which people fail to do now.

If women were expected to be dutiful, obedient, sacrificial and forgiving, then what did the masculine role constitute? Phoolo was married to a young man of fifteen when she was eleven years old in 1926. She had three children with him and as committed to the marriage until his death and afterwards, never remarrying. He unfortunately reciprocate this loyalty. A few years after their marriage, when she had two of her three children, he was employed as a foreman on a sugar estate in St. Augustine and began a lifelong habit of drinking, violent abuse, openly consorting women out of his marriage, and even having children with them. During his marriage to her, he brought very little earnings into their household and she was forced to work for a nearby cotton plantation in St. Augustine to support the family. Her reason for remaining with him was partly due to the children and partly because her family expected this from her. And what of his behaviour as it was condoned in Trinidad. Was this due to a Western influence including Trinidadian gender ideology which weakened traditions and tolerated flaunting of the Hindu marriage vows?

What does this tell us of the changes which were emerging in the construction of femininity and masculinity in Trinidad? The stories of duplicity on the part of females suggest that the emasculated Indian male in Trinidad seemed incapable of controlling his wife's libidinous instincts. Certainly the notions of what constituted masculinity would have undergone change in Trinidad, and, perhaps, what is displayed here is a male concern with their increased powerless in the sphere of sexual relations. Between mythological representations and the lived reality we find a dissonance brought on by new and challenging conditions for both sexes in the Western setting. [34] In Trinidad the concern for preserving the virtue of Indian girls and women had attained other dimensions. The character of Rawan in the *Ramayana* was portrayed as a black man as he was of Dravidian extract, and the portrayal of the myth in the Ramleela festival took on additional relevance int he setting of Trinidad where Indian women could not help but come into contact with black men. Kim Johnson again makes the following observations : 'How else can we explain the seeming preoccupation of Indian men with Indian women being seduced by black men long before such liaisons were commonplace. There must have always been a subconscious fear the women would be unable to resist Rawan's advances'. [35] Here again we see evidence of the way in which the gender systems of other groups in the society were beginning to force another influence on to the day to day choices of Indian women, despite the force of mythology and religion.

We must once more recall that in the earlier period of indentureship and up to the first few decades of the twentieth century there was a noticeably high rate of suicide among Indian men or murders of Indian wives by their husbands. One explanation of this was again rooted in the responsibility of women to ensure that male honour is preserved. Brereton suggests that, 'The man whose wife had been unfaithful suffered a disastrous loss of self-esteem, and in the absence of other mechanisms for expressing anger and self-assertion, violence directed against the other (murder or Mutilation of the woman) or against self (suicide was almost as frequent in these situations) was the only way to recover his pride.' [36] The reports on male suicides or murders performed by men are too frequent to be ignored. The year 1918 begins with an inquest into the death of one Siju who was found hanging by a rope on 4 December 1917 (*Trinidad Guardian*, 1 January 1918). Two days later another inquest is held on the death of one Sookhoo found hanging from a cocoa tree on 25 November 1917. A verdict of suicide was returned (*Trinidad Guardian*, 3 January 1918). On the same day the newspaper reported the trial and execution of another case, that of Palakdharri, a young Indian man of about 26 years who was executed for the murder of Bajbahaher, an Indian woman on the Non-Pareil Estate, Sangre Grande on Sunday, 31 October 1917. Palakdharri was an indentured immigrant form India and had been resident in the colony for a period of years. The account of the murder is instructive.

A short time before the crime took place Palakdharri and the murdered woman lived together in one of the barrack rooms on the estate and for some reason or another they fell out. It was suggested that the woman left him for some other man. His defence at the trial was that the woman, apart from being unfaithful, had him put off the estate and jeered at him when he was going away. He had a cutlass in his hand at the time and chopped her. (*Trinidad Guardian*, 3 January 1918.)

What evidence such as this confirms is that the post -indentureship period was one of great flux for the construction of both masculinity and femininity, and that this was due primarily to the shift which had taken place in the perception of the actors of themselves, and in the way in which the rest of the society was now beginning to view them. It was clearly not acceptable agin to assume that one's wife or partner was property to be disposed of at will. Certainly the Western court looked harshly on the extremes of this attitude to women as property. The fluidity of this period however gave rise to further contradictions after indentureship. Recall that women themselves colluded in the efforts to establish a stability necessary to community building and redefining and ethnic identity in Trinidad.

The task of unravelling gender identities becomes more elusive when we try to match stereotypic norm with reality as there is so much variation in real life, and many changes taking place at each historical moment. What emerges in the examination myth, and symbolic interpretations of these myths , and the range of male and female experiences during the period after 1917 and 1947, is that some aspect of the traditional roles were definitely retained by a majority of the population – on the part of many men the idea of commitment to wife, responsibility to family and so on were still part and parcel of the Indian family system and gender relations established therein. The majority of women retained the reciprocal commitment to endure whatever hardships this required, while remaining monogamous and faithful to husband, and an impeccable mother to ones children. But gender ideology had begun its imperceptible shift form mythological India to the western setting of Trinidad.

Conclusion

It is relatively simple to demolish physical structures and replace them with new ones. Our architectural tastes are perhaps more accommodating to changes. Not so with the edifices of culture which are subterranean, and thus less easily dislodged. As I have demonstrated in this essay, new symbolic understandings of masculinity and femininity emerged from the cumulated and collective challenges of individuals in the group, and from other mythmaking forms which began to recognise new behaviours for Indian men and women. The influence of African and other western ideas had begun to challenge the old ideas of gender, but the period of post-indentureship was largely one of reconstituting the recollected norms and traditions and there was insufficient mixing between groups at this time to tamper with the centuries of Indian mythological beliefs. That these ideas were nonetheless intruding is clear from the shifts we observe above in the folktales in Trinidad, the newspaper efforts to invoke traditional expectation of women's roles, and the actual practices of some men and women who did openly challenge the norms. Nonetheless, the old foundations were perpetuated, forcing the need for continuous negotiations between men and women, between institutions and individuals. Born into a particular ethnic group, even if they depart from the norms established by the group, men and women are never indifferent to the cultural boundaries defined by their community. While they push these boundaries further, they are circumscribed in their own lifetime to only creating incremental change, particularly in the sphere of gender ideology. The results of their challenges bear fruit in the next generation, thus shifting gender ideology either imperceptibly or radically based on the extent to which their historical circumstances allow. Meanwhile, the sacred texts remain the key sources informing Hinduism, the dominant Indian religion in Trinidad, adhered to by the majority of the Indian population. The stories of Ram and Sita are to this day still read as religious instruction to each new generation of Indians in Trinidad. And the pundits who interpret the sacred texts are still, primarily, men.

Notes

1. See Meera Kosambi, 'The Meeting of the Twain: The Cultural Confrontation of Three Women in Nineteenth Century Marhrashtra' in *Indian Journal of Gender Studies* 1:1 (1994). Kosambi notes in personal conversation with me, and in this paper that in her attempt to uncover women who had defied the gender norms established in Indian society, she found few examples. In this paper she looks at the lives of Pandita Ramabai (1858-1922), Anandibai (1865-1887) and Rakhmabai (1864-1955)/ Anandibai was the first woman in Western India to be trained as a medical doctor (she was trained in the United States), Rakhmabai was widely known for her court case for divorce (the first ever in India), and became the first Maharashtrian female doctor trained in England, and Pandita Ramabai figured as the sole champion of the women's cause within the reform movement, studied in England where she converted to Christianity and travelled widely in the USA to propagate her ideas before returning to India to implement her plans. Kosambi notes that 'the three women shared the same socio-cultural milieu and knew each other'.
2. Nirad C. Chaudhuri, *Hinduism* (Oxford: Oxford University Press, 1979) 135-136.
3. This notion is not as a fixed one and clearly is open to interpretation. Nonetheless, my oral history interviews or over 60 men and women in Trinidad over the age of 50 confirmed this reading of as a general notion of Hinduism shared by all Indians, including Muslims. An interview with Mrs Dassie Parsan, (now deceased) as a member of another varna and caste whose father joined the Arya Samaj movement and later she was converted to Presbyterianism, pointed out that this was the major challenge to the dominant ideas of Hinduism which prevailed in Trinidad in her experience.
4. N. C. Chaundhuri, *Hinduism*, op. cit. P.221.
5. Claude Levi-Strauss, *Structural Anthropology* (New York and London: Basic Books, 1963), p. 232.
6. As cultures are mapped across geographical space and different centuries, there are some universal aspects of gender identities in almost all known cultures: male patriarchal control, female subordination and sexual division of labour which ties women to the domestic sphere and allocates more power to men in the wider society. This universalistic expression of gender difference is also implicated in as a discussion on gender ideology, but is not the primary concern of this paper.
7. Valuable research done by Peggy Ramesar on language in Trinidad shows that the variant of Hindi which emerged as the spoken language here was Bhojpuri, the dialect which was spoken by the majority of those who came from India.
8. N. C. Chaundhuri, *Hinduism*, op. cit. pp 259-261.221.
9. Albertine Gaur, Women in India (London: The British Library, 1980) pp 22-23.
10. Because of the numerous mixtures which can be derived from the multi-racial Trinidad population the term 'mixed' is used both officially and colloquially to describe any person of mixed parentage. This did not apply to the Indian population until late in the twentieth century however, as this group was extracted from the total population and presented separately in the statistics until 1946.
11. See Bridget Brereton, *Race Relations in Colonial Trinidad 1870-1900* (Cambridge: Cambridge University Press, 1979).
12. Colin Clarke 'Spacial pattern and social interaction among Creoles and Indians in Trinidad and Tobago' in Kelvin Yelvingtyon, (ed) *Trinidad Ethnicity* (London: Macmillan Caribbean, 1993).
13. The theoretical notions developed here have emerged from the wider study from which this chapter is developed entitled 'as a Social History of Indians in Trinidad 1917-1947:

as a Gender Perspective'. This paper utilizes primary material from the larger study including oral history tapes which are assigned as a number and are to be located in the Oral History Collection of the library, University of the West Indies, St. Augustine, Trinidad.

14. Islam also had as a similar experience to that of Hinduism in that those who knew how to read the Koran became the interpreters of the religion in the new society. Sadhul explained that the village of Lengua for instance shared one Iman with many surrounding villages because he was the only one who knew how to read the Koran from Arabic, the language in which it was written (Tape 42 Oral History Collection, UWI St. Augustine library). Only when it was more organised by visiting missionaries from the Middle East by the second decade of the twentieth century it began to adopt different features from Hinduism, as for instance the cessation of dancing Muslim weddings, than the syncretism which Muslim Indians who had migrated from India would have been used to.

15. I recall the fascination I felt as as a child and adolescent in the fifties and sixties when we would visit the site in Cedar Hill village where the Ramleela festival was annually staged. The play was performed in as a natural sunken amphitheatre - as a small flat plain surrounded by gently sloping hills on two sides. The festival was also as a time of great joy and merriment, an opportunity to buy and sell the traditional Indian sweets and savouries and clearly as a public ritual celebration of as a dominant aspect of Indian culture.

16. Ramleela is the more contemporary spelling of this festival and myth which was referred to as Ramlilla in the historical sources found in Trinidad.

17. Information gleaned from an informal discussion with Dr Rosabelle Seesaran who has carried out research on Indians in Trinidad and who was also one of my oral history interviewees.

18. L. Persaud, *Butterfly in the Wind* (England: Peepal Tree Press, 1990).

19. Albertine Gaur, *Women in India* op. Cit.

20. A.L. Basham, *The Wonder That was India: as a Survey of the History and Culture of the Indian Sub-continent Before the Coming of the Muslims* (London: Sidgwick & Jackson 1967).

21. P. Duncker, *Sisters and Strangers: An Introduction to Contemporary Feminist Fiction* (Oxford UK & Cambridge USA: Blackwell Publishers, 1992) p 132.

22. This discussion which is cited from Desai and Krishnaraj is originally taken from Uma Chakravarti 'The Sita Myth' in *Samya Shakti*, Vol.1, No. 1., July 1983, p. 70.

23. L. Persaud, *Butterfly* op. cit. P.10. The Valmiki edition of the *Ramayana* predated the Persian edition.

24. L. Persaud, op.cit. p. 105.

25. S. Naipaul, *Gurudeva and Other Stories* (London: Deutsche, 1976) p. 26.

26. Kim Johnson, 'Considerations on Indian Sexuality', presented at the Third Conference on East Indians, St. Augustine, Trinidad, University of the West Indies, August 1984,. p.27.

27. K. Ramchand, 'Introduction' in as a. Maharaj, *Indo-Trinidad Folk Tales in the Oral Tradition*, (Trinidad: Indian Review Committee, 1990), p. vii.

28. 'Saga Boy' is the colloquial term used in Trinidad to refer to as a man who dresses smartly and is generally known as as a charmer of ladies. I am not aware of the derivation of the term.

29. Datwan refers to as a piece of strong vine used as as a toothbrush.

30. as a. Maharaj, *Indio-Trinidad Folk Tales* op. cit ., p. 6.

31. V. Golikheri, 'Indian Films in Trinidad', *People*, (3) 21, 1977: pp. 52-55.

32. While it is true that the literacy rate in English among Indians was low at the time, historian Brinsley Samaroo has noted that one of the reasons the *East Indian Weekly* failed to be as a viable commercial enterprise is that one or two newspapers served the

entire village as it was bought and read by the few who knew how tor read and the newspaper was read out to the wider village. Thus the written word did get around through an oral medium as well.

33. Nonetheless my reading of Indian history and fiction reveals that the classic mythology still plagued the women in India. See for instance the novel by Vickram Seth, *as a Suitable Boy* (London: Viking Press, 1995) in which the protagonist eventually makes as a choice of as a husband based on what was acceptable for her family and kin.

34. Thus far I have concentrated on the idea that the symbolism and Hinduism was the dominant one in influencing the construction of masculinity and femininity among Indians. Islam as it was later practised from the 1920s onwards grew sufficiently different in its gender imagery to warrant its own inquiry which this paper does not pretend to deal with. For instance, the gender imagery for Muslim men and women was derived from the literal interpretation of the austere writings in the Holy Koran. Nonetheless, it must be stressed that in terms of the primary definition of gender there is little difference to be found between Muslim and Hindu women. It was Christianity which long before 1917 had already begun to impose the most radical ideas (such as education for girls and deferred age of marriage) on the construction of gender within the Indian community, but these were at this time presented as largely consistent with Indian gender ideology. Thus for instance, the Presbyterians also arranged marriages for the educated Indian girls as their parents had done before.

35. K. Johnson, 1984, op. cit., p. 27.

36. Bridget Brereton, *Race Relations in Colonial Trinidad 1870-1900* (Cambridge: Cambridge University Press, 1979), p.183.

23

Contestations over National Culture in Trinidad and Tobago:

Considerations of Ethnicity, Class and Gender

Rhoda Reddock

As with other immigrant and colonial societies, a complex system of social stratification developed in Trinidad and Tobago, based on race/ethnicity, colour, class, nationality and gender. This was the result of years of plantation agriculture and waves of forced migration including slavery and bonded or indentured labour. This situation is true not only of the Caribbean region. Similar situations have been constructed in other areas of European colonialism such as Mauritius, Fiji, Sri Lanka, Malaysia, Singapore and of course South Africa, all of these (former) plantation societies. In the post-colonial era, the problems of nation, identity and culture emerge as issues for renegotiation and reconceptualisation some-times with sad and violent results.

For the subordinated peoples of these societies, be they indigenous or immigrant, there was first the problem of rejecting colonial i.e. European cultural hegemony, and later in the Trinidad and Tobago case its Euro-American variant, not a simple task. But even more difficult was the question of its replacement. In these societies there is a continuous struggle and negotiation over representation.

Intersections of Ethnicity, Class and Gender in Trinidad and Tobago

Like people in most parts of the world, I live in a society where ethnic tensions complicate the 'normal' hierarchical intersections of class and gender. Daily as we attempt to fashion a movement for social change we are confronted with the realities of these tensions of which we are all part but which we do not fully understand. Indeed Third World scholarship on the interconnections of ethnicity, class, gender and culture are largely absent, in particular with respect to relations among what North Americans refer to as 'people of colour'. This is so although ethnic tensions have been the cause of bloodshed and civil war in many of our societies. Studies of race/ethnicity and class abound but their relationship to gender is yet to be analysed.

Over the past three years, I have sought to lay the groundwork for the analysis of ethnicity, class and gender in multi-ethnic, post-colonial societies, based on the experience of my society, Trinidad and Tobago. I argued in an earlier publication that:

In the international literature on race, class and gender, little input has been made of the Caribbean experience. Indeed most of the debate has centred around the experiences of Afro-American or Afro-British women in the metropolis, African women in South Africa and Indo-British women in Britain. Within that context, therefore, race, like class and gender, becomes a basis of exploitation, discrimination and oppression of non-European (non-white) groups (Reddock 1993: 46).

I continued that: 'No contributions to these discussions have yet been made on, for example, the issue of race, class and gender in a situation where two or more non-white groups have antagonistic or non-antagonistic relations' (Reddock 1993: 46).

In battling with this complexity I have had to return to the old questions of Caribbean, i.e., how do we understand these societies? How do we define their national identities and is there a Caribbean culture? In addition, I had to now add a new question, how do issues of gender enter into this discourse? In this paper I concentrate on the Trinidad and Tobago situation, hoping to bring to you the result of some of my early efforts to conceptualise this situation.

Conceptualising Trinidad and Tobago Society

Much debate continues on how social relations in the Caribbean should be conceptualised. The two most famous of these formulations are those of Michael G. Smith (1965) with his plural society thesis and E. Kamau Brathwaite's thesis of 'Creolisation'(1977). To summarise briefly, Smith argued that Caribbean societies were characterised by 'cultural pluralism' in that they were divided into distinct cultural groups each with their own social institutions e.g. family and kinship, religion, property relations, economic patterns and recreational pursuits. These societies are held together by force or the threat of force through a dominant minority. He saw plural societies as being hierarchic, segmented or complex.

For Smith therefore, Jamaica was a plural society, divided hierarchically between 'whites', 'browns' and 'blacks', while Trinidad and Tobago was a complex plural society divided into Europeans, Africans, Indians, Chinese, Portuguese and others. In his later work, Smith developed what he called his corporation theory arguing that in plural societies groups are differentially incorporated into the societies' public domain. This could be true of ethnic groups as in South Africa, as well as for genders as in the case of Swiss women until 1987, and native peoples in the Americas. This approach has come under a great deal of critique over the years and as a result has also been amended on many occasions. Basically it has been criticised for paying inadequate attention to class differences and for ignoring the common values of the society which all groups share. An early contributor to this critique was Lloyd Braithwaite who argued that the common value held by the societies was the superiority of things European (Braithwaite 1953).

The other main approach which is very relevant to this analysis is that of Creolisation. The main proponent of this approach, Kamau Brathwaithe, saw this concept as,

a specialised version of the two widely accepted terms *acculturation* and *interculturation*: the former referring, to the process of the absorption of one culture by another; the latter to a more reciprocal activity, a process of intermixture and enrichment, each to each (Brathwaite, 1977: 11).

This process he saw as beginning during the slave system through the interaction of African and European in a 'fixed superiority/inferiority relationship' first by the adaption of both groups to their new environment, then of 'blacks to white norms' and of interculturation between both groups. In other words, Brathwaite argued that Caribbean creole society emerged both from the assimilation of blacks to the dominant European cultural norms and behaviours *and* by the inadvertent interculturation of whites into black norms and behaviours.

On the part of the African slaves this was facilitated through socialisation e.g. 'seasoning', imitation, native creation or indigenisation, language and sex and amorous relations. But what was important for Brathwaite was that this was true for whites as for blacks. In spite of that hierarchical context whites also adopted African cultural patterns, speech patterns etc. Additionally this approach rejected the view that New World Africans had lost their culture, arguing instead that in assimilating to the dominant European norms they had transformed or indigenised them, and in the process, created a creole society.

This creole society, however, was not culturally homogenous, one can speak of a cultural continuum related to class, colour and ethnicity with predominantly Euro-creole forms forming the higher, more acceptable side of the continuum and Afro-creole forms or what Brathwaite called 'folk forms' at the lower end of acceptability.

In *The Middle Passage*, published the year of Trinidad and Tobago independence, 1962, V. S. Naipaul poured scorn and disgust on what he saw as the mimicry, uncreativity and barrenness of colonial Trinidad and Tobago society. But he failed to recognise the struggle for a national identity which was beginning to dominate the scene. This is a struggle which continues to take place although the parameters of the struggle have changed over time. In my attempts to study and understand this struggle over national identity, it was necessary for me to try to under-stand processes and transformations which had taken place in this society over the last four decades since the emergence of the middle-class Afro-Trinidadian dominated nationalist movement as the first replacement of the colonial government.

The concept of creolisation is important because it is at the heart of the problem of national identity and culture in Trinidad and Tobago. The term 'creole' according to Brathwaite appears to have originated from two Spanish words *criar* meaning to create, to imagine, to establish, to found, to settle and *colón*, a colonist, founder or settler and combined in Spanish into *criollo* of which the anglicised version is 'creole'. In different parts of the colonised world the word has developed different meanings, all of them however have the connotation of 'native creation'. Originally in the Caribbean it was used to refer to all groups born in the region.

Today in Trinidad it is used in three senses (1) to refer to an amalgam of European descendants who still dominate the local economy *viz.* French Creoles and (2) primarily by Indians to refer to people of African descent. (3) To refer to aspects of the dominant Afro-Trinidadian indigenised culture e.g. creole food, creole bacchanal, etc. This is interesting as African-Trinidadians seldom refer to themselves as creoles, but as 'black people' or 'African people' or even 'negro people'. However many Indians still use the word 'creole' or 'kirwal'.

This is very interesting as, in a way, they are reflecting what is a very real situation which is that creole culture, which is today the dominant culture of the country until recently, to large extent excluded the Indian experience. With the emergence of the nationalist movement in the late

1950s, there were subsequently, creole nationalist projects based on selected aspects of creole culture. That culture was formed through imitation, but also through the native creation and indigenisation of African and European cultural forms which until recently became the accepted national culture of the country. It is important to note that this status for creole culture was achieved through great struggle, and its hold is still tenuous and constantly being challenged.[1]

Indeed, until the 1970 Black Power revolution, indigenous and African-derived art forms, belief systems, ways of life, language and even foods were still not accepted in the dominant culture. And still today its claim to be true art and culture has to be constantly validated. The increased acceptance of creole culture as a national culture therefore has to be seen as the result of years of class struggle as it was the poorest and working class who were the most creative and tenuous in their re-creation and indigenisation of cultural forms; as well as years of ethnic struggle as it was the result of struggle of African derived groups for the valorisation and acceptance of their culture by the Euro-dominated colonial and post-colonial societies, a struggle which is continuing.

It should be noted that African nationalist organisations also exist which seek to go beyond creolisation in their search for ethnic identity. The movement of Rastafarianism is a specific manifestation of this phenomenon in that it incorporates a rejection of Western consumerist culture and many aspects of creole culture. Interestingly in Trinidad some marginalised Indian youth also find sanctuary in Rastafarian culture. But this should be the subject of another study.

The position of Indians, women and men, in creole society is the issue which is now on the agenda. In the past it was assumed both by creoles and some foreign anthropologists that it was simply a matter of time before Indians were assimilated into the dominant Creole/Euro-Christian culture. Indeed there is an ongoing debate between cultural anthropologists Morton Klass (1991) and Joseph Nevadomsky (1983) as to the extent to which this has already taken place.

Today it is clear that both are correct. At the same time there has been a strong degree of cultural persistence as there have been the emergence of 'creolised' Indian forms. In some ways assimilation into the Afro-creole aspects of the dominant culture has been problematised as ethnic consciousness and religious pride have become stronger. Stephen Vertovec and others argue that the economic boom of the late 1970s and early 1980s contributed greatly to the emergence of a revitalisation movement among Hindus and Muslims (Vertovec 1992: 163). Similarly, Premdas and Sitahal record what they term the 're-indianisation' of Indian Presbyterians and an increasing pressure to indianise the rituals and hymns used in that church and to reintegrate the Presbyterian into the Hinduised and Islamicised Indian culture (Premdas and Sitahal 1991: 348).

Race and Ethnicity

So far we have spoken of distinct groups of people within the country negotiating their representation in the national culture. But it would be incorrect to continue this discussion as if those categories in themselves were not problematic. The two approaches mentioned above take as a given more or less the existence of fixed groups. What is important for us to note here is that these groups have been fashioned not biologically as 'races' but historically and socially in relation to the specific circumstances of their reality. In the words of one author,

studies of Trinidad often assume the existence of 'whites' 'East Indians', and Afro-Trinidadians', and describe these as collective individuals, composed of numerically definite populations, which occupy particular social strata and compete for political power and economic resources. One indication of the inadequacy of this approach is that at any moment in Trinidad history one finds persons who on a variety of criteria do not fit neatly within the boundaries of these groupings (Segal 1992: 2).

In similar vein another writer notes that:

Categorisations of ethnic identity that marshall a variety of historical, social and cultural dimensions in their construction may also encompass apparently contradictory images, since traits, qualities, stereotypes, and the like are not self-contained or mutually exclusive. Indeed the very fact of combination and ambiguity foregrounds fluidity of ethnic identity (Khan 1992: 181).

In other words, this paper takes the position that ethnic groups (locally described as races), are socially and historically defined and have meanings in their locations which may be meaningless outside of it. So in Trinidad and Tobago, Indians are referred to as East Indians, a term introduced in the nineteenth century to differentiate them from longer-term inhabitants who were then referred to as West Indians. As Segal notes, in popular Caribbean historiography each group has its origin outside of the region and their placement in this society fixed in the past. Europeans as colonisers and slave masters, Africans as slaves, and East Indians as indentured labourers. The fact that some Africans came as free labourers and some Indians as traders is not registered in the popular imagination.

But, as we all know, the lexicography of race does not end here. Colour descriptors were also added. Europeans were 'white', Africans were 'black' and Indians had no definite colour until recently when they became 'brown' in rejection of the hegemonic concept of 'black'. This of course was still not all, in addition to these three main 'races' there were others Chinese, Portuguese who were not considered Europeans until recently, probably because of the manner in which they entered the country, as indentured labourers; Middle Easterners usually referred to as Syrian-Lebanese and of course descendants of the original inhabitants usually referred to as Caribs. Then there were the combinations of all the above.

Scholars on the region have from time to time attempted to explain the bases of ethnic tension and difference in Trinidad and Tobago. In general one can summarise the findings as follows.

(1) At the point of the arrival of the Indian immigrants, African ex-slaves had already inculcated European values of civilised and acceptable behaviour and lifestyle. They accepted, for example, the lower value of dark skin, the superiority of Christianity over non-Christian religions; the barbarism of indigenous practices and the unacceptability of indigenous foods. In the same way that they devalued their own African cultural survivals, they also devalued the heathen and 'backward' practices of 'coolie (Indian) culture'.

(2) Indians were also seen as 'scab labour', depressing wages on the plantations and removing the labour advantages of the ex-slaves.

(3) Whereas in the case of most Africans 400 years of brutal enslavement had resulted in the transference of cultural memory from the conscious to the subconscious or unconscious realm, for Indians, Hindus and Muslims, their diverse practices, more present in their consciousness were reconstructed, recodified within the new context and continued to be part of their daily lived experience.

The cultural practices of a small but significant number of 'free Africans' who arrived after the abolition of slavery added to the store of African retentions and reinterpretations. However, they suffered immensely under the rejection of European dominated colonial society. In the post-1970s,[2] however, African-derived cultural and religious practices have been revalorised, providing African-Trinidadians, especially working-class women with a non-Christian and Afro-Christian religious experience in which they predominate.

(4) In the case of Indians, whereas in the past it was assumed that the caste system had lost its significance in the face of the realities of the plantation, and unequal sex ratios during the nineteenth century, it is now being realised that caste values which have to be seen as dynamic and not static,

continue to exist although they have been reconstructed to meet the realities of a new situation. Values such as purity and endogamy discourage racial intermarriage and sexual relations in a circumstance where 'ethnic' and religious groups e.g. Africans, Europeans, Christians, Hindus and Muslims, now take on new forms as pseudo-castes or sub-castes.

This is maintained through the continuation of arranged marriages or parental choice of marital mates. As late as 1966 Colin Clarke in his study of San Fernando found that of 96 Hindu couples, exactly half of his sample, had married caste endogamously and half exogamously. The frequency varied among castes and between women and men. Where varna exogamy did take place, it was twice as frequent between adjacent castes as between non-adjacent castes (Clarke 1986: 125-126). In my own data for 1991, based on a sample representative of the entire country, I found that 94.3 per cent of Brahmins in the sample had Brahmin fathers, 4.6 per cent Kshatriya and 1.1 per cent Sudra.[3]

This endogamous tendency is illustrated by the fact that for most of the nineteenth century and the early twentieth century, in spite of a serious shortage of women, there was no intermarriage or sexual cohabitation between Indian men and African women. Among the reasons put forward to explain this phenomenon, I would like to suggest the maintenance of caste values as most significant in this regard.

(5) Additionally, the caste system already based on a hierarchy of colour, was articulated with the colour based hierarchy already in existence in creole society. Indians therefore ascribed to the dominant Eurocentric and creole value system, in relation to skin colour and hair quality as standards of beauty, status and acceptability.

In discussing this phenomenon in Naipaul's writing, John Theime notes that while in *One Out of Many*, Santosh, likens the black woman to 'Kali, goddess of death and destruction, coal black, with a red tongue and white eyeballs and many powerful arms', in *India: A Wounded Civilisation*, Naipaul refers to Kali as 'The black one, the coal-black aboriginal goddess, surviving in Hinduism as the emblem of female destructiveness, garlanded with female skulls, tongue forever out for fresh blood, eternally sacrificed to but insatiable'. Clearly, at least for Naipaul, this combination of 'blackness' and female power present a major spiritual threat to Hindu patriarchal orthodoxy, a phenomenon which may require further exploration.

It is in this context of tension, competition and inter-relation therefore that we have to examine the contestations over national culture in

Trinidad and Tobago in the 1990s. Recognising that as these struggles take place in the larger arena, greater interconnections and intercultura-tions are taking place at another.

A Contested Arena: The struggle over a national culture

Trinidad and Tobago is known regionally and we like to think interna-tionally for its artistic and musical forms, most notably Carnival, calypso and steelband. The latter two, although not really limited to Carnival, are considered essential components of the festival. In recent times the tenuous legitimacy of this triad has been challenged both internally by the transformations in their form and content, performers and audience as well as externally in relation to their claim to be truly national forms by, among others, a revitalised Indian identity movement. The addition of 'tassa' and 'chutney' to this grouping, has had a mixed effect, the complexities of which will be explored in the discussion below.

Debate over the origins of Carnival has taken place over the years. It can be agreed however that it has two main progenitors the African masquerade of the slaves and the French pre-lenten festival of carnival which featured revelry and masquerading prior to the asceticism of lent.

For years the African component of Carnival was downplayed. It was suggested that the slaves imitated their French masters by copying their practices, which as, Brathwaite would probably agree, they probably did. However festivals based on the African masquerade emerged in all Caribbean territories but it was in the French dominated colonies that it became incorporated into the Carnival. From its inception therefore, Carnival reflected the colour and class hierarchy which was to continue to characterise Carnival itself and Trinidad and Tobago society into the future. There was always the conflict between the African-derived dances, music and other activities and middle-class European sensibilities of proper behaviour. According to Ann Lee:

The calinda, the chorus and the drum were to become integral and disturbing aspects of the post-emancipation Carnival. The entry into Carnival, after emancipation, of a mass of ex-slaves, changed not only the colour of the festival but its tone and content as well. The drums we are told replaced the fiddle as the principal instrument. The stick-fight, a ritualised blood-sport carried out to the accompaniment of drumming and singing was added to the canboulay. The carnival was celebrated with much clamour, hooting and howling in the distinctive style the whites associated with Africans and despised. Later in the century, Carnival was overrun by the jamettes, 'lewd songs', 'indecent gestures', 'sexual horseplay' and such offensive portrayals as the 'Pissenlit' or 'stinker' became the order of the day [sic] (Lee 1991: 420-421).

Although Carnival is today usually associated with Roman Catholicism, it is one of those syncretisms into Christianity which has its roots in pre-Christian festivities. Its timing which changes with the vernal equinox, is a period when in many parts of the world, fertility festivals characterised by a high female participation and a relaxation of sexual mores and patriarchal control take place.

Not surprisingly, therefore Carnival, has always been a festival when women have taken more 'freedom' than they are normally allowed at other times of the year. Although this is also true to some extent for men, it is not considered as much a challenge to the patriarchal order as it is for women. From very early in Trinidad, commentators have complained about the behaviour of women. Not only did it provide an opportunity for vulgar displays by lower-class women, but even the 'better class of young women' tended to be led astray. Calls were made for the abolition of street parades . Between 1877 and 1900 efforts were made to clean up the carnival i.e. to rid it of some of its more bawdy and African derived elements. This was met with much resistance and in annual riots and disturbances between masqueraders and the police. In 1884 the Peace Preservation Act prohibited 'public torch processions, drum beating, any dance or procession and disorderly assembly often of ten or more persons armed with sticks or weapons' (Lee 1991: 426).

By the 1950s with the gradual development of a nationalist conscious-ness Carnival came to represent the creole national spirit. According to Ann Lee:

Much of the success of a nationalist movement depends on an ideology which affirms the unity of the people and distinctiveness of the nation. Carnival easily became that symbol for the nationalist movement in the late 1940s and 1950s. It was indigenous, it cut across race class, colour and creed [as far as they understood it]. Importantly it was still a festival with which the urban masses strongly identified. More than any other festival it could express the distinctive Trinidadian style (Lee 1991: 429).

But this was not the style of all Trinidadians, for Indian nationalists this was just another example of the way in which the dominant creole culture imposed its idea of culture and identity on the entire population.

Interestingly, the Hindu 'spring' festival of *Holi* or *Phagwa* usually follows close on the heels of Carnival. Before the institutionalisation of Hinduism it was mainly a village festival. However, it is today coordinated by large organisations at major centres. In these instances, much to the chagrin of religious leaders it was referred to as 'Indian Carnival'.

There are many similarities between the two festivals. Apart from the occurrence at similar times of the year, both are characterised by gay abandon, including a reduction of customary restrictions on women and men, suggestive dances, open flirtation between the sexes and participation in collective bands'.[4] Any suggestion of a link between the two festivals is frowned upon by the Hindu orthodoxy and devotees are entreated not to turn it into a carnival. I suggest that both of these festivals have a common origin in fertility rituals of pre-Christian/pre-Hindu animist belief systems. Belief systems of agricultural peoples where women's productivity and sexuality were seen as closely linked to the productivity of the land. The suggestive dancing of women during both these festivals probably has a common source in the natural rhythms of the universe of which they may both be unaware.

Mas

The word 'mas' is usually used to refer to the masquerade, the donning of costumes as individuals or in groups or bands. The masquerade is divided into 'ole mas' and 'pretty mas'. It is in the mas bands or as individuals that masqueraders dance through the streets and 'play mas' during the two days of Carnival. The ethnic, colour and class divides still characterise the festival, but there is also a large gender divide. Carnival continues to be especially popular with women of all classes, especially middle-class women who can afford the expensive and often revealing costumes for the 'pretty ma'. While Carnival is seen as a national festival by the creole community there is some ambivalence towards it. Fundamentalist Christian groups call on their flock to stay away from its immorality and vulgarity and organise weekend trips to the beach for young people. In 1995, this reached a peak with the prolonged call for a ban on the Carnival band called 'Hallelujah' by 208 'independent' pastors.

In their rejection of Carnival as a national festival, Indian nationalists refer to this vulgarity and wanton display of sexuality which they argue is incompatible with the Indian or Hindu way of life. Indeed over the years, mas designers attempt to portray the beauty or reality of Hindu deities as with other non-western religious deities, have been met with strong protest leading to actual legislation prohibiting the use of religious symbols in the masquerade.

Indian women who participated in Carnival until recently were seen as putting a stain on their sacred womanhood. The debauchery of this festival is seen as another example of the decadence and low moral standards of creole society and the African population in particular and some have called for Indians to refrain from participation. In this situation it is the Indian women in particular who have to be watched for it is they who have the responsibility of maintaining the image of the culture.

Today there is a general concern that women are taking over the masquerade and that Carnival is becoming a woman's festival. In the past the mas as discussed in Earl Lovelace's *The Dragon Can't Dance*, was one means through which working-class African men could become a king for a day in a large and elaborate costume. Additionally these aspects of the mas are being dominated not only by men but by middle-class women, many of them independent income earners who in the increased social space enjoyed by women in these times are willing and able to purchase their own costume.

Women in these bands for two days give up responsibilities for home and children, often to men, and abandon 'decency' in a wave of abandon. Men it seems participate much more in the early Monday morning 'Jour Ouvert' with its satire, protest, transvestism, and revelling in dirt, mud and oil, but women are also very much present here. The reality is of course that women and men participate in Carnival in different ways and women's participation in the 'pretty mas' on Mondays and Tuesdays is much more noticeable.

With all of this in mind it was interesting for me to see the results of the 1991 survey. According to this survey only 6.5 per cent of the sample actually play mas which is the national festival, with almost equal proportions of males and females. Most masqueraders lived in the capital Port of Spain. Interestingly more Indian males than African males played mas and less than one-half the number of Indian women played as African women. One the other hand, many people are spectators of the festivities on the streets or look at televised coverage. More women than men stay at home during Carnival some do look at mas on television but a substantial proportion especially of Indian women stay at home but do not look at mas on television. More men also work during the days of Carnival. So the masquerade is one of those arenas where the negotiation and contestation is taking place over whose culture and who should define this culture.

Calypso

In V. S. Naipaul's book *The Middle Passage*, the calypso is the only aspect of Trinidad and Tobago society which receives honourable mention. He states:

It is only the calypso which touches reality. The calypso is a purely local form. No song composed outside of Trinidad is a calypso. The calypso deals with local incidents, local attitudes, and it does so in local language. The pure calypso is unintelligible to the outsider. (Naipaul 1962:70)

It is interesting to discuss the calypso here as not only is it yet another of these contested terrains of 'national culture', but its lyrics explore very clearly the conflicts and representations as they are perceived in everyday life. The calypso however is an art form developed among working-class, urban African men. It is therefore characterised by the sexism and racial consciousness characteristic of that group.

In the calypsonians' explorations of inter-ethnic relations male-female relations provide a spicy metaphor. And so in spite of, or probably because of, the strong feelings of endogamy present within the Indian community, African male working-class men constantly sing of relationships with Indian women.

In the 1930s and 1940s calypsonians viewed as threatening the gradual entrance of Indians into creole society. They saw them as moving from their backward 'coolie' ways to 'modern' (read Western) ways, including the practice which has since ceased of Indians adopting European surnames.

Ramjohn taking lessons daily
From a high school up in Laventille (repeat)
The first day lesson was dictation
And a little punctuation
After class he come home hungry to death
His wife eh cook Ramjohn start to fret
Whole day you sit down on your big fat comma
And you eh cook nothing up
But ah go dab dis hyphen in your semi colon
And buss up you full stop and stop.
(Mighty Skipper, Ramjohn, 1959)

In addition increasingly they began to see Indians as threats in the economic marketplace. A theme which continues to the present.

As for the men and them I must relate
Long time all they work was in a cane estate
But now they own every theatre
Yes hotel, rumshop and hired car
Long time was Ramkaisingh, Boodoo, Poodoo and Badoo
Now is David, Cooper, Johnston, Caesar, Cephas Alexander
(Mighty Killer, Indian people with creole names, 1950)

In relation to Indian women I argue in another publication (Gibbons and Reddock, nd) that calypsonians discourse on women, sexuality and inter-ethnic relations can be seen as a metaphor for Indian/African relations at a more general level. At one time Indians and by extension Indian women were seen as exotic and different; hence the calypso *Dookanii*:

> She was exotic, kind and loving too
> All her charms I could never describe to you
> When she smiled her face lit up raptuously
> Radiating joy, life and vitality
> (Attila the Hun, 1939)

But many calypsos also dealt with Indian women as the forbidden fruit, that which they desired but could not attain because of a controlling father. This can be seen as a metaphor for the lack of contact between the two ethnic groups for many years. The impression is always given that the woman is interested but if it were not for the father then the relationship would have taken place: a possible reference to the colonial leaders who through spatial and other mechanisms sought to keep the groups apart, but also to the community leaders (usually of the Brahmin caste) who discouraged social mixing among the populace.

Much reference is made to the proverbial violence of Indian men in general and towards their women in particular, a component all too real of the stereotype held by the society. African men also refer to stereotypes of themselves in these songs and the contrast is often made between the entrepreneurship of the Indian and the lack thereof of the African as we see in the following songs.

> No doolahin Ah cyah come back here again
> Suppose yuh man ketch we in the act
> Take a big stick and open me back
> So you see somebody go dead
> Ramlal eh making fun
> When he know he go use he gun
> (Melody, *Aw Nigger*, c. 1960)

or:

> Well I was in love with an Indian
> I was born in Jermingham junction
> I couldn't see eye to eye with her family

Her mother argues:

> Ramlogan house got cattle
> The Kirwal can't gie am nothing
> (Dictator, *Moonia*, 1955)

According to analyst Zeno Constance:

The mother's objections are based on facts: the creolised African cannot make a suitable match for her daughter. Economically and culturally it is a mismatch. (Constance 1991: 15-16).

The calypsonians response is of course to refer to the one thing the colonised African male perceives that he has up on men of every other ethnic group, his sexuality, which the young woman desires but her father or in this case her mother refuses to allow (Constance 1991: 16).

But another genre of calypso, usually referred to as the 'nation-building' calypso seeks to build harmony by echoing bland clichés about unity among every creed and race. Numerous of these exist and are usually played on national holidays like Independence or Republic Day. Some of them however echo sincere sentiments of hope and aspiration for a society free from ethnic tension such as this one from Indian calypsonian, Hindu Prince:

Since in the days of our forefathers
Who came from India and Africa
They inject these two races
To treat one another with disgrace
After they slave together
They still hated one another
Leaving us to carry on foolishly
With such names as nigger and coolie
Because if this racial problem should spread everywhere
We'll always be divided because of the difference in our hair.
    (*Racial Division*, 1972)

Calypsos by male African calypsonians also reflect what they feel about women of their own ethnic group. This yearning for the other in song illustrates the fact that women in Trinidad and Tobago are constantly being defined in relation to or in opposition to each other. Years ago, when I did my historical research on women in Trinidad and Tobago, it was as important to me to understand the Indian experience as it was the African experience as we had often been defined in relation to each other.

Hence one finds the calypsonian for a long time wanting the best of both worlds, the creole culture to which he is accustomed but the docility and subservience stereotypically associated with Indian women at that time but not associated with African women:

I want everybody to realize
I want a nice Indian girl that is creolise
I don't want no parata or dhal water
I want my potato and cassava

crab, callaloo and of course my manicou
And how about my stew pork and pound plantain too
I want my own vermouth and whisky
And they must agree to support my family.

And

All meh friends and family calling me stupid
Since I pick up ah Indian woman and married.
(Invader, *Maharaj Daughter*, 1939)

But he explains why:

She does wake up in the morning and cook me food
She does give me romance when I ah in the mood
Before ah go to work she does shine me shoes
That is what a Negro woman wouldn't do.
(Unity, *My Indian Wife*, 1972)

In spite of the involvement of creole women and male Indian singers in calypso, it continues to be a working-class male African form. The entrance of Indian women in recent times initially met with some consternation. The most significant of these was Drupatee Ramgoonai, a young woman from Penal, a rural town in the deep south who entered the scene in 1987.

Drupatee had previously been involved in Indian singing, of classical music and a Trinidad creation 'chutney' an Indian folk form which is discussed later in this paper. Drupatee's entrance marked a trend which had been taking place for some time but which is not explored here in detail, the incorporation of Indian words, phrases, melodic lines and instruments into the calypso, creating a new form referred to as 'chutney soca'. Indeed, the official originator of the soca, calypsonian Shorty (now known as Ras Shorty I), in a 1979 interview stated that he called the music 'Sokah', in recognition of the Indian influence which was evident in his compositions and which he incorporated into this new form of the calypso (Constance 1991: 63-64).

Returning to Drupatee, according to Constance, she was described as 'a thorn among Indian women', 'immoral and disgusting'. He continues:

The Indian community which was so prepared to defend their name when sullied by the words of the Calypsonian was not now willing to allow one of their members to be part of that tradition. 'No Indian woman has any right to sing calypso', and 'Indian women have been a disgrace to Hinduism' were cries from the fraternity (Constance 1991: 51).

Noor Kumar Mahabir, writing in the paper *Sandesh* in 1988 noted:

For an Indian girl to throw her high upbringing and culture to mix with vulgar music, sex and alcohol in Carnival tents tells me that something is radically wrong with her psyche. Drupatee Ramgoonai has chosen to worship the Gods of sex, wine and easy money (Mahabir, February 19, 1988 quoted in Constance 1991: 51).

What is interesting is that Indian men had been involved in calypso since the 1930s and, although still a small minority, their numbers have increased since the 1960s, yet similar concern was not expressed at their involvement. Clearly, for women as the bearers of tradition and locations of cultural identity, this incursion into the creole culture by a rural Hindu woman was another matter altogether. This development is captured in a poem by another Indian woman Ramjandaye Ramkissoon-Chen:

When the Hindu Woman Sings the Calypso

The moon takes on the glint of sun
Sleep flies, eyelids open
Legs supine rise to rhythm,
Past the midnight.
There, where she was born
In those early days
The village lamplight
With the cock's last crow
Was out. Feet huddled
Fast in sleep.

Strings of rhinestone now
'Purdah' her forehead
Her hair frizzled
To a 'Buss-up-shot'
The long tresses of
A long Tradition
Seared in the electricity
Of the mike's cord length

The glare of stagelights
Takes over her backyard.
There was her training
Near standpipe and river.
That was the ground where only
Girls and women danced
To 'tassa' drummings
Of pre-nuptial celebrations.
. . .

Her voice vibrates
Past stage and audience,
Through all transmissions
The whole country listens
Night insects too
Stop their churrings

As she sings and *'winds'*
To calypso and *'pan'*
With *'tassa'* blending.
    (Extract from *Creation Fire,* 1990)

In the book *The Web of Tradition*, the author John Thieme analyses V. S. Naipaul's use of the calypso in his early work *Miguel Street*. In this collection of stories, Thieme notes, quotations from ten calypsos are included in the text. Additionally Naipaul's use of allusions is similar to that of the calypsonian.

In *Miguel Street*, Naipaul deals continuously with the battle of the sexes, a phenomenon which as we have seen is a constant theme of the calypsonian. In Theime's words:

The further one reads, the clearer it becomes that, far from being a collection of only related stories, Naipaul's first book is a carefully orchestrated investigation of the concept of manliness as it obtains in Trinidad. "To be a man, among we men" the statement of one of Naipaul's characters Hat, captures the ideal of manliness which is as central to *Miguel Street* as it is to the Calypso tradition (Theime 1987: 23).

The writer argues that in the use of this calypso tradition, Naipaul related this work to the culture of the black urban populace with a degree of sympathy which he never would again in his work. His underlying conclusion being that the society, or at least the urban African society, is fundamentally matriarchal, hence the male's need to assert his threatened manhood in aggressive macho postures (Theime 1987: 26).

As Trinidadian feminist Ramabai Espinet notes: 'The Indian presence in today's calypso is very strong and there are conscious efforts at blending the musical forms of both dominant cultures in jazz, parang and calypso. The next stage will be very interesting to observe as Indians, and women in particular, assert their right to sing instead of being sung about (Espinet 1993: 54).

Pan

Steelband, that third component of the triad, emerged around the 1930s. Many factors have been given for its emergence, the ban on the use of drums during the nineteenth century, and experimentation with alternatives, the availability of oil drums from the oil industry among others. For Creoles, the pan is seen as indigenous to Trinidad and Tobago, a form of native creation. For Indians, it is primarily an African-derived form. As with the calypso, the steelband developed among the urban dispossessed males and has been aggressively defended by them over the years.

As with Carnival and to a lesser extent calypso, in the 1950s the steel band was elevated to the level of national culture by the new nationalist movement from the its previous negative, low-class status, although the status and standard of living of its practitioners has not show any significant improvement. While on the one hand there is the view reflected in the following quotation by Steumple that:

Perceptions of pan as a national art persist in spite of the fact that the majority of pannists are African. Similarly, steelband music is basically a synthesis of African and European derived traditions, with relatively little Indian input. These characteristics are significant to many Indians, particularly those in rural areas. For them steelband is not a national music but an Afro-Trinidadian music (Steumple 1990: 288).

This is so in spite of the fact that Indian arrangers and pannists have featured among some of the best in the country.

In contrast to this, research by Indian nationalists point to the significant contributions which Indians have made to the development of the pan. There is the need for further research to ascertain the claim by Noor Kumar Mahabir, for example, that Indian *tassa* drums provided a framework and a pattern for the development of the steelband, both are played with 'sticks' and initially the steelpan was suspended around the neck while playing. Pan men in St James, an urban centre with equivalent proportions of Indians and Africans, argue that *tassa* groups and steelbands have both influenced each other, where for example the *tassa* drum in some bands is used as a 'cutter', while some of the rhythms played by the *tassa* have been influenced by Afro-Trinidadian rhythms (Steumple 1990:167).

Until recently women were seldom present in the macho world of the steelband, especially during the years of steelband clashes. There was always a minority of women players and many supporters but in spite of the increasing number of female pan players, this was and predominantly still is culturally a male institution. In the 1950s a small number of all-female steelbands were formed, mainly of middle-class young women, but none of them survived. Since the 1970s according to Steumple, the number of female players has increased amounting to approximately 15 per cent of the adult bands. Additionally there is now another all-female band.

This increased entrance of women, was facilitated largely through the introduction of pan into schools, however initially men did not take to kindly to women's entry into their domains. Indeed, today women have to 'prove their mettle' to be able to make it with the men and men have admitted that the introduction of women to the panyard has altered the 'tenor' of the yard. Historically steelbands develop in communities and derive their membership and support from them. Not surprisingly therefore, this is reflected in their class and ethnic composition.

Chutney

In the contestations over national culture, efforts to create an acceptable popular Indo-Trinidadian alternative have proved more difficult. The contestation over chutney therefore presents a lucid example of the ways in which issues of gender, class, caste and nationality intersect in very specific and contentious ways.

'Chutney' is the term used locally to refer to a folk form of Indo-Trinidadian music and dance (this must be differentiated from chutney soca which was referred to earlier). Most sources suggest that it derives its tradition from Indian folk practices of the non-Brahmanical castes and rural folk as well as the ritual sensuous and suggestive dances of Hindu women at women's ceremonies on the eve of weddings (Patasar 1990; Ribiero 1992).

The chutney phenomenon grew in popularity during the 1980s with the emergence of large chutney shows in huge open spaces such as Rienzi Complex in Couva, Hi-way Inn in Charlieville, Chaguanus, Himalaya Club in San Juan, Lall's Cultural Complex in Debe and Simplex Cultural Centre in New Grant, Princes Town. They are attended by large crowds of hundreds and thousands, a significant proportion being women of all ages.

On the one hand, this phenomenon presented a cultural alternative for Indian people, especially the perceived 'vulnerable' groups, women and youth, for social and cultural enjoyment within their community. This was welcomed by Indian nationalists such as Kamal Persad who argued that this provided Indian-Trinidadians with an opportunity to engage in a peculiarly Indian kind of dance at public events, something which was not possible in other venues such as discos and Western-oriented occasions (Persad 1991: 8).

For the Brahmanical and other leadership of religious bodies, this development presented what could be termed a problem of representation. It severely challenged and undermined the mythical contrast between Indian and African-derived art and cultural forms which saw the latter as obscene, bacchanalian and characterised by loose behaviour of women and the former as its alter ego. The chutney phenomenon if anything showed that African and Indian working-class people were more similar than different in their willingness to express their free spirit with sensuousness in dance and music. It also showed that in both communities it is women especially who feel this need for self-expression and release from the responsibilities and abuses which characterise their daily lives.

In the debate which ensued, largely within the Indian community, the representation of Indian womanhood and by extension of Indian culture became a major focus. The 1990 seminar organised by the *Trinidad Guardian* and the Hindu Prachar Kendra entitled 'The Phenomenon of Chutney Singing', in the words of Indira Ribiero: 'provided a forum for healthy discussion and debate.' (Ribiero 1992).

Deo Kiernan Sharma, executive member of the National Council of Indian Culture saw chutney as the corruption of a genuine folk form through the desecration of Hindu sacred songs in an atmosphere of drunkenness, sensuality and vulgarity which had no place in East Indian culture (Ribiero 1992). Similarly respected cultural activist Narsaloo Ramaya despaired at the squandering of the Indian cultural legacy through debauchery and obscenity at the altar of commercialism. Indian singers he argued were using the sacred names of gods and goddesses in their music in the pure, undefiled form and polluting them with lewdness which now characterised the dancing at chutney shows (Ribiero 1992).

When it was pointed out that this so-called obscenity and sensuousness was a time-worn Hindu tradition still preserved in the *matikor* ceremonies on wedding nights of Indian women today, Indrani Rampersad, then president of the Hindu Women's Organisation had this to say:

Whereas Guardian-Kendra seminar on chutney recognises that women have their special forms of dancing at Friday night weddings, chathis etc. and that there is a time and place for everything, be it resolved that the dancing which accompanies Friday night, wedding nights, chathis etc. remain amongst women in their private functions and not be taken to public forms like chutney occasions and that the police enforce laws against vulgarity and obscenity throughout the land, and in this case, chutney occasions (*Express*: December 12, 1990, p. 10 quoted in Ribiero 1992).

In this case we see clearly that the contestations over representation in national culture takes place not only between ethnic groups but also within groups between genders and among classes. As late as 1995, the Hindu Women's Organisation president in a public address denounced the chutney phenomenon as a disgrace to the community. In many ways, working-class Indian women and men are defining for themselves in the commercially charged and emotionally stressful context of contemporary Trinidad and Tobago, their understanding of culture, and not accepting definitions imposed from above, something which they and their African counterparts have had to do for generations.

Conclusion

What starts to emerge from the exploration above is that in creole[5] Trinidad and Tobago, the symbols of national culture and national identity emerged from a struggle over representation and citizenship of specific classes, genders and ethnic groups. This struggle continues as other groups seek to define their presence in the society. Through a continuous struggle and contestation, the authenticity of these symbols is being challenged and in the process are being transformed. This process if allowed to continue could provide a basis for a more truly inclusive national and indeed regional identity.

Feminist scholars and activists have an understanding of marginalisation, unequal power relations, hegemony and dominance, based on our personal experiences and an increasing global awareness. In attempting to construct an alternative, we are also aware that male norms of identity formation and selfhood are problematic in that they are based on the negation of selfhood and identity to others. We therefore have a political responsibility to engage with this discourse and to transform the parameters in which cultural expression and identity formation takes place.

Notes

1. One such recent challenge was the Hallelujah controversy. This took place at Carnival 1995 when calls were made by 208 independent Christian pastors to have the name of band leader Peter Minshall's band 'Hallelujah' changed, as it was a blasphemy against the faith.
2. The 1970s was a period of Black Power revolt and black consciousness movements. These emerged among young people and spread to the wider population. One of the effects of these movements was the revalorisation of African-derived cultural artifacts as well as a revalorisation of Africa and africanness within the Caribbean.
3. National Mobility and Social Interaction survey, carried out through the Institute of Social and Economic Research (ISER), St Augustine in 1991 on a representative sample of 3,931 persons in Trinidad and Tobago based on the design of the Trinidad and Tobago CSSP (Continuous Sample Survey of the Population) of the Central Statistical Office.
4. In recent years on Hindu religious grouping the Hindu Prachar Kendra has introduced a form of Indian song competition into its celebrations of *Phagwa* known as *Pichakaree*. This has a similar characteristic of social commentary as the calypso but is not yet a generalised popular form of cultural expression.
5. Since the 1995 general elections and the accession to power of the first Indo-Trinidadian prime minister, the social context has changed somewhat. This paper has not been able to explore these new developments. It should be noted however that some analysts have begun to refer to the post-1995 era as the post-creole era.

24

Liberal Ideology and Contradictions in Caribbean Gender Systems

V. Eudine Barriteau

Liberalism has built into itself a contradiction between the ideals of individual freedom and equality in the public sphere and the assumption that women are naturally subject to men in the family. It is this contradiction that lies at the heart of its democratic theory and practice.[1]

And so, with precious few exceptions, the boys are left to languish in that desert of academic uncertainty which empowers rapidly increasing numbers of females without so much as a backward glance to appreciate the human devastation that is taking place . . . Such is their confusion that they will even take to the soap box spouting coed propaganda, completely ignoring that a school system in which, for example, 75 per cent of head teachers are female is unlikely to produce any assessment favourable to boys. Not in academic studies. Not in the humanities. Not in socialization. Not in physical education [Editorial, *Barbados Advocate News*, February 6, 1996].

Introduction

This analysis is motivated by an attempt to devise an explanatory framework for the changing nature of gender relations in the Caribbean.[2] Sharp, polarised divisions exist in the ways in which Caribbean people interpret these evolving gender relations. I also want to theorise about the surfacing and expressions of currents of misogyny in our societies. I am seeking to understand why some men and women are expressing outrage, and in some instances hatred, at women and blaming many negative developments on the changing economic and social roles of women. A common theme running through their criticism is a questioning of the ideology of gender equality and a challenge to the work of feminists and others to promote gender equality.

Public commentators now often typecast Caribbean women as the witches of medieval Europe (Anderson and Zinsser 1988: 151-173). We are responsible for the destruction of families (but not crops as yet), high rates of divorce, male economic and social marginalisation, and the comparatively poor performance of boys and men at every educational level. Repeated newspaper articles and editorials warn of the damage being done to boys by being raised in female-headed households, attending co-educational schools and being taught primarily by female teachers (Barriteau 1994: 283). According to this type of analysis Barbados is a matriarchal society and other Caribbean countries could be heading in that direction: 'Slowly but surely becoming a matriarchal society, women outnumber men, make up most of the workforce, own most of the homes' (*Advocate News*, March 6, 1996).

The search for an explanation led me to consider a key inheritance of the colonial encounter a set of social relations influenced by the Enlightenment discourse of liberalism. A significant aspect of that inheritance is the material and ideological expression of relations of gender as part of the operations of gender systems in Caribbean societies.[3] I am specifically interested in revealing how the ideological and material relations of gender interact and reinforce each other. I examine these against an assumption by policy makers and the public that the post-colonial state can introduce and manipulate changes in relations without repercussions in the ideological relations of gender or the need to pay attention to these repercussions. I examine the roles liberal ideology assigns to women in the public and private spheres of society and the assumed naturalness of women's inferior and subordinate status in the private.

I contend that the State attempts to construct or facilitate new roles for women only in the public sphere of society primarily through altering access to the resources of the state. However, when these new constructs of women's roles create either unintended or unanticipated outcomes, some men and women begin to question seriously the whole idea of women's relevance as equal citizens with a right to make equal demands on the resources of the state. I perceive and theorise the currents of misogynous behaviour as nostalgia, a longing, for women to return to their proper place in society. The opponents of women's expanded public sector participation and visibility in the non-traditional areas, imagine women's proper place as location within the private sphere of the family, households, and kinship groups.

Before post-independent states introduced equal access to resources, the opponents of women's citizenship could take comfort in a 'sexual division of labour' informed more by gendered relations than any biological functions. Among other outcomes, that division of labour ensured women received less financial and other rewards for the same and often greater levels of output. It denied women access to more rewarding and remunerative types of employment. Altogether a gendered division of labour reinforced an unequal distribution of political, economic, and social power. To support my theorising about the contradictory nature of women's experience of gender relations I analyse and juxtapose the United Nations Development Programme's (UNDP) high ranking of the Barbadian state in promoting gender equality, and the misogynous currents simultaneously existing within Barbadian society.

This paper therefore, examines some challenges posed by the continuity between the systems of beliefs we inherited and the particular manifestations of gender relations in our societies. I problematise and interrogate the philosophical inheritance of liberalism and isolate the theoretical features that create problems for women. I use examples of adverse contemporary gender relations to illustrate the playing out of the inherent negative conceptualisation of women in liberal thought. I conclude by noting that the state and society must now invest in altering negative gender ideologies about women.

Theorising Gender Relations and the Liberal Legacy

Feminist investigations of the nexus of 'the differences of class, race, sex, age, culture and nationality' (Braidotti 1991: 6) and how these affect women's lives have created many analytical tools to explain why women continuously experience persistent patterns of subordination. One of the more powerful explanatory frameworks to emerge criticises the position that the adverse experiences women have arisen in the traditional idea of biological, sexual differences. This new explanation argues women's adverse experiences originate in the socially created relations of gender. These relations of gender are multidimensional, and are influential on the symbolic level, the conceptual level, the social and institutional level, and the individual level (Kuiper 1995; Scott 1986).

Rosi Braidotti observes that theories of gender differ from 'sexual difference' theories because at the core of the former is the notion that 'gender challenges the pretense at universality and objectivity of conventional systems of knowledge and scientific discourse' (Braidotti 1991:

5-6). By using the socially constructed relations of gender rather than the concept of biologically based, unchangeable, sex differences we can pay attention to history and culture and emphasise particularity. This is important from a Caribbean perspective. The concept of gender moves feminist analyses away from the notion of Caribbean women as an undifferentiated sex class of victims experiencing a fixed, hegemonic, superstructure of patriarchal oppression. It opens the possibilities for theorising the multiple contested locations of dominations in women's lives (Barriteau 1995: 144).

Joan Acker argues that the development of the concept as an analytical category resulted from attempts to find new avenues into the diverse and complicated problems of explaining the extraordinary persistence throughout history and across societies of the subordination of women (Acker 1990: 145). Constructing this new analysis, feminists identified previous analyses of women's oppression or subordination as instances or representations of larger societal phenomena. Extending this insight, I view 'Capitalist Patriarchy', 'Biological Determinism', and 'The Subjugation of Women' as differing moments and historical and cultural expressions of the social relations of gender.

I define the concept of gender to refer to a complex system of social relations that socially creates and maintains women and men and through which they gain access to, or are allocated power, status and resources within a society (Barriteau 1994). As an analytical category, gender does not explain the socially constituted being 'woman' in relation to an autonomous, unproblematised social being 'man' (Barriteau 1994: 34). I also reject the definition of women as deficient men. In my definition, the concept of gender refers both to a system of social relations through which women and men are socially constituted and as an analytical category for examining social conditions affecting the constituted beings, women and men.

Two components of my definition the creation and maintenance of gender identities and access to resources underscore the ideological and material dimensions of relations of gender. The material dimension reveals how women and men gain access to or are allocated status, power and material resources in a given society. Feminist analyses of material relations of gender have made visible the distribution of political, economic and social power, and material resources. The ideological dimension indicates the ways in which a society constructs what it accepts (and contests) as the appropriate expression of masculinity and femininity. Combined they comprise gender systems that are networks of power relations. Gender relations constitute the continuous social, political, economic, cultural, and psychological expressions of the material and ideological aspects of a gender system. An unequal gender relation is a relation of domination. Its inequality is rooted in an asymmetry of power that has differential ideological and material outcomes (Barriteau 1996). Caribbean states either ignore or are unaware of how both dimensions of gender systems reinforce and underwrite each other. Changes in one dimension will produce alterations in the other or at the very least threaten the status quo.

I emphasise five critical points in my development and application of the concept to making sense of women's lives:

(1) Gender relations as women experience them now are power relations and relations of domination (but they do not have to be).

(2) Gender also constitutes an analytical frame with its own methodologies that enable us to interrogate social conditions affecting the constituted 'beings' (women or men).

(3) Investigators should do gender analysis with an understanding of the multiple relations of domination that women experience even as they attempt to alter these.

(4) The social relations of gender intersect with other oppressive relations such as those arising from class, race, ethnicity, age, and sexual preference.

(5) The material and ideological relations of gender reinforce and complicate each other. For analytical purposes they can be isolated, but changes in one dimension have immediate repercussions in the other.

Asymmetrical gender relations occur in all dimensions of society and affect all aspects of the lives of women. It is incorrect to isolate one dimension of women's life as more or less gendered than the other.

Along with altering how we view women that is by recognising our subjectivities and the interplay of other social relations focusing on gender enables a widening of the scope of analysis. We have a conceptual frame with which to appreciate both the interior elements of women's lives and the external social and epistemological environment in which these lives are lived. Rosi Braidotti argues that concentrating on gender results in renewed emphasis being place on the situated (local) structure of knowledge (Braidotti 1991 :6). Maintaining a simultaneous focus on the situated local structure of Caribbean feminist epistemologies and 'the multiple, messy, lived diversities of Caribbean women's lives' (Barriteau 1995: 147) has to be an ongoing project. Paying attention to relations of gender has created new conceptual and methodological openings to investigate the lives of Caribbean women. It has generated a new research agenda that feminists should address.

Feminist discourses in the Caribbean have yet to problematise and contextualise the epistemological and ideological superstructure that influences our institutions, policies and practices. We should deconstruct the foundational assumptions of liberal political ideology to reveal its gendered construction of citizenship. Our scholarship has yet to interrogate what liberal notions of political and economic participation means for women in our societies. We are yet to examine how the State's definition of citizenship and political relevance influences policies of the state and produces complications and benefits in women's lives.

Feminist scholars in industrial societies have undertaken extensive critiques of the classical liberal philosophy and of the modern liberal conception of democracy and citizenship (Siim 1988: 162). They have also examined the problems posed for women by state systems premised on liberal ideology (Pateman 1989; Pateman and Gross 1986; Elshtain 1981; Young 1990; Eisenstein 1979; Jones and Jonasdottir 1988).

Caribbean societies differ significantly from those of Europe and North America. Different historical, cultural, social, economic and political experiences shape the conditions of women's lives in the Caribbean (Beckles 1989; Reddock 1995; Barriteau-Foster 1992; Hart 1989; Mohammed 1994). Yet we share critical connections. One of the legacies of British colonialism in the Caribbean is a political and economic system derived from the Enlightenment philosophy of Liberalism. The Enlightenment legacy remained unchallenged when the political status of Caribbean countries changed from British colonies to independent nations (Howard 1989; Thomas 1988; Lewis 1968). The connections between contemporary gender relations in the Caribbean and the legacy of Enlightenment thought have not been sufficiently explored in analyzing gender relations for women.[4]

I do not identify the Enlightenment legacy to attribute blame to a colonial past for ongoing gender relations of domination. One of the reasons these continuities exist is because post-colonial states find it in their interests to maintain them. Our state systems and dominant institutions are based on and generally remain faithful to the same liberal ideological and philosophical foundations as those of northern industrialised societies. It is this foundation that we must examine because not only do the core contradictions reoccur in our societies, but they have vastly different outcomes where women's lives do not mirror the experiences of women in the North.

The colonial encounter between Europe and what are now the commonwealth states of the anglophone Caribbean created a society that is of the West, but located in the geographic south. The Caribbean became a *tabula rasa* for European powers. No indigenous traditional political, economic and social foundations survived cohesively to offer resistance to the institutions and practices transplanted from Europe. As C. L. R. James argued in the 1920s, the Caribbean is a product of the West. The states of the commonwealth Caribbean are products of European expansionism, imperialism and greed. We exist geographically in the south, but our political and economic antecedents are decidedly Western. Once European colonial penetration began in the Caribbean there was no ongoing competition between traditional (i.e. indigenous) and European institutions of state and society as happened elsewhere in Asia and Africa. As a result, in spite of creolisation our dominant values and beliefs have more in common with European traditions and practices than with any other region of the world. We need now to examine what these value systems mean to the multiple realities of Caribbean women's lives. Unless we challenge, expose and seek to alter the ideological legacy of colonial rule then the fundamental disjunctures created in the way women have been theorised into subordinate positions will continue.

Gender Relations, the Public/Private Dichotomy and Caribbean Women

Caribbean states have an ideological foundation derived uncritically from the Enlightenment discourse of Liberalism with all its inherent, embedded contradictions for women. The contemporary institutions and ongoing practices of our state are stubbornly, and for some critics (Lewis 1968: 226-256; Thomas 1984) proudly, maintained according to the tenets of liberal political and economic theory. Liberal ideology has certain foundational assumptions. Some of these are:

(1) The belief that rationality is the mechanism or means by which individuals achieve autonomy.
(2) The idea that an individual and citizen is a male household head.
(3) The separation and differentiation of society into the private and the public; the world of dependence, the family, and the world of freedom, the state and work (Flax 1990: 6).
(4) The gendering of that differentiation so that women are posed in opposition to civil society, to civilisation (Flax 1990).

The conception of society as divided into two spheres, the public and the private is a dominant and recurring feature of liberal political ideology. It is also the feature I want to emphasise as producing contradictions for Caribbean women. Carole Pateman argues that the dichotomy between the private and the public is central to almost two centuries of feminist writing and political struggle (in the North). She observes that feminist criticism is primarily directed at the separation and opposition between the public and private spheres in liberal theory and practice (Pateman 1989: 119).

In liberal ideology the public sphere is the world of the economy, civil society and the State. Although Jurgen Habermas' theorising of the public sphere is unsatisfactory from a feminist perspective, his establishment of three analytically distinct arenas of the public is useful (Habermas 1989; Fraser 1992: 199). The public sphere is therefore the realm of the formal and informal economy, public discourse, rationality, civic responsibility, freedom and equality, rights, and citizenship. Nancy Fraser's warning not to conflate the arenas of the public, or to be tempted to view these distinctions as merely a theoretical issue is relevant for the argument I am building. She notes that there are practical political consequences to any conflation. The differentiation enables us to determine whether gender issues are being subjected to the logic of the market or the state in its administrative bureaucratic function (Fraser 1992: 198). I argue that not only do we need an understanding of the different arenas of the public, but we need to recognise the fictional nature of the public/private divide, interrogate the purposes this divide serves, and expose how the issues of the public and private in fact criss-cross and transcend each sphere continuously.

The private sphere is the realm of domesticity, and for women a pivotal site for relations of domination. According to liberal political theory it comprises the world of the family, conjugal and sexual relations. The private sphere is part of civil society but it is incorporated differently. It is theorised as separate from the public world of the economy, public discourse and the state. Ruth Lister argues that one of the achievements of feminism is that it, 'has succeeded in shifting the boundaries between public and private on a number of important issues such as domestic violence and marital rape' (Lister 1995:10).

Historically the private domain has been a complex, contested location for women. Liberal ideology structured the private domain in a hierarchical manner. Women were subordinate to men, conceptually and practically. They were not considered household heads irrespective of the real dynamics of household decision making. The organisation of domestic life is a site where women generally experience some of the more punitive aspects of gender relations that are grounded in domination and a denial of agency, but it does not occur only there. Policy makers have come to accept feminist investigations that prove domestic relations for many women have largely been problematic and in some cases, life-threatening (World Bank 1995: 21-42). What they have yet to acknowledge is that the gender ideologies that underpin women's inequalities in domestic life also exist and reoccur in the public sites such as the economy and political participation.

Fundamental to my development of the concept of gender is the view that adverse gender relations also exist in the public sphere so that gender relations transcend this inherited dichotomy of liberalism. In the public/private divide, liberal ideology theorises and locates women in the private sphere and locates our activities, contributions and relevance to societies as belonging to that sphere. My central thesis is that this public/private divide is at the core of many problems women experience in liberal societies. Not only is civil society divided into these two spheres but the private is subordinate and inferior to the public.

Liberalist ideology maintains an equality of all participants in the public so that even though liberal theorists admit women may be subordinate to men in the private sphere, these theorists assume women participate as equals in the public once the State creates access. This is not true. The hierarchies embedded in the organisation of domestic life follow women into public spaces. When they resent or attempt to reject these by articulating the equality implied in the core assumptions of liberal ideology, women meet with resistance and condemnation. I illustrate this in the second part of the chapter.

Of the two competing traditions within Liberalism, freedom and equality (Lister 1995), the Caribbean post-colonial state has selected equality as a basis for redefining its relations with women. The egalitarian impulse has dominated the state's attempts to undo the structural conditions of inequality built into the fabric of social life for Caribbean women. States have done this primarily by removing structural barriers for women to participate in the economy and the polity. By so doing they have attempted to give to women an equality in some arenas of the public sphere that both the State and society deny women in the private. Theoretically and in terms of daily experiences, women remain tethered to sexual and gender differences.

Another root cause of contradictions in contemporary gender systems is the notion of equality of participation and relevance in the public, contrasted with hierarchical subordinate relations in domestic life. The post-colonial Caribbean state has gradually opened up the public sphere of the economy for women. The State attempts and successfully manipulates and alters material relations of gender for women while attempting to ignore or hold ideological relations of gender constant. I theorise that the State alters material relations of gender since these affect the market and therefore economic growth and development as defined by its model of development the modernisation paradigm. States seek to maintain ideological relations of gender as they are. They assume these relations operate primarily in the private sphere and therefore to benefit maintaining the status quo or the structures of domestic life.

The post-colonial state's primary area of intervention for women in the public arena is in the economy. It does not take the lead in public discourse on women. When it becomes involved it is usually drawn into dialogue and interventions by interest groups. As the economic expression of liberal ideology, capitalism requires a critical mass of both skilled and unskilled workers women and men. The industrialisation by invitation variant of development requires cheap, easily manipulated sources of labour. In the Caribbean that translates into women workers. As the foundation of capitalist production the market requires equality of access to whatever labour is necessary. States investing in maintaining the market will also invest in enhancing women's participation in the market.

There is a key assumption that States make that which is flawed. They believe that they can modernise Caribbean economies by following the conventional approaches to development, and retain a pre-modernisation cultural/ideological purity of rigid roles for women and men. At some point ruptures will appear and they have. States cannot willfully alter material relations of gender and assume ideological relations will remain static. I maintain that the deep divisions in relations of gender are the rupturing of ideological relations of gender.

For example, at the beginning of the twentieth century Caribbean women experienced a subordinate status in both domestic life (the private sphere) and the economy and political participation (the public sphere). Although detrimental to women at the level of the state and civil society, material and ideological relations of gender supported each other and the inferior status of women. Early twentieth-century Caribbean society did not allow women to vote (Mayers 1995), provide them with equal access to educational resources (Cole 1983), or the opportunity to participate equally as workers in the economy (Reddock 1995).[5]

I maintain this is a major source of contradictions in contemporary gender systems. The State continues to alter material relations of gender for women in the public sphere without either wanting or attempting to address the subordination of women in the private. Policy makers also disregard how ideological aspects continuously complicate attempts at material change. It is difficult to maintain a society premised on hierarchy and subordination in domestic, family, conjugal and sexual relations (the private) when there are ongoing moves towards equality of participation in the economy, public discourses, and political institutions (the public).[6]

Contradictions in Contemporary Gender Systems

How do these contradictions for women in liberal ideologies play out in Caribbean societies? How have changes in women's access to resources in the public sphere destabilised existing gender relations and instituted further complications in their lives? Gender systems in the Caribbean are riddled with contradictions and paradoxes for women and men. The 1995 Human Development Report published by the UNDP contained for the first time an index and analysis of how women and men fare in countries worldwide. The UNDP offers a Gender Development Index (GDI) and a Gender Empowerment Measure (GEM). According to this report some Caribbean states ranked high in their treatment of women. Barbados's

Table 24.1 Rank of Caribbean countries on Gender Development Index

Country	Rank in CARICOM	Rank in the world [2]
Barbados	1	11
Bahamas	2	26
Trinidad and Tobago	3	36
Jamaica	4	52
Guyana	5	70
Cuba [1]	–	47[3]
Dominican Republic[1]	–	69[3]
Haiti [1]	–	105

Source: United Nations Human Development Report 1995.

Notes:

[1] These Caribbean countries are not members of CARICOM neither are they former colonies of Britain.
There is no information for the other countries that are members of CARICOM.
[2] This is based on data for 130 countries.
[3] Note that Cuba and the Dominican Republic rank higher than Guyana, a CARICOM country.

rating is singular and most outstanding of all developing countries in the world. Barbados is ranked at number 11, on the GDI ahead of several industrialised societies (UNDP 1995: 76). Table 24.1 shows the comparative ranking of Caribbean countries within the region and worldwide with the GDI.

The GDI of the UNDP attempts to measure inequality between women and men as well as the average achievement of all people (UNDP 1995: 72). The GDI concentrates on the same variables the UNDP used to create its Human Development Index (HDI) but compares and takes note of differences in the achievement of women and men to determine a country's progress or efforts to attain gender equality. 'The methodology used imposes a penalty for inequality, such that the GDI falls when the achievement levels of both women and men in a country go down or when the disparity between their achievements increases' (UNDP 1995: 73).

The HDI measures longevity (life expectancy), knowledge (educational attainment), and access to the basic resources in a society (adjusted real income). The GDI is simply the HDI discounted or adjusted downwards for gender inequality (UNDP 1995: 73). Countries may have a high HDI ranking and fall in ranking on the GDI. This indicates that improvements in society have not benefitted women as much as men.

According to the UNDP, the GEM is their attempt to assess the extent to which women are empowered in the public sphere of their societies. It focuses on three variables. It measures women's participation in political decision making, their access to professional opportunities, and their earning power (UNDP 1995: 72). The GEM concentrates on participation, political, economic, and professional. 'While the GDI focuses on the expansion of capabilities, the GEM is concerned with the use of those capabilities to take advantage of the opportunities of life' (UNDP 1995: 73). Tables 24.2 and 24.3 present GDI and GEM indices for selected Caribbean countries. We note that the Bahamas, Trinidad and Tobago and the Dominican Republic show declines in their HDI ranking when it is adjusted for gender-related development indices. On the other hand Jamaica, Barbados, Cuba, Guyana, and Haiti improve their HDI when adjusted to incorporate gender-related indices. As Table 24.3 shows the GEM for Caribbean countries is also comparatively high. Barbados, the Bahamas, Trinidad and Tobago, Cuba, and Guyana perform much better than industrial countries in moving towards gender equality in women's political, economic and professional activities (UNDP 1995: 83).

From its analyses of these two indices the UNDP offers three salient conclusions. They note:

Table 24.2 Gender Development Index for Caribbean Countries

Country	Gender Development Index (GDI)	Share of earned income %[a]		Life expectancy (years) 1992		Adult literacy rate % 1990		Combined primary, secondary and tertiary school gross enrolment ratio (%) 1992		HDI rank minus GDI rank
		Female	Male	Female	Male	Female	Male	Female	Male	
Barbados[b]	0.878	39.4	60.6[c]	77.9	72.9	96.3	97.8	73.1	74.8	10
Bahamas[b]	0.828	28.3	71.7	77.9	68.7	97.7	98.4	76.8	71.8	-4
Trinidad and Tobago[b]	0.786	24.7	75.3[c]	74.0	69.3	96.4	98.5	67.8	67.9	-4
Cuba	0.726	27.2	72.8[c]	77.3	73.5	94.2	95.5	67.7	62.2	10
Jamaica	0.710	38.6	61.4[c]	75.8	71.4	87.2	79.4	64.6	64.5	14
Dominican Republic	0.590	12.1	87.9[c]	71.7	67.6	80.7	80.8	73.8	70.0	-1
Guyana[b]	0.584	21.2	78.8	68.0	62.4	96.8	98.3	68.2	68.1	3
Haiti	0.354	34.2	65.8	58.3	54.9	39.6	45.8	28.4	30.5	4

Source: *UNDP Human Development Report 1995*

Notes: [a] Data are for latest available year.
[b] CARICOM Countries.
[c] An estimate of 75 per cent was used for the ratio of the female non-agricultural wage to the male non-agricultural wage.

Table 24.3 Gender Empowerment Measure for Caribbean Countries

Country	Gender Empowerment Measure (GEM)	Seats held in Parliament (% women)[a] 1994	Administrators and managers (% women) 1992	Professional and technical workers (% women) 1992	Earned income share (% women)[b]
Barbados	0.545	14.3	32.6	52.3	39.4[c]
Bahamas	0.533	10.8	26.3	56.9	28.3[c]
Trinidad and Tobago	0.533	17.7	22.5	54.7	24.7c
Cuba	0.524	22.8	18.5	47.8	27.2[c]
Guyana	0.461	20.0	12.8	47.5	21.2[c]
Dominican Republic	0.412	10.0	21.2	49.5	12.1[c]
Belize	0.369	7.9	12.6	51.9	21.1[c]
Haiti	0.349	3.0	32.6	39.3	34.2[c]

Source: *UNDP Human Development Report 1995*

Notes: [a] Data are as of June 1994. A value of 0 was converted to 0.01 for purposes of calculation.
[b] Data are for latest year.
[c] An estimate of 75 per cent was used for the ratio of the female non-agricultural wage to the male non-agricultural wage.

No society treats its women as well as its men. Gender equality [*or more accurately working towards gender equality* (my words)] does not depend on the income level of a society. Significant progress has been achieved over the past two decades, though there is still a long way to go. (UNDP 1995: 77-78)

The UNDP's analysis substantiates and reflects the positive changes post-colonial Caribbean states have introduced to benefit women. It also confirms that Caribbean states target altering material relations of gender in the public sphere as the means of correcting women's historic subordination in societies.

But if things are so wonderful for Caribbean women, (and some material conditions are much better than in other parts of the world), why is there such an outpouring of ridicule, contempt and fear of the gains that women have made? The comparatively high ratings of Caribbean countries on the GDI and GEM have not altered gender ideologies that view women as subordinate to men and that have become overtly misogynist.

Barbados has the best rating of all developing countries on both the GDI and the GEM. On the latter Barbados ranks ahead of Luxembourg, Switzerland, the United Kingdom, Belgium, Ireland, Spain, Japan, Portugal, and France (UNDP 1995: 84-5). Yet there are distinct dissonances between the ideological climate of gender relations in which Barbadian girls and women exist and the officially recorded material gains women have made as reflected in the UNDP report.

In 1996, a Barbadian calypsonian composed a song whose lyrics capture this contested, unstable ideological climate. He struggles to be balanced or even fair in his assessment of the current state of gender relations but he has inculcated the ideology that when women gain economically men lose, and women are to be blamed for adverse circumstances in men's lives.

Save Our Sons

It is with a heavy heart that I come to warn
The young men of this country on the road to damnation
Gang wars, HIV, drugs, violent crimes
Make their lives more worthless than a nickel or a dime
What have they done to deserve this fate?
Are they really to blame for this sorry state?
We must reverse this trend at any cost
The manhood of this country must not be lost
Chorus
Save our sons
There is no self respect if they cannot find jobs
Save our sons

Don't be surprised if they turn to choke and rob
Save our sons
No man should be forced to live off his parents
Save our sons
From my own experience I can understand their plight
The training by their parents didn't prepare them for this fight
They treated their daughters with tender loving care
While the boys are left alone to roam 'bout everywhere
They are not taught responsibility
How they can act differently when they become men
And be proper fathers to their children

I am happy for the progress Bajan women have made
But is it worth the high price our sons have paid?
Women now play the role of mother and father too
But when you check the schools male teachers are few
In every circle females now dominate
No role models for boys to emulate
A rooster cannot teach a fowl to be a hen
It wasn't God's plan for women to teach boys to be men
    (Darwin Worrell 1996: 4)

The lyrics of this song alone can be the genesis of a thesis on contradictions in Caribbean gender systems. The lyrics also echo the view of a cross-section of the Barbadian public. The calypsonian is intervening in the arena of public discourse. He is reflecting and at the same time influencing public opinion on women's roles. He acknowledges that most women are forced to be mothers and fathers. Yet without giving them credit he blames them for doing this and invokes religion (God) as not sanctioning the raising of boys by women.

The concept of women 'fathering' is not new in Caribbean society. George Lamming addressed this in his novel, *In the Castle of My Skin* 45 years ago (Lamming 1986). This influenced social anthropologist Edith Clarke to name her seminal work, *My Mother Who Fathered me* (Clarke 1957). There was no public outrage at women raising boys 45 years ago, because women had very little presence and visibility in the public then. If they had to be responsible for both parenting roles this was merely an extension of their 'natural' roles in the private sphere.

The calypsonian holds the so-called progress of women accountable for the problems men experience and in some cases create for themselves. Caribbean men do face serious economic and social problems, some different to that experienced by women. But recognising that men, like women have problems does not mean the existence of these difficulties can be reduced to women's existence.

There are huge unproblematised spaces between the obvious crises in personal, social and economic relations that many men experience and conflating these to be the fault of women. When we seek to explore these spaces we should ask:

What are the choices men make in the construct of their masculinity?
How does the State relate to men?
What are the gender ideologies men subscribe to?
What are the contents of the concept and construct of Caribbean masculinity?
Does the former include a definition of masculinity as total control and power over women?

These are some of the conceptual issues on Caribbean masculinity we should problematise to understand how men affect relations of gender and in turn how it affects them. This may also prevent the more hysterical forms of analyses that hand to Caribbean women all the ills of our contemporary society.

What is this progress that women have made for which men are paying a high price? A release on the Report of the National Commission on the Status of Youth registers the many examples of discrimination, gender subordination and exploitation experienced by young Barbadian women. This was reported in a news story titled, 'Young Women Most Affected: Report shows Females to be Worse Off Among Youth in Barbados' (*Advocate News*, February 24, 1995, p. 3).

Ironically the study of the youth, (commonly used in the Caribbean to mean young men), was commissioned by the Barbados Government because of the plight and alleged marginalisation of the young, black, Caribbean male. Many awaited the publication of the report to provide the evidence for the widespread argument that Caribbean women had gained too much at the expense of Caribbean men. Instead the report concluded the following:

Young women attempted more suicides;
They are the lowest income earners;
They are affected by sexual harassment at the workplace;
They are more likely to be unemployed than young men; and
The young poor are primarily female.
    (*Advocate News*, February 24, 1994, p. 3).

Another argument targeted against women in Barbados is the alleged damage being done to boys in co-educational schools.[7] The opening quotation to this chapter is from a newspaper editorial. It states with conviction that boys are left to languish in a desert of academic uncertainty 'which empowers rapidly increasing numbers of females without so much as a backward glance to appreciate the human devastation taking place.' As conspiratorial as this contention may sound there is some merit to investigating the comparatively poorer performance of boys if that is the case. What is objectionable are the other charges the editorial goes on to make. It questions and undermines the professional integrity of female head teachers. It states as part of a school system where 75 per cent of heads are women, these women will not produce any assessments favourable to boys in academics, the humanities, in physical education or in socialisation.

If these public commentators had phrased these arguments in terms of race instead of gender, there would have been a national uproar. Instead this was followed by another news story some weeks later proclaiming the establishment of a new private school for 'Boys Only'. The news item stated that the school is being established for boys because the co-educational structure of secondary education 'is generally believed to have disadvantaged the boys' (*Advocate News*, March 16, 1996).

This hysterical conviction that feminists have a deliberate plot to damage the educational opportunities of young men has been around for some time. Three years ago a columnist addressed his concerns to the then Minister of Education:

Sir, I fear a great upheaval of this society may be upon us, in which women will try to usurp authority over the man. As I see it the feminists have two hurdles left how to reproduce without men; and how to deny men positions of authority in the society. Education is the vital conduit to better jobs and social advancement; and women are taking it over. Most teachers are women, and some of these expect boys to behave like nice little girls, or be considered rebels and troublemakers. And while girls are lauded for good results, boys are labelled 'nerds'. And so we end up with boys on every block turning to crime; 500-odd men in prison mostly young and uneducated: only 12 women. This then is your golden opportunity to save our young males from illiteracy, crime and unemployment and perhaps save man-kind itself. Take my advice and end coeducation, that miserable experiment. Wherever possible let male teachers teach boys. (Richard Hoad, 'Those Femme Fatales', *Daily Nation* September 17, 1993, p. 9).

It is impossible to analyse here all the articles and news items dealing with this theme in the print media but some headlines will underscore the resentment and fear about women's and girls' academic performance. 'Too Many Men on Sidelines, says Niles' (*Barbados Advocate*, May 6, 1993, p. 7); 'Co-ed Classes May Not be Best for Boys', (*Daily Nation*, July 16, 1993, p. 32); 'Will Girls Continue Dominance: Co-education and Scholarship Performance,' (*Barbados Advocate*, September 23, 1993, p. 12); 'Co-education Benefitting Girls', (*Sunday Advocate*, October 31, 1993, p.

16); 'Co-education Could Be the Cause of Boys' Poor Performance', (*Barbados Advocate,* April 7, 1993, p. 7).

If women's position in Caribbean societies is so ideal, why do women always experience higher levels of unemployment than men? Table 24.4 presents the most recent unemployment ratios in Barbados for women and men for a four-year period.

Female labour force participation has never equalled that of men. The UNDP notes that although the gaps between women and men in access to education and health care have been closing, the gaps in income have remained wide and in some cases have increased (UNDP 1995: 74).

Ironically the virulent anti-feminist stance of a female journalist in Barbados underscores the limitations of arguments explaining women's 'oppression' as originating in biological determinism. This woman uses most of her columns to castigate feminists and women in national organisations who call attention to existing negative situations for women. Her level of contempt for other women whose positions she does not agree with is so strong that her choice of language as well as the content of her arguments are abusive.

Instead we have the pressure of the fast-track career push. The I can do anything males can do better. The slut eat slut attitude that is now defining the modern female. Why is it that so many 'feminists' seem to think that one has to be a subservient female or an overpowering dictatoress. Instead of being sensitive, and loving and generous, many have become asexual or mock lesbians. Then swift on the heels of hating men for being money-grubbing, lots of women seem to be using their vaginas as cash registers. They use the very core of their biological femaleness to profit from the core of male sexuality. And the males resent being used so brashly and indiscreetly, so they make sure they get their pound of flesh for the dollar. (Dawn Morgan, *Advocate News*, March 8, 1996).

Morgan released this column as her contribution to the celebration of International Women's Day. She states, 'many feminists' perceive there

Table 24.4 Unemployment ratios in Barbados

Year	Women	Men	National average
1991	21.4	13.2	17.1
1992	25.7	20.4	23.0
1993	27.6	21.5	24.5
1994	25.7	18.2	21.9

Source: *Barbados Statistical Services 1991-94*

are only two choices available to them, dominate or be dominated. She paints a picture of 'many' feminists as motivated by hatred of women and men. She skillfully attempts to establish a causative link between lesbianism, a sexual orientation or preference for women and feminism, a political stance to expose conditions of domination or subordination for women. This she does in a society where there is both an articulated homophobia and a day to day tolerance of male homosexuality. The purpose of her tirade seems devoted to painting feminists as despicable in every aspect of their lives. It seems she raises the charge of lesbianism to derail the issues raised by feminists and have discussions instead focus on speculations about their sexuality.

Conclusion

These contradictions exist because liberal ideology cannot accommodate women's participation as equals in the public arena. The post-colonial Caribbean state has to begin to address what the World Bank calls institutionalised norms and biases that influence the organisation of life and the allocation of resources within households (World Bank 1995). Put differently, the State should acknowledge how ideological relations of gender in both the private and public spheres structure and complicate material relations of gender. Correcting biases against women to ensure access to the market through public policy does not eliminate or reduce prejudices existing against women within domestic life or the extension of these biases into many areas of women's public sector participation. Creating conditions for equal access to the resources of the state through altering material gender relations will not automatically eliminate or reduce relations of domination in the private domain. Instead, it often exacerbates adverse relations of gender in both the public and private domain. In spite of expanded opportunities for women to participate in the public domain, I contend that the archaic ideological relations of gender prevent women from exploiting these. Some women also subscribe to maintaining antiquated notions of appropriate roles and gender identities. However the greater degree of resistance comes from masculinist ideas, structures and practices that adhere to a belief in an innate inferiority of women. Without a willingness to examine how its emphasis on changes in some spheres of public life may alter domestic life, liberal ideology contributes significantly to the increasing resentment of women in the public arena.

Notes

1. Carole Pateman quoted in Birte Siim (1988: 162).
2. Caribbean in this chapter refers to the anglophone countries that were once colonies of England\Britain or are still in a dependent political relationship such as Montserrat or the British Virgin Islands. It was once called the West Indies and is now the Commonwealth Caribbean. These countries share a common colonial past, analogous political institutions, and comparable social and economic relations.
3. For a full explanation and typologies of Caribbean gender systems see, V. Eudine Barriteau, 'Gender Systems and The Project of Modernity in the Post Colonial Caribbean', paper presented at the first SEPHIS Workshop. The Forging of Nationhood and the Contest Over Citizenship, Ethnicity and History, New Delhi, February 6-8, 1996.
4. However in my dissertation I begin this examination of how the post-colonial Caribbean state shapes economic relations for women.
5. However, equality of access to the market does not necessarily mean equality in conditions of participation, that is equality in wages and benefits received or other conditions of employment. It means policy makers have removed structural barriers but ideological barriers, qualifying the degree, nature and acceptance of women's participation remain. Winston Cox observes that although women took up most of the new employment opportunities in the manufacturing sector especially after 1970, two facts qualify this occurrence. First the increase in employment opportunities in manufacturing did not translate into higher female labour force participation. Second within the manufacturing sector there were marked divergencies in the wages paid to women and men with women receiving significantly lower wages. See Cox 1982: 63-69.
6. I am not at all suggesting that women have equality in the public sphere or that states have removed or are interested in removing all barriers for women in the public. Instead I am saying that where and when the state makes concessions to women it is overwhelmingly in that area of civil society regarded as the public.
7. All government owned and operated primary schools are coeducational as are 98 per cent of government secondary schools.

Bibliography

Abelove, Henry, Michele Aina Barale, and David Halperin, eds, *The Gay and Lesbian Reader* (London: Routledge, 1993).

Abraham-Van der Mark, E. E. 'The Impact of Industrialisation on Women: A Caribbean Case' in *Women, Men and the International Division of Labor*, ed. by June Nash and Maria Fernandez-Kelly (Albany: State University of New York Press, 1983) pp. 374-386.

_____. 'Marriage and Concubinage Among the Sephardic Merchant "Elite" of Curacao' in *Women and Change in the Caribbean*, ed.by Janet Momsen (Kingston: Ian Randle Publishers; Bloomington: Indiana University Press; London: James Currey Publishers, 1993) pp. 38-49.

Abrahams, Roger, 'Patterns of Performance in the British West Indies' in *Afro-American Anthropology: Contemporary Perspectives*, ed. by N. Whitten and J. Szwed, 163-179 (New York: Free Press, 1964).

Acker, J. 'Class, Gender and the Relations of Distribution.' *Signs* 13:3 (1988) pp. 473-497.

Abu-Lughod, L. 'The Romance of Resistance: Tracing Transformations of Power Through Bedouin Women', *American Ethnologist* 17:1 (1990) pp. 41-55.

Acker, Sandra, *Gendered Education: Sociological Reflections on Women, Teaching and Feminism* (Toronto: The Ontario Institute for Studies in Education, 1994).

Adorno, Theodor W. 'Subject and Object.' in *The Essential Frankfurt School Reader*, ed. by A. Arato and E. Gebhardt (New York: Urizen Books, 1978).

Agard, John, *Mangoes and Bullets* (London: Pluto, 1985).

Agarwal, Bina, *A Field of One's Own: Gender and Land Rights in South Asia* (Cambridge University Press, 1994).

Ahye, Molly, 'Carnival, the Manipulative Polymorph: An Interplay of Social Stratification in *Social and Occupational Stratification in Contemporary Trinidad and Tobago*, ed. by Selwyn Ryan (Port of Spain: Institute of Social and Economic Research, University of the West Indies, 1991) pp. 399-416.

Alexander, Jack, 'The Culture of Race in Middle Class Kingston, Jamaica', *American Ethnologist* 4:3 (1977) pp. 413-435.

_____. 'The Role of the Male in the Middle Class of Jamaican Family: A Comparative Perspective', *Journal of Comparative Family Studies* 8:3 (1977) pp. 369-389.

Ali, Lynne A. *Hand in Hand*, Caribbean Caresses Series (Oxford: Heinemann, 1993).

Ampka, A. 'Floating Signification.' *Hybrid* 3 (1993) pp. 5-6.

Andaiye. 'Women and Poverty in Guyana'. [Paper presented at] Institute of Development Studies, University of Guyana Seminar on Poverty in Guyana: Finding Solutions, [held in] Guyana March 18-19, 1993.

Andaiye, ed. 'Working Hands: Caribbean Women Organising.' *Woman Speak* 26 and 27 (1990). Special issue.

Andaiye and B. Shiw Parsad, *Changes in the Situation of Women in Guyana: 1980-1993 (Facts and Figures)* (Georgetown: Guyana National Printers, 1994).

Andaiye and P. Antrobus, 'Towards a Vision of the Future: Gender Issues in Regional Integration.' Paper commissioned by the West Indian Commission, 1991.

Anderson, Bonnie S. *A History of Their Own: Women of Europe From Prehistory to the Present* (New York: Harper & Row, 1988).

Anderson, Patricia, 'Conclusion: Women in the Caribbean.' *Social and Economic Studies* 35:2 (1986) pp. 291-324.

Anderson, Patricia and D. Gordon, 'Labour Mobility Patterns: The Impact of the Crisis', in *Development in Suspense*, ed. by George Beckford and Norman Girvan, 184-97 (Kingston: Friedrich Ebert Stiftung, 1984) pp. 184-197.

Anderson, Robert M. *Vision of the Disinherited: The Making of American Pentecostalism* (New York: Oxford University Press, 1979).

Antrobus, Peggy and C. Deere, *et. al.*, *In the Shadows of the Sun: Caribbean Development Alternatives and U.S. Policy* (Boulder, CO: Westview Press, 1990).

Anzaldùa, G. *Borderlands/La Frontera: The New Mestiza* (San Francisco: Spinsters/Aunt Lute, 1987).

Ardener, Edwin. 'Belief and the Problem of Women' in *Perceiving Women*, ed. by S. Ardener, (London: Dent, 1975) pp. 1-17.

Arjoon, S., N. Jayaram, and K. Nurse. 'Caribbean Social Science: Review and Relevance.' Faculty of Social Science Staff Seminar Series, Institute of Social and Economic Research, University of the West Indies, St. Augustine January 25, 1996.

Armstrong, D. 'From Clinical Gaze to Regime of Total Health.' in *Health and Wellbeing: A Reader* ed. by A. Beattie, M. Gott, L. Jones, and M. Sidell. Milton (Keynes: Open University Press, 1993).

E. Arnold , 'The Use of Corporal Punishment in Child Rearing in the West Indies', *Servol News* 8:34 (1992).

Atkinson, R. L., R. C. Atkinson, D., E. E. Smith, J. Bem and E. R. Hilgar,. *Introduction to Psychology* (San Diego: Harcourt Brace and Jovanovich, 1990).

Austin-Broos, Diane J. 'Born Again and Again, and Again: Communities and Social Change Among Jamaican Pentecostalists', *Journal of Anthropological Research* 37 (1981) pp. 226-246.

_____ . 'Politics and the Redeemer: State and Religion as Ways of Being in Jamaica', *Nieuwe West-Indische Gids* 70 (1996) pp. 1-32.

_____. 'Redefining the Moral Order: Interpretations of Christianity in Post-Emancipation Jamaica' in *The Meaning of Freedom*, ed. by F. McGlynn and S. Drescher (Pittsburgh: University of Pittsburgh Press, 1992) pp. 221-245.

_____. 'Religion and the Politics of Moral Order in Jamaica' *Anthropological Forum* 6 (1991-1992) pp. 287-319.

_____. 'Pentecostals and Rastafarians: Cultural, Political and Gender Relations of Two Religious Movements', *Social and Economic Studies* 36:4 (1987) pp. 1-39.

_____. *Urban Life in Kingston, Jamaica: The Culture and Class Ideology of Two Neighbourhoods*, Caribbean Studies Series, no. 3 (New York: Gordon and Breach, 1984).

_____. 'History and Symbols in Ideology: A Jamaican Example.' *Man* n.s., 14 (1979) pp. 297-314.

_____. *Jamaica Genesis: Religion and the Politics of Moral Orders* (University of Chicago Press, 1997).

Ayodike, T. 'Images of Woman in Selected CXC Literature', Paper presented at a Gender and Education Seminar, Faculty of Education and Women and Development Studies, University of the West Indies, Mona, 1989.

Bacchus, M. K. *Education for Development or Underdevelopment?* (Ontario: Wilfrid Laurier University Press, 1980).

Bailey, Barbara, 'Gender: The Not so Hidden Issue in Language Arts Material Used at the Primary Level in Jamaica', *Caribbean Journal of Education*. (in press).

_____. 'Sexist Patterns of Formal and Non-Formal Education Programmes: The Case of Jamaica' in *Gender: A Caribbean Multidisciplinary Perspective*, ed. by Elsa Leo-Rhynie, Barbara Bailey, and Christine Barrow. Kingston, (Kingston: Ian Randle Publishers, 1997).

Bailey, Barbara and Elsa A. Leo-Rhynie, 'Factors Affecting the Choice of Science Subjects by High School Students: A Pilot Study'. Paper presented at a Gender, Science and Technology Seminar, Centre for Gender and Development Studies, University of the West Indies, Mona, 1994.

Bakker, I., ed. *The Strategic Silence* (London: Zed Books, 1994).

Bandura, A. *Social Learning Theory* (Englewood Cliffs, NJ: Prentice Hall, 1977).

Bandura, A. and R. Walters, *Social Learning and Personality Development* (New York: Holt, Rinehart and Winston, 1963).

Barbados. *Barbados Blue Book, 1911-12* (Bridgetown: Advocate Printery, 1913).

Barbados. Ministry of Agriculture. *1989 Census of Agriculture*. Bridgetown: Ministry of Agriculture, Food and Fisheries in collaboration with the Data Processing Department and Barbados Statistical Department, 1991.

Barber, Karin. 'Popular Arts in Africa.' *African Studies* 30:3 (September 1987): pp. 1-78.

Barker, David and Balfour Spence, 'Afro-Caribbean Agriculture: A Jamaican Maroon Community in Transition.' *Geographical Journal* 154:2 (1988) pp. 198-208.

Barriteau, V. Eudine. 'The Construct of a Postmodernist Feminist Theory for Caribbean Social Science Research', *Social and Economic Studies* 41:2 (1992) pp. 1-43.

_____. 'Gender and Development Planning in the Post-Colonial Caribbean: Female Entrepreneurs and the Barbadian State.' Ph.D. diss., Howard University, 1994.

_____. 'Gender Systems and the Project of Modernity in the Post-Colonial Caribbean'. Paper presented at the First SEPHIS Workshop on the Forging of Nationhood and the Contest over Citizenship, Ethnicity and History, New Delhi, India, 1996.

_____. 'Postmodernist Feminist Theorizing and Development Policy and Practice in the Anglophone Caribbean: The Barbados Case' in *Feminism, Postmodernism, Development*, ed. By Marian H. Marchand and Jane Parpart, New York: Routledge, 1995) pp. 142-158.

Barrow, Christine. 'Anthropology, the Family and Women in the Caribbean' in *Gender in Caribbean Development*, ed. by Patricia Mohammed and Catherine Shepherd, (Kingston: Women and Development Studies Project, University of the West Indies, 1988) pp. 156-169.

_____. *Family in the Caribbean: Theories and Perspectives* (Kngston: Ian Randle Publishers; Oxford: James Currey Publishers, 1996).

_____. 'Small Farm Food Production and Gender in Barbados ' in *Women and Change in the Caribbean*, ed. by Janet Momsen (Kingston: Ian Randle Publishers; Bloomington: Indiana University Press; London: James Currey Publishers, 1993) pp. 191-193.

_____. 'Finding the Support: A Study of Strategies for Survival', *Social and Economic Studies* 35:2 (1986) pp. 131-76.

_____. 'Male Images of Women in Barbados', *Social and Economic Studies* 35:3 (1986) pp. 51-64.

_____. 'Reputation and Ranking in a Barbadian Locality', *Social and Economic Studies* 25:2 (1976) pp. 106-21.

Barthes, R. *Mythologies* (New York: Jonathan Cape, 1972).

Basham, A. L. *The Wonder that Was India: A Survey of the History and Culture of the Indian Sub-Continent before the Coming of the Muslims*(London: Sidgwick and Jackson, 1967).

Bateson, Mary, *Composing a Life* (New York: Plume, 1990).

Beauvue-Fougeyrollas, Claudie, *Les Femmes Antillaises* (Paris: L'Harmattan, 1979).

Beckles, Hilary McD. 'Black Masculinity in Caribbean Slavery', *Occasional Paper 2/96*. (Bridgetown: Women and Development Unit, University of the West Indies, 1996).

_____. 'Sex and Gender in the Historiography of Caribbean Slavery' in *Engendering History: Caribbean Women in Historical Perspective*, ed. by Verene Shepherd, Bridget Brereton, and Barbara Bailey (London: James Currey Publishes; Kingston: Ian Randle Publishers, 1995)pp. 125-140.

_____. 'Kalinago (Carib) Resistance to European Colonisation of the Caribbean.' *Caribbean Quarterly* 38:2-3 (1992) pp. 1-14.

_____. *A History of Barbados. From Amerindian Settlement to Nation-State* (Cambridge University Press, 1990).

_____. *Natural Rebels: A Social History of Enslaved Black Women in Barbados* (New Brunswick, NJ: Rutgers University Press, 1989).

_____ . *Afro-Caribbean Women and Resistance to Slavery in Barbados* (London: Karnak House, 1988).

_____. 'Caribbean Anti-Slavery: The Self-Liberation Ethos of Enslaved Blacks', *Journal of Caribbean History* 22:1-2 (1988) pp. 1-19.

Beechey, Veronica, *Unequal Work* (London: Verso, 1987).

Belgrave, Valerie, *Sun Valley Romance*, Caribbean Caresses Series (Oxford: Heinemann, 1993).

Bem, S. L. 'Gender-Schema Theory: A Cognitive Account of Sex Typing.' *Psychological Review* 88 (1981) pp. 354-364.

_____, *The Lenses of Gender: Transforming the Debate on Sexual Inequality* (New Haven, CT: Yale University Press, 1993).

_____. 'The Measurement of Psychological Androgyny', *Journal of Consulting and Clinical Psychology* 42 (1974) pp. 155-162.

Beneria, L. and S. Feldman, eds *Unequal Burden: Economic Crises, Persistent Poverty and Women's Work* (Boulder, CO: Westview Press, 1992).

Bennett, J. H. *Bondsmen and Bishops: Slavery and Apprenticeship on the Codrington Plantations of Barbados, 1710-1838* (Berkeley: University of California Press, 1958).

Berleant-Schiller, Riva and William Maure, 'Women's Place Is Every Place: Merging Domains and Women's Roles in Barbuda and Dominica', in *Women and Change in the Caribbean*, ed. by Janet Momsen, (Kingston: Ian Randle Publishers; Bloomington: Indiana University Press; London: James Currey Publishers, 1993) pp. 65-79.

Bernabe, Jean, Patrick Chamoiseau, and Raphael Confiant, *L'éloge de la créolité*. Discussed by A. James Arnold, in 'The Gendering of *Créolité*: The Erotics of Colonialism' in *Penser la créolité*, eds,. Maryse Condé and Madeline Cottenet-Hage (Paris: Karthala, 1989) pp. 21-40.

Besson, Jean, 'The Creolization of African-American Slave Kinship in Jamaican Free Village and Maroon Communities' in *Slave Cultures and the Cultures of Slavery*, ed. by S. Palmie (University of Tennessee Press, 1996) pp. 187-209.

_____. 'Empowering and Engendering Hidden Histories in Caribbean Peasant Communities', in *History and Histories of the Caribbean*, ed. byThomas Bremer and Ulrich Fleischmann. Berlin. (Forthcoming).

_____. 'Consensus in the Family Land Controversy: Rejoinder to Michaeline A. Crichlow', *Nieuwe West-Indische Gids* 69:3 and 4 (1995) pp. 300-304.

_____. 'Free Villagers, Rastafarians and Modern Maroons' in *Born Out of Resistance*, ed. by W. Hoogbergen (Utrecht: ISOR Press, 1995) pp. 301-314.

_____. 'Land, Kinship and Community in the Post-Emancipation Caribbean', in *Small Islands, Large Questions*, ed. By Karen F. Olwig (London: Frank Cass, 1995) pp. 73-99.

_____. 'Religion as Resistance in Jamaican Peasant Life', in *Rastafari and Other African-Caribbean Worldviews*, ed. by B. Chevannes (London: Macmillan, 1995) pp. 43-76.

_____. 'Women's Use of ROSCAs in the Caribbean', in *Money-Go-Rounds*, ed by S. Ardener and S. Burman (Oxford: Berg, 1995)pp. 263-288.

_____. 'Reputation and Respectability Reconsidered: A New Perspective on Afro-Caribbean Peasant Women' in *Women and Change in the Caribbean*, ed. by Janet Momsen (Kingston: Ian Randle Publishers; Bloomington: Indiana University Press; London: James Currey Publishers, 1993) pp. 15-37.

_____ . 'Agrarian Relations and Perceptions of Land in a Jamaican Peasant Village' in *Small Farming and Peasant Resources in the Caribbean*, ed. by/ by John S. Brierley and Hymie Rubenstein (Winnipeg: University of Manitoba, Department of Geography, 1988) pp. 39-61.

_____ . 'Family Land as a Model for Martha Brae's New History' in *Afro Caribbean Village in Historical Perspective*, ed. by C. V. Carnegie (Kingston: African-Caribbean Institute of Jamaica, 1987) pp. 100-132.

_____ . 'Freedom and Community: The British West Indies' in *The Meaning of Freedom: Economies, Politics and Culture after Slavery*, ed by F. McGlynn and S. Drescher (University of Pittsburgh Press) pp. 183-219.

_____. 'A Paradox in Caribbean Attitudes to Land' in *Land and Development in the Caribbean* ed. by Jean Besson and Janet Momsen (London: Macmillan, 1987) pp. 13-45.

_____. 'Family Land and Caribbean Society: Toward An Ethnography of Afro-Caribbean Peasantries' in *Perspectives on Caribbean Regional Identity*, ed. by E. Thomas-Hope (Liverpool: Liverpool University Press, 1984) pp. 57-83.

_____. 'Land Tenure in the Free Villages of Trelawny, Jamaica', *Slavery and Abolition* 5:1 (1984) pp. 3-23.

Billington, Louis and Rosamund Billington, ' "A Burning Zeal for Righteousness": Women in the British Anti-Slavery Movement, 1800-1820', in *Equal or Different: Women's Politics, 1800-1914*, ed. by Jane Rendall (Basingstoke: Macmillan, 1985) pp. 82-111.

Bird, L. 'Deconstructing Your Tertiary Studies: A Brief Guide for Feminist Students' in *Growing Up: The Politics of Human Learning*, ed. by J. Morss and T. Linzey (Auckland: Longman Paul, 1991) pp. 56-70.

Blake, Judith, *Family Structure in Jamaica: The Social Context of Reproduction* (New York: Free Press, 1961).

Blumberg, Rae Lesser, 'The Political Economy of the Mother-Child Family Revisited ' in *Family Kinship in Middle America and the Caribbean*, ed. by A. F. Marks and R. A. Romer (Leiden: Royal Institute of Linguistics and Anthropology, 1975) pp. 526-575.

Blumberg, Rae Lesser with M. P. Garcia, 'The Political Economy of the Mother-Child Family: A Cross-Cultural View', in *Beyond the Nuclear Family: A Cross-Cultural Perspective*, ed. by L. L. Otero (London: Sage, 1977) pp 99-159.

Bolles, A. Lynn, 'Doing It for Themselves: Women's Research and Action in the Commonwealth Caribbean' in *Researching Women in Latin America and the Caribbean*, ed. by Edna Acosta Belin and Christina E. Bose (Boulder, CO: Westview Press, 1993) pp. 153-174.

_____, *Sister Jamaica: A Study of Women Work and Households in Kingston* (Laham, MD:University Press of Jamaica, 1996).

_____ ,'Household Economic Strategies in Kingston, Jamaica',in *Women and World Change: Equity Issues in Development*, ed. by N. Black and A. Cottrell (Thousand Oaks, CA: Sage, 1981).

_____, 'Kitchen Hit by Priorities: Employed Working Class Jamaican Women Confront the IMF ' in *Women, Men and the International Division of Labor*, ed. by June Nash and Maria P. Fernandez-Kelly (Albany: State University of New York Press, 1983) pp. 138-160.

_____, *My Mother Who Fathered Me and Others: Gender and Kinship in the English-Speaking Caribbean*, Women and International Development, no. 175 (East Lansing, MI: Michigan State University Press, 1988).

_____, 'Of Mules and Yankee Gals', *Anthropology and Humanism Quarterly* 10:4 (1985) pp. 114-19.

_____, *We Paid Our Dues: Women Trade Union Leaders in the Caribbean* (Washington, D.C.: Howard University Press, 1996).

Bolles, A. Lynn and Deborah D'Amico-Samuels, 'Anthropological Scholarship on Gender in the English-speaking Caribbean',in *Gender and Anthropology*, ed. by S. Morgen (Washington: American Anthropological Association, 1989) pp. 171-188.

Bordo, S. R. 'The Body and the Reproduction of Femininity: A Feminist Appropriation of Foucault', in *Gender, Body, Knowledge: Feminist Reconstructions of Being and Knowing*, ed. by A. M. Jaggar and S. R. Bordo (New Brunswick, NJ: Rutgers University Press, 1989).

_____, 'Reading the Male Body', *Michigan Quarterly Review* 32:4 (1993).

Bowles, S. and H. Gintis, *Schooling in Capitalist America* (New York: Basic Books, 1976).

Boyd, Derick A. C. *Socio-Economic Report: Guyana, Parts 1 and 2*. (Washington, DC: Inter-American Development Bank, 1989).

Boyd, Derick A. C. *Economic Management, Income Distribution and Poverty in Jamaica* (New York: Praeger, 1988).

Boyden, J. 'Childhood and the Policy Makers: A Comparative Perspective on the Globalization of Childhood' in *Constructing and Reconstructing Childhood: Contemporary Issues of the Sociological Study of Childhood*, ed. by A. James and A. Prout (London: Falmer Press, 1990) pp. 184-215.

Braidotti, Rosi, *Theories of Gender, or: 'Language Is a Virus'* (Utrecht: Faculteit Der Letteren Rijksuniversiteit Utrecht, Openings College, 1991).

Braithwaite, Lloyd E. 'Social Stratification in Trinidad: A Sociological Analysis.' *Social and Economic Studies* 2:2 and 3 (1953).

Brana-Shute, Gary, 'Drinking Shops and Social Structure: Some Ideas on Lower-Class West Indian Male Behaviour', *Urban Anthropology* 5:1 (1976) pp. 53-68.

_____, *On the Corner* (Assen: Van Gorcum, 1979).

Brand, Dionne, *Bread Out of Stone* (Toronto: Coach House, 1994).

_____, 'No Language Is Neutral' in *Frontiers of Caribbean Literature in English*, ed. F. Birbalsingh (London: Macmillan, Warwick University Caribbean Studies, 1996) pp. 130-137.

_____ *Sans Souci and Other Stories* (New York: Fireband Books, 1989).

Brathwaite, Farley S. and Joyce L. Cole, 'Life Among the Caribbean (Lower Class) Poor: Past Research, Present Problems and New Directions', *Journal of Caribbean Issues* 4:3 (1978) pp. 78-100.

Brathwaite, Kamau, 'Caribbean Woman During the Period of Slavery'. Elsa Goveia Memorial Lecture, University of the West Indies, Cave Hill, 1984.

_____, *Contradictory Omens: Cultural Diversity and Integration in the Caribbean* (Kingston: Savacou, 1977).

_____, *The Development of Creole Society in Jamaica 1770-1820* (Oxford: Clarendon Press, 1971).

Braverman, Harry, *Labour and Monopoly Capitalism* (New York: Monthly Review Press, 1974).

Brereton, Bridget, *Race, Relations in Colonial Trinidad 1870-1900*, (London: Cambridge University Press, 1979).

_____, 'Text, Testimony, and Gender: An Examination of Some Texts by Women on the English-speaking Caribbean, from the 1770's to the 1920's', in *Engendering History: Caribbean Women in Historical Perspective*, eds,. Verene Shepherd, Bridget Brereton, and Barbara Bailey (London: James Currey Publishers; Kingston: Ian Randle Publishers, 1995) pp. 63-94.

Brewer, Rose, 'Theorizing Race, Class and Gender: The New Scholarship of Black Feminist Intellectuals and Black Women's Labor' in *Theorizing Black Feminisms*, ed. by S. James and A. Busia (New York: Routledge, 1993) pp. 13-31.

Brierley, John S. 'A Profile of Grenadian Women Small Farmers', in *Women and Change in the Caribbean*, ed. by Janet Momsen (Kingston: Ian Randle Publishers; Bloomington: Indiana University Press; London: James Currey Publishers, 1993) pp. 194-204.

Brierley, John S. and Hymie Rubenstein, eds *Small Farming and Peasant Resources in the Caribbean*. Manitoba Geographical Studies no. 10. (Winnipeg: Department of Geography, University of Manitoba, 1988).

Brittan, A. *Masculinity and Power* (Oxford: Basil Blackwell, 1989).

Brodber, Erna. 'Family Structure and Sex Role Learning: A Study of Socialisation in Jamaica', MSc thesis, University of the West Indies, Mona, 1968.

_____ *Jane and Louisa Will Soon Come Home* (London: New Beacon, 1980).

_____ *Louisiana* (London: New Beacon, 1994).

_____. *Myal* (London: New Beacon, 1988).

_____ *Perceptions of Caribbean Women: Towards a Documentation of Stereotypes*. Introduction by Merle Hodge. Women in the Caribbean Project, Volume 4 (Bridgetown: Institute of Social and Economic Research, University of the West Indies, 1982).

_____, 'A Second Generation of Freemen in Jamaica, 1907-1944.' Ph. D. diss., University of the West Indies, Mona, 1984.

_____ *A Study of Yards in the City of Kingston* (Kingston: Institute of Social and Economic Research, University of the West Indies, 1975).

Brown, C. K. *Gender Roles in Household Allocation of Resources and Decision-Making in Ghana*, Fadep Technical Series No. 2. Legon, (Ghana: University of Ghana, 1994).

Brown, J. and B. Chevannes, 'Gender Socialisation Project of the University of the West Indies. Final Report to UNESCO', Mimeo., 1995.

Brown, J., P. Anderson, and B. Chevannes, *Report on the Contribution of Caribbean Men to the Family: A Jamaican Pilot Study* (Kingston: School of Continuing Studies, Caribbean Child Development Centre, University of the West Indies, 1993.

Brown, Susan, 'Lower Economic Sector Female Mating Patterns in the Dominican Republic: A Comparative Analysis' in *Women Cross-Culturally: Change and Challenge*, ed. by R. Rohrlich-Leavitt (The Hague: Mouton, 1975) pp. 149-162.

Bruce, J. and D. Dwyer *A Home-Divided: Women and Income in the Third World* (Stanford University Press, 1988).

Bryce, Jane, 'Reformulating the Language of Love: A World of Caribbean Romance' in *Framing the Word: Gender and Genre in Caribbean Women's Writing*, ed. by Joan Anim-Addo (London: Whiting and Birch, 1996) pp. 108-127.

Bryden, Lynne and Sylvia Chant, *Women in the Third World: Gender Issues in Rural and Urban Areas* (New Brunswick, NJ: Rutgers University Press, 1989).

Bunton, R. and R. Burrows, 'Consumption and Health in the "Epidemiological" Clinic of Late Modern Medicine' in *The Sociology of Health Promotion*, ed. by R. Bunton, S. Nettleton, and R. Burrows (London: Routledge, 1995).

Burman, E. *Deconstructing Developmental Psychology* (London: Routledge, 1994).

_____. 'Feminism and Discourse in Developmental Psychology', *Feminism and Psychology* 2(1992) pp. 45-59.

_____. 'Power, Gender and Developmental Psychology', *Feminism and Psychology* 1 (1991) pp. 141-53.

_____. 'Transforming Psychology in South Africa', *Feminism and Psychology* 4 (1994) pp. 479-482.

Bush, Barbara, *Slave Women in Caribbean Society, 1650-1838* (Bloomington: Indiana University Press, 1990).

_____, 'Towards Emancipation: Slave Women and Resistance to Coercive Labour Regimes in the British West Indian Colonies, 1790-1838', in *Abolition and Its Aftermath: The Historical Context, 1719-1916*, ed. by David Richardson (London: Frank Cass, 1985) pp. 27-54.

Buss, D. M. 'Psychological Sex Differences: Origins through Sexual Selection.' *American Psychologist* 50 (1995) pp. 164-68.

Bussey, K. and A. Bandura, 'Self Regulatory Mechanisms Governing Gender Development', *Child Development* 63 (1992) pp. 1236-1250.

Buvinic, Mayra, N. H. Youssef with B. Von Elm, *Women-Headed Households: The Ignored Factor in Development Planning* (Washington, DC: International Center for Research on Women, 1978).

Carnegie, James, *Some Aspects of Jamaica's Politics: 1918-1938* (Kingston: Institute of Jamaica, 1973).

Chakravarti, Uma, 'The Sita Myth.' *Samya Shakti* 1:1(1983) p. 70.

Chant, Sylvia, 'Single-Parent Families: Choice or Constraint? The Formation of Female-Headed Households in a Mexican Shanty Town,' *Development and Change* 16(1985) pp. 635-56.

Charles, Annette, *Love in Hiding*, Caribbean Caresses Series (Oxford: Heinemann, 1993).

Chaudhuri, Nirad C. *Hinduism* (Oxford University Press, 1979).

Chevannes, Barry, 'Jamaican Lower Class Religion: Struggles Against Oppression.' MSc. thesis, University of the West Indies, Mona, 1971.

_____, 'New Approach to Rastafari', in *Rastafari and Other African-Caribbean Worldviews*, ed. by B. Chevannes (London: Macmillan, 1995). pp. 20-42.

_____ *Rastafari: Roots and Ideology* (Syracuse University Press, 1994).

_____, 'Revivalism: A Disappearing Religion.' *Caribbean Quarterly* 24:3 and 4 (1978) pp. 1-17.

Chodorow, N. J. 'Gender as a Personal and Cultural Construction.' *Signs* 20: 3 (1995) pp. 516-544.

_____. *The Reproduction of Mothering: Psychoanalysis and the Sociology of Gender* (Berkeley: University of California Press, 1978).

Cixous, Helene, *Three Steps on the Ladder of Writing* (New York: Columbia University Press, 1993).

Clark, Victor S. *Puerto Rico and Its Problems* (Washington, DC: The Brookings Institution, 1930).

Clarke, Colin G. *East Indians in a West Indian Town: San Fernando, Trinidad 1930-1978* (London: Allen and Unwin, 1986).

_____. 'Spatial Pattern and Social Interaction among Creoles and Indians in Trinidad and Tobago' in *Trinidad Ethnicity*, ed. by Kevin A. Yelvington (London: Macmillan Caribbean, 1993) pp. 116-135.

Clarke, Errol L. 'Please Keep Edwin out of Our Schools', *Daily Nation*, November 8, 1995, p. 7A.

Clarke, Edith, *My Mother Who Fathered Me* (London: George Allen and Unwin, 1957).

_____ *My Mother Who Fathered Me: A Study of the Family in Three Selected Communities in Jamaica* 2nd. ed. (London: Allen and Unwin, 1966).

Claypole, William,. 'Land Settlement and Agricultural Development in the Liguanea Plain, 1655 to 1700', M.A. thesis, University of the West Indies, Mona 1970.

Cliff, Michelle, *Abeng* (New York: Crossing Press, 1984).

_____, *No Telephone to Heaven* (New York: Vintage Books, 1989).

Coard, Phyllis, Grenada, to Political Bureau, New Jewel Movement, Grenada, Letter. Library of Congress, Washington, D.C. Document DSI-83-C-010292. CONF.-105657.

Cockburn, C. Brothers: *Male Dominance and Technological Change* (London: Pluto Press, 1983).

Cole, Joyce, 'Official Ideology and the Education of Women in the English-speaking Caribbean, 1835-1950' in *Women and Education* (Bridgetown: Institute of Social and Economic Research, University of the West Indies, 1982) pp. 1-34.

Colleton, Lucille,. *Merchant of Dreams*, Caribbean Caresses Series (Oxford: Heinemann, 1993).

Collins, Merle, *Angel* (London: Women's Press, 1987).

_____ *Rain Darling* (London: Women's Press, 1990).

Collins, Patricia Hill, *Black Feminist Thought: Knowledge, Consciousness and the Politics of Empowerment* (New York: Routledge, 1990).

_____, 'The Social Construction of Black Feminist Thought.' *Signs* 14:4 (1989) pp. 745-773.

Colón, A. 'Feminist Research and Action in Contemporary Puerto Rico: A Trajectory of Changing Visions of Gender Relations Within the Family: A Work in Progress', ASA Miami, 1993.

Comaroff, J. *Body of Power, Spirit of Resistance* (Chicago University Press, 1985).

Conn, Charles W. *Where the Saints Have Trod: A History of the Church of God Missions* (Cleveland, Tennessee: Church of God Publishing House, 1959).

Connell, R. W. 'An Iron Man: The Body and Some Contradictions of Hegemonic Masculinity', in *Sport, Men and the Gender Order: Critical Feminist Perspectives*, ed. by M. Messner and D. F. Sobo (Champaign, IL: Human Kinetics Books, 1990).

Constance, Zeno O. *Tassa, Chutney and Soca: The East Indian Contribution to the Calypso* (San Fernando, Trinidad: Z. O. Constance, 1991).

Constantinople, A. 'Sex Role Acquisition: In Search of the Elephant,' *Sex Roles 5* (1979) pp. 121-33.

Cooper, Carolyn, *Noises in the Blood* (London: Macmillan, 1993).

Coppin, Addington, 'Female Participation in the Barbados Labour Market: A Post Independence Perspective', Institute of Social and Economic Research. Staff Seminars Series 95/06, University of the West Indies, 1995.

Council for Voluntary Social Services (CVSS), *Street Children in Jamaica*. Child Labour Series Report, no. 6. (London: Save the Children Fund, 1987).

Coward, Rosalind, *Female Desire: Women's Sexuality Today* (London: Paladin, 1984).

Cox, W. 'The Manufacturing Sector in the Economy of Barbados', in *The Economy of Barbados 1946-1980*, ed. by Delisle Worrell (Bridgetown: Central Bank of Barbados, 1982) pp. 47-80

Cozier, C. 'Conversations with a Shirt-Jac' in *Portrayals of Masculinity in the Work of Two Contemporary Trinidadian Artists*, ed. by S. Ouditt and C. Cozier. (Port of Spain: Centre for Gender and Development Studies, University of the West Indies, 1996). Paper presented at the conference on 'The Construction of Caribbean Masculinity: Towards a Research Agenda', held at the University of the West Indies, St. Augustine, January 11-13, 1996.

Craton, Michael, 'Changing Patterns of Slave Families in the British West Indies', *Journal of Interdisciplinary History* 10:1 (1979) pp. 1-35.

Crawford-Brown, C. 'What Must Be Done About Child Abuse?' *Jamaica Herald*, November 8, 1993.

Crawford, M. and J. Marace, 'Psychology Reconstructs the Female, 1968-1988', *Psychology of Women Quarterly* 13 (1989) pp. 147-165.

Croll, E. and D. Parkin, *Bush Base: Forest Farm: Culture, Environment and Development* (London: Routledge, 1992).

Cucchiari, S. 'Between Shame and Sanctification: Patriarchy and Its Transformation in Sicilian Pentecostalism.' *American Ethnologist* 17(1990) pp. 687-707.

Cuffie, Joan, 'Gender and Subject Choice in Secondary Schools.' Paper presented at a Gender and Education Seminar, Faculty of Education and Women and Development Studies, University of the West Indies, Mona, 1989.

Cumper, G. E. 'The Jamaican Family: Village and Estate', *Social and Economic Studies* 7:1 (1958) pp. 76-108.

Curtin, Philip D. 'Africa and the Wider Monetary World, 1250-1850' in *Precious Metals in the Later Medieval and Early Modern Worlds*, ed. by John F. Richards (Durham: Carolina University Press, 1982) pp. 231-268.

D'Allan, Deidre, *Fantasy of Love*, Caribbean Caresses Series (Oxford: Heinemann, 1993).

Dagenais, Huguette, 'Women in Guadeloupe: The Paradoxes of Reality' in *Women and Change in the Caribbean*, ed. by Janet Momsen (Kingston: Ian Randle Publishers; Bloomington: Indiana University Press; London: James Currey Publishers, 1993) pp. 83-108.

Dann, Graham, *The Barbadian Male: Sexual Attitudes and Practices* (London: Macmillan, 1987).

Danns, George, 'Decolonization and Militarization in the Caribbean: The Case of Guyana', in *The Newer Caribbean*, ed. by Paget Henry and Carl Stone (Philadelphia: Institute for the Study of Human Issues, 1984) pp. 63-93

Davenport, William, 'A Comparative Study of Two Jamaican Fishing Villages', Ph.D. diss., Yale University, 1956.

_____ 'The Family System in Jamaica', *Social and Economic Studies* 10: 4 (1961) pp. 420-454.

Davis, David Brion, *The Problem of Slavery in Western Culture* (Ithaca: Cornell University Press, 1966).

_____, *Slavery and Human Progress* (New York: Oxford University Press, 1984).

Davy, John. *The West Indies before and since Slave Emancipation* (London: W. Cash, 1854. Reprint, London: Frank Cass, 1971).

Dayton, Donald W. 'Theological Roots of Pentecostalism.', *Pneuma* (Spring 1980) pp. 3-21.

Deere C. et. al., *In the Shadows of the Sun: Caribbean Development Alternatives and US Policy* (Boulder:Westview Press, 1990).

De Leon, S. 'Krosfyah Singer — Ragamuffin King', *Trinidad Guardian* , January 19, 1996.

De Lisser, Herbert G. *Twentieth Century Jamaica* (Kingston: Jamaica Times, 1913).

Derrida, J. *Of Grammatology.* trans. by G. C. Spivak. (Baltimore: John Hopkins University Press, 1976).

Dhawan, N., I. J. Roseman, R. K. Naidu, K. Thapa, and S. I. Rettek, 'Self-Concepts Across Two Cultures: India and the United States', *Journal of Cross-Cultural Psychology* 26 (1995) pp. 606-621.

Dickson, William, *Letters on Slavery* (Westport: Negro University Press, 1789. Reprint, 1970).

Dirks, Robert, 'Networks, Groups and Adaptation in an Afro-Caribbean Community.' *Man* 7:4 (1972) pp. 565-585.

Dominica, *Population and Housing Census, 1991* Vols. 2 and 6 (Roseau: Statistics Office, 1994).

Dominica, *Special Tabulations* (Roseau: Statistical Office, 1995).

Donald, James and Ali Rattansi, eds,, '"Race", Culture and Difference', (London: Sage in association with Open University Press, 1992).

Douglass, Lisa, *The Power of Sentiment: Love, Hierarchy, and the Jamaican Family Elite* (Boulder, CO: Westview Press, 1992).

Drayton, Armel, 'Representations of Women in Selected Caribbean Romance', Unpublished paper towards the Literatures in English degree. University of the West Indies, Cave Hill, 1995.

Drayton, Kathleen, 'White Man's Knowledge: Sex, Race and Class in Caribbean English Language Textbooks', in *Gender: A Caribbean Multidisciplinary Perspective*, ed. by Elsa Leo-Rhynie, Barbara Bailey, and Christine Barrow (Kingston: Ian Randle Publishers, 1997) pp. 159-183

Du Tertre, Jean-Baptiste, *Histoire générale des Antilles habitées par les françois* 4 vols (Paris: Thomas Jolly, 1667-71).

Duncker, P. *Sisters and Strangers: An Introduction to Contemporary Feminist Fiction* (Oxford: Blackwell Publishers, 1992).

Durant-Gonzalez, Victoria, 'The Realm of Female Responsibility' in *Women and the Family,* ed. by Joycelin Massiah (Bridgetown: Institute of Social and Economic Research (EC), University of the West Indies, 1982) pp. 3-27.

Durkheim, Emile, *Suicide: A Study in Sociology* (London: Routledge and Kegan Paul,1952. First pub. 1897).

Dyer, R. 'Whiteness', *Screen* 29:4 (1988)

Eagly, A. 'On Comparing Women and Men', *Feminism and Psychology* 4 (1994) pp. 513-22.

Eagly, A. H. 'The Science and Politics of Comparing Women and Men', *American Psychologist* 50 (1995) pp. 145-158.

Earle, S. 'Maroon Leader I'm Under Seige', *The Gleaner*, January 5, 1996.

Eaton, George, *Alexander Bustamante and the Modern Jamaica* (Kingston Publishers, 1975).

Eckensberger, L. H. 'Activity or Action: Two Different Roads Towards an Integration of Culture into Psychology', *Culture and Psychology* 1 (1995) pp. 67-80.

Edgell, Zee, *Beka Lamb* (Oxford: Heinemann Educational Books, 1982).

Eisenstein, Z. 'Developing A Theory of Capitalist Patriarchy and Socialist Feminism', in *Capitalist Patriarchy and Socialist Feminism*, ed by Z. Eisenstein, (New York: Monthly Review Press, 1979) pp. 5-41.

Ellis, Patricia, *Women of the Caribbean* (Kingston Publishers, 1986; London: Zed Books, 1987).

Elshtain, J. B. *Public Man, Private Woman* (Oxford: Martin Robertson, 1981).

Elson, Diane and Ruth Pearson, 'Nimble Fingers Make Cheap Workers: An Analysis of Women's Employment in Third World Export Manufacturing', *Feminist Review* (1981) pp. 87-107.

Eltis, David and James Walvin, eds,, *The Abolition of the Atlantic Slave Trade: Origins and Effects in Europe, Africa and the Americas* (Madison: University of Wisconsin Press, 1981).

Enloe, C. *Ethnic Soldiers* (London: Penguin, 1980).

Ennew, J. and P. Young, *Child Labour in Jamaica*, Child Labour Series Report, no. 6 (London: Anti-Slavery Society, 1981).

Espinet, Ramabai, *Creation Fire: A CAFRA Anthology of Caribbean Women's Poetry* (Toronto: Sister Vision; Tunapuna, Trinidad: 1990).

_____, 'Representation and the Indo-Caribbean Woman in Trinidad and Tobago', in *Indo-Caribbean Resistance*, ed. by Frank Birbalsingh (Toronto: TSAR Publications, 1993).

Fage, John, 'The Effects of the Export Trade on African Populations', in *The Population Factor in African Studies*, ed. by R. P. Moss and R. J. Rathbone (London: University Press of London, 1975) pp. 15-23.

_____, 'Slave and Society in Western Africa, c. 1455-1700', *Journal of African History* 21:3 (1980) pp. 289-310.

Fanon, Frantz, *Black Skin, White Masks* (New York: Grove Press, 1982; Paris: Edition de Seuil, 1952).

_____, *Black Skin, White Masks* (London: Pluto, 1985).

Farouk, Keith, 'Nothing Womanish About Earrings', *Sun on Saturday*, (Barbados) 4 (1995) p. 13.

Fast, Irene, *Gender Identity: A Differentiation Model* (Hillsdale, NJ: Lawrence Erlbaum, 1984).

Ferguson, T. *Structural Adjustment and Good Governance: The Case of Guyana* (Georgetown: Guyana National Printers, 1995).

Fernandez-Kelly, Maria P. *For We Are Sold, I and My People: Women and Industry in Mexico's Frontier* (Albany: State University of New York Press, 1983).

Flax, Jane, 'What Is Enlightenment: A Feminist Rereading'. Paper prepared for Conference on Postmodernism and the Rereading of Modernity, University of Essex, 1990.

Folbre, N. 'Holding Hands at Midnight: The Paradox of Caring Labour', *Feminist Economics* 1: 1 (1995) p. 81.

Ford-Smith, Honor, 'Women's Place in Caribbean Social Change', in *A Caribbean Reader on Development*, ed. by Judith Wedderburn (Kingston: Friedrich Ebert Stiftung, 1986) pp. 152-176.

Foucault, Michel, *Discipline and Punish* (London: Allen Lane, 1977).

_____, 'Docile Bodies' in *The Foucault Reader*, ed. by Paul Rabinow, (New York: Pantheon Books, 1984) pp. 179-187.

_____, 'The Ethic of Care for the Self as a Practice of Freedom', in *The Final Foucault*, ed. by. A. Bernauer and D. Rasmussen (Cambridge, MA: MIT Press, 1988).

_____, *History of Sexuality. Volume One: An Introduction*, trans. by R. Hurley (London: Allen Lane, 1979).

_____, 'Nietzsche, Genealogy, History' in *The Foucault Reader*, ed. by P. Rabinow (London: Penguin Books, 1984).

_____. 'Right of Death and Power Over Life', in *The Foucault Reader*, ed. by Paul Rabinow (London: Penguin Books, 1984) pp. 258-272.

_____, 'The Subject and Power', in *Michel Foucault*, ed. by P. Dreyfus and P. Rabinow (London: Harvester, 1982).

Fox, R. *Kinship and Marriage* (Harmondsworth:Penguin Books, 1967).

Fraser, N. 'Rethinking the Public Sphere: A Contribution to the Critique of Actually Existing Democracy' in *Postmodernism and the Rereading of Modernity*, ed by Francis Barker, Peter Hulme, and Margaret Iversen (Manchester University Press, 1992) pp. 197-231.

Frazier, E. Franklin *The Negro Family in the United States* (Chicago: University of Chicago Press, 1939).

Freeman, Carla, 'Designing Women: Corporate Discipline and Barbados' Off-Shore Pink Collar Sector', *Cultural Anthropology* 8:2 (1993) pp. 169-186.

_____, 'From Higglering to High-Tech and Home Again: Barbadian Women Workers in a Transnational Arena', *Folk* 36 (1995) pp. 5-25.

_____, *High Tech and High Heels in the Global Economy: Women, Work and Off-Shore Informatics in Barbados* (Durham: Duke University Press). (Forthcoming).

French, Joan, 'Colonial Policy Towards Women After the 1938 Uprising: The Case of Jamaica.' Presented at the Conference of the Caribbean Studies Association Caracas, Venezuela, 1986.

French, Joan and Honor Ford Smith 'Women and Organisation in Jamaica, 1900-1944', *Women and Development Studies* (The Hague: Institute of Social and Economic Research, n.d).

Frieze, I. H., J. E. Parson, P. D. Johnson, D.N. Ruble, and G.L. Zellman, *Women and Sex Roles* (New York: W.W. Norton, 1978).

Garvey, Amy Jacques *Garvey and Garveyism* (London: Collier Macmillan, 1970).

Gaur, Albertine, *Women in India* (London: British Library, 1980).

Gautier, Arlette, 'Les Esclaves Femmes aux Antilles Francaises, 1635-1848', *Reflexions Historiques* 10:3 (1983)pp. 409-435.

Gearing, Margaret J. 'The Reproduction of Kinship in a Migration Society: Gender, Kinship and Household in St. Vincent, West Indies.' Ph. D. diss., University of Florida, 1988.

Gergen, K. J. 'Exploring the Postmodern: Perils and Potentials' , *American Psychologist* 49 (1994) pp. 412-416.

Giacalone, Rita, 'Caribbean Women in the 21st Century', *21st Century Policy Review*, 17, 1, 2 (1994) pp. 219-243.

Giddens, Anthony, *The Consequences of Modernity* (Cambridge: Polity Press, 1990).

_____, *Modernity and Self-Identity* (Cambridge: Polity Press, 1991).

Gill, Lesley, 'Like Veil to Cover Them: Women and the Pentecostal Movement in La Paz', *American Ethnologist* 17 (1990) pp. 708-721.

Gillett, J. and P. G. White. 'Male Bodybuilding and the Reassertion of Hegemonic Masculinity: A Critical Feminist Perspective', *Play and Culture* 5(1992) pp. 358-369.

Ginzburg, Carlo, *Ecstasies: Deciphering the Witches Sabbath* trans. by Raymond Rosenthal, ed. by Gregory Elliott (London: Hutchinson, 1989).

Gittens, Priscilla. 'Quit Dissing Positive Yuts, Old Fogies', *Sun on Saturday*, (Barbados), (1995) p. 13.

Glasgow, J. 'Science in the Jamaican Community: A Survey of Some Aspects of the Provisions for Training in Science', M.A. thesis, University of the West Indies, Mona, 1978.

Glassner, B. 'In the Name of Health' in *The Sociology of Health Promotion*, ed by R. Bunton, S. Nettleton, and R. Burrows (London: Routledge, 1995).

Golikheri, V. 'Indian Films in Trinidad', *People* 3:21 (1977) pp. 52-55.

Gomez, Ofelia and Rhoda Reddock, 'New Trends in the Internationalization of Production: Implications for Female Workers' in *International Labour and the Third World: The Making of a New Working Class*, ed. by R. Boyd, R. Cohen, and P. Gutkind (Aldershot: Auebury/Gower, 1987).

González, Nancie L. *Black Carib Household* (Seattle: University of Washington, 1969).

_____. 'Rethinking the Consanguineal Household and Matrifocality', *Ethnology* 23(1984) pp. 1-12.

_____. 'Toward a Definition of Matrifocality', in *Afro-American Anthropology: Contemporary Perspectives*, ed. by N. E. Whitten Jr. and J. F. Szwed (New York: Free Press, 1970) pp. 231-244.

Goode, William. 'Illegitimacy in the Caribbean Social Structure', *American Sociological Review* 25:1 (1960).

Goodman, G. Aubrey and C. P. Clarke, eds, *Laws of Barbados Vol. 1: 1667-1891* (Barbados: Advocate Printing, 1912).

Gopaul-McNicol, S-A. 'A Cross-Cultural Examination of Racial Identity and Racial Preference of Pre-School Children in the West Indies', *Journal of Cross-Cultural Psychology* 26 (1995) pp. 141-152.

Gordon, Derek, 'Access to High School Education in Post-War Jamaica', in *Education and Society in the Commonwealth Caribbean*, ed. by E. Miller (Kingston: Institute of Social and Economic Research, University of the West Indies, 1991) pp. 181-206.

_____, *Class, Status and Social Mobility in Jamaica* (Kingston: Institute of Social and Economic Research, University of the West Indies, 1987).

_____, 'Women, Work and Social Mobility in Post-War Jamaica', in *Women and the Sexual Division of Labour in the Caribbean*, ed. by K. Hart (Kingston: Consortium Graduate School of Social Sciences University of the West Indies, 1989) pp. 67-80

Gordon, Lindon, 'What's New in Women's History', in *Feminist Studies/Critical Studies*, ed. by Teresa de Lauretis (Bloomington: Indiana University Press, 1986) pp. 20-23.

Gordon, Shirley C. *A Century of West Indian Education* (London: Longman Group, 1963).

Gordon, W. *Self Identity Measures and Academic Achievement of Sixth Form Students in Jamaica*. Ph. D. diss, University of the West Indies, Mona, 1981.

Grant, D. R. B. *Living Conditions of Some Basic School Children: Pointers to Disadvantage* (Kingston: Bernard Van Leer Foundation, Centre for Early Childhood Education, 1974).

Grant, D. R. B., E. A. Leo-Rhynie, and G. Alexander *Household Structures and Settings* Life Style Study: Children of the Lesser World in the English-speaking Caribbean. Vol. 5. (Kingston: Bernard Van Leer Foundation, Centre for Early Childhood Education, 1983).

Greene, Cecilia, 'Historical and Contemporary Restructuring and Women in Production in the Caribbean' in *The Caribbean in the Global Political Economy*, ed. by Hilbourne A. Watson (Boulder, CO: Lynne Rienner, 1994) pp. 149-171.

Greenfield, Sidney M. *English Rustics in Black Skin: A Study of Modern Family Forms in a Pre-Industrialised Society* (New Haven, CT: College and University Press, 1961).

_____, 'Land Tenure and Transmission in Rural Barbados', *Anthropological Quarterly* 33 (1960) pp. 165-176.

_____. 'Socio-Economic Factors and Family Form', *Social and Economic Studies* 10:1 (1961) pp. 72-85.

Griffin, C. and M. Wetherell, 'Feminist Psychology and the Study of Men and Masculinity Part 2: Politics and Practices', *Feminism and Psychology* 2 (1992): pp. 133-168.

Grossman, Rachel, 'Women's Place in the Integrated Circuit', *Southeast Asia Chronicle* 55 (1979).

Grundy, S. and S. J. Hatto, 'Teacher Educators' Ideological Discourses', *Journal of Education for Teaching* 21 (1995) pp. 7-24.

Gwaltney, John L. *Drylongso* (New York: Random House, 1981).

Habermas, Jurgen *The Structural Transformation of the Public Sphere: An Inquiry into a Category of Bourgeois Society* trans. by Thomas Burger with the assistance of Federick Lawrence (London: Polity Press, 1989).

Hall, Douglas. 'The Early Banana Trade From Jamaica, 1868-1905: A Descriptive Account', in *Ideas and Illustrations in Economic History*, (New York: Holt, Rinehart and Winston, 1964) pp. 56-79.

Hall, S. *Myths of Caribbean Identity* Walter Rodney Memorial Lecture. (Coventry: University of Warwick, Centre for Caribbean Studies, 1991).

Hall, S. 'New Ethnicities', in *'Race', Culture and Difference*, ed. by J. Donald and A. Rattansi (London: Sage in association with Open University Press, 1992).

Hamilton, Marlene A. 'An Investigation into the Relationship Between Social Class, Success in the Common Entrance Examination and Performance in the GCE 'O' Level Examinations, Jamaica 1975', *Social and Economic Studies* 28:3 (1979) pp. 499-515.

_____. 'Performance Levels in Science and Other Subjects for Jamaican Adolescents Attending Single-Sex and Co-Educational High Schools', *Science Education* 64:4 (1985) pp. 535-547.

_____. 'The Prediction of Academic Success — An Interim Report', *Caribbean Journal of Education* 1 (1981) pp. 43-58.

_____. 'A Study of Certain Personality, Educational and Environmental Variables Associated with Science Orientation in a Selected Group of 5th Form Students', Ph. D. diss., University of the West Indies, Mona, 1976.

Hamilton, Marlene A. and Elsa A. Leo-Rhynie, 'Sex Roles and Secondary Education in Jamaica' in *World Yearbook of Education 1984: Women and Education*, ed. by Jacquetta Megarry, Sandra Acker, Stanley Nesbit, and Eric Hoyle (London: Kogan Page; New York: Nichols Publishing, 1984) pp.123-138

Haniff, Neisha, *Blaze of Fire* (Toronto: Sister Vision Press, 1988).

Hare-Mustin, R. T. and J. Maracek, 'Asking the Right Question: Feminist Psychology and Sex Differences', *Feminism and Psychology* 4 (1994) pp. 531-537.

_____. *Making a Difference: Psychology and the Construction of Gender* (New Haven, CT: Yale University Press, 1990).

Harré, R. 'Rules, Roles and Rhetoric', *The Psychologist* 6:1 (1993) pp. 24-28.

Harrison, F.V. 'Women in Jamaica's Urban Informal Economy: Insights from a Kingston Slur', *Nieuwe West-Indische Gids*, 62, 314 (1988) pp. 103-128.

Hart, Keith, 'Introduction' in *Women and the Sexual Division of Labour in the Caribbean*, ed. by Keith Hart (Kingston: Consortium Graduate School of Social Science, University of the West Indies, 1989).

Hart, Keith, ed. *Women and the Sexual Division of Labour in the Caribbean* (Kingston: Consortium Graduate School of Social Sciences, University of the West Indies, 1989).

Hartmann, Heidi, 'The Historical Roots of Occupational Segregation: Capitalism, Patriarchy and Job Segregation by Sex', in *Women and the Workplace*, ed. M. Blaxall and B. Reagan (University of Chicago Press, 1976) pp. 137-169.

Haug, W. F. *Critique of Commodity Aesthetics: Appearance, Sexuality and Advertising in Capitalist Society* (Minneapolis: University of Minnesota Press, 1986).

Henriques, Fernando, *Family and Colour in Jamaica* (London: Eyre and Spottiswoode, 1953).

_____, 'West Indian Family Organization', *American Journal of Sociology* 55(1949) pp. 36-37.

Henwood, K. L. 'Resisting Racism and Sexism in Academic Psychology: A Personal/Political View', *Feminism and Psychology* 4 (1994) pp. 41-62.

Herskovits, Melville J. *Life in a Haitian Valley* (New York: Octagon Books, c. 1937).

_____. *The Myth of the Negro Past* (New York: Octagon Books, 1941; Boston: Beacon Press, 1958).

Herskovits, Melville J. and Frances S. Herskovits, *SurinameFolk-Lore* (New York: Columbia University Press, 1936).

_____. *Trinidad Village* (New York: Alfred A. Knopf, 1947).

Heyrick, Elizabeth, *Appeal to the Hearts and Conscience of British Women.* (Leicester: Cockshaw, 1828).

Higman, Barry W. 'Domestic Service in Jamaica, since 1750', in *Trade, Government and Society in Caribbean History, 1700-1920. Essays Presented to Douglas Hall,* ed. by Barry Higman (London: Heinemann, 1983) pp. 117-138.

_____. *Slave Population and the Economy in Jamaica, 1807-1834* (Cambridge University Press; New York: Oxford University Press, 1976).

Higman, Barry W. *Slave Populations of the British Caribbean, 1827-1834* (Baltimore: Johns Hopkins University Press, 1984).

Hill, Frank, *Bustamante and His Letters* (Kingston Publishers, 1976).

Hill, Robert. 'Leonard P. Howell and Millenarian Visions in Early Rastafari.' *Jamaica Journal* 16 (1983) pp. 24-39.

Hintzen, P. *The Costs of Regime Survival: Racial Mobilization, Elite Domination and Control of the State in Guyana and Trinidad* (Cambridge University Press, 1989).

Hobbs, Doreen, *Jewels of the Caribbean: The History of the Salvation Army in the Caribbean Territory* (London: The General of the Salvation Army, 1986).

Hodge, Merle, 'Challenges of the Struggle for Sovereignty: Changing the World Versus Writing Stories',in *Caribbean Women Writers: Essays From the First International*

Conference, ed. by Selwyn R. Cudjoe (Wellesley, MA: Calaloux Publications, 1990) pp. 202-208

_____, *Crick Crack Monkey* (London: Heinemann Educational Books, 1970).

_____, *For the Life of Laetitia* (New York: Farrar, Straus and Giroux, 1993).

_____, 'Young Women and the Development of a Stable Family Life in the Caribbean' *Savacou* 13 (1977) pp. 39-44. Special issue 'Caribbean Women', ed. by Lucille Mathurin Mair.

Hodgkin, Thomas, 'Kingdoms of the Western Sudan', in *The Dawn of African History*, ed. by Roland Oliver (London: Oxford University Press, 1961).

Holder, Y. *Women Traders in Guyana* (Santiago: Economic Commission for Latin America and the Caribbean, Caribbean Development and Cooperation Committee, 1989).

Hollenweger, Walter J. *The Pentecostals*, trans. by R.A. Wilson (London: SCM Press, 1972).

Holmes, R. M. *How Young Children Perceive Race* (Thousand Oaks, CA: Sage, 1995).

Holmund, C. A. 'Visible Difference and Flex Appeal: The Body, Sex, Sexuality and Race in the *Pumping Iron* Films', in *Women, Sport and Culture*, ed. by S. Birrell and C. L. Cole (Champaign, IL: Human Kinetics Books, 1994).

hooks, bell, *Black Looks: 'Race' and Representation* (Boston: South End Press, 1992).

_____, 'Facing Difference: The Black Female Body', in *Art On My Mind: Visual Politics* (New York: New Press, 1995).

_____, 'Marginality as a Site of Resistance', in *Out There: Marginalization and Contemporary Cultures*, ed. by M. Gever, R. Ferguson, T. M. Trinh, and C. West (New York: New Museum of Contemporary Art and the Massachusetts Institute of Technology, 1990) pp. 341-344.

_____, 'Representing the Black Male Body', in *Art On My Mind: Visual Politics* (New York: New Press, 1995).

_____, 'Sisterhood: Political Solidarity Between Women', *Feminist Review* 23(1986) pp. 125-138.

_____, *Sisters of the Yam: Black Women and Self-Recovery* (Boston: South End Press, 1993).

Howard, Michael, *Dependence and Development in Barbados, 1945-1985*, (Bridgetown: Carib Research and Publications, 1986).

Howitt, D. and J. Owusu-Bempah, *The Racism of Psychology: Time for Change* (New York: Harvester Wheatsheaf, 1994).

Hulme, Peter, *Colonial Encounters: Europe and the Native Caribbean 1492-1797* (London: Routledge, 1986).

Hulme, Peter and Neil L. Whitehead, *Wild Majesty: Encounters with Caribs from Columbus to the Present Day* (Oxford University Press, 1992).

Hyde, J. S. 'Should Psychologists Study Gender Differences? Yes, with Some Guidelines', *Feminism and Psychology* 4 (1994) pp. 507-512.

Inikori, Joseph, *Forced Migration: The Impact of the Export Trade on African Societies* (London: Hutchinson, 1981).

Inter-American Development Bank, *Building Consensus for Social and Economic Reconstruction*. Report of IDB Pilot Mission on Socioeconomic Reform in the Co-operative Republic of Guyana (Washington, DC: IDB, 1994).

James-Reid, Olga and S. Jones. 'Who Is Running Our Schools?' Paper presented at a Gender and Education Seminar Faculty of Education and Women and Development Studies, University of the West Indies, Mona, 1989.

James, Selm, *The Ladies and the Mammies: Jane Austen and Jean Rhys* (Bristol: Falling Wall Press, 1983).

Jemmott, Carlton, 'Face It, Earrings Look Far Better on Women', *Daily Nation* (Barbados), October 12, 1995, p. 7A.

Joeckes, Susan, *Women in the World Economy: An INSTRAW Study* (New York: Oxford University Press, 1987).

Johnson, Kim 'Considerations on Indian Sexuality', presented at the Third Conference on East Indians, University of the West Indies, St Augustine, 1984.

Jolly, Dorothy,. *Heartaches and Roses*, Caribbean Caresses Series (Oxford: Heinemann, 1993).

Jones, Delmos J. 'Towards A Native Anthropology', *Human Organization* 29(1970) pp. 251-259.

Jones, Kathleen B. and Anna G. Jonasdottir, *The Political Interests of Gender: Developing Theory and Research with a Feminist Face* (London: Sage Publications, 1988).

Justus, Joyce Bennett, 'Women's Role in West Indian Society' in *The Black Woman Cross-Culturally*, ed. by Filomina C. Steady (Cambridge MA: Schenkman Publishing, 1981) pp. 431-450.

Kabeer, N. *Reversed Realities: Gender Hierarchies in Development Thought* (London: Verso, 1994).

Katzin, M.F. ' "Partners": An Informal Savings Institution in Jamaica', *Social and Economic Studies* 8, (1959) pp. 436-440.

Kaufman, G. *Shame, The Power of Caring* (Rochester: Schenkman Books, 1985).

Kaufman, M. 'A Theoretical Framework for the Study of Men and Masculinities.' Paper presented at the Construction of Caribbean Masculinity: Towards a Research Agenda. Conference organised by the Centre for Gender and Development Studies, University of the West Indies, St Augustine, January 11-13, 1996.

Kea, Ray, *Settlement, Trade and Politics in the Seventeenth Century Gold Coast* (Baltimore: Johns Hopkins University Press, 1982).

Keens-Douglas, Richardo, *La Diablesse and the Baby* (Toronto: Annick Press, 1994).

Kelly, Deirdre, *Hard Work, Hard Choices: A Survey of Women in St. Lucia's Export Oriented Electronics Factories*. Occasional Paper no. 20. (Bridgetown: Institute of Social and Economic Research, University of the West Indies, 1987).

Kerns, Virginia, *Women and the Ancestors: Black Carib Kinship and Ritual* (Urbana: University of Illinois Press, 1989).

Khan, Aisha, 'What Is "a Spanish"?: Ambiguity and "Mixed" Identity in Trinidad' in *Trinidad Ethnicity*, ed. by Kevin Yelvington (London: Macmillan Caribbean, 1993) pp. 170-207.

Kimmel, M. S. 'Masculinity as Homophobia: Fear, Shame and Silence in the Construction of Gender Identity.' Paper presented at The Construction of Caribbean Masculinity: Towards a Research Agenda. Conference organised by the Centre for Gender and Development Studies, University of the West Indies, St Augustine, January 11-13, 1996.

_____. 'Rethinking "Masculinity": New Directions in Research', in *Changing Men: New Directions in Research on Men and Masculinity*, ed. by M. S. Kimmel (Newbury Park, CA: Sage, 1987) pp. 9-24.

Kincaid, Jamaica, *Annie John* (New York: Farrar Straus Giroux, 1983).

_____, *At the Bottom of the River* (London: Pan, 1984).

_____, *Lucy* (New York: Farrar Straus Giroux, 1990).

King, I. 'Attitude to Spanish of Third and Fourth Formers of Secondary Schools in Trinidad and Tobago.' Paper presented at a Gender and Education Seminar, Faculty of Education and Women and Development Studies, University of the West Indies, Mona, 1989.

King, Ruby and Mike Morrissey, *Images in Print: Bias and Prejudice in Caribbean Textbooks* (Mona: University of the West Indies, Institute of Social and Economic Research, 1988).

Kiple, Kenneth F. *The Caribbean Slave: A Biological History* (Cambridge University Press, 1981).

Kiple, K. F. and V. H. Kiple, 'Deficiency Diseases in the Caribbean', *Journal of Interdisciplinary History* 11:2 (1980) pp. 197-205.

_____, 'Slave Child Mortality: Some Nutritional Answers to a Perennial Puzzle.' *Journal of Social History* 10 (1979) pp. 284-309.

Kitzinger, C. 'Feminism, Psychology and the Paradox of Power', *Feminism and Psychology* 1 (1991) pp. 111-29.

_____. 'Politicizing Psychology', *Feminism and Psychology* 1 (1991) pp. 49-54.

_____. 'Should Psychologists Study Sex Differences?' *Feminism and Psychology* 4 (1994) pp. 501-506.

Klass, Morton, *Singing with Sai Baba: The Politics of Revitalisation in Trinidad and Tobago* (Boulder, CO: Westview Press, 1991).

Klein, Herbert S. 'African Women in the Atlantic Slave Trade' in *Women and Slavery*, ed. by Claire C. Robertson and Martin A. Klein, (Madison: University of Wisconsin Press, 1983) pp. 29-32.

Klein, Herbert S., and Stanley L. Engerman, 'Fertility Differentials between Slaves in the United States and the British West Indies', *William and Mary Quarterly* 35 (1978) pp. 357-374.

Klein, Martin A. 'The Study of Slavery in Africa: Review Article', *Journal of African History* 19:4 (1978) pp. 599-609.

_____. 'Women in Slavery in the Western Sudan',in *Women and Slavery*, ed. by Claire C. Robertson and Martin A. Klein (Madison: University of Wisconsin Press, 1983) pp. 67-92.

Knight, Franklin W. 'Jamaican Migrants of the Cuban Sugar Industry, 1900-1934' in *Between Slavery and Free Labour: The Spanish-Speaking Caribbean in the Nineteenth Century*, ed. by M.M. Fraginals, F.M. Pons, and S.L. Engerman (Baltimore: Johns Hopkins University Press, 1985) pp. 84-114.

Kohlberg, L. A. 'Cognitive Developmental Analysis of Children's Sex Role Concepts and Attitudes' in *The Development of Sex Differences*, ed. by Eleanor E. Maccoby and Carol N. Jacklin (Palo Alto, CA: Stanford University Press, 1974) p. 171.

Kopytoff, Barbara K. 'Colonial Treaty as Sacred Charter of the Jamaican Maroons,'] *Ethnohistory* 26:1 (1979) pp. 45-64.

_____. 'The Development of Jamaican Maroon Ethnicity', *Caribbean Quarterly* 22, 2:3 (1976) pp. 33-50.

_____ . 'The Early Political Development of Jamaican Maroon Societies', *William and Mary Quarterly* 35(1978) pp. 287-307.

Kopytoff, Igor, 'Indigenous African Slavery: Commentary One', *Historical Reflections* 6 (1979) pp. 62-77.

Kopytoff, Igor and Suzanne Miers, 'African "Slavery" as an Institution of Marginality' in *Slavery in Africa*, ed. by Suzanne Miers and Igor Kopytoff (Madison: University of Wisconsin Press, 1977) pp. 1-81.

Kosambi, Meera, 'The Meeting of the Twain: The Cultural Confrontation of Three Women in Nineteenth Century Maharashtra', *Indian Journal of Gender Studies* 1:1 (1994).

Kunstadter, Peter, 'A Survey of the Consanguine Or Matrifocal Family', *American Anthropologist* 65:1 (1963) pp. 56-60.

Labat, Jean-Baptiste, *Nouveau voyage aux îles de l'Amerique* 2 vols (Paris: Cavelier, 1722).

Lamming, George, *In the Castle in My Skin* (London: Longman, 1986. First pub. London: Michael Joseph, 1953).

LaRuffa, Anthony, 'Pentecostalism in a Puerto Rican Community', in *Perspectives in Pentecostalism*, ed. by S. Glazier (Washington, D.C.: University Press of America, 1980) pp. 44-55

Lash, S. and J. Urry, *Economies of Signs and Space* (London: Sage, 1994).

Laurie, N. 'Negotiating Gender: Women and Emergency Employment in Peru', Ph.D. diss., University of London, 1995.

Lawlor, C. 'The World Turned Upside Down', *Hybrid* 3 (1993) pp. 2-4.

Layne, Anthony, 'Gender and School Achievement in Barbados.' Paper presented at a Gender and Education Seminar, Faculty of Education and Women and Development Studies, University of the West Indies, Mona, 1989.

Lazarus-Black, M. *Legitimate Acts and Illegal Encounters: Law and Society in Antigua and Barbuda* (Washington DC: Smithsonian Institution Press, 1994).

Le Franc, Elsie, 'Overview and Conclusions', in *Report of the Conference on the 'Role of Women in the Caribbean'* ed. by Joycelin Massiah (Bridgetown: Institute of Social and Economic Research, University of the West Indies, 1983) pp. 89-93.

Leach, Melissa, 'Gender and the Environment: Traps and Opportunities', *Development in Practice* 2:1 (1992) pp. 12-22.

_____, *Rainforest Relations: Gender and Resource Use Among the Mende of Gola, Sierra Leone* (Washington DC: Smithsonian Institution; Edinburgh University Press for the International African Library, 1994).

Leach, Melissa, S. Joekes, and C. Green, 'Gender Relations and Environmental Change', *IDS Bulletin* 26:1 (1995) pp. 1-8.

Lee, Ann, 'Class, Race, Colour and the Trinidad Carnival', in *Social and Occupational Stratification in Contemporary Trinidad and Tobago*, ed. by Selwyn Ryan (Port of Spain: Institute of Social and Economic Research, University of the West Indies, 1991) pp. 417-433.

Lefort de Latour, M. *Carte géometrique et géographique de l'île de Ste Lucie* (London: Colonial Office, 1787. Reprinted 1883).

Leo-Rhynie, Elsa A. 'Educational Opportunities for Jamaican Female Students: A Contemporary Perspective.' Paper presented at the First Interdisciplinary Seminar on Women and Development Studies, University of the West Indies, Mona, 1987.

_____. 'Gender Issues in Education and Implications for Labour Force Participation' in *Women and the Sexual Division of Labour in the Caribbean*, ed. by Keith Hart, (Kingston: University of the West Indies, Consortium Graduate School of Social Sciences, 1989) pp. 81-97

_____. 'Gender, Race and Class in Child Rearing in the Caribbean', in *Parent-Child Socialization in the Caribbean*, ed. by J. L. Roopnarine and J. Brown. (in press).

_____.' "Girls" Toys, "Boys" Toys: Toys as a Factor in the Formation of Gender Identity.' Paper presented at the Caribbean Studies Association Conference, Curacao, 1995.

_____. 'The Performance of Jamaican Sixth Form Students in the Cambridge 'A' Level Examination', *Caribbean Journal of Education* 5:3 (1978): pp. 153-167.

Levi-Strauss, Claude, *Structural Anthropology* (New York: Basic Books, 1963).

Lewis, Gordon K. *The Growth of the Modern West Indies* (New York: Monthly Review Press, 1968).

Lewis, Linde, 'Constructing the Masculine in the Context of the Caribbean.' Paper presented to the 19th Annual Conference of the Caribbean Studies Association, Merida, Mexico, May 23-29, 1994.

Lewis, Matthew G. *Journal of a West Indian Proprietor, Kept During a Residence in the Island of Jamaica, 1815-1817* (London: Routledge, 1929).

Lewis, Oscar, *Five Families* (New York: New American Library, 1959).

———, *La Vida* (New York: Random House, 1966).

Lewis, Rupert *Marcus Garvey: Anti-Colonial Champion* (London: Karia Press, 1987).

Ligon, Richard, *A True and Exact History of the Island of Barbados.* (London: A. Moseley, 1657).

Lim, Linda, *Women Workers in Multinational Enterprises in Developing Countries* (Geneva: International Labour Organization, 1985).

Lindsey, L. L. *Gender Roles: A Sociological Perspective.* 2nd ed (New Jersey: Prentice Hall, 1994).

Lister, Ruth 'Dilemmas in Engendering Citizenship', *Economy and Society* 24:1 (1995) pp. 1-40.

Littlewood, R. *Pathology and Identity: The Work of Mother Earth in Trinidad* (Cambridge University Press, 1993).

Lobdell, Richard, 'Women in the Jamaican Labour Force 1881-1921', *Social and Economic Studies* 37:3 (1988) pp. 203-240.

Long, Edward, *The History of Jamaica* 3 vols (London: T. Lowndes, 1774).

Lowenthal, David, *West Indian Societies* (London: Oxford University Press, 1972).

Maccoby, Eleanor E. and Carol N. Jacklin *The Psychology of Sex Differences* (Palo Alto, CA: Stanford University Press, 1974).

MacCormack, C. P. and A. Draper, 'Social and Cognitive Aspects of Female Sexuality in Jamaica' in *The Cultural Construction of Sexuality*, ed. by P. Caplan, (London: Tavistock, 1987) pp. 143-165.

Maharaj, A. *Indo-Trinidad Folk Tales in the Oral Tradition*, 6 (Trinidad: Indian Review Committee, 1990).

Mair-Fisher, S. L. 'An Investigation into the Relationship Between Social Class and the Eleven-Plus Educational Policy: Its Impact on Social Stratification, and Its Effect on Entry into High Schools Over 30 Years.' Unpublished B.Ed. Study, University of the West Indies, Mona, 1983.

Mair, Lucille Mathurin, 'A Historical Study of Women in Jamaica, from 1655 to 1844.' Ph.D. diss., University of the West Indies, Mona, 1974.

———, *The Rebel Woman in the British West Indies During Slavery*, (Kingston: Institute of Jamaica, 1974).

———, 'Recollections of a Journey to a Rebel Past', in *Caribbean Women Writers*, ed. by Selwyn R. Cudjoe (Wellesley, MA: Calaloux Publishers, 1990) pp. 51-60.

———, 'Women Field Workers in Jamaica During Slavery.' The Elsa Goveia Memorial Lecture, University of the West Indies, Mona, 1986.

Manning, Frank, *Black Clubs in Bermuda: Ethnography of a Play World* (Ithaca: Cornell University Press, 1973).

Marable, M. 'Beyond Racial Identity Politics: Towards a Liberation Theory for Multicultural Democracy', *Race and Class* 35:1 (1993) pp. 113-130.

Maracek, J. 'Gender, Politics and Psychology's Ways of Knowing', *American Psychologist* 50(1995) pp. 162-163.

Marshall, Woodville K. 'Commentary on Sidney W. Mintz, Slavery and the Rise of

Peasantries' in *Roots and Branches: Current Directions in Slave Studies*, ed. by (Toronto: Pergamon Press, 1979) pp. 243-248.

Martin, Biddy, 'Lesbian Identity and Autobiographical Difference[s]' in *The Lesbian and Gay Studies Reader*, ed. by Henry Abelove, Michele Aina Barole, and David Halperin, (London: Routledge, 1993) pp. 274-293.

Martin, C. L. and C. F. Halverson 'A Schematic Processing Model of Sex Typing and Stereotyping in Children', *Child Development* 52 (1981) pp. 1119-1134.

Martin, C. L. and J. K. Little, 'The Relation of Gender Understanding to Children's Sex Typed Preferences and Gender Stereotypes', *Child Development* 61 (1990) pp. 1427-1439.

Massiah, Joycelin, *Employed Women in Barbados: A Demographic Profile, 1946-1970* (Bridgetown: Institute of Social and Economic Research, University of the West Indies, 1984).

———, *Women as Heads of Household in the Caribbean: Family Structure and Feminine Status* (Paris: UNESCO, 1983).

———, 'Women in the Caribbean Project: An Overview', *Social and Economic Studies* 35:2 (1986)pp. 1-29.

———, 'Women's Lives and Livelihoods: A View From the Commonwealth Caribbean', *World Development* 17:7 (1989).

———, 'Women Who Head Households', in *Women and the Family*, ed. Joycelin Massiah, Women in the Caribbean Project, Vol. 2.(Bridgetown: Institute of Social and Economic Research, University of the West Indies, 1982).

Matthews, Basil, *Crisis of the West Indian Family* (Port of Spain: Extra-Mural Department, University of the West Indies, 1953).

Mattson, K. 'The Dialectic of Powerlessness: Black Identity Culture and Affirmative Action' ,*Telos* 84 (1990) pp. 177-184.

Mayers, Janice, 'Access to Secondary Education for Girls in Barbados, 1907-43: A Preliminary Analysis' in *Engendering History: Caribbean History in Historical Perspective*, ed. by Verene Shepherd, Bridget Brereton, and Barbara Bailey (Kingston: Ian Randle Publishers, 1995) pp. 258-278

McElroy, Jerome L. and Klaus de Albuquerque, 'Sustainable Small-Scale Agriculture in Small Caribbean Islands', *Society and Natural Resources* 3(1990): pp. 109-129.

McKenzie, Alecia, *Satellite City and Other Stories* (Essex: Longman, 1992).

McKenzie, H. 'The Family, Class and Ethnicity in the Future of the Caribbean' in *Race, Class and Gender in the Future of the Caribbean*, ed. by J. E. Greene, (Kingston: Institute of Social and Economic Research, University of the West Indies, 1993) pp. 75-89.

McMillan, V. 'Academic Motivation of Adolescent Jamaican Girls in Selected Single-Sex and Co-Educational Schools', M.Ed. thesis, University of the West Indies, Mona, 1982.

Measor, Lynda and Patricia J. Spikes, *Gender and Schools* (London: Cassell, 1992).

Mehra, R. *Women, Land and Sustainable Development*, Working Paper No. 1. (Washington DC: International Center for Research on Women (ICRW), 1995).

Meillassoux, Claude, 'Female Slavery' in *Women and Slavery*, ed. byClaire Robertson and Martin A. Klein (Madison: University of Wisconsin Press, 1983) pp. 49-66.

Merritt, B. and C. A. Stroman, 'Black Family Imagery and Interactions on Television', *Journal of Black Studies* 23(1993) pp. 492-499.

Midgley, Clare, *Women Against Slavery: The British Campaigns, 1780-1870* (London: Routledge, 1992).

Mies, Maria, *Patriarchy and Accumulation on a World Scale: Women in the International Division of Labour* (London: Zed Books, 1986).

Millar, A. *The Drama of the Gifted Child: The Search for the True Self* (New York: Basic Books, 1981).

Miller, Errol, 'Education and Society in Jamaica', *Savacou 5* (1971) pp. 51-70.

_____, 'Gender Composition of the Primary School Teaching Force: A Result of Personal Choice?' Paper presented at a Gender and Education Seminar, Faculty of Education and Women and Development Studies, University of the West Indies, Mona, 1989.

_____, *Marginalization of the Black Male: Insights From the Development of the Teaching Profession* (Kingston: Institute of Social and Economic Research, University of the West Indies, 1986).

_____, *Men at Risk* (Kingston: Jamaica Publishing House, 1991).

Mills, Patricia Jagentowicz, 'Marx, Dialectics and the Question of Woman' in *Feminist Interpretations of Karl Marx*, ed. by Christine di Stefano (Pittsburgh: Pennsylvania State Press) (Forthcoming).

Mintz, Sidney W. *Caribbean Transformations* (Chicago: Aldine, 1974).

_____, *Caribbean Transformations* (New York: Columbia University Press, 1989).

_____, *Goodbye Columbus: Second Thoughts on the Caribbean Region at Mid-Millennium*, Walter Rodney Memorial Lecture (Coventry: University of Warwick, Centre for Caribbean Studies, 1993).

_____, 'The Historical Sociology of Jamaican Village' in *Caribbean Transformations* (Chicago: Aldine, 1974) pp. 157-179

_____, 'The Origins of the Reconstituted Peasantries' in *Caribbean Transformations* (Chicago: Aldine, 1974) pp. 146-156.

_____, 'Peasant Markets', *Scientific American* 203:2 (1960) pp. 112-122.

Mintz, Sidney W. and R. Price, *An Anthropological Approach to the Afro-American Past: A Caribbean Perspective* (Philadelphia: Institute for the Study of Human Issues, 1976).

_____, *The Birth of African-American Culture* (Boston: Beacon Press, 1992. First pub. 1976).

Mischel, W. 'A Social Learning View of Sex Differences in Behaviour', in *The Development of Sex Differences*, ed. by Eleanor E. Maccoby (Palo Alto, CA: Stanford University Press, 1966).

Mitchell, Juliet, *Psychoanalysis and Feminism* (New York: Pantheon, 1974).

Modood, T. 'Who's Defining Who?' *New Society* (1988) pp. 4-5.

Moghaddam, F. M. 'Modulative and Generative Orientations in Psychology: Implications for Psychology in the Three Worlds', *Journal of Social Issues* 46 (1990) pp. 21-41.

Mohammed, Patricia, 'Fragments of Colonial Legacy: The Representation of Masculinity in the Caribbean Thought.' Paper presented at the Society for Caribbean Studies Annual Conference, London, Institute of Commonwealth Studies, July 5-7, 1995.

_____, 'Nuancing the Feminist Discourse in the Caribbean', *Social and Economic Studies* 43:3 (1994) pp. 135-167.

_____, 'A Social History of Post-Migrant Indians in Trinidad From 1917-1947: A Gender Perspective', Ph.D. diss., Institute of Social Studies, The Hague, 1994.

Moi, Toril, *Sexual/Textual Politics: Feminist Literary Theory* (London: Methuen, 1985).

Moitt, Bernard, 'Women, Work and Resistance in the French Caribbean During Slavery, 1700-1848' in *Engendering History: Caribbean Women in Historical Perspective*, ed. by Verene Shepherd, Bridget Brereton, and Barbara Bailey, (London: James Currey Publishers; Kingston: Ian Randle Publishers, 1995) pp. 155-175.

Momsen, Janet, 'Female Roles in Caribbean Agriculture', in *Geography of Plural Societies*, ed. by C. Peach, C. G. Clarke, and C. Leys (London: Allen and Unwin, 1984) pp. 173-192.

————, 'Gender and Environmental Perception in the Eastern Caribbean' in *The Development Process in Small Island States*, ed. by D. G. Lockhart, D. Drakakis-Smith, and J. Schembri (London: Routledge, 1993) pp. 57-70.

————, 'The Geography of Land Use and Population in the Caribbean with Special Reference to Barbados and the Windward Islands', Ph.D. diss., University of London, 1969.

————, 'Introduction' in *Women and Change in the Caribbean*, ed. by Janet Momsen (Kingston: Ian Randle Publishers; Bloomington: Indiana University Press; London: James Currey Publishers, 1993) pp. 1-12.

————, *Post-Emancipation Settlement Change in Barbados*. Seminar Paper No. 54. Department of Geography, University of Newcastle upon Tyne, 1988.

Momsen, Janet, ed. *Women and Change in the Caribbean* (Kingston: Ian Randle Publishers; Bloomington: Indiana University Press; London: James Currey, Publishers, 1993).

Monk, Janice and Charles S. Alexander, 'Migration, Development and the Gender Division of Labour: Puerto Rico and Margarita Island, Venezuela' in *Women and Change in the Caribbean*, ed. by Janet Momsen (Kingston, Jamaica: Ian Randle Publishers; Bloomington: Indiana University Press; London: James Currey, 1993) pp. 167-177.

Moore, Henrietta L. *Feminism and Anthropology*, (Cambridge: Polity Press, 1988).

————, *A Passion for Difference: Essays in Anthropology and Gender*, (Cambridge: Polity Press, 1994).

————, 'The Problem of Explaining Violence in the Social Sciences', in *Sex and Violence: Issues in Representation and Experience*, ed. by P. Harvey and P. Gow (London: Routledge, 1994).

————, *Space, Text and Gender: An Anthropological Study of the Marakwet of Kenya* (Cambridge University Press, 1986).

————, *Feminism and Anthropology* (Cambridge: Polity Press), 1988.

Moore, Henrietta L. and Megan Vaughn, *Cutting Down Trees: Gender, Nutrition and Agricultural Change in the Northern Province of Zambia, 1890-1990* (London: James Currey Publishers; Portsmouth: Heinemann; Lusaka: University of Zambia Press, 1994).

Mootoo, Shani, *Out on Main Street and Other Stories* (Vancouver: Press Gang Publishers, 1993).

Mordecai, Pamela and Betty Wilson, *Her True-True Name: An Anthology of Women's Writing From the Caribbean* (London: Heinemann, 1989).

Morgan, D. H. J. 'You Too Can Have A Body Like Mine: Reflections on the Male Body and Masculinities' in *Body Matters: Essays on the Sociology of the Body*, ed. by S. Scott and D. Morgan (London: Falmer Press, 1993).

Morgan, D. H. J. and Scott, S. 'Bodies in a Social Landscape' in *Body Matters: Essays on the Sociology of the Body*, ed. by S. Scott and D. Morgan (London: Falmer Press, 1993).

Morgen, Sandra, 'Gender and Anthropology Introductory Essay' in *Gender and Anthropology*, ed. by S. Morgen (Washington, D.C.: American Anthropological Association, 1989) pp. 1-20.

Morrell, Carol, 'Introduction' in *Grammar of Dissent: Poetry and Prose by Claire Harris, M. Nourbese Philip, Dionne Brand* (Fredericton: Goose Lane Editions, 1994).

Morris, J. 'Gender Differences in Science and Mathematics in CXC Examinations.' Paper presented at a Gender and Education Seminar, Faculty of Education and Women and Development Studies, University of the West Indies, Mona, 1989.

Morrissey, Marietta, 'Female-Headed Households in Latin America and the Caribbean', *Sociological Spectrum* 9 (1989) pp. 197-210.

_____, *Slave Women in the New World: Gender Stratification in the Caribbean* (Lawrence: Kansas University Press, 1989).

_____, 'Women's Work, Family Formation and Reproduction among Caribbean Slaves', *Review* 9 (1986) pp. 339-367.

Morrow, Betty H. 'A Grassroots Feminist Response to Intimate Violence in the Caribbean', *International Women's Studies Forum* 17:6 (1994) pp. 579-592.

Morsen, H. *The Present Condition of the British West Indies: Their Wants and the Remedy for Them* (London: 1841).

Moses, Yolanda T. 'Female Status, the Family and Male Dominance in a West Indian Community' in *The Black Woman Cross-Culturally*, ed. by Filomina C. Steady (Cambridge, MA: Schenkman Publishing, 1981) pp. 499-513.

_____. 'Female Status, the Family, and Male Dominance in the West Indian Community' in *The Black Woman Cross-Culturally*, ed. by Filomina C. Steady (Cambridge: Schenckman, 1981) pp. 499-513.

Moyne, Lord, *(1938) Report (with Appendices) of the Commission Appointed to Enquire into the Disturbance Which Occurred in Jamaica Between the 23rd May and 8th June 1938* (Kingston: Government Printing Office, 1945).

Naipaul, Seepersad, *Gurudeva and Other Stories* (London: Deutsch, 1976).

Naipaul, V. S. *The Middle Passage*. London: Andre Deutsch, 1962.

Nash, June and María P. Fernández-Kelly, eds *Women, Men and the International Division of Labour* (Albany: State University of New York Press, 1983).

Nelson, Julie, 'Holding Hands at Midnight: The Paradox of Caring Labour', *Feminist Economics* 1:1 (1995)p. 77.

Nesmith, Cathy, 'Gender, Trees and Fuel: Social Forestry in West Bengal, India', *Human Organization* 50:2 (1991) pp. 337-348.

536. Nettleford, Rex, *Mirror, Mirror: Identity, Race and Protest in Jamaica* (Kingston: Sangster's, 1972).

Nevadomsky, Joseph, 'Changes in Time and Space in the East Indian Family in Rural Trinidad' in *Overseas Indians: A Study in Adaptation*, ed. by George Kurian and Ram Srivastava (New Delhi: Vikas Publishing, 1983).

Newman, Louise M. 'Critical Theory and the History of Women: What's at Stake in Deconstructing Women's History', *Journal of Women's History* 2:3 (1991).

Newton, Velma, *The Silver Men: West Indian Labour Migration to Panama, 1850-1914* (Kingston: Institute of Social and Economic Research, University of the West Indies, 1984).

Nichols, Grace, *The Fat Black Woman's Poems* (London: Virago, 1984).

_____, *I Is a Long Memoried Woman* (London: Karnak House, 1983).

_____, *Lazy Thoughts of a Lazy Woman* (London: Virago, 1989).

Noddings, N. 'Gender and the Curriculum' in *Handbook of Research on Curriculum*, ed. by R. Jackson. (London: Macmillan, 1992).

Norris, Katrin, *Jamaica: The Search for Identity* (Oxford University Press, 1962).

Nuland, Sherwin B. *How We Die: Reflections on Life's Final Chapter* (New York: Alfred Knopf, 1994).

O'Callaghan, Evelyn, 'Interior Schisms Dramatized: The Treatment of the Mad Woman in the Work of Some Female Caribbean Novelists' in *Out of the Kumbla* ed. by Carole Boyce Davies and Elaine Savory Fido(Trenton, New Jersey: Africa World Press, 1990) pp. 89-106.

————, 'Stripping Bare the Double Standard.' Presentation on Panel: Gender and Caribbean Identity, Humanities Week, Faculty of Arts and General Studies, University of the West Indies, Cave Hill, 1994.

————, *Woman Version: Theoretical Approaches to West Indian Fiction by Women* (London: Macmillan, 1993).

Ogbu, J. 'Origins of Human Competence: A Cultural-Ecological Perspective', *Child Development* 52 (1981) pp. 413-29.

Oliver, P. ' "What Do Girls Know Anyway?" Rationality, Gender and Social Control.' *Feminism and Psychology* 1(1991) pp. 339-360.

Olssen, M. 'Producing the Truth About People: Science and the Cult of the Individual in Educational Psychology' in *Growing Up: The Politics of Human Learning*, ed. by J. Morss and T. Linzey (Auckland: Longman Paul, 1991) pp. 188-209.

Olwig, Karen Fog, *Global Culture, Island Identity* (Camberwell: Harwood Academic Publishers, 1993).

Olwig, Karen Fog, *Small Islands, Large Questions. Society, Culture and Resistance in the Post-Emancipation Caribbean* (London: Frank Cass, 1995).

————, 'Women, "Matrifocality" and Systems of Exchange: An Ethnohistorical Study of the Afro-American Family on St John, Danish West Indies', *Ethnohistory* 28:1 (1981) pp. 59-78.

Ong, Aihwa, 'Colonialism and Modernity: Feminist Representations of Women in Non-Western Societies', *Inscriptions* 3-4 (1988) pp. 79-93.

————, 'The Gender and Labour Politics of Postmodernity', *Annual Review of Anthropology* 20 (1991)pp. 279-309.

————, *Spirits of Resistance and Capitalist Discipline: Factory Women in Malaysia* (Albany: State University of New York Press, 1987).

Orloff, Ann, 'Gender and the Social Rights of Citizenship: The Comparative Analysis of Gender Relations and Welfare States', *American Sociological Review* 58 (1993) pp. 303-328.

Otterbein, K. 'Caribbean Family Organization: A Comparative Analysis', *American Anthropologist* 67 (1965) pp. 66-79.

Ottley, J. 'Some Gender Related Issues in Guidance and Counselling in Schools.' Paper presented at a Gender and Education Seminar, Faculty of Education and Women and Development Studies, University of the West Indies, Mona, 1989.

Pantin, G. 'The Religious Background to Child Punishment', *Servol News* 8:34 (1992) pp. 10-14.

Parker, I. *Discourse Dynamics: Critical Analysis for Social and Individual Psychology* London: Routledge, 1992).

Parry, Odette, 'Equality, Gender and the Caribbean Classroom' in *Twenty-First Century Policy Review*. Special ed. Institutional Development in the Caribbean. (in press).

————, 'Schooling Is Fooling: Why Do Jamaican Boys Underachieve in School?' *Gender and Education*. (in press).

Patai, D. *The Owell Mystique: A Study of Male Ideology* (Boston:Univeristy of Massachusetts Press, 1984).

Patasar, Mungal, Inaugural Address to the Seminar: 'The Phenomenon of Chutney Singing', Hindu Prachar Kendra and Trinidad Guardian, 1990.

Pateman, Carole, *The Disorder of Women: Democracy, Feminism and Political Theory* (Stanford University Press, 1989).

Pateman, Carole and E. Gross, eds *Feminist Challenges: Social and Political Theory* (Stanford University Press, 1986).

Patterson, Orlando, 'Blacklash: The Crisis of Gender Relations Among African Americans', *Transition* 62 (1993) pp. 4-26.

_____, *The Sociology of Slavery* (London: MacGibbon and Kee, 1967).

_____, *The Sociology of Slavery* (London: Granada, 1973).

_____, 'Sexuality and the Secondary School: Some Observations on Coed and Single-Sex Environments.' Paper presented at a Gender and Education Seminar, Faculty of Education and Women and Development Studies, University of the West Indies, Mona, 1989.

Payne, Monica A. 'Occupational Sex-Role Stereotyping by Barbadian Adolescents.' Paper presented at the XIVth Annual Conference of the Caribbean Studies Association, Barbados, May 23-26, 1989.

Payne, Monica A. and E. H. Newton, 'Teachers' and Students' Perception of the Major Advantages and Disadvantages of Co-Educational Secondary Schooling', *Australian Journal of Education* 34 (1990) pp. 67-86.

Peake, Linda, 'The Development and Role of Women's Political Organizations in Guyana' in *Women and Change in the Caribbean*, ed. by Janet Momsen (Kingston: Ian Randle Publishers; Bloomington: Indiana University Press; London: James Curr ey Publishers, 1993) pp. 109-131.

Pearse, A. 'Carnival in Nineteenth Century Trinidad' in *Trinidad Carnival*, ed. by A. Pearse (Port of Spain: Paria Publishing, 1988) pp. 4-41.

Pearson, Ruth, 'Gender and New Technology in the Caribbean: New Work for Women?' in *Women and Change in the Caribbean*, ed. by Janet Momsen (Kingston: Ian Randle Publishers, Bloomington: Indiana University Press; London: James Currey Publishers, 1993)pp. 287-295.

Pena, Devon, 'Tortuosidad: Shop Floor Struggles of Female Maquiladora Workers' in *Women on the US-Mexico Border: Responses to Change*, ed. by Vicki Ruiz and Susan Tiano (Winchester: Allen and Unwin, 1987).

Perez Herranz, Carmen A. 'The Impact of a Development Program on Working Women in the Garment Industry: A Study of Women and Production in Puerto Rico', Ph.D. diss., Rutgers, 1990.

Persaud, Lakshmi, *Butterfly in the Wind* (Leeds: Peepal Tree Press, 1990).

Phelps, Owen W. 'The Rise of the Labour Movement in Jamaica', *Social and Economic Studies* 9: 4 (1960) pp. 417-468.

Philip, Marlene Nourbese, *Looking For Livingstone: An Odyssey of Silence* (Toronto: Mercury Press, 1991).

_____, *Salmon Courage* (Toronto: Williams Wallace, 1983).

_____, *She Tries Her Tongue; Her Silence Softly Breaks* (Charlottetown: Ragweed, 1989).

Phillips, Peter, 'Jamaican Elites: 1938 to Present' in *Essays on Power and Change in Jamaica*, ed. by Carl Stone and Aggrey Brown (Kingston: Jamaica Publishing House, 1976) pp. 1-14.

Piaget, Jean, 'Piaget's Theory' in *Carmichael's Manual of Child Development* vol 2, ed. by P.H. Mussen (New York: Wiley, 1970).

Pineau, Gisèle, 'Ecrire en tant que noire',in *Penser la créolité*, ed. by Maryse Condé and Madeleine Cottenet-Hage (Paris: Karthala, 1995.) pp. 289-295.

Poirier, Jean and Huguette Dagenais, 'En marge, la situation des femmes dans l'agriculture en Guadeloupe: Situation actuelle, questions methologiques', *Environnement Caraïbe* 2 (1986) pp. 151-186.

Police Magistrates' Returns to Governor's Private Secretary. Accession No. 67 *List of Property Owners of One Acre or More, 1847,* Barbados Archives: 1847.

Pollard, Velma, 'Images of Woman in Some Modern Caribbean Texts.' Paper presented at Gender and Education Seminar, Faculty of Education and Women and Development Studies, University of the West Indies, Mona, 1989.

Poovey, Mary, 'Feminism and Deconstruction', *Feminist Studies* 14 (1988).

Post, Ken, *Arise Ye Starvelings: The Jamaican Labour Rebellion of 1838 and Its Aftermath* (The Hague: Martinus Nijhoff, 1978).

Potter, J. and M. Wetherell, *Discourse and Social Psychology: Beyond Attitudes and Behaviour* (London: Sage, 1987).

Powell, D. 'Caribbean Women and Their Response to Familial Experiences', *Social and Economic Studies* 35: 2 (1986)pp. 83-127

Powell, Patricia, *Me Dying Trial* (Oxford: Heinemann Caribbean Writers Series, 1993).

_____ *A Small Gathering of Bones* (Oxford: Heinemann Caribbean Writers Series, 1994).

Poynting, Jeremy, 'East Indian Women in the Caribbean: Experience and Voice' in India in the Caribbean, ed. by David Dabydeen and Brinsley Samaroo,(London: Hansib, 1987) pp. 231-263.

Premdas, Ralph, 'Race and Ethnic Relations in Burnhamite, Guyana' in *Across the Dark Waters: Ethnicity and Indian Identity in the Caribbean,* ed. by David Dabydeen and Brinsley Samaroo (London: Macmillan, 1996) pp. 39-64.

Premdas Ralph and Harold Sitahal, 'Religion and Culture: The Case of the Presbyterians in Trinidad's Stratified System' in *Social and Occupational Stratification in Contemporary Trinidad and Tobago,* ed. by S. Ryan (Port of Spain: Institute of Social and Economic Research, University of the West Indies, 1991) pp. 337-339.

Price, R. *Maroon Societies.* 2nd ed. (Baltimore: Johns Hopkins University Press, 1979).

Project on the Development of Women in the Trade Unions, *Understanding Women* (Kingston: Trade Union Education Institute, University of the West Indies, 1987).

Proudfoot, Mary, *Britain and the U.S. in the Caribbean*(New York: Praeger, 1953).

Pulsipher, Lydia M. 'Changing Roles in the Life Cycles of Women in Traditional West Indian Houseyards' in *Women and Change in the Caribbean,* ed. by Janet Momsen (Kingston: Ian Randle Publishers; Bloomington: Indiana University Press; London: James Currey Publishers, 1993) pp. 50-64.

Pyle, Jean Larson, *The State and Women in the Economy: Lessons From Sex Discrimination in the Republic of Ireland* (Albany: State University of New York Press, 1990).

Rabinow, P. ed 'Introduction' in *The Foucault Reader* (London: Penguin Books, 1984).

Ramazanoglu, C. ' "What Can You Do with a Man?": Feminism and the Critical Appraisal of Masculinity', *Women's Studies International Forum* 15(1992) pp. 339-350.

Ramchand, Kennet, 'Introduction' in *Indo-Trinidad Folk Tales in the Oral Tradition,* ed. by A. Maharaj, vii.(Port of Spain: Indian Review Committee, 1990).

Rawlins, Joan, 'Preliminary Findings: Study of Jamaican Middle Class Women.' Paper presented at the Annual Meeting of the Caribbean Studies Association, Pointe-à-Pitre, Guadeloupe, 1987.

Rebecca, M., R. Hefner, and B. Oleshansky, 'A Model of Sex Role Transcendence', *Journal of Social Issues* 32 (1976) pp. 197-206.

Reddock, Rhoda, *Elma Francois:The NWCSA and the Worker's Struggle for Change in the Caribbean* (London: New Beacon, 1988).

_____, 'Feminism and Feminist Thought: An Historical Overview' in *Gender in Caribbean Development*, ed. by Patricia Mohammed and C. Shepherd, (Kingston: Women and Development Studies Project, University of the West Indies, 1988) pp. 53-75.

_____, 'Historical and Contemporary Perspectives: The Case of Trinidad and Tobago',in *Women and the Sexual Division of Labour in the Caribbean*, ed. by K. Hart (Kingston: Consortium Graduate School of Social Sciences, University of the West Indies, 1989) pp. 47-66.

_____, 'Primacy of Gender in Race and Class' in *Race, Class and Gender in the Future of the Caribbean*, ed. by J. E. Greene (Kingston: Institute of Social and Economic Research, University of the West Indies, 1993).

_____, 'Women and Labour and Struggle in Twentieth Century Trinidad and Tobago, 1898-1960', Ph.D. diss., University of Amsterdam, 1984.

_____, 'Women and Slavery in the Caribbean: A Feminist Perspective.', *Latin American Perspectives*, Issue 44 12:1 (1985) pp. 63-80.

_____, *Women Labour and Politics in Trinidad and Tobago: A History* (Kingston: Ian Randle Publishers, 1994).

Rhys, Jean *Wide Sargasso Sea* (London: Andre Deutsch, 1966; Penguin Books, 1968).

Ribiero, Indira, *The Phenomenon of Chutney Singing in Trinidad and Tobago: The Functional Value of a Social Phenomenon* (Port of Spain: Caribbean Studies Project, University of the West Indies, 1992).

Rich, Adrienne, 'Compulsory Heterosexuality and Lesbian Existence' in *The Gay and Lesbian Studies Reader*, ed. by H. Abelove, M. A. Barale, and D. Halperin (London: Routledge, 1993) pp. 227-254.

Riger, S. 'Epistemological Debates, Feminist Voices: Science, Social Values, and the Study of Women', *American Psychologist* 47(1992) pp. 730-740.

Ríos-González, Palmira N. 'Women and Industrialization in Puerto Rico: Gender Division of Labour and the Demand for Female Labour in the Manufacturing Sector, 1950-1980', Ph.D. diss., Yale University, 1990.

Roberts, George W. *The Population of Jamaica* (Cambridge University Press, 1957).

Roberts, George W. and S. Sinclair, *Women in Jamaica: Patterns of Reproduction and Family* (Millwood, New York: KTO Press, 1978).

Robertson, Claire C. and Martin A. Klein, 'Women's Importance in African Slave Systems',in *Women and Slavery in Africa*, ed. by Claire C. Robertson and Martin A. Klein (Madison: University of Wisconsin Press, 1983) pp. 3-25.

Robertson, Claire C. and Martin A. Klein, eds, *Women and Slavery in Africa* (Madison: University of Wisconsin Press, 1983).

Rodman, Hyman, *Lower Class Families: The Culture of Poverty in Negro Trinidad* (New York: Oxford University Press, 1971).

_____, 'Marital Relationships in a Trinidad Village', *Marriage and Family Living* 23 (1961) pp. 166-70.

Rodney, Walter, 'African Slavery and Other Forms of Social Oppression on the Upper Guinea Coast in the Context of the Atlantic Slave Trade', *Journal of African History* 7:3 (1966) pp. 431-443.

_____ 'Gold and Slaves on the Gold Coast', *Transactions of the Historical Society of Ghana* 10(1969) pp. 13-28.

Roopnarine, J. L. and N. S. Mounts, 'Current Theoretical Issues in Sex Roles and Sex Typing' in *Current Conceptions of Sex Roles and Sex Typing Theory and Research*, ed. by D.B. Carter (New York: Praeger, 1987) pp. 7-31.

Rose, N. 'Individualizing Psychology' in *Texts of Identity*, ed. by J. Shotter and K. Gergen (London: Sage, 1989) pp. 119-132.

Rose, Susan D. 'Women Warriors: The Negotiation of Gender in a Charismatic Community', *Sociological Analysis* 48 (1987) pp. 245-258.

Rossi, A. 'Gender and Parenthood: An Evolutionary Perspective', *American Sociological Review* 49 (1984)pp. 1-19.

Rowe, A. C. 'Look Beyond Edwin's Dress to His Values', *Sun on Saturday* (Barbados) November 18, 1995, p. 13.

Rubenstein, H. *Coping with Poverty: Adaptive Strategies in a Caribbean Village* (Boulder, CO: Westview Press, 1987).

Rubin, Gayle, 'The Traffic in Women: Notes on the "Political Economy" of Sex' in *Toward An Anthropology of Women*, ed. by R. Reiter (New York: Monthly Review, 1975, pp. 157-210).

Ruiz, Vicki L. and Susan Tiano, eds,. *Women on the US-Mexico Border: Response to Change* (Winchester: Allen and Unwin, 1987).

Rutherford, J. 'Who's That Man?' in *Male Order: Unwrapping Masculinity*, ed. by R. Chapman and J. Rutherford (London: Laurence and Wishart, 1988).

Safa, Helen I. 'Economic Autonomy and Sexual Equality in Caribbean Society', *Social and Economic Studies* 35:3 (1986) pp. 1-22.

_____. 'The Female-Based Household in Public Housing: A Case Study in Puerto Rico', *Human Organization* 24:2 (1965)pp. 135-139.

_____. *The Myth of the Male Breadwinner: Women and Industrialization in the Caribbean* (Boulder, CO: Westview Press, 1995).

_____. 'Runaway Shops and Female Employment: The Search for Cheap Labour.' *Signs* 7 (1981) pp. 418-434.

_____. 'The Social Cost of Dependency: The Transformation of the Puerto Rican Working Class From 1960 to 1990', [Paper presented at] Caribbean Studies Association Meetings, 1993.

_____. 'Women and Industrialization in the Caribbean' in *Women, Employment and the Family in the International Division of Labour*, ed. by S. Stichter and J. Parpart (Philadelphia: Temple University Press, 1990).

Salter, V. 'Factors Affecting Female's Choice of Non-Traditional Careers in Jamaica'. Paper presented at a Gender and Education Seminar, Faculty of Education and Women and Development Studies Project, University of the West Indies, Mona, 1989.

Sampson, E. E. 'The Deconstruction of the Self.' In *Texts of Identity*, eds,. J. Shotter and K. Gergen (London: Sage, 1989) pp. 1-19.

_____. 'Identity Politics: Challenges to Psychology's Understanding', *American Psychologist* 48(1993) pp. 1219-1230.

Sangster, Alfred W. 'Common Entrance Misconceptions', *The Sunday Gleaner* (Jamaica) March 10, 1996.

Sassen, Saskia, *The Mobility of Labour and Capital: A Study of International Investment and Labour Flow* (Cambridge University Press, 1988).

_____ 'Women and Industrialization in the Caribbean' in *Women, Employment and the Family in the International Division of Labour*, ed. by S. Stichter and J. Parpart (New York: Macmillan, 1990).

Sanday, Peggy, *Female Power and Male Dominance* (Cambridge University Press, 1981).

Satchell, V. M. 'Women, Land Transactions and Peasant Development in Jamaica, 1866-1900' in *Engendering History: Caribbean Women in Historical Perspective*, ed. by Verene Shepherd, Bridget Brereton, and Barbara Bailey ; London: James Currey Publishers; Kingston: Ian Randle Publishers, 1995) pp. 213-232.

Schmidt, Elizabeth, *Peasants, Trader and Wives: Shona Women in the History of Zimbabwe, 1870-1939* (Portsmouth, N.H.: Heinemann; Harare: Baobab Books, 1992).

Schuler, M. *'Alas, Alas, Kongo': A Social History of Indentured African Immigration into Jamaica, 1841-1865* (Baltimore: Johns Hopkins University Press, 1980).

Scott, J. 'Gender: A Useful Category of Historical Analysis', *The American Historical Review* 91:5 (1986) pp. 1053-1075.

Segal, D. ' "Race" and "Colour" in Pre-Independence Trinidad and Tobago' in *Trinidad Ethnicity*, ed. by Kevin Yelvington (London: Macmillan Caribbean, 1992) pp. 81-115.

Sen, Amaryta, 'Agency and Well-Being: The Development Agenda' in *A Commitment to the World's Women: Perspectives on Development for Beijing and Beyond*, ed. by Noeleen Heyzer with Sushma Kapoor and Joanne Sandler (New York: UNIFEM, 1995).

Senior, Olive, *Working Miracles: Women's Lives in the English-Speaking Caribbean* (Bridgetown: Institute of Social and Economic Research, University of the West Indies, Published in association with London: James Currey Publishers and Bloomington: Indiana University Press, 1991).

Shepherd, Verene, 'Gender, Migration and Slavery' in *Engendering History: Caribbean Women in Historical Perspective*, ed. by Verene Shepherd, Bridget Brereton, and Barbara Bailey. (London: James Currey Publishers; Kingston, Jamaica: Ian Randle Publishers, 1995) pp. 233-257.

_____, *Women in Caribbean History* (Kingston: Ian Randle Publishers; Department of History, Social History Project, University of the West Indies) (in press).

Sherif, C. W. 'Needed Concepts in the Study of Gender Identity', *Psychology of Women Quarterly* 6 (1982) pp. 375-398.

Shiva, Vandana, *Staying Alive: Women, Ecology and Development* (London: Zed Books, 1989).

Shiw Parsad, B. and G. Danns, *Women and Domestic Violence in Guyana* (Turkeyen: University of Guyana, 1989).

Siebert, Charles, 'The DNA We've Been Dealt', *Weekend Guardian* (London), November 4, 1995 p. 22.

Siim, Birte, 'Towards a Feminist Rethinking of the Welfare State' *The Political Interest of Gender*, ed. by Kathleen B. Jones and Anna G. Jonasdottir (London: Sage Publications, 1988)pp. 160-168.

Silvera, Makeda, 'Her Head a Village' in *Voices: Canadian Writers of African Descent*, ed., by A. Black (Toronto:HarperCollins: 1992) p. 107.

Simey, Thomas S. *Welfare and Planning in the West Indies* (Oxford: Clarendon Press, 1946).

Simmonds, L. 'Slave Higglering in Jamaica 1780-1834', *Jamaica Journal* 20: 1 (1987) pp. 31-38.

Sistren with Honor Ford Smith, *Lionheart Gal: Life Stories of Jamaican Women* (London: Women's Press, 1986).

Skelton, Tracy, 'Boom Bye Bye: Jamaican Ragga and Gay Resistance' in *Mapping Desire: Geography of Sexualities*, ed. by David Bell and Gill Valentine (London: Routledge, 1995).

_____ *Women, Men and Power: Gender Relations in Montserrat* (Newcastle Upon Tyne: University of Newcastle Upon Tyne, 1989).

Slaby, R. G. and K. S. Frey, 'Development of Gender Constancy and Selective Attention to Same-Sex Models', *Child Development* 46 (1975) pp. 849-856.

Slater, Mariam, *The Caribbean Family: Legitimacy in Martinique* (New York: St Martin's, 1977).

Smith, Ashley, 'Pentecostalism in Jamaica', *Jamaica Journal* 42 (1978) pp. 3-13.

Smith, Howard L. and Mary Grenier, 'Sources of Organizational Power for Women: Overcoming Structural Obstacles', *Sex Roles* 8:7 (1982) pp. 773-846.

Smith, M. G. *Culture, Race and Class in the Commonwealth Caribbean* (Kingston: Extra Mural Department, University of the West Indies, 1984).

_____. *Kinship and Community in Carriacou* (New Haven: Yale University Press, 1962).

_____. 'Introduction' in *My Mother Who Fathered Me* by Edith Clarke (London: George Allen and Unwin, 1970).

_____. *The Plural Society in the British West Indies* (Berkeley: University of California Press, 1965).

Smith, M. G., F. R. Augier, and Rex Nettleford, *(The Rastafarian Movement in Kingston, Jamaica* (Kingston: Institute of Social and Economic Research, University of the West Indies, 1960).

Smith, P. B. and M. H. Bond *Social Psychology Across Cultures: Analysis and Perspectives* (New York: Harvester Wheatsheaf, 1993).

Smith, Raymond T. 'The Family in the Caribbean' in *Caribbean Studies: A Symposium.* 2nd. ed., ed. by Vera Rubin, (Seattle, Washington: University of Washington Press, 1960) pp. 67-79.

_____. 'Hierarchy and the Dual Marriage System in West Indian Society' in *Gender and Kinship: Essays Toward a Unified Analysis*, ed. by J. F. Collier and S.J. Yanagisako (Palo Alto, CA: Stanford University Press, 1987) pp. 163-196, 353-356.

_____. 'Introduction' in *Kinship Ideology and Practice in Latin America*, ed. by R. T. Smith (Chapel Hill: University of North Carolina Press, 1984) pp. 3-31.

_____. *Kinship and Class in the West Indies: A Genealogical Study of Jamaica and Guyana* (Cambridge University Press, 1988).

_____. 'The Matrifocal Family' in *The Character of Kinship*, ed. by J. Goody (Cambridge University Press, 1973) pp. 121-144.

_____. *The Negro Family in British Guiana: Family Structure and Social Status in Villages* (New York: Grove Press, 1956).

Sobo, Elisa J. *One Blood: The Jamaican Body* (Albany: State University of New York Press, 1993).

Solien, Nancie L. 'Household and Family in the Caribbean: Definitions and Concepts', *Social and Economic Studies* 9:1 (1960) pp. 101-106.

Spence, J. T., R. L. Helmreich, and J. Stapp, 'Ratings of Self and Peers on Sex Role Attributes and Their Relation to Self Esteem and Conceptions of Masculinity and Femininity', *Journal of Personality and Social Psychology* 32 (1975)pp. 29-39.

Squire, C. 'Empowering Women? The *Oprah Winfrey Show*', *Feminism and Psychology* 4 (1994) pp. 63-79.

St Lucia, *Population and Housing Census, 1991* vol. 2. (Castries: Statistics Department, 1994).

St Lucia, *Special Tabulations* (Castries: Statistical Office, 1995).

St Philip Parish Rate Books, 1874-1895. Barbados Archives.

St Vincent, *Population and Housing Census, 1991*. Vol. 2. Kingstown, St Vincent: Statistics Office, 1993.

St. Vincent and the Grenadines, *Special Tabulations*. Kingstown, St. Vincent: Statistical Office, 1995.

Steumple, Steve, 'The Steelband Movement in Trinidad and Tobago: Music, Politics and National Identity', Ph.D. diss., University of Pennsylvania, 1990.

Stevenson, Robert Louis, *The Strange Case of Dr. Jekyll and Mr. Hyde and O8her Stories*. edited by Jenni Calder. (London: Penguin, 1979).

Stimpson, Catharine, 'Zero Degree Deviancy: The Lesbian Novel in English' in *Writing and Sexual Difference*, ed. by E. Abel (Sussex: Harvester Press, 1982) pp. 243-259.

Stone, Carl, *Class, Race, and Political Behaviour in Urban Jamaica* (Kingston: University of the West Indies, 1973).

Stone, Carl and Aggrey Brown, eds *Essays on Power and Change in Jamaica* (Kingston: Jamaica Publishing House, 1976).

Stromquist, N. P. 'Gender Inequality in Education: Accounting for Women's Subordination', *British Journal of Sociology of Education* 11:2 (1990) pp. 137-153.

Sutton, Constance, 'Cultural Duality in the Caribbean', *Caribbean Studies* 14:2 (1974) pp. 96-101.

Sutton, Constance and Susan Makiesky-Barrow, 'Social Inequality and Social Status in Barbados' in *The Black Woman Cross-Culturally*, ed. by Filomina C. Steady (Cambridge: Schenkman, 1981) pp. 469-497.

Tanner, Nancy, 'Matrifocality in Indonesia and Africa and among Black Americans' in *Women, Culture and Society*, ed. by M. Rosaldo and L. Lamphere (Stanford University Press, 1974) pp 129-156.

Taylor, E. 'Women in School Administration: Exclusion and Isolation' in *Gender: A Caribbean Multidisciplinary Perspective*, ed. by Elsa A. Leo-Rhynie, Barbara Bailey, and Christine Barrow (Kingston: Ian Randle Publishers, 1997)pp. 183-200.

Taylor, R. D. and G. Oskay. 'Identity Formation on Turkish and American Late Adolescents.', *Journal of Cross-Cultural Psychology* 26 (1995) pp. 8-22.

Terborg-Penn, Rosalyn, 'Through an African Feminist Theoretical Lens: Viewing Caribbean Women's History Cross-Culturally' in *Engendering History: Caribbean Women in Historical Perspective*, ed. by Verene Shepherd, Bridget Brereton, and Barbara Bailey (London: James Currey Publishers; Kingston: Ian Randle Publishers, 1995) pp. 3-10.

Thieme, John, *The Web of Tradition: Uses and Allusion in V.S. Naipaul's Fiction* (London: Hansib/Dangaroo Press, 1987).

Thomas, Clive Y. *The Poor and the Powerless: Economic Policy and Change in the Caribbean* (London: Latin American Bureau, 1988).

_____. *The Rise of the Authoritarian State in Peripheral Societies.*(New York: Monthly Review Press, 1984).

Thomas-Hope, Elizabeth M. 'Caribbean Diaspora, The Inheritance of Slavery' in *The Caribbean in Europe*, ed. by C. Brock (London: Frank Cass, 1986) pp. 15-35.

Tilly, Louisa A. and Joan W. Scott, *Women, Work and Family* (New York: Holt, Rinehart and Winston, 1987).

Todorov, Tzvetan, *La conquête de l'Amerique la question de l'autre* (Paris: Seuil, 1982).

Tomich, Dale, *Slavery in the Circuit of Sugar* (Baltimore: Johns Hopkins University Press, 1990).

Trinidad and Tobago National Planning Commission, *Restructuring for Economic Independence: Medium Term Macro Planning Framework, 1989-1995* (Port of Spain: The Commission, 1990).

Trotman, David, 'The Image of Indians in Calypso: Trinidad 1946-1986' in *Social and Occupational Stratification in Contemporary Trinidad and Tobago*, ed. by Selwyn Ryan (Port of Spain:University of the West Indies, Institute of Social and Economic Research, 1991) pp. 385-399.

Trotz, D. 'Gender, Ethnicity and Familial Ideology in Georgetown, Guyana', Ph.D. diss., Cambridge University, 1995.

Trouillot, Michel-Rolph, 'The Caribbean Region: An Open Frontier in Anthropological Theory', *Annual Review of Anthropology* 21 (1992) pp. 19-42.

Unger, R. K. 'Will the Real Sex Difference Please Stand Up?' *Feminism and Psychology* 2 (1992) pp. 231-238.

United Kingdom. Public Record Office, *Calendar of State Papers*, America and the West Indies, vol. 9 (1675-1676) (London, 1893).

United Kingdom, West India Royal Commission, 1938-1939 *West India Royal Commission Report* [Chairman: W.E.G. Moyne]. Cmd. 6607. 1945.

United Nations Children's Fund, *Analysis of the Situation of Women and Children in Guyana* (Georgetown: UNICEF/Government of Guyana, 1993).

United Nations Development Programme, *Human Development Report 1995* (New York: Oxford University Press, 1995).

University of the West Indies, *Official Statistics 1993/94* (Port of Spain: Office of Policy Planning and Development, University of the West Indies, 1995).

Valentine, Charles, *Black Studies and Anthropology: Scholarly and Political Interests in Afro-American Culture* (Reading, MA: Addison-Wesley Publishing, 1972).

Vansina, Jan, *Paths in the Rainforest* (London: James Currey Publishing, 1990).

A Vindication of Female Anti-Slavery Associations (London: Female Anti-slavery Society, n.d.).

Wacquant, L. J. D. 'A Body too Big to Feel: Review Essay', *Masculinities* 2, no. 1 (1994) pp. 78-86.

Waithe, Neilson, *Caribbean Sexuality* (Bethlehem, P.A.: Department of Publications, Moravian Church, 1993).

Walby, S. *Patriarchy at Work: Patriarchal and Capitalist Relations in Employment* (Cambridge: Polity Press, 1986).

Walcott, Derek. 'A Far Cry from Africa' in *The Penguin Book of Caribbean Verse in English*, ed. by Paula Burnett (Harmondsworth: Penguin, 1986) p. 243.

Ward, J. R. *British West Indian Slavery, 1750-1834: The Process of Amelioration* (Oxford: Clarendon Press, 1988).

Ward, Kathryn, *Women Workers and Global Restructuring* (Ithaca NY: ILR Press, School of Industrial and Labor Relations, Cornell University, 1990).

Warner, Aucher, *Sir Thomas Warner Pioneer of the West Indies : A Chronicle of His Family* (London: The West India Committee, 1933).

Warner, Marina, *From the Beast to the Blonde: On Fairy Tales and Their Tellers* (London: Chatto and Windus, 1994).

_____. *Indigo* (London: Chatto and Windus, 1993).

Waters, M. *Globalization* (London: Routledge, 1995).

Watts, M. 'The Study of Literature in Schools Is Mostly for Girls: Some Implications for Curriculum Goals, Implementation and Research.' Paper presented at a Gender and Education Seminar, Faculty of Education and Women and Development Studies, University of the West Indies, Mona, 1989.

Wedenoja, William, 'Modernization and the Pentecostal Movement' in *Perspectives on Pentecostalism*, ed. by S. Glazier (Washington D.C.: University Press of America, 1980) pp. 44-65.

Weeks, Jeffrey, *Sexuality* (London: Routledge, 1986).

Weiner, G. *Feminisms in Education: An Introduction* (Milton Keynes: Open University Press, 1994).

Westwood, Sallie, *All Day, Every Day: Factory and Family in the Making of Women's Lives* (London: Pluto Press, 1984. Chicago: University of Illinois Press, 1985).

Wetherell, M. and J. Potter, *Mapping the Language of Racism: Discourse and the Legitimation of Exploitation* (New York: Harvester Wheatsheaf, 1992).

Whiteley, P. 'Equal Opportunity: Gender and Participation in Science Education in Jamaica.' Paper presented at the Third Biennial Cross-Campus Conference, University of the West Indies, Faculty of Education, Cave Hill, 1994.

_____. 'The Gender Balance of Physics Textbooks: Caribbean and British Books, 1985-91', *Physics Education*. (in press).

_____. 'The 'Gender Fairness' of Integrated Science Textbooks Used in Jamaican High Schools', *Journal of Science Education*. (in press).

_____. 'Science Education in the Caribbean: A Gender Perspective.' Paper presented at the International Science Teachers' Association Conference, Jamaica,1995.

Whitson, D. 'The Embodiment of Gender: Discipline, Domination and Empowerment' in *Women, Sport and Culture*, ed. by S. Birrell and C. L. Cole. (Champaign, IL: Human Kinetics Books, 1994).

Wilkinson, S., ed. *Feminist Social Psychology* (Milton Keynes: Open University Press, 1986).

Williams, C. H. 'The Relationship Between Academic Motivation, Academic Performance and Certain Selected Variables in a Sample of 5th Form Jamaican Students', B. Ed. Study, University of the West Indies, Mona, 1981.

Williams, Eric, *Education in the British West Indies* (New York: University Place Book Shop, 1951).

Williams, S. and G. A. Bendelow ' "Excavating the Body" ' in *The Sociology of Chronic Illness* (Coventry: University of Warwick, Department of Sociology, 1995).

Willis, William, 'Skeletons in the Anthropology Closet' in *Reinventing Anthropology*, ed. by D. Hymes (New York: Vintage Press, 1974) pp. 121-152.

Wilson, Peter J. 'Caribbean Crews: Peer Groups and Male Society', *Caribbean Studies* 10:4 (1971) pp. 18-34.

_____. *Crab Antics: The Social Anthropology of English-Speaking Negro Societies of the Caribbean* (New Haven: Yale University Press, 1973).

_____. 'Reputation and Respectability: A Suggestion for Caribbean Ethnology.' *Man* 4:1 (1969) pp. 70-84.

Wiltshire, Rosina, 'The Caribbean Transnational Family' in *Changing Family Patterns and the Role of Women in the Caribbean* (Bridgetown: Institute of Social and Economic Research (EC), University of the West Indies/UNESCO, 1986).

Wint, E and J. Brown, 'The Knowledge and Practice of Effective Parenting', *Social and Economic Studies* 37:3 (1988) pp. 253-277.

Wittig, Monique, 'One Is Not Born a Woman' in *The Gay and Lesbian Reader*, ed by Henry Abelove, Aina Barole, and David Halperin (London: Routledge, 1993) pp. 103-109.

Woolf, V. *A Room of One's Own* (London: Panther, 1977).

World Bank, *Toward Gender Equality: The Role of Public Policy* (Washington D.C.: World Bank, 1995).

Yanagisako, Sylvia and Jane Collier, 'Towards a Unified Analysis of Gender and Kinship' in *Gender and Kinship: Essays Toward a Unified Analysis*, ed. by S. Yanagisako and J. Collier (Palo Alto: Stanford University Press, 1987) pp 14-50.

Yelvington, Kevin A. *Producing Power* (Philadelphia: Temple University Press, 1995).

Yelvington, Kevin A. 'Gender and Ethnicity at Work in a Trinidadian Factory' in *Women and Change in the Caribbean*, ed. by Janet Momsen (Kingston: Ian Randle Publishers; Bloomington: Indiana University Press; London: James Currey Publishers, 1993) pp. 263-277.

Young, K. 'Notes on the Social Relations of Gender' in *Gender in Caribbean Development*, ed. by Patricia Mohammed and C. Shepherd (Kingston: Women and Development Studies, University of the West IndiesProject, 1988) pp. 97-109.

Young, K., P. White, and W. McTeer, 'Body Talk: Male Athletes Reflect on Sport, Injury and Pain', *Sociology of Sport Journal* 11(1994) pp. 175-194.

Young, Marion I. *Throwing Like a Girl and Other Essays in Feminist Philosophy and Social Theory* (Bloomington: Indiana University Press, 1990).

Young, R. J. C. *Colonial Desire: Hybridity in Theory, Culture and Race* (London: Routledge, 1995).

Youssef, N. H. and C. Hetle,. 'Establishing the Economic Conditions of Woman-Headed Households in the Third World: A New Approach' in *Women and Poverty in the Third World*, ed. by Mayra Buvinic, M. A. Lycettes, and W.P. McGreevey (Baltimore: Johns Hopkins University Press, 1983) pp. 216-243.

Contributors

Klaus de Albuquerque is a Professor of Sociology at the College of Charleston (South Carolina, USA). During the academic year 1994/5, he was a Fulbright Scholar in the Department of Government, Sociology and Social Work, University of the West Indies (Cave Hill Campus, Barbados). He has published numerous articles related to Caribbean development. The most recent on Caribbean dependent territories appears in *Social and Economic Studies*.

Caroline Allen is a Ph.D. student at the University of Warwick (UK), conducting a sociological study of health promotion and fitness culture in the Commonwealth Caribbean. She worked as a Research Fellow at the Institute of Social and Economic Studies, University of the West Indies (Cave Hill Campus, Barbados) from 1991 to 1994, on the Reproductive Health research project.

Diane Austin-Broos is Professor of Anthropology and Head of the Department of Anthropology at the University of Sydney (New South Wales, Australia). She has conducted extensive anthropological research in Jamaica and is the author of *Urban Life in Kingston, Jamaica: The Culture and Class Ideology of Two Neighbourhoods* (New York: Gordon and Breach, 1984).

Barbara Bailey is Lecturer in the Faculty of Education, University of the West Indies (Mona Campus, Jamaica) in the area of Curriculum Studies. She served as Coordinator of the Women and Development Studies Unit at that campus for the period 1992-1994 and, in 1996, was appointed to act as Regional Coordinator of the Centre for Gender and Development Studies, University of the West Indies. Her research interest is in gender issues in education and she has developed and taught undergraduate and postgraduate modules in gender and education. She is joint editor of *Gender: A Caribbean Multi-Disciplinary Perspective* (Kingston: Ian Randle Publishers, 1997).

V. Eudine Barriteau is Lecturer and Head of the Centre for Gender and Development Studies at the University of the West Indies (Cave Hill Campus, Barbados). She has been involved in research, administration and coordination of regional projects in the Caribbean. Currently she is writing on gender and development planning in the post-colonial Caribbean, and gender and economic relations. Her most recent publication is 'Postmodernist Feminist Theorising and Development: Policy and Practice in the Anglophone Caribbean' in Marianne Marchand and Jane Parpart (eds) *Feminism Postmodernist Development* (London and New York: Routledge, 1995).

Christine Barrow is a Senior Lecturer in Sociology and Head of the Department of Government, Sociology and Social Work at the University of the West Indies (Cave Hill Campus, Barbados). Her main research interests are Caribbean family, gender and rural development and her most recent publication is *Family in the Caribbean: Themes and Perspectives* (Kingston: Ian Randle Publishers, 1996). She is joint editor of *Gender: A Caribbean Multi-Disciplinary Perspective* (Kingston: Ian Randle Publishers, 1997).

Hilary Beckles is Professor of History and Dean of the Faculty of Humanities at the University of the West Indies (Cave Hill Campus, Barbados). A major research interest is gender in Caribbean slavery and he has published several articles and books on the subject, including *Natural Rebels: A Social History of Enslaved Black Women in Barbados* (New Brunswick: Rutgers University Press, 1989).

Jean Besson is Senior Lecturer in Anthropology at Goldsmith's College (University of London). She has conducted extensive fieldwork in rural Jamaica and published widely on Caribbean peasantries. She has recently contributed a Caribbean review chapter to the collection edited by S. Ardener and S. Burman entitled *Money-Go-Rounds: Women's Use of Rotating Savings and Credit Associations* (Oxford: Berg, 1995).

A. Lynn Bolles is a Professor of Women's Studies and Affiliate Faculty in Anthropology, Afro-American Studies and Comparative Literature at the University of Maryland (College Park, USA). Her research focuses on the African Diaspora, particularly the Caribbean. She is completing a project on race, class and women tourist workers in Negril, Jamaica and a textbook on Pan-Caribbean women's experiences. Her most recent publications include *We Paid Our Dues: Women Trade Union Leaders in the Caribbean* (1996) and *Sister Jamaica: Women, Work and Households in Kingston, Jamaica* (1996).

Jane Bryce worked in Nigeria from 1983 to 1988 as a freelance journalist and gained her doctorate from Obafemi Awolowo University, Ile-Ife. Since 1992, she has been a Lecturer in African Literature at the University of the West Indies (Cave Hill Campus, Barbados). Her research interests have focused on popular culture, specifically 'unofficial' women's writing such as romantic fiction in Africa and the Caribbean.

Helen Carnegie is a recent graduate of the University of the West Indies (Cave Hill Campus, Barbados) with a First Class Honours in English. She is a poet, playwright and a visual artist who specialises in surrealist feminist paintings. Her pieces have been exhibited in Barbados and the United States.

Jeniphier Carnegie is a Reference Librarian at the Main Library of the University of the West Indies (Cave Hill Campus, Barbados). She has published several bibliographies including 'Select Bibliography: Criticism and Related Work' in Carole Boyce Davies and Elaine Savory Fido eds, *Out of the Kumbla: Caribbean Women and Literature* (Trenton: Africa World Press Inc., 1990).

Merle Collins teaches at the Departments of English and Comparative Literature at the University of Maryland (USA). Her publications include two volumes of poetry and collections of short stories. He most recent work is a novel entitled *The Colour of Forgetting* (London: Virago Press, 1995).

Denise deCaires Narain is a Lecturer in English at the School of African and Asian Studies at the University of Sussex (Brighton, UK). She taught English at the University of the West Indies (Cave Hill Campus, Barbados) from 1992 to 1993. Her doctorate was on Caribbean women poets from 1940 to the present and her research interests include Caribbean literature and culture generally, feminist cultural theory and women's writing and post-colonial writing and theory.

Rhonda Ferreria Habersham was educated at the University of the West Indies (St Augustine Campus, Trinidad and Tobago). There she received a BA in French and History in 1989. In 1994, she was awarded a MEd from Regent University in Virginia, USA. She is currently living in Savannah, Georgia where she is teaching French to middle school students.

Carla Freeman has lectured at the University of the West Indies (Cave Hill Campus, Barbados) and at the University of North Carolina (Chapel Hill, USA). She is currently an Assistant Professor of Anthropology and Women's Studies at Emory University (USA). She has published several articles on her research on women workers in the transnational informatics industry. Her book entitled *High Tech and High Heels in the Global Economy* is forthcoming from Duke University Press.

Elsa Leo-Rhynie has been Professor and Regional Coordinator of the Centre for ʒender and Development Studies at the University of the West Indies since 1992. Prior to this she was Executive Director of the Institute of Management and Production and a Senior Lecturer in Educational Psychology in the Faculty of Education, University of the West Indies (Mona Campus, Jamaica). She has published extensively in the areas of education, training and gender concerns and, in 1993, delivered the Grace Kennedy Foundation Lecture on 'The Jamaican Family: Continuity and Change'. She is joint editor of *Gender: A Caribbean Multi-Disciplinary Perspective* (Kingston: Ian Randle Publishers, 1997).

Patricia Mohammed is Lecturer and Head of the Centre for Gender and Development Studies, University of the West Indies (Mona Campus, Jamaica). She was the first Coordinator of the Rape Crisis Centre in Trinidad in 1985. She has worked in gender studies at the University of the West Indies, the Institute of Development Studies at Sussex University and recently, at the Institute of Social Studies at the Hague where she completed her Ph.D. on a gender perspective of the Social History of Indians in Trinidad. Her interests are feminist theory and the history of gender relations.

Janet Momsen is Professor of Geography at the University of California-Davis. Starting in 1963, she has conducted extensive research on gender, agriculture and development in the Caribbean. She is the editor of *Women and Change in the Caribbean: a Pan-Caribbean Perspective* (Kingston: Ian Randle Publishers, Ltd., 1993).

Marietta Morrissey is Professor of Sociology at the University of Toledo (USA). She is author of *Slave Women in the New World: Gender Stratification in the Caribbean* (Lawrence: Kansas University Press, 1989). Her current research explores the impact of Caribbean and Central American state programmes on women's and children's economic statuses.

Evelyn O'Callaghan is Senior Lecturer in the Department of Language, Linguistics and Literature, University of the West Indies (Cave Hill campus, Barbados). She received her post-graduate training at Oxford University on a Rhodes Scholarship. She has published *Woman Version: Theoretical Approaches to West Indian Fiction by Women* (London: Macmillan, 1993) and numerous chapters and articles on West Indian Literature. She is currently researching early narratives of the West Indies by women.

Monica Payne worked as Lecturer in Psychology at Bayero University (Kano, Nigeria). During the 1980s she was based in the Faculty of Education, University of the West Indies (Cave Hill campus, Barbados), where she taught developmental and educational psychology and helped to establish the undergraduate programme in Women's Studies which she coordinated during 1989 to 1991. Since 1991, she has been Senior Lecturer in the Department of Education Studies at the University of Waikato (Hamilton, New Zealand). Her current research interests are in the developmental social psychology of late childhood and adolescence, with particular emphasis on issues of gender and culture.

Nan Peacocke was born in Guyana and spent her early years in Trinidad and Venezuela. She was educated in Jamaican and Canada and has worked in several Caribbean territories including St Vincent and Barbados where she was Publications Editor at the Women and Development Unit (WAND) of the University of the West Indies. She writes poetry, some of which has appeared in Canadian and Caribbean collections.

Rhoda Reddock is Senior Lecturer and Head of the Centre of Gender and Development Studies at the University of the West Indies (St Augustine campus, Trinidad and Tobago). She has been active in the national and regional women's movement for many years and is the author of a number of publications including *Elma Francois, the NWCSA and the Workers' Struggle for Change in the Caribbean* (London: New Beacon Press, 1988) and *Women, Labour and Politics in Trinidad and Tobago* (London: Zed Books, 1994).

Sam Ruark is a graduate student, planning to pursue work in demography at the Department of Sociology, College of Charleston (South Carolina, USA).

Olive Senior is the author of eight books, one of which, a short-story collection entitled *Summer Lightning* (England: Longman, 1986), won the Commonwealth Writers Prize in 1989. She also writes poetry and non-fiction including *Working Miracles: Women's Lives in the English-Speaking Caribbean* (Oxford James Currey, 1991) which was based on data from the Women in the Caribbean Project (WICP) (University of the West Indies, Barbados). She has read her work, lectured and conducted workshops in Europe, the USA and Canada as well as the Caribbean.

Alissa Trotz is a Researcher at the Centre of Latin American Studies (University of Cambridge, UK). She is currently working on gender and ethnicity in the Caribbean and completing a book on Gender, Ethnicity and Poverty in Guyana with Professor Linda Peake of York University (Canada).

Marina Warner has published four novels, the most recent being *Indigo* (London: Chatto and Windus Ltd, 1992). Her extensive studies of female myths and symbols culminate in her most recent book, *From the Beast to the Blonde: On Fairy Tales and their Tellers* (London: Chatto and Windus Ltd, 1994). In 1994 she presented the prestigious Reith Lectures for the BBC entitled *Managing Monsters – Six Myths of Our Time*. Her current research includes a study of ogres, *No Go the Bogeyman*.